Families, Carers and Professionals

Building Constructive Conversations

Gráinne Smith

John Wiley & Sons, Ltd

Telephone (+44) 1243 779777

Email (for orders and customer service enquiries): cs-books@wiley.co.uk
Visit our Home Page on www.wiley.com

Other Wiley Editorial Offices

John Wiley & Sons Inc., 111 River Street, Hoboken, NJ 07030, USA

Jossey-Bass, 989 Market Street, San Francisco, CA 94103-1741, USA

Wiley-VCH Verlag GmbH, Boschstr. 12, D-69469 Weinheim, Germany

John Wiley & Sons Australia Ltd, 42 McDougall Street, Milton, Queensland 4064, Australia

John Wiley & Sons (Asia) Pte Ltd, 2 Clementi Loop #02-01, Jin Xing Distripark, Singapore 129809

John Wiley & Sons Canada Ltd, 6045 Freemont Blvd, Mississauga, ONT, L5R 4J3

Wiley also publishes its books in a variety of electronic formats. Some content that appears in print may not be available in electronic books.

Anniversary Logo Design: Richard J. Pacifico

Library of Congress Cataloging-in-Publication Data

Smith, Gráinne, 1945–
Families, carers, and professionals : building constructive conversations / Gráinne Smith.
p. cm.
Includes bibliographical references and index.
ISBN 978-0-470-05695-0 (pbk. : alk. paper) 1. Medical personnel-caregiver relationships – United States. 2. Nursing home patients – Family relationships – United States. 3. Nursing homes – United States – Employees. 4. Older people – Medical care – United States. I. Title.
R727.47.S65 2007
610.69′6 – dc22

2007001275

British Library Cataloguing in Publication Data

A catalogue record for this book is available from the British Library

ISBN 978-0-470-05695-0

Typeset in 10/13 pt Scala and Scala Sans by SNP Best-set Typesetter Ltd, Hong Kong
Printed and bound in Great Britain by TJ International Ltd, Padstow, Cornwall
This book is printed on acid-free paper responsibly manufactured from sustainable forestry in which at least two trees are planted for each one used for paper production.

This book is dedicated to all carers, family and professional, who work to support vulnerable individuals at the centre of our care efforts.

Contents

Foreword

Gráinne Smith has unique knowledge and experience which have resulted from the many different perspectives she has lived through. In her professional life as a primary headteacher she was able to have an overview of the wide range of children's behaviours, as well as working with many parents and parenting styles. More recently, sparked by personal experience, she has been deeply involved in thinking about parental responses to challenging behaviour.

Initially fuelled by her personal family experience when her daughter was ill, she 'wrote the book she'd searched for for several years', *Anorexia and Bulimia in the Family*, offering practical ideas of how home carers can best help and support their loved ones through an eating disorder.

Immersing herself in researching this field by tapping into sources of expert knowledge, Gráinne also became part of the network of parents of troubled children and young adults and has become a resource for other parents and carers. She has played a key role in planning services for Scotland. *Anorexia and Bulimia in the Family* is informed not only by her own experiences but also by the difficulties and frustrations of the hundreds of family members and other carers she has spoken to, on local and national Eating Disorder Association telephone helplines and at meetings.

Her curiosity and creativity have now led her to explore other challenging behaviours involved in allied conditions such as autism, Asperger's syndrome, substance abuse, depression and self-harm. Again she has studied expert sources and has interviewed many family members to inform her writing. This new book therefore encapsulates what Gráinne has learnt in this new phase of her life's journey.

Clinically we see parents who feel bereft and isolated, left to manage challenging behaviours at home as best they can. They have to cope on their own; uncertain whether they are being helpful or worrying that perhaps they may be inadvertently harmful in their reactions. Books like this enable people to feel listened to and to feel connected and supported and I highly recommend it.

Janet Treasure PhD FRCP FRCPsych

Preface

A personal perspective

In 1993, my daughter Jay returned home aged 21 after a disastrous marriage. There followed two years of strong denials that anything was wrong when I expressed concern as I noticed her severe weight loss, heard her exercising for hours every evening, and became aware of the equally dramatic change in her usual 'Tigger' personality. Frequently I felt that the Jay I knew had disappeared. At 23, when the doctor warned her that she was at serious risk of a heart attack because of her low potassium level, Jay told me of the diagnosis: anorexia 'with elements of bulimia'. At the time, in my complete ignorance, I felt relieved – at least it wasn't cancer as I had feared. When I asked our GP what I could do (or avoid doing) to help my daughter who was so obviously ill, I was told that I knew as much as the doctor did.

So began the most painful, difficult and agonising years of my life and – having now seen Jay recover and resume independent life, working fulltime, enjoying friends and social life – ultimately the most satisfying.

For two years, initially handicapped by not knowing the phrase 'an eating disorder', with 'anorexia' and 'bulimia' on the very edge of my vocabulary, I searched without success for information and support until I finally discovered Eating Disorders Association UK. As I cope better when I can think of something practical to do, and being a former trained Samaritan, I became a volunteer on the EDA national telephone helpline. Through this work I talked to many family members, and discovered others living in the same area. We decided to meet, then to start a support group for others in a similar situation. Much later this small band linked with another group in Aberdeen to become NEEDS Scotland.

Later came travelling to SEDIG conferences (Scottish Eating Disorder Interest Group, mainly professionals with a few carers and former sufferers) and more information, some of which I found extremely scary: up to 20% of people with anorexia die. For years I got up every morning wondering if that day I would have to cope with the death of my beloved Jay. Yet still I had no idea of what to do to support. My daughter was legally an adult, denying the need for professional help, and I felt I was living in a nightmare. I worried endlessly about doing the wrong thing entirely and making everything worse for my daughter.

Reading whatever I could find which I thought just might give me a few answers, listening and talking to many others, along the way I found so much that was puzzling, awful, interesting, fascinating. During my search I found a few books by anorexia sufferers, who told their own, often tragic, stories; one or two by parents whose daughter had died and again told a personal story; some by professionals who I discovered often blamed parents for the whole problem. Added to the misery of not knowing what to do, I spent hours trying to work out what I could possibly have done – or not done – to cause my daughter such suffering. Not one of these books gave me a practical clue as to the best way of coping with the extreme and unpredictable rages, the hostility, the rejection, which are all part of the illness. As a former primary teacher and headteacher, with many years' experience in all sorts of difficult and occasionally threatening situations, I discovered a new meaning to the phrase 'challenging behaviour'.

Years of struggle passed slowly as I looked with increasing desperation in every bookshop both new and secondhand, in various libraries in Britain and abroad – for a practical book to support me in my efforts to help my daughter. At the end of 2000 I set out to write the book for which I had searched for so long.

Anorexia and Bulimia in the Family was published in 2004 and is based not only on my own experiences during those nightmare years but also on conversations with hundreds of other family members; much reading and research into compulsive and addictive behaviours as well as other conditions; discussions with leading professionals from the Maudsley Hospital, London, and elsewhere; many years of working with children – including some very vulnerable and troubled young people – and their families.

* * * *

Gradually I had become aware of the tragic lack of resources and services for people with eating disorders and their families, and became involved in campaigning for better. Following a NEEDS Scotland/SEDIG petition, the Scottish Health Committee undertook a major investigation of the situation, publishing their report with strong recommendations in 2005. More recently, I became aware that lack of services and resources was not only restricted to parts of the UK; I now work as part of an eight-strong Academy for Eating Disorders task-force from around the world to develop and implement a worldwide Patient/Carer Charter in Eating Disorders. Without recognition and appropriate early treatment, eating disorders can quickly become compulsive and chronic, severe and enduring, last many years and lead to individual and family tragedy.

At the same time, I was becoming aware of the gulf between many professionals and families caused by the frequent reluctance to give any information to people, even about their own bodies, let alone what might be wrong with them. Before I was 20, I'd had several major orthopaedic operations; every question I'd asked over the years about *why* they were necessary had been, very politely, ignored. I discovered that 'confidentiality' was the most frequently quoted reason given for not giving information, whether general or particular, to an individual.

With my daughter well and independent, I moved house and concentrated on my dream of writing fiction, plays and poetry, enjoyed presenting workshops in creative writing – Building a Character, Scenes and Settings, Using Dialogue and Monologue, and so on. Short stories and poems were published in various magazines and anthologies. A series of social history stories were published as a small book, then a book of poems. I continued to listen on the helpline, to support the local self-help group, and gradually other aspects of life, ignored or abandoned over the years of Jay's illness, again began to play a greater role in my life.

Then a friend told me of a very distressing and difficult meeting with some professionals, of their apparent assumption that family problems were caused by lack of parenting skills; no other explanation was considered, nor was practical help or support offered. Coincidentally I heard another friend talk of ongoing problems caused by the lack of any clear diagnosis for her son; for years she and her husband had seen a succession of professionals, each time after waiting for months for an appointment, before being told that the problems did not fit the particular speciality of the individual professional. Again no practical help or support was offered; again I heard about inferences of parental deficits being the cause. Knowing the people involved in both these situations, I felt very surprised to hear their stories, so very different yet with similarities to so many others I'd listened to on the helpline.

So I decided to write another book. Over 2006 I have interviewed many individuals, several families in depth, and professionals from several fields, as well asking three questions, of professionals and family members, to be answered anonymously if preferred. Key questions related to situations/examples of poor communication; for ideas of how situations could be resolved through better communication; and outlines of how good communications may be established. Of those who replied, several professionals gave me excellent suggestions as well as general outlines of where they thought communication might break down; two said they couldn't answer *any* questions because of confidentiality; one said they thought working with families would negatively affect therapeutic work with patients and thought working with families a very bad idea. Family members offered thoughtful insight into personally difficult home situations, as well as ideas for positively improving family–professional communications while often stressing their appreciation for the difficult circumstances and lack of resources many professionals work with. Quotes from these interviews and questionnaire responses are used throughout; most preferred to be quoted anonymously.

I hope this book will be practical in helping to 'bridge the gap' – the tragic gap – in communication and understanding between teachers, social workers, psychiatrists, psychologists and others, all of whom work to support people with conditions and illnesses involving 'challenging behaviour', and the families and other carers struggling to support them at home.

In retrospect I can recognise a few personal factors which turned out to be assets when Jay was so ill, and several turning points both for Jay and for myself. In retrospect I can see how useful some of my work experience turned out to be in understanding that my daughter was venting her intense frustration at the world in general and that I was simply in the firing line; in recognising that meekly giving in to unreasonable demands would only lead to an increase in demands and not help Jay tackle any of her problems. This is all in retrospect – at the time I felt completely helpless, struggling on a daily basis to survive personally to support my daughter.

I also feel extremely fortunate in many of the people I met along the way: Janet Treasure, Professor of Eating Disorders at the Maudsley Hospital, London, is a key figure who was willing to share information about eating disorders, willing to listen, and then to consider her own professional experience and the wider picture in eating disorders (which is, of course, far greater than mine). Only after that careful reflection does she agree, or calmly and politely disagree, then explain *why* – an excellent and much valued example of the good communication so crucial to building effective support for very vulnerable individuals. Janet Treasure kindly agreed to write the Foreword to this book as well as to *Anorexia and Bulimia in the Family*.

Most of all, watching Jay out there getting on once more with her life, I feel especially fortunate that somehow without any information, let alone support, I worked out a way to support my daughter through those nightmare years; was able to somehow avoid, through ignorance and lack of experience or training, inadvertently colluding with the illness and thereby reducing chances of Jay's recovery. It could so easily have been otherwise.

Acknowledgements

My thanks go to all the people without whose contributions, help and encouragement this project would not have been completed:

to my own family and many friends for their support;

to everyone – family and professional – who contributed by giving time, energy and thought to answer questions and by offering their own insights into communication problems between family members, between colleagues, between professionals and families;

to those professionals who have been willing to patiently answer my many questions over the last few years, who made interesting suggestions for my reading list and pointed me in new directions, most especially Janet, Ulrike, Chris, Harry and Jane;

to 'Joan' who first sparked the idea for this book and gave practical, very constructive feedback along the way;

to Gillian and her colleagues at Wiley for so ably guiding me through the process between idea, writing and print;

and most especially to the families and individuals who gave much time in interviews and afterwards, when they told their own stories with the thought that doing so might help others.

From all these people I have learned so much.

Gráinne Smith

Introduction

Family: A primary social group consisting of parents and their offspring, the principal function of which is provision for its members.

(Extended) Family: All the persons living together in one household. A group descended from a common ancestor.

Carer: A person who has accepted responsibility, without payment, for looking after a vulnerable neighbour or relative.

Caregiver: USA and Canada term for carer.

Careworker: A person who, as paid employment, provides essential care for others.

Professional: An occupation requiring special training, esp. law, theology or medicine; undertaken or performed by people who are paid; extremely competent in a job.

(*Collins English Dictionary*, 2001)

And 'challenging behaviour'? Definitions may vary depending on situation and experience; may range from infringement of school, society or home rules, from relatively minor to extreme behaviour endangering safety; may appear in childhood or later following stress, illness, accident or substance abuse; may have short-lived or long-term effects. Emerson *et al.* (1987) outline how extreme behaviour may lead to an individual being limited in reaching their full potential place in society; each contributor to this book outlines how individual challenging behaviour affects family as well as professional carers.

Challenging behaviour includes:

- *aggression to self* – including head-banging, biting, cutting, suicide attempts
- *aggression to others* – including hitting, biting, kicking, stabbing, eye poking
- *hostility and rejection of attempts to help*
- *unpredictable extreme rages*
- *destruction of property* – breaking/smashing things, throwing objects, ripping clothes
- *unacceptable verbal habits* – swearing, screaming, shouting, interrupting, saying inappropriate things in public, asking repeated questions.

This book is about building clear and constructive communication for all family members, for all carers/caregivers and careworkers, and for professionals including doctors, social workers, psychiatrists, teachers, nurses, psychologists and many others, working to support any vulnerable person with a condition which involves 'challenging' – demanding or difficult – behaviour.

In the UK alone there are estimated to be at least 6 million people, the majority of whom are parents or spouses, caring for vulnerable people who would otherwise be unable to live independently because of illness, disability or frailty; in USA an estimated 50 million. Not all of these conditions involve challenging behaviour, but many do. To a huge extent, the care of these vulnerable individuals depends on communication, between them and their home carers and between the family and the trained professionals involved in more 'official' care. Communication – effective, constructive and supportive or inadequate, difficult and destructive – depends on a wide variety of contributing factors.

With the gift of language and speech, most people believe not only that they can talk to everyone and be understood, but also that they also understand the thoughts and intentions of others.

It's an interesting exercise to ask for other people's understandings of any particular exchange or experience – all may have been physically present, but may have entirely different memories. Even in close families who have shared their lives for many years, at times of stress it is possible for misunderstandings to arise as everyone sees the problem from a different viewpoint.

Unfortunately in families – and between friends, between professionals, between tribes, clans and nations – years of misery and bad feelings have often developed because of interpretations and misinterpretations of messages.

Any human communication involves a message being sent and received, by words spoken or written, by actions or gestures. A silence long or short, a frown or a smile, a raised eyebrow, an inclined, raised or lowered head, eye contact or lack of it, a touch gentle or brutal – all can speak volumes without the use of a single word. Even these may be misinterpreted: a frown could mean bad temper, or concentration, or straining because of poor eyesight or hearing.

Other factors creep in too: tiredness perhaps, attention and concentration, assumptions and misperceptions, hearing problems which may affect understanding. Personality traits such as anxiety, aggression, rigidity or black and white thinking and their opposites, all added to individual temperament, play a part: some people seem endlessly ready to pick up any possible negative aspect to comments, while others naively believe the best of everyone, that everyone has positive intentions.

Only through being aware of at least the possibility of misunderstandings, plus talking about what another person actually intends by any particular words or actions do we find out whether or not our mutual understanding of words is the. Consider the question: 'Is your mother controlling?' (email, personal contact). The professional questioner is no doubt clear on what s/he means by 'controlling', while the client/patient's interpretation may or may not coincide. Teenagers especially think the world, and their parents in particular, spend huge amounts of time simply dreaming up rules to control their every action, get them to do boring stuff like education and chores, stop them hanging around with much more interesting people and trying out all sorts of *really cool* activities.

While individual interpretations and assumptions may or may not have important consequences in our everyday lives, they can cause particular problems in many situations both informal and formal. An effective police inquiry, for instance, where various witnesses give their own accounts to be interpreted by the officers who interview and question them, is greatly dependent on those officers' communication skills. Any effective and constructive communication – family, or workplace, or professional–family-carer – depends on the skills of those involved.

Until fairly recent times only a very few people might be involved in trying to provide such care for vulnerable members of a community. Today often whole teams of multi-skilled professionals, sometimes separated by many miles, may be involved with one troubled individual. And each person involved, whether family or professional – and sometimes professionals are also home carers – will come from their own individual viewpoint, with their own background, experiences, perceptions, memories, personality, assumptions and interpretations.

> Most people think they can read minds and know what other people mean and feel, and therefore don't really listen properly. Where professionals and carers – often distressed and exhausted and coping in fraught situations – work together to provide support, having a sense of humour and some common sense in everyday situations is just not enough. And long-term thinking is essential.
>
> [Rachel, special educational needs teacher, interview, 2006]

This book is an attempt to cross the minefield of human communication frequently encountered when several people come together on a single project – in this case, providing help to support a troubled individual. With goodwill, co-operation on all sides and much discussion, I believe it is possible to build – and rebuild – the constructive communication and relationships needed between professionals and family and other carers. These co-ordinated efforts can lead to better family–professional relationships as well as more effective support for the individuals in particular need, who are at the centre of all efforts to provide consistent and effective care.

CHAPTER ONE

Families are fascinat...

> Families are terrible things – I've got one myself.
>
> [Dr J. Morris, psychiatrist]

> Families are communities in which each member is affected by what happens to each of the others.
>
> (Marriott, 2003)

For centuries, storytellers and writers have found families a great source for their sagas, poems, ballads, short stories, plays and novels: cruel, demanding or inadequate parents, ugly bullying sisters and wicked stepmothers are a regular feature from earliest times. Unusual or horrible behaviour is much more interesting, exciting or fascinating to write about than nondescript folk going about their ordinary lives.

As Andrew Marr, writer, journalist and broadcaster, puts it:

> To work the alchemy, journalists reshape real life, cutting away details, simplifying events, 'improving' ordinary speech, sometimes inventing quotes . . . it isn't only journalists. Everyone does it, all the time, mostly unconsciously. We hear a piece of gossip and as we retell it, we improve it, smoothing away irrelevance and sharpening the point; we turn experiences of friends and relatives into bolder more heroic or tragic episodes.
>
> Remember that news is cruel. Reading the awful things that people apparently say about each other, or newspapers say about them, can be depressing.
>
> (Marr, 2004)

Given the makeup of each individual with a unique mix of personality traits, and qualities such as optimism, empathy, generosity, resilience, honesty and curiosity, each family group will also have its own unique flavour, added to which will be effects of the particular society, culture and century.

Other factors include:

- age and generation of parents, single or a couple, or living with other carers – who and why
- siblings, ages and spaces between them, position in family
- further pregnancies and births within the family
- physical, mental and emotional health of mother

physical health of the child

- health of other close family members
- death of a sibling, deaths of other close relatives and friends and effects of these on self, on parents, on siblings
- religion/atheistic/secular
- war or peace
- status, financial resources
- accommodation – flat or house, rural, urban or inner city
- community? nomadic? several family moves? reasons?
- parents' work/family commitments (caring for other family members?); experience of pets/other animals; culture – society – century; parental and society attitudes to discipline, to status, materialistic or idealistic; television/technology access and availability; leisure pursuits; exposure to advertisements; pressure to acquire and 'keep up with the neighbours'; expectations – of parents/society/self; physical affection or reserve
- genetic vulnerability (for example, hearing problems, Huntingdon's disease, Alzheimer's disease, schizophrenia and spina bifida also run in families).

Only after the publication of my book *Anorexia and Bulimia in the Family* in 2004, which triggered discussion within my extended family, did I discover that two other young women in the same generation as my daughter had also suffered from anorexia nervosa/bulimia nervosa. They too recovered. Three young women in three different countries with thousands of miles between them, and the only common link one set of great-grandparents.

Like father like son?

Like mother like daughter; like father like daughter? Watch and listen at any family gathering, large or small, and it's impossible to miss likenesses between relatives, likenesses of feature and build, gesture and movement, voice and intonation, attitudes and approaches to life.

He's sure got his grandfather's temper!
She's her Aunt V all over again.
Should stick up for herself more; just like her mother.
Awkward from first to last, just like Uncle P.
Pity, he's inherited that from his grandfather.
As alike as two peas in a pod . . . they could be twins!
He is so like his father – attitudes, personality, not taking responsibility for his own choices, not following through. No perseverance, no determination. Blame the

universe or others for all problems large and small . . . But his father left us when A was two, he's hardly ever seen his father. [K, senior social worker]

And when I asked how and why a friend had survived various major upheavals during childhood, the response was: *I have my father's temperament.*

Then there's peer pressure. And education, formal or otherwise; encouragement or otherwise. Even the weather may play a part – people are more vulnerable to depression in dark northern climates than in warmer places with more sunshine.

In every case, family and background will play a huge part in forming the adult. But what any adult makes of their life will depend just as much on how they cope with all their experiences and resilience to adversity and struggle. Two children experiencing similar difficulties in, for example, mathematics or language may cope in very different ways: – one giving up very quickly before 'going under' and the other perhaps struggling for a while, but eventually those difficulties are overcome and used towards becoming stronger emotionally.

> . . . But there is also a huge random effect that rains down on even the best parenting efforts. If you are in any way typical, you have known some intelligent and devoted parents whose child went badly off the rails. You may have also known of the opposite instance, where a child succeeds despite his parents' worst intentions and habits.
> (Levitt & Dubner, 2006)

In *Freakonomics*, Levitt and Dubner (2006) describe the stories of two boys, one white and one black. The white boy grew up outside Chicago and had a 'solid' upbringing with smart, encouraging, loving parents who stressed education and family. The black boy from Daytona Beach was abandoned by his mother, beaten by his father, and had become a gangster by his teens. So what became of the two boys?

The second child, who experienced such a tough beginning, is Roland G. Fryer Jr, the Harvard economist studying black underachievement. 'The white child also made it to Harvard. But soon after, things went badly for him. His name is [notorious killer] Ted Kaczynski' (Levitt & Dubner, 2006).

Nature and nurture?

Nature versus nurture? Nature via nurture?

The debate about whether genes or environment, or 'nature versus nurture', are the causes of life difficulties such as mental illness, alcoholism and other addictive and compulsive conditions, autism or Asperger's syndrome, attention deficit hyperactivity disorder (ADHD), post-traumatic stress disorder, reactions to various personal stresses – all frequently associated with 'challenging behaviour' – has been raging with ever greater intensity over the last century in psychiatry and other professional disciplines.

Quoting from a vast array of documented and referenced research in his 2003 book *Nature Via Nurture: Genes, Experience and What Makes us Human,* Matt Ridley outlines the effects of some of the more extreme views quoted by those who have denied any part for heredity.

> The schizophrenic is painfully distrustful and resentful of other people due to the severe early warp and rejection he encountered in important people of his infancy and childhood, as a rule mainly in a schizophrenogenic mother.
>
> (Fromm-Reichmann, 1948)

Others asserted a similar diagnosis for autism: that it was caused by an indifferent 'refrigerator mother'. According to this theory, homosexuality was caused solely by withdrawn, absent or weak fathers and a negative relationship.

Even today in the early 21st century, a few diehard supporters of this theory, often by quoting out-of-date and discredited research, feel they may assert that, for instance, manic depression, schizophrenia, eating disorders, depression, criminality, all may be laid at the door of 'unempathic care'.

Laying out the theories of either side on the nature/nurture debate, Matt Ridley notes the effects of some of these extreme views by intellectuals working in academia whose ideas were taken up with enthusiasm by the media.

> For the parents of schizophrenic youths, already under terrible stress, Freudian culpability was a blow they could have done without. The pain it was to cause to a generation of parents would have been more bearable if there was any evidence to support it. But it was soon obvious to any neutral observer that Freudian treatment was failing to cure schizophrenia.
>
> (Ridley, 2003)

Matt Ridley (2000, 2003), Judith Rich Harris (1998) and Levitt and Dubner (2006) all make the same point, that – while there is indeed a correlation between, for instance, divorcees having divorced children, criminal parents rearing criminal children, obese parents rearing obese children – this does not mean the same as causation. In Denmark, with its most detailed records of population studies, including criminal records of adoptees, research found 'a strong correlation with the criminal record of the biological parent and a very small correlation with the criminal record of the adopting parent – and even that vanished when controlled for peer-group effects' (Ridley, 2000).

> Not even lip service was being paid to this omission: correlation was routinely presented as causation.
>
> (Ridley, 2000)

Unfortunately the effects of the nurture theory, or assumption that all emotional or mental health problems – not only schizophrenia or autism – must have been caused by 'unempathic' care in childhood, have been far reaching, influencing several generations of parents. And, sadly, still do.

Is it true that there is research now which shows it's not always the fault of the mother? I read it in a magazine . . . is it true?

My daughter has been ill with anorexia nervosa, binge-purge type, for over 18 years. She is now 42 and has relapsed again following the death of her partner in a car accident. She's home again just now, I think she's heading for hospital again, and I still don't know how to help her even after all these years. I wish I did.

My husband died three years ago. We were told years ago that it's the mother's fault when someone has anorexia, but I've never been able to work out why or what I did. My husband always blamed me for our daughter's illness.

How I wish I could talk to my husband about the new research. It always caused such trouble between us before he died.

[Mary, eating disorders helpline, 2001]

I knew a couple who had a baby boy in the 1970s, born with spina bifida. When he was small he was very pretty and like a 'wooden doll'. Everyone wanted to cuddle him. As he got older the 'wooden doll' lost its attraction. The father's family blamed the mother, as this is what they were told. The father's family persuaded their son to refuse to support the mother and child as 'it was the mother's fault the boy was born like this'. The couple broke up. I don't know what happened to them afterwards. [GS, personal conversation]

The parents had a baby with a wasting disease – myopathy I think it was called – who died before he was two. They had another baby with the same condition and he died too. Both parents were tested by the doctor who said they both carried the gene so it was likely other children could have the same condition. The father's family were shocked to hear of the test results as until then they assumed the mother was to blame for the condition. [GS, personal conversation]

My mother didn't tell me until I was in my 30s that I had been diagnosed with a mild case of spina bifida; she said she too was told that It Was the Mother's Fault, and was worried that I might blame her for my leg and back problems. (Having no idea of what caused my leg and back problems, and therefore the reason for several major orthopaedic operations, I had a few (a very few!) advantages – I saw no reason why I shouldn't try to skip, ride a horse, dance, go hill walking, climb a cliff roped on top and bottom.) [GS]

With new evidence-based research becoming available, including brain scanning, and more rigorous scrutiny of current research, attitudes of the blame-and-shame 20th century are changing.

This is not to say that parents are always pure. There are indeed parents as well as other family members who treat their children – and other people – abominably. Even in my own small experience of 40 years as a primary teacher I have known of some who have, for instance, stubbed cigarettes out on bare flesh; kept a child locked in a cupboard; abused family members, including children, in all sorts of dreadful ways. A mother, addicted to drugs, lived in one room with her three children (see Chapter 2). Prostitution brought her money to feed herself, her children, and her drugs habit. Before being found those children suffered terribly, with strong suspicions that they were sexually abused, leaving all of them emotionally scarred for life. Trying to trust another human being, when every human encountered before the age of 5 years has inflicted pain and misery, must be almost impossible.

Emotional abuse occurs too. Across the world children are, for instance, sold sometimes for very small amounts and sometimes by their parents; in some countries orphaned children, who live on the streets as they have no other place to go, are targeted and shot by police or vigilantes; others are dragged or lured into exploitation and prostitution.

Parents' experience

Many parents are inexperienced in bringing up children – just as I was – and take decisions (e.g. divorce, education, move job/house/town/city/country) which turn out to have an adverse effect on one or more of their children, make many mistakes along the way – just as I did. I also believe that the vast majority do the best they can in whatever circumstances they find themselves in. Just as I tried to.

But no matter how hard anyone tries – parents, teachers, shop assistants, pilots, doctors, businessmen, psychiatrists, social workers, all walks of life – and no matter how good their intentions, the ones remembered, talked of and written about will be those whose actions give parents, shop assistants, doctors and all other walks of life a bad press. After all, a story about completely happy people in perfect circumstances and behaving always in impeccably loving and caring ways . . . interesting? Think of Dr Harold Shipman who murdered many of his patients; a nurse whose deliberate treatment of patients led to their deaths; priests who sexually abused children in their care; an aunt who kept a child in the bath and starved her because she believed the child possessed of evil spirits and social workers did not follow up on neighbours' reports of hearing crying; cruel and unfair teachers, and so on.

Watching only television news reports, reading only sensationalised headlines, it would be easy to form the opinion that all humankind is abusive rather than the exception; if an alien flew in from outer space and read only these accounts, this could well be the picture taken back and broadcast.

> Is life really so writhing with distaste, failure and loathing? Acts of kindness, generosity, forgiveness and mere friendliness are hardly ever news. (Marr, 2004)

In adulthood, very few people can say they agreed with every aspect of their upbringing and have no issues at all with their parents, who have cleaned them as babies and small children, provided for them whatever food, shelter and living conditions, education, discipline, perhaps religious training, they could, depending on their circumstances – think of life for a 21st-century child in rural Ethiopia and another in the Australian outback; northeast Scotland and urban USA. But within their own situation and circumstances, most parents do their best to try to provide for their offspring.

Only gradually as we grow up do we come to realise that our parents – those all-powerful beings with often mysterious behaviour and decisions – make mistakes, are not always right, do not hold the key to life and a direct line to the Right Thing To Do In All Circumstances. Only gradually do we realise that our parents have faults and foibles, have views and opinions we may want to question, ideas bad as well as good. That they are not always strong and capable, that they too experience sadness and pain, feel tired and low, frustrated and despondent. And even weep.

Only gradually do we realise that we may have misread or misjudged our parents' actions when we were children, their feelings and actions towards us.

My father, born in 1915 one of 12 children, was brought up on a farm in NE Scotland where hard work was simply part of life – there was no choice with beasts to be fed and mucked out, cows milked, eggs collected, fields ploughed and planted and weeded and harvested throughout the year. Holidays were not possible, and a lie-in unheard of. Warmth and affection, though there in the background, were rarely demonstrated openly. Praise for skills and abilities would be muted if shown at all, possibly mentioned by way of a jokey reference, for fear of someone getting 'too big for their boots' or being seen to show off and needing to be taken down a peg or two. Education was compulsory but with most children needed on the farm as much as possible, usually only the basics were completed; most children were delighted to finish school as early as possible, and educating girls beyond the basics at that time was seen as unnecessary.

Walking 2 miles each way every day to primary school carrying books, lunch and a piece of coal or wood for the fire, later cycling a much greater distance to secondary school, my father was the only one of the 12 who went on to further education, later to university. My father saw education as Extremely Important – not only because of his love of learning but also as a way of escaping from a gruelling life of physical work, a way of 'betterment'. His own background and upbringing was reflected in his approach to his own children – to the extent that a spelling error in a letter to him would be corrected and sent back to the writer! Having no background in showing his feelings, he concentrated on working hard to provide a comfortable house, good food (he grew all our vegetables), expressing his caring through strong encouragement to do well at school, providing outings to archaeological sites and castles, camping trips.

It is only now, long into adulthood, that I can see that my perceptions did not always accurately reflect the reality. It is only now that I can see the doll's house he made out of an old orange box, hours spent sanding, painting and giving it windows, doors and stairs plus small carved wooden furniture, as his equivalent of many hugs.

And it is only with hindsight that I can understand the whole story of how my father's background formed his own approach to parenthood – he wanted to do better for his children through stressing what he felt was really important. Just as my own upbringing formed the background to my own years of being a parent and bringing up my son and daughter.

Depending on hindsight, consciously or not, we will decide to do similar in bringing up our own children, or reject and strive to provide different.

> My mother used to lock me in the coal cellar when I was naughty. I'd never ever do something like that to any child, let alone my own, no matter what they did to annoy me – I still remember my terror in the dark, waiting for the sound of the key in the lock to let me out. I still hate the dark and sleep with the light on.
>
> [A, personal friend of GS]

The jury is still out on just what the balance is on the nature/nurture debate, or how the two work together to form an individual with strengths, skills and weaknesses, with new technologies and research pointing the way.

Getting the balance right

Watching as a child or young person heads for what we think will be certain disaster is painful, whether it is smoking behind the bike sheds, finding 'unsuitable' friends who might have different values and might even lead into the start of wrongdoing, or actual mischief or crime. Say the wrong thing and it is possible that the young person will find the activity or friend even more attractive . . . after all, don't want to be a goody-goody, do we? Say nothing at all, and we could be seen as uncaring, or even condoning.

Personal parenting

I determined to do better than my parents with my own children. As a teacher I gave many talks on the importance of 'time and talk, not telly and treats', the importance of encouragement of strengths and interests, finding practical ways of overcoming difficulties, trying to consider and respect the feelings of others. In the brilliant light of hindsight, I know I made many mistakes along the way – I had been tired, cross and grumpy at times: working full-time to support them after my marriage failed, organising meals and a home every day, not to mention trying to work out best choices for all sorts of daily big and small decisions – not easy. I did not always manage to be as fair or to give as much energy as I'd hoped, for instance to encouraging my son's great interest in sport by going to matches to watch. But I loved my kids more than anyone in the world, we'd done lots of things together over their years growing up. Stories at bedtime, songs to keep us going while walking the long road home before I passed my driving test, camping, visits and holidays. From about 11 years on, showing them how to make simple meals for which they could choose the menu, or how to set and light the fire to heat the water. While there had been rows with my daughter about homework undone, staying out late in teenage years, disagreements with my son over tidying his room and lack of organisation – which at the time seemed much like what I heard from other parents with teenagers – I thought I'd been an OK parent, thought I'd done an OK job. Not perfect but, I thought, OK.

My son went off to university to study engineering. My daughter wanted to stay closer to home to work, then to marry at 19 the young man she'd been seeing since they were 13 (the reason for the rows over undone homework and coming in later than agreed!). I continued to work full-time, write stories and plays, walk the dog.

All change. My daughter at 21 returned home, the imagined happy ending having turned out to be a nightmare. At the time it did not occur to me that, after sharing our meal at the table each night, she was going to her room via the bathroom where compulsive bulimia made sure she retained no nourishment from her food before then starting compulsive exercising all evening.

Skeletal, two years later she eventually told me of the diagnosis anorexia 'with elements of bulimia', and said she'd started having eating problems while she was married and her husband was away from home; while he was away she was forbidden to go out apart from work. Then she repeated what the doctor had told her – that at 23, her potassium level was so low she was at serious risk of a heart attack. For the next several years I lived daily with wondering if this was the day I'd lose my daughter.

It came as a tremendous shock to discover among much other information about all sorts of conditions – as I had never come across the phrase 'an eating disorder', I searched far and wide – books devoted to the idea that all parents are to blame for their children's emotional problems. Autism? = 'frigidaire parenting'. Mental illness? = abuse (mostly unspecified) in the family. Anorexia nervosa? = sexual abuse, probably in the family (Jay & Doganis, 1987). And again like many other parents I've spent hundreds of painful hours going over all aspects of my children's upbringing to try to identify what I could possibly have done to inflict such suffering on my child, or perhaps not done to prepare her adequately for the extremely stressful experiences which triggered her illness.

My family, past and present – not perfect. Is it possible for *any* family, given its kaleidoscope of individual members, to function perfectly at all times? At just what point does an individual, or a family, become 'dysfunctional'?

Job description for a perfect family

Either alone or as a group, design a job description for a perfect family. You might like to think about the following:

1 *Knowledge* of childhood milestones needed?

2 *Nurture*

- How best to support healthy development physically?
- How best to support healthy emotional development?
- How best to educate a child?
- How best to encourage a child's strengths?
- What if anything could or should be done to identify difficulties, physical, learning or emotional?
- How best to support and encourage a child in weaknesses?
- What limits/rules/boundaries should be set?
- How best to set boundaries during early childhood?

- How best to set boundaries during puberty and adolescence?
- How best to encourage responsibility towards others?
- How best to encourage responsible financial management?
- How best to prepare a child for the world they will meet beyond the doors of home?
- Other?

3 *Preparation for life* in the future: What skills will they need?

4 *What qualities* do you think are needed to properly nurture a healthy child into adulthood? How important are these qualities? What are the consequences of lack of these qualities?

Perhaps ability to provide financial support or patience or organisational skills appear, among others, on your list? Are there any limits to the extent to which a parent can or should show, say, patience? What would happen if someone had absolutely limitless patience? Limitless tolerance? Or none at all?

What could or should be done when a parent does not possess a quality you feel is crucial to healthy development?

Can one parent offer qualities to balance the shortcomings of their partner? How could this be done? Identify a possible shortcoming and think how this could be balanced and by whom.

Are there any circumstances where shortcoming(s) might be detrimental to a child's health? What might be done to mitigate the effects of these shortcomings? And how?

Any other issues you feel important for this perfect family job description?

Preparation for caring role

> Even though we had professional expertise, personal resourcefulness and knowledge of community resources, we were not able to cope very well. We felt ill prepared and inadequate for our hands-on caregiving roles. These experiences made us wonder about the fate of other family caregivers who did not have the same professional advantage we believed we had.
>
> [Dr Jack Nottingham, Psychology Professor, Georgia Southwestern College, USA, quoted in Carter (1994)]

Whatever the family circumstances, and whether or not 'prepared' in any way, professional, family and other carers working together as a supportive team will provide the best hope of most effective care for the vulnerable person at the centre of all efforts.

Questions

- At what point does an individual or family begin to struggle and then become 'dysfunctional'? Is it possible for a family to be 'functional' in every circumstance?

Every family functions differently in good times and bad. Chapter 2 gives an outline of how several families currently cope with adversity involving challenging conditions and behaviours.

CHAPTER TWO

Families coping

> To call anorexia nervosa an eating disorder is like calling cancer a cough. I've known carers bankrupt themselves financially, physically and emotionally in their efforts to provide support for their loved ones.
>
> [Professor Arthur Crisp, EDA Carers Conference, London, 2000]

For over five years I got up each day wondering if it was the day I'd lose my beloved Jay. Neither did I know what unpredictable behaviour might be triggered by, e.g. a curtain not pulled 'properly'. I felt ill with worry about possibly doing something which might make things worse. In common with many other parents, I now understood the saying 'out of my mind with worry'.

Nothing seemed to make any sense. The child I loved, had supported and brought up seemed to have vanished with Anorexia and Bulimia taking her place – very different characters who put the most relentlessly negative interpretation possible on anything and everything, and specialised in aggression and screaming over trivia (making coffee for her in the 'wrong' mug; mentioning that others in the family would like food left for breakfast).

Learning from other families

Working on both the local and national eating disorders helplines, I have talked to hundreds of parents and other carers, as well as at conferences and meetings. Further stories of people coping with eating disorders can be found in Smith (2004). One of the most common questions is: *Is it my/our fault? Is it because:*

- we moved several times because of my husband's job?
- we moved, he lost all his friends and he was bullied at school?
- we sent her to boarding school like our other children and she felt unwanted?
- we both worked and maybe she felt neglected?

- we somehow didn't set the right example?
- we were too strict?
- we were too lax?
- we expected too much because she was oldest in the family?
- we spoiled her a bit because she was much younger than our other children – she got things the others didn't?
- we sent him to a school he hated?
- maybe we didn't talk enough about things?
- our neighbour, whom we'd known for years, came to babysit and sexually abused our daughter. If only we hadn't gone out that night.

Whatever their circumstances, whatever the strengths and weaknesses within any family, when coping in adversity common themes appear.

> I do not think it would have mattered what took my daughter's life – I would have felt guilt over not being able to protect her or to save her. I think it's almost a mother's instinct. I have now met many mothers who have lost children for all sorts of reasons (some illness, some accidents, some murder, some suicide); not one of them has been spared the relentless guilt that comes with the loss of a child.
>
> (Smeltzer, 2006)

> Parents do not need to be blamed; they do a very good job of this themselves.
>
> [Kay Gavan, social worker (now retired) attached to Eating Disorders Unit, Maudsley Hospital, London]

> Relationships with parents may be part of the problem; they are also part of the solution.
>
> [Janet Treasure, Professor of Eating Disorders, Guys Hospital, London]

Family interviews, January–September 2006

Each family interviewed was coping with very different circumstances, different illnesses/conditions/disorders, and individuals coped in different ways. All faced extremely challenging situations. Some details and names have been changed.

Andy and Bea's story

Andy and Bea have three children, two daughters – Corrie and Cat – and son Dave, all teenagers. The whole family was present.

Andy: Going through my son's illness has made us much stronger as a family, the experience has brought us much closer. Before Dave's illness we were just an ordinary family with ordinary problems, going along sort of in parallel lines – doing all our own things, work and school and stuff, and we just sort of made assumptions about knowing what others in the family were thinking and their intentions. I think lots of families operate like that most of the time, it's only when something big hits that you really have to work together as a team. And we were hit by this monster of an illness when Dave was diagnosed with anorexia nervosa.

We did lots of family things before, but when Dave was really really ill it was so much more important to talk properly. When he was ill there was much more need to *say* things, actually say the words, not just assume everyone knew what we meant.

For instance, I've always been so proud of all the kids but then Dave said to me 'You see me as a trophy.' He saw it as love only if he achieved, where I thought they all knew how much I loved them, including Dave, whatever happened. But I hadn't said it in those words, I had to say the words. We've more empathy for each other now, more understanding, less naïve now, much more connected.

Communication never ever broke down completely, but it wasn't like that at first – at first we disagreed about how to tackle things. I didn't understand at first just how strong the compulsion to starve was, so strong.

Dave: Like torture.

Andy: I had to learn that trying to argue him out of it, and losing my temper, wasn't doing any good at all; achieving nothing. There's no point in trying to reason. At first the doctor thought Dave was complying with what she wanted him to do – no exercise and put on weight. But he wasn't making any headway, still losing weight because he was exercising constantly. Then she made a strict timetable – he had to take meal supplements, increase the amount . . . one a day every day by Saturday, two a day by Tuesday and so on.

It was really good that the doctor explained that below a certain weight there's a 'biological depression' and getting Dave's weight above that line was like magic. With the depression his behaviour was beyond reason and he wasn't rational. No-one warned us about the roaring like a lion because he was so frustrated and confused after eating – he knew he had to eat, but didn't want to because of the illness. Sometimes it went on for over an hour, solid . . . it was really frightening when he roared, the girls were absolutely terrified, and we worried that he might burst a blood vessel. Then when he got up to the optimum weight, the depression lifted and he was instantly much better and not anxious in the same way.

Dave: It was sort of communicating how difficult it was, explain without words. If I didn't roar I'd bang my head against the wall.

Andy: Maybe other people might scream, something to release the awful tension. It expresses terrible pain. The doctors should warn about that sort of communication, even the possibility of communication like that, it was really frightening and totally unexpected . . . and tell you that until you see the monster, you're not challenging the illness. If you don't challenge the behaviour, the monster, it's like a tape winding on, winding on – and the illness gets stronger and more comfortable. You have to actively challenge – 'energetic action'. It's no good just hoping it'll all go away, you need total active care 24 hours every day. It's very very draining, total active care. It was like going along a dark corridor, no idea where we were going or what might happen.

We had to work as a family team – the whole family knew The Plan, we discussed it together and how it was working, how we felt. Supported each other, we were very focused and that made all the difference.

Dave: You won't get better on your own. It's like a crutch, you become comfortable with false comfort. I was lucky to have such a family. And lots of friends too, they all helped me. Overall they were really dependable, wanted to help. Sufferers want to get better but they need help, can't do it on their own.

Andy: Active support . . . I took time off work for a while to support Bea – we weren't sleeping much at all, and Bea was trying to cope on her own at home during the day. Not enough just to 'be there'. If two or more in the family can work together properly, much better. If people can't work together or don't know what to do, it could make the illness worse. And you should never argue about differences in front of the sufferer – if you disagree with what someone has done or said, you wait to talk about it later, don't say anything at the time.

Dave: If you have trouble convincing someone what to do, what they have to do for the best, talk to them. Be friends. If you want to communicate, try to relate, try to understand. Don't always talk about food, talk at the right level for them.

Andy: A support structure is essential, all the time every day. The doctor was very helpful but was only there one hour a week. Tell all the people who need to know – friends and family. And the school . . . Dave was off school for 54 half days over a 6–7 week period, as needed. It's important to keep people informed – they all wanted to help, we were very lucky. And you have to give the message, 'We know you can do this!' – body language as well as the words to show you're confident of success.

One really helpful thing was when we needed distraction – you can't fight the monster every minute – we found *Buffy the Vampire Slayer* and we all watched it. We all shared it and that meant more structure which made it all easier. In *Buffy*, they're all individuals, all got issues, all fighting vampires. One was a demon, taking vengeance. In *Buffy* the antidote to the evil demon is Love – the force fighting the demon must be stronger than the illness.

And *Finding Nemo* – Nemo's father said not to swim over the edge, Nemo did and was caught. Nemo's father and his friend never ever gave up – and Nemo had to play his part too.

We used Buffy and Nemo to discuss all sorts of issues, and that made opportunities for other discussions too.

The best chance is a concerted effort. For parents, take time off if needed, either annual leave or unpaid leave. You must believe that the problem can be resolved, and that family can help and support the patient. Encourage teamwork. *Be honest, always, that's really important.* That's important in the family, and for professionals. Especially if there's a high risk of something, like suicide. Parents need to know what to expect, what might happen, what might help.

It would have helped if we'd had more information at the beginning, with simple explanations, straightforward. And about treatment, and why particular approaches were used – or not. For instance, antidepressants don't usually work with biological depression because of low weight; and about expressing pain through roaring, or screaming or self-harm in some way.

Once we had relevant information we could ask relevant questions . . . people need information, books, professionals to help. And ongoing support, suggest strategies which could be tried. When he saw we were flagging, Dave said to phone the doctor . . . Maybe older patients wouldn't be so open, might hide more.

Bea: It was very hard to try to support the girls, very difficult when we were focused on fighting the anorexia monster. And exhausted. We didn't know at first that Corrie was being bullied at school, she had a really terrible time with some girls.

Corrie: They used to be my friends, but what they did said more about them than it did about me. I had to challenge them, and I did. We're not friends now, I know who my real friends are.

Andy: I think things could have been so different. If Dave had been admitted and force fed. If there had been no communication, there would have been no development of support strategies at home in the family. It would have been almost impossible to know how to support him or what to do. Or not to do. If he'd been in hospital then discharged, we wouldn't have known what to do at all, I've heard of families like that and then the sufferer relapses.

Never want to go through it again, but we've come through. We're much stronger as a family now, more connected.

What would you to say to others in a similar situation?

Andy: Love is active, not passive.

Share information.

Teamwork, understand The Plan.

Think of strategies.

Trust and hope.

Time and effort.

Keep it simple, straightforward, honest, loving, firm – and never lose your temper.

Take a breather if and when you need it.

Sheila's story

Sheila is married with a daughter N, 18, and son C, who is 13.

Sheila: I knew C was different early on, when he was still a baby. I was a childminder, and had lots of experience with young children. Sometimes he bashed his head on concrete, and he hated being contained in any way – cot, room, bed. He didn't like being touched or cuddled. Hated having his hair washed, anything on his head even when it was freezing outside; hated anything tight round his waist. He went into screaming fits about all those things although it took me ages to work out what was the problem. He does like things round his neck, and certain materials. By the time he was three when he went to nursery he seemed much worse.

When he went to school he was sometimes very disruptive in class – he couldn't concentrate. He had ear problems too which didn't help. At school he did try hard, and he wasn't as bad as at home – he was a real 'firecracker' at home! When I went and asked for help, I was just brushed off, not taken on board at all. Often he could be fine, his behaviour was fine short term, polite and everything for a short time, he did try really hard but then something would upset him and he would be screaming again. Nobody took me seriously, no-one saw the reality at home.

Then when C was seven, he was often almost uncontrollable, really strong. One night he tried to climb out of an upstairs window. I called the emergency services. I felt I just couldn't cope any more. Then I got an appointment. But no-one could give a diagnosis, and without a diagnosis – a 'label' – there's no help and no support. Many and various suggestions were made but no diagnosis. C was seen by lots of people, there was no continuity. Every time we saw someone different, we'd go through the same story, again and again and again, never got anywhere. Then eventually a speech therapist suggested he be seen by an occupational therapist . . . who suggested dyspraxia . . . and obsessive compulsive disorder . . . ADHD . . . and Tourette's.

That's when the consultants began to take me seriously. And I've a friend who's had family experience of Asperger's syndrome, and thought some of C's behaviour could be similar. But when I mentioned this, I was told 'Don't be silly!'

This was when C was given a prescription for melatonin to help him sleep, and this really helped – and we got to sleep too. It's always the same, as soon as they feel we're coping, the consultant discharges us – to go on to the next on the waiting list – and that's that. Often it's the end of support. And sometimes things are forgotten or overlooked – when the consultant discharged C, he forgot to inform our GP that the prescription for melatonin needs to be continued. Back to square one, more appointments. Hope that'll be sorted out soon.

I was always hoping for help, but it took so long, so long to get into the system. Over all the years, we've seen social workers, doctors, consultants, you name it. And it's exhausting, really exhausting, not just coping with C but trying to get help for him, proper help.

C worries a lot, often very anxious – he was in primary 5, just nine, when he started worrying about going to secondary school. Started worrying two whole years before he actually went to secondary school.

There are lots of problems at school, always have been. Often new teachers, and specially relief teachers, aren't told about C's problems and there's no understanding let alone sympathy. His problems are just not taken on board. In primary school he was recognised with high intelligence so he wasn't given any help, not any special educational needs input. He's very eager to answer because often he knows an answer, but teachers got fed up of him. He got into a lot of trouble because of answering too soon in class, and other behaviours.

When C's nervous his tics get worse, everything gets worse. Once in primary 7, he was rubbing his lips, and the teacher shouted at him about 'not rubbing his snot all over'. All the other kids thought it hilarious, and wound him up even more.

It's been much better in secondary school, there's a guidance teacher who sees him regularly, who knows him and he can talk to her. He was given three extra days of induction at the beginning to help him get used to the new situation and feel safe. And there's a support assistant to remind everyone to get on with their work.

For a whole year he was given a support worker. Once a week he talked to her, she helped C realise how to cope in different situations. That's the only year he's come home from school smiling, with a smile and in a good mood. But others were needing help and it couldn't continue. For a while he went to see someone at the Lowitt Unit and they helped too. But that stopped for the same reason too.

'Open space' environments – PE, technical or science for instance – are difficult for C. Other kids often wind him up deliberately just to get a reaction. And get him into trouble. For instance, try to burn him with a Bunsen burner. All because he's 'different.'

If life is difficult and stressful for C, at school or outside with his friends and others maybe in the playground people sometimes like to wind him up just to get a reaction – he tries hard to control his behaviour outside. Anyway, if life is difficult outside, there'll be massive explosions at home. C calls them 'mentallers', he says he has 'mentallers'.

C is very exact, very truthful. When he's under stress, his tics get worse – swearing, rubbing, whooping noises. Any changes cause him stress – changing activities, changing class, changing teachers, changing situations, teasing – some kids are relentless, think it's funny to get a reaction. Often now he can cope, can be self controlled. Then explode again at home.

What helped?

The speech therapist who was interested and first suggested practical things which eventually led to proper diagnosis. She listened, really listened. And we've had more help from the friend I mentioned who has family experience of Asperger's and could suggest things, than from anyone else.

And the practical help that was offered:

- 'Social skills' class.

- Trying the prescription to help C sleep which helped us cope better too.
- Support worker for C to talk to about particular situations.
- When practical strategies were suggested to try.
- Talking to friends, especially my friend whose son has Asperger's; she gave up her job as a social worker to care for him.
- Good communication when we met it – when people actually sat and listened to what we were saying. It was only when C was older, when he'd communication skills to explain and discuss his problems – he's very articulate – that people began to see the real problems. Before that, often they were trying to identify what this couple had done to *cause* the problems. They often talked only to us, the couple, rarely looked at or talked to the unhappy child in the middle, C.
- When it was realised that this couple – us – were doing their best in difficult circumstances, that we were honest and open about my husband's drinking problems and his ongoing long-term battle to beat it (mostly winning now!) that's when things changed, when they realised that. And by then C was old enough to articulate his problems and frustrations.
- Honesty and openness about resources and help/no help available.

What didn't help?

- Bad communications.
- The long wait to be seen on yet another waiting list.
- Some professionals we saw gave the impression of clock watching, must be difficult when they see an endless stream of people with problems.
- Some people just didn't seem interested in C, only talked to us.
- Feeling that those same people were just interested in trying to identify what this couple – we – had done to *cause* the problems.
- Saying 'This child is traumatised' and then look no further or suggest anything.

- Years were wasted on 'Blame the parents.'
- Feeling we were 'under a microscope'.
- Not being taken seriously.
- No coordination or continuity.
- Finally when C gets help, it's a case of as soon as he's coping, Off You Go. Same for families – 'Can do no more for you. Discharge.'
- No respite, exhaustion.

What would you say to others in similar situations?

Communication is the key.

Family–Family communication. (Sometimes children see mothers are there to teach, train, guide, discipline. And they often idealise fathers who aren't always there so much, because of work and so on.)

Family–Professional

Professional–Patient/client/pupil

Professional–Family

Professional(s)–Professional(s)

Change and stress is often the problem, causes the problem behaviour. I'm already wondering about the change from Young Person's Dept to officially Adult.

What would you say to other parents?

1 Don't give up.

2 No matter what you feel about the behaviour, keep on loving your child, he or she needs you.

3 Challenge the behaviour:

- Explain.
- Three warnings, then . . .
- Keep your word.
- Talk about consequences.
- Try to calm him down.
- Cope with the fallout – when he's mad at me for challenging his behaviour, the three warnings etc, my son will spend at least half an hour banging walls, doors, head. Be prepared for it.
- Don't take it personally, no matter what he says, such as 'I don't need you'. Or whatever.
- Listen, observe, discuss, work out what helps.
- No collusion with behaviour, no letting off with unacceptable behaviour – letting him off will do him no good in the outside world.

What would you say to professionals?

- Listen. Just listen. Really listen.
- Honest communication.
- Focus on child and observe in different circumstances.
- Look at the whole picture, and long term.
- Offer practical suggestions and strategies which might help in situation, age appropriate.

I don't know how I survived. Often thought about running away but nowhere to run to. Even thought of disappearing, but what would have happened to C, and the rest of my family too?

Alan and Joan's story

Alan: We adopted our son Peter 10 years ago when he was four. We realised very quickly he had great needs. It's been a *long* journey – we feel we've achieved a lot. But it's been a major battle to find the right care for our son.

We were given very little background information, about what had happened to Peter before he came to us – and what we were told turned out to be incomplete and distorted. For instance, we weren't told about the concerns of those who were looking after our son before we adopted him.

It took a long time for us to find any help and for Peter's problems to be recognised. Reactive attachment disorder is often confused with ADHD – often 'wild', out of control, hyperactive behaviour. We now know that the core problem in this condition is that children who have been physically, mentally or sexually abused experience trauma which has very long-lasting emotional effects on behaviour – lack of trust in adults, resulting in resistance to bonding, closeness and affection. The closer the relationship, the more the resistance.

Our daughter was born about a year and a half after we adopted Peter. Mairi has never known life without Peter as part of our family.

Joan: At first no-one seemed to believe us when we tried to explain what was happening at home. When we saw a social worker – this happened over and over again, with various professionals – we were told to 'Look at your parenting skills'. And given books and leaflets about child development – *normal* child development, no mention anywhere of what we were experiencing every day. Including anal masturbation, smearing faeces which is a health and hygiene risk.

Alan: Not surprising it's confused with ADHD, and often there's a split between behaviour at home and other places. Peter behaves very differently in different circumstances. So this led to disbelief and sometimes dismissal by professionals who only saw behaviour outside the home.

Joan: Social workers appeared very judgemental of our parenting skills, we often felt all our efforts were belittled. Didn't do our self-esteem any good, that was often shredded.

Alan: And behaviour we described was often minimised by professionals.

When Peter sexually abused Mairi, the social worker's reaction was 'It's just natural experimentation, don't get so uptight about it!' When I expressed my concern re my daughter's safety after sexual abuse, a play therapist we saw told me to 'examine my attachment to my adopted son'.

The only person who really believed us and tried to help, because she's known the whole family well for years, was our GP.

Joan: Mairi has been very badly affected. I think she's afraid that if she doesn't please us or is naughty she might be sent away 'because bad children are sent away.'

Alan: Peter's been in residential care for about four years now. For about 18 months before that, we had to physically restrain him as he tried to climb out of windows on the 1st floor. At that time, he was self-harming, and masturbating in front of Mairi.

Joan: The first help was from our GP, she knew us all – she put the whole picture together, and believed us when we told her what was happening. And about what happened when Peter abused our daughter sexually. She said we must protect our daughter, be very vigilant.

Alan: The social work department assumed we were the problem, so we were sent to a child psychiatrist. After about 9 months, the psychiatrist asked to see our son. After assessment, we were told Peter needed intensive therapy, at least three times a week – and that that just wasn't available. As an experienced psychiatrist, she said Peter 'was one of the most damaged children she'd ever encountered. Only intensive therapeutic environment could give him any hope.' The best she could offer was specialist help in a department over a hundred miles away, and asked us to take Peter there twice a week.

The social work department resisted the idea of specialist residential care. They were very dismissive of the child psychiatrist's report, suggested interim care provision which we felt was completely inappropriate. He needed specialist care which we recognised we couldn't provide for him, and which wouldn't be provided by 'interim general care'.

Joan: When we asked about our son's background, we were told no records were passed on. Eventually we threatened court action. Then we were told the files were lost. And then that they were found. We discovered that concerns were expressed by the police, about when our son was injured before he was two. The social workers had told us that both injuries were unfortunate accidents. We also found out that after both these injuries Peter had been abandoned in hospital.

Alan: And later that a play worker was concerned that – if Peter was placed for adoption – he might 'act out' the abuse he'd been subjected to. We discovered that Peter's birth mother was a prostitute living in one room with several children . . . and clients visiting may have had access to the children. We understand that all Peter's siblings . . . their care placements have also broken down.

Eventually after Peter was diagnosed, we offered SW reading material about such problems in children. The social worker said 'I don't have time to read such books or to attend specialist courses.'

We feel there are no proper resources, huge lack of time, no proper training for the professionals who have seen us, they're just not equipped either in knowledge of problems or to advise.

Communication is the main problem . . . When we agreed to be interviewed we made a list.

What was unhelpful?

- People not listening properly!
- Not being believed when we described what we were living and coping with.
- Control through power but no basic respect.
- Meetings when decisions were being taken about our son, discussing his future, but we weren't allowed to be part of them – for one instance, there was a discussion between Social Work and a child psychiatrist, leaving me sitting two hours outside the room. As adoptive parents, we have full parental rights and should be involved in decisions.
- Phone calls (e.g. at 7.15 a.m. or in evening) to discuss our son when he is there and listening, also my daughter is there.
- When arrangements are changed/cancelled, statements 'I have a *real* emergency on my hands' – therefore Peter feels he is not important. He just lost trust in them.
- Some of the things said to us: 'If you really tried a bit harder . . .' 'I am a mother, therefore I know what your child needs.' 'I thought you were good parents. Now I see.'
- Sloppy record keeping, no minutes of meetings.
- No feeling of any compassion for what we were coping with, or any attempt at understanding.
- Only seemed to believe us when a professional carer reported the same behaviour we'd been coping with for years.

Joan: Over the years I've found coping with the social work department as well as Peter's behaviour, increasingly difficult, and my husband has become their main point of contact for our family. There seem to be quicker results if the father comes along to meetings as well.

When we say it's really hard to cope, we're exhausted with the struggle, they seem to hear something different – as if they hear we don't care.

When I was desperately asking for help, once the response was 'Well, you adopted a damaged child.'

What did you find helpful?

Joan: We've met a few real Angels along the way – who said they recognise the difference we have made to our son's life by trying to find the right care for him, also how hard it is to accept he needs more than we can give.

A few words of encouragement meant so much: 'You've come a long way.' 'Tell us about it – what are you coping with?' 'What can we do to help you?'

'I'll write the report and let you see what I've written.' – this meant no secrecy, accuracy checked, no feeling of Them and Us.

Not *showing* revulsion at behaviour, a matter-of-fact reaction – that made such a difference.

Recognition of how difficult it is to cope with it at home with difficult behaviour towards us and Mairi.

What would you say to professionals?

- *Listen*!
- Treat with respect another human being who has problems.
- Think how you might cope in same situation.
- Try to show interest in the individuals; how they are coping; and compassion.
- Don't act as if professionals know it all – they only know a little bit of the picture.

- Say you will support in any way you can.
- Ask what parents feel they need/how you might be able to help.
- Look for useful and practical resources in *actual* situation.
- Look for appropriate training/ideas/suggestions from other professionals.
- Offer to share minutes etc with parents, so there's no feeling of secrets.
- Meetings/communications with professionals – not at home, possibly at parents' work places? And time-limited, outwith child's hearing.
- *Resources are needed for professionals, including time, and appropriate training. Resources or rather lack of them, are a major problem.*

Alan: The dilemma of people in our situation . . . continue with care and risk the wellbeing of other children and marriage relationship? Or give up and live with guilt that you've rejected a child who has already suffered dreadfully, been removed from birth parents or been given up by them, had to cope with many major changes in life and no control or choice in any of it?

Joan: Or recognise and accept that no matter how we try to provide for our son, we don't have the resources to give him the specialist care he needs? And then find the best provision possible for those needs?

Many adoptions break down – one estimate is up to 20%. Risk factors are: older child; institutionalization; history of emotional/behavioural difficulties; history of abuse/neglect. (Source: Adoption UK)

Many marriages disintegrate under pressure from difficult behaviour, different views of how to cope/what to do in specific situations.

Young carers and siblings

Given the numbers of people of all ages struggling with all sorts of conditions which involve 'challenging behaviour', and living with family and other carers, inevitably the lives will be affected of huge numbers of siblings and 'young carers' (young carers are people under 16 who provide a substantial amount of care and support to another family member, who may be a parent, grandparent or sibling – in many cases, a young carer may be providing essential care in shopping, cooking, feeding, washing up, washing clothes, house-cleaning, planning all these).

Mairi's story

Mairi is 8. She lives with her parents and her brother Peter, 13, adopted a year before Mairi was born.

GS: Would you like to tell me a bit about your brother?

Mairi: My brother is sometimes a good brother and sometimes not. When he's a good brother he plays Monopoly, Pictionary and lots of other games. We have a celebration every year on the day he was adopted and that's good.

When he's not a good brother, he shouts at me and stops me doing things. I feel very upset when he says things in a not-nice voice. I do not trust him, I feel he doesn't like me. I'm afraid he might do something to me.

He might break things, he breaks things on purpose then tells lies, not the exact truth. In our house you have to replace things if you break them – he says it's an accident when it's not.

I asked mum if you would understand about my brother. People often don't understand so I don't talk about my brother and what he does.

It's better now I can use the new bathroom upstairs, I don't like the other bathroom because my brother uses it and he might put germs all over it. We've just got the upstairs bathroom, before that we all had to use the other one. It's better now I can use the new bathroom upstairs but sometimes if I just want to wash my hair quickly in the basin without using the shower, I have to use the one Peter still uses. And I worry about all the germs he puts all over it.

[Here Mairi hesitated for quite a while.]

He smears poo all over the middle bathroom, I don't want to use it because of the germs.

GS: Have you talked to anyone else about how you feel? Your teacher? Or the doctor? Or friends or anyone?

Mairi: No. No-one. If I talked to a teacher I'd have to go into the corridor and people might hear. They wouldn't understand. Nobody understands my brother or anything. I don't tell my friends or other children, they might call names. Then my brother would get angry and there would be more problems.

My brother is not allowed in the bathroom upstairs, it's the one I use and that makes it *much* better at home. So I don't worry.

He tried to hurt me. He used to nip me, and kick me, and try to push me down the stairs. I worry about that in case it happens again.

GS: What do you think would help?

Mairi: It would help for people who have difficult behaviour, if they could have special schools to help them and care for them.

GS: Do you think it is more difficult for families if someone has difficult behaviour?

Mairi: I don't think, *I know!* Very difficult. The bathroom. Not trusting. Worrying. Much much much more difficult.

It would help if people understood more. If other boys and girls could understand. Talk to them. If it helped, tell them what happens and how to help.

It's difficult travelling in the car all the time. Really difficult when we were taking my brother to school, hours and hours in the car to take him there, hundreds of miles every week. I was often car-sick. And I had no-one to talk to. Sometimes Mum or Dad had to go in the back to help with my brother's behaviour. Very squeezy-squeezy with him and me and Mum or Dad as well in the back.

GS: Do you think he knows and understands that he hurts and upsets you?

Mairi: I think he does. Sometimes I think in a way he can't help it – instead of paying attention to the voice in your head saying '*no*', he just does.

His new school is helping though, he's much much better since he started there. That helped.

GS: How do you think your life would be different if Peter didn't have problems?

Mairi: He would live Monday Tuesday Wednesday Thursday Friday Saturday and Sunday with us all the time.

When I was little Mum made up songs to help me get to sleep. I was really scared of the noise when Peter was screaming and I couldn't get to sleep. Sometimes he screamed for a long time.

Sometimes Mum and Dad both had to go to meetings. Meetings and meetings and meetings about Peter. So I had to have other people to look after me lots of times. Sometimes I was scared and didn't want to be left. I wanted Mum or Dad to stay with me instead of go to another meeting.

Joan (Mum): When we lived in the flat, when Mairi was small, Peter used to scream at bedtime all the time, every day, and at other times too. We shared our bedroom with Mairi, Peter had the other bedroom. There was no room to play in our room because of the beds, our bed and Mairi's. When she was small, there was often screaming in the background – it was nothing unusual. Sometimes for hours. When Peter went to the residential school, we thought Mairi would move into

Peter's room so she could have more space to play. But she wouldn't even go in, ever, without one of us with her.

Mairi: I felt it was dangerous to go in. I was scared. I'm not allowed to be alone with my brother. In case he hurts me again like he did when I was little. Mum and Dad are always near, unless we go outside – once he helped me make a huge massive snowman, that was good.

I can go into his room now, I'm not scared really now.

GS: You must have been happy to move into your new home?

Mairi: Very happy. I have a room of my own, and I got to choose the wallpaper. The old wallpaper hurt my eyes. It's changed to flowers and hearts on it now. This flat is much bigger, with an upstairs. And we have a bathroom upstairs too.

GS: How does your life change when Peter comes home?

[Mairi didn't answer.]

Joan: This is the first time Mairi has ever talked to anyone else about life with Peter.

GS: Would it help if you could talk to other people about how it feels to have a brother like Peter?

Mairi: Yes! I'd like to talk to friends, tell them how it is but even my best friend wouldn't really understand.

Amy's story

Amy, 9, has two brothers with autism.

Amy: One of my brothers, he copies actions and things he sees on DVDs and sometimes that's difficult. And when he's stressed or frustrated, he screams and screams and screams and then everyone feels stressed. And the neighbours complain, some of them moved somewhere else.

GS: What helps?

Amy: We get lots of carers to help. Different ones all the time. And Young Carers. They listen, really listen and they try to help us.

Hannah's story

Hannah, 12, lives with her mother who is disabled.

> *Hannah:* I do the housework, and the shopping and cooking and everything. I manage it. I don't like to go out too much, because I worry about my mum. In case something happens. When my mum gets stressed she forgets things, and she starts to clean and gets really exhausted, then I get stressed and we argue. Sometimes my older brothers and sisters visit but they don't help much.
>
> *GS*: What helps?
>
> *Hannah:* Young Carers – they really listen and help.

Lisa's story

Lisa's sister is disabled and has special educational needs.

> *GS*: What helps?
>
> *Lisa:* It doesn't help when the teachers don't understand when I'm tired and I can't concentrate! Young Carers – really help because they listen.

Pop Idol's story

'Pop Idol', age 12, lives with his mother.

> *Pop Idol*: My mum has depression, and schizophrenia, and a personality disorder.
>
> *GS*: How do you know all that?
>
> *Pop Idol*: Because I listen to what they say. Grownups think I don't understand but I do. I pieced it all together like a sort of jigsaw so I can understand. No-one has told me properly apart from depression. I have a social worker but they don't listen, and they don't understand properly and don't explain.
>
> *GS*: What do you find most difficult?

Pop Idol: It's really hard at school because when mum doesn't sleep it keeps me awake and I'm tired. My mum needs to keep busy and since she hasn't been working any more she doesn't sleep, her sleep patterns are all mixed up. It would be much easier if she got another job. Our car was stolen so now she can't get to her job.

It's really complicated because of mum's boyfriends. One of them made death threats and that was scary. I have high anxiety and stuff. One of them just moved out and now my little brother goes to stay with him sometimes – I don't get to go because he's not my dad. That's how I found out that he's not my dad, I've just found that out. I thought he was my dad.

GS: What helps?

Pop Idol: Maybe it'll help when we move. And sometimes I go to stay with my grandma for a sleepover, that helps. She comes to pick me up. And coming to Young Carers group helps, they listen and help.

Listening and being believed were common themes running throughout every interview – how much it meant to feel really listened to, the frustration when not.

A final word for all professionals:

Carers really need three things:
Listen with empathy and kindness and try to help.
Acknowledge what carers cope with.
Don't promise what you can't deliver.

[Mary Drever (social worker) and Angie Taylor (psychologist), Aberdeen Young Carers Project.]

CHAPTER THREE

Back to basics

The beginning of wisdom is silence; the second is listening. Listening is more than hearing.

[Unknown ancient sage]

Sensitive listening skills are rare.

(Burns, 1999)

Communication, most particularly listening or lack of it, has been a recurring theme throughout all the interviews, letters and emails involved in this book project.

Most human beings begin to talk at an early age. Usually babies, after discovering that they have a voice and hear others talking, try out sounds; a baby sometimes sounds as if s/he is having a long conversation with all sorts of inflections long before they can understand or form words. Then come single words, usually nouns such as mumumum or dadada, later come short sentences and then they're off.

And most human beings – of whatever age, in whatever situation – assume that because they can talk, they can communicate with everyone around them. They assume that what *they* think and feel is shared by others, that they immediately understand what others mean. Here is where the real skill in human communication begins, and some people are much better at it than others. And here is the root cause of so many misunderstandings and so much puzzlement. Even the use of pauses or silence, a slight change of expression or gesture, can communicate.

Many years ago Paul Watzlawick and his colleagues identified some basic axioms necessary to effective communication Watzlawick, 1978, 1983; Watzlawick *et al.*, 1967):

- *Every behaviour is a kind of communication.*
- *One cannot* not *communicate.*
- *Communication does not involve merely spoken words.* Think not only of words – observe and consider your own and others' facial expressions, body language, hand gestures, touch, tone of voice, closeness of space between people, small encouragement noises: mmmm, uhuh? Frowning? Smiling and relaxed? Eyebrows raised, eyes wide? Stony silence or warm? Pause:

thoughtful, quizzical or critical? Door slamming? Playing the martyr? Touch on shoulder or hand? Stiff body or relaxed and easy? Warm and interested or critical, rude, sarcastic, e.g. 'Oh, I'm selfish, am I?'

- *Both talker and receiver of information structure the communication flow differently*, and therefore interpret their own behaviour during communicating as merely a reaction to the other's behaviour (i.e. each partner thinks the other the cause of a specific behaviour).
- *Inter-human communication procedures are either symmetric or complementary*, depending on whether the relationship of the partners is based on difference or parity.

People with good communication skills tend to assume everyone else also has good communication – they check how people feel, they accept that they make mistakes (everyone does), they try to keep an open mind and seek out new ideas. People with good communication skills look for ways to further improve their understanding of how others feel, and what they really mean by their words.

People with poor communication skills don't see a problem, never check out how anyone else really feels, and sail through life assuming they understand how others feel – other people feel the same as they do, see the same things they do, think the world should agree with them.

To listen is to concentrate on hearing something: to take heed; pay attention. *I told you many times but you wouldn't listen.*

People with outstanding, good, adequate or poor communication skills can be found in *all* walks of life; can be carers or professionals in any field of work (sometimes both simultaneously).

> Responding with empathy is especially difficult when you feel frustrated and upset, and when you feel criticised or not listened to.
>
> The three listening skills – disarming, empathy, inquiry – capture the essence of effective listening. These skills are frequently overlooked, even by professionals whose very work demands expert communication.
>
> (Burns, 1999)

Undertaking this project has led to an evaluation of my own communication skills. As a teacher I was highly trained to teach the primary curriculum, *yet had no actual basic training in communication skills* – the teaching of language, yes, but not in human interaction.

> This is equally true of professionals – teachers, social workers, doctors, nurses – who need training to really listen properly to clients, to distressed and exhausted family members in fraught situations. (Rachel, special educational needs teacher)

The basics of good communication remain the same whatever the situation, whoever is involved. Without these, whether the conversation is in a formal situation or informal, at work in a meeting or conference setting, poor communication will lead to misunderstandings, which contributes to all relationships causing difficulties for any of the communicators.

Elements of poor communication

- *Talking at rather than to* the other person.
- *Assuming you are right* without listening to or considering discussion or others' experience.
- *Insisting you are right* and the other person is wrong.
- *Assuming blame*: it's the other person's fault.
- *Martyrdom*: you're the innocent victim.
- *Put down*: you imply the other person is a loser because he 'always' or 'never' does certain things.
- *Hopelessness*: you give up and insist that there is no point in trying.
- *Demanding*: you say you're entitled to better treatment, but don't explain what exactly would make things better for you.
- *Denial*: you insist you don't feel angry, sad, hurt, when you really do.
- Passive *aggression*: sulk or withdraw or say nothing.
- *Self-blame*: act as if an awful person instead of dealing with the problem.
- *Helping*: instead of hearing how depressed, hurt or upset the other is, you try to 'solve the problem', or 'help' him or her; don't encourage self reliance or solution seeking.
- *Sarcasm*: words or tone convey tension or hostility not openly acknowledged.
- *Scapegoating*: suggesting that other person has 'a problem' . . . and you're sane, happy or uninvolved.
- *Defensiveness*: refuse to admit any wrongdoing or imperfection.
- *Counterattack*: instead of acknowledging how the other feels, you respond by criticism.
- *Diversion*: instead of dealing with how you both feel in the here-and-now, you list grievances about past injustices.
- *The accusatory*: '*You* make me feel . . .' 'You never . . .' 'You shouldn't . . .'

- *Inflaming a difficult situation by fanning the flames into a real explosion:* shouting, face-to-face/toe-to-toe/nose-to-nose exchange, interrupting, finger pointing, teeth baring, fist clenching, threatening body language, public temper displays, bringing up past conflicts, not allowing others to talk about their own different views.
- *Tiredness and frustration* are major factors in making any conflict situation worse.

Good communication

Listening: it may be helpful to practise listening through exercises such as asking a colleague or family member to draw something you describe without naming what you are describing; gestures are not allowed.

Be conscious of your body language, facial expressions and so on and observe others' too.

Empathy – try to think how the other person feels.

Warmth and openness

- Checking out how the other feels.
- Agreeing to disagree.
- Expressing own feelings openly and respectfully.

Listening and empathy

- *Check that you have understood* – don't assume.
- *Clarification* at every step and stage is essential in all important conversations.
- *Reflect*: Am I right – is that the way you feel? Do you feel I've got that right?
- *'I feel' statements* are important: positive ('I am glad that . . .') and *most especially* when expressing negative feelings: 'I *feel* angry/criticised/put down/frustrated/misunderstood/vulnerable'; 'I *feel* sad/rejected/hurt/unloved/disappointed/ignored/inadequate/intimidated' (rather than the accusatory 'You make me feel . . .'); 'I guess you might be *feeling* frustrated with me right now, am I right?'; 'In your place I might *feel* . . . Is this the way you *feel*?'
- *Wishes and desires*: 'I'd like to spend more time with you, I want to work out this problem'; 'I really want you to keep this appointment/be on time'; 'I would like you to understand my point of view.'

- *Put yourself in the other person's shoes*: listen carefully and try to understand what they are thinking and feeling. State what you think the other person is thinking and feeling: 'It sounds like you feel . . .' Paraphrase.
- *Ask about a specific problem* and how they feel about it: ask for details, e.g. 'How often does it happen?' 'How do you feel when . . .?' 'What makes it worse or better?'
- *However, don't ask more than three or four questions in a row*, which can close down the speaker's exploration of feelings and valuable reflection on them.
- *Tone*: respectful, not challenging or critical.
- *Genuine respect* even if and when you don't agree or see things their way.
- *Be mindful of body language, your own and the other person's*: is it open and relaxed and attentive? Or showing boredom and inattention?
- *Use good eye contact* to show you are really listening.
- *Use attentive silence* to allow a speaker to reflect on thoughts and feelings.

Acronyms

Acronyms can be irritating, especially when others use them – and you aren't familiar with them! Using professional jargon while new staff members struggle to understand what's going on, or during a meeting and some there feel inadequate and patronised, is a particular bugbear for many.

However, remembering one or two acronyms can be useful when listening – OARS and LESS are just two in the world of building positive and constructive communication.

OARS

- ***O**pen questions* which require thought and explanation rather than a yes-or-no answer. (What do you feel is holding you back? How do you plan to set about this?)
- ***A**ffirmation*: stress any personal strengths and achievements. (It must have taken real guts to tackle that . . . It's great that you managed to . . .)
- ***R**eflective*: show your interest by saying what you understand the other to mean; if you've not got it quite right, this allows the other to clarify. (Am I right in thinking you . . . Sounds like you feel . . .)

- *Summarise* what has been said. Even if you get it all wrong, the opportunity to explain further helps the speaker to clarify for him/herself as well as you the listener.

LESS is more

- *Listen*: really concentrate on what is being said, as well as be aware of body language, facial expression and gestures.
- *Empathy*: focus on trying to understand the feeling and true meaning behind a person's words.
- *Share*: try to imagine how you might feel in a similar position.
- *Support*: by using *open questions and affirmation* (see OARS above) help the other person to explore fully the negatives and positives of the situation, the problem, their feelings, and any further action they might consider.

LESS focus on self and more on the other person. LESS time talking about ourselves and more listening to others.

VIEW

Use **V**ery **I**mportant **E**ncouraging **W**ords as often as possible, notice positive daily efforts, no matter how small, as often as possible, and remember to comment! In today's rushing world, it is all too easy to mention only what is irritating and annoying. ('Thank you for . . .' 'I noticed that you . . .' 'I like it when you . . .' 'You remembered to . . .' 'Great to know you . . . !')

Conflict and negotiating skills

Poor communication and lack of real listening skills may lead to conflict; sometimes conflict arrives unexpectedly and you just have to tackle it as best you may. Anger and conflict can be healthy – but unhealthy if not expressed, then it will become more intense. In either situation, poor communication will fan the flames in a deteriorating relationship.

In a conflict situation, it is not so easy to remain calm but assertive. In general.

- let others speak,
- keep hands relaxed,
- offer time-outs or an 'escape hatch',
- divert attention,
- offer choices,

- keep silent,
- refer to responsibilities as well as rights,
- use humour where possible and appropriate.

In any conflict situation where you have a choice.

- *Find a good time and place* to have a joint discussion when people are not tired or thinking about other matters.
- *Present the problem in as constructive a way as possible*: work out before what you want to say, the best way of saying it.
- *State your points and how you feel clearly.*
- *If you have a grievance, say it clearly* and how you feel. (*I feel . . .* rather than *You make me feel . . .*)
- *Listen* to what others want to say.
- *Acknowledge* that others may feel differently.
- *Check that you understand* what is being said by trying to summarise what the other has said.
- *Discuss what is different* about your positions.
- *Restate how you feel, if necessary.*
- *Look for solutions*: brainstorm. Discuss options.
- *Be prepared to compromise*: the issue is not about winning or losing. Try to find a compromise acceptable to both/all.
- *Use open questions*: How do you feel about . . . ?
- *Emphasise any common ground.*

Avoid

- *Ordering*: it will produce resentment, resistance and sabotage
- *Threatening*
- *Advice* ('You *should* do this')
- *Too much non-constructive reassurance, sympathy, consolation* (You poor thing)
- *Too many questions one after another*
- *Diverting or changing the subject*

- *Lecturing/logical argument*: stress, distress, intense emotion *don't* respond to logic.

Saints and angels

Only saints and angels never ever say the wrong thing, never ever wish they could replay a conversation. Very few saints or angels exist on Earth. Most people, including me, are simply human beings – or 'shuman beans' as a five-year-old once described them to me. When our 'shuman bean' qualities intrude, when things go wrong, all we can do is say 'Sorry, can we start again, talk it over? When would be a good time?' *And try to remember all the rules of good communication.*

There is more about communication in the chapters that follow.

CHAPTER FOUR

Consequences

Whatever the illness or problem, long-term and chronic, physical or emotional, all of these, there will be consequences in terms of lives.

> My daughter is now almost 30 and needs constant care. She's mostly incontinent and unable to dress or feed herself without help – I'm told she has a mental age of about two. Sometimes she gets very angry and frustrated and lashes out. As she's got older, and her dad died, I think her temper is worse.
>
> I do get some help, but it seems to get more and more difficult, there seems more and more to do. I'm getting older too, and what's going to happen when I'm not here? Apart from the careworker's visits no one comes now, I sometimes think I'm invisible.
>
> [P, mother of severely learning disabled girl]

Whatever their individual levels of good or poor communication, whether with or without solid information and support, with or without family and professional input, millions of family carers devote years of their lives, often putting aside their own to do so, to supporting their loved one.

In some families, more than one member needs special support. One year is 365 days; ten years is 3,650 days of coping in whatever circumstances, on good days, bad days and nightmarish days. This is love in action. Many give up their paid employment because of their home commitments – this will inevitably have financial consequences – and often struggle on through exhaustion and pain with little or no respite, sometimes to the point of collapse.

The level of coping in the family will be tested to its limits – stamina and strength as well as patience. While some carers actively seek out information and other support, others feel paralysed, powerless. As with everything else in life, there is no one answer to fit everyone.

> I've known carers bankrupt themselves financially, physically and emotionally in their efforts to provide support for their loved ones.
>
> [Professor Arthur Crisp, EDA Carers Conference, London, 2000]

As a headteacher I recognised that, given the right resources, physical and practical help was relatively simple to organise for various problems. But it was only rarely, despite regular meetings, that I felt I got an accurate glimpse of the real impact emotional or behavioural difficulties were having on the life of the child; even rarer were glimpses of the impact on other lives in the family. Parents might be defensive at meetings, or weep, or show anger – either about lack of resources, or perceived lack of sympathy for their plight, sometimes directed heatedly at whoever happened to be near.

But it was only much later as a parent and carer myself that I felt I had any real insight into their feelings of despair and helplessness, as well as grief for their child, and guilt at being unable to protect their loved one. And discovered first-hand the effects of living daily with all the associated feelings.

Consequences for the vulnerable individual

All actions big or small have consequences: breathe/stop breathing, stand, sit, run, walk, crawl, drink, eat, take, give, leave early or late, arrive early or late, travel, stay still, move, throw – every action leads to consequence of some sort. And learning about negative consequences of actions as well as positive is one of the most important lessons of childhood, and all through life. Watching a loved one of any age taking action – knowingly with understanding, even skewed understanding, or impulsively with none – which might lead to negative consequences, is one of the hardest parts of loving. Yet if or when someone is always completely protected from consequences, and *learning* from them, life – and possibly even survival – in the long term will not necessarily be enhanced. This is the dilemma many parents and other carers face when learning of an addiction and trying to decide on the best course of action.

In providing support for a troubled individual, the following aspects need to be taken into account in any assessment.

Physical health

1 *Are growth and development affected?* How does the individual's chronological age compare with mental age and development? These will be of particular concern where, for instance, a learning disability is recognised, or where the frequent regression of an eating disorder is present.

2 *Are there any likely effects*, either short or long term, on brain and organs, resulting from the individual's current problems? For instance, drugs, alcohol or an eating disorder will affect all these.

3 *Does the individual self-harm?* Some people, when feeling under stress, inflict injuries on themselves, sometimes dreadful injuries. In some cases this may involve cutting or scoring with nails or with a razor or other sharp implement, head banging until bruised and bleeding, tearing skin, biting, screaming, sometimes for hours on end.

4 *Are there any foods which trigger a negative reaction?* While diet obviously plays an important part in conditions connected with food, e.g. diabetes, diet is also an important factor in many individuals with challenging behaviour.

> I watched A, at the time a boy of seven whom I'd known well for about two years, change dramatically after having a snack at a party. Within about 15 minutes A changed from being his usual quiet and easy-going happy self to screaming, shouting, running wildly around the hall, hitting and kicking people. Anyone who tried to stop him was fought off with all his strength. When his mother arrived in response to an urgent phone call, she asked 'Has he been drinking orange juice?'
>
> [GS]

In conditions such as attention deficit hyperactive disorder (ADHD) it has been found that changing a child's diet sometimes alters behaviour too, leading to calmer behaviour and ability to concentrate.

Eating disorders such as anorexia and bulimia nervosa often have devastating physical as well as emotional consequences, e.g. mineral deficiencies and damage to body functioning, although 'It's not about food, it's about feelings' (Eating Disorders Association).

Emotional health

Frustration at the effects of their illness or disorder is often a factor in an individual's life as they become more and more aware of how a long-term condition changes many aspects of their lives. This can apply to people of any age and with a wide range of conditions including:

- learning disability
- attachment disorder (which can affect adopted or foster children as well as children who never leave their birth families, but – perhaps for medical reasons – are separated from their mothers after birth)
- an intelligent child with Asperger's syndrome
- disordered thinking due to mental illness
- other diagnosed or as-yet-undiagnosed conditions.

These individuals may not at first have an awareness of any effect of their behaviour on others, but gradually as they grow older they begin to realise that other people may avoid contact with them. The frustration, with its individual trigger perhaps involving noise, or personal contact, or dislike of particular foods or clothes, may be shown in many ways including explosions of temper, hitting and kicking and biting.

Stress and distress, whether articulated or not, leads to a flood of hormones throughout the body. Stress is a very individual affair – what stresses one person may be of little or no consequence to another, for instance G described how several sleepless nights followed a confrontation, while a colleague responded that he actively enjoyed the buzz of adrenaline a confrontation gave him – 'and I've never been bested yet!' he laughed. In each individual the response is different, with a list of Most Stressful Events including moving house, marriage, divorce, bereavement – *any* change may be experienced as stressful, even those which have a happy outcome, including getting married, moving to a better house or a promotion leading to greater responsibility.

Where a chronic condition is present, often any perceived stress – which may or may not be obvious to other people – will trigger a relapse into the challenging behaviour.

Mental disorders: with disordered thinking, in which the world seems to make no sense and is often perceived as extremely frustrating, an individual will try hard to make some sort of sense of experiences they cannot understand. Their 'making sense' may not make any sense to those around them, but given the distortion in their thinking processes it makes sense to themselves. Any particular stress or frustration, whether the perception of being thwarted or of not being able to articulate feelings or needs, will often lead to an outburst or relapse into unacceptable or inappropriate behaviour.

People with a learning disability may also be affected by any of the above. While great attention may be paid to obvious problems of motor disability or delayed development, it is often overlooked that the individual may also be suffering from depression or other emotional condition – but lack the language and verbal skills to talk about how they feel. This in itself leads to further frustration and more outbursts as the individual grows bigger and stronger.

Diagnosis

Diagnoses are great – but should be used with caution. While often being able to recognise a particular collection of symptoms as a particular illness, condition, disorder – or 'label' – means that an individual is assigned to the caseload of a particular department or professional and therefore may be offered help and treatment, there is also a danger that once a diagnosis is made and written into notes, all other investigation then ceases. Unfortunately for some individuals their problems are much more complex than one simple diagnosis; mental health problems does not mean there are no physical problems or illness, and physical illness – especially if chronic – may lead to depression, and certainly does not preclude mental health problems.

With much greater specialisation in today's medical world, it is quite possible for symptoms to be missed or ignored simply because a busy professional, no matter how caring, has no experience of them within their own specialism and therefore does not see them. Some individuals have very complex problems which fit no one specialism.

However, a diagnosis – almost any diagnosis – is often better than none. A diagnosis leads to assessment, often to being able to share information and coping strategies and support with others in a similar position, which can only lead to better care for the vulnerable individual.

Before diagnosis, an individual has to be referred, usually by a general practitioner.

> Without a diagnosis it's almost impossible to explain to teachers about my son's problems, and other children wind him up deliberately to try to get a reaction and get him into trouble – they think that's fun, don't understand his behaviour is because of his problems. When he is stressed he has tics, swearing, whooping, screaming fits, rubbing things incessantly. As a baby he used to bash his head on concrete, hated being touched or cuddled. [Sheila Gray: Sheila's story in Chapter 2]

This points to another advantage of close teamwork between professionals and other professionals in different specialisms, and between professionals and families – *families will often be the first to notice changes in behaviour*. Sadly, ignoring families' reports and pleas has sometimes led to tragedy.

Education may become problematic in many challenging conditions or disorders. Special educational facilities and individual programmes may be developed to address particular needs, and can be very successful when there is co-operation and co-ordination of effort between home and school.

The level of emotional disability is a main consideration in deciding on care as well as educational provision. Education will include teaching a much higher level of social skills than in the ordinary school curriculum, as well as the usual language, mathematics and so on.

As a child grows into adolescence and adulthood their needs and behaviour may change too. With appropriate support in place, a co-ordinated approach and structure between home and outside, many vulnerable individuals are gradually able to cope with life in the outside world or in a more sheltered environment.

Education must also be considered when an eating disorder develops and a flexible approach found; in anorexia it is not advised to attend school or college at a very low weight. Again, a flexible approach, with communication and co-operation between home and school, is needed so that the young person does not lose too much schooling at a vital time.

Loss of home and family care is sometimes a consequence for individuals whose families are no longer able to offer the level of care needed for their particular condition and difficulties. In many cases the home environment, with appropriate professional and other support, will best support the individual; in others residential education is the best option. There can be no hard-and-fast rules – each situation and needs must be examined to find what is best for the individual.

After many years of coping valiantly at home, Jane Gregory describes making the agonising decision to allow her daughter, who has multiple physical and emotional needs, to live in a residential school where highly trained carers were able to provide what Chrissie needs on a 24-hour basis – a completely calm, very structured environment with a set routine, and resources which simply are not possible in a home situation. With other children and family members at home, answering the doorbell or telephone, shopping or cooking, even going to the bathroom, may mean distracted attention from an individual who, for instance, may have no concept or understanding of danger.

Making the decision to let our son go into residential care was very very hard. We recognised we couldn't offer the level of 24-hour care he really needs, socially and emotionally. After talking to him and hearing of his early life experiences, the psychiatrist said he was one of the most damaged children she had ever seen, and he needed to live in a really intensive therapeutic environment if he was to have any chance in life. We feel by allowing him to go, his chances are better for the future. (Interview, 2006, parent of adopted son with reactive attachment disorder; see Chapter 2)

I did not give up seeing her, loving her, cuddling her, listening to her, phoning her, texting her, being her mum. Not a singles day passes without contact. Making the decision was the most difficult of my life.

[Anthea, interview]

Social implications associated with their behaviour may or may not be apparent to the challenging individual. It is only with growing awareness of self and surroundings, of reactions of others, that the person with challenging behaviour may realise the consequences of his or her behaviour.

> Challenging behaviour sealed her fate.
>
> (Gregory, 2000)

Carers often become very distressed when they talk of the impact on their loved ones' own lives of:

- inappropriate or unacceptable behaviours
- outbursts in public places as well as at home
- aggression or even violence
- self-harm
- financial problems
- crime and its consequences, court appearances and so on; possibly a criminal record which in turn may affect work opportunities
- loss of trust in home and social situations
- loss of job
- loss of spouse or partner
- friends' reactions: invitations may be rare as people are uncertain how to react, or if they can cope with difficult behaviour
- stigma: many people as well as society are often intolerant of even small, let alone greater, deviations from what is seen as the norm
- isolation.

To watch someone behaving in a way which a carer knows will have negative consequences is a particular kind of torture. No matter how exasperating, difficult or demanding, most families do indeed love their troubled family member, desperately want to help and continue seeking appropriate solutions and offering support even in the most trying circumstances. Learning what others cope with is a humbling experience.

Even the strongest and most capable families have a limit to the support they can give – and if and when that limit is reached, perhaps when a key strength dies and others can't cope – this is yet another consequence, often devastating, for the vulnerable individual at the heart of all the efforts.

Chair

by Gráinne Smith

Each day
I give you comfort.
Each day
since we came home together
I support your weight,
increasing with the years.

You should look at me you know,
be aware of the burden I carry,
feel the cracks as my skin rubs, wears.
You should attend my worn springs,
sturdy frame and broad smooth surface.

Why don't you
brush down my worn coat?
Listen to my creaks and groans?
Come here, stroke me, touch
with love these faithful arms
waiting, fearful
that you might not return.

Why don't you
feel the warmth of my heart
beating at the sound of your feet?
Why don't you,
just once,
look at me?

I am tired
of your careless demands,
the way you blindly take
and take and take and take.
One day my inner strengths
without warning
will break.

Family breakdown: care implications

When family care breaks down, when it is not possible for family carers to cope even with outside support – if and when that may be available – sometimes hospital care is needed, either short term during acute phases or for a longer spell, to stabilise the effects of the condition. In some cases the special care needed is within easy travelling distance for family members; for others this may not be an option and care is arranged hundreds of miles from home and family. When this is the case, depending on individual situations and disorders, added to the stress of the move for the individual will often be the lack of familiar faces around.

Hospital admission

Sometimes a person endangers themselves and others by their behaviour, and is therefore admitted to hospital. Sometimes this happens with the person's agreement, for example, someone suffering recurrent acute phases of their condition such as bipolar disorder or schizophrenia, or in anorexia when their eating avoidance means they are not taking in enough nourishment to preserve life.

On the other hand, thinking may be distorted and the person cannot grasp how they may endanger themselves and/or others, so that admittance is against the person's will under the Mental Health Act. Even when this is being considered, every effort to achieve agreement through persuasion and discussion with the individual is worthwhile rather than use force (Stewart & Tan, 2006).

Relapse prevention plan

Relapse prevention plans have been developed successfully in many treatment centres, with clients/patients and their treating professionals co-operating to draw up an agreement for use in the case of relapse and when admittance would or should be considered – by which time an individual's thinking may be so distorted that again danger to life is possible.

Feelings of personal guilt frequently play a strong part in many addicts' lack of self-esteem when they overcome the pre-contemplation (denial of or lack of recognition of problems), whether addicted to drugs, alcohol, eating behaviours or gambling – guilt and frustration at being unable to beat the cravings which control their behaviour, and strong feelings of their own perceived lack of willpower.

Feelings of personal guilt about effects of personal problems on family and carers often add to the misery of people with challenging behaviours when these are recognised.

Consequences for the family

My husband says he can't cope any more with my son's problems and behaviour. He says I'm no fun anymore, that I don't pay any attention to him now. I think he's seeing someone else, I think he's going to leave. My other children don't get

> half the attention from me that D does, he needs watching all the time. I'm just exhausted with it all, I don't think I can go on much longer.
>
> [M, carer of D, with severe learning disabilities and very challenging behaviour]

There may be different effects on family carers depending on the particular illness, condition or problems. For instance, a child or adult with ADHD may be physically fit and very active, while a child with a learning disability may also have a physical handicap and therefore not be as mobile while still presenting huge challenges with their behaviour; a young person with anorexia will in acute phases have very distorted and manipulative thinking as in other addictive behaviours. Obsessive compulsive behaviour may or may not be part of the overall picture.

In all families with an individually challenging member there are several common consequences to health, both for individual family members and also for the family itself as a dynamic entity.

Physical health

No matter how much they love their family member and want to provide the best support they can, individual members – especially the main carer but also anyone closely connected and sharing living space – can become physically and emotionally exhausted simply through the day-to-day struggle.

In his book, *Excessive Appetites*, Jim Orford quotes several studies of how the health of many family members was affected by a loved one's gambling:

> Most commonly reported were: suffering chronic or severe headaches (41%); irritable bowels, constipation, diarrhoea (37%); feeling faint, dizzy, having cold clammy hands, excessive perspiring (27%); hypertension, shortness of breath, rapid breathing or other breathing irregularities (23%).
>
> (Orford, 2001)

These figures relate to families affected by gambling, but the families of other carers can experience similar symptoms.

Emotional health

Many parents and other carers go through agonies of guilt, whatever the condition involved. Figures suggest that 30% feel guilty and responsible for causing or contributing to the gambling (30%), while 47% reported feeling depressed (Orford, 2001). Carers, especially parents, worry that somehow they may have done something to cause or trigger the problem.

Guilt

Carers often feel guilt about the possibility of not coping well enough, most especially if they have been unable to find information; this is a particular problem when someone who is already adult develops a condition which affects behaviour.

'What could/should I do to help my child?' was the first question I asked myself and the GP when my daughter was diagnosed with anorexia – without information it is entirely possible that a carer may inadvertently do the wrong thing, possibly with tragic consequences. For instance, when an eating disorder develops many families think – as I did at the beginning – that as the person is very obviously changed and ill, *perhaps* difficult behaviour might have to be tolerated where in other areas of life and for other members of the family as well as friends and colleagues very different rules and expectations would be the norm. *But families who give in to unacceptable behaviour because they don't know what to do for the best – whether in eating disorders, drugs or any other 'excessive appetite' problem – will soon discover that giving in simply gives the message that pushing the boundaries of what is acceptable pays dividends, at least in the short term.* Giving in to unacceptable behaviour, tiptoeing around it, playing down or ignoring the effects on the family, will have long-term consequences for the family and for the individual in their battle to overcome these difficulties (see Chapter 13).

Guilt is also a major factor when carers are torn between conflicting needs of other children, spouse and self and the troubled person.

Then there is the decision about hospital admittance. If someone is in a life-threatening condition it seems a relatively easy decision to make – but not if that person's distorted thinking leads to a battle about admission.

> I'd never ever have forgiven you if you'd made me go into hospital when I said No! I'd have done what I had to do, eat, put on weight or whatever, with hate in my heart – until I got out. And if you'd allowed it to happen, I'd never have spoken to you again. [Jay, my daughter, in discussion several years after she refused treatment aged 23, following the suggestion that she needed hospital inpatient treatment; GS]

Grief

Grief is a major feature of life for many parents whose children face major problems. Sometimes this begins at birth; sometimes, as a slow realisation that development in comparison with others of the same age is not quite as it should be; sometimes, as in schizophrenia, and in all the addictive and compulsive behaviours, with personality changes and unpredictable behaviour appearing gradually over a period of time, or suddenly; sometimes beginning with diagnosis or perhaps as the implications of that diagnosis dawn. Sometimes a diagnosis is a relief, in other cases it brings dread, or a mix of emotions. Circumstances and situations differ but the grief remains for what might have been, for lost opportunities for the affected person.

I have two daughters. One is 22, has just finished training as a physiotherapist, has started her first permanent fulltime job, has a serious relationship with her boyfriend, is planning for her future. My other daughter is 20, lives in residential care. She has a mental age of about two, is totally incontinent, dribbles constantly and can communicate at a toddler level through signs and a very few words. It breaks my heart when I visit her and think of all she is missing; and worse when I don't visit, I feel so guilty. I'm not even sure if she recognises me.

[H, carer, personal contact]

I'm at uni now, really enjoying the course and being in my own flat. Lots of friends and loads to do. I've joined the drama club, and the debating. I feel quite guilty sometimes thinking about what I'm doing and then I think about my sister. She's older than me and she'll never ever have what I have. Sometimes I feel guilty about enjoying everything so much, about not being at home to help mum after all these years. But it's a relief in lots of ways not to have to be at home and see all the stuff going on all the time. And I do go home in holidays sometimes, but not enough maybe. [L, sister of C, who is learning disabled]

Resentment

Resentment, mild or intense, about effects on a carer's own life and what might have been, and guilt about feeling so, often affects carers who offer support, sometimes over many years, through sacrificing their own lives. Many give up work outside the home because they find it impossible to juggle with all the demands on time and energy, only to face increased isolation from friends and activities. And siblings whose own lives are affected may have very strong feelings:

I get totally but totally fed up hearing about what Poor A is going through . . . how difficult her life is, all the awful stuff going on all the time at home . . . what about me, what about Dad, what about J? We have lives too! I've got exams coming up soon, but not a word about the work I'm doing, oh no! As soon as I can I'm leaving!

[O, sibling of A, who has AN/BN]

Anxiety

Anxiety about being able to support their loved one is also a common feeling. *What should I be doing? I want my child to have the best care I can give, but I'm never sure if I'm doing the right thing. What if I get it wrong?*

Long-term stress affects carers in various ways, with evidence through research showing that long-term carers have much higher incidences of physical and mental health problems (WHO, 2001). The physical and emotional exhaustion involved in 24-hours-a-day commitment will take a toll when short spells of caring for someone sick; when that commitment is over years on end, often with little or no respite, the toll can be very heavy indeed (see Chapter 16).

Endless decisions, both major and minor, have to be made on a daily basis, often with little or no idea of short- or long-term consequences for the loved one or the whole family. Priorities may change regarding actual physical arrangements, resources and organisation, education, care implications, when something changes such as a family bereavement, the illness or death of the main carer. These are, of course, in addition to ongoing household organisation to make sure there is food, clean clothes, transport, and so on, for the whole family.

Finance

Finance is a main consideration in many long-term illnesses and causes many problems. Very few families are in the position of being able to give 24-hour care for an extended period of time without counting the cost in practical money terms.

When time is regularly taken off work – to attend meetings or hospital visits, address family crises – it affects work and work relationships. Although giving up work may solve some home care issues, such as company and care for the troubled individual, it also obviously means reduced income, affecting both carer and cared-for and bringing increased isolation for the carers.

Care and support are also very much dependent on how resources are allocated, which may vary from country to country. In the UK there is a national health service funded by taxation but allocation of resources differs in different areas depending on health authorities' decisions – the 'post code lottery'. In other countries, such as the USA, treatment is mostly dependent on adequate insurance.

Decisions and reality: decisions may have to be made about how to provide costly care, with these decisions then affecting what it available for others in the family. Even when it is possible to find specialist support, this may involve outside helpers coming into the family home which will also affect financial resources.

Where care and treatment are dependent on insurance, even high levels of insurance reach an eventual limit; in this scenario, families are left with the decision of how it might just be possible to provide hospital care when the insurance company says it is no longer liable for bills.

> My husband worked in the oil industry and we enjoyed a high standard of living. When our daughter developed anorexia she needed hospital treatment several times, which was covered by our insurance. Now my husband is retired. After several years of fulltime work, my daughter has relapsed and needs hospital treatment again but the insurance company says they will no longer pay the bill for what may be a long spell. We are considering selling our house.
>
> [N, personal contact, email]

Stigma

With many illnesses or conditions, especially in mental health issues, stigma – either real or anticipated – may be a factor. Decisions will be taken as to whether and how and how much to tell friends of family problems, and the same is true with work and colleagues. To be open and honest may lead to perceived or actual stigma, while not to say anything at all about why time may be needed off work fairly regularly goes along with the blame-and-shame attitudes of the past century and more.

Ignorance can be a blessing. Having no clue as to any possible stigma, I talked at work about the diagnosis and my anxiety about Jay's future. Having done so, there seemed no point in trying to bury the information when I gradually discovered that some people, including professionals, associated 'an eating disorder' with 'abuse and malignant parenting'. And in my case at least, being open and honest about the problems caused for both my daughter and our family has led to no withdrawal of friends – rather to more awareness of the illnesses and their consequences, and to increased support and care for both me and my daughter. In many instances, my own talking of the illness and the problems seemed to 'give permission' to others to talk of their own heartaches. The situation might have been different if Jay had wanted her illness kept secret.

And while some strangers will go out of their way to offer help in difficult situations, others will be singularly unhelpful and even condemning. During one of her daughter's outbursts in a shop, Jane Gregory describes how Chrissy had to be carried out between the family, and outside, Chrissy's sister spoke of how a someone in the shop had said 'horrible things in there about you mummy, that you're not fit to be a parent' (Gregory, 2000).

For some, the decision is almost made for them by circumstances, for others it is neither clear-cut nor simple:

> My son was in hospital for months and is now attending as an outpatient for treatment for schizophrenia. He doesn't want anyone, including all our family, to know about his mental health problems, hates feeling that people are talking about him. I think most of his friends must know or at least guess. What do I say to my brother and his family who are coming home for a visit from Australia? Should I tell them why my son sometimes responds in an 'unusual' way? Or say nothing? [C, a personal contact]

Where crime is associated with conditions such as drug-taking, alcohol abuse or bulimia – for instance, stealing to support the addictive habit, or accumulating debts – or in other mental health problems, the consequences for families, parents, grandparents, siblings, even cousins or more distant relatives, of being part of the family of someone who behaves in an antisocial way may be severe in their community, as well as for the person themselves.

> Fraudster son lost £160,000 on website'
> [headline on report in *Aberdeen Press and Journal* newspaper, 16 June 2006]
>
> My younger son was beaten up at school because his brother R has been in trouble; he's been dealing drugs and the boys who beat him up have a sister who's been taking drugs and they said R had led her into it. [S, personal contact]
>
> We got a phone call threatening that if we didn't pay our son's debts for drugs, they'll come and set fire to our house. That time we gave our son the money – all our savings – to get him out of trouble, but after a while he just went back to his old ways. This time we'd have to sell our house to help him. [Pattie, interview]

Family dynamics

Family dynamics will be greatly affected by ongoing reactions to an individual's greater need for care, having huge consequences for the family as a functioning entity.

Different family members may react in very different ways to challenging behaviour again depending on individual factors – different understandings of problems depending on information given (or lack of, accurate or not), media, reactions of friends.

Depending on character and genetic or personality traits and coping abilities, one person may react as a Rhino, charging in to fix the situation. ('If you'd only listen – stop going out with your pals, they're a bad influence, that's the problem. All you have to do is stop seeing them!')

Another carer may stick their head in the sand like the Ostrich – if the problem is not acknowledged, it doesn't exist, isn't happening. Kangaroo believes that everything can be cured by love – smother love and keeping safe in a 'pouch'. Hawk may try hovering at a distance, trying to see the problems from every angle but taking no part in proceedings. (More information will be found on the reactions of Rhino, Hawk, Ostrich and Kangaroo – also Dolphin – in Treasure *et al.*, 2007, in preparation.)

Everyday communication becomes even more difficult as individuals struggle to cope. With less attention and time available for everyone else's problems, lack of attention for spouse and siblings and their activities, physical and emotional exhaustion, feelings of growing isolation with their problems, and anxiety about coping skills, even strong 'together' families feel the strain.

It is not surprising that many families under such pressure begin to disintegrate.

Siblings are often badly affected as their lives are shadowed by parents struggling to care for someone with great needs, leaving less time and energy for attention to others in the family. Although spouses and other adults will also be affected to a greater or lesser extent, they at least will (usually) have more information and insight into the reasons for all that time and energy spent on the vulnerable individual. Siblings, frequently with no explanation about these reasons, often see only that no-one seems to have time for them or their needs or interests. (In other circumstances could this be seen as neglect of the sibling?) This may be difficult when special physical care is needed; it is even more difficult when challenging behaviour is involved ('Well, P did that and you didn't say anything! *She* got away with it!').

Consequences for young carers

> This core experience, which may be near-universal – transcending culture, socio-economic circumstances, and the particular relationship of the relative to the person whose drinking they are affected by – consists of finding the excessive drinker unpleasant to live with (because of verbal or physical aggression, mood swings, lying and poor communication generally).
>
> (Orford, 2001)

> It follows that children, currently living with parents who are excessive drinkers, must exist in very large numbers indeed, probably in excess of 1 million in Britain.
>
> (Orford, 2001)

These are figures quoted for young carers affected by alcohol abuse – many more young lives are affected by living with parents with conditions involving challenging behaviours, often triggering problems such as those mentioned in the first extract above.

Often the lives of siblings – young carers – are led ir
someone with a condition which demands most or even
going.

Preparation for a caring role?

Families do not choose to be carers, they find themselves – suddenly or gradually – in that role. Although certain conditions run in families, very few parents or families have the skills to cope when, for instance, mental illness first affects a young person and often-dramatic personality changes are noticed. While feelings of inadequacy and guilt affect many – most? – such families, these feelings may be even more acute for people working in the caring professions.

The first inkling of this came as I listened and talked to a psychiatrist's wife, who was struggling to come to terms with her daughter's dramatic personality change, equally dramatic and life-threatening weight loss and compulsive exercising associated with anorexia.

> My husband has insisted that P, our daughter, must *not* be treated locally. He's arranged for treatment in [. . .], hundreds of miles away. He's afraid of his colleagues' reaction! – they'll blame the parents. Us. And he's given talks on Awful Parents in the past, as part of his job. It's what he believes.
>
> [EDA helpline, 2002]

Added to her distress about her daughter's life-threatening illness and behaviour involving rejection of any attempts at support, including denial of any problems, the lady was intensely angry about her husband's reaction and insistence on sending their daughter for treatment far from home.

Consequences for professionals

Changing views of humanity – coping exclusively with individuals who have distorted thinking, may be aggressive, paranoid or telling a distorted version of their own truth (no-one is referred to e.g. a social worker or psychiatrist unless they have Problems) – may lead to a professional forming a very distorted view of human beings in general.

Feelings of constantly being in the firing line are distressing and cause great stress, whether from someone with challenging behaviour who does not understand or appreciate efforts meant to help and support, or when a carer vents their frustration through angry words.

Social and home life may be affected – coping with distressed family members, whether showing stress through tears or anger, will inevitably be stressful for those trying to help.

> It's hard to switch off sometimes when you've heard an appalling story; everyone laughing and chatting round me and I just can't leave it behind.
>
> [M, social worker, personal contact]

Trusting bonds may be harder to form in new relationships:

> I know social workers who work with sexually abused children who won't let any man near their own kids without close supervision, ever.
>
> [Social worker, personal contact]

Changes in practice: knowing of emerging research about more effective treatments than those of the past may trigger uncomfortable feelings in some professionals; in others denial and defensiveness, possibly anger about having to cope with a backlash.

> I was involved at one time in questionnaires which now I think were not fair or balanced in their questions. Lots of assumptions were made in the past which have now been disproved by e.g neuro-imaging techniques.
>
> [Psychiatrist, personal conversation]

Keeping abreast of ongoing developments in research can take up much time, time which has to be taken from where? Time which might otherwise be used for seeing clients/patients? Personal time? Cut out lunch and other breaks? Work late again? Or just continue on auto using original basic training without seeking out better or more appropriate methods until they hit you over the head?

Difficulties with setting work/home time management: many caring professionals give huge amounts of personal time to trying to keep on top of email and other administrative jobs, attending conferences to try to keep abreast of current developments and training for these. This too can lead to reduced family time and energy.

To gain more insight into consequences for all the individuals involved, asking those individuals about their own difficulties gives a clearer knowledge and understanding of their particular situation; it also adds to the burden of despair, pain, sadness and frustration of dedicated professionals working with limited resources. Whatever resources they work with, most do their very best for those they care for (see also Chapter 8).

The Appendix contains useful information such as websites, support lines and charities.

CHAPTER FIVE

Friends and family

When someone is experiencing health problems, actions and reactions of family and friends are important to recovery; in emotional problems, even more so. Indeed, these informal reactions could be described as crucial to supporting the individual towards coping better with problems and stresses – or to supporting and/or endorsing unacceptable behaviour. This applies to close family carers – parents, grandparents, siblings, aunt or uncle – and to friends and neighbours who may be in regular or occasional contact.

In any heated exchange, in any situation when people are worried, agitated and under stress, reactions may include (depending on family members' own individual makeup):

- trying to argue logically in an attempt to demonstrate the wrongness of what their loved one believes and their actions
- trying to ignore the challenging behaviour in the hope that it will go away
- offering placatory and soothing remarks in an attempt to please and hopefully ease the situation
- trying to self-defend against unfair accusations and remarks
- trying to show unconditional love by offering food or a gift
- giving in to any demand
- losing the temper (or in Scots 'losin the heid'), shouting back; even smacking or hitting
- being paralysed by sadness and grief that someone you love could behave in such a way towards you
- breaking down in tears
- feeling completely helpless, powerless, wanting to give up
- feeling frightened, of the consequences both long and short term (for the individual, self and others)
- or? Perhaps readers can think of other possible reactions?

Think of heated situations in your own family – do you recognise any of the responses above? What would your own reaction be to aggressive or unpleasant behaviour within your own house? Treasure *et al.* (2007, in preparation) have given names to common responses:

- *Rhino response:* Rhino charges in and tries to 'fix' everything with logic and reason.
- *Kangaroo care:* Kangaroo tries to help by efforts to surround the individual with unconditional love with no constructive criticism, no guidance, no boundaries – no matter what.
- *Ostrich oblivion:* Ostrich pretends that the problem doesn't exist; if Ostrich does not acknowledge it, it isn't there.

And then there's *Dolphin*, who calmly swims alongside and tries to nudge the individual into a more constructive behaviour pattern and hopefully an understanding of why they feel such anger, frustration, fear or anxiety, or perhaps physical discomfort because of heightened senses of hearing or touch. Few people are able to be Dolphin all the time. This is true in everyday life, even more so in situations where someone shows challenging behaviour over a period of time, whether weeks or months or many years.

Jan Cullis of the Bronte Foundation, Melbourne, working independently in Australia, has worked out similar approaches for differing personalities by using ducks to humorously illustrate how someone with, for example, a high anxiety level (or high aggression, or determination) might react to a challenging situation (GS, personal conversation).

When difficult situations arise, often unpredictably and with no warning, it can be difficult to keep calm and work out what might be best. This is especially true when family members encounter behaviour they have never seen before or when the behaviour of a loved one changes, often dramatically. Only a saint responds calmly in *all* situations no matter what, and never ever loses control. Unfortunately, in common with most human beings, I'm no saint!

> Coping with the aggression, hostility and rejection – one of the most difficult aspects of eating disorders identified by families.
>
> [EDA Carers Conference, London, 2000]

When my daughter came home at 21 following an abusive marriage, I often could not recognise 'Anorexia' standing yelling at me as my beloved Jay whom I'd known all her life. As I had no information, it took me some time to work out what might – just might – help her in the long term. It felt I was living in a nightmare where nothing seemed to make sense any more. Initially I went through several of the reactions noted above:

As she was very obviously ill, maybe she couldn't help the behaviour and I just had to accept, ignore or put up with aggressive behaviour I'd never seen in my home before? [GS, Ostrich?]

Perhaps trying to ignore such behaviour (very difficult!) as much as possible, grit my teeth and bite my tongue, this might help Jay cope with her illness better? [GS, Ostrich?]

Jay's thinking was very distorted, so I tried to show her by arguing reasonably what she could/should do to be healthy again . . . I tried to remind Jay of all those lessons from an early age, that to be healthy she must eat a certain amount for her height and build – that even when we are asleep our bodies are using energy just to keep our hearts and other organs going. [GS, Rhino?]

We'd always eaten a balanced diet with lots of fruit and vegetables, fish and meat and chicken. Amounts of crisps, sweets, burgers and chips were restricted all through childhood, to the extent that my children felt they might be quite deprived in comparison to the rather different diets of some other children! Teaching the Scottish primary curriculum over many years, including Jay, it was obvious that when she was ill Jay had somehow lost all the knowledge she'd previously had about diet and nutrition. The distorted thinking of anorexia dictated her revised attitude to eating – not to eat if at all possible; if her willpower snapped and she binged, to get rid of any nourishment. [GS, Rhino?]

After her marriage broke down, planned at 18 and imagined as a Happy Ending, Jay lost all her confidence and self esteem. I tried hard, by giving many reasonable examples, to convince her that although I sometimes didn't agree with her this did not mean that I didn't love her, that the negative interpretations (very much part of any eating disorder) of friends' actions were wrong. [GS, Rhino?]

When she said horrible things to me, or accused me of not caring about her, I tried to defend myself and show with logical examples that they just were not true. [GS, Rhino?]

I made her favourite meals, tried to placate her spectacular temper over such things as the curtains not being drawn to her satisfaction (eventually I realised that our cat liked to sleep on the windowsill and often disturbed the curtains!). I tried to show in every way I could think of that I loved her, tried to help in any way I could. [GS, Kangaroo?]

When a week's shopping for food for the household disappeared overnight, I tried to excuse this complete disregard for other people's needs as part of whatever was wrong with Jay. [GS, Kangaroo?]

Frightened by the level of aggression Jay showed when she was ill, seeing her trying to control everything else around her as well as her food intake, and afraid she might actually carry through some of her threats, for a time I was definitely Kangaroo.

Now, through talking to hundreds of parents on the eating disorders helpline, at meetings and conferences, I know that sometimes people become so determined to show caring in any and every way they can possibly think of, that they become almost paralysed by terror at the thought that if they don't give in to every whim there will be terrible consequences.

> I scoured newspapers over weeks, drove hundreds of miles, to seek out just the right flat for my daughter, would drive miles to find just exactly the 'right' sort of bread my daughter insisted on, spent hundreds of pounds I couldn't afford on the bedlinen my daughter said she wanted. Nothing I did was right, ever.
>
> [S, EDA helpline]

I have heard many such stories from families with a member affected by eating disorders, or by drugs or alcohol – no matter how they tried to please, or change the behaviour by logical argument, or protect from consequences, nothing was ever enough.

Now I know that none of these reactions – all of them common – has a positive effect on the thinking of someone whose thinking is distorted, whatever the reason. Ostrich or Kangaroo or Rhino reactions, while understandable under extreme stress and distress in situations without any information or support, are not helpful in motivating someone to consider changing their unacceptable, often antisocial and self-destructive, behaviour, let alone to consider following through with action to change. As in other conditions where logical arguments are beyond the understanding of an individual, it is only through gentle guidance and much patience that change can be achieved.

Unfortunately there are no easy answers, no simple straightforward 'Do This/ Don't Do That and all will be well'. Where individuals are concerned, individual problems, perceptions and feelings have to be explored, discussed and worked through to find the right solution for the vulnerable individual needing support and all those in close contact. What works for one person may not be right for another; what works in one situation at one time may not be the answer in another.

Confrontation

While most of the time meeting confrontation with similar behaviour achieves nothing, and in some cases leads to yet more distress and retreat into even more difficult behaviours, *very occasionally* a row and venting your own feelings and frustrations with the situation and the individual's behaviour, will indeed clear the air in the way months of gentle persuasion did not. *Very occasionally* a row may clear the air – but usually meeting aggression with more aggression simply escalates the problem.

> The more someone tries to drive or push me into doing something – anything! – the less likely I am to do it.
>
> [L, interview]

> Influence is real power. Attempts to control will always be fought against.
>
> (Konstant & Taylor, n.d.)

Influencing the loved one takes time and much long-term thought and effort; there are no quick fixes.

However hard it may be, seeking a long-term answer to challenging behaviour is most effective when everyone is working together as a team to influence and convince. A single person working in isolation to try to support a troubled individual may well achieve positive change, only to see the results disappear under other influences.

> I tried to encourage my partner to achieve her lifelong ambition to go on to further study, she's well able. She'd even sent off for the application forms for university. Then her father walks in and says 'Why waste your time? Be realistic about your abilities.' I felt like clocking him!
>
> [N, personal contact]

> My dad is driving me up the wall, keeps pushing me, he wants everything to change overnight!
>
> [Personal contact]

Finding reasons

- *In case of fire, it's more important to douse the flames than to try to find the reasons*: finding the reasons can come later.
- *Identify* what you are trying to achieve and why.
- *Think through long-term aims*: discuss them with close family, friends and involved colleagues.
- *Co-ordinate and plan*: be aware of individual strengths as well as weaknesses within the team, plan to allow for or address these.
- *Review* regularly (see also Chapter 13).

With teamwork, two results will gradually appear – as the vulnerable person's needs and behaviour are better understood, their self-esteem will increase, and family harmony will improve. Remember that real change will not happen overnight; don't give up at the first hurdle.

Identify

Brainstorm a list of what behaviours negatively affect the lives of the individual and those around. The list may be written or talked through – the more ideas the better. Seek information from books or workshops; explore as fully as possible; find out from other families, from charities. If possible discuss your list with treating professionals to gain even more ideas of what might help; they will have experience which the family may lack.

For instance, in anorexia, binge/purge type:

- extreme temper tantrums
- aggression and hostility
- self-harming behaviours
- threats of suicide
- refusal, while carrying out rituals, to allow others into the only bathroom.

Jane Gregory (2000) writes about learning from watching how a member of staff dealt with a screaming episode: Chrissy was given minimal interaction and attention – no eye contact, and very brief verbal exchanges with little expression. As Chrissy renewed her efforts and outbursts to attract attention, the staff member wrapped her in a towel to contain her. When Chrissy stopped screaming, she was asked if she was ready, with gestures such as fingers on lips. Chrissy *then* received immediate access to adult attention. Successful strategies had been developed over years in this special school described by Gregory, with staff being trained in strategies to cope with extreme behaviour. Someone not trained would be unlikely to be able to cope in this way.

Such observation, such co-operation between family members and professional (and personally detached) staff, is invaluable for helping the vulnerable individual and for building carers' coping strategies.

Prioritise

What behaviour is most difficult, what needs to be worked on most urgently? Whose life/lives are being affected? In what way? In some situations, where personal danger is a factor either to the troubled individual or to others, it is necessary to take swift action to avert disaster. In others it may be possible, even essential, to ignore more minor behaviours while addressing others that are more important.

When Jay was very ill, her whims would change from day to day. One day she yelled because I left the kitchen door open while she was in the kitchen so I shut it. Next day I carefully made sure the door was shut as she'd requested – but she wanted it open.

I decided these were irritating events, I'd grit my teeth and say OK, then shut or open the door as requested, whatever she wished at that moment, rather than try to confront her unpleasantness over every trivial incident. It wasn't possible to challenge each and every situation – I had to choose my battles, decide which were essential and which could wait.

[GS – there were only so many hours in each day,
I had only so much energy.]

Long-term aims

What will be achieved for the individual? For family, friends, colleagues?

If there are several difficult behaviours, is it possible to develop a co-ordinated plan? Who will be involved? Who would it be helpful to involve? What difficulties might be encountered by trying?

Jane Gregory worked with the hospital and her daughter's school to draw up management guidelines for Chrissy's behaviour, with clearly stated aims, for instance to encourage Chrissy to learn to share adult attention with others, or to help Chrissy gain control if she is upset. Although these guidelines varied slightly between school and home, they were kept as consistent as possible – the same approaches to unacceptable behaviour. A detailed outline of strategies, such as responding in a clear, confident and calm way, having positive expectations, and 'never showing her that you are dithering' is given. And Jane Gregory describes the change in Chrissy's behaviour as the teamwork took effect: her daughter became much more confident, calm and settled, better able to cope with relationships and interactions with others.

Val Strawford, interviewed in the *Guardian* in an article describing the Meriden Project, Birmingham, run by Birmingham and Solihull Mental Health Trust, had a similar experience.

> Since the family's participation, Rob has not needed to be admitted to hospital. 'Within three months, there were improvements,' she says. 'Rob started having cups of tea with us, then joining us for meals.'
>
> (*Guardian*, 2005)

By teaching skills and confidence the project helped keep the vulnerable young man from permanent confinement in a psychiatric unit.

Review regularly

Use an ongoing regular dialogue to discuss key messages, assess progress and achievements, and acknowledge difficulties – what went wrong and why? Is there a possible flaw in the plan or was it temporary setback? Was a carer very tired and couldn't follow it through at that particular time? Are there any new features which were not initially identified?

Messages

What messages do we want to give? Are individuals being consistent in the messages? (Some family members may find it more difficult than others to stick to plan. This must be openly acknowledged and addressed, otherwise the consequence may be manipulation.) Are the messages spoken or demonstrated (perhaps by a hug, perhaps by a frown or lack of a smile, depending on situation)? For instance, *I love you very much. I don't like it when you [name the behaviour] because [. . .]. I still love you.* How else could we give the message?

Dealing with tantrums

Completely ignoring bad behaviour or pretending it doesn't exist *may* be an answer when a two-year-old is having a tantrum; giving in to every demand could give the message that shouting and screaming and kicking gets you what you want. The same message is magnified when the person being given in to is an adult. The difficulties in managing the behaviour are likewise magnified because of the greater size, strength and weight of the adult individual. Also, it does not help the person cope with life's frustrations or to gain control of their feelings and find other ways of expressing them.

Always trying to placate, whether a child or adult, gives the same message – unpleasant behaviour gets you what you want.

Kangaroo care

Trying to protect an individual, whether young person or adult, from all of life's difficulties, leads to that person being dependent which in turn often leads to lack of confidence. Kangaroo behaviour, often with the best of intentions and much love, gives the unspoken message that you don't think a person can cope.

Terry came to school at almost six unable to put his shoes on or fasten them, unable to fasten or unfasten his coat, unable to change for games or PE, unable to cut up his food, unable to go to the toilet on his own. He had great difficulty in playing with other children, or sharing activities with them. On his first day at school he stood like a penguin waiting for someone to undo his coat and take it off. He lived with his parents and grandparents who dearly loved him – and did absolutely everything for him. He was a very bright boy but it took a long time for him to settle and we had to encourage him all the time to think for himself then take action. [GS]

The same holds true in eating disorders when decision-making skills are lost and self-esteem has to be rebuilt. Prior to her illness, my daughter worked fulltime, organised her life including mortgage and bill paying, food, washing, etc for her household – yet anorexia meant she felt uncertain of any ability in any area. 'Kangaroo care' removes personal responsibility and the chance of personal growth.

Dolphin's message

What message does Dolphin give? Swimming alongside while nudging towards more constructive ways of dealing with the feelings of anger, aggression, fear, frustration or anxiety, by helping to identify the stress triggers which led to the unacceptable behaviour, can give the message, whether spoken or not, that Dolphin has faith that an individual can change.

Dolphin will acknowledge any achievements, no matter how small, and rejoice in them. Dolphin will acknowledge that change may be difficult, and stressful, that there will be setbacks, that while the unacceptable behaviour is challenged the troubled individual is still loved. Dolphin will show that the aim is not to restrict someone's life and independence but to help achieve and reach potential in the long term, enable them to lead a more fulfilling life with better relationships, to cope better with their condition or illness, to work towards recovery and/or controlling the symptoms – as well as building their self-esteem through being able to cope with the difficulties.

Dolphin will encourage open acknowledgement of problems and honest discussion. Dolphin will discourage relentless focus on negative thoughts and memories – often a part of depression as well as other mental health problems. Dolphin will encourage and stress further talk of positive thoughts or memories ('I can hear you enjoyed that . . .' 'Tell me more . . .' 'What did you like best about . . .?' 'What are you most looking forward to – e.g. in the holidays; next week; tonight on television?')

By focusing on the positive, a more positive frame of mind can often be set in train. Grab the moment wherever and whenever it appears!

Exhaustion and Dolphin

Being a Dolphin is not easy, takes much patience and practice, and can be extremely exhausting when lasting weeks, months or possibly years (the average length of time for an eating disorder is five to six years). Dolphins who support must look after themselves to ensure that they do not 'go under', leaving the vulnerable person without support (see also Chapter 16).

Rewards however can be wonderful, for the vulnerable person who gains control of their behaviour and confidence through their own efforts, and for the family members and friends who support.

> It was incredibly difficult and demanding, especially during the active phases of my son's illness, but also incredibly worthwhile and satisfying to see the change now he's beginning to recover and take real control of his life again. [Peter, carer, ED conference 2004]
>
> You have to talk about everything – if you don't, it's *so* easy to assume things. Families often go along parallel lines, assume they know the thoughts and intentions of other people round about but when you talk about it you can see how wrong you were. Or right sometimes! Before my son was ill, we did lots of family things together, but after working together to help him, as a team, we feel much more connected. We wouldn't have got through if we hadn't worked as a team.
>
> At first we weren't very sure, then we talked to our friends and teachers and everyone who was involved in any way. They were all really dedicated and helped in so many ways.
>
> We called it 'Total Active Care'. You have to see 'the monster' and challenge it. It wouldn't have worked if we'd just accepted what was happening. [Andy and family, interview: Andy and Bea's story in Chapter 2]

Exhaustion, stress and mistakes

Only a saint would never make mistakes. All human beings, especially when stressed and exhausted – and being a carer on a daily basis for anyone with challenging behaviour is extremely stressful and totally exhausting – can give way to momentary anger or inattention. Some human beings are better at controlling feelings and giving vent to irritation or anger than others.

Sorry!

Not only does saying *I'm sorry* open up lines of communication and build towards more constructive conversations, it also shows that being wrong is part of Life – if a person never apologises, even when recognising they were wrong, what message does this give? That they are always right? Or that it is OK to deny wrongdoing? *Sorry* is one of the biggest words in the world and, far from demonstrating weakness, shows strength and honesty as well as self-knowledge and empathy.

Consistency

There's no point in one person making huge efforts to support towards gaining and regaining control of emotions and actions, only to have those efforts undermined or even destroyed by Great Uncle Rhino, Second Cousin Kangaroo, or an unwitting remark by Ollie Ostrich!

The calmer and more consistent the approach and the better the teamwork, the better the chance of 24-hour best care.

CHAPTER SIX

Lies, manipulation and control freakery

> Sometimes patients tell us things which might be really important for carers to know, things to be aware of such as feelings of depression leading to the possibility of self-harm – and then tell us we mustn't tell their family. They know very well we can't pass on what might be crucial information, because of confidentiality.
>
> [Nurse therapist, eating disordered patients]

> My son told us that the social worker said stressful situations can make his drugs habit worse and that we have to make his life as easy as possible. He wants us to give him money to pay his rent again, and says if we don't it'll be our fault if he takes an overdose. I don't know what's true and what's not true any more, he's told us so many lies . . . I think he spends all the money we give him for rent or food or clothes, whatever, on drugs, but I can't bear the thought of him doing something awful.
>
> [C, mother of Pete, drug addict, personal contact]

> I've tried to get my daughter to eat, I've talked about how our bodies need nourishment, it's like fuel for a car to make it go. I've tried all that, I think she can repeat it word for word. Makes no difference. Now she says that if I don't stop talking about it, she's going to stop drinking as well. I just don't know what to do.
>
> [N, mother of Maxine, 15, who has anorexia, eating disorders helpline]

In ordinary day-to-day life it is common to find that others see things in a different way from ourselves, and sometimes we discover just how very different their picture may be. In many conditions, seeing a very distorted version of reality is part of the picture although without any deliberate intent. In others – especially those conditions connected with addictions (or 'excessive appetites' as Jim Orford, 2001, describes them) – lying, manipulating and attempts at control of all around including family, friends and professionals, is quite common.

Often the challenging individual is able to accurately identify those who are most gullible, most tender-hearted, most naive or most affected by threats of various kinds – aggression, actual violence, self-harm, suicide, perhaps bringing shame on the family – if they don't comply with the demands being made. For example, to pay a fine or perhaps a dealer, as in John's story.

> My son is in big trouble with a dealer, he can't pay him and the dealer knows he has no money unless we give it to him. John says if he doesn't pay up on Friday the dealer's going to come round here and set fire to our house. Last time we remortgaged our house. We can't do that this time. And last year we gave him money for a court fine. Every time he promises he'll give up drugs – but he doesn't.
>
> [S, mother of John, drug addict, interview]

Despair and feelings of helplessness are common among long-term carers, while some professionals are also very aware of how patients/clients in the grip of eating disorders, drugs or other addictive compulsive behaviours may be trying to manipulate them.

In John's story no professional was involved at this stage, and his parents had to decide what their options were. Consider selling their house to try to help their son financially, with little hope that promises would be kept this time any more than in the past? Or refuse to be blackmailed this time, with the knowledge hanging over them of the possibility that the dealer might indeed keep his ugly promise?

A postscript to this story: John's parents decided that there was no point in making themselves homeless by selling their house. They offered instead to support John in going to the police with his story and supporting him through whatever happened next, as well as through the battle of trying to give up his addiction. John decided on the latter course of action. Now, several years on and after a very long hard struggle, John is clear of drugs and his downward spiral in life. He regularly helps at a centre supporting others in their own similar battles. The drugs dealer is still serving his sentence.

> I didn't have a clue that he took out these loans. How could anyone know?
>
> [G, personal contact, on discovering her husband's gambling debts]

> For several wives . . . there were repeated threatening calls and harassment at home from creditors.
>
> (Orford, 2001)

Once aware of tangled stories being told – this may take quite a while especially when mutual trust has hitherto been the norm – identifying the possible causes and triggers may be the beginning of helping the individual cope better with the stresses which are part of life. Whether drugs, alcohol, over-exercising, overeating or restricting food or gambling – it is important to recognise that such behaviour may be part of *any* exchange of views, thanks to the distortion of thinking. And it is only by regular family discussions, and/or family–professional discussion, that anyone involved around the troubled individual will be able to assess what is fact and what is fiction before making what may be an important decision as to a best course of action.

> It was only when we all sat down together at the kitchen table and really talked about what was happening to our family that we realised that all the rows of the last few months were actually because May had been stirring big-time – telling me one thing, then my husband something else, and another thing to Gran. She'd ask me for money, and I'd say No, then she'd go to her dad and say that I'd said Yes but I'd no change . . . so he'd give her money. Once I gave her money for a trip with friends, then she told my mother that I was being mean and she couldn't go because it was too expensive; she knows her Gran is a soft touch . . . so she ended up with money for the trip – and I don't need to guess what the rest went on. And she took money from her brother's room . . . But we'd never have worked it out if we hadn't finally worked out what was happening and got together and tried to sort the whole mess out. Then we invited May to our next round-the-table! She wasn't very happy when she realised that we wouldn't buy her stories any more, wouldn't play her games. Those 'round-the-tables' as we called them were really hard sometimes, but it was the beginning of us getting back on track as a family, working together instead of against each other. *And* it was the beginning of May getting her eating back under control.
>
> [F, mother of May, 24, severe bulimia 3 years, at an eating disorders workshop]

Building family teamwork

Divide and rule – playing people off against each other – can only be exposed through communication. By 'stirring it', by telling 'alternative versions' – embroidering or reinterpreting incidents and telling lies about other family members, by manipulating all sorts of situations and playing on personal weaknesses, knowing that in today's rushing world people living in the same house can lead parallel lives which make for few whole-family discussions – someone can very effectively control others *as long as honest and open communication between those involved does not take place.* And all the while they avoid trying to control, sometimes even to acknowledge, their 'excessive appetite' and its effects and consequences on themselves and others. And all the while their self-esteem plummets even further.

Once a family – or group of friends perhaps – realise what is happening in their midst, it is possible to take steps to address the problems. Setting up regular meetings is a positive step to begin the difficult but necessary process, which can include asking those taking part what incidents or behaviour they would like discussed. The person whose behaviour is causing problems may be invited to attend; they may resent the idea of such a meeting to discuss their behaviour, and do their best to stop it going ahead, but few people like the idea of such a meeting going ahead and not knowing what is said about them.

Hearing family and/or friends talking openly about the problems caused by the challenging behaviour is possibly the first time the troubled individual has been faced with how their behaviour affects others. They may become distressed and tearful, shouting and aggressive, storm out with dire threats, and possibly all of these in a desperate attempt to continue controlling others.

It is unlikely to be an easy meeting, and may be compared to lancing a boil.

But just as May's mother noted, it is only when the behaviour and its effects and consequences are acknowledged can gaining control become an option; with the regaining of control comes the beginnings of renewed self-esteem as well as self-control.

Permissions and professional support

As it depends on the agreement of the troubled individual, family–professional communication may be much more difficult to achieve when someone is officially an adult – no matter at what level they may be able to function.

> Jay, at 23 and very ill with anorexia, seemed at times to regress to about age three – yet was still working fulltime. [GS]

> We feel that if information had been provided our daughter's care would have been better and her recovery quicker. If we'd known what behaviour to possibly expect, or even that certain things might be part of the picture, we'd have been so much better prepared. Even if those awful things didn't actually happen, well at least that would have been a bonus! But we never ever knew what was going to happen next, what might happen, let alone how to react.
>
> [Alison, carer, daughter with anorexia, interview]

According to the January 2006 Continuity of Care Briefing Paper (Department of Health, 2006) many mentally ill people would be happy to involve their carers. They recognise that carers need information to enable them to support them, for example when medication is changed, or to note particular behaviour which may mean that relapse is imminent. In fact, 'fewer than one-third (31%) of service users felt there were no situations where information should be shared without their consent' (Department of Health, 2006).

I've no idea what she tells the psychiatrist. Or the social worker or anyone else. She sees a dietician too. Her thinking isn't straight and there's lots of things I wish I could tell the doctors and others, but they just won't talk to us. Sometimes she tells us a bit about a meeting, but I really don't know if what she tells us is true or selected bits of what's been said. Or maybe her own made-up fantasy of what she'd like us to believe. Maybe if we knew what the dietician said or her agreed targets or whatever . . . We'd really like to help if we can but we have no idea what's the best way to help her.

[Mother of Wenda, 32; relapsing anorexia, binge-purge type, for 15 years, several hospital admissions]

Without information to enable Wenda's family to support her, it was possible for Wenda to readily agree to every suggestion professionals made to her in discussions about steps she could take to control the binge/purge aspect of anorexia – and as soon as she got home to continue as before. All her determination evaporated as soon as she was faced with eating and the compulsion again took over.

The turning point was when she was sent to a new, specialist, dietician who asked who Wenda would like to support her. She nominated me. So from then on I drove her to appointments, and I went for a walk or a coffee – then went back to collect her 15 minutes before the official end of the appointment. Between them, the dietician and Wenda explained to me what they had agreed as the Next Steps to help her control her eating. And Wenda told me what I could do to help her. For instance, if I could talk to her about – well, things we both liked doing was best, or talking about a film we'd both watched, things like that. That might help stop her immediately going to the bathroom to get rid of the food. She said it had become just a very bad habit that she had to break – it wouldn't happen overnight.

Talking about how she felt – that was the first time I'd really had any idea of how she felt about it all, how rotten she felt about not being able to be in control of her eating, how desperately worried she was about becoming fat after eating even just a bite. The obsession with what everyone else was eating. And talking about how other people, especially me as I'd stuck by her all the way through, could help her beat the illness, really seemed to help give her more determination to overcome it. It gave me a role too, instead of feeling so useless. Took a long time, she was right it didn't happen overnight, but we got there. I'm so proud of my daughter and the way she beat it. Great if I played a part, but she did the real work. And I'm so thankful to that dietician.

The turning point for Wenda in her fight against the 'excessive appetite' controlling her life was that question: '*Who* would you like to support you?' Not 'if' but '*who*'.

Very few people live in complete isolation, with absolutely no-one they'd like to support them. This person may be a parent, a grandparent, a sibling, friend. And that support, added to good and appropriate professional care, may be the crucial turning point in avoiding relapse, in working towards recovery.

> It is worth persevering and try to obtain consent for carers to be involved where appropriate.
>
> (Treasure *et al.*, 2007)

Detached viewpoints

Each family situation will be different. Sometimes people become so frustrated and locked into their own perceptions and problems that they 'can't see the wood for the trees'.

This is where someone with a more detached view, whether friend or professional, may be invaluable. The Meriden West Midlands Family Programme, mentioned earlier, is just one project currently working towards 'moving everyone forward, not just the person who is ill'. Although this project relates to the families of people with schizophrenia, the same aim is true of any family trying to support someone with challenging behaviour. Without constructive conversations it is all too easy for relationships to deteriorate further, even disintegrate.

Choice

There is, as always in life, a choice. The choice in difficult situations where relationships become fraught is: remain in the same place – what are the consequences of staying still, for the individual, for the family? Or try to look for solutions to move forward, and contemplate working towards change?

Open communication is *always* the first step to exploring the real situation, all the events, the people involved and their feelings, and the first step to positive change.

None of this is easy – energy and much commitment are needed. Not every member of every family will be able to give the same in time or energy or commitment. Some will always be able to give more than others for all sorts of reasons – age, stamina, resilience, health, temperament. However, with everyone giving what they can when they can, mindful of how others react in various situations and for the need for constant communication, appropriate breaks and support, the chances of real 'best care' developing whenever required become much greater for any vulnerable individual. The alternative is allowing the compulsive behaviour not only to negatively affect – possibly ruin – one life, but those of a whole family and beyond.

Quite apart from giving carers much-needed information and support to enable them to achieve an effective and appropriate support role, and as well as such discussion and agreement also serving as reinforcement of the individual's determination, such teamwork may also help prevent relapse. In many chronic conditions, an advance agreement to treatment with carer support if relapse *does* occur may be a key to swift treatment leading to quicker recovery.

See also Chapter 5 and Chapter 13.

CHAPTER SEVEN

Difficult scenes and destructive relationships

It's really unfair to be shouted at about something that's nothing to do with me, as if it's my fault someone lost his lunch box.

[Sandra, primary teacher]

The mum was yelling and swearing at me good-oh . . . 'Don't you tell me what I should do, you and yer [. . .] textbook babies!' And other choice phrases. Seems like a regular part of my work. [Patrick, social worker]

I think it's important that the consultant knows my son is becoming ill again. But when I try to phone he won't speak to me, the girl said it was because of confidentiality. Last time my son was ill he was quite aggressive and I'm so worried. [L, mother of F, schizophrenia]

I've been trying to cope with that behaviour for years, but it's only when someone else reports it that it's taken seriously, and believed. I'm in despair, I really dread these meetings and nothing is getting any better. [Joan, carer]

My son was a bright outgoing baby, then his behaviour changed. That was bad enough but it was really shattering to discover that the doctor thought my son's behaviour was my fault. Eventually we were told 'He's on the Asperger's spectrum.' I still find it painful to watch the videos of him as a baby, but the way some professionals treat us is much worse.

[L, personal conversation]

At six, in middle 1950s, my sister was punished for being left handed, and severely punished for getting all her sums wrong – the answers were right, but she'd written all the numbers the wrong way round. [GS]

On my first day at secondary school, 1930s, a teacher read out the register of names. When he came to my name, he said Peter B? Brother of James B? I said Yes sir. And was belted for being the brother of James.

[GS, personal contact]

> We were told 'You have to examine your parenting skills.' We were then sent to a child psychiatrist, who assumed we were the problem.
>
> [Joan; Alan and Joan's story in Chapter 2]
>
> When we went in, there were four people – all professionals, all formally dressed – sitting behind the table facing us. Apart from one of them, we had no idea who they were or why they were there. They all asked us questions. Often they talked to each other and we couldn't understand what they were saying because of lots of initials and so on. We thought we were going there to get some help and advice – yeah, right! We felt like they all looked at us as if we were criminals.
>
> [T, interview, 2006]

All of which makes for very unhappy reading, as well as very unhappy situations for professionals and carers who somehow have to find a way through the minefield in order to help and support.

History and assumptions

Anticipating blame

Anticipating that blame will be served up as part of the discussion at meetings with a child's headteacher, a psychologist, a social worker or a psychiatrist often initiates a poor beginning to any communications, with the parent being interviewed feeling nervous and possibly defensive. Indeed, the parent may be a headteacher or psychiatrist or social worker by profession, or perhaps a fisherman, airline pilot, shop assistant, hairdresser, beautician, involved in business, copy writer, journalist . . . all represented in calls to the eating disorders helplines. In some cases, unfortunately, those fears are born out by events:

> Our daughter had been ill for about three years when we were called in to see a different psychiatrist, who looked at us and said 'In our experience, this behaviour is caused by sexual abuse in the family. Now, what do you have to tell me?'
>
> [Parent at eating disorders support meeting]

This report is not unique (see, for example, Jay & Doganis, 1987, p. 142).

> Parents? I wouldn't touch them with a barge pole!
>
> [Overheard by GS at eating disorders conference]

> Peter lives in a residential school now. They have interpreted the psychologist's report of reactive attachment disorder as 'you have a broken attachment with P'. They have told us that the excrement problem is 'a home problem we just have to sort out' – even though the school has a huge problem with the same behaviour, so much so that his place there might be in jeopardy.
>
> [Alan, see Alan and Joan's story in Chapter 2]

> In today's world, a mother's place is not in the kitchen or even in the home . . . a mother's place is in the wrong. [Anon]

Given the 20th-century history of 'blame and shame', perhaps it is not surprising still to find such attitudes surviving; not everyone keeps up with or wants to know the latest evidence-based research, often involving new technology such as brain scanning, which may give a very different perspective from the past.

The feeling of even the possibility of being blamed is a barrier to the building of constructive communications.

Parents are an easy target. Not only is the individual's childhood viewed by memories possibly – probably? – skewed by illness, but stress and exhaustion will already have taken their toll while problems are recognised and diagnoses made. Added to this, individual members of any family may remember the same events in different ways depending on personality and temperament, inevitably making it even more difficult to reach a true and accurate picture of events leading up to any stress-related illness.

> I remember my childhood as really happy. We lived in a detached house in the country. Although my parents were very busy – my father with work which often took him away, and my mother was involved in lots of committees and such, and they did quite a lot of entertaining at weekends – I remember having fun with the other children on the estate. As long as we appeared for lessons and at mealtimes, we were allowed to do more or less what we pleased. I invented lots of games and liked acting out stories I wrote even then.
>
> But recently I was talking to my sister and brother and it was as if we were remembering different lives! Really different. My brother said he hated the holidays because he had no other boys for company, really didn't want to come home from school at the end of terms. He said nothing ever happened at home where we lived, apart from 'mucking about'. Couldn't wait to get back to school and his friends.
>
> My sister was five years older than me, we didn't play much together I suppose because of the age difference thing. She said she remembers feeling isolated and really lonely where we lived. All her friends lived miles away. I suppose going to boarding school meant that we didn't have much contact with most of the village children. And she wanted our mother to spend more time with us. Maybe I just liked doing things on my own much more, could fill hours on my own with the things I liked doing. Now I can be with other people, but quite happy on my own too, don't mind. And it didn't bother me that mother was not around all the time, or busy. [N, writer friend, personal contact]

Professionals too will bring their own perceptions, background, theories and ideas along to any meetings and other communications, their own complicated network of personalities, background and environmental experiences, reactions to and perceptions of events, assumptions of common feelings and attitudes.

Many problems *do* have their roots in family life, and some parents or other family members may indeed be abusive, but much also depends on individual reactions and perceptions to particular situations. One child may have struggled through a negative experience – the death of a parent, or divorce and loss, for instance – with great difficulty but then gradually came to terms with it and has been able to move on. Another might 'fall apart' altogether and be affected long-term to a much greater degree. Yet another might try to ignore intense feelings at the time but have a reaction much later in life. The example might just as well involve various kinds of abuse both verbal and physical and of varying degrees, expectations of keeping a 'stiff upper lip' or not, expectations or not of achievements in education or sport or arts; in fact in every area of family life. Personality and temperament would seem to be the key to the differing reactions and ability to cope, added to where the family live, in what circumstances and society.

> This assumption – the Freudian assumption that many people's psychological problems had been put there by their parents – became so automatic that to this day no biography is complete without a passing reference to the parental causes of the subject's quirks.
>
> (Ridley, 2003)

From observations of the thousands of children with whom I worked, from observations of their siblings as well as interactions throughout their primary school education with parents and other family members, I believe that in addition to genetic influences, peer pressure, society and culture, television and advertising assume as a combined influence at least as much if not greater importance than parents as today's children grow up.

However I hesitate to go as far as Judith Rich Harris (1995) when she wrote: 'Do parents have any important long-term effects on the development of their child's personality? This article examines the evidence and concludes that the answer is no.' Harris, in common with Ridley (2003) and Levitt and Dubner (2006), makes the point that correlation does not mean the same as causation.

Generations of professionals, meanwhile, have been trained in the idea that emotional and psychological problems of children – and adults – are caused, simply, by the wrong actions of their parents during childhood. Much research, even recently, has been based on this assumption. From the School of Psychology, University of Birmingham, I received a set of three questionnaires designed for use with people diagnosed with eating disorders: 'This study investigated the relationship between reported childhood abuse and eating disorders in late adolescence . . . This proposes that childhood abuse indirectly affects eating attitudes through other variable core beliefs' (University of Birmingham, 2005). I found the questions – and possible choices for answers – a revelation (see also p. 128 Chapter 11).

When reading research, past or present, it is interesting to think of how the results were gained, how the questions were phrased, the options and phrasing allowed for response, as well as when and where it was carried out. And of course, who was asking the questions, how many people were involved in the study and under what circumstances: perhaps a large sample of the general population? People already in treatment for depression and/or other mental illness? Hospitalised patients?

As Jim Orford writes:

> Much personality research has been post hoc, based upon examination of people whose appetitive behaviour has already come to notice as being excessive. This fact immediately gives rise to the most challenging question: Are we witnessing the causes of excess or its consequences?
>
> (Orford, 2001)

In 1965 when I started teaching, there was often an invisible line drawn across the school door to deter parents from questioning teachers about curriculum or discipline matters, just as there had been during my own schooldays; even more so in my parents' day. Most teachers lived in the community in which they worked, so much more was known about a child's background. Despite teachers sometimes being very critical of a parent's behaviour, at that time there seemed no general culture of actually blaming parents for a child's difficulties – a dramatic change in attitude in 40 years.

> I was told that my illness stemmed from my parents' upbringing of me.
>
> [C, recovered from anorexia, ED helpline, 2005]

> When I was having counselling for anxiety, this therapist tried to get me to say I hated my father because he never really *showed* his affection. I used to say: no, honestly I didn't. It was the culture we lived in, not showing our feelings, being strong, nobody else's father showed affection either at that time.
>
> [RN, interview]

As Steven Pinker, cognitive psychologist, observes:

> Patients in traditional forms of psychotherapy while away their 50 minutes reliving childhood conflicts and learning to blame their unhappiness on how their parents treated them.
>
> (Pinker, 2002)

How did we get here?

Practitioners and treatment systems have not only failed to offer family education, but in too many cases they have intentionally avoided any communication with

> families except for collecting background information about the circumstances of the disorder. Family members' questions, their very natural attempts to obtain information about what is wrong with their relative and what they can do to help, have been carefully deflected or ignored by the treating professionals.
>
> Traditionally, this failure to communicate with family members was the deliberate policy of many mental health facilities. Although its effects were cruel and often damaging to the patient and family, the policy was considered necessary for effective treatment. It was based on a model of mental illness in which recovery was viewed as evolving from a therapeutic alliance between the patent and therapist. In this model, it was felt that any communication with family members would be experienced as a breach of trust by the patient and would gravely interfere with progress in treatment. Most models, in fact, viewed the family as a source of 'toxins' rather than help.
>
> (Mueser & Gingerich, 1994, p. xi)

Some parents may face personal and very individual difficulties – poverty, long working hours, poor health – which affect their children's upbringing; some might benefit from anger or stress management at times of their lives as they struggle to cope with work, family, finance, adversity; some may have differing views on what 'best' is (differing from mine perhaps as well as often from those, in retrospect, of their offspring!) but the vast majority of parents do try their best. Though not all.

> A girl of five, taken ill in school: in the absence of a telephone contact number, staff members took the child home during their break time. The child started screaming uncontrollably when she saw that the person who opened the door was an uncle. Later it was discovered that grandmother *knew* that the uncle regularly took advantage of being left alone with the child.
>
> [GS]

Tragically, sometimes families *are* horribly abusive.

Consequences of 'assume abuse' theory

When assumptions are made on either or possibly both sides – by some professionals that parents' behaviour has caused their children's behaviour, by parents having come across such theories – it is inevitable that relationships will become fraught, may not even 'get off the ground' without hard words. Professionals, including this author, can all tell stories of aggressive parents who shout and threaten, which may affect future family–professional and professional–family relationships.

Patronising, ignoring, accusing

Many family members talk of feeling patronised and/or ignored.

> When my brother asked me to go with him for support at his first meeting with the psychiatrist, I said ok. She spoke only to me, addressed all questions about my brother to me. Although my brother was having some emotional problems, there was no reason to ignore him – and I didn't know the answers anyway. She didn't even try to find out how he was feeling, or if he could answer the questions. In the end I said to ask my brother the questions, talk to him. She looked very surprised and not too pleased.
>
> [Linda, interview]

And in a few cases, relationships are destroyed by 'cringe' conversations based on lack of training, lack of understanding or empathy.

> My friend's little girl remains dangerously ill with anorexia – weeks on the drip etc, vomiting very bad and awful problems with the drip. She's in a general ward with a 24-hour watch as she is suicidal – the specialist eating disorders programme won't take her until she's stable. In the general ward there is no psychological programme or input, she's heavily drugged now. My friend is burnt out and no-one will listen to any of her suggestions. She's been told to 'Cut the cord and go home'.
>
> [L, personal contact]

Whatever the roots of *any* problems with an emotional background, the offence caused by initial communication, operates later or established contact which destroys trust, which leave anyone feeling patronised, blamed, ignored and frustrated, *will not help in any way the young person whom both carer and professionals want to help.* They certainly did not help in any of the situations outlined in the extracts quoted from various sources for this book.

Whatever the research debates, it is not helpful to the most vulnerable people at the centre of the often unhappy picture if professional and home carers start out with preconceived suspicions about the other, let alone if the essential relationship is affected by destructive communications.

Benefits of constructive carer–professional communication

- Better chance of 24-hour 'best care'
- Better chance of continuity of care, whether at home, in the community, in outpatient or inpatient care
- Effective role for family members and other carers, leading to more family harmony and better support

- Better chance of a good outcome for vulnerable individual – quality of life, recovery, prevention or reduction of relapse episodes

Finding and laying constructive communication foundations is the best way to build towards all of the above.

CHAPTER EIGHT

Resources

Creating 24-hour best care

Whatever job we take on, whether individual or group project, to enable us to do it effectively we need resources; we need to look at what we have and then work out what we need.

Each of the following tasks needs resources. Individually or as a group, use a piece of paper to scribble down what resources you might need to do one of these jobs effectively; try to be as precise as possible.

- Planning a new dwelling
- Organising a move (home or work)
- Feeding your family for a month
- Travel to visit a long lost relation in Australia, travelling via Singapore
- You're new to an area, rural or city, and you have severe toothache – possibly an abscess – on a Sunday.

Have you included what you already have? What is on your list of new resources that you need to acquire? How are you going to find them? Who might be able to help you try to find them?

On the journey through life, sometimes if we are lucky we recognise that we already have what we need – knowledge and information, finances, tools, physical and emotional help and support. And energy. Sometimes in any job or undertaking, we have time to plan for acquiring what we may need; today we in the developed world have a vast range of ways of finding what we may need. If we're really lucky there'll be detailed instructions, if really *really* lucky we may have some relevant training or find someone with experience to teach or guide us through. At times, however, circumstances mean that resources are more make-do-and-mend – and in an emergency or very hard times we just have to cope as well as we can using whatever comes to hand.

The same is true in supporting a vulnerable individual who needs help to cope with aspects of life, whether this is a short- or long-term need, physical or emotional – for example, a diagnosis of cancer, distress over the sudden death of a loved one, or a major operation.

This also applies whether the person in supportive role is a family or professional carer. *Having adequate resources* – or the tools to enable the job, whatever it may be, to be done – *is a crucial factor in providing effective support, and in its outcome.*

Professionals, resources and providing care

> One of the biggest challenges facing [social work] professionals is how to square professional practice with the 'circle' of organisational constraints.
>
> (Adams *et al.*, 2002)

When a professional – social worker, psychologist, psychiatrist, teacher, nurse, therapist or other – meets with any condition or illness, long years of training are usually involved, plus discussions with and support from more experienced colleagues. Resources include information, literature from many sources outlining past and current thinking, equipment as up-to-date as possible, meetings and conferences, administrative support, as well as resources of time in the form of people working in the same area of expertise. Resources are developed to support all efforts in the best way possible.

Professional resources in medical and social work and teaching are rarely if ever enough. With continuing developments through research always adding to knowledge and information, and expectations growing, sometimes they are completely inadequate. This is especially true with state or public funding where a global amount is raised through taxes, allocated to support these services and then divided between all the 'competing' areas or departments.

Professionals from these departments will argue as best they can for support for their own field. Whatever the area under debate, there will be 'winners' and 'losers', with 'winners' of financial resources often coming from fields which seem more attractive to the public as well as to officials and administrators. Even the debating, arguing and negotiating skills of the professionals may be an important factor in support of their particular field of interest and expertise: e.g. medicine – maternity or mental health; teaching – nursery, primary, secondary or tertiary; transport – air, railway or road transport.

Traditionally people who displayed challenging behaviour – or indeed any behaviour outside what was considered the norm in whatever society they lived – were ostracised, including by their own families. Sometimes in earlier times people who did not conform to an accepted norm – or annoyed their neighbours? – could be accused of witchcraft or other socially condemned activities, tried summarily, and put to death. In Britain in Victorian times, institutions were set up to address the 'problem' of those who did not conform, and thousands were locked away – sometimes even for the 'crime' of being pregnant at the wrong age and in the wrong circumstances or when the girl had suffered rape.

Gradually over many years services have been developed and research carried out, but in comparison to other disciplines, mental health services were – and still are in many countries – seen as a 'Cinderella' service. This is despite any individual's good mental health underpinning physical health; if a high number of individuals suffer poor health, the whole community will be affected. Conditions which did not seem to fit into any known diagnosis were traditionally referred to mental health services. And traditionally, the public in general have little or no understanding of such services, nor patience with people who – to an outsider with no knowledge or experience of the issues involved – may seem to be simply indulging in either self-pity or bad behaviour.

Social work and mental health professionals feel keenly the endless frustration of poor resources: lack of funding for adequate manpower, of seeing waiting lists growing because there are simply not enough trained staff to offer appointments at time of need, or no-one to answer the telephone or do the administration because the admin assistant is off ill, or perhaps no replacement has yet been appointed after someone went on maternity leave. In anorexia a wait of 8 months for specialist treatment can make the difference between life or death (up to 20% die an early death), recovery or relapse, and years of chronic illness. As in any of the 'excessive appetites', by the time the professional help is offered the illness has become more entrenched and the person may have retreated again into denial. Knowing this adds to the frustration; many professionals will work longer and longer hours and even risk their own health to offer a better level of care than the resources they have available might allow.

> The reality of effective services is based on the amount of resources allocated to them. Funding (for eating disorders services for Tayside and Grampian) has been *reduced* between 2003 and 2005. Child and adolescent services often adopt a family approach from the start, whereas those who are trained in adult psychiatry and adult mental health professions do not tend to have training in family work, so any work we do with families tends to be in parallel with individual patients. That is a deficiency of our services. If we had resources we could develop work with families, we ought to develop an improved provision. Lack of resources is a big factor in provision of services or lack of them.
>
> I do not know why a dedicated unit in Aberdeen, with NHS inpatient provision for adults in a life-threatening condition, has not been achieved – you need to ask the people from the health authority.
>
> [Evidence from Dr Harry Millar, Scottish Health Committee, Eating Disorders Inquiry 2005]

Even resources such as training of primary professionals, e.g. GPs, to allow early recognition of conditions such as eating disorders are frequently missing, severely restricted or dependent on a majority vote by a professional body as to what training the group should undertake. When this is the case, despite physical health being inextricably linked to emotional and mental health, training in mental health has frequently been the loser. And often, when training is at last on offer and undertaken, lack of specialist services to which diagnosed patients may be referred causes further frustration.

Comparatively low rates of pay may also be a factor in attracting and retaining staff, but most nurses, teachers and other professionals chose their job for other reasons and go into it knowing the salary scale. Inadequate resources to do the job they want to in the best way they can for the people they want to help, is one of the most important issues which leads to able professionals leaving to work elsewhere, as is poor morale if – when? – they feel undervalued by their community.

> There is a huge difference between theory and reality. In my job I work with adult individuals, male, with extremely challenging behaviour; one is over 6 feet tall and 17 stone in weight, and lives in social care because family carers can't cope at home. Social Work *had* to find a placement for the client, and they expect the project and the placement to work.
>
> Theory says provide a 'home environment'. Theory says that violent behaviour is caused by triggers causing frustration, therefore avoid the triggers. Is it possible to avoid all violent behaviour? *No.* In reality, violent behaviour is blamed on carers triggering the behaviour. In reality, the violent client controls the project because we can't physically deny him things – we have no sanctions, he simply refuses to cooperate. But there is pressure to keep the project functioning.
>
> [E, care worker, interview]

Often professionals, having tried to develop a effectively supportive scheme and persuaded authorities to fund it, feel under pressure to *make* it work – or to make others make it work.

▶ Carers, resources and providing care

> Long-distance lorry drivers are required by law to limit the time they spend behind the wheel. When they bend the law, which from time to time they do, they often bend something else as well. Fatigue affects the way we function, and is known to be dangerous. Carers, unlike lorry drivers, are not prohibited by law from spending too long on the job.
>
> (Marriott, 2003)

Exhaustion and frustration are frequently top of any carer's list of difficulties, with knock-on effects on the quality of care which it is possible to offer.

As Hugh Marriott also points out, almost all professional carers 'have their hearts in the right place' – after all, they could probably earn much more and with far less hassle if they had chosen a different career; most genuinely do care and want to help. Although rules are necessary in all organisations, they are also a constraint when their development and application eat up financial resources.

Lack of professional resources frequently creates huge difficulties and frustration for home or 'informal' carers. Lack of proper administrative support or extra therapists or social workers or teaching support assistants means very hard choices being made. This means, for example, a doctor tries to cope without adequate notes for a patient, or spends his own precious time tracking down the relevant information; a social worker takes brief notes at an important meeting, which are not typed up or filed ready for next meetings and recommendations, and not available in what may turn out to be a critical situation or turning point. Lack of staff to cope with the numbers needing help means that adults as well as children may be put at risk.

The day started really well. We went over the timetable, including how we would change immediately after break to be ready for gym at 11 a.m. We discussed what each group was to tackle in maths and at about 9.15 everyone had settled down to work. For the first 20 minutes everything was great – two groups were doing practical work with me, Martin was in one of the other two groups doing written work. He knew what he was doing so he was quite happy, worked hard and kept on track even though Heather, the assistant who usually worked with him, was absent that day.

Then a message came from the office to say that there had been a change to the gym timetable, could we be ready for gym at 10 a.m. Most of the kids were delighted to abandon maths! But Martin became really distressed and angry; he hates being disturbed when he gets settled to a task or *any* change to what he has understood to be happening during a day. He was shouting and when I tried to calm him and explain what had happened, he hit me. Several of the other kids got involved and I had to send for the headteacher to come up. The class was in chaos, and I felt awful. The rest of the day was ruined, the whole week affected. Some of the kids aren't past trying to wind Martin up, some of the them think it's funny – and others see it as a great way of disrupting work they want to get out of doing. All my planning went down the drain.

[G, primary teacher, class of 12-year-olds]

In schools, a teaching assistant may mean the difference between a pupil with challenging behaviour coping in the classroom, or not. If the pupil becomes distressed and angry when accustomed routine changes suddenly, because they cannot understand why this has happened, and the teacher is also struggling to work with 20–30 other children, not only will the individual's education be affected but that of the whole class as well as the work and morale of the teacher.

There is no point – as well as being completely unfair – in feeling cross with a teacher or teaching assistant, or anyone else who is 'stretched to the limit', simply doing their best in difficult circumstances. As Joan (see Chapter 2) says:

> The speech therapist only works part time; the manager is off ill; his line manager is on secondment and *his* line manager is also the director for several other departments. Therefore it is often better to go straight to the top – write to your MP or MSP, put pressure on top levels about lack of resources, because your poor speech therapist (or teacher or teaching assistant) can do nothing.

Family resources

It is rare that families have much in the way of resources either in training or finances. Even professionals with long experience may find it hard to cope at home when a 'challenging' condition affects one of their own family and they find all aspects of life affected as they have to cope every day, every week, month and year.

Although professionals may have a better idea of how to set about finding basic information about the condition, for most families finding information is frequently the first, often ongoing, challenge. Some GPs are happy to accept that they know little about a particular condition brought to their surgery – and offer the name of an appropriate charity who might be able to help; others simply say they have referred a patient to the appropriate department but otherwise provide no information. This is particularly true when someone is officially an adult, over 16 or whatever the local designated age for adulthood may be. Still others simply refuse to talk to family members, quoting 'confidentiality' as the reason (see Chapter 10).

It took me two years to find the Eating Disorders Association (EDA, a UK charity) and some information about my daughter's illness, as well as a helpline and listening ear. It was only when I went to London for the EDA Carers' Conference in 2000, five years after my daughter told me of her diagnosis, that I heard professionals freely giving information about these devastating illnesses – and I began to make sense of some of the very challenging behaviour I'd struggled to cope with at home. The relief I felt was immense at hearing Professor Janet Treasure outline best practice in ED, and knowing that what I'd been doing at home was roughly what was being recommended.

I wept with that relief, travelling all the hundreds of miles home from London. Somehow, by blundering about, trial and error – many errors! – and some sort of intuition, I had found a way to support my beloved Jay in her years-long battle against the compulsive dictates of anorexia/bulimia.

Had I not somehow worked out that the best way to support my daughter was *not* to collude with the illness by giving in to her demands, nor to be so frightened by the unpredictable rages that it paralysed my responses – at times very similar challenging behaviour, I know now, to that encountered in other addictions such as drugs, alcohol, gambling – things might have turned out very differently indeed.

> On my son's discharge from hospital after an episode of acute psychosis we had no information about his condition, how he would behave, how we should react to him. We had no experience in dealing with him when unwell. We were expected to just cope – a complete nightmare!
>
> [Carer, quoted in Department of Health, 2006]

I too felt I was living in a nightmare; nothing seemed to make any sense. Today, through listening to many other family members and other carers on helplines, at meetings and conferences I know that, comparatively speaking, my daughter and I got off lightly! Everything is relative. I count myself very fortunate to be able to watch and talk to Jay, now 33 and well, living independently and working fulltime, enjoying social life with her many friends.

Resources for home carers

Without information and other resources to enable families and other carers to support their loved one, it is simply not possible to create the best care on a 24-hour basis. After diagnosis and any waiting list, there will be, it is hoped, appropriate and specialist therapeutic appointments with trained experienced professionals, or perhaps relatively short admissions for intensive treatment. Apart from these relatively very short periods of time, carers have to find ways of coping in the everyday. With chronic conditions this may mean years, even many years.

To go back to the questions at the beginning of this chapter about resources for any job or project, what would help give a carer the tools to enable them to do the job of supporting their family member? Is it possible to make a list of resources? If you were to be asked to care at home for a family member who needed a greater level of care than hitherto, what would be on your list?

Information

Up-to-date information came first on carers' lists in each and every interview: information, not about confidential discussions between patient and professionals, but about the illness or condition. For example:

- what they might have to cope with so that they might be prepared for what may happen
- what to do in certain circumstances, e.g. in a situation involving danger for the individual or for other people, or what to be watchful for as signs of possible relapse
- possible or probable duration of illness
- where to find help.

> Without information how am I expected to know what to do? I love my son so much, but I don't like this behaviour . . . and if I do the wrong thing because I don't know how to respond, what then? I'm so afraid of doing the wrong thing but how do I know?
>
> [M, carer, son with bulimia nervosa]

Support

Support came next. For example:

- coming to terms with the information and how it may affect them and other family members
- understanding all the implications of that information
- support in finding ways of best supporting the troubled individual.

> When the doctor told me my son was autistic, I just couldn't take it in at first. And that it wasn't going to go away, it wasn't just a phase.
>
> [R, carer, son with autism]

Doctors talk about how difficult it is to give bad news about possible length of illness – hearing that the average time anorexia takes to work through is five to six years (and possibly much longer) with many setbacks, is extremely distressing. Yet without this information carers may believe uninformed comments such as: 'It's just a phase, she'll grow out of it'.

Writing on autism, Drs Simon Baron-Cohen and Patrick Bolton say this:

> Any diagnostic assessment should be followed by sensitive discussion with the family about their child's problems, their severity and expected future course. Further information and support should always be provided.
>
> Doctors should try to keep information short and simple when discussing the diagnosis, and then go through the details when the parents have had a chance to recover from hearing the news.
>
> (Baron-Cohen & Bolton, 1993)

A wide range of emotions which parents may feel are outlined in their whole chapter on 'coping with the news' – loss, grief, disbelief, shock, sometimes despair and depression, coupled with anxiety about the child's future. A 'cloak of guilt' is mentioned along with the common feeling of somehow being responsible for the child's condition, feelings of embarrassment at how other people might regard their parenting skills.

> Nothing seemed real and more. He (the doctor) was certainly not real. It was as if he had just fallen to pieces in front of my eyes. Everything – my way of life, my pride, my confidence, my whole outlook – had just been totally and irrevocably shattered. The numbness was merciful. It was better that I should realise slowly how much we, and above all, Simon, had lost.
>
> (Lovell, 1978)

Empathy and understanding

'Some glimmer of understanding for what the family is going through and coping with on a daily basis' was/is often mentioned by carers. Even a simple acknowledgment of what they *may* be feeling is preferable to simple statement of facts by professionals, without further comment.

> Faced with your child turning away from you, apparently more absorbed in some repetitive activity than in you, wouldn't you feel dismayed, rejected and frustrated?
>
> (Baron-Cohen & Bolton, 1993)

Baron-Cohen and Bolton note that common patterns in coming to terms with the news often involve:

- *denial* (there must be something else, something the doctors haven't thought of)
- *anger* at the injustice (why our child?)
- *guilt* (what did we do to cause this?)
- *sadness and despair.*

Often it is only after going through all these emotions that parents come to terms with the news, followed by

- *acceptance* and
- *looking for practical ways of coping.*

Also acknowledged are extreme reactions – shock, denial, blame, endless searching for a cure, deep depression – which adds greatly to the stress already affecting family relationships. When a parent expresses blaming angry feelings by 'shooting the messenger', the doctor who gave the bad news is also included in the unhappy circle.

Talking to or meeting others coping in similar circumstances can also help. Feelings of isolation are often mentioned by carers; finding – or, better still, being given right after diagnosis – a contact number of a charity or other support group or individual can help. Sharing information, practical ideas and ways of coping can be very beneficial, as well as acknowledging the difficulties encountered in the long-term caring role (see Appendix).

Every condition is different, and every individual in every family may react in a different way.

> Psychological resilience of each parent and amount of support available from family, friends and health professionals will also be important, helping some parents (and other family members) to pass through some stages more quickly than others.
>
> (Baron-Cohen & Bolton, 1993)

Although these writers were referring to parents coping with a diagnosis of autism, the same or similar patterns can be observed in families coping with many different conditions. I have heard many echoes at meetings, interviews for this book, at conferences and on the helpline.

First steps to 24-hour best care

Draw up a list of resources already there, ideally with professionals and family members working together wherever possible.

1 *Professional*

- What can professionals do to support the family?
- What can family do to support the individual?
- What can the family do to support the professionals' work?
- What will treatment involve?
- What do professionals need from the family?
- How best to work towards operating as a team to provide the best care possible?

2 *Information*: What is already known? What is needed? How and where to find?

- Resources needed

3 *Family*: Tell family members, explain the effects of the illness/condition, and what may happen. Assess what level of information they will be able

to cope with, particularly siblings – everyone will need some information on why a loved one is behaving differently.

- What can each member do to help the individual/the main carer/the family?
- Family forum?—discussion, brainstorm.
- Encourage everyone to take part, offer ideas, discuss problems, possible solutions.

4 *Friends*: Tell your friends. Most people want to help their friends if they know what is needed, and are pleased to be asked. (You're also giving them permission for them to ask for aid when they need it.)

5 *Finance*: Existing? What may change? How will you cope?

- What help is needed? (Author's note: this became a major problem when bulimia spiralled out of control, as for many other families struggling to cope with other addictive compulsive disorders. Talking about the problems was the beginning of realisation for my daughter of how her behaviours were affecting others in our family.)

6 *Support*: Existing? (Needed? Where to find? – See below.)

7 *Respite*: Having rests to allow you to continue your journey are essential. These may involve simply arranging to have cup of coffee with a friend, or joining an enjoyable activity on a regular basis, or having an overnight, weekend or holiday break. Work out how these crucial breaks can be achieved; if necessary, consider who will look after your loved one at that time, and how such help may be found (see Chapter 16).

8 *Work issues*: Will caring roles at home have any implications for work commitments of any member of the family? If someone gives up paid employment how will this affect the household/quality of life for everyone?

9 Other?

Having identified the resources already available, now draw up another list, this time of what is still needed, again using the headings given above – professional, information, family, friends, finance; support; respite; any others?

- *If possible, discuss* the list with others – perhaps friends, or a professional, who may see something you have forgotten or haven't thought of.
- *Work out from your list how you will develop resources* in each area to enable you to offer the best care possible.

- *Make your lists, whether professional or home carer, as practical as possible.*
- *The lists – professional and carer – may be added to or changed at any time, depending on changes in circumstances.*

The more information and support that can be shared the better, not only for the professionals and carers concerned who develop a more pleasant working relationship; most importantly, better for the troubled individual everyone is trying to help. No information? The results have often led to relapse or even to tragedy.

> My son was discharged again from hospital, after intensive treatment, and they didn't inform anyone. So there was no-one in the house when he got home – what a welcome. For anyone, not just because he's my son, or because he's been ill. I know he's an adult – legally at least – but he's also very vulnerable and sometimes even at the best of times doesn't think very straight. Anyway it's a bad start – he thinks no-one cares about him, doesn't understand him or make allowances. And I hadn't much food in the house. Imagine if I'd gone off to visit my daughter and her family for a couple of weeks.
>
> [A, carer for M, schizophrenia]

An ideal world?

It is not possible to have perfect relationships in every case, there will always be problems, oversights, exceptions, things will go wrong, misunderstandings occur – as in every human endeavour. There will always be instances even within *good* relationships when things go awry.

But without even trying to work towards such co-operation the results are usually lack of understanding on all sides, poor relationships and much frustration, leading to care well short of what is possible (let alone best) for those who most need it. Just imagine what real teamwork – including co-operation, co-ordination and combining forces to push for properly developed resources – could achieve!

CHAPTER NINE

Professionals and carers

Pressures, problems and pleasures

Few jobs involve complete isolation from human company and, given the ease with which misunderstandings may occur between people in everyday life, in every conceivable situation, it is inevitable that a few of these will also be part of working life. There are workplaces where relationships are good, misunderstandings are few and far between, and workdays flow fairly smoothly – at least, most of the time. There are also workplaces where conflict, backbiting and unpleasantness seem almost an inbuilt part of the scene.

Most groups of people working on a project – whether in a shop, theatre, tourist agency, factory, school, surgery or anywhere else – fall somewhere in the middle, depending on the individual personalities of those involved. However, the more people involved in any workplace, the more likely it will be that someone somewhere will not grasp what another means in any communication; the more likely someone somewhere in the organisation will be having an 'off day'; the greater the possibility for deterioration of relationships; and the more difficult it will be to get everyone on track and pulling together again.

And when the job itself entails working with people already under stress – and their varying ways of coping with that stress – the potential for difficult relationships increases greatly.

It is not possible to list specifically here every problem encountered – whether working individually or in a team, professional or family group, tempers and tolerance are much more likely to be shorter in people already under pressures caused by lack of time/energy/resources. Therefore I intend to concentrate on those I see as main problems adding enormously to ongoing stress. (See Chapter 4 for the effects on families and other carers of stress in their caring role.)

Professional pressures and problems

Among the pressures and problems can be included time, energy, active listening, stressful encounters, home pressures, confrontations, morale (low), unrealistic expectations, and admin and record keeping (endless).

Time and energy

Time and energy are two of the most important pressures in any job – time to do the job properly, and enough personal energy to meet all the demands.

When a job involves the personal qualities and particular communication strengths of an individual (and also recognition of weaknesses) in addition to skills particular to the job, it is inevitable that increased pressure is also involved.

> I felt I couldn't run fast enough just to keep up, no matter how I tried.
>
> [P, former social worker]

> Careworkers feel that admitting to 'stress or depression' would be seen as a mark against them if this appears on their record, and that they'd be penalised in an application for promotion or a new job. The reality is stress and depression are big problems – the 'shelf life' isn't long before burnout, and there's a high sickness rate.
>
> [E, care worker]

Without proper support, resources frequently lack enough workers on the ground to cope with demand for services. Professionals' precious time may be spent on activities such as administration, answering calls, searching for records, all of which add to professional pressures.

Personal energy too fluctuates depending on activities both at work and outside, with family commitments and events.

> I ended up feeling bad about taking a long weekend off to go and visit my daughter and her husband when my first grandchild was born! I kept thinking about all the people whose appointments had to be postponed because there was just no-one else to see them.
>
> [Cathy, social worker]

Lives outside work involve family commitments, friends, hobbies, social life, perhaps further study , and these will take up varying amounts of energy depending on the professional's own age and age of their family (a young baby may involve wakeful night hours or lack of sleep; a family member may need special care; a friend's invitation to socialise). It is important that professionals have these activities to revive and refresh them at work; without them professionals like anyone else can become workaholics, risking illness and burnout.

> I got to Friday and then I got flu, spent the weekend in bed. I knew there was no-one to take my class, so I dragged myself in on Monday.
>
> [Jane, primary teacher]

This was a recurring theme when I was teaching: teachers worked flat out on preparation, actual time in class, followed by marking to enable them to prepare for next day, plus the amount of administrative work which has increased greatly over the years. Similar patterns may be found in other 'caring' professions.

Trying to be realistic about personal energy, finding a realistic work/life balance becomes a major problem for many when resources such as time and adequate support are restricted. Caring can be felt almost as a handicap when you know that not being able to offer appropriate support will inevitably affect the lives of others, and feelings of guilt can encroach during time off; the more conscientious and caring, the more you are at risk!

Therefore time out to discuss feelings, resources, realistic balance of time, energy levels, as well as to share resources and information, time out to spend with family and friends on leisure activities to renew energy levels is a necessity rather than a luxury when 'time allows' – but one of the easiest cuts to make when trying desperately to find extra time for appointments, to write up the pile of reports or work out how to allocate very restricted financial resources.

> Often I think on Sunday that it'll only take half an hour to do a catchup so I start the week ahead or at least on track – and three hours later I'm still working. My husband and kids often complain.
>
> [Cathy, social worker]

Such choices are one of the greatest pressures.

Active listening

Whether between colleagues or in family, active listening is an extremely important skill. To a few people this comes naturally – they seem to be able to 'tune in' to other people, listen and respond appropriately without really having to stop to consider what they are doing. For most, however, trying to put aside your own feelings and thoughts, *not* putting your own interpretations on events described, *not* making assumptions about mutual understanding as well as being detached and non-judgemental, for any length of time is a skill to be developed, possibly over several years.

To actively listen in *any* circumstances – even with good friends, though especially in conversations needing thought and careful response – takes concentration and focus, plus empathy and patience, all of which take energy. To do this when someone has distorted thinking due to illness or disorder is even more difficult, when that person acts in a way which is detrimental to their own health, perhaps or that of others, and possibly is very hostile to any efforts no matter how well-meant. Added to that will be decisions about level of information to give, if and when and how ideas could or should be challenged. All of which makes active listening even more draining.

Stressful encounters

Stressful encounters will deplete personal energy.

During my many years in primary teaching sometimes a meeting involved giving a parent bad news, e.g. when a child was having problems with some area of the curriculum, or perhaps a personal problem involving bullying. Sometimes a parent found it distressing and felt somehow guilty about their child's problems; others were unwilling to believe what they were being told, even in the face of several witnesses ('My child would never behave like that!'). Sometimes parents felt that the rules were unfair, or that staff were not making enough efforts, or accused witnesses of lying. And occasionally a parent would be very unpleasant; on a few occasions, actually threatening.

Expectations, realistic and unrealistic

As a primary headteacher any serious problems inevitably came to my door – therefore stressful and difficult communication experiences were indeed part of my working life.

> When I told him that the bus drivers were refusing to carry his son to school, he towered over me, yelling into my face. It was terrifying. All I could think of was to keep repeating that perhaps we should talk about this later when he was calmer. Over and over again until eventually he left. Later, when he'd gone, I started to shake.
> [GS]

Thankfully in teaching for me there were many other aspects to the job to balance these, including working with the children, watching their achievements and progress through their first years at school, and working with a great team.

> Parents just don't understand we work within limits – they seem to think we can wave a magic wand, or give out a few pills and everything will be OK. Totally unrealistic!
> [J, social worker in mental health]

In social work and for other mental health professionals, it is usually *only* during difficult times that they will be involved. Working with people at times when they are troubled and vulnerable, whether client or carer, plays a far greater part in these working lives than in most teachers' lives. Communication with distressed people at times of difficulty in their lives – who may react by crying helplessly, with defensive aggression, argue relentlessly, lack of concentration and unable to take in what is being said – is stressful for anyone who listens and cares. And when someone is very distressed it is often hard (impossible?) to remember how others may feel on the other side of the communications.

Paperwork and administration

A relentlessly growing amount is officially required, and often, in any project, the amount of time it will take for proper record keeping, letters to be sent out, appointments to be made, careful filing to enable others to find individual records, is underestimated. Further, when financial cuts are being made this is often the first soft target, leaving committed professionals struggling even more to keep adequate records in order.

Machines may make all sorts of things easier – legible writing, presentation, information sharing, communication both formal and informal – but they have also increased the amount of contact and other expectations. For the volume of email can be such that many professionals now dread the amount of time they'll have to give to dealing with it on return from even a short break; there may be hundreds of messages to deal with, only some of them really important – and they all need to be opened and read before deciding what needs to be given time and responded to in depth. Ignore them and a professional may miss some vital piece of information; the decision on how much time to devote to such administration then becomes a stress in itself.

> I'd hundreds of emails – I'd only been away a week! Some were relating to a car left in the wrong place in the car park, or headlights left on, some-one looking for a reference book, that sort of thing. Others were important to my work . . . but every single one had to be opened to check, and dealt with. Takes so much time, email, time I want to use for what I think really matters – but I still have to deal with them, decide how important each one is, before I can delete any of them. Is it worth having a holiday?!
>
> [K, co-ordinator of public health project, personal contact]

Confrontation

Finding personal strength to cope with conflict and confrontation can be a huge pressure using much energy. I can recall occasions of being yelled at about incidents which had nothing to do with me – I happened to be there, available, and in the firing line when someone reached the end of their tether, and vented their frustration at the world in general on whoever happened to appear. The last straw might have been a letter about headlice (the school nurse who had issued the letter was long gone) or a lost dinner ticket, and a new ticket would have to be paid for.

Then there were instances where bullying was involved. Unfortunately bullying behaviour has been a part of human life for many centuries and shows no sign of disappearing.

It is distressing to discover that your child has been the victim of bullying; perhaps even more distressing to be told that your child has subjected others to bullying. As always with human beings, reactions will vary ('What can I do to help?' 'Wait till I get the little . . . home!' 'My child would never behave like that – I don't believe you no matter how many [. . .] people say they saw it happen.') Some parents, no matter what the evidence, seem programmed to 'defend' their children come what may: if they feel denying a problem is needed, that's exactly what they will do. If unable to dismiss the evidence they may even find reasons why the unacceptable behaviour was necessary, blaming anyone who happens to be in the firing line.

> She was yelling at me as if it was all my fault, swearing and threatening. All I could do was to ask her to leave and come back when she's calm. I kept repeating it, over and over. Finally she ran out of steam and left.
>
> [J, social worker]

Whatever the circumstances or scene, workplace or home, it is extremely unpleasant to be shouted at, let alone threatened, most especially when the reaction seems unfair.

Morale

Many people are willing to do a job with few resources, are willing to settle for fewer material rewards, *if they feel valued*. As in every place of work, shop or shipyard, office or factory, there are indeed also inadequate teachers in schools whose actions and their effects are remembered for many years and deserve all the criticism, but generally teachers care much for those for whose education and welfare they are responsible, work long hours to try to provide the best start in life possible – and take home relatively poor financial reward in comparison with many other workers. The same is true of social workers, care home workers and nurses. Yet most of the stories read in newspapers are not about the hard work of the many but about the truly dreadful actions of the few – endorsing the distorted view of these professions.

> 'If it bleeds, it leads' is an old newsroom adage. Newspapers don't do 'proportionate'. It was ever thus.
>
> (*Sunday Herald*, 2006)

This relentless stress on the negative with very few mentions of the hard work and commitment of the vast majority of both professionals and families has had quite an effect. With inadequate resources, lack of time and depleted energy all making their contributions to pressures, many professionals feel the lack of value placed on their efforts as the last straw. With morale at rock bottom many leave the profession they trained so hard for, conscious that by doing so they leave an even more difficult job with even fewer resources of time for those left behind. A recently published report in Scotland gives depressing figures for recruitment of social workers – in only one area are all social work posts filled, with most seeking staff to fill up to 30% of vacancies. Finding teachers, including promoted staff, is also a problem in many areas.

> The family seemed hostile at first. Took a while to break the ice. I think they expected criticism.
>
> [Mary, psychologist]

> I get really fed up with telling the same story over and over again, for years now, every time we have to see yet another professional – there have been so many changes of staff, so many different professionals, while they tried to decide what the diagnosis is for my son.
>
> [Sheila Gray, carer]

Pressures and problems for carers

- Read this chapter again.
- Where you read 'professionals', substitute 'families and carers'.
- Everything on the list above – time and energy, active listening, stressful encounters, confrontations, morale, lack of resources, expectations – also applies to home carers, on a 24-hour basis.
- Read *The Selfish Pig's Guide to Caring* by Hugh Marriott (2003).

Breaking the cycle

- Stressful confrontations build on the pressures of time and energy, can easily become a vicious circle – difficult meetings and confrontations, whatever the triggers or reasons – for professionals can lead to a very jaundiced view of families in general as unreasonable, unrealistic and displaying awful personality traits . . .
- . . . which in turn may lead to unfair judgements and handicap beginnings with new or inherited clients and their families . . .
- . . . while families may get a very unfair picture of professionals who to them just seem not to care whether or not the family actually has the resources needed to provide home support sometimes for many years let alone offer the necessary information and support to enable them to fulfil their caring role . . . [GS]

How can this cycle be broken?

Both family members and professionals have a part to play in breaking this destructive cycle, by trying to understand the pressures and problems of each other – lack of resources or 'tools of the trade' to do the job of support. This is not easy, most especially with media stress on the most horrific cases of negligent professionals and relentless criticism of families, even exaggerating in order to 'spice up' a story.

> I actively started looking for another job after a particular story I wrote – I'd interviewed the family about what had happened with their son and after the court case, and written a piece with their agreement. Then the editor changed all sorts of details, gave it a headline which wasn't accurate, to 'Spice It Up' he said. And I was the one who had to pick up the pieces with the family who contacted me and were extremely upset. If I'd been the family I'd have been upset too – furious!
>
> [L, personal contact]

Small words

> Children – and people – are like plants. When a plant is struggling, a small change can make all the difference – more or less light or shadow, more or less water, more or less space.
>
> [Rachel]

Thank you

> When someone writes to say how much I helped them – even though they didn't show it at the time – it makes such a difference. I got a letter last week . . . Maybe I'll frame it to remind me why I do this job, so often all I hear is complaints and the things that go wrong. Makes it all worthwhile when someone says thank you!
>
> [C, psychiatrist]

It is so easy in our rushing world to forget to notice out loud what others do for us. As a former primary head teacher, I could have written the psychiatrist's words above – and I still have, tucked away in a chocolate box, some much valued and appreciated cards and letters which I received from pupils and from parents. Trying to remember to notice and comment when anyone – at work or home – does some small thing which makes things easier for us, is one good way of easing the pressures and problems ('Thanks for bringing in the washing . . . thanks for putting laundry in the right place . . . for laying the table . . . for remembering my favourite piece of music . . . for taking the time/trouble to meet . . . for your help . . . your understanding').

Sorry

This small word, in whatever language, is one of the biggest in the world – and difficult sometimes to say, to admit our mistakes, perhaps believing that others might think less of us if we do.

The social worker said sorry that our appointment had to be changed last week . . . my husband had taken time off work to be there, I had asked my mother to babysit and she'd changed her shift. It was very awkward to have to rearrange another time. But he apologised, and explained what had happened and why it was changed. That made a difference, just having that sorry, and him telling us why.

[V, carer]

I was annoyed as well as taken aback over the incident when a mum was so angry with me over being sent – by the school nurse, not me – a letter referring to headlice. The lady came in to apologise a couple of days later, telling me about how the letter had been her 'last straw' on a difficult day. Far from thinking less of her, her words and gesture were very much appreciated – I thought it took guts to come in to say she had been in the wrong.

Sorry I haven't been able to give you the information you need; maybe we could go over a few things I think might help?

Sorry, I was tired when we last met, perhaps I misunderstood?

Sorry, I haven't had time to do that.

Sorry, I forgot.

Sorry, I think maybe I got that wrong.

Sorry you've had to wait, we're working short staffed and things are a bit difficult.

Sorry, I felt very upset when you told me that – and I shouldn't have got cross.

Sorry, I felt angry when . . . I shouldn't have said what I did.

A sincere apology may be the first step in breaking the cycle and starting to repair and rebuild constructive communication.

Remembering that everyone makes mistakes – including ourselves, whether carer or professional, parent or child, carer or cared for – and that admitting them and possibly giving a reason for them, is a sign of strength rather than weakness. Seeing and appreciating the difference such openness may bring to a relationship is a great pleasure which can make up for coping with many of the pressures and problems.

Acknowledging the difficulties of another person, and their efforts even when they are not as successful as they hoped, is not only important for vulnerable and troubled individuals, they are also important for *everyone* concerned with that individual's care and support – and can go a long way to building and rebuilding constructive conversations, better relationships and a smoother path all round. Building and rebuilding bridges can only be positive in its effects on the 'best care' efforts for the person at the centre of all those efforts.

And it will lead to more pleasures in the job of caring to balance the pressures and problems.

Pleasures

Surely, you are saying, *in such circumstances of restricted resources, stress and low morale, the pressures and problems far outweigh any possible pleasures!*

In my job I have worked with all ages and stages and from all walks of life, children with great gifts, abilities and spirit; children who had been born with huge difficulties to overcome before they could even start to achieve their potential in other ways; and I worked with their families, writing formal reports as well as meeting informally to discuss individual progress and problems. One of the main joys of my job was the variety of experience as well as people I met, celebrating achievements and trying to make a positive difference when things went wrong – the positive experiences, with children and their families, with the many colleagues I worked with along the way, far outweighed the negative.

Sadly it is possible that when people are tired, lack often-vital resources, when relationships have deteriorated over a period of time, for whatever reason (perhaps a lack of desperately-needed information or openness, perhaps different perceptions/interpretations of confidentiality, perhaps through misunderstandings) and with a lack of confidence or trust on either or both sides, relationships may be felt to be beyond retrieval. But trying, repeatedly, to find a way to a new beginning through better communication on both sides can only help the people we are trying to support.

Trying to find positives – let alone identify pleasures – in difficult situations is often hard but always worthwhile. Try sharing a plate of 'crap sandwiches' with a friend, a colleague: for every negative you mention (the filling) it must be sandwiched between two positives (the slices of bread). The positives may include, for instance, a blue sky above, the wind on your face when you went outside. Try it on a particularly bad day, after a meeting you felt was less than successful, sadness, despair and frustration. The sharing is often a way of coping with the yucky filling in the middle, no matter how awful, and the start of thinking towards trying to resolve the situation.

A personal 'crap sandwich':

> Peter's smile when he got every sum right – success at last!
> Yelling mouth shouts awful words, all referring to me and all my defects.
> Sun shining on harvest field.
>
> [GS]

(More uses for 'crap sandwiches' are described in Chapter 14.)

Peer support

Recognising the stressful effects of being in support mode, many supporters, paid or unpaid, doing telephone work such as Samaritans or EDA, organise regular times to talk about how they feel – what may be known as 'supervision' – to try to ensure that they and other colleagues or volunteers have a space in which to talk and thereby not risk burnout. A more experienced teacher will support or 'mentor' a younger one.

Sharing or writing a few crap sandwiches – some days perhaps even a whole plateful! – after a difficult day/week may help put things into a better perspective.

The same is true for family or friends in a support role; finding others to share the load can be crucial to survival in a 24-hours-a-day situation. Such support may be found through organisations such as charities or foundations; perhaps along with a chat over a cup of coffee or a distracting activity with a friend or relative or colleague. By sharing the problems and pressures with others, we give permission to them to share their own, whether present or in the future.

Jane Gregory writes of the toughest challenge she ever faced – bringing up Chrissy, and her joy in watching Chrissy finally reach her potential and find contentment and serenity (see Gregory, 2000).

* * * *

Watching my own daughter back out there in the Big Bad World, getting on with her life again independently, working fulltime with lots of friends, her own home again, making her own decisions . . . it is simply wonderful. Every day I feel so thankful for having got through those nightmare years when I wondered every day if I'd lose her to anorexia. I look back on those years and wonder too how we got through, how I survived at all. I'd never want to repeat them, wouldn't wish them on my worst enemy, but I've also met so many great people I wouldn't otherwise have met, both carers and professionals. And without those experiences, neither of us – Jay nor myself – would be the people we are today.

Whether professional or family carer, the very greatest pleasure is in seeing someone making progress in coping with the hard deal life has thrown at them, and the feeling that we may have had a positive part to play.

CHAPTER TEN

Confidentiality

A thorny issue

> I might be disciplined or even lose my job if someone thinks I've broken confidentiality rules.
>
> [H, psychiatrist]

Many relationships – in families, between friends, between professional and client/patient – have been broken by different understandings of confidentiality and its importance. The more sensitive the information, the greater the importance of confidentiality, of not discussing the information with people who may then pass it on to others. Confidentiality, its varying definitions and interpretations, causes huge problems on both sides of any relationship between professionals and parents or other carers.

In many illnesses and conditions, such as diabetes, cancer, orthopaedic disease or heart disease, carers are seen as an important part of the care team. For instance, when a friend's (adult) daughter was diagnosed with diabetes, my friend was given a helpline number, with the instruction: 'Call any time you are at all worried about your daughter.'

However, in the field of mental health and emotional problems, confidentiality and even the possibility of involvement of carers is a very thorny issue indeed.

> On my son's discharge from hospital after an episode of acute psychosis we had no information about his condition, how he would behave, how we should react to him. We had no experience in dealing with him when unwell. We were expected to just cope – a complete nightmare!
>
> [Carer, quoted in Department of Health, 2006]

> We feel that if information had been provided our son's care would have been better and his recovery quicker.
>
> [Carer, quoted in Department of Health, 2006]

Between family and friends it is important to think about wider issues of definition – what for instance is the right thing to do if you have been asked by a friend or relative not to pass on information about their lawbreaking? Or their intention to break the law, or hurt someone else? Or if you think that their own behaviour is going to cause future problems for them, for instance, at the worst extreme, if someone tells of plans to commit suicide? Do you then say 'Well, it's up to you, it's your life', or do you try to persuade the person to seek medical or other help to try to resolve their problems? Do you break their confidence and seek medical help with the thought that they are not thinking rationally and you want to save your friend or relative's life? If you decide that trying to save their life is more important than the confidentiality issue, do you inform them of your decision before doing so?

Professional dilemmas

Doctors, psychologists, psychiatrists, mental health nurses, social workers and other professionals want to offer best care for their patients and clients – yet often fear they may breach confidentiality rules. Therefore they feel they must err on the side of extreme caution when interpreting confidentiality rules. In the very narrowest definition, it is interpreted as never ever having contact with family or other carers as this might be interpreted as possibly affecting the trust between them and their patients/clients. Yet without relevant information about the condition and what might be expected, with support where needed, families are handicapped in effectively supporting their loved one.

Most of the people who choose to train in the caring professions – teachers, social workers, nurses, doctors and others – do so because they want to help people, to contribute to best care for more vulnerable individuals:

> I wanted to try and make a difference to the world. I know that's quite a cliché. But that's why I started – and I suppose why I'm still here.
>
> [D, social worker]

> I joined to have that person-to-person contact. Unfortunately that's not always possible. When so many agencies are involved, someone has to make sure they all work together. That's me.
>
> [Gilroy, social worker, quoted in *Big Issue*, 2006]

> I love working with kids, never considered any other job but teaching. When I can explain something new, which puzzles and presents challenge to someone, it gives me a real buzz when light and understanding dawns. [GS]

> Always wanted to be a doctor; helping my mum when my brother was ill maybe made up my mind. And paediatrics just seemed the right field for me, I love it.
>
> [R, personal contact]

Along with interesting and absorbing work in these professions comes much responsibility – the decisions of doctors often have long-term life-affecting consequences for their patients; sometimes those decisions mean life or death. Social workers and mental health workers become involved in their clients' lives only when there are problems, sometimes serious problems with major repercussions. Again they are involved in making choices and decisions with inevitable long-term consequences, such as removing a child from a difficult or *potentially* difficult situation with all the associated stress for that child and the family. In the interests of child safety, they err on the side of caution. A headteacher has responsibility for the education and welfare of all the pupils in a school; in my case, for about 240 ranging in age from 3-year-olds in nursery to 11–12-year-olds in their final year before the move to secondary education.

Just as individuals very rarely live in complete isolation, neither do professionals operate in a vacuum. They, and others working in similar fields, also have a responsibility to colleagues. Ultimately their work – good long-term decisions and mistakes included – affects the community within which they work, as well as society as a whole. Decisions, all actions whether minor choices or major, have consequences and some will be unforeseen.

Autonomy

When someone reaches legal adulthood they will be assumed able to take responsibility for making responsible life choices in all areas. They are then given autonomy over their own lives, along with the right to confidentiality.

No account is taken of maturity at the legal age of adulthood – some young people are indeed ready to marry, to organise their own lives and homes, competent to take sensible decisions which affect their futures. They are seen as responsible enough to drive and operate machinery; to undergo various training. They are seen as ready to serve in armies and navies, and to fight for their country.

Others, although legally recognised as adult, are a long way from the same maturity, also making choices and decisions which also inevitably affect their futures; those choices and decisions may or may not be sensible or practical. Their choices may lead to much unhappiness not only for themselves but also affect many other lives around them.

> The moving finger writes; and having writ,
>   Moves on: nor all your Piety nor Wit
>   Shall lure it back to cancel half a Line
>   Nor all your Tears wash out a Word of it.
>
> [*The Rubáiyat of Omar Khayyám of Naishápur*, trans. Edward Fitzgerald (1809–1883)]

No matter how we wish it, we cannot wipe out any decisions, words or actions – good, bad or indifferent. We have to live in the future with consequences of today's actions (one of the hardest lessons of growing up).

And if someone has an emotional or mental health problem those decisions at whatever age, made with stressed, impaired thinking, may have very far-reaching consequences for their own lives as well as others. The fact that depression, eating disorders, schizophrenia, or any other mental health problem may fluctuate from day to day, month to month, year to year, makes it even more complicated for both professionals and carers who help those who suffer.

Sometimes family and friends may only gradually become aware that someone's behaviour is changing; at other times the onset of problems may be more dramatic. Whatever the timescale, whatever the problem, help is now sought. In school, confidentiality regarding a child or family's wellbeing usually meant discussing the problems only with people who would be directly affected, who needed to know in order to continue working effectively with the child. In teaching, any problems a child had which affected his or her life in school – educational, social, emotional, discipline, or health and welfare issues – would be discussed with parents in an attempt to help and support a child through the problems. Any teacher or headteacher could cause huge distress as well as anger simply by breaking confidentiality, through careless chat, as could other professionals who indulged in the same.

On reaching official adulthood, people are legally awarded autonomy over their own lives, and legally they may instruct professionals that no information is to be given to their family regarding them or any problems they may have. As adults they are expected to be mature human beings, self-sufficient people with independent reasoning skills. This issue has caused debate for centuries – often families watch as loved ones self-destruct, head for disaster through drugs misuse, eating disorder, and so on, and doctors are bound legally to respect a patient's wishes if they state that their family is not to be given any information.

> A patient said she wanted to make a complaint about the staff treating her, 'who seemed to think she had a mental health problem.'
>
> [A, nurse working with eating disordered patients]

> Sometimes patients know perfectly well we can't tell their families anything because of confidentiality, and that families can't check things with us. Sometimes patients use that to stir trouble between staff and home.
>
> [B, mental health nurse]

Definitions

Definitions of what constitutes confidentiality vary; interpretations and definitions even vary between doctors and departments and over time. Recently there have been legal developments in the UK regarding the right to autonomy of people who develop, say, Alzheimer's disease, whose thinking and decision-making abilities are affected by the condition, and whose quality of

life is inevitably linked and interrelated to those who care for
1993).

It was only when I was 37 that my mother unexpectedly to
diagnosis of spina bifida occulta, made when I was 5. My GP co
but nothing more. Confidentiality – the interpretation that information about patients was classified and must not be shared with anyone including the patient whose body and life were affected – had always been quoted as the reason for not answering my past questions about back and leg problems, the need for several major operations.

Years later a young doctor unexpectedly brought my medical file with him to an examination, opened it – and, even more unexpectedly, assumed that I would be interested! Some of the comments and information were recorded in a very personal way. One letter was headed The British Cripples Association, and the young doctor, embarrassed, exclaimed 'Very non-PC', and assured me that 'Things have changed a bit since those days.'

> It is only very recently that patients were told of a diagnosis by doctors, psychiatrists and so on, let alone tell other professionals involved in their care – like social workers!
>
> [J, senior social worker]

Transition to adult services

When the young person reaches legal adulthood, carers often suddenly find themselves excluded from any discussion.

The 'no information of any kind' definition not only causes much frustration and unhappiness to family members, it can also be detrimental to many patients. Without even general information, it is quite possible that many attempts at therapeutic work in clinics and hospitals could be inadvertently affected negatively by actions and reactions, or words, of stressed family members leading to increased possibility of relapse.

Under this definition of confidentiality, someone with Alzheimer's disease, for instance, would be deemed to be able to make decisions despite impaired and deteriorating reasoning skills. Under this definition, a patient over 18 with, say, anorexia—where there can be a discrepancy between chronological age and 'functioning age' because of impaired reasoning and decision-making skills—might be discharged after hospital treatment in a safe and understanding environment where it is possible to insist that proper meals are eaten to maintain health and medication can be administered, out into the 'real world' where the same patient is expected to be able to cope without any real day-to-day support if the people they live with have no clue as to how to help, what to do or just as important, what is best to try to avoid doing. In anorexia, developmental stages are often delayed, and decision-making skills and competence often badly affected as part of the regression of the illness (see Tan *et al.*, 2003).

> It's a revolving door, home for a while then gradually all the good intentions fade. Then relapse, long waiting lists and hospital again – years and years my daughter has been ill. When she comes home, there's no follow-up to assess how she's doing. I've never had any guidance from the staff as to how I could help, it breaks my heart every time.
>
> [V, mother of Y, anorexia nervosa]

In recent times focus has begun on the ethics of involving carers as part of 'best care'. Most family members do not want or need personal details which may be discussed in patient–professional meetings, but without information families are severely handicapped in trying to provide the best care possible for their loved one. If families don't know what to do for the best, and inadvertently do the wrong thing no matter how good their intentions – a wrong words, tone of voice, misunderstanding – months of good professional work may well be undone (see Treasure *et al.*, 2005).

Questions and developments

It is now beginning to be recognised that it may be in the best interests of patients and clients to ensure that the people they spend most of their lives with are equipped to support them.

The question is now being asked – and mental health provision and laws examined – about to how to protect as much privacy and autonomy as possible, and how to provide the very best care both in and outside the treatment centre, for people who for any reason have lost the competence to make decisions which will affect their future lives, who spend relatively short time in professional care – an hour a week? a week in hospital then discharge? – and most of their lives in the community, at home with family and other carers.

> A key problem for the health professional may be in identifying who the main carer is, and what to do if there are concerns that the carer's relationship with the service user is abusive . . .
>
> The operational guidance that exists (guidance that tells people not just what to do, but how to do it) is both inconsistent and scattered throughout many documents – both nationally and in local guidance . . .
>
> Fear about breaching patient confidentiality has frequently created a barrier to effective involvement of carers in mental health care.
>
> (Department of Health, 2006)

Relapse prevention

In some areas discussions are further on than in others.

> I think it should be written down when the client is well, stable, somewhere prominent the things they want done when they're ill and things they don't want done. Come the time when they're ill it's too late to start collecting consent.
>
> [Service user, in Department of Health, 2006]

First step?

The first step in trying to find a way through this minefield of misunderstandings and frustrations on both sides could be simply to *ask* those people for whom both families and professionals are trying to work towards 24-hour best care: *not* 'Do you want someone to support you?' but '*Who* would you like to support you?'

Bearing in mind that 'it is too late when someone is ill to start collecting consent', asking the 'Who?' question at an initial assessment could be both a major step to establishing more constructive communication with carers and also the start of better support outside a clinic or hospital setting, as well as leading to more continuity of care.

According to the Department of Health (2006) 'only 12% of services users reported that they are routinely asked by professionals for consent to share personal information'. Yet, as noted earlier, general information about the particular illness or condition, what might happen and best ways to react, is what is asked for and needed by carers rather than information confidential between patient and professional.

If met with refusal, gently exploring the reason could be the answer:

> When the issue of meeting his parents was raised with Tim, he said he did not want them involved. His key nurse on the ward took time to sit down to discuss his concerns with him. It transpired that Tim's main concern was that he would have to disclose the fact that he had taken drugs in the past. He was happy for other information to be shared, in fact he was pleased that someone wanted to offer support to his parents whom he knew were finding it hard to understand what was going on.
>
> (Royal College of Psychiatrists, 2004)

Small wonder that relationships are frequently difficult! A fresh start, as well as much goodwill and effort to build constructive communication, are needed to ensure that positive change is possible.

CHAPTER ELEVEN

More assumptions, perceptions and interpretations

> When I was small I used to watch the coalman with his face and hands all dusty, smeared and black, deliver coal every week, heaving the big bags into our coal bunker, and think about how the coalman spent the rest of the week underground digging more coal up for us the next week when he made deliveries. I thought what a really hard job he had, how immensely strong he was.
>
> [Jim, personal contact]

As a child Jim did what we all do: put together our experience with what we know at any given time – and our understanding of that knowledge – to make some sort of sense in our own minds. It is only with more experience, more knowledge and understanding that later we can make different sense of the same information. In Jim's case, very much later – he simply assumed for many years that his interpretations were right.

When working together as a team, any team, it is extremely important that everyone understands all communications between them. Mention 'gossip' for instance: everyone has a shared definition and understanding of gossip, yes? Gadget-obsessed status-seeking individual professional?

One of the most common complaints of parents is of feeling puzzled or patronised by professionals, who may use words, abbreviations and terms – jargon – they don't understand. It is very easy for a teacher for instance to say to a parent, 'Sorry, can't manage to see you after school today, I've got a PAT meeting.' (This is a Planned Activity Time, an after-school staff meeting – but not to the puzzled parent!)

While professionals may be so used to hearing and using jargon words and terms that it never occurs to them that not everyone shares their vocabulary, parents and other carers may understand a completely different working definition of a particular word and therefore not even think of asking for the professionals' definition; or because of shyness or embarrassment or perhaps a hesitation about showing what might be perceived as ignorance, an explanation is not asked for.

And so misunderstandings between individuals can easily build up to a very unhappy picture and contribute to poor relationships.

One such word is 'perfectionism'. This word has almost come to be a term of abuse in some circles, to such an extent that some people deliberately don't correct a spelling error when they notice it in case others might imagine them as a perfectionist! Until very recently my own understanding of a perfectionist involved people who do lots of housework, e.g. cleaning windows after every shower of rain, washing pan scrubbers in a washing machine, arranging everything around them in order of size or shape, carpeting their garage and cleaning the tyres before driving the car in, hanging out washing in strict order of size! I've met or heard of people who do all these things as part of their daily routines. To me, a perfectionist meant someone to whom order and cleanliness was really *really* important, what seemed to me obsessively so. As a result, looking at the state of my windows, my haphazard arrangement on the washing line organisation, and dust on various surfaces at home, if anyone asked if I was a perfectionist I could honestly reply 'No'.

> As a primary teacher I know that some children are naturally tidy and like order, others less so, and still others are happily messy – they don't see what to others is mess. Some children are fortunate enough to be naturally neat and have good co-ordination, therefore present neat work at all times – and where presentation counts some lose out from day one. Some people like order around them, others live in happy chaos, still others like order but only make efforts to clear the chaos after a certain point of irritation.
> [GS]

It was only after working with psychiatrists over some time, and becoming extremely puzzled over comments about perfectionist traits, that it began to dawn on me that perhaps they meant something different from my own working definition. Eventually I asked for their understanding of the word – which involved someone who thinks it possible to create perfection in everything they do, get 100% in examinations with anything else seen as failure, win every game or race, set impossibly high personal standards, paying obsessional attention to all sorts of detail, which may or may not involve cleaning.

Although the different definitions caused me a bit of puzzlement, and probably the same for those with whom I was working, no particular harm was caused by this misunderstanding. Unfortunately this is not always the case.

It must come as a particular shock to many professionals – social workers, psychiatrists, psychologists, teachers and others – who have worked with 20th-century nature/nurture theory for years and accepted it as gospel, to discover that their own children are not immune from mental health problems including schizophrenia, anorexia nervosa, depression, addictions, bipolar disorder, autism and other distressing conditions. Thanks to some interpretations of that theory, many people make all sorts of assumptions about *all* families whose children develop stress-related problems.

Definitions

All definitions are from *Collins English Dictionary*, 21st century edition (2001).

Abuse

> *Abuse:* verb, to use incorrectly or improperly; misuse; to maltreat, esp. physically or sexually; to speak insultingly or cruelly to; to revile.

Abuse and *abusive* are almost guaranteed to raise a strong reaction, while individual definitions are often vague and unspecified. Estimates of abuse vary widely depending on how 'abuse' is defined by the researchers. When parents – or anyone – rightly or wrongly feel that they stand accused of abuse, whether through word or perceived attitude, their reactions may vary from open hostility and refusal to work with the professionals involved, to feelings of overwhelming despair, and everything in between.

> In our experience anorexia nervosa means sexual abuse in the family. Now, what have you to tell me?
>
> [A psychiatrist, see Chapter 7]

Depending on definition, and perhaps the intention behind the words used, abuse may now be defined to include rudeness, or ridicule of some sort; may range from teasing seen by the teaser as some sort of joke through to various types of bullying; verbal abuse; punishment varying from 'a naughty corner' to a light smack to brutal beating with a belt or implement; gross sexual abuse, sexual games between siblings, relatives or friends; emotional distance; physical neglect; being called names; being left alone unsupervised for minutes, hours or days; excessive and unfair blame or punishment for perceived wrong behaviour. Have I left anything out?

These could all be called forms of abuse, although each may vary in intensity (e.g. gross physical abuse sexual or torture to light smacking, vicious verbal bullying to passing reference to physical attributes such as hair or teeth). Without discussion of an exact definition – for instance with people filling in a questionnaire, reading a newspaper report, or in a meeting between family and professional – it will depend on an individual's definition of what they think of as abuse – and usually the most negative assumption is made. If someone has already been diagnosed with a mental health problem, their thinking will already be distorted.

Dysfunctional

> *Dysfunctional:* adjective, not functioning normally.
>
> My mother is dysfunctional.
>
> [L, social worker, personal conversation]

Before using this word, 'normally' needs to be defined . . . which may be difficult as every family functions differently on an everyday basis, under 'stress' individuals may react in very different ways, and adverse events may affect one, a few or all the family members.

Dysfunctional, in relation to family or individual, involves making subjective judgements – assumptions – of what 'normal' 'functional' family life means as well as answering the question at the end of Chapter 1.

Designer research recipes

Main ingredients

1 idea or opinion, well publicised in media for many years.

3 questionnaires, either as suggested below or adapted to suit taste.

Recipe 1: Home environment

Ingredients

The questionnaire should contain references, as preferred, to punishment, abuse, unhappy, ridicule, maltreatment, unpredictability, traumatic, dislike, loneliness, alone, stressful, angry, physical mistreatment, sexual maltreatment, blame, afraid.

At no time should ingredients include references to love, kindness, giving, laughter, warmth.

At no time should any reference be made to acceptance, happiness, gifts, warmth, unreserved love at any time past or present, by any family member.

At no time discuss definitions of the above ingredients.

Sprinkle generously with references to troubles, difficulties, desperation, suspicions, ulterior motives, hurt, betrayal, alienation, embarrassment, uptight, pressure, constraint, frustration, abandonment.

Stir well in a large vessel. Turn out onto A4 paper and print smoothly. Bake thoroughly at cool and intellectual temperature.

Serving instructions

'Where a question inquires about the behaviour of both your parents and your parents differed in their behaviour, please respond in terms of the parent whose behaviour was the more severe or worse.' (University of Birmingham, 2005)

Recipe 2: Personality

Ingredients

Number of ingredients may vary; usually works well with about 75 ingredients.

The questionnaire should contain selected statements from can't, haven't, don't fit, afraid, worry, shouldn't, unworthiness, incompetence, no choice, must, and so on.

Recipe 3: Eating

Ingredients

The questionnaire should contain numerous negative statements – self-denial, trapped, weaknesses, suffering, ashamed, and so on, with repeated references to weight, feelings about size of hips, stomach, buttocks, and so on.

Results

The reader may like to guess what the results would show.

By restricting choice to relentless negativity with no mention anywhere of even *possible* positive memories of any family members – strong, coping, warmth, laughter, competent, loving – administered to people already depressed and with distorted thinking because of their illness, it is hard to see how such questionnaires could give anything other than skewed results. Even the strongest among us can remember negative comments and actions from childhood; and as a parent it is very easy to be less than perfect – even grumpy! – when tired and distracted.

Added to this already unhappy and very tangled story, over recent years the debate has grown over so-called 'false memory syndrome' where people have asserted that a therapist has urged them to find memories of childhood abuse.

It is *extremely* unfortunate that such skewed research has led not only to stigma and much misery, but also to some people questioning good evidence-based research conducted rigorously under the most stringent circumstances.

> Most of these hypotheses suffered from one great drawback: they were extrapolations from observations made during therapy. Far more desirable, from a scientific viewpoint, are studies of large groups of people over a period of several years, to see who among them eventually comes down with the problem.
>
> (Goleman, 1996)

According to Dr Stephen Rosenman, Centre for Mental Health Research, Australia National University, research carried out with psychiatric patients into childhood experiences leads to 'biased results'. Therefore his research into possible connections between what he termed 'childhood adversity' and the later development of mental health problems,was carried out over many years with people in the general population with regular follow-up into adulthood. Over 60% of this general population sample of approx 7,500 reported some childhood adversity including domestic conflict, physical or sexual abuse, and withdrawal of love (BBC, 2005).

Apart from the possibility of biased results, it is also possible that in filling in a 'designer research recipe' questionnaire with no mention anywhere of positive qualities which might have co-existed in their childhood with another parent or close relative, could actually be *iatrogenic.*

> *Iatrogenic* – adjective, Medical – of an illness or symptoms induced in a patient as a result of a physician's words or action.

In other words, making people who already have emotional problems feel even worse than they did before, dwelling on each and every past experience they might define or redefine as fitting what the research suggests, while also forgetting or dismissing any more positive experiences or relationships.

Without defining what a psychiatrist – or anyone else – has in mind as abuse, or what the people answering questions think of as abuse, or what those who read of such research may imagine is abuse, or newspapers wanting to sell more copies, it is small wonder that there are so many interpretations and misunderstandings.

Implications for today's professionals and carers

The label 'abusive' is frequently felt by all members of a family, whatever their particular relationship with the person having problems; if serious abuse by a relative has indeed been a factor in developing mental health problems, all members of the family feel blamed – and indeed in some cases have been. Added to the common exclusion of parents leading to many other misunderstandings, it is understandable that families and vulnerable individuals have been reluctant to speak in public, sometimes even to close friends, of emotional and behavioural problems, let alone mental illness in the family.

> 1 in 4 people did not find out about their friend's mental distress until they went into hospital. 5% found out about their friend's mental distress following their suicide attempt. 1 in 3 friends (33%) talked about wanting to help their friend, 25% of their concern for them. 'Shocked and worried. Appalled at the state of the hospital. Felt as if my friend had died and I was grieving for them.'
>
> (Mental Health Foundation, 2001)

Despite the recent recognition that individual reactions to different kinds of stress acting on brain activity may be the trigger for emotional, behavioural and mental health problems, and campaigns to tackle public perceptions, families whose members suffer such problems – including professionals – still feel the weight of stigma in many quarters.

As Dr Rosenman's research study shows, added to many years' observations in primary schools, few children go through childhood without some adverse events. Depending on temperament and personality, children cope in different ways with the same adverse events. For instance, if a family member makes remarks about, say, red hair, or ears, teeth or any other physical attribute, one child may react with rage and fists, perhaps retaliate in kind, but then be able to forget the incident afterwards with no lasting effects; while another might dwell on the same as a huge insult which leads to long-term feelings of insecurity. The actual words may be intended as insult by the person who spoke them, may be the beginning of more intense bullying, might be used to provoke a particular reaction which is perceived as extreme, or might be due to an unfortunate and thoughtless sense of humour and not truly intended to hurt. Bruises and even broken bones will mend, while unkind words can be a lifetime memory for some; some people can quote words said to them in the school playground, or at home, 50 or more years later. Those words may only have been said once or twice, but were so upsetting at the time that they lodged in the memory while more positive ones were often lost in the mists of time.

> When I was 10, I still had a bad limp after an operation. A group of girls – about 3 or 4 – surrounded me in the playground and shouted 'Cripple!' at me. I think it only happened the one time yet (50 years later!) I can clearly remember how upset I felt at the time. I also remember lots of friends at school, who helped me, often walked with me at my pace rather than their usual run – but none of the words they said to me. Why has that one word, that one nasty incident, lasted in my mind for so long while the many other kind words have disappeared? [GS]

There is a world of difference in accepting that 'adverse events' in childhood may well affect a child into adulthood, interwoven with individual perceptions, reactions and stress – and the inference of abusive behaviour by parents.

KISS: keep it simple and straightforward

> I was meeting a public relations officer from the National Australia Bank when she volunteered that banks were full of TLAs. We'd just been talking about the danger of jargon masking what we're attempting to say. For a few seconds, I lost the train of what she was saying as I mulled over what TLAs might be.
>
> 'Oh, by the way,' she then concluded, 'TLAs are Three Letter Acronyms'. We use Three Letter Acronyms all the time, then forget that you first had to learn what they meant before understanding them. And that means that whoever you're speaking to is lost until they too learn the TLA's meaning.
>
> (McFarlan, 2003)

All professionals, all workplace teams, use jargon and shortcut words in daily communication. Do you recall PAT at the beginning of this chapter, and what it stands for? (Bill McFarlan devotes a whole chapter to KISS, which should be required reading for everyone, whatever their field of work). Not only do people have to learn what the acronyms mean, they must remember them. To people working with the same abbreviations every day this may be easy when everyone understands the same. For families and other carers, most of whom are already under stress and often distressed, careless use of language without ensuring mutual understanding of what is meant can lead to – at best – misunderstandings and ineffective discussion at cross purposes. At worst, it may lead to feelings of being deliberately patronised, excluded, and of being made to feel inadequate. It may lead to actions which are less than helpful to the troubled individual whom everyone is trying to help.

Without clear language and understanding of what might help their loved one, carers are handicapped in knowing how to relate with their family member, let alone in knowing how to support them. Unless words are used with a common understanding of meaning, professionals may be working with skewed pictures and incomplete information relating to the lives of those they are trying to help.

There may be many other words or abbreviations liable to misunderstanding by either family members or professionals.

It is therefore essential to check, ask questions, explore, and discuss at every stage of meetings or treatment so that everyone *there has the same understanding.*

CHAPTER TWELVE

Constructive professional–carer conversations

> We knew from early on that our son had great needs.
>
> [Alan, see Chapter 2]

> We noticed over months that he had changed – little things. Each one on their own wouldn't have mattered, but all together they built up to Something Was Wrong.
>
> Sheila (see Chapter 2)

> First she stops her afternoon snack. Then her morning one. Always with a reason – she'll have it later or something. Then she stops eating with us, always busy doing something when we're eating. Same pattern every time. [V]

> I can tell the minute he gets in the door, if he's had a good day or bad at school, even before he speaks. Just the way he opens and closes the door . . . if he slams the door so hard the house shakes, throws his bag, stamps his feet – etc – I know to watch out! [Sheila, see Chapter 2]

These are the words of family carers, coping with loved ones with very different challenging conditions.

Yet with an individual's behaviour unlikely to be the same in every circumstance or situation, liable to change depending on surroundings and people whether work or home, formal or informal, friendly and relaxed, supportive or not, as well as feelings, tiredness and so on, it is inevitable that professionals have only a limited picture of life, circumstances and behaviour of their clients outside the structured and secure environment of their clinic, hospital or office.

Early signs and symptoms, sometimes very small changes, are often first noticed by those living with or close to an individual, whether with a physical condition such as diabetes or with any condition or disorder involving challenging behaviour. The same is also often true when an individual, after a spell of stability, starts sliding into relapse.

Even very young children will behave in very different ways depending on whether at home with family members, or in class or outside at break times; the same is true of all human interactions – those closest to an individual, especially those living with them, will probably know that individual best. (Although there are no guarantees: it's still possible for an individual to keep parts of their life completely hidden for quite a time.)

If these important clues and observations are passed on early and acted on, it is possible that with appropriate support, treatment timescales may be reduced; relapse might be shorter in duration or even averted. In some tragic cases carers have tried without success to alert professionals and sometimes authorities that their family member is deteriorating, e.g. into paranoia, which in the past has caused dangerous consequences for the individual or for others; or in anorexia, their loved one has been refusing to drink liquid as well as refusing food. Having unfortunately been through the whole cycle before, possibly several times, they have recognised all the early signs.

Whatever the condition, physical, behavioural or emotional, the people living with the troubled individual need:

- to know the possible or probable course to be expected
- to know possible problems to be aware of; at least knowing what might happen, even the worst, it is possible to prepare; if the worst doesn't happen – a major bonus!
- support in coming to terms with a diagnosis of possibly long-term problems
- information about best ways to support an individual in tackling their problem behaviour and its consequences
- help in coping with specific situations, e.g. aggression, lying
- support to enable carers to provide long-term support on a daily basis
- to know when to call for help
- support in an emergency situation.

Reliable and practical information is needed all along the way.

Realistic expectations

Some carers have very unrealistic views of what we can offer. In any one day I have clients to meet, meetings with colleagues to discuss everything from what a particular client needs to finance and ways of providing what is needed, to answering the phone to writing reports and minutes of meetings, to trying to keep up with email to . . . the list is just endless! Not to mention all the changes in rules and regulations. And research, etc. And we're short staffed. I'm in the office at eight every morning, often work evenings.

I just don't have time to sit and talk to everyone who comes through the office door; I wish I had!

[J, senior social worker]

Parents have to accept that we have no magic pill. [V, social worker]

Without any information at all, how was I supposed to know what to do – by osmosis?! [Parent]

On the professionals' side, perhaps they assume that families will somehow just *know* how to respond, calmly and in a considered manner, to behaviour which a family probably has never met before and finds extremely difficult to cope with within the home. It is very easy to forget that their own calm and considered responses have been built through initial interest plus years of training and experience (not only of their own particular experience but the accumulated experience of many others gained through study, training and conferences) while a family member may be struggling to cope – as I did – with dramatic changes. For example, when Jay became ill with anorexia changes in personality and behaviour involved real aggression over trivial irritations, perhaps the kitchen door being left open when she wanted it shut while she made coffee, though the day before she'd wanted that same door shut while making coffee.

Carers may believe that the professionals are experts who hold all the answers, while many professionals are only too aware that whatever they might be able to achieve will be limited by the resources they are working with.

Family–professional co-operation wherever possible offers a chance to learn the skills and abilities, strengths as well as difficulties on each side – and to plan the best way of building on those strengths, skills and abilities while addressing any weaknesses and needs. Recognition by both professionals and carers of the contributions each can make to the whole support structure can go a long way to building constructive communications: professionals with their greater experience in their chosen field of expertise, and carers with their greater experience and the knowledge and information they can offer about how the troubled individual copes with ordinary life in the world outside.

But this depends on everyone knowing and being realistic about the whole picture, which can only be viewed through open and honest dialogue.

Realism and research

With research continuing and growing, many ideas and beliefs of the past have been proved, or disproved. Most professionals try hard to keep up with research and developments in their own field, while also working 'at the coalface' to provide for their patients/clients. Professionals may indeed be leaders in their field with in-depth information on the latest research and treatments on offer – and also aware that all that research may be overtaken by current or future developments.

This is true in any work – medicine, education, social work and nursing have all changed dramatically just in the last century; and looking back over a few centuries the changes in working practices are quite amazing. In the field of mental health, for instance, many practices which were common a relatively short time ago are now regarded as draconian and punitive e.g. withdrawal of all privileges in an attempt to force someone with anorexia to eat. Rather than succeeding in the aim, attempts at control are now recognised to be more likely to drive the patient further into resistance.

Realism and changes

> In education, my own field, when my father was growing up in early 20th century in Scotland, discipline both at home and school was usually based on 'spare the rod and spoil the child'. In Scottish schools a leather belt, called the tawse, was applied by teachers to the hands of pupils as punishment (not all used it – some relied on the power of their personality to create order and motivation – but many did). There are many stories about sadistic teachers being not only unfair at times but also using their authority to inflict pain frequently.
>
> In every profession or work, there will always be strong characters who are memorable because of their empathy and ability to do a good job and others who are memorable for all the wrong reasons. Unfortunately such teachers have left a legacy for other teachers to overcome; the same is true of doctors, social workers, psychiatrists, shop assistants, drivers . . . the poorest of the profession give the others a bad name.
>
> [GS]

Each professional will do the job within the rules and guidelines to 'best practice' according to time and place.

While this is true for professions and professionals, it is equally true of family members. Being realistic, not every single member of every single family is equipped or able to offer support to another individual let alone a troubled and vulnerable one. Everyone can only do their best within their capabilities. But often people can surprise themselves as well as others when given ideas, support and the opportunity to try.

Being realistic about resources, with both professional and carer having realistic expectations, can only be achieved through open discussion and exchange of information.

Information

What information can professionals give?

(See Chapter 10 for issues of confidentiality.)

For many years, information was not even shared with the patient whose body (and mind) was being discussed. This is changing.

Families and other supporting professionals involved were similarly handicapped. It is only gradually, over recent times, that information has become more freely available with the advent of wider access to books, the internet, and other ways of finding information as well as a realisation that families as well as individuals plus other professionals involved in supporting an individual *need* certain information to enable them to provide support.

What information can carers expect from professionals?

When a diagnosis is given, carers may then research basic information on the condition, may be directed to the best sources by the professionals, may even be given some time to ask questions and discuss general problems associated with that condition. But a doctor or social worker, with respecting individual confidentiality written into their contract, may not discuss information specific to the patient or client without permission from that individual.

How can carers find the information they need to enable them to provide effective caring?

> It was obvious how very ill she was – Jay's behaviour was totally unpredictable, her reactions made no sense, yelling and screaming over complete trivia – the curtains, the wrong plate. Nothing made any sense. And I'd no idea what to do. [GS]

'Living in a nightmare' is a phrase used by many of the carers I've come across. Without information there is a constant, real fear of somehow making everything worse, added to the other most common feeling – guilt – that somehow the carer was unable to protect, that somehow they must be responsible for the suffering.

A sense of personal guilt – that she could not somehow protect her daughter from developing bulimia following the breakdown of a relationship, that she could not prevent her daughter's sudden death, alone, from heart failure – is a recurring theme throughout Doris Smeltzer's book *Andrea's Voice*. Finally a counsellor asked her:

> 'Do you really believe you are that powerful, Doris?' I could finally hear the words – that when we look back at the 'should haves' and 'if onlys' we tend to see them in the stagnant one-dimensional realm. We forget the dynamics of the situation,

> the many factors involved in our decisions and in others' reactions, and how truly complicated and intricate is the reality of Then.
>
> (Smeltzer, 2006)

How, then, can carers obtain information? *For any professional the rights of their client or patient must always come before any other consideration* (see Chapter 10). However, by not asking their patients *who* they might indeed like as support, unanticipated consequences may follow:

> When the anorexia is strong I'm not myself, I'm someone else. I listen to what people say, including my mum, including the doctors and the dietician, and I really mean to try to beat the anorexic thoughts, then I do something else – Anorexia wins.
>
> [S, anorexia patient]

While many professionals may recognise the need of family and other carers for information and even have goodwill towards them, constraints such as lack of time and resources may conspire against providing this. Carers can also help themselves, by exploring ways of finding information in various ways.

Finding information

Books

For many years it was only through having access to a good library that most people could find information, and then only if the library had or could obtain a copy of a relevant book; sometimes such information was held only in medical books – kept in medical libraries inaccessible to the general public.

Bookshops, including secondhand, and libraries now carry many more non-fiction books; in every case care must be taken that information is up-to-date and accurate. For instance, I have come across articles and books making sweeping or general statements on eating disorders by writers who, to anyone with experience of the illnesses, have a very limited knowledge of the subject – yet might be taken seriously by people at the start of the long road of discovery and recovery.

Several things have changed the information situation – charities, magazines and newspapers, radio and television, and the internet – and quite a few professionals have been taken aback in recent years, and perhaps felt disconcerted, by the level of knowledge that patients and many families may have.

Internet/websites

Finding much information at one time depended on knowing the right words to look for, access to libraries with the right books, being able to read and understand difficult medical language and jargon. With the advent of the internet, it is now possible to key in search terms to lead you to the information you need – for instance, keying in 'anorexia' or 'bulimia' into a search engine would quickly lead to 'an eating disorder'.

Not only is it possible to find general information on the internet, on a vast range of topics, it is also possible to do a much more detailed search and find information relating to, for instance, support available in your own area. Many charities now have their own websites. (For example, by keying in eating disorders, north east and Scotland, you'd find North East Eating Disorders Support Scotland at www.needs-scotland.org).

Internet regulation: One downside of the internet is that it is unregulated. Therefore it is possible to find some rubbish – occasionally dangerous rubbish – among all the information available. Anyone, anywhere, can publish anything on the internet, therefore it is inevitable that some wrong information is published by people with good intentions but little real knowledge, by people with strong opinions but little real knowledge; and – sadly – people with strong opinions and ill intent. Without any knowledge at all, it is difficult to sift the good and useful from the rubbish, *therefore it is important to seek a range of information through as many reputable sources as possible.*

Many people feel they lack the skills to use the internet, perhaps because they did not have such access in their younger days. In this case, consider asking a friend to help.

For some useful websites see the Appendix.

Charities

Over the last century or so, many charities have been formed by people who have recognised the need for information, support and help. Often these have been built up by a few passionate individuals willing to give time, effort and energy to find funds to offer what they found was missing when they – or perhaps someone close to them – needed help. A list of charities may be available at your local library, or perhaps a friend, colleague or acquaintance might know of one which might give the information needed. Awareness-raising is also an important part of charity work.

Many charities organise support helplines and groups who meet to offer mutual help, sometimes with speakers offering information – when you find a contact number, get in touch and find out what is available. If there is little or nothing in your own area, consider ways of travelling to find what you need, or perhaps even consider what you would need to start a group or helpline yourself. Talking to others in the same or similar situation can be very therapeutic and helpful in surviving tough times, with sharing of information as well as personal support. Often others will be found with experience of different stages of an illness or condition, who can give hope for the future.

The Appendix contains more about charities.

Magazines and newspapers

Some magazines are published which relate to a particular or specialist interest, and many general magazines and newspapers contain articles on health issues, as well as 'problem pages' to which readers may write. For many years mental health issues were ignored, but gradually this has changed with the recognition of how emotional and mental health underpin physical wellbeing. Look in bookshops at the racks of magazines and newspapers, and study the health section in libraries. Write to a regular health page and ask for information, or suggest a topic for future inclusion.

Radio and television

Radio and television programmes cover a wide variety of subjects, and regular series as well as occasional programmes are made on health issues – search out what you are looking for, write and ask for information, suggest topics for future programmes.

What can professionals realistically offer?

What are the problems in providing information to carers?

Very few adults live completely isolated lives; most have families, friends, colleagues and acquaintances. Living alone, and coping alone with life's ups and downs, is difficult enough for those who are well and strong. For anyone who has problems, either physical or emotional or possibly both, living alone is even more difficult. Asking a new patient – or even an established one – *who* they would like to support them could be the first step to finding the support they need to tackle their illness and give the best chance of successful living. (Note – *who* they would like to support them, not *if* they would like someone for support.) Most people know at least one person, either family or friend or other carer, they'd like to help them and think are capable of providing the support they need – and most people are happy to feel needed, that they have been thought capable of providing such support.

> I think sometimes staff are worried about saying the wrong thing. They don't know what language to use, are frightened of upsetting the carer, and aren't sure what they can and cannot share. [Community psychiatric nurse]
>
> I object to information sharing without my being told what information is being shared so that I can correct errors. [Service user]
>
> I think it should be written down when the client is well, stable, somewhere prominent the things they want done when they are ill and things they don't want done. Come the time when they're ill it's too late to start collecting consent. [Service user]
>
> The study summarised in this briefing paper managed to identify only a handful of good policies advising on how to share information with carers. Too many

policies concentrated on the negative effects of sharing information with carers, rather than the benefits.

[Extracts from Department of Health, 2006]

When support is refused

Some very vulnerable and troubled individuals may refuse even the thought of involving others in their care – perhaps seeing any expressions of concern or even interest as intrusion, or unable to cope with any close contact with anyone at all, or possibly because of some perceived problem with those offering that help – but many are pleased to feel that more support is indeed a possibility and on offer to help them cope.

The first step for professionals in maximising carers' strengths and using them to better support a troubled individual is therefore to ask the individual who they would like to help them.

Respecting a person's wishes about family contact while recognising their need for support is an extremely difficult balance to find for both professionals and for family members. In *Relative Stranger: A Life After Death*, Mary Loudon, writing after learning of the death of her older sister, gives a painfully vivid picture of her own feelings and those of her parents and other family members towards a much-loved sister and daughter who had suffered from schizophrenia for most of her adult life, and who cut herself off from her family and all close contact with other people.

> When Catherine left home she went to India for a year where she became seriously ill, suffered the breakdown from which she never fully recovered, and then vanished. After a fraught search by the Foreign Office and our father she was found but vanished for a second time. Some time later, she finally returned to England, broken.
>
> (Loudon, 2006)

During her final illness, knowing she had inoperable advanced cancer, Catherine 'had stated, very firmly, that she had no next of kin. Two parents, four brothers and sisters, each with spouses and children. No next of kin?' (Loudon, 2006). It was only when the authorities went into her flat that they found an unopened letter with an address, and contacted Catherine's family.

No matter how much someone is loved, no matter how people want to offer all sorts of support, both physical and emotional, it is the right of an adult to refuse such support – and this inevitably causes much pain for mothers, fathers, other family members who care, who see ways in which help is needed, only to have all offers of help rejected.

Coping with changes in behaviour, caused by distorted thinking or chemical changes due to drugs or alcohol, which may involve aggression, paranoid negative interpretations of all words and actions, rejection of any offer of help or support no matter how well intentioned, is very painful. When delegates at the EDA Carers Conference, 2000, were asked what they found most difficult, 'coping with aggression, hostility and rejection' was top of the list.

Such a refusal of help also causes problems for professionals who are bound to recognise the rights of an adult individual to choice over how they wish to live their life.

> Legally, if someone is an adult, they can choose to commit suicide, or self harm. All we can do is try to persuade.
>
> [C, social worker]

Refusal of support can also cause friction between carers and professionals when carers, wanting to help their loved one, try to find out how and what they can do to help. For highly trained and caring professionals whose daughter or son or other family member is affected by mental health problems, unable to get information and rejected when they try to offer help, this may be even more difficult to accept; Catherine's father was a GP (Loudon, 2006). Unable to cope with close contact, Catherine chose to lead her life far from her family and, while replying to letters, often refused visits. She had many friends in the area where she chose to settle, who could accept the very limited contact Catherine could cope with.

> I was so proud of her then, proud of the nurses too, for looking after her psychologically and emotionally in the way that they did: for not mocking or judging her; for being kind to Stevie [Catherine's preferred name] and not questioning him; above all, for understanding that the maintenance of others' dignity often amounts to no more than the tact and insight to leave them alone.
>
> (Loudon, 2006)

Accepting this may be extremely difficult for carers to come to terms with, especially for parents, but perhaps better to accept reduced contact than none at all.

Carers may have to learn to stand back, no matter what their own feelings. Simply, gently and regularly letting their loved one know that they are loved, that the carer is there, and willing to help if asked to do so, may be the best thing. At times, any contact – no matter how gentle or well meant – might be read as pressure, and might lead to even more efforts at distance. Sometimes standing back, allowing the individual their own choice of (what may seem to others incomprehensible) isolation, accepting that what one individual may need and want is not the same as another person no matter the relationship, respecting individual dignity with tact and insight as noted by Mary Loudon, *may* lead later to increased trust and renewed contact.

There are no easy answers, no short-cuts to building any relationship; even established relationships may change. There is no one right way to suit every troubled or vulnerable individual, or every carer whether family or professional. Finding the best way to provide 24-hour care for any individual with their individual needs depends on many factors.

The one common factor in providing that care is the need to build constructive communication by all involved whether by letter, telephone, email or – if possible – meeting. All these depend first of all on what the adult individual finds acceptable.

Contact with professionals: what can carers expect?

As we have seen, information may be given by a professional on the illness, or it may be found through books, websites and charities, but for contact with family members much depends on what the vulnerable individual wants – as well as whether treating professionals think meetings involving family or other carers would help their patient/client and enable carers to offer more effective support. (Being realistic, though most family members want and are able to help, some do not and a few unfortunately cause further stress.)

A first step to gain an individual's agreement to carer involvement may be taken by professionals, only to be met with failure. If this is the case, the individual's rights to privacy must be respected, with the paramount consideration being to preserve and build communication with the patient, no matter how much support the carers may be able and willing to offer. Further attempts to obtain agreement may be tried later.

> Where a patient is not able to make rational decisions for their long-term health and benefit, their competence to make decisions in question, it is worth trying to gently persuade – through giving clear information rather than attempts to control.
>
> (Stewart & Tan, 2006)

> Often gentle persuasion, patience and being willing to listen and talk, works when assertiveness or other approaches fail.
>
> [J, senior social worker]

Without constructive communication, relationships between carers and professionals may deteriorate fast.

Constructive or cringe conversations?

What can both professionals and carers do to build constructive rather than cringe communications? How can carers get professionals to listen? And how can professionals obtain and give valuable information without breaking confidentiality rules?

> *Professional*: It's so unpleasant when someone shouts at me. I have to work within guidelines and rules and not enough resources.

Carer: All I need is some information about how to help my son! Can no-one tell me what to do or not to do – I'm out of my mind with worry!

Frustrations for both sides may well carry over into other professional–carer interactions, with judgements, assumptions and stress all playing their part in deteriorating relationships – none of which will help in any way the vulnerable individual everyone wishes to help.

Practical ideas for professionals and carers

At meetings

- *Try to start afresh at each meeting.* Whether carer or professional, try hard not to carry with you any possible past resentments or preconceived ideas of the behaviour of the people you are about to meet.

  Key thought: Everyone at the meeting wants to support the vulnerable individual, may have different approaches but also have strengths to offer (as well as a few human weaknesses to work on).

- *With limited time available, an outline* of what is to be discussed is essential from the lead professional at the beginning of a meeting, with carers asked if they have any particularly important issues they wish to add. Without asking this, it is quite possible for carers to have a really important issue which is causing huge problems to their loved one and/or themselves, to be thinking of this rather than being able to concentrate on what professionals have on their agenda.

- *Any deviation from the agreed outline* may either be added when it comes up, or postponed for later discussion.

- *Listen carefully* to what other people are saying.

  Key thought: Lack of listening is the most frequently mentioned problem in any discussion about communication.

- *Try to keep calm and concentrate,* which can be much more difficult when you are under stress.

  Key thought: Remember that professionals often cope with lack of resources and time pressures, and carers with exhaustion and worry – it is inevitable that stress will take its toll.

- *A 5-minute 'time out' break* may be suggested by anyone if frustration and stress cause emotions to overwhelm.

  Key thought: Try to be aware of how others may be feeling; think of the long-term benefits the meeting has been set up to try to achieve.

- *If something is not clear*, ask for an explanation. If you don't, it is more than likely that lack of common understanding may cause problems at a later date.
- *Spend a short time at the end of the meeting to review progress*, achievements and what went well, setbacks and what needs further discussion, new topics for another meeting.

These bullet points are easy to write or to say, but are often difficult to put into practice when personal feelings are involved. Carers may be handicapped by love and unable to be objective; affected by stress reactions such as tearfulness or anger; want to hear that there is a 'magic pill' or cure for their loved one; and frequently exhausted with struggling to cope 24 hours a day, every day. While professionals may be more detached and objective, they too may be under great stress through unrealistic workloads, lack of resources, and personal problems.

Differences of opinion

Differences of opinion are inevitable in all areas of human life, most especially when there is a lack of information, communication and honest open discussion.

Note for carers: Remember that no matter how you may disagree with what's being said, no-one likes to be shouted at. Unpleasant behaviour or aggression not only spoils the atmosphere for everyone at the meeting, it rarely accomplishes anything other than bad feeling. If you lose your cool, you'll quite possibly lose credibility (and probably confirm all sorts of stereotyped opinions about parents!). Ask for a five-minute break if you feel you need it.

Note for professionals: It is important to judge the best way to foster a long-term constructive atmosphere. Bear in mind how carers may feel, consider their individual reactions and suggest a short break if necessary.

Language

Notes for professionals

Avoid jargon or long words unless unavoidable. Where unavoidable, explain the word or term and make sure your meaning is understood. Remember KISS: keep it short and straightforward.

Notes for carers

- Think beforehand about any important information you want to pass on or anything you want to ask or clarify.

- Rehearse and practise what you want to say, how you want to say it, the questions you want to ask (see below, Choosing the right words). Make a list, write it down if necessary, think of how you will ask.
- If you don't understand something, ask politely for it to be explained again.

Note for carers and professionals

Remember that it is very easy to assume understanding, or to hesitate or even to forget to ask for clarification.

Written communications

Letters are a useful aid to constructive communications: a busy GP, consultant, headteacher, social worker, or any other professional working with many people and probably surrounded by paperwork may not have time or may forget to add a note to a particular file following a telephone conversation.

These are general principles for both carers and professionals: it is easy to forget that clear simple and straightforward communication makes for understanding all round. Although not all the following notes will apply to everyone reading this book, it is worth reading them all through.

The Appendix contains a basic layout for letters and some useful phrases.

Notes for carers

- Write a polite, dated letter (remember about losing credibility if you lose your cool – no sarcasm or swear words) outlining all the information and points you feel the professionals/carers need to be aware of. Do not post it yet.
- Keep the letter at least overnight, then check it over. Never write and post a letter in the heat of the moment. Is this what you want to say? Is there anything you'd like to add, change or delete?
- Letters will be kept in a file for future reference; this is particularly helpful for new professionals who may not have worked with your loved one in the past.
- Keep a copy for your own records to which you may refer in future. Unfortunately, sometimes pieces of paper do get lost in busy offices and clinics.
- Either send your letter, or take it with you to a meeting and leave it for the professionals to discuss and file.

Choosing the right words: written

When writing a letter, think carefully about who will read the letter. For instance, if it is to tell some family news to someone you know very well, the letter may be written on an informal card or writing paper, may use familiar in-jokes and words. This will be very different from more formal communications needed at work. As a teacher, I once received a brief absence note written on toilet paper (quite appropriate in the circumstances as the absence was caused by an upset stomach).

Whatever the correspondence, whoever the writer or recipient, clarity and meaning are most important.

Notes for professionals and carers

The most effective letters:

- are short and to the point
- find the right tone – calm and concerned, or carping and critical?
- say exactly what you intend
- are clear and legible
- have care taken over spelling (checked in a dictionary or spellchecker)
- have pages numbered in case they get separated after leaving you
- have pages fastened together with a paper clip or staple.

Reread your letter and if possible wait for a day or two before posting. Ask yourself: Does my letter say what I want to say? How does it sound – serious and considered, concerned, calm – or cross and critical? Is this the way I want to sound? Have I missed out anything important? Will this letter make the impression I want it to make, make a positive – or a negative – difference to the situation? Will this letter help the person most needing help?

Remember that letters (and emails) can be used as legal documents.

Choosing the right words: spoken

At meetings

Any meeting when you feel it is important to present your thoughts, worries or problems and wish to offer information in a constructive way which will be taken seriously may be nerve-wracking. This can be as true for professionals as for anyone else when discussing possibly difficult issues involving a loved one's behaviour and how it affects others. Some people find it more difficult than others to keep calm; some become angry, some become weepy and incoherent, some withdraw into silence. This is particularly true when anyone is under stress and exhausted.

What can carers do to help constructive conversations at meetings?

- *Support at the meeting?* If carers feel that they may be unable to explain their feelings or worries clearly, or are possibly not sure if they will be able to keep to all the good intentions about remaining calm even despite careful preparations – remember about probably losing your credibility if you lose your temper! – it might be worth considering asking a trusted friend or family member, or even seeking out a professional experienced in mediation work, to come with you for support. (A Carers' Centre, found in many big and even smaller cities and towns, may be able to help.)
- *Preparation* might include deep breathing, listening to music; running or other exercise to use up some adrenaline; or meditation.
- *Make notes* of what you want to say.
- *Practising* with a friend or mirror can be very helpful.

What can professionals do to encourage positive communications with carers?

At meetings:

- *Impressions are important:* think carefully about the setting for a meeting. Whether doctor, teacher, social worker or other professional, many or most of the people you will see will be feeling nervous, uncomfortable or unhappy and may have a negative image of your profession based on hearsay, the media, or previous experience.
- *The setting may make or break the atmosphere* and how constructive or otherwise it may turn out to be. Formal or informal? 'For some people a desk is associated with a position of authority and can trigger feelings of weakness or hostility. When a listener sits behind a desk, the interaction is more likely to be role-to-role rather than person-to-person' (Bolton, 1979).
- *On either side of a table or desk or at right angles at the corner* of the same table or desk? Facing each other without a table or desk? Around a conference table, or coffee table? With a larger number, your chair facing a line of others? Or in a circle? Height of chairs – if a professional sits on a much higher chair than anyone else at the meeting, what message does that give? What is on the walls: a few professional posters, fire regulations, and otherwise bare? Or a few pictures or photos? You may be so used to the

office or room where you work that you may not see ho others; ask a friend or colleague – or families? – to comme see and feel on entry to your room.

- *Greetings are important* for setting the tone – a smile and h handshake, makes a *much* better start to any meeting than s behind a desk who looks up briefly then goes back to note reading before asking the first question, making the first comment. This is especially true for people who feel nervous or hesitant about their ability to cope with professionals, possibly because of past experiences or the fear of being judged or blamed in some way.
- *Introduce yourself and any colleagues,* with reminders of *why* everyone is attending the meeting. Don't assume that others will simply somehow 'know'.
- *Outline what's to be discussed, ask for any pressing issues carers would like discussed.* Be realistic about time available: if it's really not possible to include a new topic in the time, offer to include it next time. Or ask which are the most important issues. If something cannot be discussed because of lack of time, find out what is the issue of least importance, always bearing in mind the best long-term benefit of the vulnerable individual at the centre for whom everyone is there to try to develop 24-hour best care.
- *Use language which everyone in the room can understand.* Carers feel patronised and helpless if professionals use words or jargon they are unable to access easily.
- *Don't assume things: check that everyone is following what is being said.* Misunderstandings not only cause frustration as well as feelings of being patronised, they may also in some cases lead to tragedy.
- *Assume best intentions: many carers feel they are under suspicion and are defensive as a result.* Whatever the problems, whatever the individual strengths and weaknesses, family members and other carers are there because they care and want to support: they probably wouldn't turn up otherwise. Many may need reassurance that this is recognised.
- *Encourage expressions of personal coping strengths,* e.g. patience, empathy.
- *Gently encourage recognition of weaknesses* which may be detrimental to relationships, e.g. short temper and impatience. Humour can sometimes be used to talk about awkward topics: it's often a great way to gently lead into discussion of personality traits – Rhino response, Ostrich, Kangaroo care and so on (Treasure *et al.*, 2007).

- *Gently suggest practical ways of trying to address weaknesses,* e.g. where someone gives in easily because they are nervous of aggression, perhaps suggest they find a local assertiveness course.

- *With a family where there has been abuse,* physical, emotional or sexual, causing stress leading to an individual developing challenging behaviour, remember that other family members still need support – even more support? – in coming to terms with this, *as well as* with the illness or condition and the challenging behaviour of the individual at its centre.

- *Give information if at all possible when asked a question.* Most carers don't want information which may be confidential between professional and patient/client; most want to feel equipped to help and support their loved one at home. General information about illnesses and disorders which affect behaviour may be found in books or leaflets distributed by charities (see also the Appendix). By simply offering the names of relevant organisations which might be helpful, especially in the local area, by showing an openness and willingness to help and support, much can be achieved in establishing good relationships with carers to enable them to care effectively. All of which aids constructive communication.

- *If it is not possible to give the information sought* for whatever reason, *say so.* If the information is really confidential and divulging it would break the trust between you and the person you are trying to help, *say so.* Much frustration is felt by carers when they feel that professionals are simply hiding information without any good reason.

- *If you do not know the answer to a question, say so.* Some professionals may appear patronising rather than knowledgeable if they brush off questions; it's much better to say you don't know the answer but could try to find out (if you really can keep to that – don't raise false hopes). Or suggest a possible way the carer might be able to find out.

- *When working with carers of legally adult people,* ask your patient/client *who* they feel would best be able to support them, then suggest gently that person could attend part of some future meetings to learn how best to give that support. When agreement has been given, that person can then be invited along to an agreed part of meetings, perhaps for the last summarising part of an appointment; e.g. in eating disorders, if an eating plan has been agreed with a dietician, the support person could be invited to discuss how best to help a patient keep to that plan, any possible problems which may be encountered, and so on.

- *Try to think how family and friends might be able to support your work* when your patient/client is not with you. This could make or break your patient/client's efforts to stick to the agreed plan of action – and also gives carers a valuable role to play. All of which could lead to enhanced progress for your patients/clients, as well as better relationships all round.

- *Never promise what you can't deliver.* Doing so raises expectations and disappointment leads to negative feelings for future relationships.
- *Endings are as important as beginnings.* Summarise, outline any decisions and suggestions, check mutual understanding, end on a positive constructive note, and set the tone for support for the troubled individual, for future teamwork towards 24-hour best care.

How can professionals get necessary information (without breaking confidentiality)?

Living together on a day-to-day basis, family and other carers often hold huge amounts of information about all sorts of factors relevant to a troubled individual. By noticing small changes in routine or behaviour, they will often be the first to realise that all is not well with their friend or family member.

> My daughter is beginning to restrict her food intake again, she's stopped eating the snack I leave for her in the afternoons – I only found out when I went into her room with some ironing and saw them in her waste bin. And she's much snappier and moodier than she's been since she was discharged from hospital . . . I'm really worried about her relapsing again. I don't know what to do.
>
> [Val, EDA support line]

These are a few ideas which have been found useful.

Crisis management

> Crisis can be seen as part of 'normal' human experience, likely to occur, for example, at certain developmental stages and in response to common, but distressing life events. More complex or psychiatric crises can then be seen as one end of a continuum.
>
> A 'social crisis' could not be objectively measured – one person's major problem could be another person's small inconvenience. It was important not to trivialise people's distress or the causes of it. At the same time, staff at the social crisis service located social crisis as part of 'normal' experience, something which happens to all of us.
>
> Social crisis services are intended to have a preventative role, provide an alternative to hospital admission, an opportunity for assessment and promotion of recovery.
>
> (Stalker *et al.*, 2005)

One possibility is an extension of the long-established Samaritans, who offer telephone and face-to-face support to anyone, for any reason, in distress.

Direct helpline

Setting up a system for carers to offer confidential information through an agreed contact (perhaps a member of staff who will be available for consultation and support at a set time each week), or through encouraging carers to write down and send their concerns, may be very worthwhile. Lack of time and staff resources may make this difficult to organise, but in the long run it may be a way of actually saving time and resources by offering outpatient or other support at an early stage. In chronic conditions (for example, eating disorders such as anorexia; schizophrenia; bipolar disorder) which often follow a long pathway involving periods when the individual is well followed by a spell of illness, such early help can shorten a relapse or in some cases avoid relapse altogether.

Relapse management plan

An agreed plan of action including contact agreements between sufferers, carers and professionals, made when a sufferer is well, can also be very beneficial in tackling a possible relapse at the early stages rather than waiting. In some hospitals relapse management plans, worked out with an individual while well and coping – to give clear instructions and guidance as to what the individual would like to happen if and when relapse occurs, who they would like to be involved (or not) – have been very successfully developed.

Recent developments in mental health services have included research into alternatives to inpatient treatment where possible. Offering personal support at an early stage, through telephone lines or a 'crisis meeting' – someone sitting down and listening, considering options, working out a best course of action – is frequently valued by an individual experiencing what may be described as a 'social crisis', and has an important part to play in lessening the effects of individual personal distress as well as reducing admissions.

Journals

Writing is a well-established alternative to talking for many, including myself. When sad, angry or agitated I find writing out all those feelings through factual description, short story or poem really helps put things into a better perspective. There is a reason for writing being a particularly good way of addressing intense feelings – while thinking of ordering the words being written, to express exactly the sadness, anger, agitation felt about a particular event, all those emotions are also being ordered.

The writing may or may not be shared with someone else. It may be shared, then shredded. It may be thrown in the fire. Or it may be the start of a novel (with characters suitably disguised)!

Journals may also be developed as a two-way communication system between professionals and patients/clients and between professionals and carers, and used as a record of progress and achievements as well as noting setbacks along the way and any particular concerns.

Giving bad news

Being told that a child or young person has a condition, disorder or illness, whether autism, learning difficulties, Asperger's syndrome, ADHD, anorexia or any other mental health problem, can be extremely difficult for a parent or other carer to take in and accept.

> The paediatrician came to see me. He asked me if I actually had any idea what was wrong with my son. I replied that my father-in-law and one of my friends had both suggested that he might be mildly autistic, though I myself had no real idea what the word meant. He nodded. 'I'm afraid they are right,' he told me gently. 'Simon is autistic. I am afraid you have a long hard road ahead of you.' I looked at him. Nothing seems real any more. He was certainly not real. It was as if he had just fallen to pieces in front of my eyes. Everything – my way of life, my pride, my confidence, my whole outlook – had just been totally and irrevocably shattered. The numbness was merciful. It was better that I should realise slowly how much we, but above all, Simon, had lost.
>
> (Lovell, 1978)

> Any diagnostic assessment should be followed by sensitive discussion with the family about their child's problems, their severity and expected future course. Further information and support should always be provided.
>
> (Baron-Cohen & Bolton, 1993)

A whole chapter in *Autism: The Facts* is devoted to helping parents cope with the news, describing common feelings of parents as loss and grief, disbelief and shock, feeling overwhelmed, sometimes depression and despair coupled with anxiety about the child's future. Also present are a 'cloak of guilt, feelings of being somehow responsible for their child's condition, feelings of shame and embarrassment' (Baron-Cohen & Bolton, 1993). Feelings of failure are also common.

> Faced with your child turning away from you, appearing more absorbed in some repetitive activity than in you, who wouldn't feel dismayed, rejected and frustrated?
>
> (Baron-Cohen & Bolton, 1993)

Feelings of rejection, and the difficulty in coming to terms with hostility and aggression, are mentioned by almost all carers as the greatest causes of distress for them. The same authors outline how doctors should:

- try to keep information short and simple when giving or discussing a diagnosis

- later go through the details, when parents have had a chance to recover from hearing the news.

They note that recognisable patterns of behaviour in coming to terms with such news can often be seen – shock and a period of denial perhaps, anger at the injustice, possibly guilt ('What did we do to cause this?'), sadness. Followed finally by acceptance, with more realistic assessment of practical ways of coping at home.

> The psychological resilience of each parent and amount of support available from family, friends and health professionals will also be important, helping some parents to pass through some stages more quickly than others.
>
> (Baron-Cohen & Bolton, 1993)

Extreme reactions

> Occasionally very extreme reactions may be encountered, where a parent becomes stuck in denial, blaming others and searching for answers.
>
> (Baron-Cohen & Bolton, 1993)

Many people find it very difficult to accept that despite the huge range of modern medicines and treatments, for some conditions, disorders and mental illnesses there are often no known cures – it really is a case of accepting the reality and finding practical ways of coping to support not only the vulnerable and very troubled individual but also to ensure that other members of a family cope.

> Some parents get very angry, seem to think it's my fault that their child has an eating disorder and I can't give any easy solutions – the average time for recovery is several years. They just don't want to hear that and some can't accept it. Sometimes they can be very unpleasant.
>
> [Dr J. Morris, psychiatrist, young people's unit]

Although Drs Bolton and Baron-Cohen's book is about autism, and refers to giving the news to families faced with such a diagnosis, they could well be describing the feelings common to almost all families and other carers with a family member affected by any condition involving challenging behaviour.

The situation becomes even more difficult when a young person is legally an adult and differing definitions of confidentiality may be involved – carers may then be left struggling not only to cope with difficult behaviour at home but also lacking information about the particular condition and strategies to support that individual . . . not to mention the very real fear that if they inadvertently do or say the wrong thing their loved one might become even worse . . . while the troubled individual is faced with a world which because of unusual or distorted thinking often makes little sense, and lack of understanding of events and other people's words and actions. All of which can cause much frustration and distress.

How can professionals offer support?

Small things can make a big difference.

A willingness to offer whatever is realistically possible is a very good start: an information sheet; recommended reading and where to find it; recommended information and charity websites; telephone helpline numbers; local support available through a charity; local authority support such as through social work departments; visit from community nurses or community psychiatric nurses.

Information about particular behaviours or patterns involved in a condition and what might be expected are very helpful, plus if possible suggestions of ways to cope with these, e.g. many carers find aggression really difficult to deal with – a gentle suggestion about trying to find a class to help them cope through developing more assertiveness could be seen as helpful.

Be realistic about resources: don't offer what you can't deliver. If a carer or family ask for information or resources or meetings or discussion which are simply not possible for whatever reason – confidentiality, lack of time or staffing resources – explain *why* rather than risk the possibility of being seen as uncaring or unsympathetic by the people who support your clients or patients in the world outside.

Constructive approaches

Stress the following:

- all sorts of approaches may be tried and may work for an individual
- what works for one family in one case may not work for someone else: a family has not failed because something they tried was unsuccessful
- perhaps depending on tiredness, stress levels and other factors, what works one day at one time may not work on another day
- everyone in the family will have strengths they can offer; not everyone will have the same strengths but they can work together to maximise patience, empathy, listening, humour and so on
- help family members to recognise their own strengths and what they can bring to supporting their loved one
- any perceived weaknesses can be worked on for the benefit of everyone, especially that of their loved one

- teamwork, a common approach and constructive whole-family awareness and support of each other can achieve much more than isolated efforts.

> Small things can really help – just a simple acknowledgement of how distressing it is can give me strength to go on.
>
> [Joan, see Chapter 2]

There really are, unfortunately, no easy answers. Each family and each carer must find their own way of practical coping, and constructive searching for this through reading and other research is well worth tackling. However, by offering small nuggets of information to support finding ways of family coping, professionals can go a long way towards initiating constructive communication. Simply acknowledging, even while unable for any reason to offer all that anyone is hoping for, that the family's or individual's situation is causing distress shows caring and concern.

Record keeping – and sharing?

When a child is involved, discussing relevant information will be part of ongoing support structures at home.

When a patient is an adult, before any record is shared, of course their agreement must be sought (see Chapter 10). Some patients when asked for such consent, where it is relevant to developing appropriate support, readily agree when it is explained that it is important to their carers to enable them to provide best care for them. Other patients refuse for a variety of reasons.

> Gentle persuasion can work where attempts at control will fail.
>
> [J, senior social worker]

After an initial refusal, such persuasion can be really important in gaining support for an individual. Practical suggestions are invaluable where carers have had no previous experience, e.g. *how* a carer is expected to supervise eating plans in anorexia; or with chronic bulimia *how to* try to distract a loved one from visiting the bathroom immediately after a meal or snack.

What can professionals offer a family?

Practical suggestions

Any practical suggestions to ease the burden of 24-hour care, 365 days a year, every year.

Honesty and trust

Some professionals perhaps feel that by fudging the truth, by not mentioning the most difficult aspects of, for example, mental illness, it might somehow protect carers.

> . . . provides a practical guide as well as suggestions for parents and other carers . . . an excellent addition to the literature . . . based on many carers' stories as well as her own . . . This book is not for the fainthearted.
>
> [Extract from review of Smith, 2004 http://edr.org.archives/2004/02/04]

> Not for the fainthearted?! They haven't a clue!
>
> [E, carer at eating disorders support meeting]

> What on earth do professionals think we have to cope with at home?!
>
> [S, carer at eating disorders support meeting]

> Maybe they think that somehow they're protecting us by not telling us, not talking about the behaviour . . . My son caused £300 of damage in our kitchen last week when he had one of his rages.
>
> [C, carer at eating disorders support meeting]

> After long years of experience in primary school, I thought I'd encountered the whole range of behaviours. These included, for instance, being punched and having my shins kicked black and blue by an out-of-control five-year-old from a farm who had never had much contact with children or adults, terrified by the idea of having to stay with a whole class of strange people and one adult whom he didn't know; being shouted and sworn at; restraining a hefty ten-year-old from climbing out of a window; being yelled at at close range by an enraged father when he heard that drivers were refusing to carry his son on the school bus.
>
> Yet when my adult daughter developed anorexia I found those years of experience no help at all in knowing what to do. I found the level of out-of-control aggression and rage absolutely terrifying and had no real idea what reaction from me might ease or make worse the behaviour. A 'way over-the-top, out-of-control, Hairy Jamaica' was my daughter's description at a much later stage of the spectacular aggression and screaming tempers which were part of her illness. [GS]

Discussion of the above 'faint hearted' quote

During training, professionals learn all about the very worst aspects of illnesses and conditions families may have to cope with, yet professionals in mental health in the past have felt that families will somehow 'know' how to do what they have spend years in training to do.

Ignorance is bliss? In common with many carers I've talked to, I certainly wish it had not been necessary to learn over years – the hard way – of behaviours such as the 'Hairy Jamaicas', common when someone suffers from an eating disorder, and to have to work out what might, just might, help in the long run. And What Definitely Will Not Help.

Without any information about the possible paths of anorexia, binge-purge type, the outcome for Jay as well as myself could so easily have been very different.

Supportive preparation

Whatever the disorder, it is better to be supportively prepared for The Worst, The Very Worst, regarding possible behaviour and timescale and then not need the information, than to be faced with the unexpected, to be totally unprepared, not having a clue what to do or not do, and feel totally unable to cope.

It may be too late to give relevant information after a certain behaviour appears and a carer, without information, preparation or guidance, reacts in a way which may turn out to be less than helpful.

And if – when – one carer collapses or becomes ill, who will be there to support and help?

CHAPTER THIRTEEN

Challenging the behaviour

What do you do when you are faced with 'challenging' behaviour? Crumble? Panic? Shout back? Run? Try to be louder? Bigger and more aggressive? Walk away? Stay calm and try to reason? Ignore for as long as possible, then any of the former?

> Challenging behaviour must be challenged.
>
> [J, social worker, 2006]

Agreed. Unacceptable behaviour – whether at home, in school, at work or elsewhere – needs to be challenged. And it needs to be actively challenged. Almost always.

> Hello dear.
> *Hello mother.*
> How are you dear?
> *Fine, mother.*
> And how's your sister?
> *Fine, mother.*
> And how's your cousin?
> *Fine, mother.*
> And how's your friend?
> *Fine, mother.*
> And how's your mother?
> *Fine, mother.*
>
> My mother had Alzheimer's in the last years of her life. Although I could recognise some humour in the above conversation, I could have wept. And had to accept that my mother as I knew her was gone. Sadly she could not recognise me nor the effect of her words or behaviour, sometimes unpleasant and aggressive and completely out of character for her, on me or others. Nor could she do anything to control that behaviour. I am so glad that my mother, who had given me such love and care over so many years, had no knowledge or understanding of what happened to her in the last years of her life.
>
> [GS]

In most other situations involving challenging behaviour, it is not enough to simply 'be there' in support, even when you feel the person is ill, nor to try to ignore its effects on yourself or others (see Chapter 16).

The question is how to challenge that behaviour in the particular situation. Perhaps you've had some useful training to help you cope?

> I used to be very bombastic . . . then I was trained in Motivational Interviewing techniques about how to really listen and reflect what someone's saying, to raise questions in their own mind about their behaviour, and how that behaviour is affecting their life.
>
> [Psychiatrist, workshop, 2006]

By nature some temperaments seem better able to cope than others with difficult scenes, and in some lives, households, neighbourhoods and workplaces there is more 'rough and tumble', more rows, more confrontation of varying intensity, to be dealt with – this could be seen as a form of 'training' for meeting situations in later life. Some people are given some training as part of their work, where they may have to deal with difficult situations; some after being involved in notable incidents, perhaps leading to court action, may be advised to undertake anger management to help control a quick temper or aggressive nature. But most – like me – have only their own experiences in life as 'training', and cope as best they can.

Growing up in a quiet household with lots of play activities and outings and with little obvious conflict might be a handicap later in not knowing how to react to and deal with confrontation when it comes to your door. Finding ways of coping with unreasonable behaviour in unexpected situations can be seen as part of life: some actual training in such situations would certainly have been extremely useful in my work, and also in coping during the years of my daughter's illness with the dramatic changes in her personality and behaviour.

Luckily some experiences at work, which at the time I had to work out ways of coping with, had providing me with at least a glimmer of what might help my daughter: actively challenging unacceptable behaviour *while still assuring her that I loved her. No matter how I loved her, it was the behaviour I wouldn't accept.* I would not accept it from other people, and certainly not in my own home.

Triggers for challenging behaviour

Challenging behaviour – whether aggressive and personally threatening, unpleasant manipulation, prolonged screaming, throwing things, destruction of property, self-harm, or threat of suicide (either seriously, or possibly emotional blackmail to get you to cave in and do what someone wants, usually short term and with no thought for long-term consequences) – may have all sorts of individual triggers, including:

- fear
- frustration
- feelings of loss of control

- lack of understanding of what is happening
- feelings of no control of a particular situation
- feelings of being under threat.

Frustration

Frustration may be:

- at being unable to do something
- at being unable to understand what's going on
- at being unable to find the right words
- at not being able to meet personal standards e.g. when personal willpower is overcome by physical craving for and dependency on nicotine, drugs or alcohol, or by entrenched habits.

Fear

Fear may be:

- of the unknown
- of being wrong
- of being unable to cope
- of deteriorating faculties
- of loss of control
- of being unable to control a situation
- of being unable to understand
- of being under threat
- of being abandoned.

Anxiety may apply to any of the fear factors above.

In some cases there may be a hair-trigger temper trait from childhood; in others emotional distress in certain situations; or a particularly stressful experience leads to dramatic changes in personality. In yet other cases a brain injury or a learning disability means intense frustration for an individual, or a lack of understanding of other people's reactions, or, as in Alzheimer's disease, a loss of being able to make sense of the world, loss of recognition of loved ones, loss of being able to distinguish between strangers and family.

Do any of these ring a bell? Perhaps you can add to this list?

Just as the trigger may vary with the individual, so too may the most effective way to react, tackle and – it is hoped – eventually change it or manage it better. It would be wonderful to say Do This or Don't Do That, and all will be well – but unfortunately there is no magic wand. *There is no One Right Way to fit all circumstances; it really does depend on individuals, circumstances and situation.*

Although circumstances, the physical situation where the behaviour takes place, and resources all need to be considered, the unpredictable nature of much challenging behaviour often makes it difficult to respond in a considered way. Sometimes, as with Alzheimer's disease or Huntingdon's disease, relentlessly deteriorating mental faculties are the reason for the behaviour, and working out strategies to ensure survival of the carer is the best option (see Hugh Marriott's account of caring for his wife over many years: Marriott, 2003).

At times, when someone is aggressive and seriously threatening family or others, the best thing may be to try talking gently and calmly; or simply to withdraw and look for help. When there is a history of such incidents, whatever the trigger(s), perhaps better to acknowledge that professional help is needed, and the situation may be beyond what a single carer can manage.

However, in most conditions, it is a very worthwhile exercise to try to identify individual triggers and what particular circumstances may lead to an outburst. This is often the first step in helping the individual having difficulties in coping. This usually involves careful observation over a period of time; in the meantime, families and others have to cope with the behaviour and its consequences.

A chicken-and-egg situation: later we discuss trying to identify what situations affect an individual and lead to the challenging behaviour and consequences.

> Sometimes families don't challenge the behaviour.
>
> [J, social worker, 2006]

Agreed. This may or may not be true when the child is very small and tantrums may be considered part of growing up or testing the rules, or in the teenage years where testing all known and previously agreed boundaries is part of the picture. Learning what happens when rules are broken, learning self-control, is also part of growing up and usually, as a child grows beyond being a toddler, tantrums become a thing of the past. Once teenage years are past and peer pressure recedes in importance, behaviour (mostly) calms.

Part of growing up?

Unfortunately, because some difficult behaviour may be simply part of the growing-up process, early clues are often missed. Many families describe taking a child to a doctor, outlining their concerns that all is perhaps not as it should be – only to be given bland reassurance or their worries treated as fussing over trivia. Perhaps they are given a book on parenting skills. ('Don't worry, it's a phase. They'll grow out of it.')

Though well-meant, such reassurance over a child who is showing early symptoms of troubling behaviour may lead to a loss of the early intervention which might have meant a big difference in outcome for the individual, more understanding in nursery or school situations, an easier pathway through various situations causing major problems for both individual and carers struggling to cope. And in anorexia it could mean the difference between recovery, the illness becoming entrenched and chronic over many years, or with its high mortality, early death.

Jane Gregory, in *Bringing Up a Challenging Child at Home: When Love is Not Enough*, describes how her health visitor arranged a GP appointment to discuss her concerns about Chrissy's development and behaviour. He allowed plenty of time but did not appear to listen, leading to Jane Gregory's strong feelings of being patronised and misunderstood. Later she read his comments in Chrissy's medical notes: 'Mum says is miserable at home. Throughout this long consultation, Christina was happy and playing in the room. Looks well. Further reassurance.'

Chrissy's behaviour at that time included self-injurious behaviour such as eye-poking, head-banging or biting own hands; aggression towards others, biting, kicking or hair pulling; destruction of property including breaking windows, throwing objects, stripping off and ripping clothes; sleep problems; swearing.

> Behaviour we described was frequently minimised by professionals who gave us casual parenting advice about normal childhood development, offered us books and tapes – none of which mentioned the behaviour we were coping with at home. Perhaps if we'd had more information at the beginning we'd have been able to help him more, or maybe some professionals could have helped him and he wouldn't have developed so many problems later on. If he'd had the right help sooner.
>
> [Alan, parent of adopted son, reactive attachment disorder, see Chapter 2]

> If the professionals don't see the actual behaviour, often they don't believe that the charming child in front of them can be a nightmare at home.
>
> I think if he'd had help earlier, things could have been much better for C.
>
> [Sheila Gray, see Chapter 2]

Working with children with individually difficult behaviour in a class situation can be very challenging for any teacher, as well as challenging for carers at home if behaviour is similar in all situations – which may or may not be the case.

As a teacher, I met many different and very challenging behaviours; in primary teaching – at that time at least – I was given no training in how to best support any child who had special educational needs. Teachers were simply expected to know how to respond to unpredictable challenging behaviour which could, and often did, disrupt the planned work of the class. At times these incidents were relatively minor, at others it was only after months – and in a few cases years – of reporting difficult incidents that finally appropriate support was put in place.

> D's behaviour was often unpredictable, and when he couldn't cope in class he was very disruptive. That day he'd had a good day in class, and at the end of the afternoon D settled with the others for a story and singing before home time. All was well until all the children were packing up. Suddenly D said 'I'm going to throw this chair.' And did, right across the room. [GS]

With many others in the same class, perhaps some also with special educational needs, added to various educational targets in language, mathematics and so on which teachers are expected to meet with their pupils, plus other parents worried about the effects of distractions on the attainments of their own offspring, small wonder the situation can often become fraught and stressful for everyone concerned! The longer the time taken to recognise problems and their possible origins and or triggers, and then to find help and support, the more difficult the situation becomes for the vulnerable person in the middle as well as for others in the class and the teachers.

Many people, including parents and other family members, have great difficulty in 'challenging challenging behaviour' or in extreme situations knowing even how to respond to behaviour they've never encountered before. Sometimes onset is sudden:

> My daughter T aged eight went in a matter of weeks from being a happy-go-lucky, healthy child doing well at school to having prolonged screaming fits at the slightest thing – for instance, being asked to tidy up, always been part of our routine, never been a problem before. Or when her sister knocked a bottle of tomato sauce off the table and it broke. When that happened, T started screaming that a splash of tomato sauce was on her leg, it would poison her, she was really terrified.
> [S, father of T, diagnosed with anorexia nervosa]

With a first child, recognising that all may not be well may take longer because parents are perhaps more unsure about what might be considered 'normal' development.

Home situation: adulthood

The home situation often grows even more fraught as the troubled individual grows to adulthood, or is already legally an adult when the condition or disorder develops.

Overt rudeness, swearing, verbal aggression and threatening body language, out-of-control rages, violence towards property or people are hard enough to cope with at work, out driving, at the supermarket or in the street. To meet such behaviour in your own home, perhaps especially when it has never previously been part of the picture, is even more difficult.

Schizophrenia, eating disorders or bipolar disorder, often appear, though not always, in the teens or early twenties with a preceding stressful experience sometimes thought to be the trigger: leaving home for the first time, even for positive reasons, e.g. to study or start work; bullying; moving house and losing friends and activities; bereavement; any sort of abuse. Sometimes unfortunately the stress is within the family. Experimenting with drug taking and alcohol, or problems with gambling in various forms (all becoming much more easily accessible in Western society) may be part of the picture; for those with a genetic vulnerability, trying to gain control of any of the 'excessive appetites' can prove a huge stumbling block to development of an individual pathway through life.

Whatever the cause of the behaviour, at whatever age, in whatever situation, families are expected to cope. The question is how?

A few ideas

Tackle the flames first

When coping with a difficult situation, it's a bit like tackling a fire – deal with the flames first, look for causes afterwards.

A colleague once told me that he 'enjoyed a good run-in', and he'd 'never been bested yet!' This is where a temperament which enjoys an adrenaline rush sparked by 'a good run-in', or training, is useful. For the rest of us, looking for practical ideas and strategies is the best we can do.

Reactions to challenging behaviour

It may be a very understandable human reaction to unfair and upsetting behaviour to want to shout back, try to argue logically, dissolve into tears, or feel totally helpless – but this is not helpful to the person you want to help and support. It also achieves nothing apart from building further on existing stress.

Read through the following ideas and strategies which, after thinking about your own situation, its background and progress, you may like to try perhaps with some adaptation. There will obviously be differences depending on the illness or condition, age or stage – try to identify what might be helpful for you. Or use them as a basis to look for other possibilities – perhaps discussing the problems and how you feel with family, friends or a professional might help, or they may know of useful reading materials.

Look again at the list of possible triggers earlier in the chapter: frustration, fear, anxiety. In ordinary daily home life, whatever the trigger for regular displays of unreasonable temper – whether fear, frustration and/or anxiety, or a mix of any or all of these – it is important to try to tackle it as soon as possible.

Identifying the trigger(s)may be as simple as ABC: the Antecedents, the Behaviour and the Consequences.

Observation

Observe in order to identify any pattern in what leads up to (or the *Antecedents* to) an incident.

Keep a record of incidents in diary or notebook; try to identify what might particularly upset the troubled individual. For example, an unexpected change of activity is a problem for many children who have settled down, and most especially for anyone on the autism/Asperger's continuum. They are engrossed in one activity and expect to continue when quite suddenly the understood plan is changed and they are expected to transfer their attention to something else. Even worse if the Something Else is an activity they dislike or don't think half as important as the one they were initially engaged in.

Small things can make a big difference

A simple timetable

A simple timetable or outline of activities, including meal breaks, discussed at the beginning of a day or any other period, can be useful, followed up by regular reminders such as: 'Only a few minutes left now, then you'll have to tidy up. We'll be moving on to [. . .] next.' Talking about what time an activity will draw to a close, where the clock hands will be pointing, setting a timer to sound just before finishing time, may all be useful strategies to try.

Special occasions

In eating disorders such as anorexia and bulimia, a social situation involving decisions around food – e.g. Christmas, parties, wedding reception – can cause stress; in other conditions a special occasion with various unknown, unexpected stimuli can be the trigger. Once conscious of the possibility of such an anxious reaction, carers may be able to talk through the feelings in preparation and ask what might help during the stressful situation.

Other triggers

- *Unknown or misunderstood language or vocabulary?* Increase sign language and gestures? Simplify instructions? Repetition?
- *Hearing problems?* Try making sure you face the person; speak very clearly. Don't shout: this distorts lip movements. Repeat as necessary, use hand gestures. Write. Lipreading classes can be invaluable.

- *Dislike of touch or particular materials?* Try experimenting with different materials.
- *Dislike of certain noises?* Try experimenting to see if this causes problems.
- *New or unknown people or situations?* Try talking through as before, in preparation.

Is there a common thread you can recognise, a situation perhaps which causes particular stress?

Trivial triggers – or not?

Remember that what may be trivial to you may be a big source of stress to someone else, and that stress shows in different ways for individuals: some people cope well in exam situations, others go to pieces and never achieve their potential; some people cope easily with change, others find the same change (moving activity, moving house, change of surroundings) difficult; some people feel heightened reactions to and are affected by particular materials, sounds, light. Some individuals with serious mental health problems may experience psychosis, paranoia or feelings of persecution; their reactions may be extreme to *their perceptions* of what is happening around them – words, people, events – rather than what others are experiencing.

Sometimes, in some situations, it is possible to find a fairly simple cause, and to find an approach which can make quite a dramatic difference.

> After a good start in a new class, I started playing up. When I'd been in endless trouble at school for not listening, for behaving in all sorts of annoying ways in class, a child psychologist was called in to test me and identify the problem. It was discovered that my hearing had been seriously affected by illness a few months previously! And I couldn't hear instructions or even sometimes when someone said my name.
>
> [W, personal contact]

Try also

- Use of *simple hand signs* to accompany words (thumbs up, or shake of head?).
- *Makaton.*
- *Flashcards* with e.g. a happy face, sad face or other simple expression or instruction.
- Considering *tone of voice* is also worthwhile: a carer showing their irritation can cause what may start as a trivial incident to escalate.

An individual mix of these or other ideas can make a huge difference to understanding and removing many frustrations for some individuals. All are worth exploring.

Identifying what causes individual behaviours, in addition to trying to work out how to lessen and cope with the effects, is well worth the effort both for that individual and for encouraging a more positive atmosphere at home. Simple ideas such as testing the hearing, using simpler vocabulary or hand signs, and so on, is worth trying if only to exclude them and look for other possibilities.

- *Music, noise or lack of noise, aromatherapy, bright or soft lighting*: all these may enhance or affect atmosphere and are worth trying.

This is where professional and family working together as a team to provide continuity of approach can really make an enormous difference for an individual – and often for carers too.

Catch the moment

If possible – and not possible in all circumstances – try to find a good time to discuss the unacceptable *behaviour* and its *consequences* (B and C in ABC).

In many disorders and conditions, identifying a 'good time' for discussion of problems both for the individual and how they affect other people may again make a huge difference in supporting the individual to try to change the behaviour. This is particularly true in all the compulsive addictive behaviours: drugs, alcohol, eating disorders, gambling. There is little point in bringing up problem behaviour when someone has been drinking or is high on drugs.

Formal or relaxed and informal? This depends on the situation, the time available, who is or may be around – Sunday morning sitting around reading the papers or watching television in pyjamas, when we were both relaxed, turned out to be a good time for talking when my daughter was ill. Or it might be during a walk or drive, around the table or in passing at the top of the stairs. You might want to find a time when you're guaranteed the house will be empty or the phone won't ring.

If you've tried to identify a Good Time to Talk but the response is negative, ask the individual if they can think when might be a good time. Stress that you're concerned about the behaviour, its effects on the individual, and would really like an opportunity to talk it over. *Don't ignore* the behaviour and hope it will go away. If the response is negative, *don't give up* first time; every so often, calmly mention your observations, what you've noticed, how concerned you are for your loved one. Talk about the possible consequences that you worry about for the individual.

And when you have found a mutually agreed time to talk, ask how you can help.

Think and prepare

- What do you want to discuss?
- What words will you use? Practise saying them, with a family member, a friend, in front of the mirror.
- How will you say those words? Body and facial language are important, gentle discussion and reassurance of concern are more likely to be effective than criticism and attempts to control.
- Reread Chapter 3.

Useful phrases

- 'I've noticed . . .'
- 'I'm concerned that . . .'
- 'I'm a bit worried about . . .'
- 'What might help?'
- 'Is there anything I can do?'

(See also Chapter 4)

When the response is positive

- Make the most of it! Build on it.
- Help your loved one make a list of possible actions which might help or those which might not be a good idea.
- Writing the list serves as a reminder and may be tacked to a door, or carried in purse or pocket; and also helps when it comes to reviewing progress and achievements and tackling any setbacks.
- Encourage any mention of positive action. ('How are you going to set about . . .?')
- Encourage any talk of positive feelings. ('Tell me more about . . .')
- Encourage any mention of happy memories.
- Think of all those very important encouraging words you might use to motivate.
- Accentuate the positive, eliminate the negative.

Be prepared for adverse reactions

Especially when someone, on any level, realises that their behaviour is unacceptable, they may become defensive and even abusive.

A loved one may be able to control their irritation or temper or other negative reactions and feelings for only a short time; *make best use of the short time rather than prolong a less productive interaction.*

Don't walk away from a negative reaction and then ignore it: 'I've said what I feel, you maybe feel different . . . I think we should leave this just now and talk about it later on when we're both calm.'

If someone reacts strongly, begins to shout and there's a risk of losing your temper, try hard to resist this. Keep repeating that you've said your piece and the matter may be discussed later, and now you are going to go and wash the car; do some gardening; listen to music – and do exactly as you say.

'I beg your pardon? I *beg* your pardon? I – BEG – YOUR PARDON?' When someone's temper has got the better of them and they are shouting out of control, try saying these four words. Said quietly, the words can mean you didn't quite catch what was said. With different emphasis, that you can't *quite* believe they said what you thought you heard. Try it with flashing eyes and strong body language; it might just make someone pause long enough to draw breath and give an opportunity to say 'I think we should talk about this when we are both calm'.

Think about words and phrases you might find useful in various situations, practise with a friend or assertiveness class, while walking the dog (preferably in a quiet or rural setting!), or in the mirror – so that they are ready and there for use when needed.

Motivation

As with reactions to stress, motivation towards change will also be individual; what motivates one will draw little or no reaction from someone else. For some, money seems to be the driving force: money to buy a more impressive car – or house or clothes or jewels or art works – than a neighbour or colleague; if no money is involved they see no reason to make any effort. ('He wouldn't even get out of bed for less than a thousand . . .') For others, status or power of various kinds, which may or may not be connected to impressing friends, neighbours or colleagues with money and position; while yet others find it much more satisfying to feel that they are contributing to the wellbeing and happiness of their neighbours or family, even defining 'neighbours' and 'family' in the widest possible way – the family of mankind. And some want only to express themselves through writing or music or art – and as long as they can eat and keep themselves adequately warm, choose to live very frugally to allow them the time needed to follow their dreams.

Having observed carefully to find individual triggers – whether stress caused by a particular situation, by certain sounds or flashing lights, by feelings of lack of control or understanding – for challenging behaviour, finding what motivates an individual to consider changing their behaviour is then the next step. As with everything else concerning human beings, each situation will vary. What will motivate Abigail may not be relevant to Bryan; Chrissie and Don may well need different approaches again.

Identifying individual motivation is crucial to any hope of success, with a first step being to ask: what reward will motivate this person?

What will be the reward if I make the change?

Depending on the individual, an understanding of the negative effects of their challenging behaviour may or may not be possible, but *to motivate towards change there need to be perceived benefits for that individual.* These may include: increased loving attention; better health; reduced negative effects on future health; smoother interactions with others.

And if I don't?

In some situations the perceived benefits of continuing the situation may appear greater than those for change, for example, where an individual feels in control by using negative behaviour to gain short-term needs and doesn't really much care about effects of his or her behaviour on self or others. These may include the initial 'high' felt with smoking, drugs, alcohol, over-exercising or any other addictive habit which becomes compulsive. They may include enjoying feelings of power and being in control whether in a work situation, at home or anywhere else.

> The whole project is being controlled by this individual because no sanctions can be applied – he's well over six feet tall and heavily built. Asking or even telling him to help with chores or make any positive contribution to the household just doesn't work because if he doesn't want to help with the dishes or anything else there really isn't anything staff can do to make him – and he knows that. Bribery doesn't work, because he worked out that if he complies with whatever and he gets some sort of reward he then wants bigger and better and more next time . . . his height, weight, sheer size and strength make it incredibly difficult to even negotiate with him in any way. He just says 'No!' if he doesn't want to do or not do anything, and that's it.
>
> [E, care worker in residential home]

In a few individuals behaviour unacceptable and difficult for other people and society, sometimes with violent or tragic consequences, seems to be hardwired into the brain. As with every other personality trait, lack of insight or understanding of others' reactions varies, and may or may not be possible for the individual; sometimes a reaction of fear or pain, physical or emotional, even seems to give pleasure – a case of any reaction rather than none? (See also Chapter 4.)

Am I able to change?

Before change is possible, most individuals not only have to perceive personal benefits but also need to be convinced that they can follow through on the effort needed, which may be physical or emotional and mental or a mix. Family and friends can play a crucial role here in building or blighting motivation, by their words and actions. Just think of a situation where someone said words, positive or negative, which made a major difference in your motivation towards following a course of action.

> R had worked hard, felt that he had built up knowledge and experience as well as good relationships, and was now considering applying for further training towards future job prospects and possible promotion. His application was written and ready to post, all he needed was a stamp. Before he'd got around to buying the stamp he met his father. When R told his father what he was planning his father's response was 'What makes you think you're good enough to go any further? Be realistic!'
>
> [GS, personal contact]

R quietly forgot about the application, despite the encouragement of others.

With just a few different words, R's motivation and decision was changed. With just a few different words, R's working – and possibly personal – life might have followed a different path.

The few words – careless and damaging, or supportive and motivating – may be from any family member, from a friend, a teacher, a neighbour (or indeed from a casual conversation with someone met on a train!). When supporting a vulnerable individual encountering problems – or their families trying to support – it is even more important to choose words carefully to encourage and motivate rather than knock down thoughts and determination towards positive action. In everyday life it may not be possible to vet every single word for possible consequences, but simply being more aware of other people's feelings is a good beginning.

What resources are needed for change?

Exploring possibilities and resources – physical and emotional, plus determination and guts to follow through a personally difficult course of action – is another step towards motivation which close contacts can sometimes help with.

Offers of active help may be valued and accepted ('Would you like me to come with you to the doctor/clinic/therapist?' 'I've found this interesting website/article/book – you might like to have a look at it?')

The person may wish to – and need to – 'go it alone': it is important to allow the individual to choose and follow their own path, thereby building self-confidence. Don't take away the opportunity of personal growth by trying to do everything for any individual (and smothering the spark of initiative). Here, simply being alongside in a passive but supportive role will be most valuable. (Dolphin, see also Chapter 5)

A mix of either or both may be needed at different stages of the journey. Or the individual may not be ready to contemplate change, and will deny that the behaviour causes them any problem.

Action: getting there

Whatever the condition, whatever the personal situation, constant calm and consistent encouragement – especially when the going gets tough and the temptation is strong to revert to former patterns – will be important.
That encouragement may be through:

- hugs and kisses
- smiles and obvious pleasure at success in following through with more acceptable behaviour
- simple spoken words: 'I knew you could do it!'
- written and tangible reward through a card or letter: 'I'm so proud of you!' A card or letter has the added bonus of being kept to treasure and remind of success, which may lead to further encouragement and motivation
- a treat or gift of flowers, a special meal or outing to celebrate success, no matter how small
- distraction when needed – a walk, playing a card or board game, sharing a film or video
- reassurance that any setback does not inevitably mean the end of the battle towards eventually surmounting the problem
- encouragement to keep trying.

Sometimes progress is achieved through a long series of small steps forward interspersed with minor and major setbacks. Sometimes a plateau seems to have been reached, then no more progress for some time. And sometimes sudden regression to a much earlier stage shatters carers' dreams of change.

Whatever the individual journey, motivation towards change must be ongoing throughout. Occasionally motivation and the beginnings of real work towards change come unexpectedly and for unforeseen reasons.

Christmas 1999 was the worst ever in our house. After eight months of relentless episodes of screaming rages ('Hairy Jamaicas' as Jay later called these) over trivia – a door shut or open, curtains not drawn 'properly', the 'wrong' mug – plus all the seasonal difficulties for anyone struggling with an eating disorder, with lots of food around for family and guests, my daughter again accused me of not loving her. She showed me pills and again threatened to commit suicide, a threat I took very seriously, and stormed out of the house. As I waited, and waited, and listened to the wind rising I wondered how I could possibly cope if she followed through on her threat, how could I live with the thoughts of not being able to protect her from the awful effects of her illness. Eventually the dog raised her head and listened, followed footsteps on the stairs – I knew Jay was back. I went upstairs and asked what she had taken, then rang the doctor who reassured me Jay would sleep off the effects.

After over five years of struggle, I reached breaking point. Two days later I repeated what I'd said during our most recent confrontation – how much I loved Jay, how hard I'd tried to help and support her, how difficult I found her behaviour since she'd been ill, said that I'd tried really hard to understand but really couldn't accept in my own house such behaviour which I wouldn't accept from anyone else. Therefore if she couldn't accept that everyone in the house – including me – was worthy of respect, perhaps she should consider finding other accommodation.

And two days further on again, Jay told me that she'd decided that perhaps after all she needed professional help. The wait on the list for an appointment was agonising – would Jay change her mind? No. Jane, a specialist dietician, helped Jay at monthly appointments over the next two years to bring her eating behaviour under control.

Jay turned her formidable willpower to fight against the twin horrors of anorexia and bulimia and their effects on her life, instead of fighting all around her who loved her and tried to help. Anorexia still showed her nasty face occasionally but Jay brought her under control too.

Having had a ringside seat watching the battle, I am extremely proud of my daughter.

The motivation to finally change, to fight the illness instead of everyone around, appears to have been the thought of leaving constant love, security and support, or having it possibly withdrawn. [GS]

However, there were no guarantees that this might happen. Looking back I wonder how exactly I might have reacted had Jay returned to the clutches of the terrible twins, Anorexia and Bulimia, and the behaviour which led me to the edge of collapse.

How long?

Whether screaming fits or aggression, getting drunk or high on drugs, self-harm through not eating or overeating, change will not happen overnight – most especially when the behaviour has been endorsed by years of practice, brain patterns have been worn to a groove and become entrenched by repetition of the behaviour many many times.

The longer the timescale involved before tackling the problem the more difficulty in changing, the more time needed, the more effort against the temptation to revert, will be required in the long term – and the more setbacks along the way . . . all these before any individual can feel they have beaten the illness. Even then vigilance is needed to ensure that a recurrence is not triggered by future stress.

There are no guarantees, ever. Carers can only do their best, try to find strategies to help their loved ones, and make sure they survive to continue caring (see Chapter 16.)

Therefore family and other carers should prepare for a very long road; a shorter journey than average or expected is a major bonus (see Chapter 14).

Don't give up, keep on trying: your loved one's health and wellbeing could be at stake.

Try again, going through the above suggestions, ask for other ideas from family, friends, professionals, colleagues – anyone with whom you feel you may share. Look for the help you need – and keep looking.

CHAPTER FOURTEEN

Communications in difficult days (decades?)

Days or decades?

Wouldn't it be wonderful if, when we meet a problem, we could put – like a 'best before' date – an 'in the past' date on it, a date when that particular problem will be left behind? By finding and collecting all relevant and necessary information plus following the right formula, we would be equipped to work through The Problem in a given time, perhaps a month or a year, three months or three years, and we would know that on a given date in the future we would have successfully solved whatever-it-is. And when the due date arrives for stamping '*In the Past*' or '*Discard if not used by . . .*' on The Problem, we can tick it off our list and move on.

Life, unfortunately, is rarely like that.

Usually in mathematics and science a formula may be found which, when applied to a defined problem in a logical way, will solve that problem. However, even here it is possible that unexpected snags arise to trip up the mathematician or scientist who thinks they have found a clear answer: try asking a mathematician or scientist to explain how sounds form a logical musical scale!

With some illnesses it is possible to find out what is causing the problem, perform an operation, perhaps use medicine or other therapeutic practice, and give a timescale in which most people will recover. Recovery may still vary, but in general it is often possible to predict how an average person may progress. There are always exceptions – circumstances and reactions unforeseen, depending on age, fitness and condition, diet and nutrition, support from family, friends, professionals, and a vast array of individual living factors.

With challenging behaviour, it is impossible to predict accurately how any individual will progress, simply because it is impossible to say how any individual will react to variable factors dependent on treatment – which in turn is dependent on individuals.

To maximise an individual's chances of surmounting their problems and reach their potential in life, it is therefore necessary to mobilise all the positive forces possible – whatever they are and from even the most unlikely quarters – over the long and short term.

At every step and stage, constructive communication is crucial. Without this, the chances of overcoming often-massive problems are – at best – much reduced.

Communication with the troubled individual

(See also Chapter 13.)

As with any communication, it is important to identify what level of communication is appropriate: – unless the right level is found, whether at home or school, hospital or clinic, talking to a child or adult with restricted understanding and vocabulary will lead only to increased frustration. Exactly the same is true whether professional–child, professional–parent, parent–child communication; again, LESS is more in understanding the problems: – Listen, Empathy, Share and Support.

All too often a pupil, finding difficulty (as I did) with mathematics, will meet with total incomprehension of the problem – because to the adult teacher, with specialist degrees, long years of practice and experience in mathematics, the mathematical problems set were 'Simple, girl! Why can't you just apply yourself?!' She simply could not understand anyone having difficulty with something so completely obvious to her. To anyone who has understanding and ability in any area, it is hard to understand why everyone doesn't feel the same . . . a musician can't comprehend why others may not be able to hear a scale let alone sing in tune; being unable to hear the beat is unimaginable for dancers; some find spelling and grammar rules, or multiplication tables, or maths or science formulae, easy to learn and remember – while others struggle. Generations of children have told of similar situations throughout school careers.

Consider experiments set up to explore the development of children's language and understanding:

> Those who study such topics are, for the most part, accustomed to abstract and formal modes of thought to the point where they find it hard to appreciate that degrees of abstractness which present no kind of difficulty to them may render a task senseless and bewildering to a child. In other words, the research worker may fail to 'decentre'. (Donaldson, 1978)

The same is true throughout all human communication: true listening, and the ability to understand another's difficulties, depends on being able to think outside one's own feelings, emotions, and assumptions of similar on the other side.

Often very simple changes and awareness can make a big difference; finding the right ones to work in individual situations may take time, with no one approach fitting everyone. The following are a few suggestions which might be useful and could be adapted to fit individual circumstances.

Steps towards constructive communication with the vulnerable individual

Language, vocabulary, level of understanding

Try to work out, preferably in a calm moment, what level of vocabulary is understood. Don't assume that because a year ago, or even more recently, someone understood your language, vocabulary and meaning that your words will be understood now as you intend them. Finding the right level becomes even more important when trying to help someone with challenging behaviour as a reaction to a lack of understanding of the world around them.

> It was only when a new speech specialist realised that my daughter often didn't understand what was going on and *why* something happened – and therefore felt threatened – and tried using Makaton communication with her, that things began to improve. So simple, but no-one else had thought of it. The change just by using very simple signs and words, instead of ordinary sentences, has been remarkable. Now my daughter can make her needs known – and does! – without screaming. [H, mother of K, 9, interview]

> My daughter seemed to regress to infancy/toddler when she developed anorexia after leaving a very unhappy marriage – at 23, she came into my bed to be cuddled and comforted like a small child, something she hadn't done since she was very small. I'll never forget holding the frail, freezing-cold body as she cuddled into me.
>
> During her 2-year marriage she had efficiently run a house, organised meals, shopping, mortgage and bill paying, continued working fulltime . . . yet under the ghastly impact of her illness she had lost all sense of being able to cope with everyday life. It was only gradually over several years that she regained her confidence and 'grew up' all over again. [GS]

It took me some time to work out, for instance, that what I meant as concern Jay took as criticism and interference, which led to anger and defensiveness, so that any small action like leaving a door open might be interpreted in a totally unintended way. A frequent reaction was a 'totally over-the-top, out-of-control, real Hairy Jamaica', as she later described the rages which were part of life when she was ill. Sometimes the HJ was over in minutes, sometimes not.

And it took some time for me to see that my everyday communications had to be carefully structured to enable my daughter to actually *hear*, spelled out in so many words, how much I loved her – it was no longer enough to simply say what I wanted to say and assume that she would understand the words and phrases I'd habitually used for many years. Given her extremely unpredictable behaviour at the time, even asking her for help in clearing up after a meal (always part of our 'before anorexia' routine), became a request which might ignite that spectacular – and frightening – temper.

Explore possible avenues for help, for example, a speech therapist or other professional with specialist knowledge of language difficulties. Support groups of other carers with similar experiences can be a source of all sorts of ideas, strategies, techniques, and so on, which people at a more recent level of caring may not have thought of.

Don't make assumptions: appearances may be very deceptive. I worked with several children with dyslexia, who had particular problems with reading and written language yet whose logic and reasoning and spoken language was unaffected; what they needed instead of pencil and paper was a tape recorder for answering questions.

And I worked with D who could read fluently from very complicated adult books and newspapers, yet had no understanding whatsoever of the meaning of the item being read. Throughout the years of compulsory education there have been many children who were wrongly assumed to have or to lack various capabilities; I can remember classmates as well as some of my own pupils who had difficulty with various aspects of formal education who would now be recognised as having, for example, dyslexia or ADHD.

Straightforward language

While some conditions distort understanding developed over years, for children with autism or Asperger's syndrome or somewhere on the continuum – often undiagnosed – the world around them often makes little or no sense: they have great difficulty in 'reading' other people's expressions and actions. What can appear as naughtiness may be due to misunderstanding or misreading language, facial and other cues such as a yawn or a puzzled, irritated or shocked expression.

Whereas straightforward language is important in any conversation, it becomes even more absolutely essential when anyone has difficulty in understanding what most people take for granted and probably don't even notice in daily interactions. Remember KISS: Keep It Simple and Straightforward.

Interpretations

Jokes and metaphors, common phrases and sayings may be taken literally and cause problems ('Keep your hair on!' 'It's a blue day today . . .' 'You've got your grandma's eyes . . .' 'I've changed my mind . . .' 'Keep your eye on the ball . . .' 'You're pulling my leg . . .'). Some people understand words *only* in the literal sense, finding it incomprehensible when figures of speech or complicated references are used. Trying to work out what anyone means when they ask 'Has the cat got your tongue?', or assuming what it might mean, may cause intense frustration and even worry (and lead to fear, anxiety and challenging behaviour).

Here are some suggestions:

- Think of how your words may be interpreted.
- Explain what you mean, or what other people mean, to help avoid problems.
- Teach cues of when and how to greet people, how to ask or reply to particular common questions. ('How are you?' 'Would you like a cup of tea or coffee?' 'I'd like to go to the toilet please.')
- Consider using flashcards, sign language – and explore other possibilities – to help explain facial expressions ('When someone frowns it means . . .').

Physical touch

Sometimes physical touch of any kind causes problems: people have different ways of showing affection and feel comfortable with different levels of contact. When physical contact is difficult – a particularly painful area to accept for parents and others who want to show affection – an individual may feel under threat and that things are out of their control, no matter how kindly and loving the thought behind the touch. And again, the result can be intense frustration, sometimes expressed in aggression or violence towards others.

Be aware: observe, then try to work out, and discuss if possible, what is acceptable.

Heightened response to sound

For some individuals, sounds are magnified to a great intensity which can cause pain and distress – while most children love balloons, the sound of a balloon bursting, or fireworks, can be really frightening for some, as can other more everyday sounds which are usually taken for granted to the extent they often go unnoticed (e.g. vacuum cleaner, engines, aeroplanes, hammering and banging). For some people, sounds which cannot even be heard by others – even in another room or part of the building – will be amplified to a distressing extent.

Be aware: observe closely and make allowances. If possible try to work out ways of lessening the problem of specific noises which cause distress – for instance, if the sound of the vacuum cleaner causes distress, it may be possible to use it when the affected individual is out of the building.

Heightened sensitivity to texture

Certain materials can cause problems, particularly in clothing – what may be insignificant to most people may feel like sandpaper to their skin. Sheila Gray described how her son screamed when anything was put on his head as a baby, and when washing his hair wondered if the neighbours might report her for child abuse (see Chapter 2).

Heightened sensitivity to smell, pain, temperature, or particular foods may all cause problems for some individuals, which may vary in intensity from day to day.

In all of these situations, be aware: observe, make allowances and look for solutions to the problems caused.

Wherever possible, talking about any problem in straightforward language, about how it affects the individual and explaining how others around them feel and are affected, often brings change as well as easing communication for everyone involved. Without at least trying to talk about most problems it is unlikely that anything will change.

Knowing when and how to ask for help, when to say 'I don't know', 'I don't understand', or 'I don't like this', are particularly important.

Routine and habit

While routine and habit are part of most people's lives – a favourite chair, place at table? – routine becomes much more important for anyone affected by autism or Asperger's syndrome. A clear outline or timetable of what will happen at certain times of day – morning routine, mealtimes, after school, bedtime – can be very helpful, as can discussion of what will happen in certain circumstances.

> When we get up we . . . go to the toilet. We have to get washed. We get dressed. We eat our breakfast. Then we . . .
>
> You're getting on really well with that jigsaw/activity . . . nearly finished. Soon it'll be time for our break/next activity.
>
> We'll have our snack when the bell rings/the clock says eleven.

Repetition and reminders

Frequently it is not enough simply to mention a problem once and hope it will then disappear. Often when behaviour has become habitual it will take time to change. Regular gentle good-humoured reminders may be the key to avoiding frustration.

Giving restricted choices

> Would you like to eat [e.g. a banana] or [perhaps a yogurt]? Would you like to drive your toy cars into the garage now or just before we eat? Would you like to wear the red sweater or the blue one?

The choice is *not* will we or won't we eat or put away toys or get dressed. The choice is *What* or *When*. This can be particularly important in some conditions, for instance anorexia nervosa where a loved one is restricting food intake; or when anyone has found that certain behaviours (or refusing to do something) gives actual, or the illusion of, controlling people and events around them.

Calm, consistency and structure

Many people find change, even very small changes, distressing when they don't understand the reason for it; this is as true for an 8-year-old as for a 38- or 78-year-old. Consistency and structure help in many situations, as well as talking in advance about what will be happening in the future. For one person being told 'It's time to put your game away now, it's almost lunchtime', or being given a restricted choice of *when* to put the cards in the box, may save a tantrum; for another, knowing a timetable of events over the morning or the day with frequent references to what is going to happen next, and what s/he'll do then, means the difference between coping peacefully with the day and finding changes of activity incomprehensible and distressing.

Teach how other people feel and appropriate reactions

For someone with a problem in grasping what the actions and reactions of people mean, the use of drawings of faces with simple expressions to show how other people also feel, for instance, sadness or anger, can help explain situations. Then what the appropriate response might be can be discussed. This can be followed up by giving rules of behaviour as to what to do or not do in various given situations.

> You feel hurt if someone hurts you. Marty feels hurt if you hit him and if you hit anyone, they might hit you back. Marty hit you because he felt hurt and upset.
>
> If Julie is cross with you she'll frown like this. When Julie is pleased and happy she'll smile and laugh, like this.

Remember, KISS at all times.

'Have your say and walk away'

(See also 'When not to walk away' below.)

In dealing with some people with challenging behaviour, 'Have your say and walk away' may work.

- Try to identify the situations you find most difficult.
- Practise what you would like to say, perhaps with a friend or another family member, or in the mirror or when out walking, so that the words are there ready to be used when you next need them.

- Keep repeating these prepared words calmly as you walk away. Perhaps 'I love you very much. I don't like it when you shout at me. I still love you and would like you to think about your behaviour.' Or 'I've heard what you say, and I don't agree. I think we should discuss this when we are both calm. This is really not a good time to discuss this, let's discuss it later. Now I'm going to go out for a walk.'
- Keep repeating calmly your prepared words.
- Do exactly what you say you are going to do, go for that walk or out to the shed or listen to music in another room.

When not to walk away

Do not walk away if you assess the situation as possibly dangerous, either to your loved one or to other people.

Where someone is engaged in an activity which could be dangerous – playing with a knife, matches or electricity for example, or perhaps trying to climb out of a window – it would be wrong to walk away. Try to talk calmly about why this activity is dangerous, and ask them to give the matches or other item to you.

Threatening you?

- Try to keep calm.
- Keep talking calmly. If possible try to reason, talk about possible consequences of such threats.
- Use persuasion rather than using threats yourself.
- Adopt relaxed body language.
- Move slowly – no sudden movements to startle.
- Get help as soon as possible.

Threats of suicide?

All carers, whether professional or family, dread this scenario; trying to work out the best thing to do is extremely difficult, especially when you love the person making those threats. Is this threat serious? Or an attempt at emotional blackmail? What is the best way to react? There are no easy or simple answers; in a situation like this, love may even feel like a handicap.

When someone is very unhappy, often with distorted thinking, ending all their problems by committing suicide may indeed seem a possible option and this must be taken seriously.

Again, LESS is more.

- Talk calmly to them.
- Ask them to explain what has happened, how you can help them.
- Perhaps mention all the people who care about them, people who would miss them if they were gone, their pets; all these might help.
- You may be able to suggest trying to make an appointment with someone who has more experience than you have and may be able to help – a doctor, a psychiatrist, a trusted friend – and offer to help them make the arrangements if they would like this; you could even accompany them if this would be helpful.
- Reassure of your concern, your wish to help.
- If possible, keep them talking.
- Suggest who might be able to help: Samaritans? A trusted and known professional/team/care centre?
- If they tell you of a plan to kill themselves, suggest they contact emergency services for help.
- Ask how you can support them, if they'd like you to go with them to provide support (*if* you can do that, don't promise or suggest what you can't follow through.)

You may be able to persuade the troubled individual to talk through and consider other possibilities than suicide.

Emotional blackmail?

However, in many instances the troubled person is at least partly aware of how distressing their behaviour is, and is using a threat of suicide as the ultimate in emotional blackmail.

> I said to a client who had made many threats of suicide in the past, 'It's up to you if you kill yourself, I can't stop you. Your choice. I've done all I can to help you, now it's up to you.' Then I left. I saw him again the following week.
>
> [J, social worker]

For a professional with long training in mental health issues perhaps it is possible to make a detached judgement of how serious the threat is. For family carers, when love and long years of shared life are in the background, it is *much* more difficult. Even when threats have been made and not followed through in the past, it's possible they might just mean it this time. ('What if . . .? But if they're bluffing and I give in, it'll happen again. And then again.')

When Jay was ill, she felt that no-one could possibly love her, let alone her mother who didn't give in to what I considered unreasonable demands, and also complained about what I considered unreasonable behaviour. Her scruples, her thoughtfulness and respect for others all seemed to have vanished, buried under her illness.

Then the day came, at the end of 1999 and following 9 months of relentless daily rages over trivia – being given coffee in the 'wrong' mug, the curtains not drawn to her satisfaction – when there was yet another explosion of rage. My daughter said 'You don't care. You've never cared. You don't understand, you never do. I've got pills' – she showed me them in her hand – 'I'm going to take these then throw myself in the harbour. And then you'll be sorry!'

Again she stormed out, this time slamming the front door so hard that the house shook. I knew I couldn't catch her no matter how hard I tried. So I waited, feeling sick and ill with worry, as the wind rose. What if . . .? How could I live with myself if . . .? The only practical thing I could think of doing was to phone our GP who calmly asked if she had made such threats before, to get in touch again if and when she returned. I waited. And waited. Eventually the dog raised her head and seemed to listen. Watching my dog following sounds up the stairs and then hearing the floorboard creak above, told me that my daughter had quietly let herself in and gone upstairs to bed. She was very drowsy, so I shook her to ask what she had taken. She told me. Again I rang our doctor who said she'd just sleep off the effects.

Two days later we talked about the incident. I talked about respect for others in the house, including me, and her choice to live elsewhere . . . and Jay said that she realised that she wouldn't be able to beat the twin horrors of anorexia and bulimia on her own, the endless cycle of compulsively starving herself until her willpower broke as her body screamed for nourishment and she binged, got rid of all the food and the cycle took over again. The months of waiting to see the specialist dietician seemed to last forever; I was terrified that by the time the date arrived my daughter would have changed her mind, again retreat into denial of the problems. Those monthly appointments with Jane, from then on for two years, were enough to support Jay in her battle to control at last her self-destructive cycle of binge eating/not eating/over-exercising.

There were many battles, many setbacks, along the way towards recovery – but Jay eventually won the war against anorexia and bulimia.

[GS]

Again, a major turning point – but there was never any guarantee that she would not carry out her threats of suicide. *There never is a guarantee.*

Discussing such incidents with a trained professional, who might be able to help assess the risk, may help. But it is the person there at the time who has to make the decisions as to what best to do – and live with the stress of waiting to know the outcome. Only that has a guarantee: the stress for family and other carers will be incredibly high.

Discussing unpleasant behaviour

Many people breathe a sigh of relief because a difficult incident is over, then ignore it. However by doing this a pattern may be set up, a message given that by creating enough fuss and aggravation, the challenging behaviour can be useful in getting (what is usually) a short-term aim. It will simply happen again. And again.

If you feel the person is able to understand what you say, even though they may not like it – prepare to *come back to the incident later.* No matter how you feel, prepare what you want to say, try to choose a good moment, and say something like 'I'd like to talk over what happened earlier. Is this a good moment for you?' If the answer is negative, as it may well be, don't give up; ask 'When would be a good time for you? What about e.g. Saturday at 5 p.m.?'

Again, preparation may be the key to talking about the effects of the incident and the unacceptable behaviour – on you, and perhaps on others too – calmly. Think out exactly what you want to say, and how you will say it. Practise what you will say, and the tone of voice you want to say it in. Some patterns may have suddenly developed because of the effects of illness, others may have grown up over a period of time; and an unhealthy pattern will not change overnight.

Coping with setbacks

As already noted, it is not easy to work with long-term aims in mind: energy, time, resilience and commitment are all needed. You are helping break established bad habits, helping to set up a new and more acceptable pattern, a pattern not only more acceptable for you and other family and friends but also more healthy for the individual who needs help to control their outbursts. Without your help that individual will never understand how and why their behaviour affects others, let alone make efforts to change it. And that new understanding of the how and why, plus their own efforts towards effective change, can be the beginning of new and renewed self-control and self-esteem.

It would be unrealistic to think that every pattern of behaviour can be changed completely – but without your efforts to support someone towards at least trying to change, neither you nor the loved individual you are supporting will ever have the chance to find out. Worth the risk, worth the effort?

No progress after how long?

And if despite all efforts over years, there is no understanding, no motivation and no change of behaviour? How long do we go on trying? Only family carers can really answer such questions, depending on individual and family resilience.

In some situations (for instance, Alan and Joan's story, see Chapter 2) years of patience and loving efforts to motivate seem to have brought no change in some very distressing behaviour which affects family life greatly. All that can be done here is for carers to try to find practical ways of coping: Alan and Joan moved house to enable them to have an extra bedroom, to install a separate bathroom, and have worked out practical ways of dealing with Peter's distressing and seemingly-entrenched toilet habits.

> We are very matter of fact when we find poo on things: 'Peter, come here please, there's poo on this floor. Please will you get an antibacterial wipe and clean the whole floor and I will come back in a minute to check that I'm happy you've cleaned it all up.' This helps Peter confront his own behaviour, although he's very far from being able to know that he's doing it at the time or even afterwards. I think being very calm and factual also helps us survive this regular occurrence and not let it overshadow our lives.

Perhaps sometime in future the right person or situation will arrive to give Peter the individual motivation he needs to want to change.

Giving feedback

Positive

It is all too easy in the rush of life to comment only on the unpleasant, the irritating, the unacceptable, and forget to mention the interesting, the helpful, the supportive. ('You've left the top off the toothpaste again!' 'Why don't you put your dirty washing into the basket for goodness' sake, I've asked you a million times?!' 'Can't you *ever* remember which day is bin day when it's your turn to put out the rubbish?') Yet when the top is replaced on the tube, the washing put in the right place, the bin is put out on the right day at the right time, often these actions are never mentioned, perhaps not even noticed until they have been missed.

Giving credit wherever due (it must be sincere, and earned) is an important key to developing good relationships, whether at work, at school, at home, with friends. Try to find *at least* five (more if possible) positive things you can say every single day. Say 'Thank you!' Smile. Acknowledge small helpful gestures ('I can see you're trying hard').

Everyone, of any age or stage or situation in life, needs to know that their efforts, no matter how small, are appreciated.

Remember VIEW: Very Important Encouraging Words, whenever earned, whenever possible, for everyone. ('Thank you for remembering to . . .' 'Great that you . . .' 'I noticed that you . . .' 'Tell me more about . . .') Perhaps set a notional target to VIEW each day for your family, your friends and colleagues?

And negative

People have varying levels of response to annoying situations in their lives – what upsets or worries or angers one person may have little or no effect on another – but it is not possible to go through life without ever feeling irritation, anger, sadness or horror, at the actions or reactions of other people.

Some people try to ignore what upsets them, gritting their teeth and building up resentments perhaps for days, months or even years. Others seem on a perpetual 'short fuse', may shout, swear and even physically attack at the slightest provocation. Both these extreme reactions have consequences on the lives, relationships and health of those who respond by pretending a particular incident didn't happen, didn't affect them, or at the other extreme exploding in frequent rage. Most people come somewhere between these extremes, and most people react in varying ways which may depend on mood, levels of tiredness and personal stress.

Try to give negative feedback calmly and as positively as possible.

Giving negative feedback positively

It is possible to find ways of giving negative feedback in a constructive rather than a destructive way. One of the most effective, and most especially useful where communication is fraught, is the 'crap sandwich' (Thanks to Carol who introduced me to this idea.)

The crap sandwich: Whatever the situation or behaviour you want to comment on, try to sandwich the negative comment between positives.

- 'I love you so much. I don't like it when you [shout at me, threaten, snatch things – *specifically name the behaviour*]. When you do that I feel [describe exactly how you feel – upset, miserable, angry]. Even though I feel [. . .] I really love you and want to do the best for you.'
- 'I care so much about you. Please try not to [*name the behaviour*], it upsets me/makes me feel [. . .]. I am concerned for you, that is why I tell you this, not because I do not care.'

- 'I can see you're trying hard to [*name it* – control your temper or your eating or exercising or drinking or . . .]. I can see how difficult it is for you and appreciate all your efforts. I'd like you to try to [. . .] because when this happens I feel [*name it!*]. I am so concerned about you and really want to see you beat this. Tell me how to help.'

As ever, *preparation and practice* are often the key – think out what you want to say, how best to say it, work out ways of keeping calm, and what you could do if you feel in danger of losing your cool.

If you feel your planned calmness being threatened under pressure, be prepared to take 'time out' and return later to the discussion. ('I think it's best to leave this discussion and come back later when we are both calm. Let's leave it just now, we can talk again later when we've had time to reflect.') (If the other person continues to shout and so on, keep repeating while *you* leave.)

Keeping calm under provocation

Some people seem to be able to react calmly in almost every circumstance. No matter what the provocation they are able to respond without losing their temper, they may be able to use humour to defuse a situation, and the incident does not lead to major upset for them. I have known several such individuals at various points of my life, and wish I could be one of them.

Many people have to cope with situations at work where others behave in a less than acceptable way. These situations may be really annoying and have to be coped with in the best way possible. Some people are given training in how to react assertively, rather than aggressively and inflame the situation further – there are many books and courses available on assertiveness. However, it is one thing reacting 'by the book' at work; at home where we want to relax, to be cared for and appreciated, is a very different story. And when a family member displays challenging behaviour for any reason, and particularly over a long period of time, even those who cope well at work in difficult situations find such intrusions in their own personal space and relaxation time almost impossible to cope with.

Preparation: more ABC

Careful thought, discussion if possible, and preparation are the keys. Can you work out what are possible triggers (*Antecedents*), or what happened before the *Behaviour* in the problem situation (the *Consequences*)? Is there a way of changing things to avoid these triggers, before they lead to unacceptable behaviour and its consequences? How best to respond to change the situation for the better and help the individual in the long term? What happens just now when I respond by . . . (Think through how you actually respond, is this helpful?) Is there a better way? What would happen if I . . .? Consider as many options as possible; you may find some suggestions in this or other books, or through discussion with friends or professionals.

Identify what you need, prepare and practise what you want to say: choosing the right words, keeping a calm tone of voice and relaxed body language may be the key to a successful outcome.

Preparation time: personal

Finding a time to take some time out to do this – either alone, or with others who experience the same situation and behaviour – is important. And as always, easier said than done when again faced with the upsetting behaviour, especially when you may be tired, hungry or preoccupied. As well as observation and trying to discover a pattern of what may trigger certain behaviour, preparing words or phrases for use when under pressure and need to keep calm, personal preparation for (possible) confrontation is also important. Meditation, deep breathing, yoga or tai chi, listening to music, walking, running: try to find a strategy to help you prepare mentally.

It is simply not possible to prepare for every stressful situation – some come without warning. However, when you know that broaching a subject which may well cause an adverse reaction, it is worth investing time to prepare as much as possible. And if no adverse reaction appears, if your loved one reacts calmly and pleasantly and is willing – or even relieved – to discuss whatever problem has been identified, this is a bonus.

Listening, as always, is the key

> People need to tell their story. And if they are really allowed to tell it, then they tell it fully, and it stops hurting. As they tell it, they sort it out in their own minds. They slot each piece in place and give it new meaning. They make it more real, and less painful, by sharing it.
>
> (Quilliam, 1998)

Listening is one of the most valued gifts we can give to another. Acknowledging and accepting someone else's different reality is another gift one can give.

It is easier to offer patient listening while a friend or family member shares their pain and grief, than to listen when that same person is angry and upset – most especially when that anger or upset is directed (rightly or wrongly) at you and we feel criticised and rejected by their hostility as they take out their feelings on whoever is nearest.

> The hardest part in the years of my daughter's illness, apart from working out how best to react and cope in various situations I'd never met before, was experiencing

> all the feelings of despair at Jay's rejection of whatever I tried to do to help, the frequent hostility and rages no matter how hard I tried or what I did. [GS]

When you are in the direct firing line of unadulterated hostility, being yelled at, threatened with all sorts of dire consequences, told your perceived faults in graphic detail, it all seems extremely unfair. No matter how hard it may be to take a detached view of what is happening, *that is exactly what may help in the long run, not only help you to cope and get through but also to help the troubled person.* Preparation for this sort of listening does not start during any particular incident, *it begins with recognising the need to try hard to step back. It begins with thinking about how listening for any underlying message might help.*

Think of what your own most common response to difficult behaviour is: do you respond in kind to aggression and criticism? Burst into tears? Walk away? There may be varying responses depending on mood, energy and so on; do you feel your response is helpful in shortening the incident or not, in helping avoid such incidents in the past, in trying to set up more constructive patterns of behaviour?

Think now about a time when someone seemed really sharp tempered and out-of-sorts, which is quite unusual for that person, and later you discovered that the reason for the grouchiness had nothing to do with you personally. This often happens when caring long term for a troubled individual: the people in the firing line of their frustration with life will be those nearest.

Creating the right atmosphere

Many people react strongly to music – I'm one of them – or perhaps to colour or temperature or lighting. Try playing gentle and soothing music. Strong colours (red, blue, black, dark brown) or patterns, even dim lighting, when used in decoration may all trigger or endorse a negative mood in some individuals – might this be a factor in your own situation? If so, consider whether the use of softer shades might make a positive difference to atmosphere and to behaviour. Explore how aromatherapy might help: soothing oils such as lavender can be used in candle burners (being mindful of the safety aspect) or on a hanky or pillow.

Resisting Rhino response

It is all too easy when under pressure to jump in immediately and react to the personal criticism ('*I* think you need to . . . !' 'How can you say . . . !' 'You'd better . . . !' 'You should . . .' 'How dare you . . . !') or to offer your opinion, to blame or to give advice; some people use sarcasm and barbed remarks. None of these is helpful – rather they are likely to escalate the confrontation while not seeking or addressing the real roots of the problem.

- *Let it go, let it flow.* Whether or not you can identify any particular trigger, *simply acknowledge the feelings of anger/frustration.* ('You're upset.' 'You sound really cross.') It doesn't matter if you guess wrongly the actual trigger – this will offer an opportunity for clarification. 'You sound upset', on its own, without any other reaction may defuse the worst of the emotional pain and shorten the incident, and again offer the chance to clarify and talk about intense feelings.
- *Sounds difficult for you.* Rather than giving the instruction *Calm down!* – not easy for anyone when upset and experiencing intense emotions – *listen, acknowledge, and just be there until it gradually passes.* ('You're upset.' 'You're angry.')
- When feeling under heavy fire in the shape of personal criticism, try saying 'I can see you feel strongly about this – it's not the way I feel but I accept that you see things differently.'
- 'Let's talk about this later when we are both feeling calm.'
- *Not responding in kind* – not 'meeting fire with fire', anger with more anger – often means that confrontation fizzles out much more quickly.

Listening noises

Mmm-mmm and other empathetic listening noises as someone lets off steam are useful, as are deep breathing and avoiding too much eye contact – preparing food or a snack, picking up knitting or other occupation to which you may be able to give some attention from time to time, to allow a breathing space, can also help.

And simply keep on listening, keep on repeating your prepared phrases. Eventually, without a response to keep the incident on the boil and feelings raging, the storm will run out of energy. This is definitely not easy when you feel under attack – but worth a try?

Redirection of focus

Sometimes after recognition, acknowledgement and open discussion about temper tantrums or other unpleasant behaviour, and their consequences for self and others, a loved one makes great efforts to control that temper or behaviour. They may need help in an actual situation, when their feelings threaten to overwhelm them.

- Try to find a strategy to redirect thinking and focus:

  'I can see you feel upset/angry. Try to breathe deeply, really deeply. That's it, count the breaths, one – two – three – four – five – six. Back to one again – two – three –'

  'I can see you feel [. . .] Look out of the window/down at that stone/up at that tree/the sky (focus on anything in the room or immediate area). What colour is the sky/stone/tree? Put your hand on the wood/glass/bark/stone – does it feel smooth? Cold? Rough? Rub your fingers on it, is it getting warm, changing in any way?'

  'Keep breathing deeply, keep going. Now stretch your arms wide, then as high as you can, bend and touch the ground.'

  'Let's put on the music you find helpful when you feel upset.'

- After the intense reaction has passed, ask if this redirection helped? What might be even better?
- Whenever possible allow time to talk through the feelings, the incident and what led to it; simply listen and try to reflect or paraphrase what you hear and understand.

Building and rebuilding self-esteem

When someone lacks confidence in their own abilities and their place in what may seem a very hostile world, they may try to bolster themselves using criticism to convince themselves of the mistakes of others, including those closest to them.

When someone at last accepts that their own behaviour is causing problems not only for their own health and welfare but also for those around them, and they find it difficult if not impossible to change what they thought was under their control, that lack of control will be added to their internal list of items that drag down their sense of self-esteem.

Very important encouraging words

Very Important Encouraging Words – VIEW – frequently and from all angles?

In most families, most of the time everyday life trundles along, with everyone busy with work or school, family activities, friends and social life. We often assume that others know what we feel, that they pick up the signals we think are obvious.

> We were like lots of families, we were doing our own stuff every day but not really ever talking about feelings, how we felt about things, all the similarities and differ-

ences we recognise more now after Dave's illness. We did things together quite often at weekends – but really we were leading sort of parallel lives.

[Andy, father of Dave, 13, anorexia, see Chapter 2]

In daily life, how often do we remember to say thanks for, or even to mention little things we hardly notice? – ironing a shirt, laying the table, helping prepare vegetables, putting laundry in the machine or basket, carrying out the rubbish – small actions which may simply be taken for granted every day. Apart from at an early stage when my children were small and were praised when they began to help with chores, it soon became part of the routine; and actually saying the words 'Thank you for . . .' were often forgotten; I assumed that they knew I appreciated the help. Taking things for granted, making assumptions, are a frequent part of human relationships, perhaps especially in family life.

But when anorexia and bulimia – or any other mental health problem – enter the scene, life is no longer 'everyday'. I found it even more important not just to think or even show what I felt, but to actually *say* words to express those feelings. It was even more important to hug, to stress and focus on any positives, to use 'crap sandwiches' when negative 'stuff' appeared. This was not a one-off event, but an ongoing process of reassurance, encouragement and motivation which I believe helped my daughter on her long road to recovery.

Try to VIEW at least several times a day. These phrases may be useful and/or help you think of your own words.

- When things go wrong

  'I love you very much. I don't like your behaviour [name it, e.g. shouting and screaming; throwing things; not telling the truth]. I still love you.' (Crap sandwich – negative between two positives.)

  'I love you very much and really like it when you [name it, e.g. help me tidy up; keep your room tidy; bring in the washing; put out the bin – anything which you can praise, no matter how small]' (Positive feedback)

  'Thank you for . . .' (Positive feedback)

  'I can see you're trying hard.' (Positive feedback)

  'I know how difficult this is for you [name it – e.g. finishing a meal or snack, refraining from visiting the bathroom immediately after a meal, cleaning up after a binge] and really appreciate how hard you are trying.' (Crap sandwich)

  'Don't give up!'

  'Tomorrow is a new day – didn't beat it this time, try again tomorrow!' (Crap sandwich)

'I'd like to talk about [. . .]. When would be a good time for you? Is just now a good time?'

'I'd like to help. Tell me what I can do to help.'

'I'd like to hear more about . . . (pick up and stress *positive* thoughts/memories when mentioned)'

- Try to identify positive feedback and 'crap sandwiches' in your own communications with your loved one several times a day at least.

  '*I'm sorry*. I was tired/cross/irritated/angry because [. . .], and I shouldn't have [. . .].'

  (*Be specific* – and if you can say you feel you got something wrong, it gives the message that all human beings can make mistakes in the heat of the moment, you do too and so can your loved one; it's OK to be wrong, everyone is sometimes.)

- Focus as much as possible on anything positive.

The words are powerful and effective face to face, but need not always be spoken directly – texting, telephone, email can also be used.

> My dad used to text me around lunchtime – he knew it was a difficult time for me, I got anxious in the canteen.
> [G, anorexia]

A shared journal

Consider investing in a notebook and start a 'shared journal' where two or more people may make entries – this could be daily or weekly or occasionally. For small children, ask them what they'd like to contribute and offer to write it for them; they or others could also illustrate their entries.

- 'Good things that happened today/this week were . . . The best bit of today was . . .'
- 'I felt sad/upset/angry when . . .'
- 'It was really good when . . .'

Think again of the crap sandwich – for each bit of rubbish or crap in the middle, try to find at least two positives. Some days or weeks you may need a whole plateful of crap sandwiches!

Discuss the entries.

In a rational and positive mood?

Occasionally, even in the most difficult times and situations involving challenging behaviour, a rational moment or even several may bring more opportunity to discuss problems or a way forward. Sometimes this may be a time which you can recognise and actually *begin to plan for.*

> Weekdays, with everyone in the household working or engaged in all the many other activities which make up modern life, everyday exchanges took place mostly about practicalities of day-to-day living.
>
> Once I'd realised that on a Sunday morning, sitting around in dressing gowns, was almost always a relaxed time in our house, when conversations were also relaxed – a good time to talk and explore issues, review problems, and sometimes even identify possible ways forward – I began to sit around for longer and wait to see what might happen. If there was an issue I wanted to talk over, perhaps about a difficult scene during the week just past, this I realised was the best time to broach the subject . . . Working out what might be effective did not happen overnight. Rather, trial and error (many errors!) seemed to be the key; sometimes things which seemed to be effective on one occasion did not work the next time. [GS]

Having a ringside seat when someone you love is heading for disaster, and trying to avoid telling anyone what to do or not do is extremely difficult when it seems obvious that Any Reasonable Person would see what you see . . . Try to remember that the harder you try to reason, the harder you try to push anyone into seeing the reason or the solution you can see so clearly, the harder they'll push back and deny any possible truth in what you're saying.

Useful phrases in a calm tone will give the impression that things can change and choices might be an option, that nothing is 'set in stone'.

- 'You're not clear *yet* about the best way forward.'
- '*At the moment* things aren't going as well as you'd like.'
- 'You *sometimes* feel . . .'

Encouraging motivation

(Also see above: giving positive and negative feedback, building and rebuilding self-esteem, VIEW.)

Consistently noticing efforts and giving praise for any progress and all attempts at control and change, as well as offering any negative feedback in a constructive way, are all keys to encouraging and motivating someone to control and change their behaviour. Rather than just occasionally commenting, as often as you can think of something – no matter how small – to praise. The praise must be earned; you will soon be found out it is false or insincere.

Here are some words for responding to setbacks.

- 'The higher the mountain the more the sense of achievement.'
- 'Tomorrow is a new day, try again.'

- 'Anything worth having is worth fighting for.'
- 'The lowest ebb is the turning of the tide.'
- 'Yesterday is history. Tomorrow is a mystery. Today is a gift. That's why it's called the present.'
- 'Rome wasn't built in a day.'
- 'Beat it next time!'

Encourage talk about the future and any future plans. Encourage positive memories and looking forward to doing the same thing again, seeing friends.

No path will be straightforward. Try to keep calm, be consistent, show that you appreciate any effort no matter how small. Keep encouraging. Don't give up. It's not easy, often exhausting in the face of difficult behaviour – but your loved one's health and wellbeing are at stake.

VIEW can use up huge amounts of energy – so give yourself regular breaks. Look for signposts and support along the way (see Chapter 16).

Review regularly

Practice makes perfect – or at least easier.

- Acknowledge successes – and celebrate.
- Acknowledge any setback.
- How are individuals coping? main carer? partners? siblings? young carers? And the vulnerable individual – how does s/he feel?
- Does the original plan need to be changed or adapted? Is the timescale for progress realistic? Are there any new developments to be considered?
- Plan for the future.
- Keep on looking for what might be helpful in your own situation.

None of these strategies is a quick fix

Nothing will change overnight – consistency, calmness, co-operation and co-ordination of individual and family efforts are all needed, not just once or twice but as ongoing and daily. Regular family forums – Sunday morning? Friday evening? Saturday after lunch? – are important, at an agreed time when everyone can talk through highs and lows, problems and setbacks as well as achievements and positive change.

Difficult professional–carer communications

(See also Chapter 12.)

Unfortunately, in a world of human beings, whether within a family or between friends or colleagues, things will sometimes go wrong even in the best of relationships. The same is true of carer–professional relationships. Sometimes this is due to different interpretations of events, or a genuine difference as to what the best course of action might be. Sometimes, as with family or any other communication, it's down to simple misunderstanding of what the other is saying.

As ever, the only way to sort things out is by open discussion and explanation which, because of resources and pressures on time, may be very difficult to organise. Telephone conversations may help, but again time pressures have to be taken into consideration. Email and letters can play a part but have drawbacks when words may be interpreted in a different way from that intended. Once written and sent, words can boomerang and cause much more damage than those spoken even in anger. Today, spoken words causing offence may be the trigger for legal action or official complaint; written words, including anything sent by email, may be used as a legal document.

Keeping a record

Even a brief account can be important in difficult situations at home when communication is fraught, can be discussed at a meeting, and also serve to remind of progress or signs of possible relapse.

A record can be equally important in home–professional communication – for both carers and professionals – and when things go wrong, can become even more important. Asking if it might be possible to tape-record a meeting is one option, or jotting down brief notes during it can simply serve to remind of what was said. When more than one person takes notes, it is quite possible they will record slightly different things (or from a slightly different angle!) but between them are more likely to produce an accurate minute of what happened and was said than relying on memory. Having more than one person noting important points may also help if one set of notes becomes lost.

Crisis contact numbers

When professionals give a contact number for carers to use when they feel the need of support or advice – whether one connected to someone available at certain times of day/week in the clinic/hospital (when my friend's daughter was diagnosed with diabetes the family was given a contact number with the instruction *Call this number at any time if you are worried*), or perhaps a charity support telephone line – it not only gives carers something practical to do when they feel unsure or desperate and sick with worry, it also gives carers a feeling that their role is being acknowledged as a difficult one.

> Sometimes Dave saw we were unsure, exhausted and flagging, and he'd say to go and call the special number. It made such a difference just to know there was someone experienced and detached to talk to.
>
> [Andy, see Chapter 2]

Constant, open and honest communication wherever possible is the best way to resolve problems wherever they appear, whoever they involve – family–family, professional–professional, family–professional. Without it, no matter how good the intentions, it is much more possible that destructive misunderstandings sneak in and poison relationships – and of course, the person most affected is the one at the centre of 'best care' efforts who most needs support.

Given difficulties with resources such as time and staff, not to mention different communication styles, and human energy and mood for both carers and professionals all under stress of one sort or another, there will inevitably be hiccups along the way. But goodwill, effort, energy and a willingness to try to empathise and understand respective problems – as well as make some allowances for human weakness – can only improve that 'best care'.

Remember that small things such as a word or two of encouragement or a short telephone call may make a huge difference out of all proportion to the time spent.

Working as a team, whether in a family or professional situation, can achieve so much more than individual efforts to support the individual at the centre of all our efforts. This is particularly important during really difficult days; despite all best efforts, individual stress outside family control may lead to crisis. Planning for these possible emergencies may make coping with them easier all round.

Crisis planning

Given the wide range of conditions outlined in this book, it is inevitable that crises will also vary. Particular crises which may arise in schizophrenia, eating disorders, drugs or any other condition will differ, and ideas for helpful and positive action are better sought from specialists in these fields. For instance, a crisis in anorexia where someone collapses because of mineral imbalances (lack of potassium can lead to heart failure) or severe undernourishment will be different from a crisis involving out-of-control aggression. (A whole chapter is devoted to assessing medical risk in anorexia in Treasure *et al.*, 2007, in preparation).

Having a plan ready for action in any emergency – at home, work, travelling – is very worthwhile. Preparing a list of contacts and the steps to follow, and keeping it near the telephone, means valuable time can be saved in a crisis, when time may be crucial and calm thinking much more difficult under stress. Professional–carer crisis planning can be very valuable, as can discussion with a self-help or support group. If it turns out that the plan never needs to be used, what a bonus!

Make a list of telephone numbers

Treatment teams, crisis hotline, suicide hotline, emergency services, police, plus any others you think might be helpful. Keep the list near the telephone; it is much easier to have them easily available rather than having to look them up in the middle of a crisis.

Behave calmly

- Remain calm – panicking, shouting and hysteria can upset people even more. Keeping calm will provide more effective support and may shorten the crisis.
- Breathe deeply, speak slowly and clearly.
- Keep communication brief.
- State your concern.

Evaluate the urgency of the situation

Many situations are distressing, but are not crises.

Ask yourself – Has anyone been hurt? Is anyone in danger of physical harm? Has property been damaged – does it appear likely this may happen? Does the crisis indicate a serious relapse?

If the answer to these questions is Yes, the situation is a crisis.

Get help in handling the situation if possible

Try to enlist a family member, one of the treatment team, a neighbour or friend to help – working with another person lightens the burden and may help you respond more effectively.

Make a specific plan for managing a crisis

List step 1, step 2, step 3. Keep it simple and realistic, list what resources you need – information, telephone numbers, people. For example:

1 Call GP/treatment team/named professional/emergency services

2 Arrange evaluation

3 Arrange transport to evaluation if needed

4 Help your relative remain calm while waiting for appointment by remaining with him or her; listen to favourite music.

Keep safety in mind

In some conditions, during a crisis there may be increased chance of aggression or violence. If your relative feels threatened it's best to avoid blocking your own or your relative's way out of the room.

Review the plan

- Review while the crisis is still fresh in your mind.
- Try to take a positive, constructive approach towards better planning for any possible future crises.
- When things have gone wrong it is not helpful to angrily blame and find fault: gather information towards building a better plan.
- Helpful questions in review:

  What was happening before the crisis? (ABC) Try to identify any particular changes or stresses – e.g. loss, argument, disappointment, drugs or alcohol, depression, routine.

  What were the early signs? e.g. behaviour changes, appearance, feelings expressed, relationship changes, sleep, thinking or eating patterns disturbed.

  What part did everyone play? What helped? What was not helpful?

  How might a similar future crisis be avoided?

  How might a similar crisis be resolved if it occurs?

CHAPTER FIFTEEN

Active help for carers

Main carers

For many professional carers – as well as some family carers out working to put bread on the family table, or perhaps engaged in education – who aren't experiencing on a relentless 24-hour basis all the problems they may or may not be aware of, it may be difficult to appreciate how very exhausting such coping is. They may only be aware of the picture gained within the structured, secure walls of the treatment centre; or the detrimental effect the situation has had on a central relationship in their lives.

Even in the best of circumstances with information, some support and possibly some useful experience to draw on, for family carers it is difficult to come home after a tiring day at work or studying, only to encounter further and more difficult situations at home:

> I sometimes feel I've become invisible – we're not professionals, we haven't had a course in how to cope with this, yet we're supposed to cope with endless crises and know what to do and what not to do. And our family all seem to find other things to do if I ask them to come and help. I think they feel helpless, anyway they don't want to know. My other son sends a card for my birthday and Christmas and Mother's Day – often a bit late, but at least he remembers. But he never visits now, too far, too busy. And apart from one, my friends have just melted away. I feel so isolated.
>
> [Pauline, carer for her son D who has schizophrenia]

Some people find themselves in a completely isolated situation caring single-handedly for a loved one, in addition to trying to earn a living and support a household.

> My husband's illness has completely changed our relationship. He's very moody and often badtempered. Very unpredictable. Sometimes I feel as if I have a third child to look after instead of a husband, the man I still love in spite of everything, all the awful behaviour when he goes through a bad patch. I have to make all the decisions, look after the kids, and cope with everything. Our families live hundreds of miles away, our friends have drifted away – I don't think they know how to react. I suppose he's not the person they knew, he was fun before. I miss him too. Sometimes I wonder what will happen in the future.
>
> [Catherine cares for her husband (who has post-traumatic stress disorder), interview]

> My mother had Alzheimer's disease. Then my daughter, 23, told me she had been diagnosed with anorexia. Worry and exhaustion took their toll and I came very very close to complete collapse several times. Sometimes I took a couple of nights away from home just to sleep. Not to do anything else – activities or seeing friends or whatever – just sleep. I knew I had to survive to help my daughter.
>
> [GS]

> All the neighbours know, they've seen the police here when D got into trouble. It was all in the paper, and then he came home because he'd nowhere else to go. It's difficult in the house, he's so . . . and I find it hard to go out, go to the shops, everyone in the village knows. I just feel so alone.
>
> [Jane's son has a drugs problem which has caused major social problems in his own life as well as for his mother]

For the main carer – parent, spouse, sibling, daughter or son – the struggle to try to provide proper support for one individual with challenging behaviour may bring them to breaking point. Without acknowledgement and support this breaking point may become a reality. And unfortunately many relationships, and families, disintegrate under the pressure, leaving the main carer facing an even greater struggle. Added to the pressure of offering physical and emotional care, there is the knowledge that if the main carer were to disappear for any reason; who would be left for the vulnerable individual?

> It may be the old invisibility trick: nobody knows we're there. Or it could be that they're vaguely aware of us and are confident we're doing okay. Why should we need help? We're the ones who *give* help. We shouldn't need help . . . Whatever the reason, we remain stuck in solitary, unnoticed and with very little prospect of remission.
>
> (Marriott, 2003)

Dr Chris Williams of Glasgow University (Williams, 2006) outlines ways in which a family frequently changes under the pressure brought by illness:

- accommodation to illness needs
- restructuring of family routines
- delay in decision-making
- imbalance in resource distribution
- invasion/disruption of family rituals
- distortion of family identity

all of which lead eventually – or quickly depending on illness, condition and circumstances – to

- illness becomes a central organising principle.

This is especially true when challenging behaviour is part of the unhappy picture.

Supporting each other, and being seen to support each other is really important. If or when a disagreement on approach occurs, it is vital to at least appear united. Any disagreement over an individual reaction should be discussed – but not in front of others unless both, after discussion, agree on this. Find a quiet time as soon as the difference of approach is recognised and talk it over; often factors one partner has not been aware of will surface and an agreed way forward can be found.

If at all possible, find a common approach. If this proves difficult or impossible, aim for a compromise where one partner can allow the other to deal with the particular behaviour or situation in future. Such ongoing discussions can help to avoid possible differences of perceptions, as well as the possibility of any disagreements between partners being used to 'divide and rule' by anyone else in the family. This can often be a significant factor in challenging behaviour where one person manipulates another to set up and encourage friction between them, as a way of having their short-term wants met.

'Dad, my pal has asked me to a party at the disco, can you give me my birthday money early (or lend it)? Please Dad? *Everyone's* going. Please Dad?' Without open and ongoing discussion, only later Dad might find out that Mum had already vetoed such a request as she'd advanced the loan a week before which had not been repaid . . . such a pattern of behaviour very easily becomes established, even in families without any particularly challenging behaviour due to a specific illness or condition in their midst, with one individual playing the others off against each other and causing untold numbers of rows and much bad feeling. This will grow if it is not recognised and addressed by everyone involved.

Using a child-centred or person-centred approach

For anyone who has little or no experience of this way of working with a troubled child or adult, this approach may be explained as working with the troubled person to examine, diagnose and address his or her difficulties. For the person concerned this is indeed good news: their problems will be given careful examination in professional efforts to help them, sometimes involving several professionals with different skills and experience. It is not only good news, it is also necessary before any progress can be made in attempting to offer support.

However, by concentrating all efforts solely on identifying and trying to address that child or young person's needs, often another problem is created: little or no attention is given to others in the family – parents, siblings, close others – and their needs.

Supporting siblings and young carers

In the UK alone, conditions involving challenging behaviour – including all mental health problems, addictions, special educational needs, Alzheimer's disease, Huntingdon's disease – affect the lives of millions of young people as siblings and young carers. These numbers can only be estimated. Some cannot remember a time when their parent did not have, for example, depression, or their sibling did not need high levels of support; carers as young as 12 may shoulder the main burden of care for a parent from an early age, providing physical support in the form of shopping, cooking and housework, as well as emotional support. Years of childhood may pass in an early caring role which restricts their own choices as well as leading to feelings of great responsibility, reluctance to go out in case 'something happens', and possible later difficulties with relationships (see Chapter 2).

Even in conditions *without* any associated behavioural problems, no matter how families love their especially vulnerable members they may struggle at times to cope with the physical demands of someone who perhaps must be lifted regularly, who needs feeding, frequent hospital visits and other ongoing individual attention. Exhaustion can take a heavy toll on parents and other carers, which in turn will reduce the attention available for others in the family, and play a part in reducing the effectiveness of home care.

Childhood only happens once

Siblings of a person born with a condition involving behavioural aspects lead their lives in the shadow of having to accept that adults around may not have much time to pay them individual attention. Jane Gregory (2000) describes the problems encountered over many years as she struggled to support her daughter Chrissy and cope physically and emotionally with daily behaviour which might include prolonged screaming, self-mutilation, stripping off her clothes – incidents which could take place at home, at school, in public places – and also her feelings of despair and guilt as she recognised the effects those struggles had on her other children.

When mental health problems or perhaps drugs, anorexia or bulimia enter family life, siblings may have very mixed feelings as they watch a brother or sister, known over the years, whose personality and behaviour changes.

> They don't ask their friends home now – I think they feel embarrassed, worry about their sister's behaviour. Maybe in case she has a tantrum while their friends are there. And sometimes I feel all cross and out of sorts over just small things, I get so tired of it all.
>
> [H, mother of A, diagnosed anorexia, interview, 2006]

> I'm at Uni now. When I phone home all Mum goes on about is what my brother is doing. She never asks what I'm doing, about my exams, and friends and stuff. I used to phone much more often but not now.
>
> [Siobhan, personal contact; her brother is receiving treatment for drug addiction]

> We used to do loads together but not now, not since she's been ill. I feel as if I've lost one of my best friends and I miss her and the fun we used to have, dressing up and stuff. I do try to help her, I know it's not her fault but it's hard. None of my friends understand, and Mum and Dad are always fighting. Sometimes Dad doesn't come home now. I'm worried they'll get a divorce.
>
> [Tracy's sister has anorexia]

Siblings and young carers may start 'acting out' themselves in an attempt to get attention or because they feel no-one is really interested in what they're doing, or they may start staying out or staying away from home, or find companions or activities which may or may not be beneficial to their long-term welfare.

> I have four sons, all late teens/early twenties. Two of them have mental health problems . . . one has been diagnosed with schizophrenia and has had two admissions to hospital, the other with bipolar disorder. The others are waiting for the sky to fall on them too – not deliberately awkward, they seem to do things as if there's no tomorrow, and maybe that's because they're afraid of what tomorrow might bring them.
>
> [F, interview]

Sometimes parents are only too aware of how their inevitably divided attention may be affecting other siblings – and feel powerless to change the situation: there are only so many hours in any day, only so much energy and they have to deal with priorities which mean very hard and unwanted choices. Lack of sleep, constantly dealing with unpredictable incidents over a long period, often without remission or respite, may affect their temper, their coping skills and even their judgement.

Making the difference

Age-related information

Without any acknowledgement of the effects on family life, in particular on young people in their own formative years, not only are these young lives badly affected but in many cases it's possible that important support for the troubled individual is lost. Without age-related information as to the problems and if no-one takes time to explain as far as possible – to ask what might help the siblings, to offer time and appropriate support – not only will family friction develop and grow but often new problems for other young family members arise. Many young people, once they have some understanding of their relative's problems, can make a significant difference to the individual problems by offering valuable support from a very different viewpoint from that of parents or other adults.

Being able to play such a part and feel acknowledged as part of a team can in turn play a part in reducing sadness or perhaps resentment and anger, as well as offer some support.

Although the specific problems may vary with the illness or condition, the major effects on young lives and feelings are often remarkably similar when they are asked to describe them. The following are the most common feelings mentioned:

- *Fear* when a sibling or relative is being aggressive or abusive.
- *Anxiety* about possible future unpredictable incidents.
- *Frustration*: a sibling or young carer will often recognise the problems as needing special attention, at the same time feeling unhappy about what they perceive as unfair division of time and attention.
- *Deep unhappiness* when their relative, who with thinking distorted by e.g. anorexia, or drugs, tells a different story about an incident and is believed, sometimes without question.
- *Deep unhappiness* about perceived lack of interest in e.g. their school work, hobbies and interests, achievements, as parents respond to yet another crisis.
- While often recognising the effects of lack of sleep on parents, on time, temper and responses, feelings of *depression and despondency*.

> There's no time for me, nobody notices, I'd have to do something truly awful for anyone to notice. Nobody really cares.
>
> My mum doesn't sleep at night, her sleeping patterns are all upset just now. I find it really difficult sometimes to concentrate in school. The teachers don't really understand, they just get cross.
>
> ['Pop Idol', 12, young carer, see Chapter 2]
>
> I try to help my sister as much as I can, I love her so much and its unfair she's got this horrible illness (anorexia). It could have been me, I know that. I want to help her, I really do, but I get so fed up when she screams at me and it's really unfair what she says. It's as if she twists everything I say so it sounds bad when that's not what I said or meant. And once she took my pocket money and never paid it back. She tells mum and dad things that just aren't true but if I try to tell them they just believe her, don't listen to me. And when it's my Parents Evening

at school, or when I was in the concert, or anything I'm doing, she hates that so she makes a big fuss and then my mum has to stay with her and no-one else can come to see the teachers or me when I'm singing in the choir. I'm just fed up with it all, mum's always tired and cross, and there's no time for me. Now I feel bad about saying all that, I love her I really do. But I just get fed up sometimes. [L, sibling, primary age, EDA helpline]

I want to do well in my finals, but it's so hard to study now with everything going on in the house. Mum gets upset when there's a row, there's always rows when my sister's is at home, if she's in a bad mood she just makes a row. Nobody's interested in what I'm doing any more, it's all what my sister wants, what she needs. Maybe I'll just move out.
[M, sibling, student, EDA support line]

I don't like going to the bathroom my brother uses, it smells even after mum has cleaned and cleaned it. And I worry about germs. He puts . . . you know . . . on the walls and things. It's much better since we've got the new shower room beside my bedroom, now I use that and my brother uses the old one downstairs. I don't like it when he stares at me – I think he doesn't like me, wants to really hurt me. I know he's not allowed to be with me unless an adult is there too, all the time. But the good bit is that we celebrate the day mum and dad adopted him, every year we go and do something special. So that's a good bit.
[Sibling, primary age, interview 2006: see Chapter 2]

We used to have great fun, my brother and me, we've always shared our room. Now all he thinks about is going out and doing drugs, raves and stuff like that. He asked me to go too, but often he's horrible now and I just don't want to be like that. He thinks I'm stupid and scared but I don't care. Sometimes he's really really mean to me, takes my stuff. There're always rows now all the time and when he doesn't come home mum cries. The police were here about something too . . . mum was really upset about that. Some of the neighbours were talking about it and she was upset about that too. I think he has to go to court. I don't know what will happen, I'm a bit scared really. [D, sibling, early teens, interview]

She (Chrissy) knew exactly how to wind Jamie up. She learned from an early age how to annoy people of all ages. One day, when Chrissy was about five and Jamie three, I heard this awful screeching coming from the kitchen. My heart pounding, I rushed to investigate and saw Jamie pinned, red-faced, up against the wall by nothing more than his own indignation as Chrissy repeated his name – 'Jamie, Jamie!' with different intonations. It was as if she had a high-pressure hose turned on him. Chrissy was grinning at his reaction, delighted. (Gregory, 2000)

> When my brother gets upset he screams. Sometimes he screams for ages and ages and ages. [A, sibling of C who has autism]

Every aspect of life is changed when seriously challenging behaviour enters the picture and not only for that individual. The age of the individual, their siblings and other family members may be a factor in how each member copes, but it is inevitable that each young person, of whatever age, will have to work out ways of coping with much reduced attention time for them as the adults around them focus on the individual who needs most support. Constant supervision when behaviour may be abusive or dangerous – to the troubled child or young person, or to others – is also a factor to be considered. And how to find the 'manpower', time and energy to cope with this when also trying to carry through the practicalities of making a meal, answering the door or telephone, going shopping.

> The first duty of any commercial organisation is to stay in business. Not to go bust. Well, the first duty of a carer is to go on caring. Caring is long term. It's physically tough, emotionally draining, and financially difficult. It's all too easy to run out of energy and to burn out. When that happens, you stop caring.
>
> (Marriott, 2003)

Translating awareness into action

What can families do to avoid burnout or disintegration?

Families can help themselves and each other by discussion of:

- Sharing the caring role.
- Working out a supportive role for each family member: to support the vulnerable individual; to support other family members, e.g. sharing time for activities or helping with homework and so on; dividing household chores such as laying the table, putting washing in laundry basket/machine, taking in washing, answering phone at certain times; *any* contribution to running of home is important, no matter how small, means one less for the main carer to cope with.
- Look out for each other by being aware of others' feelings, state of energy or exhaustion.
- Acknowledgement of the problems for other members of the family is really important in reducing feelings of personal isolation.
- Actively plan for individual respite time – friends and older relatives may be able to offer some time to help – ask for suggestions at a family forum (see below).

Be aware of the effects on siblings:

- physical or emotional aspects, often including grief when a constant and loved companion becomes ill or withdraws from the relationship because of their illness
- worry about getting the condition or illness themselves
- worry about not knowing what to do
- guilt if or when they express resentment or anger
- worry about whether they too may have to go into hospital or special unit
- adults' lack of time to pay attention to their own interests and activities
- adults' lack of time to attend school events; sports events; graduation; performance in concerts, plays and other activities
- adults' lack of time to play, to listen to problems and worries
- adults' lack of energy for any non-essential activities
- worry that if 'naughty' they may be sent away
- needing regular reassurance that the adults are aware of all their feelings, take account of them, that the adults are in charge of the situation and are actively looking for ways through the difficult times.

> Our son now lives in a residential home because we were no longer able to cope on a fulltime basis, he comes home at weekends and holidays. When he gets frustrated he can be aggressive and occasionally even violent. Our daughter has become really anxious and clingy.
>
> [Parent of D, no clear diagnosis, interview, 2006]

Remember that sometimes siblings and other young carers will understand and simply begin to accept that there just isn't any time for their own lives and concerns. Siblings and other young carers may simply withdraw and endure. All the feelings – sadness, frustration, resentment – will have their effect.

Family forum

Try to set up a weekly family conference to discuss any issues which may need airing, and include young members wherever possible. It may be possible to plan for a regular time, or it may only be possible to fit it in on an ad hoc basis. The important thing is for everyone to feel that there will be a time when their individual concerns will be listened to (and, it is hoped, some sort of solution found).

Choosing a meeting leader

Perhaps more than one might be able to do this and take turns? Perhaps someone in the family – or even outside the family, a close friend maybe? – is particularly good at staying calm. A detached view is better than passionate or possibly upset; who is best at achieving such an approach?

Involving the family

Often the troubled young person will be able to attend, and may be invited to do so.

- Where cognitive ability is affected by their vulnerable member's problems, the family may decide to meet together and make arrangements for their loved family member to be looked after at that time, or meet while s/he is asleep.
- Where drugs, or alcohol, eating disorder, or any other addictive compulsive behaviour are part of the problem, often the problems are denied by the sufferer. However, as part of attempts to address the problems, it is important that the sufferer understands how their behaviour affects the lives of others around them. Most, although initially reluctant to attend, agree to take part – if only because they can't resist wanting to hear what is being said about them!

Once a time is found, try to involve as many in the family and close others as possible. This may mean that some family members might need to rearrange their schedule for work or school (e.g. dad might have to go in to work late and leave later, or a grandparent might offer to babysit for the youngest member of the family, or brother skip going to the gym) to enable them to attend.

Once the idea is established, ask for ideas and suggestions for discussion for the next roundtable get-together – no matter how small the matter may seem, if some-one has raised it don't ignore or belittle whatever it is; if it matters to anyone in the family, it is affecting their lives and feelings.

Have a rough agenda worked out if possible beforehand.

Discuss where the conference will be: around the kitchen table? In the lounge, with no television? Around the garden table? Somewhere else?

Discuss how formal or informal it will be: over a cup of tea/can of juice/drink?

It's a good idea to choose an item, perhaps a shell or other small object – which the person speaking holds, then passes on when their turn to speak is over. The more discussion and agreement beforehand between all who might be involved, the more likely to be successful the conference will be.

The chairperson's part

- Welcome everyone who is there; acknowledge efforts to be there.
- Talk about the rough agenda, ask for any late additions.
- Set the rules: only one voice speaking at a time; if you use a small object to signify whose turn it is to speak, remind anyone trying to interrupt that their turn will come too – they must be patient and when it's their own turn, no-one may interrupt them either.
- No interruptions when someone is talking about their feelings.
- Set a time limit for an individual contribution (by doing so, people hopefully will think about what they want to say and come prepared rather then waffle on too much).
- Say when you think the conference will end so that others can then plan their follow-on activities.
- Consider all suggestions. Where a particular behaviour or incident is brought up, ask for suggestions as to possible solutions – 'brainstorming' to find as many ideas as possible, which may range from funny and OTT to serious. Discuss reasons why they might – or might not – be a good idea.
- Ask for any feedback about how people felt about the meeting, any particular outcomes – good or bad – and use these to adjust arrangements for another time.
- Try gently to help younger members to express their comments, feelings and ideas, possibly remind them of significant incidents they might want to mention. Often young children can be very perceptive indeed, and add perspectives no-one else has thought of.

Reactions to a family forum

When difficult behaviour is or has become part of the family scene, difficult feelings for other family members are likely to be part of the scene too. *Therefore it is important to discuss and follow the rules agreed beforehand.* If the behaviour has been part of the scene for a long period with no prior acknowledgement of the problems caused for others in the family, establishing such conferences may be quite difficult. Unexplored pain and resentment may have built up, just waiting to explode given the opportunity. In this case, the chairperson's part becomes even more crucial – and help may be sought from someone more detached.

Everyone needs to feel valued and loved. Expressing that love, interest and value in an individual may be done in so many ways, some extravagant and wonderful, but equally important – perhaps even more so – through finding small ways. (See VIEW – Very Important Encouraging Words (Chapters 3 and 4)

Small things

Remembering someone's liking for a particular meal or a treat – a game perhaps, a video, time for a walk or to go watch sport, any shared time – no matter how small, remembering to ask 'How do you feel about . . .' is showing how much you value the person, as well as spending time with them, really listening and talking through with each individual family member any feelings they have expressed at a family conference. Finding time to do this, finding time to go to another child's important event – a match, a concert, school parents' evening, graduation – may be difficult but could make all the difference to that child's perception of how much a parent cares.

Actively look for help. If necessary, ask a relative or friend to take over for a while and explain exactly why you need some time. If at times you really must be at home and simply cannot leave due to a specific situation, perhaps arrange for a grandparent or other relation, or a friend, to take other children out for some 'quality time' such as a trip to the beach, cinema, theatre, sport.

Planning for quality time

- *Work out a plan*, then discuss.
- *Who* might help – grandparents and other family, friends, colleagues, neighbours?
- *What* could be or needs to be done: brainstorming with others to find as wide a range of ideas as possible is often useful.
- *How* to make it a practical reality: make a list of any resources needed, including time (*When*), and energy.
- *Actively seek resources*, including time for respite and relaxation, recharging of batteries.
- *Write down* your plan, keep it in a safe place where it can be checked, and *review* to check progress regularly with everyone who helped make it.
- *Little and often is more effective* than lack of attention most of time and then an out-of-the-blue big demonstration with lots of attention, followed by a return to the same situation as before. *Just 15 minutes or half an hour daily could make a huge difference – if an hour or two isn't possible.* Activities don't have to be expensive: sharing time together is the most important part of any activity; even walking to the bus stop or local shop takes on a different

meaning if you discuss surroundings, or perhaps sharing and discussion of a television programme or film, or helping with and discussing home/ school work.

Spouses need time and attention

'Time out' for a meal, a day out or weekend away from home is important for the survival of any relationship; when coping with all the difficulties involved in supporting a troubled family member, it becomes absolutely crucial – but even more difficult to organise. Here is where grandparents, uncles and aunts, other family and friends can play a valuable role.

Ask for help, even for a short while to allow you and your spouse to go out for an uninterrupted drink or a cup of tea: it may actually save your relationship as well as help carers regain enough energy to cope better with the next problem. Even if unable to offer much in the way of time or practical help, because of work or other commitments, most people like to be given the opportunity of being able to help in any small way, like to feel that you could ask for help when needed, and may be able to suggest other ways of finding spaces in a difficult situation to enable the main carers to continue coping.

Communication, as we have seen, is the main key and can be the difference between survival or disintegration of a relationship or a whole family.

Plan for survival, review regularly, and change if and when necessary. (See Chapter 16.)

How can professionals help?

> This assumes that siblings and young carers might be included in discussions with professionals. This is not our experience – while discussions went on about our son, our daughter had to sit outside with strangers. The 'child-centred approach' has no mechanism whatsoever for including siblings.
>
> [Alan and Joan, see Chapter 2]

One of the most valuable things professionals can do is to listen and acknowledge how difficult life is at home.

Simple questions

Simple questions can make a big difference:

- 'How are you coping with the effects of X's difficulties on your own life?'
- 'What aspect of X's condition do you find most difficult to cope with?'
- 'Is there anything you would like to know about X's condition?'

- 'Is there anything you feel the professional team should be aware of?'
- 'Is there anything in particular the professional team could help you and/or the family with?'
- 'Do you have any ideas of what might help X?'

Simple suggestions

Simple suggestions are often seen as helpful:

- Assertiveness training to help cope with aggression when someone finds constant confrontation difficult to cope with
- Counselling when grief about the change in or loss of the known and loved personality is overwhelming
- Anger management to help cope with frustrations
- Suggestions for respite and relaxation.

Words of encouragement

Simple words of encouragement can mean the difference between burnout, disintegration, giving up – for individuals or a whole family – and coping/getting through.

- 'Keep up the good work, you're making all the difference to X!'
- 'Without you, X wouldn't be able to cope.'
- 'Without your efforts and support, X wouldn't be making such progress.'

Good communication

The rules of good communication always apply.

- *Keep it Simple and Straightforward (KISS) at all times:* no jargon and give information at a level siblings or any other family carers can understand.
- *Be honest:* if you don't see things in the same way, say so. Give information about the illness/condition and all its aspects, recognised behaviours no matter how difficult, wherever you can without breaking confidentiality. Explain the reason, if you can't give certain information.
- *Be compassionate:* how would you and your family cope with such a situation over long periods of time, often years?

- *Listen carefully:* remember that you are talking with and listening to another human being, one experiencing huge problems with which you may be able to help.
- *Be patient:* people, including children and young adults, living under long-term stress may have difficulty concentrating, may have difficulty expressing themselves, may feel angry, sad and emotional, may have difficulty taking in what you are saying.
- *Answer as honestly as possible*; say so if you can't give particular information, and why.
- *Check understanding* at intervals throughout a meeting.
- *Allow time at the end* to summarise what has been discussed.
- *Check if there are any questions:* if no time left this time say so, and offer another time to talk.
- *Don't promise what can't be delivered.*

CHAPTER SIXTEEN

Put on your own mask first

It's as if you were stuck on a bus going round and round, and when asked how you might be helped, you just think, 'Well, more comfortable seats and maybe a sunshade.' It doesn't occur to you any longer that the most helpful thing would be to get off the bus for a while, if only to stretch and have a break!'

[Joan, see Chapter 2]

When travelling with a child or invalid, in the event of an emergency put on your own mask first. If you do not, you will be unable to help the child or invalid.

[Airline notice]

In other words, look after yourself first – if carers don't take care of themselves, if they collapse or 'go under' and become ill, who will be there to cope? Who will look after the troubled individual? Home carers provide crucial support to their loved ones, often for years and under very difficult circumstances, yet often by focusing all their care on another they neglect their own wellbeing and health, both physical and emotional. (Recognising this, UK carers are now legally entitled to have their own needs assessed.)

Professional carers, people working in caring professions and volunteers working on telephone helplines (e.g. Samaritans, EDA) all recognise that their work is with human beings who are experiencing troubles and trauma, and they make sure of personal support through regular 'supervision'. *Taking active steps to ensure physical and emotional health so that they can continue effective support for others is also essential for home carers.*

It was like living in a nightmare. His behaviour was totally unpredictable. Sometimes when he was frustrated he was really aggressive to me as well as P, J and J – my other children – and they were frightened. I don't know how I coped for all those years. Even trying to get shopping – really awful, I'd have needed eyes in the back of my head, ten hands. No holidays, no breaks . . . my mum babysat once, my mother-in-law just couldn't cope. Then my husband couldn't cope with it all. He left us. I really don't know how I got through.

[F, mother of boy with learning difficulties]

Reactions to stress

Carers' reactions to stress are individual. Feelings of stress may be a reaction to problems, perhaps financial, emotional, health, organisational, work, or too many things to do and not enough time. Machines may have made communication and cleaning, for example, easier than ever before – water no longer has to be physically carried every day, heating doesn't involve finding and carrying heavy wood or coal, carpets don't have to be beaten daily – but they have also created much higher standards. Email correspondents expect a fast reply; handwritten or hand-drawn presentations are rarely acceptable; clothes must be washed and ironed much more often – all of which disposes rather effectively of the time gained by the appliances' invention! These daily routines and expectations can become relentless pressures when added to increased stress in personal situations. And individual carers will each cope differently, with more or less resilience, varying with progress or setbacks.

Some stress is beneficial: adrenaline makes sure we move quickly in dangerous situations, which is how and why cavemen survived animal attacks at least for long enough to become our ancestors. In these circumstances, or when giving our opinion in a highly charged situation, or defending ourselves under personal attack, our heart rate will increase for a while before settling down to its normal rhythm. It is when stress becomes overwhelming that carers are in danger of collapse, with inevitable consequences for those they care for.

A Mencap report (*Adoption Today* 2006) quotes 7 out of 10 families caring for disabled children at or close to breaking point because of lack of short term respite; that the same number provide more than 15 hours of care every day . . . and point out that since their last 'Breaking Point' report in 2003, nothing has changed. The same point is made by Marriott (2003).

Small things can make a huge difference, either way.

> I really don't know how we're going to cope. Our son smokes. Our regular respite carers, who have given us a break for years, say that the new No Smoking ban means that they can't have him to stay any more. I really don't know what to do, I haven't had a break at all for months now, I'm just absolutely whacked.
>
> [P, interview]

Time for relaxation

Life video

Imagine rewinding a video of your life, to a time when you were carefree. How did you spend your leisure time? Imagine your surroundings – who was there, what were you (and any companions) wearing, what were you doing, any smells or sounds around? Imagine a specially happy occasion; feel the joy, the laughter, the warmth – perhaps an outing, a dance, a garden, a barbecue, a walk, taking part in a joint effort, watching a sunset with a loved one, luxuriating in a long bath.

Now make a list of some of the ways in which your life has changed; list anything you feel you no longer have time or energy to do.

Identifying stress

Palpitations, headaches, nausea, tremors, aches and pains, dizziness, fainting, indigestion, stomach spasms, muscle tension especially in neck, sexual dysfunction, dry mouth, cold sweats, clammy hands, aggression, poor driving, withdrawal, poor time management, accidents, loss of humour, lack of interest in/deterioration of personal hygiene, loss of appetite, nightmares, anger, panic attacks, feelings of anxiety, failure, embarrassment, helplessness, depression, shame, guilt, the list is endless.

Rather than trying to avoid stress, identifying what is causing the stress becomes important – understanding what is happening and why. There may be one major worry – money worries, work pressure, family problems, lack of understanding of situations, feelings of helplessness – or at times in our lives there may be several stressful situations happening all at the same time.

Careful observation and looking for situations which may trigger stress, then trying to avoid those situations, may help to reduce carers' stress (see also Chapter 13).

> Before I realised that my son absolutely hated anything on his head – maybe a hat or hood when it was cold or windy – he would scream for hours. When I finally put two and two together, it meant I could try to work out what else I could do to keep him warm enough. Washing his hair was another major problem – I reckon the neighbours thought I was murdering him – and that was with doors and windows shut! He hated anything tight round his waist too, I had to find trousers with elasticated waists. [Sheila Gray, interview, 2006]

When stress triggers or causes can be identified and addressed, especially when respite can be found, strategies can often be put in place to cope with the situation. Talking to a friend or seeking a counsellor, phoning the Samaritans or other helpline, attending a meeting, finding information or someone who been through similar circumstances – all these may be enough to get through a difficult time. However, recognising and identifying a problem and then finding appropriate support can be quite time-consuming:

> When my husband started drinking after his business went bust I made excuses for him. I let him get away with all sorts of things, being late or just not turning up for important occasions – he missed most of the Parents' Evenings at school for our children, and their concerts, and I had to go on my own even though he'd promised he'd be there. He even completely missed a family wedding once. I even made excuses for him when he hit me.

> It was only when he did some real damage, I went to our GP and I was in a real state and for once told him what was really happening (he was a friend of my husband's) . . .well, things changed. He gave me Al-Anon's number, didn't do anything for a while because things were always better for a while.
>
> Then he didn't come home again, he was drinking again . . . anyway I went to a meeting – and suddenly I understood what was happening. I was actually 'giving him permission' to go on behaving like a rat just by letting him off with it, by making excuses for him. They called it 'collusion'. Things changed then, he began to really try to control his drinking. I don't know where we'd be if I hadn't seen our GP, told him the truth that day.
>
> [M, interview, 2006]

Unpredictability – of mood, of behaviour, of responses – can cause major problems for carers, and many may postpone discussing a problem when they think things might remain calm for a while.

> Despite refusing any professional help, after several years of holding her own in her battle against anorexia and bulimia, not losing any more weight, yet not gaining much – my daughter's mood also seemed more stable and it was again possible sometimes to have pleasant conversations with Jay. I became hopeful of the worst being behind us, even of persuading Jay that professional help might support her . . . 1999 started reasonably well. Then came May and, without any warning, another complete change – Anorexia was back and took over with a vengeance.
>
> Months later – November – a friend phoned; I forgot the time as I enjoyed a pleasant relaxed chat. Before I'd finished the conversation, Anorexia stormed into the room and started yelling and screaming about how little I loved her. Continued after I'd replaced the phone.
>
> Then quite suddenly the screaming stopped and my daughter looked at me. Her body sagged and Jay's face appeared, to replace Anorexia's which a moment before had been contorted with rage.
>
> 'Can I have a hug Mum?' Jay said in a child's voice. Braced against more aggression, I hesitated. As I put my arms around her, I asked 'Why?'
>
> 'What do you mean?' my daughter asked, leaning into my shoulder, her arms wound tightly around me.

'It really upsets me' I said, 'All the screaming and shouting. Why? I want to know why?'

And Jay said in a frightened voice, 'I don't know why Mum, I'm out of control. I'm scared.'

For the rest of that evening we talked quite rationally, sitting together on the sofa. They were rare moments of calm in a truly bleak year. Next day Anorexia came back. (Smith, 2004)

The longer a problem and its effects remain unrecognised or unacknowledged, the longer the problem and the stress that it causes will persist, and the longer it will take to challenge the unacceptable behaviour.

Don't ignore problems and hope they'll go away. Actively look for helpful strategies, for information, for support; plan to avoid personal burnout.

By no longer excusing her husband's behaviour, M helped her husband begin his long road to regaining control. Not only did this save their marriage and turn around M's own life, she may well have saved her husband's life – had he gone on drinking and behaving aggressively to her, not only would she probably have left him but he might well have died an early death in very miserable circumstances.

'Tough love': effects on carers

It can be difficult for carers to recognise how badly affected their lives are by someone whom they love showing aggression, hostility, rejection – and takes much energy to consistently make efforts over time to support while offering 'tough love': not giving in to short-term pressure, but reassuring, demonstrating love and support.

Getting through

A key question for carers to ask themselves is: 'What would happen if I collapsed, if I just wasn't here?'

Coming from a different angle, professionals may ask the same question about home carers: What would happen to my client/patient without any support at home?

Now think about going on a journey or on holiday or starting a project at work, or a campaign, military or charity or environmental: what would make it successful? (Information? Planning? Support and resources?)

Make a list of things which might possibly help carers cope in their home situations. Look for as many ideas as possible from as many sources, perhaps brainstorm round the table: family and friends, both personal and professional, and colleagues, might suggest extra things. Perhaps find a stress management workshop.

> When my daughter was ill over several years, I came very close to collapse. At one point, coping without information or support with the aggression and hostility which are often part of the intense frustration people suffering from an eating disorder experience, and my feelings of rejection resulting from this behaviour in some-one I loved and wanted to support, at times I felt suicidal. Reading all sorts of articles about parents being responsible for emotional difficulties, or not coping with life experiences, I agonised helplessly over what I could possibly have done to cause my daughter such suffering.
>
> Wondering what might happen to my daughter – who would support her if I wasn't around, how would she cope with her feelings of guilt if I committed suicide? – stopped me following through on those thoughts. The thoughts however made me realise that if I wanted to help anyone at all, I had to plan for my own survival. My own list of what might help included music, having a meal out of the house once a week (sometimes alone in a café as often I was so exhausted I couldn't cope with having to talk to anyone at all, even a friend), sharing a walk or coffee with a friend as often as possible, relaxation and breathing exercises, walking the dog, and writing. Once a month, while I was still working and could afford it, I booked into a bed-and-breakfast to sleep – rather than with friends as often I was too tired to concentrate, or to talk.
>
> [GS, personal experience]

Carers might put on their list things they used to enjoy before their lives were taken over by caring, and also consider new activities. From discussions at conferences with people who have put their own lives on hold in their efforts to care for their family members, these are a few activities to help get such a list started:

- music, choir, drama club
- massage – shiatsu, reiki, Swedish, many others: why not try them all?!
- aromatherapy and other alternative techniques

- dance
- watching or taking part in sport: swimming, running, aerobics, exercise
- yoga, tai chi, breathing and relaxation
- hobbies: woodwork, tapestry, painting, gardening
- writing: journal, letters, stories, poems, 'crap sandwiches'
- a personal haven: bedroom, study, bath, the shed.

Strategies need not cost much: sitting with a cat purring on your lap is very peaceful; going for a short walk; standing in a garden listening to birds or watching a squirrel; sharing time for a chat or a joke with a neighbour or friend – all can really help.

- Friends, colleagues, acquaintances: sometimes distraction is needed, sometimes sharing problems. When appropriate, explain the situation to people you see regularly, say how you are feeling, ask for help – most people are glad to feel they may be able to offer help; it also means that they feel easier about talking about their own problems, asking for your support when needed. Offers of short respite times may be suddenly available, a cup of tea or a meal out, supportive telephone conversations, invitations. If you are willing to share your problems, friends will feel they can talk to you when they have a problem to share.
- Regular breaks – daily, weekly, monthly and so on. Any or all of these may be needed.
- Assertiveness training and/or anger management training may help with difficulties in coping with aggression.

Actively look for and plan for whatever is needed to get through. Even finding one or two ways of keeping up strength and coping skills may be enough. In many UK cities there are now Carer Centres; find out where the nearest one is – they may be able to suggest avenues of support no-one else has suggested, or put you in touch with support workers.

Actively help family members, especially siblings and young carers, to find ways of coping.

- Try to develop a signal for when things get really difficult for them, a *What to do if you're worried/scared/want to talk to me,* an unobtrusive signal which may be used in front of the person with challenging behaviour. It could be something like *If you feel scared came over and take my hand and I'll know how you're feeling.* Or *Ask if we need to fill the bird-feeders, then I'll try to arrange that we can be alone to talk*. Or *If you sit in that chair, where you never usually sit, I'll know you want a 'Time-out'*. Develop ideas, as Joan and Alan did to help M cope (see Chapter 2) through discussion with those affected.

- Discuss the importance of seeing friends, of continuing hobbies and interests – and try to make sure that time is found to follow up the discussion. This is where friends and relatives can be invaluable (unfortunately not everyone has relatives living locally); sometimes the fact that they know very little about what is happening in home life is a benefit in focusing on other interests.
- Reassure that parents are still in charge.
- Encourage young carers to try out new ideas such as the visualisation below, and find their own coping strategies.

  We have a cuddle (M likes being in the middle) where we bring up worries and talk about them. Then we reaffirm that we're all in this together. (Joan)

Not only are carers helping themselves, by looking after their own health and emotional wellbeing, they are also helping those they care for by not risking burnout.

> I didn't realise I'd given up so much of my own life . . . . . .I used to play golf, sing in a choir, go to ballroom dancing classes, helped with the local pantomime. I don't think giving up my life actually helped my daughter, and it certainly didn't help me cope. I came very very close to going under completely. [Mary-Ann]

Visualisation exercise

Make yourself comfortable, in a quiet room – or outside – where you know you won't be disturbed for a while.

Sit down, close your eyes and begin to breathe gently and regularly. Be aware of the air passing through your nose. Don't try to control it in any way, simply be aware of it. Rest like this for some time, breathing gently and regularly.

When you feel ready, begin to count your breaths. *One – two – three – four – five – six*. Now return to one, and begin again. *One – two – three – four – five – six*.

Repeat this several times. If you find your mind wandering, simply notice the thought then return to *one* and start counting your breaths again. *One – two – three – four – five – six*. Continue like this for some time, breathing gently and regularly and counting your breaths.

When you are ready, replace the counting with:

In – out
Deep – slow

Calm – ease
Rest – release
In this moment
Precious moment.

Continue like this for some time.

When you feel ready, imagine you are opening a gate or door. You follow a path slowly: what kind of path is it? Smooth or rough and stony? Sandy perhaps? Are there weeds on this path or is it well tended? Look at what is at each side of the path: what can you see? Are there flowers, perhaps? Trees?

Keep breathing gently and regularly as you take your time along the path. There is no hurry, take your time.

Follow the path until you find a peaceful quiet place to sit, perhaps a place you already know well. It might be on a beautiful beach. Imagine your surroundings: can you hear the waves? The gulls? What else can you hear? Can you see any boats or birds? What else can you see? Can you smell the sea? What else are you aware of?

Or it might be on a hillside. Can you hear the wind? What else can you hear? What can you hear or see or smell?

Or perhaps you are in a lovely garden, surrounded by flowers. Perhaps you open that door or gate and set off on a regular run to a local park.

Choose your own place and carefully examine your surroundings. Imagine as many details as possible.

Continue breathing gently and regularly. Feel the peace all around you.

In – out
Deep – slow
Calm – ease
Rest – release
In the moment
Precious moment.

When you feel ready, look back at the path you followed to your special place. Try to see it clearly. Is it sloping or level, through trees, paved or rough? How far can you see along it?

When you can see the path clearly, imagine a friend or very wise person is coming towards you, following the path. Is the person male or female? Short or tall? Old or young?

Slowly your friend is drawing nearer, until that person is beside you. S/he sits down beside you. Together and in peace, you rest there side by side for some time in silent companionship.

In – out
Deep – slow
Calm – ease
Rest – release
In this moment
Precious moment.

Without words, your friend understands all your feelings, any sadness and pain you feel, things you find difficult to cope with.

Gently your friend takes a round stone from a deep pocket. The stone gleams with a brilliant silver light. Your friend holds it out to you and gives it to you. Your hand closes over the stone.

In your hand you feel the stone, smooth and warm, glowing with energy. Can you feel it? How big is it? Feel its surface all over, feel the weight of it in your hand. Slowly you become aware of how warm it is, of how the warmth and weight feels in your hand. Cover it with your other hand, and feel how both your hands feel warm. They are becoming warmer.

In – out
Deep – slow
Calm – ease
Rest – release
In this moment
Precious moment.

Breathe gently. Feel the warmth, the warmth in your hands. The warmth and the light energy begins to travel through your hands and up your arms. The warmth and light energy travels slowly, slowly, slowly into your body, each rib, your lungs, your abdomen, your legs, your feet, every bone and tissue. Slowly, slowly, very slowly, the light is filling your body.

When the light energy finds any tension in your body it stops, focuses on the stress causing the problem. Imagine that stress: how does it look? Snarly and bad-tempered? What colour is it? Imagine that light with its intense warmth. Imagine how that intense warmth shines brilliantly onto the stress, imagine your stress beginning to fade. Keep focusing on that stress, the effect of the light, the effect of that brilliant energy.

In – out
Deep – slow
Calm – ease
Rest – release
In this moment
Precious moment.

Some stress needs much energy, much light, to destroy reduce it. Continue to breathe and focus that weight, that warmth, that light energy, on any unwelcome tensions in your body. Keep breathing slowly, gently.

When you feel ready, slowly focus your attention on returning the light to your hand, give it slowly back to your friend. Sit for as long as you wish to with your friend, lean on the strength of your friend.

When you are ready, bring your breathing back to normal, and open your eyes.

Return to your special place as often as you can, watch for your special friend, let your friend give you the special stone with the warm and energy light. Feel its effect on your hands, on your skin, on your bones, on every part of your body.

Visualisation: variation

Return to your special place, on your beautiful beach or it might be a hillside, in a lovely garden surrounded by flowers, or a peaceful park.

When you can see the path clearly, look for your very wise person coming towards you, following the path. Now this person has with them an empty bag. Imagine the bag swinging in a strong hand, or perhaps over a shoulder.

Slowly s/he draws near, sits down beside you. Together and in peace, you rest there side by side for some time in silent companionship. Without words, the wise person understands all your sadness and pain, the extent of your burden.

Think of the burden you have been carrying; name that painful heavy burden. Gently the wise person puts a hand on your shoulder, then opens the bag, invites you to give up your burden.

Into the bag you put whatever has been troubling you. You give up your burden, put in into the bag.

Your wise friend picks up the bag with the burden. The bag is really, really heavy and needs two hands to haul it onto his or her back. Very slowly, carrying the bag with your burden, your friend walks away along the path, and you watch as your burden is carried away. Watch how heavy the bag is, how difficult it is to carry. Watch until the wise person with your burden disappears.

When your burden is no longer in sight, bring your attention back to your breathing. Sit quietly for as long as you like, breathing gently and regularly, before opening your eyes.

In – out
Deep – slow
Calm – ease
Rest – release
In this moment
Precious moment.

Some burdens are so enormous and you have carried them for so long that they may not disappear in one visit, in one bag. Return to your special place as often as you want to, watch for your special friend who carries the bag, let your friend carry your burdens, your pain and grief, away.

The magic worry stone

Look for a small smooth stone. Find one which will fit in your hand easily. Choose one – from beach, garden, river – which feels good when you hold it in one hand and stroke it with your thumb. Try out a few until you find just the right one for you.

Sit in a comfortable place, if possible where you will be undisturbed for some time. Slow and count your breaths as before.

Think about a particular problem. Any problem. Think carefully about every aspect, about all your feelings – sadness, grief, pain, helplessness, anger, being overwhelmed.

As you concentrate on your problem, go right into the feelings. Name them as you stroke the stone. The stone has been around for thousands and thousands of years. It has seen and absorbed all sorts of pain, tears and misery, from its surroundings and from people who have passed by or walked over it. Thousands and thousands and thousands of years.

Keep stroking the stone. Name all your problems one by one, and ask the stone to absorb them as it has done others over so many many years. Feel the soothing smoothness, the warmth in your hand, between and on your fingers. Feel the love, the peace and joy it has also absorbed to counteract the pain.

Keep the stone in your pocket, in your purse, perhaps under your pillow. Carry it with you to use and help you through when you have to cope with stress caused by your problems. Hold it and use it at any time of day.

* * * *

Actively plan for survival to enable effective long term caring. Look for what you and other carers need to enable you to keep going.

Final words

> I was feeling at the end of my rope and I said to my social worker, 'I think I'm going to have a breakdown. What would happen to us then?' He just looked right through me. No answer. People think that carers are like robots or machines and can carry on endlessly without a break.
>
> Rose Fernandez, 45, is a widow and mother of four, including Crystal 20 who is severely autistic. Rose's mother, 77, has dementia and also lives with Rose who feeds, clothes, cleans and manages both of them around the clock, supervising Crystal's education programme and ensuring her mother takes all her medication.
>
> (Cochrane, 2006)

Research suggests that despite a policy drive in recent years towards supporting carers in their caring role, many carers continue to feel marginalised and often believe that their own particular health and social care needs are overlooked. Identified barriers to accessing support include:

- lack of recognition amongst some professionals of the carers' role and the needs of carers;
- prioritising the needs of the care recipient to the detriment of the carer;
- lack of training in carers' issues amongst some health and social care staff;
- carers' lack of knowledge and individual beliefs about health promotion;
- carers provided with insufficient knowledge about where and how to access services;
- professionals' concerns with confidentiality and disclosing information to carers.

(*Equality and Inequalities in Health and Social Care: a Statistical Overview*, DHSSPS (UK) 2004)

> Yesterday is history.
> Tomorrow is a mystery.
> Today is a gift.
> That's why it's called the present. (Anon)

To look forward with hope that collaboration between professionals and informal home carers can make a difference to supporting the vulnerable people at the centre of all our efforts – is this possible? Given the history of the 20th century, when various factors collided, frequently leading to a lack of of co-ordinated and consistent professional/home support, especially when adults needed special help – is this probable?

Such combined efforts can have very positive effects on 24-hour care; without teamwork, it is difficult to see how support for those we all try to help could be anything other than fragmented.

With much goodwill all round, through building constructive conversations between professional and informal home carers, I believe the answer is 'Yes'. We can all make a real contribution to bringing about a more positive tomorrow.

Appendix

Relationships and communications with carers, both home and professional, are critical to the lives of vulnerable people who need extra support to allow them to fulfil their potential. Over the last several years, this ongoing support – and the importance of these supportive relationships and communications being as constructive as possible – has been acknowledged and highlighted in many reports. When this support breaks down for any reason, sadly the person who will most lose out will be the vulnerable person at the centre of all efforts whom everyone wants to help.

> COAT has been developed as a way of working with carers to identify their need for support and to plan, agree and evaluate the help they receive. We hope that COAT will make an important contribution to fostering partnerships between family carers and formal support systems.
>
> (*Coat Outcome Agreement Tool (COAT)*, 2006)

> She had a very difficult time trying to look after him after the first admission. He became very negative about her. He was using illicit drugs and alcohol which she thought made him worse. She had been trying to get an appointment to speak to his consultant about his current illness. However she had been told that this was impossible for reasons of confidentiality.
>
> By the time they get in touch with us, relatives and carers may have become very frustrated in trying to get information and have their views heard. Sometimes the family and the mental health service have developed extremely polarised views, and sometimes their relationship has become bitterly adversarial.
>
> (*Carers and Confidentiality*, 2005)

> Eating disorders can involve and affect families and carers in a profound way. These disorders often involve issues of medical safety and it would be unreasonable not to share risks with those in a caring role. Healthcare professionals need to be sensitive to this. (*Eating disorders in Scotland, 2006*)

> Patients, and where appropriate, carers should be provided with education and information on the nature, course and treatment of eating disorders.
>
> (*National Institute of Clinical Excellence*, 2004)

These are only a very small sample of the research, many documents and reports I have come across now available which show that collaborative care, appropriate information and support for those caring at home can lead to improved outcomes for vulnerable individuals who need extra support.

It is not possible to give complete information about all the conditions which may include, as part of their presentation, physically or emotionally 'challenging behaviours', let alone the individual mix of conditions which sometimes appear.

General points

Listen for the message behind the behaviour. Try to be:

- specific
- realistic
- consistent
- patient
- calm

Use this book as a practical 'starter kit'. Look for other resources.

From these small beginnings professional and home carers may then explore what might help in their own situations. Search libraries and bookshops, both secondhand and new; try key words to help you search the internet; ask others for help. Where resources are lacking, consider developing what's needed to add to support already available.

The resources listed are those resources which I have come across, or which have been particularly recommended to me.

Samaritans

The Samaritans hold a wide range of helpful contacts, offer a listening ear and operate in many UK towns and cities.

www.samaritans.org.uk
Telephone (UK) 0845 909090

For home carers

www.carers.org
www.carersonline.org
www.livinglifetothefull.com
www.parentlineplus.co.uk
www.womensaid.co.uk

Especially for young carers

Children's Legal Centre: Email: clc@essex.ac.uk
NSPCC: www.nspcc.org.uk
www.youngcarers.org.uk
Youth Access: Email: admin@youthaccess.org.uk
Young Minds: www.youngminds.org.uk

Books

The Art of Happiness: A Handbook for Living by HH the Dalai Lama & Dr Howard C Cutler. Hodder & Stoughton, London, 1998 (paperback 1999).

The Feeling Good Handbook by Dr David Burns. Plume/Penguin Books, New York, revised editions Plume, 1990, 1999.

The '*Overcoming*...' series, published by Constable and Robinson, London UK, includes books on overcoming Anxiety, Anger and Irritability, Childhood Trauma, Compulsive Gambling, Depression, Low Self Esteem, Mood Swings, Panic, Traumatic Stress, Anorexia Nervosa, Bulimia Nervosa and Binge-Eating, and many more. Also *Overcoming Depression and Low Mood: A Five Areas Approach* by C.J. Williams. Hodder Arnold, London, 2006.

Resources for specific conditions

Grief and bereavement

The Compassionate Friends (TCF): www.compassionatefriends.org
Cruse Bereavement Care: www.crusebereavementcare.org.uk
Online grief support: www.GriefNet.org, www.KidSaid.com

Autism

> Autism is a condition that affects some children either from birth or infancy, and leaves them unable to form social relationships or to develop normal communication. As a result the child may become isolated from human contact and absorbed in a world of repetitive obsessional activities and interests.
>
> (Baron-Cohen & Bolton, 1993)

Key characteristics

- Obsessive behaviour
- Extreme social naivete shown by 'embarrassing behaviours' not done deliberately to annoy, for instance touching or smelling or grabbing a stranger, responding in an unusual way socially, 'saying the wrong thing' e.g.

commenting on personal characteristics such as dyed hair or body fat, staring at people, masturbating in public.

- Because children with autism are unable to understand other people's reactions and actions, these can seem very confusing.
- Tantrums and aggression because of confusion, frustration and anger.
- Lack of understanding of emotional impact on others.

Asperger's syndrome

Coming under the broad umbrella of autism, Asperger's syndrome is a milder form which can cause social handicap due to difficulties in relating to other people. For instance, someone with AS – sometimes highly intelligent and gifted in language – may miss social cues such as a bored yawn or shocked expression, which may lead to many misunderstandings. Before recognition and diagnosis, these may be interpreted as 'bad behaviour' by parents and school.

Books

Asperger's Syndrome: A Guide for Parents and Professionals by Tony Attwood. Jessica Kingsley, London and Philadelphia, 1998, reprinted 1999, 2000.
Eating an Artichoke: A Mother's Perspective on Asperger Syndrome by Echo R. Fling. Jessica Kingsley, London and Philadelphia, 2000.
Pretending to be Normal: Living with Asperger's Syndrome by Liane Holliday Willey. Jessica Kingsley, London and Philadephia, 1999.
Supporting Communication Disorders: A Handbook for Teachers and Teaching Assistants by G Thompson. David Fulton, London, 2003.
Understanding and Teaching Children with Autism by Rita Jordan & Stuart Powell. John Wiley & Sons, Chichester, UK, 1995.

Support

National Autistic Society, email nas@nas.org.uk

Attention deficit hyperactivity disorder (ADHD)

> The core deficit that ADHD children experience is a thick barrier between themselves and life's consequences.
>
> [Michael Gordon (1991), quoted in O'Regan 2005]

Key characteristics include poor attention span, disorganization, forgetfulness, being easily distracted, difficulty in sustaining attention in tasks or play activities, excessive impulsivity – having trouble playing quietly, interrupting others, hyperactivity – fidgeting, always 'on the go'.

ADHD is a chronic disorder which can begin in infancy and continue throughout adulthood. Although most people will vary in attention span depending on tiredness and activity, those with ADHD will experience the key characteristics with great intensity. ADHD may be found at every IQ level, though many individuals are of average or above average intelligence. ADHD may mask high intelligence leading to gifted children underachieving, and low self-esteem, with negative effects on life in school, at home and in the community. These may include unpredictable and even dangerous behaviour, leading sometimes in adult life to difficulties with employment and relationships with others.

ADHD often overlaps with other conditions such as *dyslexia, dyspraxia, conduct disorder* (aggression to people and animals, destruction of property, initiating physical fights, stealing, fire setting, lying, violating rules, running away, truanting causing clinically significant impairment of social, academic or occupational functioning) and *oppositional defiant disorder* (ODD), a pattern lasting more than 6 months and occurring more frequently than typically observed in others of comparable age, of negative, hostile and defiant behaviour involving frequent loss of temper, arguing with adults, defying or refusing to comply with adults or rules, deliberately annoying people, often angry or resentful, spiteful and vindictive).

Severity may range from mild through moderate to severe.

Books

ADHD by Fintan J. O'Regan. Continuum, London and New York, 2005.

Attention Training Systems. GSI Publications, USA. email addgsi@aol.com

Children with Special Needs – Assessment, Law and Practice: Caught in the Acts by J. Friel. Jessica Kingsley, London, 4th edition 1997.

Educating Children with ADHD by P. Cooper & F. O'Regan. Routledge Falmer Press, UK, 2001.

First Star I See by J. Caffrey. Verbal Images Press, 1997.

How to Teach and Manage Children with ADHD by F. O'Regan. LDA, Wisbech, UK, 2002.

Managing ADHD in the Inclusive Classroom by J. Metcalf & J. Metcalf. David Fulton, London, 2001.

Overcoming Dyslexia: A Guide for Families and Teachers by B. Hornsby. Vermilion, London, 1996.

Understanding ADHD, by C. Green. Doubleday Press, 1997.

Support

ADDISS Information Services: www.addiss.co.uk

Afasic: www.afasic.org.uk

British Dyslexia Association: www.bda.dyslexia.org.uk

Dyspraxia Foundation, 8 West Alley, Hitchin, Herts SG5 1EG

Hyperactive Children's Support Group: www.hacsg.org.uk
National Association for Special Educational Needs (NASEN): www.nasen.org.uk

Reactive attachment disorder

Individual adverse preverbal experiences are embedded, resulting in varying degrees of difficulty with and/or resistance to bonding, closeness and affection, including:

- children who have been separated early from their mother, e.g. because of medical factors, may have difficulty later with normal development of attachments;
- children who have been physically, mentally or sexually abused experience trauma which has very long lasting emotional effects on behaviour — lack of trust in adults;
- children who have been abused may 'act out' what they have been subjected to. The closer the relationship, the more the resistance. This is often confused with ADHD – out of control, 'wild' behaviour, hyperactive.

Books

Building the Bonds of Attachment: Awakening Love in Deeply Troubled Children by D. Hughes. Jason Aronson, Inc., Northvale, NJ, 2006.
Facilitating Developmental Attachment: The Road to Emotional Recovery and Behavioral Change in Foster and Adopted Children by D. Hughes. Jason Aronson, Inc., Northvale, NJ, 1997.
First Steps in Parenting the Child who Hurts: Tiddlers and Toddlers by C. Archer. Jessica Kingsley, London, 1999.
New Families, Old Scripts: A Guide to the Language of Trauma and Attachment in Adoptive Families by Caroline Archer. Jessica Kingsley, London, 2006.

Support

Adoption UK, 46 The Green, South Bar Street, Banbury OX16 9AB, UK. www.adoptionuk.org
Family Futures Consortium Ltd, 35 Britannia Row, London N1 8QH. www.familyfutures.co.uk

Addictions

An addiction, or an 'excessive appetite' to be more precise, is the same whether its object is alcohol, gambling, heroin, tobacco, eating or sex. It is best thought of as an over-attachment to a drug, object or activity, and the process of overcoming it is largely a naturally occurring one.

(Orford, 2001)

Drugs and alcohol

Alcoholics Anonymous: www.aa-uk.org

Al Anon hold meetings for family members – information from www.al-anon.org.uk. The same website gives links to Alateen, for young carers over 12.

For professionals working with families: www.ma-al-anon-alateen.org/aso/pdf; email: LDCofMA@aol.com

Recovering Together: How to Help an Alcoholic Without Hurting Yourself by Arthur Wassmer. Henry Holt & Co., New York, 1989.

www.drugsaction.co.uk

www.drugscope.org.uk/dworld

www.lifebytes.gov.uk

www.mindbodysoul.gov.uk

Narcotics Anonymous: www.ukna.org

National Drugs Helpline: www.ndh.org.uk

www.recovery.org.uk

www.thesite.org/drinkanddrugs

Gambling

Gamblers Anonymous: www.gamblersanonymous.org

Mental health

> Severe mental health seems to have no simple cause. It is often suggested that several factors work together to produce it. However, there are people who are subject to all these factors but who never become mentally ill. Equally, there are people with mental illness who seem to have none of the risk factors.
>
> Some of the factors thought to be involved: biochemistry; brain damage; cannabis; diet, allergies, infections; family environment; genetics; hormones; life experiences; personality; pregnancy and birth complications; psychological factors; viruses.
>
> [*Mental Health Care,* Institute of Psychiatry, London]

To these I would add the possibility of stress hormones in adverse experiences interacting with individual make-up and resilience, including genes and personality traits.

Sometimes an individual with one challenging problem may also be affected by another – for instance developing bulimia nervosa or schizophrenia or any other mental health problem does *not* mean immunity to the effects of alcohol or drugs; a learning disability means no immunity to severe depression.

Schizophrenia

> Any of a group of psychotic disorders characterized by progressive deterioration of the personality, withdrawal from reality, hallucinations, delusions, social apathy, emotional instability.
>
> (*Collins English Dictionary*, 2001)

> Schizophrenia refers to a specific psychiatric illness characterized by severe problems in social functioning and self care skills and difficulty distinguishing reality.
>
> (Mueser & Gingerich, 1994)

Bipolar disorder

Bipolar affective disorder is also known as manic depression. It is a mood disorder, meaning that someone with the condition experiences very high moods (mania) and very low moods (depression).

Eating disorders

An eating disorder is a serious illness that affects the physical and psychological health of the sufferer. Food is used in some way to try to control or block out stress, depression and low self-esteem following an experience difficult or traumatic for a vulnerable individual. Anorexia nervosa, bulimia nervosa, binge eating disorder, as well as individual mixes of these (EDNOS: eating disorders not otherwise specified) are all eating disorders.

> To call anorexia nervosa an eating disorder is like calling cancer a cough.
>
> [Professor Arthur Crisp (2000), EDA Carers Conference, London 2000]

As it is only recently that eating disorders have been recognised as serious mental health problems, leading to physical as well as psychological damage, I have included a greater number of resources for these illnesses than for schizophrenia or bipolar disorder, where there are more readily accessible resources.

Books

Andrea's Voice: Silenced by Bulimia by D. Smeltzer. Gurze Books, Carlsbad, CA, 2006.

Anorexia and Bulimia in the Family by G. Smith. John Wiley & Sons, Chichester, UK, 2004.

Anorexia Nervosa: A Survival Guide for Parents, Friends and Sufferers by J. Treasure. Psychology Press Ltd, Hove, UK, 1997.

Bronte's Story by B. Cullis & S. Bibb. Random House, Australia, 2004.

Eating Disorders: Helping Your Child Recover edited by S. Bloomfield. Eating Disorders Association, Norwich, UK, 2006.

Eating With Your Anorexic by L. Collins. McGraw-Hill, 2005.

Getting Better Bit(e) by Bit(e): A Survival Kit for Sufferers from Bulimia Nervosa and Binge Eating Disorders by U. Schmidt & J. Treasure. Psychology Press Ltd, Hove, UK, 1993.

Support

International

The Academy for Eating Disorders is an international organisation, aimed primarily at health professionals; it promotes effective treatment, develops prevention initiatives, stimulates research, and launched a worldwide Patient/Carer Charter in Eating Disorders in 2006 at international conference in Barcelona. www.aedweb.com

UK

www.b-eat.co.uk
Eating Disorders Association: www.edauk.com
www.eatingresearch.com – the website of the Eating Disorders Unit at the Institute of Psychiatry offers sections for health professionals, carers and service users with information on a wide range of topics including early recognition, risk management, confidentiality issues, current research and legal matters.
North East Eating Disorder Support Scotland: www.needs-scotland.org

Australia

www.the brontefoundation.com.au

Canada

Family and Friends Against Disordered Eating – FADE: www.fade-on.ca

USA

The Anna Westin Foundation: www.annawestinfoundation
Andrea's Voice Foundation: www.andreasvoice.org
www.findingbalance.com
www.gurze.com
National Eating Disorders Association – NEDA: www.nationaleatingdisorders.org
www.open-mind.org
www.opheliasplace.org
Overeaters Anonymous – OA: www.oa.org
www.womenshealth.gov/bodyimage/bodywise/index.cfm

Mental illness

Alzheimers Association: www.alzheimers.org.uk
Breathing Space Scotland: www.breathingspacescotland.org.uk
Community Care: www.communitycare.co.uk
Depression Alliance: www.depressionalliance.org
Institute of Psychiatry: www.iop.kcl.ac.uk
MDF – The Bipolar Organisation: www.mdf.org.uk
Mental Health Care: www.mentalhealthcare.co.uk
Mental Health Foundation: www.mentalhealth.org.uk
MIND: www.mind.org.uk
National Self Harm Network: www.nshn.co.uk
Rethink – information for anyone affected by severe mental illness: www.rethink.org
Schizophrenia Association of Great Britain: www.sagb.co.uk
Scottish Association of Mental Health: www.samh.org.uk

Letter writing tips

Remember: letters, whether sent by email or ordinary mail, are important. Letters may be filed, kept, may be read by several/many professionals, may be used as evidence.
Decide:

- Size/type of paper? Lined or plain?
- Typed or handwritten?
- Any help needed? If so, who can help?
- General layout. There are different acceptable layouts – see below for basics. Giving your address and the date written are important. If possible, address the letter to someone whose name you know.
- Plan, make notes on what you want to write about.
- Write the letter:

  Give facts and observations, with dates if possible, clearly.

  Use separate paragraphs with a space between them for each point you want to make.

  Some useful sentence beginnings are given below.

  When giving observations you have made, be specific about dates and times, frequency of the behaviour(s).

  Think of the tone of the letter, how it will be read by others.

Remember – Keep It Short and Simple.

Sign your letter and print your name alongside/underneath your signature

- Read and reread to make sure you've said exactly what you want to, and included all the points you want considered.
- Keep a copy.
- Delay posting to check tone, nothing has been forgotten, etc. Rewrite if necessary.
- When satisfied, post letter.
- If no acknowledgment – and you feel the information you give is important and urgent – consider a follow up letter or phone call to check that your letter has arrived. Consider if checking acknowledgment is essential – can it wait until a next appointment? (Remember to allow for holidays, etc.)

General layout

(Name of house)	The Mansion
(Street)	1 Any Street
(Town)	Sunlit Town
(Postcode)	AB12 3CD
(Country)	Neverland
	Date

Dear

I write to express my concern about . . . (Remember – Keep It Short and Simple)
I am worried that . . .
On . . . (dates and approx times) *I observed/noted that . . .*
These incidents worry me because . . . (e.g. last time this happened frequently it was a sign of relapse/increased aggression/agitation/deterioration in . . . condition)
I feel it is important that . . .
I would like this matter discussed at . . .
I look forward to your reply.

(Very formal) *Yours faithfully*
(Informal) *Yours sincerely*
(Informal and friendly) *Best wishes*

Alison Brown (your signature)
ALISON BROWN (Printed)

References and bibliography

Aberdeen Press and Journal (2006) 'Fraudster son lost £160 000 on website', *Aberdeen Press and Journal*, 16 June 2006.

Adams, R., Dominelli, L. and Payne, M. (eds) (2002) *Social Work: Themes, Issues and Critical Debates*, 2nd edition. Basingstoke, UK: Macmillan Palgrave.

Agich, G.J. (1993) *Autonomy and Long-Term Care*. Oxford, UK: Oxford University Press.

Archer, C. (1999) *Next Steps in Parenting a Child Who Hurts: Tykes and Teens*, 2nd edition. London: Jessica Kingsley.

Baron-Cohen, S. and Bolton, P. (1993) *Autism: The Facts*. Oxford, UK: Oxford University Press.

BBC (2005) Interview with Dr Stephen Rosenman, Centre for Mental Health Research, Australian National University, BBC Radio 4 programme *All in the Mind*. 23 August 2005.

Beattie, M. (1987) *Codependent No More: How to Stop Controlling Others and Start Caring for Yourself*. Center City, MN: Hazelden Foundation.

The Big Issue (2006) 22/28 June 2006.

Bloomfield, S. (ed.) (2006) *Eating Disorders: Helping Your Child Recover*. Norwich, UK: Eating Disorders Association.

Bolton, R. (1979) *People Skills*. New York: Simon & Schuster.

Breaking Point – Families Still Need a Break (2006) Mencap Report. Mencap, London.

Burns, D.D. (1999) *The Feeling Good Handbook*, revised edition. New York: Plume The Penguin Group.

Carers and Confentiality – Developing Effective Relationships between Practitioners and Carers (2005) Edinburgh, UK: Mental Welfare Commission for Scotland.

Carter, R. (1994) *Helping Yourself to Help Others*. New York: Times Books.

Coat Outcome Agreement Tool (COAT) – A New Approach to Working with Family Carers (2006) Aldre Vast, Sjuharad Research Centre, University of Boras, and Socialstyrelsen, National Board of Health and Welfare, Sweden; Community, Ageing and Rehabilition/Department of Nursing and Midwifery, The University of Sheffield, UK.

Cochrane, K. (2006) 'Special report: Who cares about carers?' *New Statesman Magazine*. 12th June 2006.

Collins English Dictionary (2001) London: HarperCollins Publishers.

Cullis, B. and Bibb, S. (2004) *Bronte's Story. Tears, Trials and Triumphs: A Personal Battle with Anorexia*. Sydney: Random House Australia.

Daley, D.C. (1991) *Kicking Addictive Habits Once and For All: A Relapse Prevention Guide*. San Francisco, CA: Jossey-Bass Inc.

Department of Health (2001) *The Expert Patient: A New Approach to Disease Management for the 21st Century*. London: Department of Health.

Department of Health (2006) *Sharing Mental Health Information with Carers: Pointers to Good Practice for Service Providers, Continuity of Care Briefing Paper.* London: Department of Health.

Donaldson, M. (1978) *Children's Minds.* London: Harper Perennial; Fontana Press.

Eating Disorders in Scotland – Recommendations for Management and Treatment (2006) Edinburgh: NHS Quality Improvement Scotland.

Emerson, E., Toogood, A., Mansell, J., Barrelt, S. and Bell, C. (1987) Challenging Behaviour and Community Services: Introduction and Overview. *Mental Handicap* **15**(4), 166–169.

Forward, S. (1989) *Toxic Parents: Overcoming Their Legacy and Reclaiming Your Life.* London: Bantam Books.

Fromm-Reichmann, F. (1948) Notes on the development of treatment of schizophrenics by psychotherapy. *Psychiatry*, **11**, 263–273.

Goleman, D. (1996) *Emotional Intelligence.* London: Bloomsbury.

Goleman, D. (2003) *Destructive Emotions – and how we can overcome them: A Dialogue with the Dalai Lama.* London: Bloomsbury.

Gregory, J. (2000) *Bringing up a Challenging Child at Home: When Love is Not Enough.* London and Philadelphia: Jessica Kingsley.

Guardian (2005) Peace Talks – How intervention therapy helps heal wounds when schizophrenia leads to total breakdown in families [a description of the Meriden Project, Birmingham, run by Birmingham and Solihull Mental Health Trust]. *Guardian*, 28 September 2005.

Harris, J.R. (1998) *The Nurture Assumption.* London: Bloomsbury.

Harris, J.R. (1995) *Psychological Review*, **102**, 458–459.

HH the Dalai Lama and Cutler, H.C. (1998) *The Art of Happiness: A Handbook for Living.* London: Hodder & Stoughton.

James, O. (2003) *They F*** You Up.* London: Bloomsbury.

Jay, M. and Doganis, S. (1987) *Battered.* London: Weidenfeld & Nicolson.

Konstant, T. and Taylor, M. (n.d.) *Mental Space: how to find clarity in a complex life.* www.yourmomentum.com

Levitt, S.D. and Dubner, S.J. (2006) *Freakonomics: A Rogue Economist Explores the Hidden Side of Everything.* Harmondsworth, UK: Penguin Books.

Lorig, K. *et al.* (2001) *Chronic Disease Self-Management Program.* School of Medicine, Stanford University, CA.

Loudon, M. (2006) *Relative Stranger: A Life After Death.* Edinburgh, UK: Canongate.

Lovell, A. (1978) *In a Summer Garment.* London: Secker & Warburg.

Marr, A. (2004) *My Trade: A Short History of British Journalism.* Basingstoke, UK: Macmillan.

Marriott, H. (2003) *The Selfish Pig's Guide to Caring.* Clifton-upon-Teme, UK: Polperro Heritage Press.

McFarlan, B. (2003) *Drop the Pink Elephant: 21 Steps to Personal Communication Heaven.* Oxford, UK: Capstone Publishing Ltd.

Mearns, D. and Thorne, B. (1999) *Person Centred Counselling in Action.* London: Sage Publications.

Mental Health Foundation (2001) Is Anybody There? A Survey of Friendship and Mental Health, *The Mental Health Foundation Updates,* **2**(16).

Mueser, K.T. and Gingerich, S. (1994) *Coping with Schizophrenia.* Oakland, CA: New Harbinger Publications Inc.

Myers, R.J. and Smith, J.E. (1995) *Clinical Guide to Alcohol Treatment: The Community Reinforcement Approach.* New York: The Guilford Press.

National Institute of Clinical Excellence (2004) *Eating Disorders, Quick Reference Guide.* London, UK.
O'Regan, F.J. (2005) *ADHD.* London and New York: Continuum.
Orford, J. (2001) *Excessive Appetites: A Psychological View of Addictions,* 2nd edition. Chichester, UK: John Wiley & Sons.
Pinker, S. (2002) *The Blank Slate: The Modern Denial of Human Nature.* New York: Viking.
Prochaska, J.O. and DiClemente, C.C. (1992) *The Transtheoretical Model for Change: Handbook of Psychotherapy Integration.* New York: Basic Books.
Quilliam, S. (1998) *The Samaritans book of What to Do When You Really Want to Help But Dont Know How.* Hutton, Brentwood, Essex, UK: Transformation Press.
Ramsay, R., Gerada, G., Mars, S. and Szmukler, G. (eds) (2001) *Mental Illness: A Handbook for Carers.* London: Jessica Kingsley.
Ridley, M. (2000) *Genome.* London: HarperCollins.
Ridley, M. (2003) *Nature Via Nurture: Genes, Experience and What Makes us Human.* London: HarperCollins.
Royal College of Psychiatrists (2004) *Partners in Care* leaflet. London: Royal College of Psychiatrists.
Rutter, M. (1975) *Helping Troubled Children.* Harmondsworth, UK: Penguin.
Schmidt, U., Williams, C., Eisler, I., Fairbairn, P., McCloskey, C., Smith, G. and Treasure, J. (2006). *Overcoming Anorexia: Effective Caring.* London: Routledge.
Schmidt, U., Williams, C., Eisler, I., Fairburn, P., McCloskey, C., Smith, G. and Treasure, J. (2007) *Overcoming Anorexia: Effective Caring – CD-Rom.* Leeds, UK: Media Innovations.
Scottish Executive (2004) *Changing Lives.* Edinburgh, UK: Scottish Executive.
Scottish Health Committee (2005) Dr Harry Millar, in evidence to Eating Disorders Inquiry, Scottish Health Committee.
Skinner, R. and Cleese, J. (1989) *Families and How to Survive Them.* London: Mandarin.
Smeltzer, D. (2006) *Andrea's Voice: Silenced by Bulimia.* Carlsbad, CA: Gurze Books.
Smith, G. (2004) *Anorexia and Bulimia in the Family.* Chichester, UK: John Wiley & Sons.
Stalker, K., Paterson, L. and Ferguson, I. (2005) *Some-one to Talk to: A Study of Social Crisis Services.* Sitrling, UK: Department of Applied Social Science, University of Stirling.
Stewart, A. and Tan, J. (2006) *Treatment decision-making and the consideration of competence in anorexia nervosa: clinical decision-making frameworks derived from empirical medical ethics research.* AED Workshop, 2006 International Conference for Eating Disorders, Barcelona, Spain.
Sunday Herald (2006) Editorial, 27 June 2006.
Tan, J., Hope, T. and Stewart, A. (2003) Competence to refuse treatment in anorexia nervosa. *International Journal of Law and Psychiatry,* **26**(6), 697–707.
Tannen, D. (1992) *You Just Dont Understand: Men and Women in Conversation.* London: Virago Press.
Treasure, J., Gavan, K., Todd, G. and Schmidt, U. (2003a) Changing the environment in eating disorders: working with families to improve motivation and facilitate change. *European Eating Disorders Review,* **11**(1), 25–37.
Treasure, J., Schmidt, U. and van Furth, E. (2003b) *Handbook of Eating Disorders: Theory, Treatment and Research,* 2nd edition. Chichester, UK: John Wiley & Sons.

Treasure, J., Schmidt, U. and Hugo, P. (2005) Mind the gap: service transition and interface problems for patients with eating disorders. *British Journal of Psychiatry*, **187**, 398–400.

Treasure, J., Smith, G. and Crane, A. (2007) *Skills-based learning for caring for a loved one with at an eating disorder. The new Maudsley method.* London: Routledge/Psychology Press.

University of Birmingham (2005) Set of 3 questionnaires. School of Psychology, University of Birmingham, UK.

Velleman, R. and Orford, J. (1999) *Risk and Resilience: Adults Who Were the Children of Problem Drinkers.* London, Harwood.

Wassmer, A. (1989) *Recovering Together: How to Help an Alcoholic Without Hurting Yourself.* New York: St Martins Press.

Watzlawick, P. (1978) *The Language of Change: Elements of Therapeutic Communication.* New York: Basic Books.

Watzlawick, P. (1983) *The Situation is Hopeless, but not Serious.* New York: W.W. Norton.

Watzlawick, P., Beavin, J., Helmick and Jackson, D.D. (1967) *Pragmatics of Human Communication: A Study of Interactional Patterns, Pathologies, and Paradoxes.* New York: W.W. Norton.

Williams, C. (2005) Stages leading to family reorganisation around illness A Five Areas Approach .

World Health Organization (2000) *World Health Organization Guide to Mental Health in Primary Care.* London: Royal Society of Medicine Press.

Index

ERVING GOFFMAN

FORMS OF TALK

Basil Blackwell · Oxford

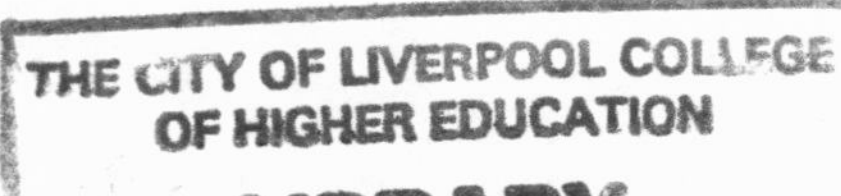

First published in 1981 by
Basil Blackwell Publisher
108 Cowley Road
Oxford OX4 1JF
England

British Library Cataloguing in Publication Data

Goffman, Erving
Forms of talk.
1. Communication
I. Title
402 P91.25

ISBN 0-631-12788-7

Printed in the United States of America

CONTENTS

INTRODUCTION

I

The five papers in this volume were written between 1974 and 1980, and are arranged in order of their completion. All deal with talk, and mainly the speaker's side of it. The first three were published as journal articles; they have been slightly revised. The last two are printed here for the first time. The three published papers are analytic and programmatic, leading to the very general statement in the third, the paper called "Footing." The two new papers could stand as substantive application of notions developed in the analytic ones. All the papers (least so the first) are written around the same frame-analytic themes, so the whole has something more than topical coherence. The whole also contains a very considerable amount of repetition. I state this last without much apology. The ideas purport to be general (in the sense of always applicable), and worth testing out. This is the warrant for repeated approaches from different angles and the eventual retracing of practically everything. Yet, of course, none of the concepts elaborated may have a future. So I ask that these papers be taken for what they merely are: exercises, trials, tryouts, a means of displaying possibilities, not establishing fact. This asking may be a lot, for the papers are proclamatory in style, as much distended by formulary optimism as most other endeavors in this field.

II

Everyone knows that when individuals in the presence of others respond to events, their glances, looks, and postural shifts carry all kinds of implication and meaning. When in these settings words are spoken, then tone of voice, manner of uptake, restarts, and the variously positioned pauses similarly qualify. As does manner of listening. Every adult is wonderfully accomplished in producing all of these effects, and wonderfully perceptive in catching their significance when performed by accessible others. Everywhere and constantly this gestural resource is employed, yet rarely itself is systematically examined. In retelling events—an activity which occupies much of our speaking time—we are forced to sketch in these shadings a little, rendering a few movements and tones into words to do so. In addition to this folk transcription, we can employ discourse theatrics, vivifying the replay with caricaturized reenactments. In both cases, we can rely on our audience to take the part for the whole and cooperatively catch our meaning. Thus, in talk about how individuals acted or will act, we can get by with a small repertoire of alludings and simulations. Fiction writers and stage performers extend these everyday capacities, carrying the ability to reinvoke beyond that possessed by the rest of us. But even here only sketching is found.

So it remains to microanalysts of interaction to lumber in where the self-respecting decline to tread. A question of pinning with our ten thumbs what ought to be secured with a needle.

III

With my own thumbs, in this volume I want to hold up three matters for consideration. First, the process of "ritualization"—if I may slightly recast the ethological version of that term. The movements, looks, and vocal sounds we make as an unintended by-product of speaking and listening never seem to remain innocent. Within the lifetime of each of us these acts in varying degrees acquire a specialized communicative role in the stream of our behavior, looked to and provided for in connection with the displaying of our alignment to current events. We look simply to see, see others looking, see we are seen looking, and soon become knowing and skilled in regard to the evidential uses made of the appearance of looking. We clear our throat, we pause to think, we turn attention to a next doing, and soon we specialize these acts, performing them with no felt contrivance right where others in our gestural community would also, and like them, we do so apart from the original instrumental reason for the act. Indeed, gestural conventions once established in a community can be acquired directly, the initial noncommunicative character of the practice (when there is such) serving merely as a guide in our acquiring gestural competency, ensuring that our learning how to be unthinkingly expressive won't be entirely rote. The purpose and functions of these displays cannot of course be caught by the term "expression," but only by closely examining the consequence each several gesture commonly has in samples of actual occurrences—with due consideration to the sorts of things that might be conveyed in the context had no such gesture been offered.

Second, "participation framework." When a word is spoken, all those who happen to be in perceptual range of the event will have some sort of participation status relative to it. The codification of these various positions and the normative specification of appropriate conduct within each provide an essential background for interaction analysis—whether (I presume) in our own society or any other.

Third, there is the obvious but insufficiently appreciated fact that words we speak are often not our own, at least our current "own." Who it is who can speak is restricted to the parties present (and often more restricted than that), and which one is now doing so is almost always perfectly clear. But although who speaks is situationally circumscribed, in whose name words are spoken is certainly not. Uttered words have utterers; utterances, however, have subjects (implied or explicit), and although these may designate the utterer, there is nothing in the syntax of utterances to require this coincidence. We can as handily quote another (directly or indirectly) as we can say something in our own name. (This embedding capacity is part of something more general: our linguistic ability to speak of events at any remove in time and space from the situated present.)

IV

So three themes: ritualization, participation framework, and embedding. It is their interplay that will be at issue. Every utterance and its hearing have gestural accompaniments, these under some control of the actors. Every utterance and its hearing bear the marks of the framework of participation in which the uttering and hearing occur. All these markings we can openly mimic, mime, and reenact, allowing us dramatic liberties. Thus, when we speak we can set into the current framework of participation what is structurally marked as integral to another, enacting a dozen voices to do so. (For example, in describing a conversation, we, as speaker, can enact what had been our unstated response as *listener.*)

In what follows, then, I make no large literary claim that social life is but a stage, only a small technical one: that deeply incorporated into the nature of talk are the fundamental requirements of theatricality.

1

REPLIES AND RESPONSES

This paper examines conversational dialogue.[1] It is divided into four parts. The first presents arguments for dialogic analysis, the second lists some failings, the third applies this critical view to the notion of a "reply"; the final part is an overview.

PART ONE

I

Whenever persons talk there are very likely to be questions and answers. These utterances are realized at different points in "sequence time." Notwithstanding the content of their questions, questioners are oriented to what lies just ahead, and depend on what is to come; answerers are oriented to what has just been said, and look backward, not forward. Observe that although a question anticipates an answer, is designed to receive it, seems dependent on doing so, an answer seems even more dependent, making less sense alone than does the utterance that called it forth. Whatever answers do, they must do this with something already begun.

1. Grateful acknowledgment is made to *Language in Society,* where this paper first appeared (5[1976]:257–313). Originally presented at NWAVE III, Georgetown University, 25 October 1974. A preprint was published by the Centro Internazionale di Semiotica e di Linguistica, Università di Urbino. I am grateful to Theresa Labov, William Labov, Susan Philips, and Lee Ann Draud for critical suggestions, many of which have been incorporated without further acknowledgment. I alone, therefore, am not responsible for all of the paper's shortcomings.

In questions and answers we have one example, perhaps the canonical one, of what Harvey Sacks has called a "first pair part" and a "second pair part," that is, a couplet, a minimal dialogic unit, a round two utterances long, each utterance of the same "type," each spoken by a different person, one utterance temporally following directly on the other; in sum, an example of an "adjacency pair." The first pair part establishes a "conditional relevance" upon anything that occurs in the slot that follows; whatever comes to be said there will be inspected to see how it might serve as an answer, and if nothing is said, then the resulting silence will be taken as notable—a rejoinder in its own right, a silence to be heard (Sacks 1973).

On the face of it, these little pairings, these dialogic units, these two-part exchanges, recommend a linguistic mode of analysis of a formalistic sort. Admittedly, the meaning of an utterance, whether question or answer, can ultimately depend in part on the specific semantic value of the words it contains and thus (in the opinion of some linguists) escape complete formalization. Nonetheless, a formalism is involved. The constraining influence of the question-answer format is somewhat independent of *what* is being talked about, and whether, for example, the matter is of great moment to those involved in the exchange or of no moment at all. Moreover, each participating utterance is constrained by the rules of sentence grammar, even though, as will be shown, inferences regarding underlying forms may be required to appreciate this.

II

What sort of analyses can be accomplished by appealing to the dialogic format?

First, there is the possibility of recovering elided elements of answers by referring to their first pair parts, this turning out to be evidence of a strength of sentence grammar, not (as might first appear) a weakness. To the question "How old are you?" the answer "I am eleven years old" is not necessary; "I am eleven" will do, and even, often, "Eleven." Given "Eleven" as an answer, a proper sentence can be recovered from it, provided only that one knows the question. Indeed, I believe that elements of the intonation contour of the underlying grammatical sentence are preserved, supplying confirmation to the interpretation and assurance that an appeal to the grammatically tacit is something more than the linguist's legerdemain. If, then—as Gunter has shown—the right pair parts are aptly chosen, answers with very strange surface structures can be shown to be understandable, and what seemed anything but a sentence can be coerced into grammatical form and be the better off for it. What is "said" is obscure; what is "meant" is obvious and clear:

A: "Who can see whom?"
B: "The man the boy." [Gunter 1974:17]

The same argument can be made about dangling or interrupted sentences, false starts, ungrammatical usage, and other apparent deviations from grammatical propriety.

Note that answers can take not only a truncated verbal form but also a wholly nonverbal form, in this case a gesture serving solely as a substitute—an "emblem," to use Paul Ekman's terminology (1969:63–68)—for lexical materials. To the question "What time is it?" the holding up of five fingers may do as well as words, even better in a noisy room. A semantically meaningful question is still being satisfied by means of a semantically meaningful answer.

Second, we can describe embedding and "side-sequence" (Jefferson 1972) features, whereby a question is not followed directly by an answer to it, but by another question meant to be seen as holding off proper completion for an exigent moment:

A_1: "Can I borrow your hose?"
B_2: "Do you need it this very moment?"
A_2: "No."
B_1: "Yes."

or even:

A_1 [To trainman in station] : "Have you got the time?"
B_2 : "Standard or Daylight Saving?"
A_3 : "What are you running on?"
B_3 : "Standard."
A_2 : "Standard then."
B_1 : "It's five o'clock."

Which, in turn, leads to a central issue so far not mentioned: the question of how adjacency pairs are linked together to form chains. For "chaining" presumably provides us with a means of moving analysis forward from single two-part exchanges to stretches of talk. Thus, one might want to distinguish the two-person interrogative chain:

A_1
B_1
A_2
B_2
etc.

whereby whoever provides a current question provides the next one, too (this turning out to have been a presupposition of the current utterance all along [Schegloff 1968:1080–81]), from the two-person sociable chain, whereby whoever provides a second pair part then goes on to provide the first pair part of the next pair:

A_1
B_1/B_2
    A_2/A_3
etc.

Combining the notion of ellipsis with the notion of chaining, we have, as Marilyn Merritt (1976) has suggested, the possibility of eliding at a higher level. Thus the typical:

i(a)A: "Have you got coffee to go?"
    B: "Milk and sugar?"
    A: "Just milk."

can be expanded to display an underlying structure:

i(b)A_1: "Have you got coffee to go?"
  [B_1] B_2: "Yes/Milk and sugar?"
        A_2: "Just milk."

an elision presumably based on the fact that an immediate query by the queried can be taken as tacit evidence of the answer that would make such a query relevant, namely, affirmation. Nor does expansion serve only to draw a couplet pattern from a three-piece unit. Thus:

ii(a) A: "Are you coming?"
B: "I gotta work."

can be viewed as a contraction of:

ii(b) A_1: "Are you coming?"
B_1: "No."
A_2: "Why aren't you?"
B_2: "I gotta work."

illustrating one interpretation (and the example) of the practice suggested by Stubbs,[2] namely, that an answer can be replaced by a reason for that answer. I might add that in what is to follow it will be useful to have a term to match and contrast with adjacency pair, a term to refer not to a question-answer couplet but rather to the second pair part of one couplet and the first pair part of the very next one, whether these parts appear within the same turn, as in:

A_1 : "Are they going?"
B_1/B_2: "Yes./Are you?"
A_2: "I suppose."

or across the back of two turns, as in:

A_1: "Are they going?"
B_1: "Yes."
A_2: "Are you?"
B_2: "I suppose."

I shall speak here of a "back pair."

III

Observe now that, broadly speaking, there are three kinds of listeners to talk: those who *over*hear, whether or not their unratified participation is inadvertent and whether or not it has been encouraged; those (in the case of more than two-person talk) who are ratified participants but are not specifically addressed by the speaker; and those ratified participants who *are* addressed, that is,

2. Stubbs (1973:18) recommends that a simple substitution rule can be at work not involving deletion.

oriented to by the speaker in a manner to suggest that his words are particularly for them, and that some answer is therefore anticipated from them, more so than from the other ratified participants. (I say "broadly speaking" because all sorts of minor variations are possible—for example, speaker's practice of drawing a particular participant into an exchange and then turning to the other participants as if to offer him and his words up for public delectation.)

It is a standard possibility in talk that an addressed recipient answers the speaker by saying that the sound did not carry or that although words could be heard, no sense could be made of them, and that, in consequence, a rerun is required, and if not that, then perhaps a rephrasing. There are many pat phrases and gestures for conveying this message, and they can be injected concerning any item in an ongoing utterance whensoever this fault occurs (Stubbs 1973:21).

All of this suggests that a basic normative assumption about talk is that, whatever else, it should be correctly interpretable in the special sense of conveying to the intended recipients what the sender more or less wanted to get across. The issue is not that the recipients should agree *with* what they have heard, but only agree with the speaker *as to what* they have heard; in Austinian terms, illocutionary force is at stake, not perlocutionary effect.

Some elaboration is required. Commonly a speaker cannot explicate with precision what he meant to get across, and on these occasions if hearers think they know precisely, they will likely be at least a little off. (If speaker and hearers were to file a report on what they assumed to be the full meaning of an extended utterance, these glosses would differ, at least in detail.) Indeed, one routinely presumes on a mutual understanding that doesn't quite exist. What one obtains is a working agreement, an agreement "for all practical purposes."[3] But that, I think, is quite enough.

3. The student, of course, can find another significance in this working agreement, namely, evidence of the work that must be engaged in locally on each occasion of apparently smooth mutual understanding and evidence of how thin the ice is that everyone skates on. More to the point, it seems that such cloudiness as might exist is usually located in higher order laminations. Thus, A and B may have the same understanding about what A said and meant, but one or both can fail to understand that this agreement exists. If A and B both appreciate that they both have the same understanding about what A said and

The edging into ambiguity that is often found is only significant, I think, when interpretive uncertainties and discrepancies exceed certain limits or are intentionally induced and sustained (or thought to be by hearers), or are exploited after the fact to deny a legitimate accusation concerning what the speaker indeed by and large had meant. A serious request for a rerun on grounds of faulty reception is to be understood, then, not as a request for complete understanding—God save anyone from that—but for understanding that is on a par with what is ordinarily accepted as sufficient: understanding subject to, but not appreciably impaired by, "normatively residual" ambiguity.

Observe that the issue here of "normatively residual" ambiguity does not have to do with the three kinds of speech efficiency with which some students have confused it. First, the matter is not that of deixis or, as it is coming to be called, indexicality. An indexical such as "me" or "that one" can be rather clear and unambiguous as far as participants in the circle of use are concerned, the ambiguity only occurring to readers of isolated bits of the text of the talk. Second, ellipsis is not involved, for here again participants can easily be quite clear as to what was meant even though those faced with a transcribed excerpt might not agree on an expansion of the utterance. Finally, the issue is not that of the difference between what is "literally" said and what is conveyed or meant. For although here, too, someone coming upon the line out of the context of events, relationships, and mutual knowingness in which it was originally voiced might misunderstand, the speaker and hearers nonetheless can be perfectly clear about what was intended—or at least no less clear than they are about an utterance meant to be taken at face value.[4] (Indeed, it is in contrast to these three forms of mere laconicity that we can locate *functional* ambiguities, difficulties such as genuine uncertainty, genuine misunderstanding, the simulation of these difficulties, the suspicion that real difficulty has occurred, the suspicion that difficulty has been pretended, and so forth.)

meant, one or both can still fail to realize that they both appreciate that they both have the same understanding.

4. A useful treatment of the situated clarity of apparently ambiguous statements is available in Crystal (1969:102–3). The whole article contains much useful material on the character of conversation.

Given the possibility and the expectation that effective transmission will occur during talk, we can ask what conditions or arrangements would facilitate this and find some obvious answers. It would be helpful, for example, to have norms constraining interruption or simultaneous talk and norms against withholding of answers. It would be helpful to have available, and oblige the use of, "back-channel"[5] cues (facial gestures and nonverbal vocalizations) from hearers so that *while* the speaker was speaking, he could know, among other things, that he was succeeding or failing to get across, being informed of this while attempting to get across. (The speaker might thereby learn that he was not persuading his hearers, but that is another matter.) Crucial here are bracket-confirmations, the smiles, chuckles, headshakes, and knowing grunts through which the hearer displays appreciation that the speaker has sustained irony, hint, sarcasm, playfulness, or quotation across a strip of talk and is now switching back to less mitigated responsibility and literalness. Useful, too, would be a hold signal through which an addressed recipient could signal that transmission to him should be held up for a moment, this hold signal in turn requiring an all-clear cue to indicate that the forestalled speaker might now resume transmission. It would also be useful to enjoin an addressed recipient to *follow* right after current speaker with words or gestures showing that the message has been heard and understood, or, if it hasn't, that it hasn't.

Given a speaker's need to know whether his message has been received, and if so, whether or not it has been passably understood, and given a recipient's need to show that he has received the message and correctly—given these very fundamental requirements of talk as a communication system—we have the essential rationale for the very existence of adjacency pairs, that is, for the organization of talk into two-part exchanges.[6] We have an understanding of why any next utterance after a question is examined for how it might be an answer.

More to the point, we have grounds for extending this two-

5. See Yngve (1970:567–78); and Duncan (1972:283–92).
6. See Goffman (1967:38); and Schegloff and Sacks (1973:297–98).

part format outward from pairs of utterances which it seems perfectly to fit—questions and answers—to other kinds of utterance pairs, this being an extension that Sacks had intended. For when a declaration or command or greeting or promise or request or apology or threat or summons is made, it still remains the case that the initiator will need to know that he has gotten across; and the addressed recipient will need to make it known that the message has been correctly received. Certainly when an explanation is given the giver needs to know that it has been understood, else how can he know when to stop explaining? (Bellack et al. 1966: 2). And so once again the first pair part co-opts the slot that follows, indeed makes a slot out of next moments, rendering anything occurring then subject to close inspection for evidence as to whether or not the conditions for communication have been satisfied.

Given that we are to extend our dialogic format—our adjacency pairs—to cover a whole range of pairs, not merely questions and answers, terms more general than "question" and "answer" ought to be introduced, general enough to cover all the cases. For after all, an assertion is not quite a question, and the rejoinder to it is not quite an answer. Instead, then, of speaking of questions and answers, I will speak of "statements" and "replies," intentionally using "statement" in a broader way than is sometimes found in language studies, but still retaining the notion that an initiating element is involved, to which a reply is to be oriented.

Once we have begun to think about the transmission requirements for utterances and the role of adjacency pairing in accomplishing this, we can go on to apply the same sort of thinking to sequences or chains of statement-reply pairs, raising the question concerning what arrangements would facilitate the extended flow of talk. We could attend the issue of how next speaker is selected (or self-selects) in more-than-two-person talk (Sacks, Schegloff, and Jefferson 1974:696–735), and (following the structuring the above have nicely uncovered) how utterances might be built up to provide sequences of points where transition to next speaker is facilitated and even promoted but not made mandatory, the speaker leaving open the possibility of himself continuing on as if he had not encouraged his own retirement from the speaker role. We could also examine how a speaker's restarts and pauses (filled and otherwise) might function both to allow for his momentary failure to obtain listener attention and to remind intended recipients of their inattention.[7] And after that, of course, we could pose the same question regarding the initiating and terminating of a conversation considered as a total unit of communication.[8] We would thus be dealing with talk as a communications engineer might, someone optimistic about the possibility of culture-free formulations. I shall speak here of system requirements and system constraints.

A sketch of some of these system requirements is possible:

1. A two-way capability for transceiving acoustically adequate and readily interpretable messages.
2. Back-channel feedback capabilities for informing on reception while it is occurring.
3. Contact signals: means of announcing the seeking of a channeled connection, means of ratifying that the sought-for channel is now open, means of closing off a theretofore open channel. Included here, identification-authentication signs.
4. Turnover signals: means to indicate ending of a message and the taking over of the sending role by next speaker. (In the case of talk with more than two persons, next-speaker selection signals, whether "speaker selects" or "self-select" types.)
5. Preemption signals: means of inducing a rerun, holding off channel requests, interrupting a talker in progress.

7. C. Goodwin (1977).

8. In this paper, following the practice in sociolinguistics, "conversation" will be used in a loose way as an equivalent of talk or spoken encounter. This neglects the special sense in which the term tends to be used in daily life, which use, perhaps, warrants a narrow, restricted definition. Thus, conversation, restrictively defined, might be identified as the talk occurring when a small number of participants come together and settle into what they perceive to be a few moments cut off from (or carried on to the side of) instrumental tasks; a period of idling felt to be an end in itself, during which everyone is accorded the right to talk as well as to listen and without reference to a fixed schedule; everyone is accorded the status of someone whose overall evaluation of the subject matter at hand—whose editorial comments, as it were—is to be encouraged and treated with respect; and no final agreement or synthesis is demanded, differences of opinion to be treated as unprejudicial to the continuing relationship of the participants.

6. Framing capabilities: cues distinguishing special readings to apply across strips of bracketed communication, recasting otherwise conventional sense, as in making ironic asides, quoting another, joking, and so forth; and hearer signals that the resulting transformation has been followed.
7. Norms obliging respondents to reply honestly with whatever they know that is relevant and no more.[9]
8. Nonparticipant constraints regarding eavesdropping, competing noise, and the blocking of pathways for eye-to-eye signals.

We can, then, draw our basic framework for face-to-face talk from what would appear to be the sheer physical requirements and constraints of any communication system, and progress from there to a sort of microfunctional analysis of various interaction signals and practices. Observe that wide scope is found here for formalization; the various events in this process can be managed through quite truncated symbols, and not only can these symbols be given discrete, condensed physical forms, but also the role of live persons in the communication system can be very considerably reduced. Observe, too, that although each of the various signals can be expressed through a continuum of forms—say as "commands," "requests," "intimations"—none of this is to the point; these traditional discriminations can be neglected provided only that it is assumed that the participants have jointly agreed to operate (in effect) solely as communication nodes, as transceivers, and to make themselves fully available for that purpose.

IV

No doubt there are occasions when one can hear:

A: "What's the time?"
B: "It's five o'clock."

as the entire substance of a brief social encounter—or as a self-contained element therein—and have thereby a naturally bounded unit, one whose boundedness can be nicely accounted

9. In the manner of H. P. Grice's "conversational maxims," deriving from the "cooperative principle" (Grice 1975).

for by appealing to system requirements and the notion of an adjacency pair. But much more frequently something not quite so naked occurs. What one hears is something like this:

(i) A: "Do you have the time?"
(ii) B: "Sure. It's five o'clock."
(iii) A: "Thanks."
(iv) B: [Gesture] " 'T's okay."

in which (i) albeit serving as a request, also functions to neutralize the potentially offensive consequence of encroaching on another with a demand, and so may be called a "remedy"; in which (ii) demonstrates that the potential offender's effort to nullify offense is acceptable, and so may be called "relief"; in which (iii) is a display of gratitude for the service rendered and for its provider not taking the claim on himself amiss, and may be called "appreciation"; and in which (iv) demonstrates that enough gratitude has been displayed, and thus the displayer is to be counted a properly feeling person, this final act describable as "minimization" (Goffman 1971:139–43). What we have here is also a little dialogic unit, naturally bounded in the sense that it (and its less complete variants) may fill out the whole of an encounter or, occurring within an encounter, allow for a longish pause upon its completion and an easy shift to another conversational matter. But this time actions are directed not merely to system constraints; this time an additional set apply, namely, constraints regarding how each individual ought to handle himself with respect to each of the others, so that he not discredit his own tacit claim to good character or the tacit claim of the others that they are persons of social worth whose various forms of territoriality are to be respected. Demands for action are qualified and presented as mere requests which can be declined. These declinables are in turn granted with a show of good spirit, or, if they are to be turned down, a mollifying reason is given. Thus the asker is hopefully let off the hook no matter what the outcome of his request.

Nor are these ritual contingencies restricted to commands and requests. In making an assertion about facts, the maker must count on not being considered hopelessly wrongheaded; if a greeting, that contact is wanted; if an excuse, that it will be acceptable; if an avowal of feeling and attitude, that these will be credited; if a summons, that it will be deferred to; if a serious offer, that it won't be considered presumptuous or mean; if an overgenerous one, that it will be declined; if an inquiry, that it won't be thought intrusive; if a self-deprecating comment, that it will be denied. The pause that comes after a tactfully sustained exchange is possible, then, in part because the participants have arrived at a place that each finds viable, each having acquitted himself with an acceptable amount of self-constraint and respect for the others present.

I have called such units "ritual interchanges."[10] Ordinarily each incorporates at least one two-part exchange but may contain additional turns and/or additional exchanges. Observe that although system constraints might be conceived of as pancultural, ritual concerns are patently dependent on cultural definition and can be expected to vary quite markedly from society to society. Nonetheless, the ritual frame provides a question that can be asked of anything occurring during talk and a way of accounting for what does occur. For example, back-channel expression not

10. Goffman (1967:19–22). The notion of ritual interchange allows one to treat two-part rounds, that is, adjacency pairs, as one variety and to see that ritual as well as system considerations have explanatory power here; that ritual considerations help produce many naturally bounded interchanges that have, for example, three or four parts, not merely two; and that delayed or nonadjacent sequencing is possible.

The term "ritual" is not particularly satisfactory because of connotations of otherworldliness and automaticity. Gluckman's recommendation, "ceremonious" (in his "Les rites de passage" [1962:20–23]), has merit except that the available nouns (ceremony and ceremonial) carry a sense of multiperson official celebration. "Politeness" has some merit, but rather too closely refers to matters necessarily of no substantive import, and furthermore cannot be used to refer to pointed offensiveness, "impoliteness" being too mild a term. The term "expressive" is close because the behavior involved is always treated as a means through which the actor portrays his relation to objects of value in their own right, but "expressive" also carries an implication of "natural" sign or symptom.

A compendium of ritual interchanges analyzed in terms of the "second assessments" which follow first pair parts, such as evaluative judgments, self-deprecations, and compliments, has recently been presented in Pomerantz (1975).

only lets the speaker know whether or not he is getting across while he is trying to, but also can let him know whether or not what he is conveying is socially acceptable, that is, compatible with his hearers' view of him and of themselves.

Note that insofar as participants in an encounter morally commit themselves to keeping conversational channels open and in good working order, whatever binds by virtue of system constraints will bind also by virtue of ritual ones. The satisfaction of ritual constraints safeguards not only feelings but communication, too.

For example, assuming a normatively anticipated length to an encounter, and the offensiveness of being lodged in one without anything to say, we can anticipate the problem of "safe supplies," that is, the need for a stock of inoffensive, ready-to-hand utterances which can be employed to fill gaps. And we can see an added function—the prevention of offensive expressions—for the organizational devices which reduce the likelihood of gaps and overlaps.

In addition to making sure someone (and only one) is always at bat, there will be the issue of sustaining whatever is felt to be appropriate by way of continuity of topic and tone from previous speaker's statement to current speaker's, this out of respect both for previous speaker (especially when he had provided a statement, as opposed to a reply) and, vaguely, for what it was that had been engrossing the participants.[11]

As suggested, communication access is itself caught up in ritual concerns: to decline a signal to open channels is something like declining an extended hand, and to make a move to open a channel is to presume that one will not be intruding. Thus, opening is ordinarily requested, not demanded, and often an initiator

11. We thus find that participants have recourse to a series of "weak bridges"—transparent shifts in topic hedged with a comment which shows that the maker is alive to the duties of a proper interactant: "reminds me of the time," "not to change the subject," "oh, by the way," "now that you mention it," "speaking of," "incidentally," "apropos of," etc. These locutions provide little real subject-matter continuity between currently ending and proposed topic, merely deference to the need for it. (Less precarious bridges are found when one individual "matches" another's story with one from his own repertoire.)

will preface his talk with an apology for the interruption and a promise of how little long the talk will be, the assumption being that the recipient has the right to limit how long he is to be active in this capacity. (On the whole, persons reply to more overtures than they would like to, just as they attempt fewer openings than they might want.) Once a state of talk has been established, participants are obliged to temper their exploitation of these special circumstances, neither making too many demands for the floor nor too few, neither extolling their own virtues nor too directly questioning those of the others, and, of course, all the while maintaining an apparent rein on hostility and a show of attention to current speaker. So, too, withdrawal by a particular participant aptly expresses various forms of disapproval and distance and therefore must itself be managed tactfully.

Instead, then, of merely an arbitrary period during which the exchange of messages occurs, we have a social encounter, a coming together that ritually regularizes the risks and opportunities face-to-face talk provides, enforcing the standards of modesty regarding self and considerateness for others generally enjoined in the community, but now incidentally doing so in connection with the special vehicles of expression that arise in talk. Thus, if, as Schegloff and Sacks suggest (1973: 300 ff.), a conversation has an opening topic which can be identified as its chief one, then he or she who would raise a "delicate" point might want to "talk past" the issue at the beginning and wait until it can be introduced at a later place in the conversation more likely to allow for lightly pressed utterances (say, as an answer to a question someone else raises), all of which management requires some understanding of issues such as delicacy. Participants, it turns out, are obliged to look not so much for ways of expressing themselves, as for ways of making sure that the vast expressive resources of face-to-face interaction are not inadvertently employed to convey something unintended and untoward. Motivated to preserve everyone's face, they then end up acting so as to preserve orderly communication.

The notion of ritual constraints helps us to mediate between the particularities of social situations and our tendency to think in terms of general rules for the management of conversational interplay. We are given a means of overcoming the argument that any generalization in this area must fall because every social situation is different from every other. In brief, we have a means of attending to what it is about different social situations that makes them relevantly different for the management of talk.

For example, although a request for coffee allows the counterman to elect to elide an answer and move directly into a question of his own, "Milk and sugar?", this option turns out, of course, to be available only in limited strategic environments. When an individual asks a salesperson whether or not a large object is in stock—such as a Chevy Nova with stick shift or a house with a corner lot—the server may well assume that he has a prospective customer, not necessarily an actual one, and that to omit the "Yes" and to go right into the next level of specification, i.e., "What color?" or "How many rooms?", might be seen, for example, to be snide. For a purchase at this scale ordinarily requires time and deliberation. The server can assume that whatever remarks he first receives, his job is to establish a selling relationship, along with the sociability-tinged, mutually committed occasion needed to support an extended period of salesmanship. The salesman will thus take the customer's opening remarks as a call for an appreciable undertaking, not merely a bid for a piece of information. At the other extreme, the question, "Do you have the time?" is designed never to be answered in such a way that another utterance, "Can you tell me it?" will be necessary—so much so that the setting up of this second request becomes available as an open joke or a pointed insult.

May I add that a feature of face-to-face interaction is not only that it provides a scene for playing out of ritually relevant expressions, but also that it is the location of a special class of quite conventionalized utterances, lexicalizations whose controlling purpose is to give praise, blame, thanks, support, affection, or show gratitude, disapproval, dislike, sympathy, or greet, say farewell, and so forth. Part of the force of these speech acts comes from the feelings they directly index; little of the force derives from the semantic content of the words. We can refer here to interpersonal verbal rituals. These rituals often serve a bracketing function, celebratively marking a perceived change in the physical and social accessibility of two individuals to each other (Goffman 1971: 62–94), as well as beginnings and endings—of a day's activity, a social occasion, a speech, an encounter, an interchange. So in addition to the fact that any act performed during talk will carry ritual significance, some seem to be specialized for this purpose—ritualized in the ethological sense—and these play a special role in the episoding of conversation.

We might, then, for purposes of analysis, try to construct a simple ritual model, one that could serve as a background for all those considerations of the person which are referred to as "ego," "personal feelings," *amour-propre,* and so forth. The general design, presumably, is to sustain and protect through expressive means what can be supportively conveyed about persons and their relationships.

1. An act is taken to carry implications regarding the character of the actor and his evaluation of his listeners, as well as reflecting on the relationship between him and them.
2. Potentially offensive acts can be remedied by the actor through accounts and apologies, but this remedial work must appear to be accepted as sufficient by the potentially offended party before the work can properly be terminated.
3. Offended parties are generally obliged to induce a remedy if none is otherwise forthcoming or in some other way show that an unacceptable state of affairs has been created, else, in addition to what has been conveyed about them, they can be seen as submissive regarding others' lapses in maintaining the ritual code.

And just as system constraints will always condition how talk is managed, so, too, will ritual ones. Observe that unlike grammatical constraints, system and ritual ones open up the possibility of corrective action as part of these very constraints. Grammars do not have rules for managing what happens when rules are broken (a point made by Stubbs [1973:19]). Observe, too, that the notion of ritual constraints complicates the idea of adjacency pairs but apparently only that; the flow of conversation can still be seen as parcelled out into these relatively self-contained units, the relevance of first slot for second slot appreciated—but now all this for added reasons.

PART TWO

System constraints reinforced by ritual constraints provide us with an effective means of interpreting some of the details of conversational organization. This is no longer news. The point of having reviewed the arguments is to question the adequacy of the analysis that results. For although a focus on system and ritual constraints has considerable value, it also has substantial limitations. It turns out that the statement-reply format generating dialoguelike structures covers some possibilities better than others. Consider, then, some problems introduced by this perspective.

I

First, the embarrassing question of units.

The environing or contextual unit of considerable linguistic concern is the sentence—". . . an independent linguistic form, not included by virtue of any grammatical construction in any larger linguistic form"[12]—in which the contained or dependent units are morphemes, words, and more extended elements such as phrases and clauses. In natural talk, sentences do not always have the surface grammatical form grammarians attribute to the well-formed members of the class, but presumably these defectives can be expanded by regular editing rules to display their inner normalcy.

The term "sentence" is currently used to refer to something that is spoken, but the early analysis of sentences seemed much caught up in examination of the written form. The term "utterance" has therefore come into use to underscore reference to a spoken unit. In this paper I shall use the term "utterance" residually to refer to spoken words as such, without concern about the naturally bounded units of talk contained within them or containing them.

Now clearly, a sentence must be distinguished from its interactional cousin, namely, everything that an individual says

12. Bloomfield (1946:170). His definition seems to have been a little optimistic. Grammatical elements of well-formed sentences can be dependent on neighboring sentences. See Gunter (1974:9–10).

during his exercise of a turn at talk, "a stretch of talk, by one person, before and after which there is silence on the part of the person."[13] I shall speak here of talk during a turn, ordinarily reserving the term "turn" or "turn at talk" to refer to an opportunity to hold the floor, not what is said while holding it.[14]

Obviously the talk of a turn will sometimes coincide with a sentence (or what can be expanded into one), but on many occasions a speaker will provide his hearers with more than a one sentence-equivalent stretch. Note, too, that although a turn's talk may contain more than one sentence-equivalent, it must contain at least one.

Now the problem with the concepts of sentence and talk during a turn is that they are responsive to linguistic, not interactional, analysis. If we assume that talk is somehow dialogic and goes on piecing itself out into interchange spurts, then we must obtain our unit with this in mind. As suggested, a sentence is not the analytically relevant entity, because a respondent could employ several in what is taken to be a single interactionally relevant event. Even something so glaringly answer-oriented and so dear to the grammarian's heart as a well-formed question regarding fact can be rhetorical in character, designed to flesh out the speaker's remarks, adding a little more weight and color or a terminal dollop, but not meant to be specifically answered in its own right. (In fact, so much is a rhetorical question not to be specifically answered that it becomes available as something the apt answering of which is automatically a joke or quip.)

But just as clearly, the talk during an entire turn can't be used either—at least not as the most elementary term—for, as suggested, one of the main patterns for chaining rounds is the one in which whoever answers a question goes on from there to provide the next question in the series, thereby consolidating during one turn at talk two relevantly different doings. And indeed, a question may be shared by two persons—one individ-

13. By which Zellig Harris (1951:14) defines utterance. Bloomfield (1946) apparently also used "utterance" to refer to talk done during one turn.

14. Susan Philips (1974:160) has suggested use of the term "a speaking" in this latter connection, and I have in places followed her practice, as well as Sacks' locution, "a turn's talk."

ual stepping in and finishing off what another has begun—all for the edification of a third party, the addressed recipient (Sacks 1967), who does not thereby lose a beat in the sequencing of his own reply. Thus, the talk during two different turns can yet function as one interactional unit. In fact, an addressed recipient can step in and help a slow speaker find the word or phrase he seems to be looking for, then follow this with a reply, thereby combining in one turn at talk some of two *different* parties' contribution to the dialogue. In general, then, although the boundary of a sequence-relevant unit and the boundary of a speaking commonly coincide, this must be seen as analytically incidental. We are still required to decide which concern will be primary: the organization of turns *per se* or the sequencing of interaction.[15] And we must sustain this discrimination even though the two terms, turn and interaction sequence, seem nigh synonymous.

In order to attack this problem, I propose to use a notion whose definition I cannot and want not to fix very closely—the notion of a "move."[16] I refer to any full stretch of talk or of its substitutes which has a distinctive unitary bearing on some set or other of the circumstances in which participants find themselves (some "game" or other in the peculiar sense employed by Wittgenstein), such as a communication system, ritual constraints, economic negotiating, character contests, "teaching cycles" (Bellack et al. 1966:119–20), or whatever. It follows that an utterance which is a move in one game may also be a move in another, or be but a part of such other, or contain two or more such others. And a move may sometimes coincide with a sentence and sometimes with a turn's talk but need do neither. Correspondingly, I redefine the notion of a "statement" to refer to a move characterized by an orientation to some sort of answering to follow, and the notion of "reply" to refer to a move characterized by its being seen as an answering of some kind to a preceding matter that has been raised. Statement and reply, then, refer to moves, not to sentences or to speakings.

15. A point also made, and made well, by Sinclair et al. (1970–72:72).

16. See Goffman (1961:35), and (1972:138 ff.). Sinclair et al. (1972), following Bellack et al. (1966), uses the term "move" in a somewhat similar way.

The notion of move gives some immediate help with matters such as types of silence. For example, there will be two kinds of silence after a conversational move has been completed: the silence that occurs between the back-pair moves a single speaker can provide during one turn at talk, and the one that occurs between his holding of the floor and the next person's holding.[17]

II

Although it is clear that ritual constraints reinforce system ones, deepening a pattern that has already been cut, qualifications must be noted. A response will on occasion leave matters in a ritually unsatisfactory state, and a turn by the initial speaker will be required, encouraged, or at least allowed, resulting in a *three*-part interchange; or chains of adjacency pairs will occur (albeit typically with one, two, or three such couplets), the chain itself having a unitary, bounded character.

Moreover, standard conflicts can occur between the two sets of conditions. Ritual constraints on the initiation of talk, for example, are likely to function one way for the superordinate and another for the subordinate, so that what is orderliness from the superior's position may be excommunication from the inferior's.

Cultural variation is important here as well. Thus it is reported of Indians on the Warm Springs reservation in Oregon that because of obligations of modesty, young women may have answers they can't offer to questions (V. Hymes 1974: 7–8), and questioning itself may be followed with a decorum a communications engineer might well deplore:

> Unlike our norm of interaction, that at Warm Springs does not require that a question by one person be followed immediately by an answer or a promise of an answer from the addressee. It *may* be followed by an answer but may also be followed by silence or by

17. Silences *during* the completion of a move differently figure, recommending concern for cognitive, as much as ritual, matters. Thus there appears to be a difference between a "juncture pause" occurring after an encoding unit such as a "phonemic clause," and one occurring during such a unit. The first is likely to be easily disattendable, the second is more likely to be seen as a break in fluency. Here see Boomer (1965:148–58); and Dittmann (1972:135–51).

> an utterance that bears no relationship to the question. Then the answer to the question may follow as long as five or ten minutes later. [ibid., p.9]

Also when utterances are not heard or understood, the failing hearer can feel obliged to affect signs of comprehension, thus forestalling correction and, in consequence, forestalling communication. For to ask for a rerun can be to admit that one has not been considerate enough to listen or that one is insufficiently knowledgeable to understand the speaker's utterance or that the speaker himself may not know how to express himself clearly—in all cases implying something that the uncomprehending person may be disinclined to convey.

III

Once we have considered the differential impact of system and ritual constraints upon talk we can go on to consider a more complicated topic, namely, the inversionary effects of both these sets of constraints.

When, during a conversation, communication or social propriety suddenly breaks down, pointed effort will likely follow to set matters right. At such moments what ordinarily function as mere constraints upon action become the ends of action itself. Now we must see that this shift from means to ends has additional grounds.

Although rerun signals are to be initially understood in obvious functional terms, in fact in actual talk they are much employed in a devious way, a standard resource for saying one thing—which propositional content can be withdrawn to if needs be—while meaning another. The same can be said of apparent "unhearings" and misunderstandings, for these also provide the apparently beset recipient a means of intentionally breaking the flow of the other's communication under the cover of untendentious difficulty.

What is true here of system constraints is, I think, even more true of ritual ones. Not only will conventional expressions of concern and regard be employed transparently as a thin cover for allusions to one's own strengths and others' failings, but just what might otherwise be protected by tact can delineate the target of abuse. As if on the assumption that other's every move is to be taken as something requiring remedial correction (lest one be seen as lax in the exaction of justice to oneself), assertions can be followed by direct denials, questions by questioning the questioner, accusations by counter-accusations, disparagement by insults in kind, threats by taunting their realization, and other inversions of mutual consideration. Here adjacency pairing and the normative sequence of remedy, relief, appreciation, and minimization continue to provide a scaffold of expectations, but now employed as a means for rejecting blame, according it without license, and generally giving offense. Neatly bounded interchanges are produced, well formed to prevent at least one of the participants from establishing a tenable position.[18]

IV

Having accounted for the prevalence of the two-person dialogic format by reference to the effective way in which it can satisfy system and ritual constraints, we can go on to examine organization that doesn't fit the format.

1. There are, for example, standard three-person plays:

> 1st speaker: "Where is this place?"
> 2nd speaker: "I don't know. You know, don't you?"
> 3rd speaker: "It's just north of Depoe Bay." [Philips 1974:160]

in which the third speaker's reply will bear a relation to first speaker's question, but a complicated one. Also to be noted are

18. Close recordings and analysis of chronic set-tos are available in M. Goodwin (1978). See also M. Goodwin (1975). An attempt at structural analysis of some standard adult gambits is made in Goffman (1971:171–83). Polite forms of these inversionary tactics constitute the repartee in plays and other literary texts, these neat packagings of aggression being taken as the essence of conversation, when in fact they are probably anything but that. Note, it is children more than adults who are subject to open blaming and given to making open jibes, so it is children who are the mature practitioners here. In any case, the great catalogue of inversionary interchanges was published some time ago in two volumes in connection with children by Lewis Carroll, thereby providing the Englishry with linguistic models to follow in the pursuit of bickering as an art form.

standard arrangements, as, for example, in classrooms, in which a speaker obliges a number of persons to cite their answers to a problem or opinions on an issue. In such cases, second respondent will wait for first respondent to finish, but second respondent's reply will not be an *answer* to first respondent, merely something to follow in sequence, resulting at most in a comparative array. This is but an institutionalized form of what is commonly found in conversation. As Clancy suggests, a speaker can answer to a topic or theme, as opposed to a statement:

> A large number of interruptions, however, do not appear to be so specifically precipitated by the preceding message. Instead, the interrupting speaker says something brought to mind by the whole general topic of conversation. In this case, speaker ignores the immediately preceding sentences to which he has proudly not paid attention since his idea occurred to him, and he interrupts to present his idea despite the non-sequitur element of his sentence. [1972:84]

Further, there is the obstinate fact that during informal conversation, especially the multiperson kind, an individual *can* make a statement such that the only apparent consequence is that the next speaker will allow him to finish before changing the topic, a case of patent disregard for *what* a person says. And, of course, when this happens, a third participant can decide to reply not to the last statement, the adjacent one, but to the one before, thus bypassing last speaker (Philips 1974:166). And if the first speaker himself reenters immediately after receiving a nonreply, he will be well situated to continue his original statement as if he had not terminated it, thus recognizing that a nonreply has occurred (Clancy 1972:84).

2. It is also an embarrassing fact that the ongoing back-channel cues which listeners provide a speaker may, as it were, "surface" at episodic junctures in the speaking, providing, thus, a clear signal that understanding and sympathy have followed this far. *Gee, gosh, wow, hmm, tsk, no!* are examples of such keep-going signals. Now these boosterlike encouragements could be counted as a turn at talk, yet obviously the individual who provides them does not "get the floor" to do so, does not become the ratified speaker. Thus, what is perceived as a single speaking, a

single go at getting something said, a single period of having the floor, can carry across several of these looked-for and appreciated interruptions.

Furthermore, it appears that the possibility of speaking *without having the floor or trying to get it* can itself be pointedly used, relied upon, in conveying asides, parenthetical remarks, and even quips, all of whose point depends upon their not being given any apparent sequence space in the flow of events. (Asides cause their maker embarrassment if ratified as something to be given the floor and accorded an answer, indeed such a reception becomes a way of stamping out the act, not showing it respect.)

All of which leads to a very deep complaint about the statement-reply formula. Although many moves seem either to call for a replying move or to constitute such a move, we must now admit that not all do, and for the profoundest reasons. For it seems that in much spoken interaction participants are given elbow room to provide at no sequence cost an evaluative expression of what they take to be occurring. They are given a free ride. (The surfacing of back-channel communication is but one example.) Thereby they can make their position felt, make their alignment to what is occurring known, without committing others to address themselves openly to these communications. (The common practice, already mentioned, whereby a teacher uses an answer to his question as an occasion for evaluating the merit of the reply suggests how institutionalized this can become.) Although such "reacting" moves—to use Bellack's term (1966: 18–19)—may be occasioned by, and meant to be seen as occasioned by, a prior move, they have a special status in that the prior speaker need not take it from their occurrence that his statement has been replied to. Nor need anyone who follows the reacting move take it that a reply to it is due. (Which is not to say that evaluative responses are not often pressed into service as replies.)

PART THREE

I want now to raise the issue of replies and responses but require a preface to do so.

I

It is a central property of "well-formed" sentences that they can stand by themselves. One can be pulled out at random and stuck on the board or printed page and yet retain its interpretability, the words and their order providing all the context that is necessary. Or so it seems.[19]

It can be recommended that the power of isolated, well-formed sentences to carry meaning for students of language and to serve so well for so many of the purposes of grammarians is a paradoxical thing. In effect, it is not that the grammarian's perspective can make sense out of even single, isolated sentences, but that these sentences are the *only* things his perspective can make sense out of. Moreover, without the general understanding that this effort is an acceptable, even worthy, thing to do, the doing could not be done. The functioning of these sentences is as grammarians' illustrations, notwithstanding that due to the residual effects of unpleasant exercises in grade school, large sections of the public can construe sentences in the same frame. The mental set required to make sense out of these little orphans is that of someone with linguistic interests, someone who is posing a linguistic issue and is using a sample sentence to further his argument. In this special context of linguistic elaboration, an explication and discussion of the sample sentence will have meaning, and this special context is to be found anywhere in the world where there are grammarians. But

19. Of course, sentences can have structural ambiguity. "Flying airplanes can be dangerous" has two quite different possible meanings. But like a reversing picture, these two possibilities are themselves clearly established solely by the sentence itself, which thus retains the power all on its own to do the work required of it as an illustration of what linguistic analysis can disambiguate. The same can be said for deictic terms. Their analysis treats *classes* of terms whose members carry meanings that are situation-locked in a special way, but the analysis itself apparently is not hindered in any way by virtue of having to draw on these terms as illustrations, and instead of being constrained by indexicals is made possible by them. "The man just hit my ball over there" leaves us radically ignorant of whose ball was hit, when, and where it went, unless we can look out upon the world from the physical and temporal standpoint of the speaker; but just as obviously this sentence all by itself can be used as an apparently context-free illustration of this indexical feature of "just," "my," and "there."

present one of these nuggets cold to a man on the street or to the answerer of a telephone, or as the content of a letter, and on the average its well-formedness will cease to be all that significant. Scenarios *could* be constructed in which such an orphaned sentence would be meaningful—as a password between two spies, as a neurologist's test of an individual's brain functioning, as a joke made by and about grammarians, and so forth. But ingenuity would be required. So all along, the sentences used by linguists take at least some of their meaning from the institutionalization of this kind of illustrative process. As Gunter suggests:

> A deeper suspicion suggests that all isolated sentences, including those that linguists often use as examples in argumentation, have no real existence outside some permissive context, and that study of sentences out of context is the study of oddities at which we have trained ourselves not to boggle. [1974:17]

What can be said about the use of sample sentences can also be said about sample dialogue. A two-part interchange—an adjacency pair—can be put on the board or printed in a book, recommended to our attention without much reference to its original context, and yet will be understandable. Exchanges provide self-contained, packaged meaning. The following illustrates:

A: "What's the time?"
B: "It's five o'clock."

I suggest that as grammarians display self-sufficient sample sentences, apparently unembarrassed by the presuppositions of doing so, so interactionists display self-sufficient interchanges. Nor are interactionists alone in the enjoyment of this license. Those who give talks or addresses or even participate in conversations can plug in riddles, jokes, bon mots, and cracks more or less at their own option at the appropriate points on the assumption that these interpolations will be meaningful in their own right, apart from the context into which they have been placed, which context, of course, is supposed to render them apt or fitting. Thus the same little plum can be inserted at the beginning or end of quite different speakers' quite different talks with easy aptness. Stage plays provide similar opportunities in allowing for the performance of "memorable" exchanges, that is, sprightly bits of dialogue that bear repeating and can be repeated apart from the play in which they occurred.

Yet we must see that the dialogic approach inherits many of the limitations of the grammarian's, the sins of which, after all, it was meant to correct. I refer to the sins of noncontextuality, to the assumption that bits of conversation can be analyzed in their own right in some independence of what was occurring at the time and place.

First, an obvious but important point about single sentences. The reproduction of a conversation in the printed text of a play or in a novel or in a news account of an actual event satisfies the condition of any body of print, namely, that *everything* readers might not already know and that is required for understanding be alluded to, if not detailed, *in print.* Thus, a physical event may be relevant without which the talk that follows does not make sense, but inasmuch as the medium is print, a description, a *written* version of the event, will be provided in the text, in effect interspersing talk and stage directions—materials from two different frames. Cues for guiding interpretation which are imbedded in the physical and interpersonal setting are therefore not denied, at least on the face of it. And yet, of course, these unspoken elements are necessarily handled so as to sustain a single realm of relevant material, namely, words in print. To draw on these materials as sources in the analysis of talk is thus to use material that has already been systematically rendered into one kind of thing—words in print. It is only natural, therefore, to find support from sources in print for the belief that the material of conversations consists fundamentally of uttered words.

I think the same strictures can be suggested regarding "conversational implicature," that is, indirectly conveyed understanding. As with grammatical ambiguities and indexicals, it appears that a cited sentence can be used in and by itself as a pedagogic example of what can be meant but not said, conveyed but not directly—the difference, in short, between locutionary content and illocutionary force. Yet, of course, here the sentence in itself is quite clearly not enough. A bit of the context (or possible contexts) must be sketched in, and is, by the analyst, using more sentences to do so. It is these verbally provided stage directions which allow the writer correctly to assume that the reader will be able to see the point. And ordinarily these sketchings are not themselves made a subject of classification and analysis.[20]

When we turn from the analysis of sentences to the analysis of interchanges, matters become somewhat more complicated. For there are intrinsic reasons why any adjacency pair is likely to be considerably more meaningful taken alone than either of its pair parts taken alone. Some elaboration is required.

As suggested, the transcript or audio tape of an isolated statement plucked from a past natural conversation can leave us in the dark, due to deixis, ellipsis, and indirection, although auditors in the original circle of use suffered no sense of ambiguity. But there is a further matter. As Gunter (1974: 94ff.) has recently recommended, what is available to the student (as also to the actual participants) is not the possibility of predicting forward from a statement to a reply—as we might a cause to its effects—but rather quite a different prospect, that of locating in what is said now the sense of what it is a response to. For the individual who had accepted replying to the original statement will have been obliged to display that he has discovered the meaningfulness and relevance of the statement and that a relevant reaction is now provided. Thus, for example, although his perception of the phrasal stress, facial gestures, and body orientation of the speaker may have been necessary in order for him to have made the shift from what was said to what was meant, the *consequence*

20. An encouraging exception is provided by those attempting to formulate rules for the "valid" performance of various speech acts (such as commands, requests, offers) and therefore generalizations concerning circumstances in which alternate meanings are imputed. See Grice (1975); Searle (1975); Gordon and Lakoff (1971:63–84); Labov and Fanshel (1977, chap. 3); and Ervin-Tripp (1976:25–66). One problem with this line of work so far is that it tends to end up considering a sort of check list individuals might apply in the rare circumstances when they are genuinely uncertain as to intended meaning—circumstances, in short, when usual determinants have failed. How individuals arrive at an effective interpretation on all those occasions when the stream of experience makes this easy and instantaneous is not much explored, this exploration being rather difficult to undertake from a sitting position. Most promising of all, perhaps, is the argument by Gordon and Lakoff (1971:77) that what is conveyed as opposed to what is said may be marked grammatically through the distribution of particular words in the sentence. Whether such a distribution determines the reading to be given or merely confirms it might still be an open question, however.

of this guidance for interpretation can well be made evident in the *verbal* elements of the reply, and so in effect becomes available to we who review a verbal transcript later. In the same way the respondent's special background knowledge of the events at hand can become available to us through his words. Indeed, the more obscure the speaker's statement for his original auditors, the more pains his respondent is likely to have taken to display its sense through his own reply, and the more need we who come later will have for this help. Second pair parts turn out, then, to be incidentally designed to provide us with some of what we miss in first pair parts in our effort to understand them, and respondents in one circle can turn out to be ideally placed and knowing explicators for later circles. Admittedly, of course, laconicity can be answered with laconicity; but although matters therefore are not necessarily improved for us, they can hardly be worsened, any words being better than none.

But note that although the one who had accepted replying had had to come to a usable interpretation of the statement *before* providing evidence that he had caught the speaker's meaning, we who later examine an isolated excerpt will find the key to hand even as we find the door. By quietly reading (or listening) on, we may find just the help we need. Quite systematically, then, we students obtain a biased view of uttered sentences. Unlike the self-sufficient sample sentences referred to by traditional grammarians, excerpts from natural conversations are very often unintelligible; but when they *are* intelligible, this is likely to be due to the help we quietly get from someone who has already read the situation for us.

However, even in spite of the fact that there are deep reasons why adjacency pairs are more excerptible than first pair parts, we will still find that sample interchanges are biased examples of what inhabits actual talk.

With this warning about the dangers of noncontextuality, let us proceed to the theme, replies and responses.

Take as a start rerun signals, whether made with words or gestural equivalents. He who sends such a signal can be demonstrating that he is, in fact, oriented to the talk, but that he has not grasped the semantic meanings the speaker attempted to convey. He thus addresses himself to the *process* of communication, not to *what* was communicated—for, after all, he professes not to have understood that. Differently put, the recipient here abstracts from the sender's statement merely its qualifications as something to be heard and understood. It is to the situation of failed communication, not to what is being communicated, that the recipient reacts. To call these signals "replies" seems a little inappropriate, for in the closest sense, they do not constitute a reply to what was said; the term "response" seems better.

Take, then, as a basic notion the idea of *response,* meaning here acts, linguistic and otherwise, having the following properties:

1. They are seen as originating from an individual and as inspired by a prior speaker.
2. They tell us something about the individual's position or alignment in what is occurring.
3. They delimit and articulate just what the "is occurring" is, establishing what it is the response refers to.
4. They are meant to be given attention by others now, that is, to be assessed, appreciated, understood at the current moment.

And assume that *one* type of response is what might be called a *reply,* namely, a response in which the alignment implied and the object to which reference is made are both conveyed through words or their substitutes; furthermore, this matter addressed by the response is itself something that a prior speaker had referred to through words. Replies, I might note, are found in the artful dialogue of the theater and in novels, part of the transmutation of conversation into a sprightly game in which the position of each player is reestablished or changed through each of his speakings, each of which is given central place as the referent of following replies. Ordinary talk ordinarily has less ping-pong.

II

Consider now the properties of responses in general, not merely replies in particular.

1. Recall that in the couplets so far considered, the second pair part incidentally can be seen as a reply to something of its own generic kind, namely, a brief spurt of words whose semantic

(or propositional) meaning is to be addressed, a restriction to same generic type to be seen when one move in a game of chess calls forth another move or one strike at a ping-pong ball calls forth another. A case simply of tit for tat. (Indeed, not only will a reply here answer a statement, but also it will be drawn from the same discourse-type, as in question-answer, summons-acknowledgment, etc.)

A minor qualification was admitted, namely, that words alone are not involved. We have, for example, a special way of knotting up the face to convey the fact that we do not understand what it is a speaker seems to be trying to convey, and that a rerun is in order. And gestures obviously can also be freighted with ritual significance. In both cases, we deal with signals that can also be conveyed by words, indeed are very often conveyed by both words and gestures, presenting, incidentally, no particular need to question the relevance of system and ritual constraints in the analysis of talk. Here I only want to suggest that although it is plain that such gestures figure in conversation, it is much easier to reproduce words than gestures (whether vocal, facial, or bodily), and so sample interchanges tend to rely on the verbal portion of a verbal-gestural stream or tacitly substitute a verbal version of a move that was entirely gestural, with consequent risk of glossing over relevant moves in the sequence. And what is true of gesture is true also of scenic contributions. In consequence, words themselves, including the most perfunctory of them, can conceal the interactional facts. Thus the transcription:

A: "Have you got the time?"
B: "Yes, it's 5:15."

suggests that the "Yes" is rather redundant, being replaceable by a good-tempered mention of the time alone. But in fact a scene is possible in which B, walking past A, who is in a parked car, wants it known that he, B, will honor the request, yet finds that the time taken to get at his watch removes him a couple of steps from the car and opens up the possibility of his being seen as declining to acknowledge the contact. The "Yes" then becomes an immediately available means of showing that an encounter has been ratified and will be kept open until its work is done.

Note, too, that ritual concerns are not intrinsically a matter of talk *or* talklike gestures. Talk is ritually relevant largely insofar as it qualifies as but another arena for good and bad conduct.[21] To interrupt someone is much like tripping over him; both acts can be perceived as instances of insufficient concern for the other, mere members of the class of events governed by ritual considerations. To ask an improperly personal question can be equivalent to making an uninvited visit; both constitute invasions of territoriality.

Of course, talk figures in an added way, because challenges given to someone seen as not having behaved properly can neatly be done with words. Moreover, if something is to be offered that is physically absent from the situation or not palpable, and this offering is to be accepted, then offering and acceptance may *have* to be done with words or emblems.

So, too, if past conduct—verbal or behavioral—is to be cited for the purposes of demanding corrective action or bestowing praise, then again words will be necessary. (And in both the latter cases, the little interpersonal rituals likely to accompany the transaction will be verbal in a sense.) Nonetheless, ritual is concerned with the expressive implication of acts, with the sense in which acts can be read as portraying the position the actor takes up regarding matters of social import—himself, others present, collectivities—and what sentences say constitutes but one class of these expressions.

It follows that events which are not themselves verbal in character, but which, for example, raise questions of propriety, may have to be verbally addressed, and will thereby be thrust into the center of conversational concern. In sum, once the exchange of words has brought individuals into a jointly sustained and ratified focus of attention, once, that is, a fire has been built, any visible thing (just as any spoken referent) can be burnt in it.

Here a terminological clarification is required. Utterances are inevitably accompanied by kinesic and paralinguistic gestures

21. Grice (1975) argues for a distinction between conventional maxims and conversational ones, the latter presumably special to talk. However, although the maxims that seem special to an effective communication system allow us to account for certain presuppositions, implications, and laconicities in speech—a reason for formulating the maxims in the first place—other maxims of conduct allow for this accounting, too.

which enter intimately into the organization of verbal expression. Following Kendon, one may refer here to the gesticulatory stream and also include therein all nonverbal gestures that have acquired an emblematic function, replacing words and replaceable by them. However, conversation involves more than verbal and gesticulatory communication. Physical doings unconnected with the speech stream are also involved—acts which for want of a better name might here be called nonlinguistic.

So conversation can burn anything. Moreover, as suggested, the conventionalized interpersonal rituals through which we put out these fires or add to the blaze are not themselves sentences in any simple sense, having speech-act characteristics quite different from, say, assertions about purported facts.

Observe, too, that something more than thrusts from the physical world into the spoken one are possible. For quite routinely the very structure of a social contact can involve physical, as opposed to verbal (or gestural) moves. Here such words as do get spoken are fitted into a sequence that follows a nontalk design. A good example is perfunctory service contacts. A customer who comes before a checkout clerk and places goods on the counter has made what can be glossed as a first checkout move, for this positioning itself elicits a second phase of action, the server's obligation to weigh, ring up, and bag. The third move could be said to be jointly accomplished, the giving of money and the getting of change. Presumably the final move is one the shopper makes in carrying the bag away. Simultaneously with this last move, the server will (when busy) begin the second move of the next service contact. Now it turns out that this sequence of moves may or may not be bracketed by a greeting-farewell ritual, may or may not be embroidered with simultaneously sustained small talk, may or may not be punctuated at various points with thank you—you're welcome exchanges. Obviously, talk can figure in such a service contact and quite typically does. Moreover, should any hitch develop in the routine sequence, words will smoothly appear as correctives as though a ratified state of talk had all along existed—giving us some reason to speak of a service encounter, not merely a service contact. But just as obviously, talk and its characteristic structure hardly provides a characterization of the service sequence in progress, this servicing being a game of a different kind. In the serious sense, what is going on is a service transaction, one sustained through an occasion of cooperatively executed, face-to-face, nonlinguistic action. Words can be fitted to this sequence; but the sequencing is not conversational.

With the strictures in mind that relevant moves in a conversation need be neither verbal nor gesticulatory, let us examine more closely the workings of some perfunctory interchanges.

A query concerning the time can be signalled by a phrase or by a gesture, such as pointing to the other's watch or one's own bare wrist. (Under many circumstances both verbal and nonverbal methods will be used to assure effectiveness.) The response to this query can be a verbal reply ("It's five o'clock") or a verbal substitute (five fingers held up). Both modes of response satisfy system and ritual constraints, letting the asker know that his message has been correctly received and seen as proper—as would, incidentally, the excuse, "I'm sorry, I don't have a watch." But in addition, the recipient of the query can react by showing his watch to the questioner—a tack common in multilingual settings. Here, too, the standard system and ritual constraints are satisfied, the implication clearly being that the person offering access to the time has correctly received the message and, in complying with its demands in good spirit, believes the request to have been proper. But, again, this answering action is not a reply in the strict sense: words are being addressed but what they are addressed by is not words or their gestural substitute but a physical doing, a nonlinguistic deed which complies with a request. So, too, when in reaction to being asked for the salt, the asked person passes it.[22] Here words may accompany the respon-

22. And, of course, standard sequences could involve a nonlinguistic doing, *then* a verbal response. Indeed, under the term "completives," Jerome Bruner has recently argued that the sequence consisting of a nonlinguistic act by an infant and an affirming comment by a parent is a very basic way in which the child is induced to articulate the stream of behavior into repeatable, identifiable, terminally bracketed segments. (See Bruner [1974: 75]). In later years the parent will monitor the child's behavior, ready to respond with a verbal or gestural sanction each time a lapse in acceptable conduct occurs. Ontogenetically, then, it could be argued that one basic model for talk (in addition to a greeting version of statement and reply) is deed and evaluative comment. And what we take to be a tidy adjacency pair is often a three-part interchange, the first part being a bit of improper or exemplary conduct.

sive action, but need not. (Of course, when such a request must be denied for some reason or temporarily put off, then words are likely to be necessary in order to provide an account, and when the request is for an action in the future—and/or in another place—words in the form of a promise are often the best that can be provided.) Indeed, a case might be made that when a speaker responds to a rerun signal by recycling his statement, *that* act is a doing, too, a deed—in this case, the making of a picture, a hieroglyph—and not in the strictest sense a reply (Quine 1962: 26).

A moment's thought will make it obvious that there are lots of circumstances in which someone giving verbal orders or suggestions expects something nonlinguistic as a response ("On your mark, get set, go"). Thus, one group of sociolinguists studying classroom interaction has even had cause to make a basic distinction between "elicitations" and "directives," the first anticipating a verbal response, the second a nonlinguistic one (Sinclair and Coulthard 1975:28). As already suggested, in starting a foot race or a classroom exercise (or a service transaction), the triggering words constitute a move in an action pattern that is not necessarily enclosed within a state of talk at all, but is rather something with a different character—a game of a different kind—whether involving a single focus of attention or a set of actions each supporting its own, albeit similar, focus of attention. The point to be made here, however, is that while some scenes of face-to-face interaction are set up specifically for nonlinguistic responses, no face-to-face talk, however intimate, informal, dyadic, "purely conversational," or whatever, precludes nonlinguistic responses or the inducing of such responses. Incidentally, it might be argued that children learn to respond with actions before they learn to respond with words.[23]

2. Another feature of responses in general, as opposed to replies in particular, must be addressed: their "reach." A contrast between answering a query regarding the time by words and by demonstration has just been argued. But the matter needs further consideration. If we take the case of verbal answers (or their emblematic substitutes), even here we find that

23. See Shatz (1974).

matters may not be merely verbal. Again look at answering a question about the time. What the respondent does is to look at his watch and then answer. His response, properly speaking, involves a strip of behavior which includes both these phases. Were he *not* to precede the verbal part of his answer with a glance at his watch, he could not answer in the same way. Should it happen that the queried person unbeknownst to the asker has just looked at his watch for an independent reason and now knows the time, making a second look (at that moment) unnecessary, it is quite likely that either he will make this unnecessary look or, if not, will express by gesture or words that there is something special in his response, namely, that he appreciates that he might appear to be answering irresponsibly—without checking, as it were—but that this is not actually so. (For similar reasons, if the time happens to be a round number, the respondent may feel it prudent to answer in a way calculated to forestall the interpretation that he is answering only roughly; thus, "It's *exactly* five o'clock.")

All of this is even more clear in other perfunctory interchanges. For example, when someone trips over another, offers an apology, and has that apology graciously accepted, the acceptance is not simply a reply to the apology; it is also a response to an apologized-for delict. (Again observe that the initial delict, although clearly a nonlinguistic act, is as fully a part of the interchange as are the words that follow the trouble in attempting to deal with it.) And the same would apply if the delict were not a physical event, such as a tripping over, but a statement that is badly managed, or untactful, or whatever.

C: [Telephone rings]
A: "Hello."
C: "Is this the Y?"
A: "You have the wrong number."
C: "Is this KI five, double four, double o?"
A: "Double four, double *six*."
→ C: "Oh, I am sorry."
A: "Good-bye." [Hangs up]

Here (in this verbatim record of an actual phone call) the caller's statement, "Oh, I am sorry," patently refers to his having caused someone to come to the phone without warrant; the answerer's immediately previous statement is merely the clincher and is not, all in itself, the object of the caller's remedial action. The object here stretches back to include the whole call.

Another example. In conversation it is obviously possible for a third person to contribute a comment—say, of exasperation—concerning the way in which two other participants have been handling an extended exchange between themselves; and an individual may even choose to comment about what has been happening in a conversation up to the current moment between himself and another party, the immediately prior statement now being read as merely the final one in a sequence, the sequence as a whole being the subject. Thus, the juncture of turn-taking, the management of interruption, and the like, may indeed support a formalistic analysis, showing the bearing with respect to timing of current statement on immediately completed one; but the semantic content of the response can still pertain to something that extends back in time.

The backward reach of responses is illustrated again in the interaction associated with storytelling. A very common feature of informal interaction is an individual's replaying of a bit of his past experience in narrative form (Goffman 1974:503–6). Such replays are commonly only a few sentences long, but sometimes considerably longer, more like, for example, a paragraph than a sentence. And very often listeners are not meant to *reply* to what they have heard, for what form could a reply take? What they are meant to do is to give signs of appreciation, and these may be very brief indeed. In any case, the appreciation shown—like the applause at the end of a play—is not for the last sentence uttered but rather for the whole story and its telling. Thus we can account for something already described, a "rhetorical question" that takes the question-asking form but is not delivered with the intent of eliciting a specific answer; for often this sort of questioning is meant to be heard as but one element in a longer statement, the longer one being the move to which the speaker intends his recipients to address their responses. (So, too, when one individual uses up a turn by directly or indirectly quoting a statement purportedly made by an absent person, the listener cannot, strictly speaking, respond with a reply, but, at least ordinarily, only with an expression of his "reaction" or attitude to such a statement, for the original speaker would have to be produced if a reply in the full sense is to be offered.) Another illustration is the "buried query": wanting to obtain a bit of information but not wanting this to be known, an individual can set up a question series such that the answer he seeks is to one member of the class of questions, here seen as merely part of a series, not symptomatic in itself. The very possibility of employing this dodge assumes that a question series that elicits a string of answers will be perceived, first off, as addressed to the sequence as a whole.[24] Finally, observe that it is possible for a recipient to respond to a speaker by repeating his words, derisively mimicking his style of delivery, this response performing the subtle—but nonetheless common—shift in focus from *what* a speaker says to his saying it in this way, this being (it is now implied) the *sort* of thing he as a speaker would say in the circumstances.

Just as we see that a response may refer to more than a whole statement, so, of course, we must see that it can refer to something less—say, the way the last word is pronounced.

To say that the subject of a response can extend back over something more or less than the prior turn's talk is another way of saying that although a *reply* is addressed to meaningful elements of whole statements, *responses* can break frame and reflexively address aspects of a statement which would ordinarily be "out of frame," ordinarily part of transmission, not content—for example, the statement's duration, tactfulness, style, origin, accent, vocabulary, and so forth.[25] And as long as the respondent can make listeners understand what he is responding to and ensure that this expression is ritually tolerable, then that might be all that is required. Thus the practice during idle talk of abstracting from a just-finished sentence something that can be

24. Another expression of this possibility is found in the tendency, noted by Shuy (1974:21) for a respondent to provide increasingly truncated same-answers to progressive items in a series of questions, the series coming thus to function somewhat as a single whole.

25. "It's time for you to answer now," the Queen said, looking at her watch: "open your mouth a *little* wider when you speak, and always say 'your Majesty.' "

"I only wanted to see what the garden was like, your Majesty—"

"That's right," said the Queen, patting her on the head, which Alice didn't like at all. . . .

punned with or jokingly understood in "literal" form or made explicit in the face of anticipated elision; thus, too, the joking or disciplining practice of ratifying another's asides and rhetorical questions as something to be officially addressed.

This skittish use of more or less than a speaker's whole statement may, of course, be something that the speaker induces. Thus, as Roger Shuy has recently suggested, when a doctor asks two questions at the same time, it is likely that the patient will have the rather enforced option of deciding which to answer:

D: "Well, how do you feel? Did you have a fever?"
P: "No."
D: "And in your family, was there any heart problem? Did you wake up short of breath?"
P: "No."[26]

Further, statements can be made with the clear understanding that it is not their ordinary meaning that is to be addressed but something else—an ironic or sarcastic interpretation, a joking unseriousness, the accent in which they are delivered, and a host of other "keyings," the transformative power of which seems to have largely escaped linguistic effort at appreciation, let alone conceptualization, until relatively recently.[27] In brief, statements very often have a demand function, establishing what aspect or element of them is to be responded to.

But of course, speaker's implied interpretation demands can often be left unsatisfied as long as some sort of meaningful response is possible. A response that casts backward in time beyond the prior statement, or abstracts an aspect of a statement, or focuses on a particular piece of a statement—all this without encouragement or even anticipation on the part of the initial speaker—can nonetheless leave him with the sense that he has satisfied system constraints, that the response he evoked has done so, too, and, further, that the ritual considerations have been satisfied—or at least not unacceptably violated. When, therefore, I earlier suggested that cited interchanges might be meaningful because whoever originally supplied the second pair part has

26. See footnote 24.

27. A useful current statement may be found in Gumperz (forthcoming). See also Crystal (1969:104).

done our job of uncovering the initial speaker's meaning, I was uncritical. A respondent cannot make evident that he has understood *the* meaning of a statement, because in a sense there isn't one. All he can do is respond to what he can display as *a* meaning that will carry—although, of course, he may effectively sustain the impression (and himself believe) that his *a* is the *the*.

It should be apparent that an encounter itself can be a subject for response. Thus, when a "preclosing" has been given, the recipient can respond by introducing a fresh statement in a manner suggesting that his remark is knowingly being introduced out of order (Schegloff and Sacks 1973:319–20). The preclosing is the immediate stimulus of the last-minute contribution, but, behind this, concern is being directed to the closing that is being postponed.

3. Another characteristic of responses. An individual can, and not infrequently does, respond to himself. Sometimes this will take the form of an actual verbal reply to the semantic content of his own utterances:

> "Do you think they would do that for you?" [Pause, ostensibly for recipient's possible reply, and then with rising stress] "They certainly would not!"[28]

More commonly a "reflexive frame break" is involved, the individual responding "out of frame" to some aspect of his own just-past utterance:

> "Also there's a guy at Princeton you should talk to. Richard . . . (Christ, I'm bad with names. I can see his face now and I can't remember his last name. I'll think of it soon and tell you.)."[29]

28. It should be added that performers of all kinds—including, interestingly, auctioneers—can find it impractical for various reasons to engage in actual repartee with members of the audience, and so as a substitute end up feeding themselves their own statements to reply to or making a statement in the name of a member of the audience, to which they can then respond. Engendered, thus, on situational grounds, is expropriation of the dialogic other.

29. Out-of-frame comments open up the possibility of being incorrectly framed by recipients, in this case heard as part of the unparenthesized material. Here speakers will be particularly dependent on obtaining back-channel expressions from hearers confirming that the reframing has been effectively conveyed. And here radio speakers will have a very special problem, being cut off from this source of confirmation. They can try to deal with this issue by laughing at their own out-of-frame comments, assuming in effect the role of the listener,

All this, perhaps, is only to be expected, for "self-responding" seems to satisfy a basic condition of meaningful communication; a move in the form of a statement occurs and the next move demonstrates that the prior one has been heard and seen to be interpretable and relevant. Note, we have added reason for distinguishing the notion of "move" from that of a speaking, since here, once again, the same turn contains more than one move. Moreover, it is evident that the notions of speaker and respondent can get us into trouble unless we keep in mind that they refer not to individuals as such, but to enacted capacities. Just as a listener can self-select himself as next speaker, so, too, apparently, can speaker.

The self-responses described here may strike one as uncommon, but there is a form of self-response that is found everywhere, namely, self-correction. Requesting suffrance for muffing a word or apologizing for inadvertently stepping on relevant toes very often occurs "immediately" after the delict, the speaker providing a remedy before his hearers have had a chance to feel that they themselves, perhaps, should take some kind of priming action. Moreover, once a gaffe of some kind has been made, it can have a referential afterlife of considerable duration; an hour or a day later, when topic and context give some assurance that those present will be able to understand what incident is being referred to, the speaker in passing can gratuitously inject an ironic allusion, showing that chagrin has been sustained, which demonstration reaches back a goodly distance for its referent.

4. All of which should prepare us for the fact that what

---

but this tack will have the effect of interrupting the flow of utterances and of underlining a joke, the merit of which is often dependent on its striking the hearer as a well-timed throwaway line, an interjection that the interjector can make offhandedly and without missing a stroke. In consequence there has emerged the "displaced bracket." The speaker makes no pause after his aside has terminated, gets established in the next line of his main text, and then, part way through this, and while continuing on with this text, allows his voice to bulge out a little with a laugh, a laugh his hearers ideally would have contributed right after the frame-breaking remark, were they in the studio with him. What is thus accomplished, in effect, is a parenthesized parenthesis. The announcer's little laugh allows him to stand back from the person who saw fit to dissociate himself by means of a wry aside from the text he was required to read. Alas, this distancing from distance sometimes takes the speaker back to the position the script originally afforded him.

appears to be an anomalous statement-reply form may not be anomalous at all simply because replying of any kind is not much involved. Thus the basic pair known as a greeting exchange. It turns out that the two parts of such a round can occur simultaneously or, if sequenced in time, the same lexical item may be employed:

A: "Hello."
B: "Hello."

The reason for this apparent license is that the second greeting is not a *reply* to the first; *both* are reactive responses to the sudden availability of the participants to each other, and the point of performing these little rituals is not to solicit a reply or reply to a solicitation but to enact an emotion that attests to the pleasure produced by the contact. And no disorganization results from the apparent overlapping or repetition; indeed, if circumstances can be seen to prevent one of the participants from easily performing his part, then the exchange can be effected through a single person's single offering. Nor, then, need the following greeting-in-passing be as strange as it looks:

A: "How are you?"
B: "Hi."

for in the underlying ritual structure a question is not being asked nor an answer provided.

5. And so we can turn to the final point. If a respondent does indeed have considerable latitude in selecting the elements of prior speaker's speaking he will refer to, then surely we should see that the respondent may choose something nonlinguistic to respond to. Respondent can coerce a variety of objects and events in the current scene into a statement to which he can now respond, especially, it seems, when the something derives from someone who could be a speaker.

A: [Enters wearing new hat]
B: [Shaking head] "No, I don't like it."

If such a remark is seen to leave matters in a ritually unresolved state, then the retroactively created first speaker can properly close out the interchange more to his satisfaction:

A: [Enters wearing new hat]
B: "No, I don't like it."
A: "Now I know it's right."

giving us a standard three-move interchange, albeit one that started out with something that need not have been treated as a statement at all and must be somewhat coerced into retrospectively becoming one. In general, then, to repeat, it is not *the* statement of a speaker which his respondent addresses, nor even *a* statement, but rather anything the speaker and the other participants will accept as a statement he has made.

Bringing together these various arguments about the admixture of spoken moves and nonlinguistic ones, we can begin to see how misleading the notion of adjacency pair and ritual interchange may be as basic units of conversation. *Verbal* exchanges may be the natural unit of plays, novels, audiotapes, and other forms of literary life wherein words can be transcribed much more effectively than actions can be described. Natural conversation, however, is not subject to this recording bias—in a word, not subject to systematic transformation into words. What is basic to natural talk might not be a conversational unit at all, but an interactional one, something on the order of: mentionable event, mention, comment on mention—giving us a three-part unit, the first part of which is quite likely not to involve speech at all.

III

I have argued that the notion of statement-reply is not as useful as that of statement-response in the analysis of talk. Now we must see that the notion of a statement itself is to be questioned.

True, a statement is something worth differentiating from a response. As suggested, statements precede responses in sequence time. Statements orient listeners to the upcoming; responses, to what has come up. Conversationalists seem more at liberty to choose a statement than to choose a response. And most important, a speaker can be free to make statements about matters that theretofore have not been presented in the talk, whereas he who makes a response must more attend to something that has just been presented, although, of course, he may construe this material in an unanticipated way. Statements elicit; responses are elicited.

Nonetheless, there are problems. Persons who provide responses, no less than those who provide statements, attend to back channel effects for a continuous guide to the reception of their contribution. And in both cases, one must wait for the actor to decide what to address himself to before one can know what is going to be said. And just as an immediately prior statement may be needed if one is to make sense out of the response which follows, so the response which follows will often be necessary if —as an unaddressed recipient—one is to make sense out of a statement now before oneself.

Moreover, beyond the constraint of intelligibility there are others. There is the question of topicality: Often the subject matter must be adhered to, or a proper bridge provided to another. There is the question of "reach" and the etiquette concerning it: Just as an addressed recipient can—whether encouraged to or not—respond to something smaller or larger than the speaker's statement, or to only an aspect of it, or even to nonlinguistic elements in the situation, so, too, a statement can be addressed to something more than the immediately expected response. Thus, the opening statement, "Have you got a minute?" can anticipate, and receive, such a reply as, "Of course," but this is certainly not all that the request implied. For the intent is to open up a channel of communication which stays open beyond the hoped-for reply that ratifies the opening. Indeed, a statement that bears on the management of some phase transition of the business at hand may anticipate no specific response, at least of an overt kind. Thus, Sinclair's recent suggestion about classroom tasks: the bracket markers employed to voice the fact that a task episode has terminated or is about to begin (e.g., "Well, okay, now then") may be employed not to elicit a response but to help with the cadence and pulsing of activity.[30] (Here, along with asides and "reacting moves," we have another example of utter-

30. Sinclair and Coulthard (1975:22). These writers use the term "frame" here. A general treatment of bracket markers may be found in Goffman (1974: 251–69).

ances that fall outside the statement-response format.) In sum, given the conversational demands of intelligibility, topicality, episode management, and the like, statements serving as brackets themselves provide an appropriate coping, seen as such, and in a sense thereby constitute responses to these demands.

To complicate matters even more, we find that responses themselves can be acceptably read as calling for a response to them, as when a question is answered with a question, and this second asking is accepted as an answering to the first. (It is even the case that should two individuals meet under circumstances in which both know that one of them is waiting for the other's answer to a particular question, the other may *open* the conversation with the awaited response.)

It follows that the term "statement" itself might be a little ill-suited, and we might want to look for a word encompassing all the things that could be responded to by a person presenting something in the guise of a response. Call this the "reference" of the response. Our basic conversational unit then becomes reference-response, where the reference may, but need not, center in the semantic meaning of the talk just supplied by previous speaker. And now the issue of how chaining occurs in conversation becomes that of how reference-response units are (if at all) linked.

You will note that this formulation rather oddly recommends a backward look to the structuring of talk. Each response provides its auditors with an appreciation not only of what the respondent is saying, but also of what it is he is saying this about; and for this latter intelligence, surely auditors must wait until the respondent has disclosed what his reference is, since they will have no other way of discovering for sure what it will be. It is true, of course, that some verbal pronouncements can be seen to condition responses closely, especially, for example, when social arrangements have underwritten this, as in interrogation sessions; but this mode of constraint is precisely what provides these occasions with their special and individual character. And it is true, of course, that when we examine or present a *record* of a conversation—real, literary, or got up—and read or listen backwards and forwards in it, the indeterminacy I am speaking of will be lost to our senses. For as suggested, in many cases we need only read on (or listen on) a little and it will be clear that the reference proves to be only what we readers expected, thus encouraging the illusion that its selection was determined all along. But, of course, the issue had not really been settled until the moment the purported respondent provided his purported response. Only then could the actual auditors (let alone we readers) actually have known who the person then beginning to speak was to be and what he has hit upon to respond to out of what had already gone on. Even when listeners can properly feel that there is a very high probability that the forthcoming response will address itself in a certain way to a certain aspect of what has been stated, they must wait for the outcome before they can be sure.[31] A similar argument is to be made concerning place of transition from one speaker to another. If a speaker may provide additional transition points after his first one is not taken up, so it follows that he will not know which of his offers is to be accepted until it has been, and we, upon reading a transcript, will only know which possible

31. Schegloff and Sacks (1973:299), provide an extreme statement:

> Finding an utterance to be an answer, to be accomplishing answering, cannot be achieved by reference to phonological, syntactic, semantic, or logical features of the utterance itself, but only by consulting its sequential placement, e.g., its placement after a question.

One problem with this view is that in throwing back upon the asker's question the burden of determining what will qualify as an answer, it implies that what is a question will itself have to be determined in a like manner, by reference to the sequence it establishes—so where can one start? Another issue is that this formulation leaves no way open for disproof, for how could one show that what followed a particular question was in no way an answer to it? Granted, an utterance which appears to provide no answer to a prior question can fail pointedly, so that part of its meaning is, and is meant to be, understood in reference to its not being a proper answer—an implication that the adjacency pair format itself helps us to explicate. But surely assessments about how pointed is the rejection of the claims of a question can vary greatly, depending on whether it is the questioner or nonanswerer to whom one appeals, and in fact there seems to be no absolute reason why an individual can't deliver a next remark with no concern at all for its failure to address itself to the prior question. Finally, to say that an answer of a sort can certainly be provided to a prior question without employing the conventional markers of an answer (and that the slot itself must be attended, not what apparently gets put into it) need not deny that answers will *typically* be marked phonologically, syntactically, semantically, etc., and that these markers will be looked to as a means of deciding that what has been said is an answer.

transition point was taken up, not why an earlier actual one or later possible one was not used. Nor is that the end of it. For after it has been disclosed who will be speaking, and at what precise point he will take up his speaking, and what reference his speaking will address itself to, there is still the open question of *what* he will say—and no interchange is so perfunctory as to allow a first pair part to totally constrain a second pair part in that connection.

In sum, we can find lots of strips of verbal interaction which clearly manifest a dialogic form, clearly establishing a difference between statements and replies (and consequently jumping along, an interchange at a time), but this differentiation is sometimes hardly to be found, and in any case is variable. Instead of replies, we have less tidy responses. Such responses can bear so little on the immediate statement that they are indistinguishable from statements; and statements can be so closely guided by understandings of what constitutes an appropriate topic as to be reduced to something much like a response.

It follows, then, that our basic model for talk perhaps ought not to be dialogic couplets and their chaining, but rather a sequence of response moves with each in the series carving out its own reference, and each incorporating a variable balance of function in regard to statement-reply properties. In the right setting, a person next in line to speak can elect to deny the dialogic frame, accept it, or carve out such a format when none is apparent. This formulation would finally allow us to give proper credit to the flexibility of talk—a property distinguishing talk, for example, from the interaction of moves occurring in formal games—and to see why so much interrupting, nonanswering, restarting, and overlapping occurs in it.

We could also see that when four or more persons participate, even this degree of flexibility is extended, for here statements and replies can function as part of the running effort of speakers either to prevent their recipients from getting drawn into another state of talk or to extend the cast of their talk, or contrariwise, to induce a division. (Thus, a speaker who has obtained the attention of one participant may shift his concern to the next person in line, neglecting someone who can be assumed to be committed in favor of someone not yet recruited.) Similarly, an addressed recipient can turn from the addressor to initiate what he hopes will be a separate state of talk with another party, minimizing any tendency to reply in order to invoke the boundary required by the conversation he himself is fostering. Nor does the issue of splitting end it. Two out of three or more coparticipants can enter a jocular, mocked-up interchange in which each loyally plays out his appropriate part, ostensibly providing appropriate statements and ostensibly responding with appropriate replies, while all the while the other participants look on, prepared to enter with a laugh that will let the jokesters off the hook, assuring them that their set piece was appreciated—and with this tactful appreciation provide a response to a statement which is itself an unserious dialogue embedded in a less lightly toned encounter.[32] Here instead of a story being narrated, it is—in a manner of speaking—enacted, but no less to be treated as an embedded whole.) More commonly, the difference between what is said and what is meant, and the various different things that can be meant by what is said, allow a speaker to knowingly convey through the same words one meaning to one auditor and a different meaning (or additional meanings) to another. For if statements or responses can draw their interpretability from the knowingly joint experience of speaker and hearer, then a speaker with more than one hearer is likely to be able to find a way of sustaining collusive communication with one of them through the winks and under-the-breath remarks that words themselves can be tricked into providing. (This three-party horizontal play can be matched in two-person talk through the use of innuendo, the common practice of phrasing an utterance so that two readings of it will be relevant, both of which are meant to be received as meanings intended but one deniably so.)

So, too, we would be prepared to appreciate that the social setting of talk not only can provide something we call "context" but also can penetrate into and determine the very structure of the interaction. For example, it has been argued recently that in classroom talk between teacher and students it can be understood

32. Another glimpse of this sort of complexity can be found in Jefferson's illustration of the "horizontal," as opposed to the "vertical," interplay of moves in a multiperson conversation. See Jefferson (1972:306).

that the teacher's purpose is to uncover what each and every pupil has learned about a given matter and to correct and amplify from this base. The consequence of this educational, not conversational, imperative is that classroom interaction can come to be parcelled out into three-move interchanges:

Teacher: Query
Pupil: Answer
Teacher: Evaluative comment on answer

the word "turn" here taken to mean sequencing of pupil obligations to participate in this testing process; furthermore, it is understood that the teacher's concern is to check up on and extend what pupils know, not add to her knowledge from their knowledge, and that it would not be proper for a pupil to try to reverse these roles.[33]

IV

Given an interactional perspective that recommends "move" as a minimal unit, that is concerned with ritual constraints as well as system ones, and that shifts attention from answers to replies and then from replies to responses in general, we can return to perfunctory interchanges and make a closer pass at analyzing them.

1. Take, for example, a standard rerun signal. A simple embedding can apparently result, this involving a "side sequence" whereby one two-part exchange is held open so that another can occur within it:

A_1: "It costs five."
B_2: "How much did you say?"
A_2: "Five dollars."
B_1: "I'll take it."

33. Sinclair et al. (1972:88, 104). Shuy (1974:12), also provides examples of three-move play. Riddles might be thought to have a three-move structure: (1) question, (2) thought and give-up, (3) answer. Again, the purpose of the asked person's move is not to inform the asker about the answer but to show whether he is smart enough to uncover what the asker already knows. But here the interaction falls flat if indeed the correct answer is uncovered (unlike the asking done by teachers) or if, upon being told the answer, the asked person does not do an appreciable "take," this latter constituting a fourth move.

This is (apparently) an "unhearing." In the case of a misunderstanding, something less tidy can result, something less neatly parceled into two-part exchanges:

(i) D: "Have you ever had a history of cardiac arrest in your family?"
(ii) P: "We never had no trouble with the police."
(iii) D: "No. Did you have any heart trouble in your family?"
(iv) P: "Oh, that. Not that I know of."[34]

The structural difference between an unhearing and a misunderstanding is to be found in terms of how the difficulty gets corrected. With unhearings, the recipient signals there is trouble; with misunderstandings, the speaker. Consequently, unhearings can be nicely managed with turns containing only one move, but misunderstandings lead to a two-move third turn, its first part signalling that trouble has occurred, and its second providing a rerun. Therefore (iii) could be seen as an elision and contraction of something like this:

iii(a) D: "No, that's not what I said."
P: "What did you say?"
D: "Did you have any heart trouble in your family?"

and its collapse into one turn perhaps based on the maxim that in serious matters, anyone who misunderstands another will rather be corrected than protected. Note that (iv) is more complicated than (iii). For although elision does not seem involved in what the speaking accomplishes, it still seems that three different kinds of work are ventured, indeed, three different moves, two involving system constraints and one involving ritual ones. A gloss might go like this:

1. "Oh." [Now I see what you really said and I tell you that I do.]
2. "That." [Although I didn't get you the first time around, what you said comes from a corpus of questions not unfamiliar to me that I can readily deal with.]
3. "Not that I know of." [An answer to the now correctly heard question.]

34. The first two lines are drawn from Shuy (1974:22), and are real; the second two I have added myself, and aren't.

Here, resolving the interchange into two-move couplets doesn't help very much. For although (i) and (ii) can be seen as a two-part exchange of sorts, (iii) is a rejection of (ii) and a restatement of (i), and (iv) is a redoing of (ii) along with a defense against (iii). Observe that an admitted failure to hear (an unhearing) need expose the unhearing recipient to nothing more deprecatory than the imputation of inattentiveness. A misunderstanding, however, causes the misunderstanding recipient to expose what he thinks the speaker might have said and thereby a view both of what he thought might be expected from the speaker and what the recipient himself might expect to receive by way of a question—all this to the possible embarrassment of the definition of self and other that actually comes to prevail.

2. In examining (iv) we found that different moves within the same turn at talk were sustained by *different* words, a convenient fact also true of the chaining examples given at the beginning of the paper. But there is no reason why this must be so. The *same* words can embody different moves in different games. This dismal fact allows us to return to the five dollar unhearing example and examine some of its complications.

There is a way of saying "How much did you say?" so as to imply a "literal" reading, that is, a reading (whether actually literal or not) that stresses what is taken to be the standard meaning of the sentence—its propositional content—and suppresses all other possibilities. But work and care will be required to secure this locutionary effect, as much, perhaps, as would be required to speak the line with any of its other freightings.

About these other freightings. Obviously, in context, "How much did you say?" can mean "That's an awfully high price"—at least in a manner of speaking.[35] And when it does,

35. Two kinds of qualifications are always necessary. First, the translation from what is said to what is meant is necessarily an approximation. One should really say, ". . . can mean something like 'That's an awfully high price.' " But I take this to be an instance of "normatively residual" ambiguity. More important, an utterance designed to be made a convenience of, that is, intended to be accepted solely for what it indirectly conveys, never has *only* this significance —apart from the inherent ambiguity of this significance. For, as suggested, a directly made statement inevitably leaves its maker in a different strategic position from the one in which an indirectly equivalent statement would leave him. For example, if a recipient takes violent exception to what a speaker meant

the fact that a move of this kind has been made, a move which questions the honesty and integrity of the informant, will show up in the rerun that comes at the next turn, for then that line ("Five dollars") is likely to be spoken in an apologetic way, its speaker commiserating with the unhearer for the way prices are now; or in a slightly taunting tone, meeting the implied accusation head on and not giving way before it; or, most complicated of all, in what amounts to a serious mimicking of a straightforward standard rerun, providing thereby the functional equivalent of a silence produced and heard as something to take note of. Observe, the practicality of the customer using a sarcastic or ironic phrasing of a rerun signal not only depends on there being a rerun signal to overlay in this way, but also upon there being a conventionalized interchange into which the server's response to this sally can be neatly fitted—whether "directly," by openly addressing the implied meaning of the customer's query, or "indirectly," by inducing through intonation and stress a special reading of what is otherwise a standard response to a standard request for a rerun. Note that the same general interchange format will allow the customer to begin the display of disgruntlement in another way, namely, by means of an utterance such as "You gotta be kidding," which in its turn can lead on to "I know what you mean," or (straight-faced), "No, that's what it really costs," and we are back once again to the same position: a customer who reserves the right to complete a transaction even as he injects note of the fact that he feels the pricing is out of line. May I add that an important possibility in the analysis of talk is to uncover the consequence of a particular move for the anticipated sequence; for that is a way to study the move's functioning (Goffman 1971:171–83). One should examine, then, the way in which a move can precipitously bring an interchange to an end before its initial design would have prefigured or extend the interchange after its termination had been expected or induce an interchange without using up the first slot to do so or cause a "break in step," as when he who gives up the floor in a manner to ensure getting it back after the

to convey indirectly, the speaker can always take the line that he meant the literal meaning all along.

next turn finds that the person who obtained the floor has managed matters so as to undercut the built-in return, or when someone being presented at court asks the royal personage questions instead of merely answering them, thereby committing *lèse-majesté* linguistically, for although monarchs may deign to penetrate a commoner's preserve conversationally, the understanding is that the exposure is not to be reciprocated.

3. Consider now that just as interchanges can incorporate nonlinguistic actions along with verbal utterances concerning these actions, so interchanges can incorporate references to past doings as occasions for now doing praise or blame, thereby placing responses to wider circumstances before or after verbal reference to these circumstances and thus bringing them into the interchange:

> B comes home from work, apparently not having brought what he promised to bring, and shows no sign that he is mindful of his failure.
> A_1: "You forgot!" [An utterance whose propositional form is that of an assertion of fact, but here can be understood as blame-giving]
> B_1: "Yes. I *am* sorry."
> A_2: "You're always doing it."
> B_2: "I know."

However, because the accuser cannot be sure of the accused's situation, a tactful hedge may be employed, and sometimes with good reason:

> A_1: "Did you forget?"
> B_1: "No."
> A_2: "Where is it?"
> B_2: "It's in the car."
> A_3: "Well?"
> B_3: "I'm on my way out to get it."

an interchange that can be nicely managed in a more elliptical form:

> A_1 :"Did you forget?"
> $B_1/B_2/B_3$: "No, it's in the car; I'm just on my way to get it."

Observe that the accuser can extend this sort of strategic hedging by asking a question, the affirmative answer to which constitutes an acceptable excuse for the action at fault, thereby giving the apparent offender an easy opportunity either to demonstrate that indeed this (or a similarly effective accounting) can be given or to initiate an admission of guilt (along with an apology) without actually having been asked for either. Thus:

> A: "The store was closed by the time you got out?"
> B: "Darn it. I'm afraid it was."
> etc: . . .
> A: "The store was closed by the time you got out?"
> B: "It was open but they won't have any 'til next week."
> etc: . . .

are possibilities (as initial rounds) the asker leaves open while actually priming the following self-rebuke, thereby allowing the blameworthy person first slot in an apology interchange:

> A: "The store was closed by the time you got out?"
> B: [Striking head] "God. I'm sorry. I'm hopeless."
> etc: . . .

4. Finally, observe how passing interchanges can bear on nonlinguistic actions and balance the claims of different games off against each other, presenting us with utterances that are routine yet functionally complex:

> At an airport a man approaches a stranger, a woman, who is seated at one end of a three-seat row. He places his small bag on the far seat of the three and prepares to walk away to a distant ticket counter.

The basic alternatives open to the man seem to be:

a. Leave his bag, civilly disattend the sitter (thus neither obliging her to do anything nor presuming on her in any other manner), and go on his way, leaving his bag at risk.
b. Openly approach the sitter in the manner of someone politely initiating talk with an unacquainted cross-sexed other, saying, for example, "Excuse me, Ma'am, I'll only be gone a minute. If you're going to be here, would you mind keeping an eye on my bag?" (to which the response would likely be a granting of the request or the provision of an explained decline).

With these possibilities as part of the actual situation confronting the two, the following interchange can easily transpire:

He: [Laconically, almost *sotto voce,* as if already lodged in conversation with the recipient]: "Don't let them steal it."
She: [Immediately utters an appreciative conspiratorial chuckle as speaker continues on his way.]

Here a man is taking license to treat a woman with whom he is unacquainted as though they were in a state of "open talk," i.e., the right but not the obligation to initiate brief states of talk at will. But the price for taking this liberty—and what neutralizes it as a liberty and therefore permits it—is that the speaker not only thereby forgoes the outright possibility of obtaining a formal commitment concerning the guarding of his bag, but also physically removes himself from the possibility of further threatening the sitter with an extension of the contact. The recipient responds with a laugh patently directed to the sally—the little joke that is to bring the two momentarily together in acknowledgment of the theft level at the airport—and not to the man's underlying need to have his bag guarded. But the sitter's response does not deny outright that she will indeed be responsive to the man's unstated hope, that prospect being scrupulously left open. The little laugh that follows the unserious command is, then, not merely a sign of appreciation for a joke made, but also evidence of a strategic position which neither denies nor accepts the buried request. (Thus, she is free to leave before the man returns and is free to help out without formally having to accept talk from a stranger.) And this hedged response to the man's deeply hedged request is what he was all along ready to settle for, namely, a hope, not a promise. Thus, an interchange that is entirely verbal and apparently unserious can yet draw upon and implicate wider nonlinguistic matters, such as guardianship, the rules for initiating spoken contact between strangers, and the like. Different orders of interaction, different interaction games, are simultaneously in progress, each involving a different amalgam of linguistic and nonlinguistic doings, and yet the same stretch of words must serve. Note that here the words that realize a move in one game can do so because they can be presented as realizing a move in another.[36]

36. Puns and other "double meanings" are not mere double meanings, for without the occurrence of the straight meaning in the context in which it occurs

V

1. Ordinary language philosophers have recently brought help in the study of the structure of interchanges, for these units of interaction appear to contain and to meld what students of Austin would refer to as quite different speech acts. Drawing on John Searle's analysis (1976:1–23), consider that the following argument is possible.

In theory at least, a speaker should be able to present a statement that solely reports pure fact (an "assertion") and receive a reply that simply attests to system constraints having been satisfied:

(i) A: "I think I'll do the wrapping."
B: "Oh."

Very often, in contrast, a speaker presents a "directive," that is, words whose point (or illocutionary force) is to urge the hearer to do something, the urging varying in degree from gentle requests to harsh commands.

One basic kind of directive is aimed at inducing the hearer to impart verbal information on a particular matter, giving us again the question-answer pair.[37]

ii(a) A: "Is that the parcel I'm supposed to start with?"
B: "Yes."

Observe that instead of speaking simply of system and ritual constraints, we might want to see B's "Yes" as a move in three different games; the requested information is provided but *also* (by implication) assurance is given that the question was correctly heard, *and* that it was not intrusive, stupid, overeager, out of order, and the like. Consequently the following recovery of two preliminary exchanges is thinkable:

(and thus in the context which allows it to occur) the sophisticated meaning could not be introduced. There is thus a hierarchical ordering of the two meanings, that is, of the unmarked and marked forms; one must be introducible before the other can be introduced.

37. A directive in the sense that "I request that you tell me" is implied. See Gordon and Lakoff (1971:66); Searle (1976:11).

A_1: "Can you hear and understand me?"
B_1: "Yes."
A_2: "Is it all right to ask you a question about the wrapping?"
B_2: "Yes."
A_3: "Is that the parcel I'm supposed to start with?"
B_3: "Yes."

The possibility that the asker needs assurance either that he has gotten across or that his question is proper seems quite remote here, and consequently the argument for elision seems extremely labored. But, of course, there are lots of circumstances in which these two considerations (especially the ritual one) are acutely problematic, being expressed either explicitly in preliminary exchanges or tacitly through intonation and stress.

Move on now to a second basic kind of directive, to the request or command for a nonlinguistic doing:

iii(a) A: "Would you put your finger on the knot?"
B: [Puts finger on knot]

Here again the response (a doing) performs triple work: it does what was requested and simultaneously affirms that the request was correctly heard and deemed to be in order. But now we can see more readily that directives involve (among other things) a timing condition, and this can imply a tacit back pair, or at least the expansion is thinkable in which this underlying possibility is exhibited:

iii(b) A: "Would you put your finger on the knot when I say now?"
B: "Yes."
A: "Now."
B: [Puts finger on knot]

which almost surfaces in the following:

iii(c) A: "Would you put your finger on the knot nnnnnnnnow!"
B: [Puts finger on knot]

The examples given here of requests for information and requests for nonlinguistic doings are simpler than ordinarily found in nature, for there quite commonly what is *meant* as a request for information or action is *said* as a request for yes/no information either about having information or being able to perform an action. ("Do you know the time?"; "Can you reach the salt?") So in many examples of both kinds of directives a further expansion is thinkable in order to recover another elided back pair:

A_1: "Do you know the time?"	A_1: "Can you reach the salt?"
B_1: "Yes."	B_1: "Yes."
A_2: "What is it?"	A_2: "Would you?"
B_2: "Five o'clock."	B_2B_3: "Yes." [Gets it, gives it]
	A_3: "Thanks."

Furthermore, although what is "literally" said in these cases can be so thoroughly a dead issue as to provide the basis for joking "literal" replies, there will, as suggested, be other occasions when both understandings are relevant, allowing for the possibilities of one utterance figuring as a move in four games: a request for evidence that one is being correctly heard; a request for information about possessing information or ability; a request for divulgence of the information or performance of the capacity; a stand taken concerning the social propriety of making these requests.

Now just as directives aim at inducing words or actions from the addressed recipient, so we can anticipate a class of speech acts through which speaker commits himself to a course of action—"commissives," in Searle's phrasing—comprising promises, pledges, threats, offerings, and the like (1976:17–18).

Commissives are similar to directives in that interchanges involving either can intimately interweave words and actions. Further, both commissives and directives raise the issue of the character of the ritual tags typically associated with them, namely, some variant of please and thank you. Thus:

Directive A_1: "Would you put your finger on the knot?"
B_1: [Does so]
A_2: "Thanks."
B_2: "'t's okay."

Commissive A_1: "Would you like me to put my finger on the knot?"
B_1: "Yes."
A_2: [Puts finger on knot]
B_2: "Thanks."

Although these politeness forms consist of lexicalized verbal utterances, the feeling with which they are spoken is always an important element; as already suggested, the point of employing these forms is not so much to state something as to exhibit feeling. In turn, we might want to distinguish this sort of verbal doing from a second sort, the sort identifiable as involving classic performatives, whereby uttering a formulaic statement in the proper circumstances accomplishes the doing of something, the formula and the circumstances being required, not the feelings of the speaker.[38]

2. A classification of speech acts—such as the one recommended by Searle—provides us with an opportunity to see that how an interchange unfolds will depend somewhat on the type of speech act involved, especially upon the type that initiates the interchange. Thus, a simple declarative statement of fact (if indeed there is such a thing in natural talk) creates a quite different second pair part from a request for information, and such a request has different sequencing implications from a request for a nonlinguistic doing. A "commissive" has still other sequential consequences. And an interpersonal ritual such as a greeting proves to be linked with a matching expression, but now much more loosely than is true of other adjacency pairs.

But if a typology of speech acts is to guide us, we must see that something equally fundamental is presumed.

In English, speech acts tend to be identified with particular syntactic structures (such as imperative and interrogative forms) and particular lexical items (such as "please" and "pardon"), the position being that here the locutionary form "directly" conveys a speech act. It is said that the speech form can "literally" express or realize the corresponding speech act.[39] It is then rea-

38. Note that all classical performatives are moves in at least two games, one that of informing hearers about, say, the name to be given, the bid to be made, the judgment to be rendered, and the other that of achieving this naming, bidding, judging (see Searle [1975]). Words are not alone in having this capacity. Every move in a board game similarly figures, both informing what move the player is to take and committing him to having taken this move. See Goffman (1961:35).

39. "Literal" here is a wonderfully confusing notion, something that should constitute a topic of linguistic study, not a conceptual tool to use in making studies. Sometimes the dictionary meaning of one or more of the

soned that a particular speech form may be routinely employed in accomplishing a speech act different from the one that would be performed were the speech form to be understood literally, that is, taken directly. So a given speech form can come to have a standard significance as a speech act different from its literal significance as a speech act.[40] Only one more step is needed to appreciate that in a particular context, a speech form having a standard significance as a speech act can be employed in a still further way to convey something not ordinarily conveyed by it —whatever, of course, it happens to say. (Indeed, on occasion the special meaning conveyed by a speech form may consist of its "literal" meaning, as when James Bond leaves his recently shot dancing partner at a stranger's table, saying that she is dead on her feet.)

Given all of this, an attempt must be made to uncover the principles which account for whatever contrast is found on a particular occasion between what is said (locutionary effect), what is *usually* meant by this (standard illocutionary force), and what in fact is meant on that particular occasion of use. Further, consideration must be given to the fact that in some cases, standard meaning is closely dependent on literal meaning, in other cases not; in some cases, particular force is closely dependent on the standard one (either as a contrast or as something that can retroactively be claimed as what was intended), in other cases there seems hardly any relation at all between them.[41]

One problem with this perspective is that a set of prear-

---

words of the utterance is meant, although how *that* meaning is arrived at is left an open question. And the underlying, commonsense notion is preserved that a word *in isolation* will have a general, basic, or most down-to-earth meaning, that this basic meaning is sustained in how the word is commonly used in phrases and clauses, but that in many cases words are used "metaphorically" to convey something that they don't really mean.

40. In fact, as recently suggested (Shatz 1974), indirect significance may be learned *before* literal meaning is appreciated.

41. A good example of this latter, one that did not show respect for linguistic doctrines of the time, can be found in the once-popular John-Marsha record, wherein a male voice repeating only the female name and a female voice repeating only the male name managed to convey through timing, stress and other paralinguistic cues a complete seduction. Dostoyevsky's version is reviewed in Vološinov (1973:103–5); and Vygotsky (1962:142–44).

ranged harmonies tends to be assumed. Speech forms are taken to be of the same number and kind as are standard speech acts; and the latter are taken to provide a matching for the variety of meanings that occur in particular contexts. The same list of possibilities is assumed to be found in each of the three classes of cases, the only issue being which instances of this list are to appear together, as when, for example, a question is said but an order is meant or an order is said but an offer is meant or an offer is what is usually meant but in this case a request is intended.[42] (A similar argument can be made about the issue of "strength"; the "strength" of an utterance is ordinarily attached to, and indicated by, a set speech form, but in context a particular usage can convey much less or much more force.)[43] The point, of course, is that although standard speech acts may form a relatively small, well-demarcated set, this applies largely to what is said; what is meant seems to draw on additional sets of meanings, too. For example, the interruptive utterance, "What?", presents the proposition that something has not been heard and the illocutionary intent of inducing a rerun. But in very many cases of actual use, these possibilities are the cover for some sort of boggling at what is occurring, and these various bogglings don't aptly fit into the standard speech act boxes.

Further, there is a degenerative relation between what is said and what is conveyed, for the special use to which a standard speech act is put on occasion can after a time become itself a standard overlayed meaning, which can then, in turn, allow for a second-order use to be employed for still other purposes. For example, "I shall hate you if you do not come to my party" has

42. Here, as Ervin-Tripp (1976) suggests, misunderstandings are to be located; so also seriously pretended misunderstandings, openly unserious misunderstandings, concern by speaker about misunderstanding, etc.

43. Linguists seem to have a special commitment to the analysis of directives. They start with a series that is marked syntactically and phonetically, beginning with imperative forms and then on to the various "mitigations" until something like a vague wish is being said. And there does seem to be a general social understanding that such a series exists; witness the fact that the series is drawn upon as a resource when formulating joking moves. But what sort of series, if any (and if only one), any particular social circle of users actually employs and what relation this may have, if any, to the grammarian's stereotypes is an open question, no doubt to be differently answered by every group one might study. Here see the useful analysis in Ervin-Tripp (1976).

to do with issuing strong invitations, not with warning of strong dislike consequent on failure to perform a particular act. But what is here conveyed as opposed to what is said may well itself be employed in a mock voice as mimicry of refinement. And some of these mockeries have themselves become rather standardized, opening up the prospect of a still further twist between what is said and what is meant. Moreover, two different standardized meanings may be established. For example, rerun signals very commonly constitute a sanctioning move against a speaker, pointedly giving him a chance to recast the way he has said something or to proceed now to account for why he did what he has just reported having done; however, the same signals are also used in their more "literal" sense to accomplish improved communication.

3. Commonly, critiques of orthodox linguistic analysis argue that although meaning depends on context, context itself is left as a residual category, something undifferentiated and global that is to be called in whenever, and only whenever, an account is needed for any noticeable deviation between what is said and what is meant. This tack fails to allow that when no such discrepancy is found, the context is still crucial—but in this case the context is one that is usually found when the utterance occurs. (Indeed, to find an utterance with only one possible reading is to find an utterance that can occur in only one possible context.) More important, traditionally no analysis was provided of what it is in contexts that makes them determinative of the significance of utterances, or any statement concerning the classes of contexts that would thus emerge—all of which if explicated, would allow us to say something other than merely that the context matters.

Here Austin has helped. He raises the question of how a speech act can fail to come off and suggests an analysis: there are infelicities (including misfirings and abuses), restrictions on responsibility, misunderstandings, and etiolations, namely, the reframings illustrated when an act turns out to be embedded in a report, a poem, a movie, and so on (Austin 1965:12–24). In asking how a speech act can fail, Austin points to conditions that must be fulfilled if the act is to succeed, this in turn suggesting how contexts might be classified according to the way they affect the illocutionary force of statements made in them. And indeed, the prospect is implied that a whole framework might be uncovered which establishes the variety of ways in which an act can be reread and a determinative account of the relations among these several bases for reinterpretation.

Say that there is in any given culture a limited set of basic reinterpretation schemas (each, of course, realized in an infinite number of ways), such that the whole set is potentially applicable to the "same" event. Assume, too, that these fundamental frameworks themselves form a framework—a framework of frameworks. Starting, then, from a single event in our own culture, in this case, an utterance, we ought to be able to show that a multitude of meanings are possible, that these fall into distinct classes limited in number, and that the classes are different from each other in ways that might appear as fundamental, somehow providing not merely an endless catalogue but an entree to the structure of experience. It will then seem obvious that the schema of schemas applicable to (and even derived from) the possible meanings of our chosen event will similarly apply to any other event. Of course, the shape of such a metaschema need only be limned in to provide the reader with a focus for easy complaint; but complaints can lead to what we are looking for.

Start, then, with a conventionalized, perfunctory social litany, one that begins with A's "Do you have the time?" and restricting ourselves to B's verbal response, consider the following unfoldings:

A. Consensual

1. The "standard" response, comprising variants of a more or less functionally equivalent kind:
   "Five o'clock."
   "Yes I do. It's five o'clock."
   "Sorry, my watch isn't working."
   "There it is" [pointing to big wall clock].
2. A standard schema of interpretation fundamentally different from the one pertaining to clocks proves to be the one that both participants are applying:
   "No, but I still have the *Newsweek.*"
   "Sure. Anyway, what you want won't take but a minute."
   "No, I left it with the basil."
3. A mutually and openly sustained full transformation of the original (a "keying") proves to prevail:

Director to actress: "No, Natasha. Turn your head or you'll never reach beyond the footlights."
Librarian: "No, that wasn't the title, but it was something like that."[44]
Language teacher: "That's just fine, Johann. A few more times and you'll have the 't' right."

4. Indirect meaning given direct reply:
"Stop worrying. They'll be here."
"All right, all right, so I did lose your present."
Prospective john: "How much for the whole night?"

B. Procedural problems holding off illocutionary concerns

1. System constraints not satisfied:
"What did you say?"
"Bitte, ich kann nur Deutsch sprechen."
"What dime?"

2. Ritual constraints not satisfied:
"I'm sorry, we are not allowed to give out the time. Please phone TI 6-6666."
"Nurse, can't you see I'm trying to tie off this bleeder?"
"Shh, that mike carries."

C. Addressing ritual presuppositions so that the illocutionary point of the initial statement is denied at least temporarily, and a side sequence is established in which the erstwhile respondent becomes the initiator:

44. Borrowed from Fillmore (1973:100), who not only provides some illustrations (in connection with his article's title), but also goes on to offer an injunction:

> We must allow ourselves, first of all, to disregard the infinite range of possible situations in which the sentence was *mentioned* or merely *pronounced*, rather than *used*. It may be that somebody was asked, for example, to pronounce four English monosyllables, putting heavy stress and rising intonation on the last one, and he accidentally came up with our sentence; or a speaker of a foreign language might have been imitating an English sentence he once overheard; or a librarian might have been reading aloud the title of a short story. Since the properties of this infinitely large range of possibilities are in no way constrained by the structure or meaning of this particular sentence, this whole set of possibilities can safely be set aside as an uninteresting problem.

Here I think Fillmore is overdespairing, confusing members and classes. There is an unmanageable number of different ways a sentence can figure, but perhaps not so many *classes* of ways it can figure, and the delineation of these classes can be an interesting problem. That different students will be free to come up with different classes does not undermine the value of examining various attempts to see which seems currently the most useful.

"Why the formality, love?"
"Could I ask where you learned your English?"
"Don't you remember me?"

D. Warranted or unwarranted treatment of asker's move as trickery—in this particular case the assumption being that once a claim is established for initiating talk, it will come to be exploited:
"No." [Not meeting the asker's eyes and hurrying away from him on the assumption that the question might be an instance of the now standard ploy to ready a robbery]
"Say, are you trying to pick me up?"
"Never mind the time, Peterkins, you know you're supposed to be in bed."

E. Jointly sustained fabrication relative to passers-by; e.g.:
[Spy recognition signal] "Yes. Do you happen to have a match?"

F. Unilateral use of features of interaction for the open purpose of play or derision:
1. Failure to perform anticipated ellipsis:
"Yes, I do. . . ."
2. Use of unanticipated schema of interpretation:
"Yes, do you have the inclination?"
[In mock Scots accent] "And may I ask what you want it for?"
3. Anything covered in A through E but reframed for playful use, e.g.:
[Huge, tough-looking black in black neighborhood, on being asked the time by a slight middle-class, white youth, looks into youth's eyes while reaching for watch] "You ain' fixin' to rob me, is you?"

It is some such framework of frameworks that we must seek out; it is some such metaschema that will allow us to accumulate systematic understanding about contexts, not merely warnings that in another context, meaning could be different.

PART FOUR

What, then, is talk viewed interactionally? It is an example of that arrangement by which individuals come together and sustain matters having a ratified, joint, current, and running claim upon attention, a claim which lodges them together in some sort of intersubjective, mental world.[45] Games provide another example, for here the consciously intended move made by one participant must be attended to by the other participants and has much the same meaning for all of them. A sudden "striking" event can constitute another source for this joint arrangement; for at such moments, and typically only for a moment, a common focus of attention is provided that is clearly not the doing of the witnesses, which witnessing is mutually witnessed, the event then having the power to collapse persons theretofore not in a state of talk into a momentary social encounter. But no resource is more effective as a basis for joint involvement than speakings. Words are the great device for fetching speaker and hearer into the same focus of attention and into the same interpretation schema that applies to what is thus attended. But that words are the best means to this end does not mean that words are the only one or that the resulting social organization is intrinsically verbal in character. Indeed, it is when a set of individuals have joined together to maintain a state of talk that nonlinguistic events can most easily function as moves in a conversation. Yet, of course, conversation constitutes an encounter of a special kind. It is not positional moves of tokens on a board that figure as the prime concern; it is utterances, very often ones designed to elicit other utterances or designed to be verbal responses to these elicitations.

Now when an individual is engaged in talk, some of his utterances and nonlinguistic behavior will be taken to have a special temporal relevance, being directed to others present as something he wants assessed, appreciated, understood, *now.* I have spoken here of a move. Now it seems that sometimes the

45. An argument recently pressed by Rommetveit (1974:23):

> Once the other person accepts the invitation to engage in the dialogue, his life situation is temporarily transformed. The two participants leave behind them whatever were their preoccupations at the moment when silence was transformed into speech. From that moment on, they became inhabitants of a partly shared social world, established and continuously modified by their acts of communication. By transcribing what they say into atemporal contents of utterances, moreover, we clearly disregard those dynamic and subjective aspects of their discourse which Merleau Ponty seems to have in mind when referring to "synchronizing change of . . . own existence" and "transformation of . . . being."

speaker and his hearers will understand this move to be primarily a comment on what has just been said, in that degree allowing us to speak of a response; at other times the move will be primarily seen as something to which a response is called for, in which degree it can be called a statement.

And the possibility of each leaves radically open another possibility, namely, that some mixture of the two will occur and in such a way as to discourage the value of the differentiation in the first place. Left open also will be the status of the reference and also the question as to whether or not the move involves action or talk or both. What we are left with, then, is the conversational move carving out a reference, such that the reference and the move may, but need not, be verbal. And what conversation becomes then is a sustained strip or tract of referencings, each referencing tending to bear, but often deviously, some retrospectively perceivable connection to the immediately prior one.

In recommending the notion of talk as a sequence of reference-response moves on the part of participants, such that each choice of reference must be awaited before participants can know what that choice will be (and each next speaker must be awaited before it can be known who he is), I do not mean to argue against formalistic analysis. However tortured the connection can become between last person's talk and current speaker's utterance, that connection must be explored under the auspices of determinism, as though all the degrees of freedom available to whosoever is about to talk can somehow be mapped out, conceptualized, and ordered, somehow neatly grasped and held, somehow made to submit to the patterning-out effected by analysis. If contexts can be grouped into categories according to the way in which they render the standard force of an utterance inapplicable and principles thus developed for determining when this meaning will be set aside, then such must be attempted. Similarly, sequencing must be anticipated and described. We must see, for example, that current speaker's shift from the ordinarily meant meaning of last speaker's statement to an ordinarily excluded one, with humorous intent, can lead to a groan intoned jointly and simultaneously by all other participants and then return to seriousness; or the maneuver can lead to the temporary establishment of a punning rule, thus encouraging an answering pun from next speaker. Standard sequences are thus involved, but these are not sequences of statement and reply but rather sequences at a higher level, ones regarding choice with respect to reach and to the construing of what is reached for. (A compliment seems totally different from an insult, but a likeness is involved if each has been elicited by its kind.) It is thus that uniformities might be uncovered in regard to reference selection, including how standard utterances will be construed as a reference basis for response. In this way we could recognize that talk is full of twists and turns and yet go on to examine routinized sequences of these shiftings. Conversational moves could then be seen to induce or allow affirming moves or countermoves, but this gamelike back-and-forth process might better be called interplay than dialogue.

And with that, the dance in talk might finally be available to us. Without diffidence, we could attend fully to what it means to be in play and we could gain appreciation of the considerable resources available to a speaker each time he holds the floor. For he can use what he is pleased to of the immediate scene as the reference and context of his response, provided only that intelligibility and decorum are maintained. His responses themselves he can present with hedges of various sorts, with routine reservations, so that he can withdraw from the standpoint, and hence the self, these remarks would ordinarily imply. Part-way through his turn he can break frame and introduce an aside, alluding to extraneous matters, or, reflexively, to the effort at communication now in progress—his own—in either case temporarily presenting himself to his listeners on a changed footing. And after he is ostensibly finished speaking, he can beat his listeners to the punch by gesturing a final bracketing comment on what he has just said and upon the person who would engage in such a saying, this comment, too, requiring a shift in stance, the taking up of a new relationship to, a new footing with, his audience. And in artfully managing this sequence of altered footings, he can but succeed, however else he fails, in extending the choices in depth available to the speakers who follow—choices as to what to address their own remarks to. Every conversation, it seems, can raise itself by its own bootstraps, can provide its participants with something to flail at, which process in its entirety can then be made the reference of an aside, this side remark then responsively provoking a joking refusal to disattend it. The box that conversation stuffs us into is Pandora's.

But worse still. By selecting occasions when participants have tacitly agreed to orient themselves to stereotypes about conversation, we can, of course, find that tight constraints obtain, that, for example, a statement by A will be followed by a demonstration from B that he found this statement meaningful and within bounds, and here supplies a response that displays the relevance of this statement and relevance for it. And we can collect elegantly structured interchanges, whether by drawing on occasions when incidental mutual impingement is handled by perfunctory politeness on both sides, or conversely, when two individuals are positioned to sustain having a verbal go at each other, or better still, by drawing on literary texts. But there are other arrangements to draw upon. Individuals who are on familiar, ritually easy terms can find themselves engaged close together (whether jointly or merely similarly) in a nonlinguistic doing that claims their main attention. While thusly stationed, one amongst them may occasionally speak his passing thoughts aloud, half to himself, something equivalent to scratching, yawning, or humming. These ventings call on and allow the license available to those sustaining an open state of talk. An adjacent hearer can elect to let the matter entirely pass, tacitly framing it as though it were the stomach rumblings of another's mind, and continue on undeflected from his task involvements; or, for example, he can hit upon the venting as an occasion to bring the remaining company into a focus of conversational attention for a jibe made at the expense of the person who introduced the initial distraction, which efforts these others may decline to support, and if declining, provide no display of excuse for doing so. In these circumstances the whole framework of conversational constraints —both system and ritual—can become something to honor, to invert, or to disregard, depending as the mood strikes. On these occasions it's not merely that the lid can't be closed; there is no box.

REFERENCES

Austin, J. L. 1965. *How to do things with words.* New York: Oxford University Press.

Bellack, Arno A.; Kliebard, H. M.; Hyman, R. T.; and Smith, F. L. 1966. *The language of the classroom.* New York: Columbia Teachers College Press.

Bloomfield, Leonard. 1946. *Language.* New York: Henry Holt & Co.

Boomer, Donald S. 1965. "Hesitation and grammatical encoding." *Language and Speech* 8:148–58.

Bruner, Jerome. 1974. "The ontogenesis of speech acts." In *Social rules and social behavior,* edited by Peter Collett. Oxford: Department of Experimental Psychology, Oxford University, multigraph.

Clancy, Patricia. 1972. "Analysis of a conversation." *Anthropological Linguistics* 14: 78–86.

Crystal, David. 1969. "The language of conversation." In *Investigating English style,* edited by David Crystal and Derek Davy, pp. 95–124. Bloomington: Indiana University Press.

Dittmann, Allen T. 1972. "The body movement–speech rhythm relationship as a cue to speech encoding." In *Studies in dyadic communication,* edited by A. W. Siegman and B. Pope, pp. 135–51. New York: Pergamon Press.

Duncan, Starkey, Jr. 1972. "Some signals and rules for taking speaking turns in conversations." *Journal of Personality and Social Psychology* 23:283–92.

Ekman, Paul, and Friesen, Wallace. 1969. "The repertoire of nonverbal behavior: Categories, origins, usage and coding." *Semiotica* 1:63–68.

Ervin-Tripp, Susan. 1976. "Is Sybil there? The structure of American directives." *Language in Society* 5:25–66.

Fillmore, Charles J. 1973. "May we come in?" *Semiotica* 9:97–116.

Gluckman, Max. 1962. "Les rites de passage." In *Essays on the ritual of social relations,* edited by Max Gluckman. Manchester: Manchester University Press.

Goffman, Erving. 1961. *Encounters.* Indianapolis: Bobbs-Merrill, Inc.

———. 1967. *Interaction ritual.* New York: Anchor Books.

———. 1971. *Relations in public.* New York: Harper and Row.

———. 1974. *Frame analysis.* New York: Harper and Row.

Goodwin, Charles. 1977. Ph.D. dissertation, University of Pennsylvania.

Goodwin, Marjorie. 1975. "Aspects of the social organization of children's arguments: Some procedures and resources for restructuring positions." Unpublished paper.

———. 1978. "Conversational practices in a peer group of urban black children." Ph.D. dissertation, University of Pennsylvania.

Gordon, David, and Lakoff, George. 1971. "Conversational postulates." In *Papers of the Chicago Linguistic Society,* pp. 63–84. Chicago: Department of Linguistics, University of Chicago.

Grice, H. Paul. 1975. "Logic and conversation." In *syntax and semantics: Speech acts,* vol. 3, edited by Peter Cole and Jerry L. Morgan, pp. 41–58. New York: Academic Press.

Gumperz, John J. Forthcoming. "Language, communication and public negotiation." In *Anthropology and the public interest: Fieldwork and theory,* edited by Peggy R. Sanday. New York: Academic Press.

Gunter, Richard. 1974. *Sentences in dialog.* Columbia, S.C.: Hornbeam Press.

Harris, Zellig. 1951. *Structural linguistics.* Chicago: University of Chicago Phoenix Books.

Hymes, Virginia. 1974. "The ethnography of linguistic intuitions at Warm Springs." Paper presented at NWAVE III, Georgetown University, October 25, 1974.

Jefferson, Gail. 1972. "Side sequences." In *Studies in social interaction,* edited by David Sudnow. New York: The Free Press.

Labov, William, and Fanshel, David. 1977. *Therapeutic discourse: Psychotherapy as conversation.* New York: Academic Press.

Merritt, Marilyn. 1976. "Resources for saying in service encounters." Ph.D. dissertation, Department of Linguistics, University of Pennsylvania.

Pomerantz, Anita May. 1975. "Second assessments: A study of some features of agreements/disagreements." Ph.D. dissertation, University of California, Irvine.

Philips, Susan U. 1974. "The invisible culture: Communication in classroom and community on the Warm Springs Reservation." Ph.D. dissertation, Department of Anthropology, University of Pennsylvania.

Quine, Willard van Orman. 1962. *Mathematical logic.* Rev. ed. New York: Harper and Row.

Rommetveit, Ragnar. 1974. *On message structure: A framework for the study of language and communication.* New York: John Wiley and Sons.

Sacks, Harvey. 1967. Unpublished lecture notes. University of California, Irvine.

———. 1973. Lecture notes. Summer Institute of Linguistics. Ann Arbor, Michigan.

Sacks, Harvey; Schegloff, Emanuel; and Jefferson, Gail. 1974. "A simplest systematics for the organization of turn-taking for conversation." *Language* 50: 696–735.

Schegloff, Emanuel. 1968. "Sequencing in conversational openings." *American Anthropologist* 70:1075–95.

Schegloff, Emanuel, and Sacks, Harvey. 1973. "Opening up closings." *Semiotica* 8:289–327.

Searle, John R. 1975. "Indirect speech acts." In *Syntax and semantics,* edited by Peter Cole and Jerry L. Morgan, pp. 59–82. New York: Academic Press.

———. 1976. "A classification of illocutionary acts." *Language in Society* 5:1–23.

Shatz, Marilyn. 1974. "The comprehension of indirect directives: Can two-year-olds shut the door?" Paper presented at the Summer Meeting, Linguistic Society of America, Amherst, Massachusetts.

Shuy, Roger. 1974. Problems of communication in the cross-cultural medical interview. *Working Papers in Sociolinguistics,* no. 19, December 1974.

Sinclair, J. McH., and Coulthard, R. M. 1975. *Towards an analysis of discourse: The English used by teachers and pupils.* London: Oxford University Press.

Sinclair, J. McH., et al. 1972. The English used by teachers and pupils. Unpublished Final Report to SSRC for the period September 1970 to August 1972.

Stubbs, Michael. 1973. Some structural complexities of talk in meetings. *Working Papers in Discourse Analysis,* no. 5. University of Birmingham: English Language Research.

Vološinov, V. N. 1973. *Marxism and the philosophy of language.* New York: Seminar Press.

Vygotsky, L. S. 1962. *Thought and language.* MIT Press and John Wiley and Sons.

Yngve, Victor H. 1970. On getting a word in edgewise. In *Papers from the Sixth Regional Meeting, Chicago Linguistic Society,* edited by M. A. Campbell et al., pp. 567–78. Chicago: Department of Linguistics, University of Chicago.

2
RESPONSE CRIES

Utterances are not housed in paragraphs but in turns at talk, occasions implying a temporary taking of the floor as well as an alternation of takers.[1] Turns themselves are naturally coupled into two-party interchanges. Interchanges are linked in runs marked off by some sort of topicality. One or more of these topical runs make up the body of a conversation. This interactionist view assumes that every utterance is either a statement establishing the next speaker's words as a reply, or a reply to what the prior speaker has just established, or a mixture of both. Utterances, then, do not stand by themselves, indeed, often make no sense when so heard, but are constructed and timed to support the close social collaboration of speech turn-taking. In nature, the spoken word is only to be found in verbal interplay, being integrally designed for such collective habitats. This paper considers some roguish utterances that appear to violate this interdependence, entering the stream of behavior at peculiar and unnatural places, producing communicative effects but no dialogue. The

1. Grateful acknowledgment is made to *Language,* where this paper first appeared (54[1978]:787–815). Without specific acknowledgment I have incorporated a very large number of suggestions, both general and specific, provided by John Carey, Lee Ann Draud, John Fought, Rochel Gelman, Allen Grimshaw, Gail Jefferson, William Labov, Gillian Sankoff, Joel Sherzer, W. John Smith, and an anonymous reviewer. I am grateful to this community of help; with it I have been able to progress from theft to pillage. Comments on broadcasters' talk are based on a study reported in this volume.

paper begins with a special class of spoken sentences, and ends with a special class of vocalizations, the first failing to qualify as communication, the second failing not to.

I

To be all alone, to be a "solitary" in the sense of being out of sight and sound of everyone, is not to be alone in another way, namely, as a "single," a party of one, a person not in a *with,* a person unaccompanied "socially" by others in some public undertaking (itself often crowded), such as sidewalk traffic, shopping in stores, and restaurant dining.[2]

Allowing the locution "in our society," and, incidentally, the use of *we* as a means of referring to the individual without specifying gender, it can be said that when we members of society are solitary, or at least assume we are, we can have occasion to make passing comments aloud. We kibitz our own undertakings, rehearse or relive a run-in with someone, speak to ourselves judgmentally about our own doings (offering words of encouragement or blame in an editorial voice that seems to be that of an overseer more than ourselves), and verbally mark junctures in our physical doings. Speaking audibly, we address ourselves, constituting ourselves the sole intended recipient of our own remarks. Or, speaking in our own name, we address a remark to someone who isn't present to receive it. This is self-communication, specifically, "self-talk." Although a conversationlike exchange of speaker-hearer roles may sometimes occur, this seems unusual. Either we address an absent other or address ourselves in the name of some standard-bearing voice. Self-talk of one type seems rarely replied to by self-talk of the other. I might add that the voice or name in which we address a remark to ourselves can be just what we might properly use in addressing a remark to someone else (especially someone familiar enough with our

2. This easy contrast conceals some complications. For a *with*—a party of more than one—can be solitary, too, as when a lone couple picnics on a deserted beach. Strictly speaking, then, a *single* is a party of one present among other parties, whereas a solitary individual is a party of one with no other parties present.

world to understand cryptic references), or what another might properly use in talking to us. It is not the perspective and standards that are peculiar or the words and phrases through which they are realized, but only that there are more roles than persons. To talk to oneself is to generate a full complement of two communication roles—speaker and hearer—without a full complement of role-performers, and which of the two roles—speaker or hearer—is the one without its own real performer is not the first issue.

Self-talk could, of course, be characterized as a form of egocentricity, developmentally appropriate in childhood years and only reappearing later "in certain men and women of a puerile disposition" (Piaget 1974:40). Common sense, after all, recommends that the purpose of speech is to convey thoughts to others, and a self-talker necessarily conveys them to someone who already knows them. To interrogate, inform, beseech, persuade, threaten, or command oneself is to push against oneself or at best to get to where one already is, in either case with small chance of achieving movement. To say something to someone who isn't there to hear it seems equally footless.

Or worse, self-talk might appear to be a kind of perversion, a form of linguistic self-abuse. Solitary individuals who can be happily immersed in talking to themselves need not in that degree seek out the company of their fellows; they need not go abroad to find conversational company, a convenience that works to the general detriment of social life. Such home consumption in regard to the other kind of intercourse qualifies either as incest or masturbation.

A more serious argument would be that self-talk is merely an out-loud version of reverie, the latter being the original form. Such a view, however, misses the sense in which daydreaming is different from silent, fuguelike, well-reasoned discussion with oneself, let alone the point (on which Piaget [1962:7] and Vygotsky [1962:19–20] seem to agree) that the out-loud version of reverie and of constructive thought may precede the silent versions developmentally. And misses, too, the idea that both the autistic and constructive forms of "inner speech" are considerably removed from facially animated talk in which the speaker overtly gives the appearance of being actively engrossed in a spirited exchange with invisible others, his eyes and lips alive with the proceedings.

In any case, in our society at least, self-talk is not dignified as constituting an official claim upon its sender-recipient—true, incidentally, also of fantasy, "wool gathering," and the like. There are no circumstances in which we can say, "I'm sorry, I can't come right now, I'm busy talking to myself." And anyway, hearers ordinarily would not *reply* to our self-talk any more than they would to the words spoken by an actor on the stage, although they might otherwise *react* to both. Were a hearer to say, "What?", that would stand as a rebuke to conduct, not a request for a rerun, much as is the case when a teacher uses that response to squelch chatter occurring at the back of the room; or, with a different intonation, that the self-talk had been misheard as the ordinary kind, a possibility which could induce a reply such as, "Sorry, I was only talking to myself."

Indeed, in our society a taboo is placed on self-talk. Thus, it is mainly through self-observation and hearsay that one can find out that a considerable amount goes on. Admittedly, the matter has a Lewis Carroll touch. For the offense seems to be created by the very person who catches the offender out, it being the witnessing of the deed which transforms it into an improper one. (Solitary self-talkers may occasionally find themselves terminating a spate of self-talk with a self-directed reproach, but in doing so would seem to be catching *themselves* out—sometimes employing self-talk to do so.) In point of fact, the misdoing is not so much tied up with doing it in public as *continuing* to do it in public. We are all, it seems, allowed to be caught stopping talking to ourselves on one occasion or another.

It is to be expected that questions of frames and their limits will arise. Strictly speaking, dictating a letter to a machine, rehearsing a play to a mirror, and praying aloud at our bedside are not examples of self-talk, but should others unexpectedly enter the scene of this sort of solitary labor, we might still feel a little uneasy and look for another type of work. Similarly, there are comedy routines in which the butt is made vulnerable by having to sustain a full-blown discussion with someone who is hidden from general view. And there are well-known comic gestures by which someone caught talking to himself attempts to transform the delict into a yawn or into the just-acceptable vocalizations of whistling, humming, or singing.[3] But behind these risible issues of frame is the serious fact that an adult who fails to attempt to conceal his self-talk, or at least to stop smartly on the appearance of another person, is in trouble. Under the term verbal hallucination we attribute failure in decorum here to "mental illness."[4]

Given the solitary's recourse to self-addressed remarks well into adult life, and that such talk is not merely a transitional feature of primary socialization (if, indeed, a natural phase of childhood development), one is encouraged to shift from a developmental to an interactional approach. Self-talk, when performed in its apparently permissible habitat—the self-talker all alone—is by way of being a mimicry of something that has its initial and natural provenance in speech between persons, this in turn implying a social encounter and the arrangement of participants through which encounters are sustained. (Such transplantation, note, is certainly not restricted to deviant activity; for example, a writer does it when he quotes in the body of his own single sentence an entire paragraph from a cited text, thereby pseudomorphically depositing in one form something that in nature belongs to another.)

With self-talk, then, one might want to say that a sort of impersonation is occurring; after all, we can best compliment or upbraid ourselves in the name of someone other than the self to whom the comments are directed. But what is intended in self-talk is not so much the mere citation or recording of what a

3. Nor should the opposite framing issue be neglected. A man talking to himself at a bar may cause the bartender to think him drunk, not peculiar, and if he wants to continue drinking may suffer more hardship from the first imputation than the second. (An instance is reported to me of a barroom self-talker being misframed as always having had too much and temporarily solving this threat to his drinking rights by retreating to the tavern's telephone booth to do his self-talking.)

4. I leave open the question of whether the individual who engages in verbal hallucination does so in order to create an impression of derangement, or for other reasons, and is merely indifferent to how he appears, or carries on in spite of some concern for the proprieties. And open, too, the question of whether in treating unabashed self-talk as a natural index of alienation, we have (in our society) any good grounds for our induction.

monitoring voice might say, or what we would say to another if given a chance, but the stage-acting of a version of the delivery, albeit only vaguely a version of its reception. What is set into the ongoing text is not merely words, but their animator also—indeed, the whole interactional arrangement in which such words might get spoken. To this end we briefly split ourselves in two, projecting the character who talks and the character to whom such words could be appropriately directed. Or we summon up the presence of others in order to say something to them. Self-talk, then, involves the lifting of a form of interaction from its natural place and its employment in a special way.

Self-talk described in this way recommends consideration of the soliloquy, long a feature of western drama, although not currently fashionable.[5] An actor comes stage center and harangues himself, sometimes at enormous length, divulging his inner thoughts on a pertinent matter with well-projected audibility. This behavior, of course, is not really an exception to the application of the rule against public self-talk. Your soliloquizer is really talking to self when no one is around; we members of the audience are supernatural, out-of-frame eavesdroppers. Were a character from the dramatized world to approach, our speaker would audibly (to us) self-direct a warning:

> But soft, I see that Jeffrey even now doth come. To the appearance of innocent business then.

and would stop soliloquizing. Were he to continue to self-talk, it would be because the script has instructed him to fail to notice the figure all the rest of us have seen approach.

Now, if talking to oneself in private involves a mocking-up of conversation and a recasting of its complementarity, then the production of this recasting on the stage in the bloated format of a soliloquy obviously involves a further insetting, and a transformation of what has already been transformed. The same could be

5. Never necessary in novels and comics where the author has the right to open up a character's head so the reader can peer into the ideas it contains, and technologically no longer necessary in the competing modes of commercial make-believe—movies and television plays. In these latter a voice-over effect allows us to enter into the inner thoughts of a character who is shown silently musing.

said, incidentally, about a printed advertisement which features realistically posed live models whose sentiments are cast into well-articulated inner speech in broken-line balloons above their heads, providing a text that the other figures in the pictured world can't perceive but we real people can, to be distinguished from the continuous-line balloon for containing words that one figure openly states to another.

Here, I believe, is a crucial feature of human communication. Behavior and appearance are ritualized—in something like the ethological sense—through such ethologically defined processes as exaggeration, stereotyping, standardization of intensity, loosening of contextual requirements, and so forth. In the case under question, however, these transformations occur to a form of interaction, a communication arrangement, a standard set of participant alignments. I believe that any analysis of self-talk (or for that matter, any other form of communication) that does not attend to this nonlinguistic sense of embedding and transformation is unlikely to be satisfactory.

II

These parables about self-talk provide entrance to a mundane text. First, definitions: by a *social situation* I mean any physical area anywhere within which two or more persons find themselves in visual and aural range of one another. The term "gathering" can be used to refer to the bodies that are thus present. No restriction is implied about the relationship of those in the situation: they may all be involved in the same conversational encounter, in the sense of being ratified participants of the same state of talk; some may be in an encounter while others are not, or are, but in a different one; or no talk may be occurring. Some, all, or none of those present may be definable as together in terms of social participation, that is, in a "with."

Although almost every kind of mayhem can be committed in social situations, one class of breaches bears specifically on social situations as such, that is, on the social organization common to face-to-face gatherings of all kinds. In a word, although many delicts are *situated,* only some are *situational.* As for social situations as such, we owe any one in which we might find ourselves evidence that we are reasonably alive to what is already in it, and furthermore to what might arise, whether on schedule or unexpectedly. Should need for immediate action be required of us, we will be ready; if not mobilized, then able to mobilize. A sort of communication tonus is implied. If addressed by anyone in the situation we should not have far to go to respond, if not to reply. All in all, a certain respect and regard is to be shown to the situation-at-large. And these demonstrations confirm that we are able and willing to enter into the perspective of the others present, even if no more than is required to collaborate in the intricacies of talk and pedestrian traffic. In our society, then, it is generally taboo in public to be drunken, to belch or pass wind perceptibly, to daydream or doze, or to be disarrayed with respect to clothing and cosmetics—and all these for the same reason. These acts comprise our conventional repertoire, our prescribed stock of "symptoms," for demonstrating a lack of respectful alertness in and to the situation, their inhibition our way of "doing" presence, and thereby self-respect. And the demonstration can be made with sound; audible indicators are involved as well as visual ones.

It is plain, then, that self-talk, in a central sense, is situational in character, not merely situated. Its occurrence strikes directly at our sense of the orientation of the speaker to the situation as a whole. Self-talk is taken to involve the talker in a situationally inappropriate way. Differently put, our self-talk—like other "mental symptoms"—is a threat to intersubjectivity; it warns others that they might be wrong in assuming a jointly maintained base of ready mutual intelligibility among all persons present. Understandably, self-talk is less an offense in private than in public; after all, the sort of self-mobilization and readiness it is taken to disprove is not much required when one is all alone.

This general argument makes sense of a considerable number of minor details. In a waiting room or public means of transportation, where it is evident that little personal attention to pedestrian traffic is required, and therefore less than a usual amount of aliveness to the surround, reading is allowed in our society, along with such self-withdrawal to a printed world as this makes possible. (Observe that reading itself is institutionalized as something that can be set aside in a moment should a reason present itself, something that can be picked up and put down without ceremony, a definition that does not hold for all of our pleasures.) However, chuckling aloud to ourselves in response to what we are reading is suspect, for this can imply that we are too freely immersed in the scene we are reading about to retain dissociated concern for the scene in which our reading occurs. Interestingly, should we mouth the read words to ourselves and in the process make the mouthings audible, we will be taken to be unschooled, not unhinged—unless, of course, our general appearance implies a high educational status and therefore no "natural" reason for uncontained reading. (This is not to deny that some mumbled reading gives the impression of too much effort invested in the sheer task of reading to allow a seemly reserve for the situation-at-large.)

In public, we are allowed to become fairly deeply involved in talk with others we are with, providing this does not lead us to block traffic or intrude on the sound preserve of others; presumably our capacity to share talk with one other implies we are able to share it with those who see us talking. So, too, we can conduct a conversation aloud over an unboothed street phone while either turning our back to the flow of pedestrian traffic or watching it in an abstracted way, without the words being thought improper; for even though our coparticipant is not visually present, a natural one can be taken to exist, and an accounting is available as to where, cognitively speaking, we have gone, and, moreover, that this "where" is a familiar place to which the others could see themselves traveling, and one from which we could be duly recalled should events warrant.[6]

Observe also that we can with some impunity address words in public to a pet, presumably on the grounds that the animal can

6. I once saw an adolescent black girl collapse her male companion in laughter on a busy downtown street by moving away from him to a litter can in which she had spied a plastic toy phone. Holding the phone up to her mouth and ear while letting the cord remain in the can, and then, half-turning as if to view the passing parade in a dissociated manner (as one does when anchored to an open telephone kiosk), she projected a loud and lively conversation into the mouthpiece. Such an act puts on public order in a rather deep way, striking at its accommodative close readings, ones we all ordinarily support without much awareness.

appreciate the affective element of the talk, if nothing else. We extend the same sort of regard to infants. Although on both these occasions a full-fledged recipient is not present to reply to our words, it is clear that no imagined person or alien agency has captured our attention. Moreover, special forms of talk are involved: for example, the praising/admonishing sort of evaluative utterance that routinely leads to no verbal reply when employed in talk between competents, or mimicked babytalk projected as the talk the incompetent would employ were it able to speak ("say-foring"). Should a pet or infant be addressed in quite ordinary speech, then, of course, something would be heard as very odd indeed. Incidentally, to be seen walking down the street alone while *silently* gesticulating a conversation with an absent other is as much a breach as talking aloud to ourselves—for it is equally taken as evidence of alienation.

Finally, there are the words we emit (sometimes very loudly) to summon another into talk. Although such a speaking begins by being outside of talk with actual others, its intended recipient is likely quickly to confirm—by ritualized orientation, if not by a verbal reply—the existence of the required environment, doing so before our utterance is completed.[7] A summons that is openly snubbed or apparently undetected, however, can leave us feeling that we have been caught engaging in something like talking to ourselves, and moreover very noticeably.[8]

To say that self-talk is a situational impropriety is not to say

7. A pet or a small child can be repeatedly summoned with a loud cry when it is not in sight, with some disturbance to persons in range; but a "mental" condition is not ordinarily imputed. Typically it is understood that the words are merely a signal—a toy whistle would do—to come home, or to come into view to receive a message, not to come into protracted conversation from wherever the signal is heard.

8. Such an occurrence is but one instance of the deplorable class of occasions when we throw ourselves full face into an encounter where none can be developed, as when, for example, we respond to a summons that was meant for someone behind us, or warmly greet a total stranger mistakenly taken to be someone we know well, or (as already mentioned) mistakenly reply to someone's self-talk. The standard statement by which the individual whom we have improperly entangled sets us right, for example, "Sorry, I'm afraid you've . . . ," itself has a very uneasy existence. Such a remark is fully housed within a conversational exchange that was never properly established, and its purpose is to deny a relationship that is itself required for the remark to be made.

that it is a *conversational* delict—no more, that is, than any other sounded breach of decorum, such as an uncovered, audible yawn. Desisting from self-talk is not something we owe our fellow conversationalists as such; that is, it is not owed to them in their capacity as coparticipants in a specific encounter and thus to them only. Clearly it is owed to all those in sight and sound of us, precisely as we owe them avoidance of the other kinds of improper sounds. The individual who begins to talk to himself while in a conversational encounter will cause the other participants in the encounter to think him odd; but for the same reason and in the same way those not in the encounter but within range of it will think him odd, too. Clearly, here the conversational circle is not the relevant unit; the social situation is. Like catching a snail outside its shell, words are here caught outside of conversations, outside of ratified states of talk; one is saved from the linguistic horror of this fact only because the words themselves ought not to have been spoken. In fact, here talk is no more conversational than is a belch; it merely lasts longer and reflects adversely on a different part of personality.

So a rule: *No talking to oneself in public.* But, of course, the lay formulation of a rule never gets to the bone, it merely tells us where to start digging. In linguistic phrasing, *No talking to oneself in public* is a prescriptive rule of communication; the descriptive rule —the practice—is likely to be less neat and is certain to be less ready to hand, allowing, if not encouraging, variously grounded exceptions. The framework of normative understandings that *is* involved is not recorded, or cited, or available in summary form from informants. It must be pieced out by the student, in part by uncovering, collecting, collating, and interpreting all possible exceptions to the stated rule.

III

An unaccompanied man—a single—is walking down the street past others. His general dress and manner have given anyone who views him evidence of his sobriety, innocent intent, suitable aliveness to the situation, and general social competency. His left foot strikes an obtruding piece of pavement and he stumbles. He instantly catches himself, rights himself more or less efficiently, and continues on.

Up to this point his competence at walking had been taken for granted by those who witnessed him, confirming their assessment of him in this connection. His tripping casts these imputations suddenly into doubt. Therefore, before he continues he may well engage in some actions that have nothing to do with the laws of mechanics. The remedial work he performs is likely to be aimed at correcting the threat to his reputation, as well as his posture. He can pause for a moment to examine the walk, as if intellectually concerned (as competent persons with their wits about them would be) to discover what in the world could possibly have caused him to falter, the implication being that anyone else would certainly have stumbled, too. Or he can appear to address a wry little smile to himself to show that he himself takes the whole incident as a joke, something quite uncharacteristic, something that can hardly touch the security he feels in his own manifest competency and therefore warranting no serious account. Or he can "overplay" his lurch, comically extending the disequilibrium, thereby concealing the actual deviation from normal ambulatory orientation with clowning movements, implying a *persona* obviously not his serious one.

In brief, our subject externalizes a presumed inward state and acts so as to make discernible the special circumstances which presumably produced it. He tells a little story to the situation. He renders himself easy to assess by all those in the gathering, even as he guides what is to be their assessment. He presents an act specialized in a conventional way for providing information—a *display*—a communication in the ethological, not the linguistic, sense. The behavior here is very animal-like, except that what the human animal seems to be responding to is not so much an obvious biological threat as a threat to the reputation it would ordinarily try to maintain in matters of social competence. Nor is it hard to catch the individual in a very standard look—the hasty, surreptitious survey sometimes made right after committing a fleeting discreditable deed. The purpose is to see whether witnessing has occurred and remedial action is therefore necessary, this assessment itself done quickly enough so that a remedy, if necessary, can be provided with the same dispatch as occurs when there is no doubt from the start that it will be necessary.

However, instead of (or as a supplement to) engaging in a choreographed accounting that is visually available, our subject may utter a cry of wonderment, such as *What in the world!* Again he renders readily accessible to witnesses what he chooses to assign to his inward state, along with directing attention to what produced it, but this time the display is largely auditory. Moreover, if nonvocal gestures in conjunction with the visible and audible scene can't conveniently provide the required information, then self-talk will be the indicated alternative. Suddenly stopping in his tracks, the individual need only grimace and clutch at his heart when the issue is an open manhole at his feet; the same stopping consequent on his remembering that he was supposed to be somewhere else is more likely to be accounted for by words. (Presumably the more obscure the matter, the more extended the self-remarks will have to be and perhaps the less likely is the individual to offer them.)

I am arguing here that what in some sense is part of the subject matter of linguistics can require the examination of our relation to social situations at large, not merely our relation to conversations. For apparently verbalizations quite in the absence of conversations can play much the same role as a choreographed bit of nonvocal behavior. Both together are like other situational acts of propriety and impropriety in that they are accessible to the entire surround and in a sense designed for it. They are like clothing more than like speech. However, unlike clothing or cosmetics, these displays—be they vocal or in pantomime—are to be interpreted as bearing on a passing event, an event with a limited course in time. (What we wear can certainly be taken as an indication of our attitude to the social occasion at hand but hardly to specific events occurring during the occasion.) Necessarily, if unanticipated passing events are to be addressed, a marker must be employed that can be introduced just at the moment the event occurs, and withdrawn when concern for the event has been.

IV

It has been argued that there is a prohibition against public self-talk, and that breachings of this rule have a display character; yet also that there are social situations in which one could expect self-talk. Indeed, I think that the very force which leads us to refrain from self-talk in almost all situations might itself cause us to indulge in self-talk during certain exceptional ones. In this light, consider now in greater detail a few environments in which exposed self-talk is frequently found.

On our being "informed" of the death of a loved one (only by accident are we "told," this latter verb implying that the news might be conveyed in passing), a brief flooding out into tears is certainly not amiss in our society. As might be expected, it is just then that public self-talk is also sanctioned. Thus Sudnow (1967:141) describes the giving of bad news in hospitals:

> While no sympathy gestures are made, neither does the doctor withdraw from the scene altogether by leaving the room, as, for example, does the telegram delivery boy. The doctor is concerned that the scene be contained and that he have some control over its progress, that it not, for example, follow him out into the hall. In nearly all cases the first genuine interchange of remarks was initiated by the relative. During the period of crying, if there is any, relatives frequently "talk." Examples are: "I can't believe it," "It's just not fair," "Goddamn," "Not John . . . no. . . ." These remarks are not responded to as they are not addressed to anyone. Frequently, they are punctuated by crying. The physician remains silent.

The commonsense explanation here is that such informings strike at our self so violently that self-involvement immediately thereafter is reasonable, an excusable imposition of our own concerns upon everyone else in the gathering. Whatever the case, convention seems to establish a class of "all-too-human" crises that are to be treated as something anyone not directly involved ought yet to appreciate, giving us victims the passing right to be momentary centers of sympathetic attention and providing a legitimate place for "anything" we do during the occasion. Indeed, our utter self-containment during such moments might create uneasiness in others concerning our psychological habitat, causing them to wonder how responsive we might be to ordinary situated concerns directly involving them.

Not all environments which favor self-talk are conventionally understood to do so. For example, podium speakers who suddenly find themselves with a page or line missing from their texts or with faulty microphones will sometimes elect to switch from talking to the audience to talking to themselves, addressing a full sentence of bewilderment, chagrin, or anger for their own ears and (apparently) their own benefit, albeit half-audibly to the room. Even in broadcast talk, speakers who lose their places, misplace their scripts, or find themselves with incoherent texts or improperly functioning equipment, may radically break frame in this way, apparently suddenly turning their backs on their obligations to sustain the role of speaker-to-an-audience. It is highly unprofessional, of course, to engage in *sotto voce,* self-directed remarks under just those microphonic conditions which ensure their audibility; but broadcasters may be more concerned at this point to show that some part of them is shocked by the hitch and in some way not responsible for it than to maintain broadcasting decorum. Also, being the sole source of meaningful events for their listeners, they may feel that the full text of their subjective response is better than no text at all. Note, there are other social situations which provide a speaker with an audience that is captive and concerned, and which thereby encourage self-talk. Drivers of buses, taxis, and private cars can shout unflattering judgments of invasive motorists and pedestrians when these have passed out of range, and feel no compunction about thus talking aloud to themselves in the presence of their passengers. After all, there is a sense in which their contretemps in traffic visibly and identically impinge on everyone in the vehicle simultaneously.[9]

9. And, of course, there will be occasions of equivalent license for nonverbal signs, both vocal and gesticulatory. In trying on a shoe we can emit all manner of grimaces and obscure sounds, for these signs provide running evidence of fit, and such information is the official, chief concern at that moment of all parties to the transaction, including the shoe clerk. Similarly, a sportsman or athlete is free to perform an enormous flailing-about when he flubs; among other reasons for this license, he can be sure (if anyone can) that his circumstances are fully attended and appreciated by everyone who is watching the action. After all, such clarity of intent is what sports are all about.

That drivers may actually wait until the apparent target of their remarks cannot hear them points to another location for self-talk, which is also suggested by the lay term "muttering." Frustrated by someone's authority, we can mutter words of complaint under the breath as the target turns away out of apparent conversational earshot. (Here is a structural equivalent of what children do when they stick out their tongues or put their thumbs to their noses just as their admonisher turns away.) For these subvocalizations reside in the very interstice between a state of talk and mere copresence, more specifically, in the transition from the first to the second. And here function seems plain. In muttering we convey that although we are now going along with the line established by the speaker (and authority), our spirit has not been won over, and compliance is not to be counted on. The display is aimed either at third parties or at the authority itself, but in such a way that we can deny our intent and the authority can feign not hearing what we have said about him. Again a form of communication that hardly fits the linguistic model of speaker and addressed recipient; for here we provide a reply to the speaker that is displaced from him to third parties and/or to ourselves. Instead of being the recipient of our reply, the initial speaker becomes merely the object or target of our response. Observe, as with tongue-sticking, muttering is a time-limited communication, entering as a "last word," a post-terminal touch to a just-terminated encounter, and thus escapes for incidental reasons the injunction against persisting in public self-talk.

Consideration of self-talk in one kind of interstice recommends consideration of self-talk in others. For example, if we are stopped for a moment's friendly chat just before entering or leaving an establishment or turning down a street, we may provide a one-sentence description of the business we are about to turn to, this account serving as a rationale for our withdrawing and as evidence that there are other calls upon our time. Interestingly enough, this utterance is sometimes postponed until the moment when the encounter has just finished, in which case we may mumble the account half-aloud and somewhat to ourselves. Here again is self-talk that is located transitionally between a state of talk and mere copresence, and again self-communication that is self-terminating, although this time because the communicator, not the hearer, is moving away. Here it is inescapably clear that the self-talker is providing information verbally to others present, merely not using the standard arrangement—a ratified state of talk—for doing so.

Finally, it must be allowed that when circumstances conspire to thrust us into a course of action whose appearance might raise questions about our moral character or self-respect, we often elect to be seen as self-talkers in preference. If we stoop to pick up a coin on a busy street, we might well be inclined to identify its denomination to ourselves aloud, simultaneously expressing surprise, even though we ourselves are no longer in need of the information. For the street is to be framed as a place of passage not—as it might be to a child or a vagrant—a hunting ground for bits of refuse. If what we thought was a coin turns out to be a worthless slug, then we might feel urged to externalize through sound and pantomime that we can laugh at the fools we have made of ourselves.[10] Trying to open the door of a car we have mistaken for our own and discovering our mistake, we are careful to blurt out a self-directed remark that properly frames our act for those who witness it, advertising inadequate attentiveness to deny we are a thief.

With these suggestions of where self-talk is to be found, one can return and take a second look at the conventional argument that children engage in it because they aren't yet socialized into the modesties of self-containment, the proprieties of persondom. Vygotsky, responding to what he took to be Piaget's position, long ago provided a lead ([1934], 1962:16):

10. Picking money off the street is, of course, a complicated matter. Pennies and even nickels we might well forgo, the doubt cast on our conduct of more concern to us than the money. (We accept the same small sums in change when paying for something in a shop, but there a money transaction is the official business at hand.) Should another in our sight drop such a coin, we might well be inclined to retrieve and return it, for we are allowed a distractive orientation to the ground we walk on so long as this is patently in the interests of others. (If we don't retrieve our own small coins, then we run the risk of others doing so for us and the necessity, therefore, of showing gratitude.) If the sum is large enough to qualify as beyond the rule of finders keepers, we might quickly glance around to see if we have been seen, carefully refraining from saying or gesturing anything else. Covert also may be our act whenever we spy a coin of any denomination to see if any others are not to be found, too.

> In order to determine what causes egocentric talk, what circumstances provoke it, we organized the children's activities in much the same way Piaget did, but we added a series of frustrations and difficulties. For instance, when a child was getting ready to draw, he would suddenly find that there was no paper, or no pencil of the color he needed. In other words, by obstructing his free activity we made him face problems.
>
> We found that in these difficult situations the coefficient of egocentric speech almost doubled, in comparison with Piaget's normal figure for the same age and also in comparison with our figure for children not facing these problems. The child would try to grasp and to remedy the situation in talking to himself: "Where's the pencil? I need a blue pencil. Never mind, I'll draw with the red one and wet it with water; it will become dark and look like blue."[11]

The implication is that self-talk serves a self-guidance function, and will be most evident, presumably, when the child senses that task performance is problematic. Given that Vygotsky's early work required an adult observer to be within listening distance, one could go on to suggest an additional interpretation, namely that for children the contingencies are so great in undertaking any task, and the likelihood so strong that they will be entirely discounted as reasonably intentioned persons if they fail (or indeed that they will be seen as just idling or fooling around anyway), that some voicing of what they are about is something

11. Piaget, as his reply (1962:3–4) to a reading of Vygotsky's manuscript suggests, apparently meant "egocentricity" to refer to speech (or any other behavior) that did not take into consideration the perspective of the other in some way, and only incidentally (if at all) to speech not openly addressed to others, the latter being what Vygotsky described, and which I call "self-talk." (Piaget's concept of egocentricity has led to another confusion, a failure to discriminate two matters: taking the point of view of the other in order to discover what his attitude and action will be, and accepting for oneself, or identifying with, the perspective of the other. The classic con operation illustrates how fully the first form of sympathy may be required and produced without leading to the second.) It is probably the case that there is a whole array of different forms of talk that are not fully other-involving, that some of these decrease with age, some increase to a point, and still others are not especially age-related. For a review of some of the possibilities, the Piaget-Vygotsky debate, and the developmental literature on self-talk in general (under the perhaps better title, "Private Speech"), see Kohlberg et al. (1968).

they are always prepared to offer. An adult attempting to learn to skate might be equally self-talkative.[12]

Some loose generalizations might be drawn from these descriptions of places for self-talk. First, when we address a remark to ourselves in public, we are likely to be in sudden need of reestablishing ourselves in the eyes and ears of witnesses as honest, competent persons not to be trifled with, and an expression of chagrin, wonderment, anger, and so forth would seem to help in this—at least establishing what our expectations for ourselves are, even if in this case they can't be sustained. Second, one could argue that self-talk occurs right at the moment when the predicament of the speaker is evident to the whole gathering in a flash or can be made so, assuring that the utterance will come as an understandable reaction to an understood event; it will come from a mind that has not drifted from the situation, a mind readily tracked. The alien world reflected in hallucinatory talk is therefore specifically avoided, and so, too, therefore, some of the impropriety of talking outside the precincts of a ratified conversation. Nor is "understandable" here merely a matter of cognition. To appreciate quickly another's circumstances (it seems) is to be able to place ourselves in them empathetically. Correspondingly, the best assurance another can have that we will understand him is to offer himself to us in a version with which we can identify. Instead, then, of thinking of self-talk as something blurted out under pressure, it might better be thought of as a mode of response constantly readied for those circumstances in which it is excusable. Indeed, the time and place when our private

12. Recently Jenny Cook-Gumperz and William Corsaro have offered a more compelling account (1976:29): "We have found that children consistently provide verbal descriptions of their behavior at various points in spontaneous fantasy in that it cues other interactants to what is presently occurring as well as provides possibilities for plugging into and expanding upon the emerging social event." The authors imply that if a fantasy world is to be built up during *joint* play, then words alone are likely to be the resource that will have to be employed, and an open recourse to self-talk then becomes an effective way to flesh out what is supposed to be unfolding for all the participants in the fantasy.

A purely cognitive interpretation of certain action-oriented, self-directed words ("nonnominal expressions") has also been recently recommended by Alison Gopnik (1977:15–20).

reaction is what strangers present *need* to know about is the occasion when self-talk is more than excusable.[13]

V

Earlier it was suggested that when an unaccompanied man stumbles, he may present his case by means of self-talk instead of silent gesture. However, there is another route to the advertisement of self-respect. He can emit one or two words of exclamatory imprecation, such as *hell* or *shit.* Observe, these ejaculatory expressions are nothing like the pointed shout of warning one individual might utter to and for another, nor even like an openly directed broadcast to all-in-hearing, such as a street vendor's cry or a shriek for help. Talk in the ordinary sense is apparently not at issue. In no immediate way do such utterances belong to a conversational encounter, a ritually ratified state of talk embracing ratified participants, nor to a summoning to one. First speaker's utterance does not officially establish a slot which second speaker is under some obligation to fill, for there is no ratified speaker and recipient—not even imaginary ones—merely actor and witness. To be sure, an interjection is involved, but one that interrupts a course of physical action, not an utterance.

When, unaccompanied, we trip and curse ourselves (or the walk, or the whole wide world), we curse *to* ourselves; we appear to address ourselves. Therefore, a kind of self-remarking seems to be involved. Like the publicly tolerated self-talk already considered, imprecations seem to be styled to be overheard in a gathering. Indeed, the styling is specific in this regard. With no one present in the individual's surround, I believe the expression is quite likely to be omitted. If women and children are present, your male self-communicator is quite likely to censor his cries accordingly—a man who utters *fuck* when he stumbles in a

13. Understandably, stage soliloquies occur only when the character's personal feelings about his circumstances are exactly what we members of the audience require to be privy to if we are to be properly positioned in the drama unfolding.

foundry is quite likely to avoid that particular expletive should he trip in a day-nursery. If we can see that persons very close by can see what we have just done (or failed to do), then whispered expletives are possible; if witnesses are far away, then shouted sounds will be required. "Recipient design" is involved (to use Harvey Sacks's term) and so quickly applied as to suggest that continuous monitoring of the situation is being sustained, enabling just this adjustment to take place when the moment requiring it comes. Of course, in any case we will have taken the time to encode our vocalization in the conventional lexicon of our language (which is, incidentally, likely to be the local one), a feat that is instantaneously accomplished even sometimes by bilinguals who in addition must generally select their imprecations from the language of their witnesses.[14] (This is not to say that bilinguals won't use a harsh imprecation from one language in place of a less harsh one drawn from the language in use, foreignness apparently serving as a mitigation of strength.) Significantly, here is a form of behavior whose very meaning is that it is something blurted out, something that has escaped control, and so such behavior very often is and has; but this impulsive feature does not mark the limits to which the utterance is socially processed, rather the conventionalized styling to which it is obliged to adhere.

It is plain that singles use imprecations in a variety of circumstances. Racing unsuccessfully to enter a turnstile before it automatically closes, or a door before it is locked for the evening, may do it; coming up to what has just now become a brick wall, we may exhibit frustration and chagrin, often with a curse. (Others, having formulated a possible reading of the precipitous rush we have made, can find that our imprecations are a way of confirming their interpretation, putting a period to the behavioral sentence we have played out, bringing the little vignette to a close, and reverting us to someone easily disattendable.) Precariously carrying too many parcels, we may curse at the moment they fall. The horse we have bet on being nosed out at the finish line, we may damn our misfortune while tearing up our tickets;

14. It would be interesting to know whether or not bilingual children who self-talk select the code likely to be employed by the others in their presence.

our cause for disappointment, anger, and chagrin amply evident, or at least easily surmisable, we have license to wail to the world. Walking along a wintry street that carries a record-breaking snow now turned to slush, we are in a position to cry *God!* in open private response, but as it happens we do so just at the point of passing another, the cause of our remark and the state of our mind perfectly plain and understandable. It might be added that the particular imprecations I have so far used as illustrations seem in our society to be the special domain of males—females, traditionally at least, employing softer expressions. Nor, as is now well known, is this gender convention impervious to rapid politically inspired change.

Finally, I want to recommend that although imprecations and extended self-remarks can be found in much the same slot, do much the same work, and indeed often appear together, raising the question as to why they should be described separately, judgment should be reserved concerning their equivalence. Other questions must be considered first.

VI

The functioning of imprecations raises the question of an allied set of acts that can be performed by singles: *response cries,* namely, exclamatory interjections which are not full-fledged words. *Oops!* is an example. These nonlexicalized, discrete interjections, like certain unsegmented, tonal, prosodic features of speech, comport neatly with our doctrine of human nature. We see such "expression" as a natural overflowing, a flooding up of previously contained feeling, a bursting of normal restraints, a case of being caught off guard. That is what would be learned by asking the man in the street if he uses these forms and, if so, what he means by them.

I am assuming, of course, that this commonsense view of response cries should give way to the co-occurrence analysis that sociolinguists have brought to their problems. But although this naturalistic method is encouraged by sociolinguists, here the subject matter moves one away from their traditional concern. For a response cry doesn't seem to be a statement in the linguistic sense (even a heavily elided one), purportedly doing its work through the concatenated semantic reference of words. A remark is not being addressed to another, not even, it seems, to oneself. So, on the face of it at least, even self-communication is not involved, only a simpler sign process whereby emissions from a source inform us about the state of the source—a case of exuded expressions, not intentionally sent messages. One might better refer to a "vocalizer" or "sounder" than to a speaker. Which, of course, is not to deny the capacity of a well-formed, conventionally directed sentence to inform us about the state of the protagonist who serves as its subject, nor that the speaker and protagonist can be the "same"—for indeed through the use of first-person pronouns they routinely are. Only that this latter arrangement brings us information through a message, not an expression, a route fundamentally different from and less direct than the one apparently employed in response cries, even though admittedly such cries routinely come to be employed just in order to give a desired impression. Witnesses can seize the occasion of certain response cries to shake their heads in sympathy, cluck, and generally feel that the way has been made easy for them to initiate passing remarks attesting to fellow-feeling; but they aren't obliged to do so. A response cry may be uttered in the hope that this half-license it gives to hearers to strike up a conversation will be exercised; but, of course, this stratagem for getting talk going could not work were an innocent reading not the official one. As might be expected, the circumstances which allow us to utter a response cry are often just the ones that mitigate the impropriety of a different tack we could take, that of opening up an encounter by addressing a remark to an unacquainted other; but that fact, too, doesn't relieve one of the necessity to distinguish between this latter, fully social sort of comment and the kind that is apparently not even directed to the self.

A response cry is (if anything is) a ritualized act in something like the ethological sense of that term. Unable to shape the world the way we want to, we displace our manipulation of it to the verbal channel, displaying evidence of the alignment we take to events, the display taking the condensed, truncated form of a discretely articulated, nonlexicalized expression. Or, suddenly able to manage a tricky, threatening set of circumstances, we deflect into nonlexicalized sound a dramatization of our relief and self-congratulation in the achievement.

VII

Consider now some standard cries.

1. The *transition display.* Entering or leaving from what can be taken as a state of marked natural discomfort—wind, rain, heat, or cold—we seem to have the license (in our society) to externalize an expression of our inner state. *Brr!* is a standard term for wind and cold upon leaving such an atmosphere. (Other choices are less easily reproduced in print.) *Ahh!* and *Phew!* are also heard, this time when leaving a hot place for a cool one. Function is not clear. Perhaps the sounding gives us a moment to orient ourselves to the new climatic circumstances and to fall into cadence with the others in the room, these requirements not ordinarily a taxing matter and not ordinarily needful, therefore, of a pause for their accomplishment. Perhaps the concentration, the "holding ourselves in" sometimes employed in inclement places (as a sort of support for the body), gets released with a flourish on our escaping from such environments. In any case, we can be presumed to be in a state of mind that any and all those already safe might well appreciate—for, after all, weather envelops everyone in the vicinity—and so self-expression concerning our feelings does not take us to a place that is mysterious to our hearers. Incidentally, it appears that, unlike strong imprecations, transition displays in our society are not particularly sex-typed.

2. The *spill cry.* This time the central examples, *Oops!* and *Whoops!,* are well-formed sounds, although not in every sense words, and again something as much (perhaps even more) the practice of females as males. Spill cries are a sound we emit to follow along with our having for a moment lost guiding control of some feature of the world around us, including ourselves. Thus a woman, rapidly walking to a museum exit, passes the door, catches her mistake, utters *Oops!,* and backtracks to the right place. A man, dropping a piece of meat through the grill to coals below, utters *Oops!* and then spears the meat to safety with his grill fork.

On the face of it, the sound advertises our loss of control, raising the question of why we should want to defame ourselves through this publicity. An obvious possibility is that the *Oops!* defines the event as a mere accident, shows we know it has happened, and hopefully insulates it from the rest of our behavior, recommending that failure of control was not generated by some obscure intent unfamiliar to humanity or some general defect in competence. Behind this possibility is another: that the expression is presumably used for *minor* failings of environmental control, and so in the face of a more serious failure, the *Oops!* has the effect of downplaying import and hence implication as evidence of our incompetence. (It follows that to show we take a mishap *very* seriously we might feel constrained to omit the cry.) Another reason for (and function of) spill crying is that, a specific vocalization being involved, we necessarily demonstrate that at least our vocal channel is functioning and, behind this, at least some presence of mind. A part of us proves to be organized and standing watch over the part of us that apparently isn't watchful. Finally, and significantly, the sound can provide a warning to others present that a piece of the world has gotten loose and that they might best be advised to take care. Indeed, close observation shows that the *oo* in *Oops!* may be nicely prolonged to cover the period of time during which that which got out of control is out of control.

Note, when we utter *Oops!* as we slip on the ice, we can be making a plea to the closest other for a steadying hand and simultaneously warning others as to what they themselves should watch out for, these circumstances surely opening up our surround for vocalizations. When in fact there is no danger to the self, we may respond to *another's* momentary loss of control with an *Oops!* also, providing him a warning that he is in trouble, a readied framework within which he can define the mishap, and a collectively established cadence for his anticipated response. That some sort of help for others is thus intended seems to be borne out by the fact that apparently men are more likely to *Oops!* for another when that other is a child or a female, and thus definable as someone for whom responsibility can be taken. Indeed, when a parent plucks up a toddler and rapidly shifts it from one point to another or "playfully" swings or tosses it in the air, the prime mover may utter an *Oopsadaisy!,* stretched out to cover the child's period of groundlessness, counteracting its feeling of being out of control, and at the same time instructing the child in the terminology and role of spill cries. In any case, it is apparent that *oopsing* is an adaptive practice with some survival value. And the fact that individuals prove (when the occasion does arise) to have been ready all along to *oops* for themselves or an appropriate other suggests that when nothing eventful is occurring, persons in one another's presence are still nonetheless tracking one another and acting so as to make themselves trackable.

3. The *threat startle,* notably *Eek!* and *Yipe!* Perhaps here is a response cry sex-typed (or at least so believed) for feminine use. Surprise and fear are stated—in lay terms, "expressed"—but surprise and fear that are very much under control, indeed nothing to be really concerned about. A very high open stairwell, or a walk that leads to a precipice, can routinely evoke *yipes* from us as we survey what might have been our doom, but from a position of support we have had ample time to secure. A notion of what a fear response would be is used as a pattern for mimicry. A sort of overplaying occurs that covers any actual concern by extending with obvious unseriousness the expressed form this concern would take. And we demonstrate that we are alive to the fearsome implications of the event, albeit not overthrown by them, that we have seen the trouble and by implication will assuredly control for it, and are, therefore, in need of no warning, all of this releasing others from closely tracking us. And the moment it takes to say the sound is a moment we can use actually to compose ourselves in the circumstances. In a very subtle way, then, a verbal "expression" of our state is a means of rising above it—and a release of concern now no longer necessary, coming after the emergency is really over.

Here an argument made earlier about multiple transformations can be taken up. Precipitous drops are the sorts of things that an individual can be very close to without the slightest danger of dropping over or intent to do so. In these circumstances it would seem that imagery of accident would come to the fore or at least be very readily available. It is this easily achieved mental set that the response cry in question would seem to participate in. Thus the uncompelling character of the actual circumstances can be nicely reflected in the light and almost relaxed character of the cry. One has, then, a warning*like* signal in dangerous*like* circumstances. And ritualization begins to give way to a copy of itself, a playful version of what is already a formalized version, a display that has been retransformed and reset, a second order ritualization.

4. *Revulsion sounds,* such as *Eeuw!,* are heard from a person who has by necessity or inadvertence come in contact with something that is contaminating. Females in our society, being defined as more vulnerable in this way than males, might seem to have a special claim on the expression. Often once we make the sound, we can be excused for a moment while decontamination is attempted. At other times, our voice performs what our physical behavior can't, as when our hands must keep busy cleaning a fish, leaving only the auditory and other unrequired channels to correct the picture—to show that indelicate, dirty work need not define the person who is besmeared by it. Observe, again there is an unserious note, a hint of hyperritualization. For often the contamination that calls forth an *Eeuw!* is not *really* believed to contaminate. Perhaps only germ contamination retains that literal power in our secular world. So again a protectivelike cry is uttered in response to a contaminatinglike contact.

VIII

So far response crying has been largely considered as something that could be available to someone who is present to others but not "with" any of them. If one picks accompanied individuals, not singles, the behavior is still to be found; indeed, response crying is, if anything, encouraged in the circumstances. So, also, response cries are commonly found among persons in an "open state of talk," persons having the right but not the obligation to address remarks to the other participants, this being a condition that commonly prevails among individuals jointly engaged in a common task (or even similarly engaged in like ones) when this work situates them in immediate reach of one another.

1. The *strain grunt.* Lifting or pushing something heavy, or

wielding a sledgehammer with all our might, we emit a grunt at the presumed peak and consummation of our fully extended exertion, the grunt so attesting. The sound seems to serve as a warning that at the moment nothing else can claim our concern, and, sometimes, as a reminder that others should stand clear. No doubt the cry also serves as a means by which joint efforts can be temporally coordinated, as is said to be true of work songs. Observe that these sounds are felt to be entirely unintentional, even though the glottis must be partially closed off to produce them and presumably could be fully opened or closed to avoid doing so. In any case, it could be argued that the expression of ultimate exertion these sounds provide may be essentially overstated. I might add that strain grunts are routinely guyed, employed in what is to be taken as an unserious way, often as a cover for a task that is reckoned as undemanding but may indeed require some exertion, another case of retransformation. Note, too, that strain grunts are also employed during solitary doings that can be construed as involving a peaking of effort. The rise and falling away of effort contoured in sound dramatizes our acts, filling out the setting with their execution. I suppose the common example is the vocal accompaniment we sometimes provide ourselves when passing a hard stool.

2. The *pain cry, Oww!* (or *Ouch!*).[15] Here the functioning of this exclamation is rather clear. Ensconced in a dentist's chair, we use a pain cry as a warning that the drill has begun to hurt. Or when a finger is firmly held by a nurse, we *ouch* when the needle probing for a sliver goes too deep. Plainly the cry in these cases can serve as a self-regulated indicator of what is happening, providing a reading for the instigator of the pain, who might not otherwise have access to the information needed. The meaning, then, may not be "I have been hurt," but

15. Solitarily experiencing a bout of intense pain, we sometimes follow its course with a half-moaned, half-grunted sound tracing, as though casting the experience in a sort of dialogic form were a way of getting through the moment and maintaining morale. We sometimes also employ such sound tracings when witnesses are perceivedly present, producing in these circumstances a real scene-stopper, implying that our current inner acutely painful state is the business everyone should be hanging on.

rather, "You are just now coming to hurt me." This meaning, incidentally, may also be true of the response that a dog or cat gives us when we have begun to step accidentally on its tail, although *that* cry often seems to come too late. In any case, these are good examples of how closely a vocalizer can collaborate with another person in the situation.

4. The *sexual moan.* This subvocal tracking of the course of sexually climactic experience is a display available to both sexes, but said to be increasingly fashionable for females—amongst whom, of course, the sound tracing can be strategically employed to delineate an ideal development in the marked absence of anything like the real thing.

5. *Floor cues.* A worker in a typing pool makes a mistake on a clean copy and emits an imprecation, this leading to, and apparently designed to lead to, a colleague's query as to what went wrong. A fully communicated statement of disgust and displeasure can then be introduced, but now ostensibly as a reply to a request for information. A husband reading the evening paper suddenly brays out a laugh or a *Good God!,* thereby causing his wife to orient her listening and even to ease the transition into talk by asking what is it. (A middle-class wife might be less successful in having her floor cues picked up.) Wanting to avoid being thought, for example, self-centered, intrusive, garrulous, or whatever, and in consequence feeling uneasy about making an open request for a hearing in the particular circumstances, we act so as to encourage our putative listeners to make the initial move, inviting us to let them in on what we are experiencing. Interestingly, although in our society married couples may come to breach many of the standard situational proprieties routinely when alone together—this marking the gradual extension of symmetrical ritual license between them—the rule against persisting in public self-talk may be retained, with the incidental consequence that the couple can continue to use response crying as a floor cue.

6. *Audible glee.* A lower-middle-class adolescent girl sitting with four friends at a table in a crowded crêperie is brought her order, a large crêpe covered with ice cream and nuts. As the dish is set before her, she is transfixed for a moment, and wonder and

pleasure escape with an *Oooooo!* In a casino an elderly woman playing the slots alongside two friends hits a twenty-dollar payoff, and above the sound of silver dropping in her tray peeps out a *Wheee!* Tarzan, besting a lion, roars out a Hollywood version of the human version of a lay version of a mammalian triumph call.

IX

It is important, I believe, to examine the functioning of response cries when the crier is a ratified participant of ongoing conversation, not merely someone copresent to others or in an open state of talk. Walking along saying something to a friend, we can, tripping, unceremoniously interrupt our words to utter *Oops!*, even as the hand of our friend comes out to support us; and as soon as this little flurry is passed, we revert back to our speaking. All that this reveals, of course, is that when we are present to others as a fellow conversationalist we are also present to them —as well as to all others in the situation—as fellow members of the gathering. The conversational role (short of what the telephone allows) can never be the only accessible one in which we are active.

Now let us move on to a closer issue. If these responses are to be seen as ritualized expressions, and some as standardized vocal comments on circumstances that are not, or no longer, beyond our emotional and physical control, then there is reason to expect that such cries will be used at still further remove, this time in response to a *verbally presented* review of something settled long ago at a place quite removed. A broker tells a client over the phone that his stock has dropped, and the client, well socialized in this sort of thing, says *Yipe!* or *Eek!* (The comedian Jack Benny made a specialty of this response cry.) A plumber tells us what our bill will be and we say *Ouch!* Indeed, response cries are often employed thrice removed from the crisis to which they are supposed to be a blurted response: a friend tells us about something startling and costly that happened to him and at the point of disclosure we utter a response cry on his behalf, as it were, out of sympathetic identification and as a sign that we are fully following his exposition. In fact, we may offer a response cry when he recounts something that happened to someone *else.* In these latter cases, we are certainly far removed from the exigent event that is being replayed, and just as far removed from its consequences, including any question of having to take immediate rescuing action. Interestingly, there are some cries which seem to occur more commonly in our response to another's fate (good or bad) as it is recounted to us than they do in our response to our own. *Oh wow!* is an example.

And we can play all of these response games because our choice of vocalization allows the recipient, or rather hearer, to treat the sound as something to which a specific spoken reply is not required. To the plumber we are precisely not saying: "Does the bill have to be that high?"—*that* statement being something that would require a reply, to the possible embarrassment of all.

Having started with response cries in the street, the topic has been moved into the shelter of conversations. But it should not be assumed from this that the behaviors in question—response cries—have somehow been transmuted into full-fledged creatures of discourse. That is not the way they function. These cries are conventionalized utterances which are specialized for an informative role, but in the linguistic and propositional sense they are not statements. Obviously, information is provided when we utter response cries in the presence of others, whether or not we are in a state of talk at the time. That is about the only reason we utter them in the first place and the reason why they are worth studying. But to understand how these sounds function in social situations, particularly during talk, one must first understand where the prototype of which they are designed to be a recognizable version is seated. What comes to be made of a particular individual's show of "natural emotional expression" on any occasion is a considerably awesome thing not dependent on the existence anywhere of natural emotional expressions. But whatever is made of such an act by its maker and its witnesses is different from what is made of openly designed and openly directed communication.

X

At the beginning of this paper it was argued that extended self-talk, if discovered, reflects badly on the talker. Then it was recommended that elements in the situation can considerably mitigate the impropriety of talking to ourselves publicly, and that in any case we are prepared to breach the injunction against public self-talk when, in effect, to sustain this particular propriety would go even harder on our reputation. Much the same position could be taken with respect to interjected imprecations. In both cases, one can point to some hitch in the well-managed flow of controlled events and the quick application of an ostensibly self-directed pronouncement to establish evidence—a veneer —of control, poise, and competency. And although response cries do not on the surface involve words uttered even to oneself, being *in prototype* merely a matter of nonsymbolic emotional expression, they apparently come to function as a means of striking a self-defensible posture in the face of extraordinary events—much as does exposed self-talk. However, there is one source of trouble in the management of the world which is routine, and that, interestingly enough, is in the management of talk itself. So again response cries occur, but this time ones that are constantly uttered.

First, there is the well-known filled pause (usually written *ah* or *uh* or *um*) employed by speakers when they have lost their places, can't find a word, are momentarily distracted, or otherwise find they are departing from fluently sustained speech. Response *cries* seems an awkward term for such unblurted subvocalizations, but nonetheless they do, I think, function like response cries, if only in that they facilitate tracking. In effect, speakers make it evident that although they do not now have the word or phrase they want, they are giving their attention to the matter and have not cut themselves adrift from the effort at hand. A word search, invisible and inaudible in itself, is thus voluntarily accompanied by a sound shadow—a sound, incidentally, that could easily be withheld merely by otherwise managing the larynx—all to the end of assuring that something worse than a temporary loss of words has not happened, and incidentally holding the speaker's claim on the floor.[16] (Interestingly, in radio broadcasting, where visual facial signs of a word search can't be effective, the filling of pauses by a search sound or a prolongation of a vowel has much to recommend it, for speakers are under obligation to confirm that nothing has gone wrong with the studio's equipment, as well as their own, the floor in this case being a station. And if only inexperienced broadcasters employ filled pauses frequently, it is because professionals can manage speech flow, especially aloud reading, without the hitches in encoding which, were they to occur, would equally give professionals reasons to ritualize evidence of what was occurring.)

In addition to the filled-pause phenomenon, consider the very standard form of self-correction which involves the breaking off of a word or phrase that is apparently not the one we wanted, and our hammering home of a corrected version with increased loudness and tempo, as if to catch the error before it hit the ground and shattered the desired meaning. Here the effect is to show that we are very much alive to the way our words should have come out; we are somewhat shocked and surprised at our failure to encode properly an appropriate formulation the first time round, the rapidity and force of the correct version presumably suggesting how much on our toes we really are. We display our concern and the mobilization of our effort at the expense of smooth speech production, electing to save a little of our reputation for presence of mind over and against that for fluency. Again, as with filled pauses, one has what is ostensibly a bit of pure expression, that is, a transmission providing direct evidence (not relayed through semantic reference) of the state of the transmitter, but now an expression that has been cut and polished into a standard shape to serve the reputational contingencies of its emitter.

16. A case can be made that in some English-speaking circles the familiar hesitation markers are systematically employed in slightly different ways, so that, for example, *uh* might be heard when the speaker had forgotten a proper name, *oh* when he knew a series of facts but was trying to decide which of them could be appropriately cited or best described for the hearers. The unfilled or silent pause participates in this specialization, giving one reason, alas, to think of it as a response cry, too. Here see the useful paper by James (1972).

XI

Earlier it was suggested that imprecations were somewhat like truncated, self-addressed statements but not wholly so. Later these lexicalized exclamations were shown to function not unlike response cries. Now it is time to try to settle on where they belong.

Say, for example, someone brings you the news that they have failed in a task you have seriously set them. Your response to the news can be: "I knew it! Did you have to?" In the styling I have in mind, this turn at talk contains two moves and a change of "footing": the first move (uttered half under the breath with the eyes turned upward) is a bit of self-talk, or something presented in that guise—the sort of open aside that adults are especially prone to employ in exasperated response to children, servants, foreigners, and other grades who easily qualify for moments of nonperson treatment. The second move ("Did you have to?") is conventionally directed communication. Observe that such a turn at talk will oblige its recipient to offer an apology or a counteraccount, locking the participants into an interchange. But although the recipient of the initial two-move turn will be understood to have overheard the self-addressed segment, he will have neither the right nor the obligation to reply to it specifically, at least in the sense that he does in regard to the conventionally communicated second portion.

Now shift from extended self-talk to the truncated form—imprecation: "Shit! Did you have to?" Given the same histrionics, one again has a two-move turn with a first move that must be oriented to as something that can't be answered in a conventional way. If the recipient does address a remark to this blurted-out portion, it will be to the psychic state presumably indexed by it—much as when we comfort someone who has burst into tears or when we upbraid them for loss of self-control. Or the respondent may have to venture a frame ploy, attempting to counter a move by forcing its maker to change the interpretative conventions that apply to it—as in the snappy comeback, *Not here,* injected immediately after the expletive. In all of this, and in the fact that standard lexicalizations are employed, *I knew it!* and *Shit!* are similar. However, although *I knew it!* follows grammatical constraints for well-formed sentences, *Shit!* need not, even if one appeals to the context in order to see how it might be expanded into a statement. *Shit!* need no more elide a sentence than need a laugh, groan, sob, snicker, or giggle—all vocalizations that frequently occur except in the utterances ordinarily presented for analysis by linguists. Nor, I think, does it help understanding very much to define *Shit!* as a well-formed sentence with *NP!* as its structure. Here, of course, imprecations are exactly like response cries. For it is the essence of response cries that they be presented as if mere expression were involved, and not recipient-directed, propositional-like statements, at least on the face of it.

Imprecations, then, might best be considered not as a form of self-talk at all, but rather as a type of response cry. Whereas unlexicalized cries have come to be somewhat conventionalized, imprecations have merely extended the tendency, further ritualizing ritualizations. Religious life already setting aside a class of words to be treated with reserve and ranked with respect to severity, response crying has borrowed them. Or so it would seem.

Insofar as self-talk is structurally different from the normal kind, imprecatory utterances (like other response cries) are too, only more so. And because of this sharp underlying difference between conventionally directed statements and imprecatory interjections, the two can be given radically different roles in the functioning of particular interaction systems, serving close together in complementary distribution without confusion.

Consider tennis. During the open state of talk sustained in such a game, a player who misses an "easy" shot can response cry an imprecation loudly enough for opponents and partner to hear. On the other hand, a player making a "good" shot is not likely to be surprised if an opponent offers a complimentary statement about him to him. (As these two forms of social control help frame his own play, so he will participate in the two forms that frame his opponents'.) But, of course, good taste forbids a player addressing opponents in praise of his own efforts, just as they must allow him elbowroom and not reply directly to his cries of self-disgust. A player may, however, use directed, full-fledged statements to convey self-castigation and (when directed to his partner) apology. Response cries and directed statements here comprise a closely working pair of practices, part of the ritual resources of a single interaction system. And their workings can be intermingled because of their structural difference, not in spite of it. Given this arrangement, it is understandable that a player will feel rather free to make a pass at ironically praising himself in statements made to opponents or partner, correctly sensing that his words could hardly be misframed as literal ones. (That he might employ this device just to induce others to communicate a mitigated view of his failure merely attests again to the various conveniences that can be made of forms of interaction.)

And just as response cries can form a complementary resource with conventionally directed statements, so they can with self-directed ones. For example, in casino craps, a shooter has a right to preface a roll, especially a "come out," with self-encouraging statements of a traditional kind directed to the fates, the dice, or some other ethereal recipient. This grandstanding (as dignified gamblers call this self-talk) sometimes serves to bring the other players into a cadence and peaking of attention. When, shortly, the shooter "craps out," he is allowed a well-fleshed imprecation coincidental with the dissolution of the table's coordinated involvement. So again there is complementarity and a division of labor, with self-talk located where collective hope is to be built up, and imprecatory response cry where it is to be abandoned.

DISCUSSION

1. Written versions of response cries seem to have a speech-contaminating effect, consolidating and codifying actual response cries, so that, in many cases, reality begins to mimic artifice, as in *Ugh!, Pant pant, Gulp, Tsk tsk,* this being a route to ritualization presumably unavailable to animal animals.[17] This easy change is

17. The carryback from the written to the spoken form is especially marked in the matter of punctuation marks, for here writing has something that speaking hasn't. Commonly used lexicalizations are: "underline," "footnote,"

only to be expected. For response cries themselves are by way of being second order ritualizations, already part of an unserious, or less than serious, domain.

Here cartoons and comics are to be taken seriously. These printed pictures must present entire scenarios through a small number of "panels" or frozen moments, sometimes only one. The cartoonist has great need, then, for expressions that will clearly document the presumed inner state of his figures and clearly display the point of the action. Thus, if individuals in real life need response cries to clarify the drama of their circumstances, cartoon figures need them even more. So we obtain written versions of something that could be thought originally to have no set written form. Moreover, cartoon figures portrayed as all alone must be portrayed acting in such a way as to make their circumstances and inner states available to the viewer (much as real persons do when in the presence of others), and included in this situational-like behavior are response cries. (So also in the case of movies showing persons ostensibly all alone.) In consequence, the practice of emitting response cries when all alone is tacitly assumed to be normal, presumably with at least some contaminating effect upon actual behavior when alone.

2. A point might be made about the utterances used in response cries. As suggested, they seem to be drawn from two sources: taboo but full-fledged words (involving blasphemy and —in English—Anglo-Saxon terms for bodily functions) and from the broad class of nonword vocalizations ("vocal segregates," to employ Trager's term [1958:1–12]), of which response cries are one, but only one, variety.

There is a nice division of linguistic labor here. Full-fledged words that are well formed *and* socially acceptable are allocated to communication in the openly directed sense, whereas taboo words and nonwords are specialized for the more ritualized kind of communication. In brief, the character of the word bears the mark of the use that is destined for it. And one has a case of complementary distribution on a grand scale.

"period," "question mark," "quotes," "parenthetically." Written abbreviations (such as British *p* for *pence*) also enter the spoken domain. Moreover, there is a carryback to the spoken form of the pictorial-orthographic form of the presumed approximated sound effects of an action: *Pow! Bam!* are examples.

Nonwords as a class are not productive in the linguistic sense, their role as interjections being one of the few that have evolved for them. (Which is not to say that a particular vocal segregate can't have a very lively career, quickly spreading from one segment of a language community to others; the response cry *Wow!* is a recent example.) Many taboo words, however, are considerably productive, especially in the tradition maintained in certain subcultures, where some of these words occur (if not function) in almost every syntactical position.[18] Furthermore, curse words are drawn from familiar scales of such words, and choice will sharply reflect (in the sense of display, negotiate, etc.) the terms of the relationship between speaker and hearer; nonwords don't function very effectively in this way.

Nonwords, note, can't quite be called part of a language. For example, there tends to be no canonical "correct" spelling. When and where convention clearly does begin to establish a particular form and spelling, the term can continue to be thought of as not a word by its users, as if any written version must continue to convey a rough-and-ready attempt at transcription. (I take it here that in our society a feature of what we think of as regular words is that we feel the written form is as "real" a version as the spoken.) Further, although we have efficient means of reporting another's use of an expletive (either literally or by established paraphrastic form), this is not the case with nonwords. So, too, the voiced and orthographic realizations of some of these constructions involve consonant clusters that are phonotactically irregular; furthermore, their utterance can allow the speaker to chase after the course of an action analogically with stretches, glides, turns, and heights of pitch foreign to his ordinary speech. Yet the sound that covers any particular nonword can stand by itself, is standardized within a given language community, and varies from one language community to another, in each case as

18. Admittedly, even in these productive cases, taboo words are not entirely vulnerable to syntactical analysis. Saying that *the fuck* in a sentence like *What the fuck are you doing?* is adjectival in function, or that *bloody* in *What are you bloody well doing?* is an adverb, misses something of the point. In such cases specific syntactic location seems to be made a convenience of, for somehow the intensifying word is meant to color uniformly the whole of the utterance some place or other in which it occurs. Here see Quang Phuc Dong (1971).

do full-fledged words.[19] And the nonwords of a particular language comply with and introduce certain of the same phonotactic constraints as do its regular words (Jefferson 1974:183–86). Interestingly, there is some evidence that what one language community handles with a nonword, other language communities do, too.

On the whole, then, nonword vocalizations might best be thought of as semiwords. Observe that the characterization provided here (and by linguists) of these half-caste expressions takes no note that some (such as *Uh?* and *Shh!*) are clearly part of directed speech, and often interchangeable with a well-formed word (here *What?* and *Hush!*), but others (such as the *uh* as filled pause) belong to a radically different species of action, namely, putatively pure expression, response crying. (Imprecations and some other well-formed interjections provide an even more extreme case, for exactly the same such word may sometimes serve as an ostensibly undirected cry, and at other times be integrated directly into a recipient-directed sentence under a single intonation contour.) Here, again, one can see a surface similarity covering a deep underlying difference, but not the kind ordinarily addressed by transformationalists.

Apart from qualifying as semiwords, response cries can be identified in another way, namely, as articulated free-standing examples of the large class of presumed "natural expressions," namely, signs meant to be taken to index directly the state of the transmitter. (Some of those signs, like voice qualifiers, can paralinguistically ride roughshod across natural syntactical units of speech.) I might add that although gender differences in the basic semantic features of speech do not seem very marked in our society, response cries and other paralinguistic features of communication are. Indeed, speech *as a whole* might not be a useful base to employ in considering gender differences, cancelling out sharp contrasts revealable in special components of discourse.

3. Earlier it was suggested that a response cry can draw on the cooperation of listeners, requiring that they hear and under-

19. Quine (1959:6) has an example: " 'Ouch' is not independent of social training. One need only to prick a foreigner to appreciate that it is an English word."

stand the cry but act as though it had not been uttered in their hearing. It is in this way that a form of behavior ostensibly not designed for directed linguistic communication can be injected into public life, in certain cases even into conversations and broadcasts. In brief, a form of response perceived as native to one set of circumstances is set into another. In the case of blasphemous cries, what is inserted is already something that has been borrowed from another realm—semantic communication—so the behavior can be said to have been returned to its natural place, but now so much transformed as to be little like a native.

This structural reflexivity is, I believe, a fundamental fact of our communicative life. What is ritualized here, in the last analysis, is not an expression but a self-other alignment—an interactional arrangement. Nor, as earlier suggested, is that the bottom of embedding. For example, when a speaker finds he has skated rather close to the edge of discretion or tact, he may give belated recognition to where his words have gone, marking a halt by uttering a plaintive *Oops!,* meant to evoke the image of someone who has need of this particular response cry, the whole enactment having an unserious, openly theatrical character. Similarly, in the face of another's reminder that we have failed in fulfilling some obligation, we can utter *Darn it!* in an openly mock manner as a taunting, even insolent, denial of the imprecation we might normally be expected to employ in the circumstances. In brief, what is placed into the directed discourse in such cases is not a response cry but a mocked-up individual uttering a mocked-up response cry. (All of this is especially evident when the cry itself is a spoken version of the written version of the cry, as when a listener responds to the telling of another's near disaster by ungulpingly uttering the word *Gulp.*) So, too, the filled pause *uh,* presumably a self-expression designed to allow hearers to track speaker's engagement in relevant (albeit silent) production work, can apparently be employed with malice aforethought to show that the word that does follow (and is ostensibly the one that was all along wanted), is to be heard as one about which the speaker wants it known that he himself might not be naturally inclined to employ it (Jefferson 1974:192–94). In this case a "correction format" has been made a convenience of, its work set into an environment for which it was not originally designed. Similarly, on discovering that he has said "April the 21st" instead of "May the 21st," an announcer may (as one type of remedial work) repeat the error immediately, this time with a quizzical, speaking-to-oneself tone of voice, as though this sort of error were enough of a rarity to cause him to break frame; but this response itself he may try to guy, satirizing self-talk (and self-talkers) even as he engages in it, the retransformation confirmed by the little laugh he gives thereafter to mark the end to error-making *and* playful correction.

The moral of the story is that what is sometimes put into a sentence may first have to be analyzed as something that could not occur naturally in such a setting, just as a solitary's self-comments may first have to be analyzed as something exclusively found in social intercourse. And the transformations these alien bits of saying undergo when set into their new milieu speak as much to the competence of ethologists as of grammarians.

A turn at talk that contains a directed statement *and* a segment of self-talk (or an imprecation or a nonlexicalized response cry) does not merely involve two different moves, but *moves of two different orders.* This is very clear, for example, when someone in or out of a conversation finds cause to blurt out *Shit!* and then, in apparent embarrassment, quickly adds *Excuse me,* sometimes specifically directing the apology to the person most likely to have been offended. Here, patently, the first move is an exposed response cry, the second, a directed message whose implied referent happens to be the first. The two moves nicely fit together—indeed, some speakers essay an imprecation knowing that they will have a directed apology to compensate for it; but this fit pertains to how the two moves function as an action-response pair, self-contained within a single turn at talk, and not to any ultimate commonality of form. So, too, when an announcer coughs rather loudly, says *Excuse me* with greater urgency of tone than he likes, and then follows with a well-designed giggle; except here he gives us a three-move sequence of sounded interference, directed statement, and response cry, the second move a comment on the first, the third move a comment on the second move's comment. Any effort to analyze such strips of talk linguistically by trying to uncover a single deep structure that accounts for the surface sequence of words is destined to obscure the very archaeological issues that the generative approach was designed to develop. A blender makes a mush of apples and oranges; a student shouldn't.

And a student shouldn't, even when there is no obvious segmentation to help with the sorting. For now it is to be admitted that through the *way* we say something that is part of our avowedly directed discourse, we can speak—ostensibly at least—for our own benefit at the same time, displaying our self-directed (and/or nondirected) response to what is occurring. We thereby simultaneously cast an officially intended recipient of our propositional-like avowals into an overhearer of our self-talk. The issue is not merely that of the difference between what is said and what is meant, the issue, that is, of implicature; the issue is that one stream of information is conveyed as avowedly intended verbal communication, whilst simultaneously the other is conveyed through a structural ruse—our allowing witnesses a glimpse into the dealings we are having with ourselves. It is in this way that one can account for the apparently anomalous character of imprecations of the *Fuck you!* form. It might appear as if one person were making a directed verbal avowal to another by means of an imperative statement with deleted subject; in fact the format is restricted to a relatively small list of expletives, such as *screw,* and none qualifies as an ordinary verb, being constrained in regard to embedded and conjoined forms in ways in which standard verbs in the elided imperative form are not (Quang Phuc Dong 1971).

Nor is this analysis of the unconversational aspects of certain conversational utterances meant to deny the traditional conception of transformation and embedding; rather the power of the latter is displayed. Waiting with her husband and a friend for the casino cashier to count down her bucket of silver, a happy player says, "And when I saw the third seven come up and stop, I just let out 'Eeeee!' " Here, through direct quotation, the speaker brings to a well-circumscribed, three-person talk what was, a few minutes ago, the broadly accessible eruption of a single. This shows clearly that what starts out as a response cry (or starts out, for that matter, as any sounded occurrence, human, animal, or inanimate) can be conversationally replayed—can be reset into ordinary directed discourse—through the infinite coverage of sound mimicry.

CONCLUSION

The public utterance of self-talk, imprecations, and response cries constitutes a special variety of impulsive, blurted actions, namely, vocalized ones. Our tacit theory of human nature recommends that these actions are "purely expressive," "primitive," "unsocialized," violating in some way or other the self-control and self-possession we are expected to maintain in the presence of others, providing witnesses with a momentary glimpse behind our mask.

However, the point about these blurtings is not that they are particularly "expressive." Obviously, in this sense of that word, ordinary talk is necessarily expressive, too. Naked feelings can agitate a paragraph of discourse almost as well as they can a solitary imprecation. Indeed, it is impossible to utter a sentence without coloring the utterance with some kind of perceivable affect, even (in special cases) if only with the emotionally distinctive aura of affectlessness. Nor is the point about segmented blurtings that they are particularly unsocialized, for obviously they come to us as our language does and not from our own invention. Their point lies elsewhere. One must look to the light these ventings provide, not to the heat they dispel.

In every society one can contrast occasions and moments for silence and occasions and moments for talk. In our own, one can go on to say that by and large (and especially among the unacquainted) silence is the norm and talk something for which warrant must be present. Silence, after all, is very often the deference we will owe in a social situation to any and all others present. In holding our tongue, we give evidence that such thought as we are giving to our own concerns is not presumed by us to be of any moment to the others present, and that the feelings these concerns invoke in ourselves are owed no sympathy. Without such enjoined modesty, there could be no public life, only a babble of childish adults pulling at one another's sleeves for attention. The mother to whom we would be saying, "Look, no hands," could not look or reply for she would be saying, "Look, no hands," to someone else.

Talk, however, presumes that our thoughts and concerns will have some relevance or interest or weight for others, and in this can hardly but presume a little. Talk, of course, in binding others to us, can also do so for protracted periods of time. The compensation is that we can sharply restrict this demand to a small portion of those who are present, indeed, often to only one.

The fugitive communications I have been considering constitute a third possibility, minor no doubt, but of some significance if only because of what they tell us about silence and talk. Our blurtings make a claim of sorts upon the attention of everyone in the social situation, a claim that our inner concerns should be theirs, too, but unlike the claim made by talk, ours here is only for a limited period of attention. And, simply put, this invitation into our interiors tends to be made only when it will be easy for other persons present to see where the voyage takes them. What is precipitous about these expressions, then, is not the way they are emitted but rather the circumstances which render their occurrence acceptable. The invitation we are free to extend in these situations we would be insane to extend in others.

Just as most public arrangements oblige and induce us to be silent, and many other arrangements to talk, so a third set allows and obliges us momentarily to open up our thoughts and feelings and ourselves through sound to whosoever is present. Response cries, then, do not mark a flooding of emotion outward, but a flooding of relevance in.

There is linguistic point to the consideration of this genre of behavior. Response cries such as *Eek!* might be seen as peripheral to the linguist's domain, but imprecations and self-talk are more germane, passing beyond semiword vocal segregates to the traditional materials of linguistic analysis. And the point is that all three forms of this blurted vocalization—semiword response cries, imprecations, and self-talk—are creatures of social situations, not states of talk. A closed circle of ratified participants oriented to engaging exclusively with one another in avowedly directed communications is not the base; a gathering, with its variously oriented, often silent and unacquainted members, is.

Further, all three varieties of this ejaculatory expression are conventionalized as to form, occasion of occurrence, and social function. Finally, these utterances are too commonly met with in daily life, surely, to justify scholarly neglect.

Once it is recognized that there is a set of conventionalized expressions that must be referred to social situations, not conversations, once, that is, it is appreciated that there are communications specifically designed for use outside states of talk, then it is but a step to seeing that ritualized versions of these expressions may themselves be embedded in the conventionally directed talk to be found in standard conversational encounters. And appreciating this, then to go on to see that even though these interjections come to be employed in conversational environments, they cannot be adequately analyzed there without reference to their original functioning outside of states of talk.

It is recommended, then, that linguists have reason to broaden their net, reason to bring in uttering that is not talking, reason to deal with social situations, not merely with jointly sustained talk. Incidentally, linguists might then be better able to countenance inroads that others can be expected to make into their conventional domain. For it seems that talk itself is intimately regulated and closely geared to its context through nonvocal gestures which are very differently distributed from the particular language and subcodes employed by any set of participants—although just where these boundaries of gesture-use *are* to be drawn remains an almost unstudied question.[20]

20. On the geographical boundaries of some nonvocal gestures, see Morris et al. (1979). A useful critique of this work is Kendon (forthcoming).

REFERENCES

Cook-Gumperz, Jenny, and Corsaro, William. 1976. "Social-ecological constraints on children's communicative strategies." In *Papers on Language and Context* (Working Paper 46), edited by Jenny Cook-Gumperz and John Gumperz. Berkeley: Language Behavior Research Laboratory, University of California.

Gopnik, Alison. 1977. "No, there, more, and allgone: Why the first words aren't about things." *Nottingham Linguistic Circular* 6:15–20.

James, Deborah. 1972. "Some aspects of the syntax and semantics of interjections." In *Papers from the Eighth Regional Meeting, Chicago Linguistic Society,* pp. 162–72.

Jefferson, Gail. 1974. "Error correction as an interactional resource." *Language in Society* 3:181–200.

Kendon, Adam. Forthcoming. "Geography of gesture." *Semiotica.*

Kohlberg, Lawrence; Yaeger, Judy; and Hjertholm, Elsie. 1968. "Private speech: Four studies and a review of theories." *Child Development* 39: 691–736.

Morris, Desmond; Collett, Peter; Marsh, Peter; and O'Shaughnessy, Marie. 1979. *Gestures: Their origins and distribution.* New York: Stein and Day.

Piaget, Jean. 1956. The language and thought of the child. 4th ed. Neuchâtel. [Translated by Marjorie Gabain. New York: Meridian, 1974.]

———. 1962. "Comments on Vygotsky's critical remarks concerning *The language and thought of the child,* and *Judgment and reasoning in the child.*" In *Thought and language,* edited by Lev Semenovich Vygotsky. MIT Press and John Wiley and Sons.

Quang Phuc Dong. 1971. "English sentences without overt grammatical subject." In *Studies out in left field,* edited by A. M. Zwicky et al., pp. 3–9. Edmonton: Linguistic Research, Inc.

Quine, W. Van. 1959. *Word and object.* New York: Wiley.

Sudnow, David. 1967. *Passing on: The social organization of dying.* Englewood Cliffs, N.J.: Prentice-Hall.

Trager, George L. 1958. "Paralanguage: A first approximation." *Studies in Linguistics* 13:1–12.

Vygotsky, Lev Semenovich. 1962. *Thought and language.* Translated by Eugenia Hanfmann and Gertrude Vakar. MIT Press and John Wiley and Sons.

3
FOOTING

I

Consider a journalistically reported strip of interaction, a news bureau release of 1973 on presidential doings.[1] The scene is the Oval Office, the participants an assemblage of government officers and newspaper reporters gathered in their professional capacities for a political ritual, the witnessing of the signing of a bill:

> WASHINGTON [UPI]—President Nixon, a gentleman of the old school, teased a newspaper woman yesterday about wearing slacks to the White House and made it clear that he prefers dresses on women.
>
> After a bill-signing ceremony in the Oval Office, the President stood up from his desk and in a teasing voice said to UPI's Helen Thomas: "Helen, are you still wearing slacks? Do you prefer them actually? Every time I see girls in slacks it reminds me of China."
>
> Miss Thomas, somewhat abashed, told the President that Chinese women were moving toward Western dress.
>
> "This is not said in an uncomplimentary way, but slacks can do something for some people and some it can't." He hastened to add, "but I think you do very well. Turn around."
>
> As Nixon, Attorney General Elliott L. Richardson, FBI Director Clarence Kelley and other high-ranking law enforcement officials smiling [*sic*], Miss Thomas did a pirouette for the President. She was wearing white pants, a navy blue jersey shirt, long white beads and navy blue patent leather shoes with red trim.

1. Grateful acknowledgment is made to *Semiotica,* where this paper first appeared (25[1979]:1–29).

> Nixon asked Miss Thomas how her husband, Douglas Cornell, liked her wearing pants outfits.
> "He doesn't mind," she replied.
> "Do they cost less than gowns?"
> "No," said Miss Thomas.
> "Then change," commanded the President with a wide grin as other reporters and cameramen roared with laughter. [*The Evening Bulletin* (Philadelphia), 1973]

This incident points to the power of the president to force an individual who is female from her occupational capacity into a sexual, domestic one during an occasion in which she (and the many women who could accord her the role of symbolic representative) might well be very concerned that she be given her full professional due, and that due only. And, of course, the incident points to a moment in gender politics when a president might unthinkingly exert such power. Behind this fact is something much more significant: the contemporary social definition that women must always be ready to receive comments on their "appearance," the chief constraints being that the remarks should be favorable, delivered by someone with whom they are acquainted, and not interpretable as sarcasm. Implied, structurally, is that a woman must ever be ready to change ground, or, rather, have the ground changed for her, by virtue of being subject to becoming momentarily an object of approving attention, not—or not merely—a participant in it.

The Nixon sally can also remind us of some other things. In our society, whenever two acquainted individuals meet for business, professional, or service dealings, a period of "small talk" may well initiate and terminate the transaction—a mini version of the "preplay" and "postplay" that bracket larger social affairs. This small talk will probably invoke matters felt to bear on the "overall" relation of the participants and on what each participant can take to be the perduring concerns of the other (health, family, etc.). During the business proper of the encounter, the two interactants will presumably be in a more segmental relation, ordered by work requirements, functionally specific authority, and the like. Contrariwise, a planning session among the military may begin and end with a formal acknowledgment of rank, and in between a shift into something closer to equalitarian decision-making. In either case, in shifting in and out of the business at hand, a change of tone is involved, and an alteration in the social capacities in which the persons present claim to be active.

Finally, it might be observed that when such change of gears occurs among more than two persons, then a change commonly occurs regarding who is addressed. In the Nixon scene, Ms. Thomas is singled out as a specific recipient the moment that "unserious" activity begins. (A change may also simultaneously occur in posture, here indeed very broadly with Mr. Nixon rising from his desk.)

The obvious candidate for illustrations of the Nixon shift comes from what linguists generally call "code switching," code here referring to language or dialect. The work of John Gumperz and his colleagues provides a central source. A crude example may be cited (Blom and Gumperz 1972:424):

> On one occasion, when we, as outsiders, stepped up to a group of locals engaged in conversation, our arrival caused a significant alteration in the casual posture of the group. Hands were removed from pockets and looks changed. Predictably, our remarks elicited a code switch marked simultaneously by a change in channel cues (i.e., sentence speed, rhythm, more hesitation pauses, etc.) and by a shift from (R) [a regional Norwegian dialect] to (B) [an official, standard form of Norwegian] grammar.

But of course, an outsider isn't essential; the switch can be employed among the ethnically homogeneous (ibid., p. 425):

> Likewise, when residents [in Hemnesberget, northern Norway] step up to a clerk's desk, greetings and inquiries about family affairs tend to be exchanged in the dialect, while the business part of the transaction is carried on in the standard.

Nor need one restrict oneself to the formal, adult world of government and business and its perfunctory service relationships; the schoolroom will do (ibid., p. 424):

> Teachers report that while formal lectures—where interruptions are not encouraged—are delivered in (B) [an official standard form of Norwegian], the speaker will shift to (R) [a regional Norwegian

dialect] when they want to encourage open and free discussion among students.

By 1976, in unpublished work on a community where Slovene and German are in active coexistence, matters are getting more delicate for Gumperz. Scraps of dialogue are collected between mothers and daughters, sisters and sisters, and code shifting is found to be present in almost every corner of conversational life. And Gumperz (1976) makes a stab at identifying what these shifts mark and how they function:

1. direct or reported speech
2. selection of recipient
3. interjections
4. repetitions
5. personal directness or involvement
6. new and old information
7. emphasis
8. separation of topic and subject
9. discourse type, e.g., lecture and discussion

More important for our purposes here, Gumperz and his coworkers now also begin to look at code-switchinglike behavior that doesn't involve a code switch at all. Thus, from reconstituted notes on classroom observations, the Gumperzes provide three sequential statements by a teacher to a group of first-graders, the statements printed in listed form to mark the fact that three different stances were involved: the first a claim on the children's immediate behavior, the second a review of experiences to come, and the third a side remark to a particular child (Cook-Gumperz and Gumperz 1976:8–9):

1. Now listen everybody.
2. At ten o'clock we'll have assembly. We'll all go out together and go to the auditorium and sit in the first two rows. Mr. Dock, the principal, is going to speak to us. When he comes in, sit quietly and listen carefully.
3. Don't wiggle your legs. Pay attention to what I'm saying.

The point being that, without access to bodily orientation and tone of voice, it would be easy to run the three segments into a continuous text and miss the fact that significant shifts in alignment of speaker to hearers were occurring.

I have illustrated through its changes what will be called "footing."[2] In rough summary:

1. Participant's alignment, or set, or stance, or posture, or projected self is somehow at issue.
2. The projection can be held across a strip of behavior that is less long than a grammatical sentence, or longer, so sentence grammar won't help us all that much, although it seems clear that a cognitive unit of some kind is involved, minimally, perhaps, a "phonemic clause." Prosodic, not syntactic, segments are implied.
3. A continuum must be considered, from gross changes in stance to the most subtle shifts in tone that can be perceived.
4. For speakers, code switching is usually involved, and if not this then at least the sound markers that linguists study: pitch, volume, rhythm, stress, tonal quality.
5. The bracketing of a "higher level" phase or episode of interaction is commonly involved, the new footing having a liminal role, serving as a buffer between two more substantially sustained episodes.

A change in footing implies a change in the alignment we take up to ourselves and the others present as expressed in the way we manage the production or reception of an utterance. A change in our footing is another way of talking about a change in our frame for events. This paper is largely concerned with pointing out that participants over the course of their speaking constantly change their footing, these changes being a persistent feature of natural talk.

As suggested, change in footing is very commonly language-linked; if not that, then at least one can claim that the paralinguistic markers of language will figure. Sociolinguists, therefore, can be looked to for help in the study of footing, including the most subtle examples. And if they are to compete in this heretofore literary and psychological area, then presumably they must find a structural means of doing so. In this paper I want to make a pass at analyzing the structural underpinnings of changes in footing. The task will be approached by reexamining the primitive notions of speaker and hearer, and some of our unstated presuppositions about spoken interaction.

2. An initial statement appears in Goffman (1974:496–559).

II

Traditional analysis of saying and what gets said seems tacitly committed to the following paradigm: Two and only two individuals are engaged together in it. During any moment in time, one will be speaking his own thoughts on a matter and expressing his own feelings, however circumspectly; the other listening. The full concern of the person speaking is given over to speaking and to its reception, the concern of the person listening to what is being said. The discourse, then, would be the main involvement of both of them. And, in effect, these two individuals are the only ones who know who is saying, who is listening, what is being said, or, indeed, that speaking is going on—all aspects of their doings being imperceivable by others, that is, "inaccessible." Over the course of the interaction the roles of speaker and hearer will be interchanged in support of a statement-reply format, the acknowledged current-speaking right—the floor—passing back and forth. Finally, what is going on is said to be conversation or talk.

The two-person arrangement here described seems in fact to be fairly common, and a good thing, too, being the one that informs the underlying imagery we have about face-to-face interaction. And it is an arrangement for which the terms "speaker" and "hearer" fully and neatly apply—lay terms here being perfectly adequate for all technical needs. Thus, it is felt that without requiring a basic change in the terms of the analysis, any modification of conditions can be handled: additional participants can be added, the ensemble can be situated in the immediate presence of nonparticipants, and so forth.

It is my belief that the language that students have drawn on for talking about speaking and hearing is not well adapted to its purpose. And I believe this is so both generally and for a consideration of something like footing. It is too gross to provide us with much of a beginning. It takes global folk categories (like speaker and hearer) for granted instead of decomposing them into smaller, analytically coherent elements.

For example, the terms "speaker" and "hearer" imply that sound alone is at issue, when, in fact, it is obvious that sight is organizationally very significant too, sometimes even touch. In the management of turn-taking, in the assessment of reception through visual back-channel cues, in the paralinguistic function of gesticulation, in the synchrony of gaze shift, in the provision of evidence of attention (as in the middle-distance look), in the assessment of engrossment through evidence of side-involvements and facial expression—in all of these ways it is apparent that sight is crucial, both for the speaker and for the hearer. For the effective conduct of talk, speaker and hearer had best be in a position to *watch* each other. The fact that telephoning can be practicable without the visual channel, and that written transcriptions of talk also seem effective, is not to be taken as a sign that, indeed, conveying words is the only thing that is crucial, but that reconstruction and transformation are very powerful processes.

III

The easiest improvement on the traditional paradigm for talk is to recognize that any given moment of it might always be part of *a* talk, namely, a substantive, naturally bounded stretch of interaction comprising all that relevantly goes on from the moment two (or more) individuals open such dealings between themselves and continuing until they finally close this activity out. The opening will typically be marked by the participants turning from their several disjointed orientations, moving together and bodily addressing one another; the closing by their departing in some physical way from the prior immediacy of copresence. Typically, ritual brackets will also be found, such as greetings and farewells, these establishing and terminating open, official, joint engagement, that is, ratified participation. In summary, a "social encounter." Throughout the course of the encounter the participants will be obliged to sustain involvement in what is being said and ensure that no long stretch occurs when no one (and not more than one) is taking the floor. Thus, at a given moment no talk may be occurring, and yet the participants will still be in a "state of talk." Observe, once one assumes that an encounter will have features of its own—if only an initiation, a termination, and a period marked by neither—then it becomes plain that any cross-sectional perspective, any instantaneous slice focusing on talking, not *a* talk, necessarily misses important features. Certain issues, such as the work done in summonings, the factor of topicality, the building up of an information state known to be common to the participants (with consequent "filling in" of new participants), the role of "preclosings," seem especially dependent on the question of the unit as a whole.

Giving credit to the autonomy of "a talk" as a unit of activity in its own right, a domain *sui generis* for analysis is a crucial step. But, of course, only new questions are opened up. For although it is easy to select for study a stretch of talk that exhibits the properties of a nicely bounded social encounter (and even easier to assume that any selected occasion of talk derives from such a unit), there are apparently lots of moments of talk that cannot be so located. And there are lots of encounters so intertwined with other encounters as to weaken the claim of any of them to autonomy. So I think one must return to a cross-sectional analysis, to examining *moments* of talk, but now bearing in mind that any broad labeling of what one is looking at—such as "conversation," "talk," "discourse"—is very premature. The question of substantive unit is one that will eventually have to be addressed, even though analysis may have to begin by blithely plucking out a moment's talk to talk about, and blithely using labels that might not apply to the whole course of a conversation.

IV

Turn first, then, to the notion of a hearer (or a recipient, or a listener). The process of auditing what a speaker says and following the gist of his remarks—hearing in the communication-system sense—is from the start to be distinguished from the social slot in which this activity usually occurs, namely, official status as a ratified participant in the encounter. For plainly, we might not be listening when indeed we have a ratified social place in the talk, and this in spite of normative expectations on the part of the speaker. Correspondingly, it is evident that when we are not an official participant in the encounter, we might still be following the talk closely, in one of two socially different ways: either we have purposely engineered this, resulting in "eavesdropping," or the opportunity has unintentionally and inadvertently come about, as in "overhearing." In brief, a ratified participant may not be listening, and someone listening may not be a ratified participant.

Now consider that much of talk takes place in the visual and aural range of persons who are not ratified participants and whose access to the encounter, however minimal, is itself perceivable by the official participants. These adventitious participants are "bystanders." Their presence should be considered the rule, not the exception. In some circumstances they can temporarily follow the talk, or catch bits and pieces of it, all without much effort or intent, becoming, thus, overhearers. In other circumstances they may surreptitiously exploit the accessibility they find they have, thus qualifying as eavesdroppers, here not dissimilar to those who secretly listen in on conversations electronically. Ordinarily, however, we bystanders politely disavail ourselves of these latter opportunities, practicing the situational ethic which obliges us to warn those who are, that they are, unknowingly accessible, obliging us also to enact a show of disinterest, and by disattending and withdrawing ecologically to minimize our actual access to the talk. (Much of the etiquette of bystanders can be generated from the basic understanding that they should act so as to maximally encourage the fiction that they aren't present; in brief, that the assumptions of the conversational paradigm are being realized.) But however polite, bystanders will still be able to glean some information; for example, the language spoken, "who" (whether in categorical or biographical terms) is in an encounter with whom, which of the participants is speaker and which are listeners, what the general mood of the conversational circle is, and so forth. Observe, too, that in managing the accessibility of an encounter both its participants and its bystanders will rely heavily on sight, not sound, providing another reason why our initial two-party paradigm is inadequate. (Imagine a deaf person bystanding a conversation; would he not be able to glean considerable social information from what he could see?)

The hearing sustained by our paradigmatic listener turns out to be an ambiguous act in an additional sense. The ratified hearer in two-person talk is necessarily also the "addressed" one, that is, the one to whom the speaker addresses his visual attention and to whom, incidentally, he expects to turn over the speaking role. But obviously two-person encounters, however common, are not the only kind; three or more official participants are often found. In such cases it will often be feasible for the current speaker to address his remarks to the circle as a whole, encompassing all his hearers in his glance, according them something like equal status. But, more likely, the speaker will, at least during periods of his talk, address his remarks to one listener, so that among official hearers one must distinguish the addressed recipient from "unaddressed" ones. Observe again that this structurally important distinction between official recipients is often accomplished exclusively through visual cues, although vocatives are available for managing it through audible ones.

The relation(s) among speaker, addressed recipient, and unaddressed recipient(s) are complicated, significant, and not much explored. An ideal in friendly conversation is that no one participant serve more frequently, or for a longer summation of time, in any one of these three roles, than does any other participant. In practice, such an arrangement is hardly to be found, and every possible variation is met with. Even when a particular pair holds the floor for an extended period, the structural implication can vary; for example, their talk can move to private topics and increasingly chill the involvement of the remaining participants, or it can be played out as a display for the encircling hearers—a miniature version of the arrangement employed in TV talk shows, or a lawyer's examination of a witness before a jury.

Once the dyadic limits of talk are breached, and one admits bystanders and/or more than one ratified recipient to the scene, then "subordinate communication" becomes a recognizable possibility: talk that is manned, timed, and pitched to constitute a perceivedly limited interference to what might be called the "dominating communication" in its vicinity. Indeed, there are a great number of work settings where informal talk is subordinated to the task at hand, the accommodation being not to another conversation but to the exigencies of work in progress.

Those maintaining subordinate communication relative to a dominant state of talk may make no effort to conceal that they are communicating in this selective way, and apparently no pointed effort to conceal what it is they are communicating. Thus "byplay": subordinated communication of a subset of ratified participants; "crossplay": communication between ratified participants and bystanders across the boundaries of the dominant encounter; "sideplay": respectfully hushed words exchanged entirely among bystanders. Nature is a pedant; in our culture each of these three forms of apparently unchallenging communication is managed through gestural markers that are distinctive and well standardized, and I assume that other gesture communities have their own sets of functional equivalents.

When an attempt *is* made to conceal subordinate communication, "collusion" occurs, whether within the boundaries of an encounter (collusive byplay) or across these boundaries (collusive crossplay) or entirely outside the encounter, as when two bystanders surreptitiously editorialize on what they are overhearing (collusive sideplay). Collusion is accomplished variously: by concealing the subordinate communication, by affecting that the words the excolluded can't hear are innocuous, or by using allusive words ostensibly meant for all participants, but whose additional meaning will be caught by only some.

Allied to collusion is "innuendo," whereby a speaker, ostensibly directing words to an addressed recipient, overlays his remarks with a patent but deniable meaning, a meaning that has a target more so than a recipient, is typically disparaging of it, and is meant to be caught by the target, whether this be the addressed recipient or an unaddressed recipient, or even a bystander (Fisher 1976).

A further issue. In recommending earlier that a conversation could be subordinated to an instrumental task at hand, that is, fitted in when and where the task allowed, it was assumed that the participants could desist from their talk at any moment when the requirements of work gave reason, and presumably return to it when the current attention requirements of the task made this palpably feasible. In these circumstances it is imaginable that the usual ritualization of encounters would be muted, and stretches of silence would occur of variable length which aren't nicely definable as either interludes between different encounters or pauses within an encounter. Under these conditions (and many others) an "open state of talk" can develop, participants having the right but not the obligation to initiate a little flurry of talk, then relapse back into silence, all this with no apparent ritual marking, as though adding but another interchange to a chronic conversation in progress. Here something must be addressed that is neither ratified participation nor bystanding, but a peculiar condition between.

There remains to consider the dynamics of ratified participation. Plainly, a distinction must be drawn between opening or closing an encounter, and joining or leaving an ongoing one; conventional practices are to be found for distinguishably accomplishing both. And plainly, two differently manned encounters can occur under conditions of mutual accessibility, each bystanding the other.[3] At point here, however, is another issue: the right to leave and to join, taken together, imply circumstances in which participants will shift from one encounter to another. At a "higher" level, one must also consider the possibility of an encounter of four or more participants splitting, and of separate encounters merging. And it appears that in some microecological social circumstances these various changes are frequent. Thus, at table during convivial dinners of eight or so participants, marked instability of participation is often found. Here a speaker may feel it necessary to police his listenership, not so much to guard against eavesdroppers (for, indeed, at table overhearing hardly needs to be concealed), as to bring back strays and encourage incipient joiners. In such environments, interruption, pitch raising and trunk orientation seem to acquire a special function and significance. (Note how a passenger sitting in the front seat of a taxi can function as a pivot, now addressing his fellow passengers in the back seat, now the driver, effectively trusting the driver to determine whether to act as a nonperson or an addressee, and all this without the driver's taking his eyes off the road or depending on the content of the remark to provide participation instructions.) Another example of structural instability is to be observed when couples meet. What had been two "withs" provide the personnel for a momentarily inclusive encounter, which can then

3. One standard arrangement is mutual modulation presented as equally allocating the available sound space; another (as suggested), is differential muting, whereby those in one of the encounters unilaterally constrain their communication in deference to the other, or even bring it to a respectful close.

bifurcate so that each member of one of the entering withs can personally greet a member of the other with, after which greeting, partners are exchanged and another pair of greeting interchanges follows, and after *this,* a more sustained regrouping can occur.

Consider now that, in dealing with the notion of bystanders, a shift was tacitly made from the encounter as a point of reference to something somewhat wider, namely, the "social situation," defining this as the full physical arena in which persons present are in sight and sound of one another. (These persons, in their aggregate, can be called a "gathering," no implications of any kind being intended concerning the relationships in which they might severally stand to one another.) For it turns out that routinely it is relative to a gathering, not merely to an encounter, that the interactional facts will have to be considered. Plainly, for example, speakers will modify how they speak, if not what they say, by virtue of conducting their talk in visual and aural range of nonparticipants. Indeed, as Joel Sherzer has suggested, when reporting on having heard someone say something, we are likely to feel obliged to make clear whether we heard the words as a ratified participant to the talk of which they were a part or whether we overheard them as a bystander.

Perhaps the clearest evidence of the structural significance of the social situation for talk (and, incidentally, of the limitation of the conventional model of talk) is to be found in our verbal behavior when we are by ourselves yet in the immediate presence of passing strangers. Proscriptive rules of communication oblige us to desist in use of speech and wordlike, articulated sounds. But in fact there is a wide variety of circumstances in which we will audibly address statements to ourselves, blurt out imprecations, and utter "response cries," such as *Oops!, Eek!,* and the like (Goffman, "Response Cries," 1978 and this volume). These vocalizations can be shown to have a self-management function, providing evidence to everyone who can hear that our observable plight is not something that should be taken to define us. To that end the volume of the sounding will be adjusted, so that those in the social situation who can perceive our plight will also hear our comment on it. No doubt, then, that we seek some response from those who can hear us, but not a specific reply. No doubt the intent is to provide information to everyone in range, but without taking the conversational floor to do so. What is sought is not hearers but overhearers, albeit intended ones. Plainly, the substantive natural unit of which self-directed remarks and response cries are a part need not be a conversation, whatever else it might be.

Finally, observe that if one starts with a particular individual in the act of speaking—a cross-sectional instantaneous view—one can describe the role or function of all the several members of the encompassing social gathering from this point of reference (whether they are ratified participants of the talk or not), couching the description in the concepts that have been reviewed. The relation of any one such member to this utterance can be called his "participation status" relative to it, and that of all the persons in the gathering the "participation framework" for that moment of speech. The same two terms can be employed when the point of reference is shifted from a given particular speaker to something wider: all the activity in the situation itself. The point of all this, of course, is that an utterance does not carve up the world beyond the speaker into precisely two parts, recipients and non-recipients, but rather opens up an array of structurally differentiated possibilities, establishing the participation framework in which the speaker will be guiding his delivery.

V

I have argued that the notion of hearer or recipient is rather crude. In so doing, however, I restricted myself to something akin to ordinary conversation. But conversation is not the only context of talk. Obviously talk can (in modern society) take the form of a platform monologue, as in the case of political addresses, stand-up comedy routines, lectures, dramatic recitations, and poetry readings. These entertainments involve long stretches of words coming from a single speaker who has been given a relatively large set of listeners and exclusive claim to the floor. Talk, after all, can occur at the town podium, as well as the town pump.

And when talk comes from the podium, what does the hearing is an audience, not a set of fellow conversationalists. Audiences hear in a way special to them. Perhaps in conjunction with the fact that audience members are further removed physically from the speaker than a coconversationalist might be, they have the right to examine the speaker directly, with an openness that might be offensive in conversation. And except for those very special circumstances when, for example, the audience can be told to rise and repeat the Lord's Prayer, or to donate money to a cause, actions can only be recommended for later consideration, not current execution. Indeed, and fundamentally, the role of the audience is to appreciate remarks made, not to reply in any direct way. They are to conjure up what a reply might be, but not utter it; "back-channel" response alone is what is meant to be available to them. They give the floor but (except during the question period) rarely get it.

The term "audience" is easily extended to those who hear talks on the radio or TV, but these hearers are different in obvious and important ways from those who are live witnesses to it. Live witnesses are coparticipants in a social occasion, responsive to all the mutual stimulation that that provides; those who audit the talk by listening to their set can only vicariously join the station audience. Further, much radio and TV talk is not addressed (as ordinary podium talk is) to a massed but visible grouping off the stage, but to *imagined* recipients; in fact, broadcasters are under pressure to style their talk as though it were addressed to a single listener. Often, then, broadcast talk involves a conversational mode of address, but, of course, merely a simulated one, the requisite recipients not being there in the flesh to evoke it. And so a broadcast talk may have a "live" audience and a broadcast audience, the speaker now styling his projection mainly for the one, now for the other, and only the music of language can lull us into thinking that the same kind of recipient entity is involved.

Still further multiplicities of meaning must be addressed. Podiums are often placed on a stage; this said, it becomes plain that podiums and their limpets are not the only things one finds there. Stage actors are found there, too, performing speeches to one another in character, all arranged so they can be listened in on by those who are off the stage. We resolutely use one word, "audience," to refer to those who listen to a political speech and those who watch a play; but again the many ways in which these two kinds of hearers are in the same position shouldn't blind one to the very important ways in which their circumstances differ. A town speaker's words are meant for his audience and are spoken to them; were a reply to be made, it would have to come from these listeners, and indeed, as suggested, signs of agreement and disagreement are often in order. It is presumably because there are so many persons in an audience that direct queries and replies must be omitted, or at least postponed to a time when the speech itself can be considered over. Should a member of the audience assay to reply in words to something that a speaker in midspeech says, the latter can elect to answer and, if he knows what he's about, sustain the reality he is engaged in. But the words addressed by one character in a play to another (at least in modern Western dramaturgy) are eternally sealed off from the audience, belonging entirely to a self-enclosed, make-believe realm—although the actors who are performing these characters (and who in a way are also cut off from the dramatic action) might well appreciate signs of audience attentiveness.[4]

I have suggested that orators and actors provide a ready contrast to a conversation's speaker, the former having audiences, the latter fellow conversationalists. But it must be borne in mind that what goes on upon the platform is only incidentally—not analytically—talk. Singing can occur there (this being another way words can be uttered), and doings which don't centrally involve words at all, such as instrument playing, hat tricks, juggling, and all the other guileful acts that have done a turn in vaudeville. The various kinds of audiences are not, analytically speaking, a feature of speech events (to use Hymes's term), but of stage events.

And from here one can go on to still more difficult cases. There are, for example, church congregations of the revivalist type wherein an active interchange is sustained of calls and answers between minister and churchgoers. And there are lots of

4. Maintaining a rigid line between characters and audience is by no means, of course, the only way to organize dramatic productions, Burmese traditional theatre providing one example (Becker 1970), our own burlesqued melodrama almost another.

social arrangements in which a single speaking slot is organizationally central, and yet neither a stage event with its audience, nor a conversation with its participants, is taking place. Rather, something binding is: court trials, auctions, briefing sessions, and course lectures are examples. Although these podium occasions of binding talk can often support participants who are fully in the audience role, they also necessarily support another class of hearers, ones who are more committed by what is said and have more right to be heard than ordinarily occurs in platform entertainments.

Whether one deals with podium events of the recreational, congregational, or binding kind, a participation framework specific to it will be found, and the array of these will be different from, and additional to, the one generic to conversation. The participation framework paradigmatic of two-person talk doesn't tell us very much about participation frameworks as such.

VI

It is claimed that to appreciate how many different kinds of hearers there are, first one must move from the notion of a conversational encounter to the social situation in which the encounter occurs; and then one must see that, instead of being part of a conversation, words can be part of a podium occasion where doings other than talk are often featured, words entering at the beginning and ending of phases of the program, to announce, welcome, and thank. This might still incline one to hold that when words pass among a small number of persons, the prototypical unit to consider is nevertheless a conversation or a chat. However, this assumption must be questioned, too.

In canonical talk, the participants seem to share a focus of cognitive concern—a common subject matter—but less simply so a common focus of visual attention. The subject of attention is clear, the object of it less so. Listeners are obliged to avoid staring directly at the speaker too long lest they violate his territoriality, and yet they are encouraged to direct their visual attention so as to obtain gesticulatory cues to his meaning and provide him with evidence that he is being attended. It is as if they were to look into the speaker's words, which, after all, cannot be seen. It is as if they must look at the speaker, but not see him.[5]

But, of course, it is possible for a speaker to direct the visual attention of his hearers to some passing object—say, a car or a view—in which case for a moment there will be a sharp difference between speaker and both cognitive and visual attention. And the same is true when this focus of both kinds of attention is a person, as when two individuals talking to each other remark on a person whom they see asleep or across the street. And so one must consider another possibility: when a patient shows a physician where something hurts, or a customer points to where a try-on shoe pinches, or a tailor demonstrates how the new jacket fits, the individual who is the object of attention is also a fully qualified participant. The rub—and now to be considered—is that in lots of these latter occasions a conversation is not really the context of the utterance; a physically elaborated, nonlinguistic undertaking is, one in which nonlinguistic events may have the floor. (Indeed, if language is to be traced back to some primal scene, better it is traced back to the occasional need of a grunted signal to help coordinate action in what is already the shared world of a joint task than to a conversation in and through which a common subjective universe is generated.[6])

One standard nonlinguistic context for utterances is the perfunctory service contact, where a server and client come together momentarily in a coordinated transaction, often involving money on one side and goods or services on the other. Another involves those passing contacts between two strangers wherein the time is told, the salt is passed, or a narrow, crowded passageway is negotiated. Although a full-fledged ritual interchange is often found in these moments, physical transactions of some kind form

5. Overlayed on this general pattern is a very wide range of practices bearing on the management of interaction. Frequency, duration, and occasion of mutual and unilateral gaze can mark initiation and termination of turn at talk, physical distance, emphasis, intimacy, gender, and so forth—and, of course, a change in footing. See, for example. Argyle and Dean (1965).

6. A useful review of the arguments may be found in Hewes (1973); a counterview in Falk (1980).

the meaningful context and the relevant unit for analysis; the words spoken, whether by one participant or two, are an integral part of a mutually coordinated physical undertaking, not a talk. Ritual is so often truncated in these settings because it is nonconversational work that is being done. It is the execution of this work, not utterances, that will ordinarily be the chief concern of the participants. And it is when a hitch occurs in what would otherwise have been the routine interdigitation of their acts that a verbal interchange between them is most likely.

A similar picture can be seen in extended service transactions. Take, for example, mother-child pediatric consultations in Scottish public health clinics, as recently reported by Strong (1979, esp. chap. 6). Here a mother's business with a doctor (when she finally gets her turn) is apparently bracketed with little small talk, very little by way of preplay and postplay, although the child itself may be the recipient of a few ritual solicitudes. The mother sits before the doctor's desk and briefly answers such questions as he puts her, waiting patiently, quietly, and attentively between questions. She is on immediate call, poised to speak, but speaking only when spoken to, almost as well behaved as the machine that is of so much use to airline ticketers. The physician, for his part, intersperses his unceremoniously addressed queries with notetaking, note-reading, thoughtful musings, instruction to students, physical manipulation of the child, verbal exchanges with his nurse and colleagues, and movements away from his desk to get at such things as files and equipment—all of which actions appear warranted by his institutional role if not by the current examination. The mother's answers will sometimes lead the doctor to follow up with a next question, but often instead to some other sort of act on his part. For his social and professional status allows him to be very businesslike; he is running through the phases of an examination, or checklist, not a conversation, and only a scattering of items require a mother's verbal contribution. And indeed, the mother may not know with any specificity what any of the doctor's acts are leading up to or getting at, her being "in on" the instrumentally meaningful sequence of events in no way being necessary for her contribution to it. So although she fits her turns at talk, and what she says, to the doctor's questionings (as in the organization of talk), what immediately precedes and what immediately follows these exchanges is not a speech environment. What is being sustained, then, is not a state of talk but a state of inquiry, and it is this latter to which utterances first must be referred if one is to get at their organization significance.

Or take the open state of talk that is commonly found in connection with an extended joint task, as when two mechanics, separately located around a car, exchange the words required to diagnose, repair, and check the repairing of an engine fault. An audio transcription of twenty minutes of such talk might be very little interpretable even if we know about cars; we would have to watch what was being done to the car in question. The tape would contain long stretches with no words, verbal directives answered only by mechanical sounds, and mechanical sounds answered by verbal responses. And rarely might the relevant context of one utterance be another utterance.

So, too, game encounters of the kind, say, that playing bridge provides, where some of the moves are made with cards, and some with voiced avowals which have been transformed into ideal performatives by the rules of the game.

And indeed, in the White House scene presented initially, the colloquy between Mr. Nixon and Ms. Thomas is not an embedded part of a wider conversation, but an embedded part of a ritualized political procedure, the ceremonial signing of a bill.

One clearly finds, then, that coordinated task activity—not conversation—is what lots of words are part of. A presumed common interest in effectively pursuing the activity at hand, in accordance with some sort of overall plan for doing so, is the contextual matrix which renders many utterances, especially brief ones, meaningful. And these are not unimportant words; it takes a linguist to overlook them.

It is apparent, then, that utterances can be an intimate, functionally integrated part of something that involves other words only in a peripheral and functionally optional way. A naturally bounded unit may be implied, but not one that could be called a speech event.

VII

Beginning with the conversational paradigm, I have tried to decompose the global notion of hearer or recipient, and I have incidentally argued that the notion of a conversational encounter does not suffice in dealing with the context in which words are spoken; a social occasion involving a podium may be involved, or no speech event at all, and, in any case, the whole social situation, the whole surround, must always be considered. Provided, thus, has been a lengthy gloss on Hymes's admonition (1974:54): "The common dyadic model of speaker-hearer specifies sometimes too many, sometimes too few, sometimes the wrong participants."

It is necessary now to look at the remaining element of the conversational paradigm, the notion of *speaker.*

In canonical talk, one of the two participants moves his lips up and down to the accompaniment of his own facial (and sometimes bodily) gesticulations, and words can be heard issuing from the locus of his mouth. His is the sounding box in use, albeit in some actual cases he can share this physical function with a loudspeaker system or a telephone. In short, he is the talking machine, a body engaged in acoustic activity, or, if you will, an individual active in the role of utterance production. He is functioning as an "animator." Animator and recipient are part of the same level and mode of analysis, two terms cut from the same cloth, not social roles in the full sense so much as functional nodes in a communication system.

But, of course, when one uses the term "speaker," one very often beclouds the issue, having additional things in mind, this being one reason why "animator" cannot comfortably be termed a social role, merely an analytical one.

Sometimes one has in mind that there is an "author" of the words that are heard, that is, someone who has selected the sentiments that are being expressed and the words in which they are encoded.

Sometimes one has in mind that a "principal" (in the legalistic sense) is involved, that is, someone whose position is established by the words that are spoken, someone whose beliefs have been told, someone who is committed to what the words say.

Note that one deals in this case not so much with a body or mind as with a person active in some particular social identity or role, some special capacity as a member of a group, office, category, relationship, association, or whatever, some socially based source of self-identification. Often this will mean that the individual speaks, explicitly or implicitly, in the name of "we," not "I" (but not for the reasons Queen Victoria or Nixon felt they had), the "we" including more than the self (Spiegelberg 1973:129–56; Moerman 1968:153–69). And, of course, the same individual can rapidly alter the social role in which he is active, even though his capacity as animator and author remains constant—what in committee meetings is called "changing hats." (This, indeed, is what occurs during a considerable amount of code switching, as Gumperz has amply illustrated.) In thus introducing the name or capacity in which he speaks, the speaker goes some distance in establishing a corresponding reciprocal basis of identification for those to whom this stand-taking is addressed. To a degree, then, to select the capacity in which we are to be active is to select (or to attempt to select) the capacity in which the recipients of our action are present (Weinstein and Deutschberger 1963:454–66). All of this work is consolidated by naming practices and, in many languages, through choice among available second-person pronouns.

The notions of animator, author, and principal, taken together, can be said to tell us about the "production format" of an utterance.

When one uses the term "speaker," one often implies that the individual who animates is formulating his own text and staking out his own position through it: animator, author, and principal are one. What could be more natural? So natural indeed that I cannot avoid continuing to use the term "speaker" in this sense, let alone the masculine pronoun as the unmarked singular form.

But, of course, the implied overlaying of roles has extensive institutionalized exceptions. Plainly, *reciting* a fully memorized text or *reading aloud* from a prepared script allows us to animate words we had no hand in formulating, and to express opinions, beliefs, and sentiments we do not hold. We can openly speak *for* someone else and *in* someone else's words, as we do, say, in reading a deposition or providing a simultaneous translation of a speech—the latter an interesting example because so often the original speaker's words, although ones that person commits himself to, are ones that someone else wrote for him. As will later be seen, the tricky problem is that often when we do engage in "fresh talk," that is, the extemporaneous, ongoing formulation of a text under the exigency of immediate response to our current situation,[7] it is not true to say that we always speak our own words and ourself take the position to which these words attest.

A final consideration. Just as we can listen to a conversation without being ratified hearers (or be ratified to listen but fail to do so), so as ratified listeners—participants who don't now have the floor—we can briefly interject our words and feelings into the temporal interstices within or between interchanges sustained by other participants (Goffman 1976:275–76, and this volume, pp. 28–29). Moreover, once others tacitly have given us the promise of floor time to recount a tale or to develop an argument, we may tolerate or even invite kibitzing, knowing that there is a good chance that we can listen for a moment without ceasing to be the speaker, just as others can interrupt for a moment without ceasing to be listeners.

VIII

Given an utterance as a starting point of inquiry, I have recommended that our commonsense notions of hearer and speaker are crude, the first potentially concealing a complex differentiation of participation statuses, and the second, complex questions of production format.

The delineation of participation framework and production format provides a structural basis for analyzing changes in footing. At least it does for the changes in footing described at the beginning of this paper. But the view that results systematically simplifies the bearing of participation frameworks and production formats on the structure of utterances. Sturdy, sober, socio-

7. David Abercrombie (1965:2) divides what I here call fresh talk into conversation, involving a rapid exchange of speaker-hearer roles, and monologue, which involves extended one-person exercises featuring a vaunted style that approaches the formality of a written form.

logical matters are engaged, but the freewheeling, self-referential character of speech receives no place. The essential fancifulness of talk is missed. And for these fluidities linguistics, not sociology, provides the lead. It is these matters that open up the possibility of finding some structural basis for even the subtlest shifts in footing.

A beginning can be made by examining the way statements are constructed, especially in regard to "embedding," a tricky matter made more so by how easy it is to confuse it with an analytically quite different idea, the notion of multiple social roles already considered in connection with "principal."

You hear an individual grunt out an unadorned, naked utterance, hedged and parenthesized with no qualifier or pronoun, such as:

> a directive: Shut the window.
> an interrogative: Why here?
> a declarative: The rain has started.
> a commissive: The job will be done by three o'clock.

Commonly the words are heard as representing in some direct way the *current* desire, belief, perception, or intention of whoever animates the utterance. The current self of the person who animates seems inevitably involved in some way—what might be called the "addressing self." So, too, deixis in regard to time and place is commonly involved. One is close here to the expressive communication we think of as the kind an animal could manage through the small vocabulary of sound-gestures available to it. Observe that when such utterances are heard they are still heard as coming from an individual who not only animates the words but is active in a *particular* social capacity, the words taking their authority from this capacity.

Many, if not most, utterances, however, are not constructed in this fashion. Rather, as speaker, we represent ourselves through the offices of a personal pronoun, typically "I," and it is thus a *figure*—a figure in a statement—that serves as the agent, a protagonist in a *described* scene, a "character" in an anecdote, someone, after all, who belongs to the world that is spoken about, not the world in which the speaking occurs. And once this format is employed, an astonishing flexibility is created.

For one thing, hedges and qualifiers introduced in the form of performative modal verbs (I "wish," "think," "could," "hope," etc.) become possible, introducing some distance between the figure and its avowal. Indeed, a double distance is produced, for presumably some part of us unconditionally stands behind our conditional utterance, else we would have to say something like "I think that I think. . . ." Thus, when we slip on a word and elect to further interrupt the flow by interjecting a remedial statement such as, "Whoops! I got that wrong, . . ." or "I meant to say . . .," we are projecting ourselves as animators into the talk. But this is a figure, nonetheless, and not the actual animator; it is merely a figure that comes closer than most to the individual who animates its presentation. And, of course, a point about these apologies for breaks in fluency is that they themselves can be animated fluently, exhibiting a property markedly different from the one they refer to, reminding one that howsoever we feel obliged to describe ourselves, we need not include in this description the capacity and propensity to project such descriptions. (Indeed, we cannot entirely do so.) When we say, "I can't seem to talk clearly today," *that* statement can be very clearly said. When we say, "I'm speechless!", we aren't. (And if we tried to be cute and say, "I'm speechless—but apparently not enough to prevent myself from saying that," our description would embody the cuteness but not refer to it.) In Mead's terms, a "me" that tries to incorporate its "I" requires another "I" to do so.

Second, as Hockett (1963:11) recommends, unrestricted displacement in time and place becomes possible, such that our reference can be to what we did, wanted, thought, etc., at some distant time and place, when, incidentally, we were active in a social capacity we may currently no longer enjoy and an identity we no longer claim. It is perfectly true that when we say:

I said shut the window

we can mean almost exactly what we would have meant had we uttered the unadorned version:

Shut the window

as a repetition of a prior command. But if we happen to be recounting a tale of something that happened many years ago, when we were a person we consider we no longer are, then the "I" in "I said shut the window" is linked to us—the person present—merely through biographical continuity, something that much or little can be made of, and nothing more immediate than that. In which case, two animators can be said to be involved: the one who is physically animating the sounds that are heard, and an embedded animator, a figure in a statement who is present only in a world that is being told about, not in the world in which the current telling takes place. (Embedded authors and principals are also possible.) Following the same argument, one can see that by using second or third person in place of first person we can tell of something someone *else* said, someone present or absent, someone human or mythical. We can embed an entirely different speaker into our utterance. For it is as easy to cite what someone else said as to cite oneself. Indeed, when queried as to precisely what someone said, we can reply quotatively:

> Shut the window

and, although quite unadorned, this statement will be understood as something someone other than we, the current and actual animator, said. Presumably, "He (or "she") said" is implied but not necessarily stated.[8]

Once embedding is admitted as a possibility, then it is an easy step to see that multiple embeddings will be possible, as in the following:

> To the best of my recollection,
> (1) I think that
> (2) I said
> (3) I once lived that sort of life.

where (1) reflects something that is currently true of the individual who animates (the "addressing self"), (2) an embedded

8. Some generative semanticists have argued that *any* unadorned utterance implies a higher performative verb and a pronoun, e.g., "I say," "aver," "demand," etc., the implication being that all statements are made by figures mentioned or implied, not by living individuals. See, for example, Ross 1970.

animator who is an earlier incarnation of the present speaker and (3) is a doubly embedded figure, namely, a still earlier incarnation of an earlier incarnation.[9]

Although linguists have provided us with very useful treatments of direct and indirect quotation, they have been less helpful in the question of how else, as animators, we can convey words that are not our own. For example, if someone repeatedly tells us to shut the window, we can finally respond by repeating his words in a strident pitch, enacting a satirical version of his utterance ("say-foring"). In a similar way we can mock an accent or dialect, projecting a stereotyped figure more in the manner that stage actors do than in the manner that mere quotation provides. So, too, without much warning, we can corroborate our own words with an adage or saying, the understanding being that fresh talk has momentarily ceased and an anonymous authority wider and different from ourselves is being suddenly invoked (Laberge and Sankoff 1979, esp. sec. 3). If these playful projections are to be thought of in terms of embeddings, then stage acting and recitation must be thought of as forms of embedded action, too. Interestingly, it seems very much the case that in socializing infants linguistically, in introducing them to words and utterances, we from the very beginning teach them to use talk in this self-dissociated, fanciful way.[10]

9. It would be easy to think that "I" had special properties uniquely bridging between the scene in which the talking occurs and the scene about which there is talking, for it refers both to a figure in a statement and to the currently present, live individual who is animating the utterance. But that is not quite so. Second-person pronouns are equally two-faced, referring to figures in statements and currently present, live individuals engaged in hearing what a speaker is saying about them. Moreover, both types of pronoun routinely appear embedded as part of quoted statements:

> She said, "I insist you shut the window."

in which case the individual who had served as a live, currently present animator has herself become a figure in a lower-order statement. The bridging power of "I" remains, but what is bridged is an embedded speaker to the figure it describes. The scene in which speaking and hearing is currently and actually occurring does not appear except through implicature: the implication that everyone listening will know who is referred to by "she."

10. In play with a child, a parent tries to ease the child into talk. Using "we" or "I" or "baby" or a term of endearment or the child's name, and a lisping sort of baby talk, the parent makes it apparent that it is the child that is being

It should be clear, then, that the significance of production format cannot be dealt with unless one faces up to the embedding function of much talk. For obviously, when we shift from saying something ourselves to reporting what someone else said, we are changing our footing. And so, too, when we shift from reporting our current feelings, the feelings of the "addressing self," to the feelings we once had but no longer espouse. (Indeed, a code switch sometimes functions as a mark of this shift.)

Final points. As suggested, when as speaker we project ourselves in a current and locally active capacity, then our coparticipants in the encounter are the ones who will have their selves partly determined correspondingly. But in the case of a replay of a past event, the self we select for ourself can only "altercast" the other figures *in the story,* leaving the hearers of the replay undetermined in that regard. *They* are cast into recipients of a bit of narrative, and this will be much the same sort of self whomsoever we people our narrative with, and in whatsoever capacity they are there active. The statuses "narrator" and "story listener," which would seem to be of small significance in terms of the overall social structure, turn out, then, to be of considerable importance in conversation, for they provide a footing to which a very wide range of speakers and hearers can briefly shift.[11] (Ad-

talked *for,* not to. In addition, there are sure to be play-beings easy to hand—dolls, teddy bears, and now toy robots—and these the parent will speak for, too. So even as the child learns to speak, it learns to speak for, learns to speak in the name of figures that will never be, or at least aren't yet, the self. George Herbert Mead notwithstanding, the child does not merely learn to refer to itself through a name for itself that others had first chosen; it learns just as early to embed the statements and mannerisms of a zoo-full of beings in its own verbal behavior. It can be argued that it is just this format that will allow the child in later years to describe its own past actions which it no longer feels are characteristic, just as this format will allow the child to use "I" as part of a statement that is quoted as something someone else said. (One might say that Mead had the wrong term: the child does not acquire a "generalized other" so much as a capacity to embed "particularized others"—which others, taken together, form a heterogeneous, accidental collection, a teething ring for utterances and not a ball team.) It strikes me, then, that although a parent's baby talk (and the talk the child first learns) may involve some sort of simplification of syntax and lexicon, its laminative features are anything but childlike. Nor do I think parents should be told about this. A treatment of this issue in another culture is provided by Schieffelin (1974).

11. One example: A few years ago, the BBC did an hour-length TV documentary on backstage at the Royal Household. The show purported to

mittedly, if a listener is also a character in the story he is listening to, as in the millions of mild recriminations communicated between intimates, then he is likely to have more than a mere listener's concern with the tale.)

Storytelling, of course, requires the teller to embed in his own utterances the utterances and actions of the story's characters. And a full-scale story requires that the speaker remove himself for the telling's duration from the alignment he would maintain in ordinary conversational give and take, and for this period of narration maintain another footing, that of a narrator whose extended pauses and utterance completions are not to be understood as signals that he is now ready to give up the floor. But these changes in footing are by no means the only kind that occur during storytelling. For during the telling of a tale (as Livia Polanyi has nicely shown [1977]), the teller is likely to break narrative frame at strategic junctures: to recap for new listeners; to provide (in the raconteur's version of direct address) encouragement to listeners to wait for the punch line, or gratuitous characterizations of various protagonists in the tale; or to backtrack a correction for any felt failure to sustain narrative requirements such as contextual detail, proper temporal sequencing, dramatic build-up, and so forth.[12]

---

display the Queen in her full domestic round, including shopping and picnicking with her Family. Somehow the producers and stars of the program managed to get through the whole show without displaying much that could be deemed inadvertent, revealing, unstaged, or unself-conscious, in part, no doubt, because much of royal life is probably managed this way even in the absence of cameras. But one exception did shine through. The Queen and other members of the Family occasionally reverted to telling family stories or personal experiences to their interlocutor. The stories no doubt were carefully selected (as all stories must be), but in the telling of them the royal personages could not but momentarily slip into the unregal stance of storyteller, allowing their hearers the momentary (relative) intimacy of story listeners. What could be conceived of as "humanity" is thus practically inescapable. For there is a democracy implied in narration; the lowest rank in that activity is not very low by society's standards—the right and obligation to listen to a story from a person to whom we need not be in a position to tell one.

12. Interestingly, the texts that folklorists and sociolinguists provide of everyday stories often systematically omit the narrative frame breaks that very likely occurred throughout the actual tellings. Here the student of stories has tactfully accepted the teller's injunction that the shift in footing required to introduce a correction or some other out-of-frame comment be omitted from the official record. Often omitted, too, is any appreciation of the frequency with

IX

It was recommended that one can get at the structural basis of footing by breaking up the primitive notions of hearer and speaker into more differentiated parts, namely, participation framework and production format. Then it was suggested that this picture must itself be complicated by the concept of embedding and an understanding of the layering effect that seems to be an essential outcome of the production process in speaking. But this complication itself cannot be clearly seen unless one appreciates another aspect of embedding, one that linguistic analysis hasn't much prepared us for, namely, the sense in which participation frameworks are subject to transformation. For it turns out that, in something like the ethological sense, we quite routinely ritualize participation frameworks; that is, we self-consciously transplant the participation arrangement that is natural in one social situation into an interactional environment in which it isn't. In linguistic terms, we not only embed utterances, we embed interaction arrangements.

Take collusion, for example. This arrangement may not itself be common, but common, surely, is apparently unserious collusion broadly played out with winks and elbow nudges in the obviously open presence of the excolluded. Innuendo is also a common candidate for playful transformation, the target of the slight meant to understand that a form is being used unseriously —a practice sometimes employed to convey an opinion that could not safely be conveyed through actual innuendo, let alone direct statement. The shielding of the mouth with the hand, already a ritualized way of marking a byplay during large meetings, is brought into small conversational circles to mark a communication as having the character of an aside but here with no one to be excluded from it. (I have seen an elderly woman in a quiet street talking about neighborhood business to the man next door and then, in termination of the encounter, bisect her mouth with the five stiff fingers of her right hand and out of one side remark on how his geraniums were growing, the use of this gesture,

which hearers change footing and inject in passing their own contribution to the tale (Goodwin 1978, esp. chap. 3 and chap. 4, pt. 5).

apparently, marking her appreciation that to play her inquiry straight would be directly to invoke a shared interest and competency, not a particularly masculine one, and hence a similarity her neighbor might be disinclined to confront.) Or witness the way in which the physical contact, focusing tone, and loving endearments appropriate within the privacy of a courtship encounter can be performed in fun to an unsuitable candidate as a set piece to set into the focus of attention of a wider convivial circle. Or, in the same sort of circle, how we can respond to what a speaker says to an addressed recipient as though we weren't ratified coparticipants, but bystanders engaged in irreverent sideplay. Or, even when two individuals are quite alone together and cannot possibly be overheard, how one may mark the confidential and disclosive status of a bit of gossip by switching into a whisper voice. I think there is no doubt that a considerable amount of natural conversation is laminated in the manner these illustrations suggest; in any case, conversation is certainly vulnerable to such lamination. And each increase or decrease in layering—each movement closer to or further from the "literal"—carries with it a change in footing.

Once it is seen that a participation framework can be parenthesized and set into an alien environment, it should be evident that all the participation frameworks earlier described as occurring outside of conversation—that is, arrangements involving an audience or no official recipient at all—are themselves candidates for this reframing process; they, too, can be reset into conversational talk. And, of course, with each such embedding a change of footing occurs. The private, ruminative self-talk we may employ among strangers when our circumstances suddenly require explaining, we can playfully restage in conversation, not so much projecting the words, but projecting a dumbfounded person projecting the words. So, too, on such occasions, we can momentarily affect a podium speech register, or provide a theatrical version (burlesqued, melodramatic) of an aside. All of which, of course, provides extra warrant—indeed, perhaps, the main warrant—for differentiating various participation frameworks in the first place.

It is true, then, that the frameworks in which words are spoken pass far beyond ordinary conversation. But it is just as true that these frameworks are brought back into conversation, acted out in a setting which they initially transcended. What nature divides, talk frivolously embeds, insets, and intermingles. As dramatists can put any world on their stage, so we can enact any participation framework and production format in our conversation.

X

I have dealt till now with *changes* in footing as though the individual were involved merely in switching from one stance or alignment to another. But this image is itself too mechanical and too easy. It is insufficiently responsive to the way embedding and ritualization work. For often it seems that when we change voice —whether to speak for another aspect of ourselves or for someone else, or to lighten our discourse with a darted enactment of some alien interaction arrangement—we are not so much terminating the prior alignment as holding it in abeyance with the understanding that it will almost immediately be reengaged. So, too, when we give up the floor in a conversation, thereby taking up the footing of a recipient (addressed or otherwise), we can be warranted in expecting to reenter the speaker role on the same footing from which we left it. As suggested, this is clearly the case when a narrator allows hearers to "chip in," but such perceivedly temporary foregoing of one's position is also to be found when storytelling isn't featured. So it must be allowed that we can hold the same footing across several of our turns at talk. And within one alignment, another can be fully enclosed. In truth, in talk it seems routine that, while firmly standing on two feet, we jump up and down on another.

Which should prepare us for those institutional niches in which a hard-pressed functionary is constrained to routinely sustain more than one state of talk simultaneously. Thus, throughout an auction, an auctioneer may intersperse the utterances he directs to the bidding audience with several streams of out-of-frame communication—reports on each sale spoken through a microphone to a recording clerk in another room, instructions to assistants on the floor, and (less routinely) greetings to friends and responses to individual buyers who approach with quiet requests for an updating. Nor need there be one dominant state of talk and the rest styled as asides respectfully inserted at junctures. For example, in a medical research/training facility (as reported in a forthcoming paper by Tannen and Wallat), a pediatrician may find she must continuously switch code, now addressing her youthful patient in "motherese," now sustaining a conversation-like exchange with the mother, now turning to the video camera to provide her trainee audience with a running account couched in the register of medical reporting. Here one deals with the capacity of different classes of participants to by-stand the current stream of communication whilst "on hold" for the attention of the pivotal person to reengage them. And one deals with the capacity of a dexterous speaker to jump back and forth, keeping different circles in play.

XI

To end, let us return to the Nixon scene that formed the introduction to this paper. When Helen Thomas pirouetted for the president, she was parenthesizing within her journalistic stance another stance, that of a woman receiving comments on her appearance. No doubt the forces at work are sexism and presidents, but the forces can work in this particular way because of our general capacity to embed the fleeting enactment of one role in the more extended performance of another.

When Helen Thomas pirouetted for the president, she was employing a form of behavior indigenous to the environment of the ballet, a form that has come, by conventional reframing, to be a feature of female modeling in fashion shows, and she was enacting it—of all places—in a news conference. No one present apparently found this transplantation odd. *That* is how experience is laminated.

The news report of this conference itself does not tell us, but from what is known about Nixon as a performer, a guess would be that he switched from the high ritual of signing a bill to the joshing of Ms. Thomas not merely as a bracketing device, a signal that the substantive phase of the ceremony was over, but to show he was a person of spirit, always capable of the common touch.

And I surmise that although his audience dutifully laughed loudly, they may have seen his gesture as forced, wooden, and artificial, separating him from them by a behavioral veil of design and self-consciousness. All of that would have to be understood to gain any close sense of what Nixon was projecting, of his alignment to those present, of his footing. And I believe linguistics provides us with the cues and markers through which such footings become manifest, helping us to find our way to a structural basis for analyzing them.

REFERENCES

Abercrombie, David. 1965. *Conversation and spoken prose: Studies in phonetics and linguistics.* London: Oxford University Press.

Argyle, Michael, and Dean, Janet. 1965. "Eye contact, distance and affiliation." *Sociometry* 28:289–304.

Becker, A. L. 1970. "Journey through the night: Notes on Burmese traditional theatre." *The Drama Review* 15/3:83–87.

Blom, Jan-Peter, and Gumperz, John J. 1972. "Social meaning in linguistic structure: Code-switching in Norway." In *Directions in Sociolinguistics,* edited by John J. Gumperz and Dell H. Hymes. New York: Holt, Rinehart and Winston.

Cook-Gumperz, Jenny, and Gumperz, John. 1976. "Context in children's speech." In *Papers on Language and Context* (Working Paper 46), by Jenny Cook-Gumperz and John Gumperz. Berkeley: Language Behavior Research Laboratory, University of California, Berkeley.

The Evening Bulletin (Philadelphia), August 7, 1973.

Falk, Dean, "Language, handedness, and primate brains: Did the Australopithecines sign? *American Anthropologist* 82 (1980): 78.

Fisher, Lawrence E. 1976. "Dropping remarks and the Barbadian audience." *American Ethnologist* 3/2:227–42.

Goffman, Erving. 1974. *Frame analysis.* New York: Harper and Row.

———. 1976. "Replies and responses." *Language in Society* 5:257–313.

———. 1978. "Response cries." *Language* 54/4.

Goodwin, Marjorie. 1978. "Conversational practices in a peer group of urban black children." Ph.D. dissertation, Department of Anthropology, University of Pennsylvania, Philadelphia, Pennsylvania.

Gossen, Gary H. 1976. "Verbal dueling in Chamula." In *Speech play,* edited by Barbara Kirshenblatt-Gimblett, pp. 121–46. Philadelphia: University of Pennsylvania Press.

Gumperz, John. 1976. "Social network and language shift." In *Papers on Language and Context* (Working Paper 46), by Jenny Cook-Gumperz and John Gumperz. Berkeley: Language Behavior Research Laboratory, University of California, Berkeley.

Hewes, Gordon W. 1973. "Primate communication and the gestural origin of language." *Current Anthropology* 14:5–24.

Hockett, Charles. 1963. "The problem of universals in language." In *Universals of language,* edited by Joseph Greenberg, pp. 1–29. Cambridge: MIT Press.

Hymes, Dell H. 1974. *Foundations in sociolinguistics.* Philadelphia: University of Pennsylvania Press.

Laberge, Suzanne, and Sankoff, Gillian. 1979. "Anything *you* can do." In *Discourse and syntax,* edited by Talmy Givón and Charles Li. New York: Academic Press.

Moerman, Michael. 1968. "Being Lue: Uses and abuses of ethnic identification." In *Essays on the problem of tribe,* edited by June Helm, pp. 153–69. Seattle: University of Washington Press.

Polanyi, Livia. 1977. "Not so false starts." *Working Papers in Sociolinguistics,* no. 41. Austin, Texas: Southwest Educational Development Laboratory.

Ross, John Robert. 1970. "On declarative sentences." In *Readings in English transformational grammar,* edited by Roderick A. Jacobs and Peter S. Rosenbaum, pp. 222–72. Waltham, Mass.: Ginn and Company.

Schieffelin, Bambi B. 1979. "Getting it together: An ethnographic approach to the study of the development of communicative competence." In *Studies in developmental pragmatics,* edited by Elinor O. Keenan. New York: Academic Press.

Spiegelberg, Herbert. 1973. "On the right to say 'we': A linguistic and phenomenological analysis." In *Phenomenological sociology,* edited by George Psathas, pp. 129–56. New York: John Wiley and Sons.

Strong, P. M. 1979. *The ceremonial order of the clinic.* London: Routledge and Kegan Paul.

Tannen, Deborah, and Wallat, Cynthia. Forthcoming. "A sociolinguistic analysis of multiple demands on the pediatrician in doctor/mother/child interaction."

Weinstein, Eugene, and Deutschberger, Paul. 1963. "Some dimensions of altercasting." *Sociometry* 26/4:454–66.

4

The following paper was originally presented as the Katz-Newcomb Memorial Lecture, University of Michigan, 1976. It was designed to be spoken, and through its text and delivery to provide an actual instance—not merely a discussion—of some differences between talk and the printed word. Nevertheless, with a modest amount of editorial work, the original format could have been transformed. Reference, laconic and otherwise, to time, place, and occasion could have been omitted; footnotes could have been used to house appropriate bibliography, extended asides, and full identification of sources mentioned in passing; first-person references could have been recast; categoric pronouncements could have been qualified; and other features of the style and syntax appropriate to papers in print could have been imposed. Without this, readers might feel that they had been fobbed off—with a text meant for others and a writer who felt that rewriting was not worth the bother. However, I have refrained almost entirely from making such changes. My hope is that as it stands, this version will make certain framing issues clear by apparent inadvertence, again instantiating the difference between talk and print, this time from the other side, although much less vividly than might be accomplished by publishing an unedited, closely transcribed tape recording of the initial delivery, along with phrase-by-phrase parenthetical exegesis of gesticulation, timing, and elisions. (This latter would be useful, but requires a bit much by way of warrant for public self-dissection.) I venture this plea without confidence, because it provides the obvious (albeit the only valid) excuse for obliging readers to suffer a text that has not been reworked for their mode of apprehending it. Of course, both this abuse of readers and what they can learn about framing from being thus abused are somewhat weakened by the fact that the original speaking was not extemporaneous talk, merely aloud reading from a typed text, and that all spontaneous elaborations added to the script on that occasion (and on others when the paper was reread) have been omitted—a standard practice in almost all conversions from talk to print. The punctuation signs employed are those designed for written grammar, being the same as those employed in the typed text from which the talk was read; however, the version of this order that appeared in sound arises from the original in unspecified ways—at least unspecified here. (For example, quotation marks that appear in the reading typescript appear also in the present text, but the reader is not informed as to how the words so marked were managed in the speaking, whether by prosodic markers, verbal transliteration ["quotes" . . . "unquote"], or/and finger gestures.) Moreover, here and there I have not foreborne to change a word or add a line (indeed, a paragraph or two) to the original, and these modifications are not identified as such. Finally, a prefatory statement has been added, namely, this one, along with the bibliographical references which allow me to acknowledge help from Hymes (1975) and Bauman (1975), all of which is solely part of the printed presentation. Thus, however much the original talk was in bad faith, this edited documentation of it is more so. (For a parallel discussion of the spoken lecture, and a parallel disclaimer regarding the written version, see Frake [1977].)

THE LECTURE

I

My topic and my arguments this afternoon are part of the substantive area I work in, the naturalistic study of human foregatherings and cominglings, that is, the forms and occasions of face-to-face interaction. The particular form in question incidentally provides scope for what I call "frame analysis." No other justifications are offered, but these are. Therefore, I hope you will reserve judgment and will not immediately assume that my selection of the lecture as a topic proves I am yet another self-appointed cut-up, optimistically attempting a podium shuck. I am not trying to wriggle out of my contract with you by using my situation at the podium to talk about something ready to hand, my situation at the podium. To do so would be to occupy a status for purposes other than fulfilling it. Of that sort of puerile opportunism we have had quite enough, whether from classroom practitioners of group dynamics, the left wing of ethnomethodology, or the John Cage school of performance rip-offs. (He who says he is tearing up his prepared address to talk to you extemporaneously about what it is like to address you or what it is like to write talks, or to formulate sentences in the first place, has torn up the wrong prepared address.) That I am transmitting my remarks through a lecture and not, say, in print or during a conversation, I take to be incidental. Indeed, a term like "paper" in its relevant sense can refer equally to something that is printed and something that is delivered.

Surely nothing I can want to say about lectures can have the effect of questioning the opportunity they give to purposely impart a coherent chapter of information, including, in my own case, imparting something about lecturing. One necessary condition for the validity of my analysis is that I cannot avoid its application to this occasion of communicating it to you; another is that this applicability does not, in turn, undermine either the presentation or the arguments. He who lectures on speech error and its correction will inevitably make some of the very errors he analyzes, but such an unintended exhibition attests to the value of the analysis, however it reflects upon the speaking competence of the analyst. More still, he who lectures on discourse presuppositions will be utterly tongue-tied unless unself-consciously he makes as many as anyone else. He who lectures about prefaces and excuses might still be advised to begin his talk with an apologetic introduction. And he who lectures about lectures does not have a special excuse for lecturing badly; his description of delivery faults will be judged according to how well the description is organized and delivered; his failure to engross his listeners cannot be reframed retrospectively as an illustration of the interactional significance of such failure. Should he actually succeed in breaching lecturing's constraints, he becomes a performing speaker, not a speaker performing. (He who attempts such breaching, and succeeds, should have come to the occasion dressed in tights, carrying a lute. He who attempts such evasion and fails—as is likely—is just a plain schmuck, and it would be better had he not come to the occasion at all.) Which is not to say that other sorts of frame break might be as clearly doomed; for example, a reference at this point to the very questionable procedure of my employing "he" in the immediately preceding utterances, carefully mingling a sex-biased word for the indefinite nominal pronoun, and an unobjectionable anaphoric term for someone like myself.

However, it is apparent that lecturing on lectures is nonetheless a little special. To hold forth in an extended fashion on lecturing to persons while they have to sit through one, is to force them to serve double time—a cruel and unusual punishment. To claim authority on lectures before an audience such as this one is to push forward into that zone where presumption shades into idiocy. Moreover, much as I argue that my avowals can, should, and must be firmly contained within the lecture format, something is likely to leak out. Indeed, I know that before this talk is over I will have turned more than once on my own immediately past behavior as an illustration of what is currently being said; for certainly I can inadvertently exhibit a thing better than I can consciously mock up a version for illustrative presentation. But there is a limit to how much of this sort of turning in one's tracks is allowable. Illustrations themselves raise questions. He who reports jokes, in a lecture on humor, has a right, and perhaps the obligation, to tell bad ones, for the punch line is properly to be found in the analysis, not in the story; he can allow data jokes to spark his presentation, but not to burn his thought down. Similarly, lecturing linguists can do a glottal stop or an alveolar flap as an illustration of it, and ornithologists a bird call, without particularly threatening the definition that it is lecturing that is going on. In a lecture on the grey-legged goose, slides of threat behavior are perfectly in order, words and slides being somehow equally insulated from the situation in which they are presented. In fact, medical lecturers can bring in the goose itself, providing it is a human one, and only the goose need be embarrassed. And yet, were the speaker to use the whole of his body to perform an illustration of grey-leg threat behavior—as I have seen Konrad Lorenz do—then something else begins to happen, something of the sort that only Lorenz can get away with doing, and he not without leaving a confirming residue in his reputation.

Trickier still: if an impropriety is enacted as an illustration of an impropriety, the enactment being, as it were, in quotes, how much extra insulation does that provide? In lectures on torture, speakers understandably hesitate to play tapes of actual occurrences; with how much less risk could I play such a tape as an illustration of what can't be played? Would that twice removal from actual events suffice to keep us all within the unkinetic world that lecturing is supposed to sustain? And finally, given that the situation *about* which a lecture deals is insulated in various ways from the situation *in* which the lecturing occurs, and is obliged to be insulated in this way, can an illustrated discussion of this disjunctive condition be carried on without breaching the very line that is under scrutiny? And if all of the presentation which is to follow is a single, extended example of the vulnerability of the line between the process of referring and the subject matter that is referred to, and I so state it to be from the beginning, am I giving a lecture or a lecture-hall exhibition? And is it possible to raise that question directly without ceasing to lecture? In reporting in this way about the goose, don't I become one?

You will note that I have eased you into a discussion of the lecture by talking about the lecturer. Indeed, I will continue to do so. Balance could only come from what I won't provide, an analysis of the intricacies of audience behavior.

II

A lecture is an institutionalized extended holding of the floor in which one speaker imparts his views on a subject, these thoughts comprising what can be called his "text." The style is typically serious and slightly impersonal, the controlling intent being to generate calmly considered understanding, not mere entertainment, emotional impact, or immediate action. Constituent statements presumably take their warrant from their role in attesting to the truth, truth appearing as something to be cultivated and developed from a distance, coolly, as an end in itself.

A platform arrangement is often involved, underlining the fact that listeners are an "immediate audience." I mean a gathered set of individuals, typically seated, whose numbers can vary greatly without requiring the speaker (typically standing) to change his style, who have the right to hold the whole of the speaker's body in the focus of staring-at attention (as they would an entertainer), and who (initially, at least) have only the back channel through which to convey their response.

Those who present themselves before an audience are said to be "performers" and to provide a "performance"—in the peculiar, theatrical sense of the term. Thereby they tacitly claim those platform skills for lack of which an ordinary person thrust upon the stage would flounder hopelessly—an object to laugh at, be embarrassed for, and have massive impatience with. And they tacitly accept judgment in these terms by those who themselves need never be exposed to such appraisal. The clear contrast is to everyday talk, for there, it is felt, no elevated role is being sought, no special competency is required, and surely only morbid shyness or some other unusual impediment could prevent one from delivering the grunts and eyebrow flashes that will often suffice. (Which is not to say that in conversational settings individuals may not occasionally attempt a set piece that asks to be judged as entertainment, not talk, and unlike talk is *relatively* loosely coupled to the character and size of the listening circle.) In any case, in talk, all those who judge competency know themselves to be thus appraised.

Face-to-face undertakings of the focused kind, be they games, joint tasks, theater performances, or conversations, succeed or fail as interactions in the degree to which participants get caught up by and carried away into the special realm of being that can be generated by these engagements. So, too, lectures. However, unlike games and staged plays, lectures must not be frankly presented as if engrossment were the controlling intent. Indeed, lectures draw on a precarious ideal: certainly the listeners are to be carried away so that time slips by, but because of the speaker's subject matter, not his antics; the subject matter is meant to have its own enduring claims upon the listeners apart from the felicities or infelicities of the presentation. A lecture, then, purports to take the audience right past the auditorium, the occasion, and the speaker into the subject matter upon which the lecture comments. So your lecturer is meant to be a performer, but not merely a performer. Observe, I am not saying that audiences regularly do become involved in the speaker's subject matter, only that they handle whatever they do become involved in so as not to openly embarrass the understanding that it's the text they are involved in. In fact, there is truth in saying that audiences become involved in spite of the text, not because of it; they skip along, dipping in and out of following the lecturer's argument, waiting for the special effects which actually capture them, and topple them momentarily into what is being said—which special effects I need not specify but had better produce.

In the analysis of all occasions in which talk figures largely —what Hymes has called "speech events"—it is common to use the term "speaker," as I will also. But in fact the term "speaker" is very troublesome. It can be shown to have variable and separable functions, and the word itself seems to demand that we use it because of these ambiguities, not in spite of them. In the case of a lecture, one person can be identified as the talking machine, the thing that sound comes out of, the "animator." Typically in lectures, that person is also seen as having "authored" the text, that is, as having formulated and scripted the statements that get made. And he is seen as the "principal," namely, someone who believes personally in what is being said and takes the position that is implied in the remarks. (Of course, the lecturer is likely to assume that right-thinking persons also will take the position he describes.)

I am suggesting that it is characteristic of lectures (in the sense of common to them and important for them) that animator, author, and principal are the same person. Also, it is characteristic that this three-sided functionary is assumed to have "authority" —intellectual, as opposed to institutional. By virtue of reputation or office, he is assumed to have knowledge and experience in textual matters, and of this considerably more than that possessed by the audience. And, as suggested, he does not have to fight to hold the floor—at least for a stipulated block of time— this monopoly being his, automatically, as part of the social arrangements. The floor is his, but, of course, attention may not be. As would also be true if instead of a lecturer at stage center we had a singer, a poet, a juggler, or some other trained seal.

Following the linguist Kenneth Pike, it can be said that lectures belong to that broad class of situational enterprises wherein a difference clearly occurs between game and spectacle, that is, between the business at hand and the custard of interaction in which the business is embedded. (The custard shows up most clearly as "preplay" and "postplay," that is, a squeeze of talk and bustle just before the occasioned proceedings start and just after they have finished.) The term "lecture" itself firmly obscures the matter, sometimes referring to a spoken text, sometimes to the embracing social event in which its delivery occurs—an ambiguity, also, of most terms for other stage activities.

The arrangement we have been looking at—the laminated affair of spectacle and game—itself will come in various formats:

as a one-shot event, or one of a series involving the same arrangements but different speakers, or one session of a course, the latter a sequence of lectures by the same speaker.

The spectacle, the environing social fuss in which a lecture is delivered, sometimes qualifies as a celebrative occasion. By "celebrative occasion" I mean a social affair that is looked forward to and back upon as a festivity of some kind whose business at hand, when any is discernible, is not the only reason for participation; rather import is intendedly given to social intercourse among the participants gathered under the auspices of honoring and commemorating something, if only their own social circle. Moreover, there is a tendency to phrase participation as involving one's total social personality, not merely a specialized segment. (The first and last night of a theatrical run according to this definition could be a celebrative occasion, but not likely the showings in between; a day at the office is not a special occasion, but the Christmas party hopefully is.) One-shot lectures "open to the public" involving a speaker otherwise inaccessible to the audience (and an audience otherwise inaccessible to him) are often embedded in a celebrative occasion, as are talks to private audiences in a serial format. Lectures that are part of a college course delivered by a local person tend to go unmarked in this particular way, except sometimes the opening and closing ones. Course lectures have another marginal feature: listeners can be made officially responsible for learning what is said—a condition that strikes deeply at the ritual character of performances. There note taking can occur, the lecturer accommodating in various ways to facilitate this, the note taker preferring to come away with a summary instead of an experience. (May I add, celebrative occasions seem to be a fundamental organizational form of our public life, yet hardly any study has been given to them as such.)

The recruitment of an audience through advertising, announcements to members, class scheduling, and the like; the selection and payment of the speaker; the provision of requisite housekeeping services—all these presuppose an organizational base which takes and is accorded responsibility, allowing one to speak of the "auspices" or sponsors of the lecture. A committee of some kind, a division of a university, a professional association, a government agency—any of these can serve. Characteristically this sponsoring organization will have a life and a purpose extending beyond the mounting of the lecture itself. Insofar as the lecture is itself embedded in a celebrative occasion, the occasion will celebrate the auspices of the talk even as it celebrates the speaker and his topic. (A rock concert may have auspices whose life is restricted to the mounting of this one event, and the event itself may little celebrate its auspices—in this case its promoters—these persons hoping for rewards of a more palpable kind.) In celebrative occasions in which a lecture is to occur, transition from spectacle to game, from hoopla to business at hand, is routinely divided (as you have recently witnessed) into two parts, the first part enacted by a representative of the auspices introducing the speaker, and the second part by the speaker introducing his topic. Sometimes the introducer's part of the introduction is itself split in two, the introducer himself being introduced, as though the organizers felt that the contribution of this slot to their various concerns could best be used by inserting more than one candidate.

Observe, the interests of the organizers will lie not only with the actual lecture delivery, but also with the photographic, taped, and textual record thereof, for such a record can serve organizational interests as much as or more than the talk itself. (The clear case here is the sort of charity ball that is held for a worthy organization, where commonly the costs of mounting the ball are barely offset by the monies gained from tickets, the real underlying purpose being to give newspapers a warrant for coverage.) Patently, to advertise a lecture is also to advertise its auspices; to obtain coverage of the lecture by the press has the same consequence. (Campus newspapers are interesting in this connection. They are ostensibly designed as independent, if not dissident, expressions of inmate opinion. But they appreciably function as vanity presses for administrations, providing coverage for what might otherwise, mercifully, go unrecorded.)

Here there is an obvious link between formal organizations and the "star system." Sponsoring organizations frequently judge themselves dependent on some degree of public support and approval, some recognition of their presence and their mission, even though their financial resources may have a more circumscribed base. A principal way of bringing the name of the sponsorship before the public is to advertise some commemorative event and to obtain press coverage of it. To make such an event significant to a wide public, it is apparently helpful to schedule one or more well-known names—personages—to make an appearance. This helps give members of the public who are far afield warrant for the journey in to witness the occasion. In a sense, then, an institution's advertising isn't done in response to the anticipated presence of a well-known figure; rather, a well-known figure is useful in order to have something present that warrants wide advertising. So one might also say that large halls aren't built to accommodate large audiences but rather to accommodate wide advertising. Of course, a speaker's prestige is relevant in another way: he lends his weight to the sponsoring organization and to its social occasions, on the assumption, apparently, that worthies only affiliate with what is worthy. For thus lending his name, the speaker receives publicity and an honorarium—rewards apart from a warm reception for his words and the opportunity to spread them. In all of this we see a glimmering of the links between social affairs and social structures, a glimpse of the politics of ceremony—and another way in which preeminence derives less from differential achievement than from the organizational needs of sponsors and their occasions.

There can be, then, between auspices and speaker a tacit, some would say unholy, alliance. And this alliance may be sustained at the expense of the lecture itself—the lecture as a means of transmitting knowledge. The speaker is encouraged to pitch his remarks down to fit the competence of a large audience—an audience large enough to warrant the celebration and cost that is involved. He is encouraged to fit his remarks into the stretch of time that such an audience might be ready to forebear, and to employ mannerisms which ensure audience involvement. And he is encouraged to accept all manner of rampant intrusion from interviewers, photographers, recording specialists, and the like—intrusions that often take place right in the middle of the heat of the occasion. (If at any moment you should get the notion that a speaker really is fully caught up in talking to you, take note of his capacity to treat photographers as though they weren't interrupting his talk. Such apparent obliviousness can, of course, come from his involvement with you, as opposed to his commitment to publicity, but don't count on it.)

Finally it should be said that although a lecture can be the main business of the social occasion in which it is embedded—an arrangement that speakers presumably find ideal—other settings are common. In the United States, for example, there is the institution of the lunch speaker, and the understanding that a membership's regular get-togethers for a meal cannot be complete without a guest speaker; who, or on what topic, need not be a first consideration—anyone in the neighborhood who does talks for a fee will often do. (In many cases, of course, we might find it more natural to speak of such luncheon performances as giving a talk, not a lecture, the critical difference somehow involving the matter of systematic topic development.) And just as an occasion can make a convenience of a speaker, so a speaker can make a convenience of an occasion, as when a political figure graces a local gathering but his main concern is the transmission of his talk to media audiences.

III

What I have said so far about lectures is obvious and requires no special perspective; we move now to more intimate matters.

In our society we recognize three main modes of animating spoken words: *memorization, aloud reading* (such as I had been doing up to now), and *fresh talk.* In the case of fresh talk, the text is formulated by the animator from moment to moment, or at least from clause to clause. This conveys the impression that the formulation is responsive to the current situation in which the words are delivered, including the current content of the auditorium and of the speaker's head, and including, but not merely, what could have been envisaged and anticipated. Memorization is sometimes employed in lectures, but not admittedly. (Theatrical parts present a more complicated picture: they are delivered as though in fresh talk, and although everyone knows they are thoroughly memorized, this knowledge is to be held in abeyance, and fresh talk is to be made-believe.) In lectures, aloud reading is a frequent mode of delivery. Fresh talk is perhaps the general ideal and (with the assistance of notes) quite common.

Memorization, aloud reading, and fresh talk are different production modes. Each presupposes its own special relation between speaker and listener, establishing the speaker on a characteristic "footing" in regard to the audience. Switches from one of the three forms to another, that is, "production shifts," imply for the speaker a change of footing, and, as will be seen, are a crucial part of lecturing. The critical point that will later be addressed is that a great number of lectures (because of my incompetence, not including this one) depend upon a fresh-talk illusion. Radio announcing, I might add, is even more deeply involved in maintaining this precarious effect.

It might be noted that fresh talk itself is something of an illusion of itself, never being as fresh as it seems. Apparently we construct our utterances out of phrase- and clause-length segments, each of which is in some sense formulated mentally and then recited. Whilst delivering one such segment one must be on the way to formulating the next mentally, and the segments must be patched together without exceeding acceptable limits for pauses, restarts, repetitions, redirections, and other linguistically detectable faults. Lecturers mark a natural turning point in the acquisition of fresh-talk competence when they feel they can come close to finishing a segment without knowing yet what in the world the next will be, and yet be confident of being able to come up with (and on time) something that is grammatically and thematically acceptable, and all this without making it evident that a production crisis has been going on. And they mark a natural turning point in fresh talking *or* aloud reading a lecture when they realize they can give thought to how they seem to be doing, where they stand in terms of finishing too soon or too late, and what they plan to do after the talk—without these backstage considerations becoming evident as their concern; for should such preoccupation become evident, the illusion that they are properly involved in communicating will be threatened.

Earlier I recommended that a lecture contains a text that could just as well be imparted through print or informal talk. This being the case, the content of a lecture is not to be understood as something distinctive to and characteristic of lecturing. At best one is left with the special contingencies of delivering any particular text through the lecture medium. At best the interface, the bonding between text and situation of delivery. One is left with the form, the interactional encasement; the box, not the cake. And I believe there is no way to get at these interactional issues without directing full and sustained attention to the question of the speaker's handling of himself—a question that is easy to write about circumspectly but hard to lecture on without abusing one's podium position. I have a right to obtain and direct your attention to some relevant topic, including myself if I can manage to work that particular object into some topical event or opinion. I have the right, indeed the obligation, to back up this communicative process (whether what is said includes me as a protagonist or not) with all due manner of gesticulatory accompaniment and seemly jumping up and down. However, if, because of what I say, you focus your attention on this supportive animation; if, because of what I refer to, you attend the process through which I make references, then something is jeopardized that is structurally crucial in speech events: the partition between the inside and outside of words, between the realm of being sustained through the meaning of a discourse and the mechanics of discoursing. This partition, this membrane, this boundary, is the tickler; what happens to it largely determines the pleasure and displeasure that will be had in the occasion.

IV

Now consider footing and its changes. Differently put, consider the multiple senses in which the self of the speaker can appear, that is, the multiple self-implicatory projections discoverable in what is said and done at the podium.

At the apparent center will be the textual self, that is, the sense of the person that seems to stand behind the textual statements made and which incidentally gives these statements authority. Typically this is a self of relatively long standing, one the speaker was involved in long before the current occasion of talk. This is the self that others will cite as the author of various publications, recognize as the holder of various positions, and so forth. As often the case in these matters, the speaker may use the term "I" or even "we" to refer to the capacity that is involved and the alignment to the audience that this particular self subtends, but this pronominal explicitness need not occur. Allied with this scholarly voice will sometimes be found a relevant historical-experiential one, the one that figures in a replay the speaker may provide of a strip of personal experience from his or her own past during which something of textual relevance occurred. (The lecture that a returning war correspondent or diplomat gives will be full of this sort of thing, as will lectures by elder academicians when they recount their personal dealings with historic personages of their field.) Observe, this textual self, presupposed by and projected through the transmission of either scholarship or historically relevant personal experience, can be displayed entirely through the printable aspects of words; it can appear in full form in a printed version of the lecture's text, an emanation from the text itself and not, say, from the way in which its oral delivery is managed on any occasion. Characteristically, it is this self that can still be projected even though the writer falls sick and a stand-in must deliver his address.

In truth, however, the interesting and analytically relevant point about the lecture as a performance is not the textual stance that is projected in the course of the lecture's delivery, but the additional footings that can be managed at the same time, footings whose whole point is the contrast they provide to what the text itself might otherwise generate. I speak of distance-altering alignments, some quite briefly taken, which appear as a running counterpoint to the text, and of elaborative comments and gestures which do not appear in the substance of the text but in the mechanics of transmitting it on a particular occasion and in a particular setting.

First, there are overlayed "keyings." The published text of a serious paper can contain passages that are not intended to be interpreted "straight," but rather understood as sarcasm, irony, "words from another's mouth," and the like. However, this sort of self-removal from the literal content of what one says seems much more common in spoken papers, for there vocal cues can be employed to ensure that the boundaries and the character of the quotatively intended strip are marked off from the normally intended stream. (Which is not to say that as of now these paralinguistic markers can be satisfactorily identified, let alone transcribed.) Thus, a competent lecturer will be able to read a remark with a twinkle in his voice, or stand off from an utterance by slightly raising his vocal eyebrows. Contrariwise, when he enters a particular passage he can collapse the distance he had been maintaining, and allow his voice to resonate with feeling, conviction, and even passion. In sensing that these vocally tinted lines could not be delivered this way in print, hearers sense they have preferential access to the mind of the author, that live listening provides the kind of contact that reading doesn't.

Second, consider text brackets. You will note that papers destined to be printed, not spoken, are likely to have some sort of introduction and closing. These bracketing phases will be presented in a slightly different voice from the one employed in the body of the text itself. But nothing elaborate by way of a shift in footing is likely—although such change *is* likely, I might add, in full-length books. In the case of *spoken* papers, however, text brackets are likely to involve some fancy footwork. The introduction, as is said, will attempt to put into perspective what is about to be discussed. The speaker lets us know what else he might have chosen to talk about but hasn't, and what reservations he places on what he is about to say, so that should we judge what follows as weak, limited, speculative, presumptuous, lugubrious, pedantic, or whatever, we can see that the speaker (he hopes) is not to be totally identified thereby; and in addition to the vaunted self implied in addressing a group at considerable length on a sober topic, he is to be seen as having an ordinary side—modest, unassuming, down-to-earth, ready to forego the pomp of presentation, appreciative that, after all, the textual self that is about to emerge is not the only one he wants to be known by, at least so far as the present company is concerned.

Closing comments have a similar flavor, this time bringing speaker back down from his horse, allowing him to fall back from his textual self into one that is intimately responsive to the current situation, concerned to show that the tack taken in the lecture is only one of the tacks he could have taken, and generally bringing him back to the audience as merely another member of it, a person just like ourselves. Comparatively speaking, a conclusion is part way between the curtain call through which a stage actor finally appears outside of the character he has been portraying, and the coda (to use Labov's term) by which a storyteller throws up a bridge between the situation he was in as protagonist in the narrative, and his current situation as someone who stands before his listeners. As part of this down-gearing, the speaker may, of course, shift into the intimacies and informalities of question and answer, through which some members of the audience are allowed to come into direct conversational contact with him, symbolizing that in effect he and all members of the audience are now on changed terms. Responding to questions, after all, requires fresh talk. In other words, question answering requires a production shift from aloud reading to fresh talk, with the speaker often marking the shift by means of bracket rituals, such as lighting a cigarette, changing from a standing to a sitting position, drinking a glass of water, and so forth. As suggested, introductions and closings, that is, bracket expressions, occur at the interface between spectacle and game, in this case, occasion and lecture proper. Question period apart, prefatory and closing comments are likely to be delivered in fresh talk or a more serious simulation of this than the body of the lecture itself provides. And these comments are likely to contain direct reference to what is true only of this current social occasion and its current audience. Observe, when several speakers share the same platform, mini versions of opening and closing brackets can occur *during* a presentation, sometimes with the reengagement of a presiding figure, all this marking the transfer of the speaking role from one person to another.

So there are text brackets. Third, there are text-parenthetical remarks. Again, if one starts from a *printed* text—one meant to be read, not heard—one will find that the author exercises the right to introduce parenthetical statements, qualifying, elaborating, digressing, apologizing, hedging, editorializing, and the like. These passing changes in voice, these momentary changes in footing, may be marked in print through bracketings of some kind—parenthetical signs, dashes, etc. Or the heavy-handed device of footnotes may be employed. (So fully are footnotes institutionalized for this change in voice that someone other than the writer, namely, the editor or translator, can use footnotes, too, to comment on the text in what is patently a voice totally different from the textual one.) Through all of these devices, the writer briefly changes footing relative to his text as a whole, coming to the reader in consequence from a slightly different angle. Observe, these elaborations ordinarily extend the "production base" for the reader, giving him more of a grounding in the writer's circumstances and opinions than the naked text might allow.

Turning from a printed text to a spoken one, aptly printable parenthetical remarks remain, but now much amplified by ones that are unlikely to appear in a printed version of the talk. (Admittedly advertisers sometimes employ the device of adding in the margins of a printed text remarks in print-script that are presumably to be taken as sprightly afterthoughts, and thus providing a keying of a communication not destined for print in the first place, a communication destined to be labored and cute.) In brief, during his talk, the speaker will almost inevitably interject remarks in passing to qualify, amplify, and editorialize on what the text itself carries, extending the parenthetical comments which would appear in a printed version. Although these remarks may be perfectly scholarly and contributed in a serious vein, they nonetheless introduce a somewhat changed alignment of speaker to hearer, a change in footing that in turn implies a facet of self different from the one theretofore projected. What results can only be partly captured through the nearest equivalents available in print, namely, parenthetical sentences and footnotes.

Text parenthetical remarks are of great interactional interest. On one hand, they are oriented to the text; on the other, they intimately fit the mood of the occasion and the special interest and identity of the particular audience. (Observe, unlike lectures, conversations appear to be scripted a phrase or clause at a time, allowing the speaker to build sensitivity to the immediately current circumstances through the very words selected to realize the main text itself.) Text-parenthetical remarks convey qualifying thoughts that the speaker appears to have arrived at just at the very moment. It is as if the speaker here functioned as a broker of his own statements, a mediator between text and audience, a resource capable of picking up on the nonverbally conveyed concerns of the listeners and responding to them in the light of the text and everything else known and experienced by the speaker.

More so even than bracketing comments, text-parenthetical ones had best be delivered in fresh talk, for by what other means could the speaker expect to respond to the trajectory of the *current* situation? Note that although only politicians and other desperadoes of the podium simulate fresh-talk replies to questions that they themselves have planted in the audience, a great number of speakers simulate fresh talk in conveying text-parenthetical remarks. The speaker will have reviewed some of these remarks beforehand and may even have inscribed them in his reading copy in note form as a reminder of the footing to be employed in delivering them. In all of this, observe, lectures are like stories or jokes: a teller can (and is encouraged to) throw himself into his telling as if this telling were occurring for the first and only time. The only constraint is that no one in the audience should have already heard his performance. And, in fact, every communication fosters a little of this "first and only" illusion.

There is an irony here. There are moments in a lecture when the speaker seems most alive to the ambience of the occasion and is particularly ready with wit and extemporaneous response to show how fully he has mobilized his spirit and mind for the moment at hand. Yet these inspired moments will often be ones to most suspect. For during them the speaker is quite likely to be delivering something he memorized some time ago, having happened upon an utterance that fits so well that he cannot resist reusing it in that particular slot whenever he gives the talk in question. Or take as a heavy-handed example the parenthetically interjected anecdote. It is told in a manner to imply that its telling was not planned, but that the story has now become so apropos that the speaker can't forebear recounting it even at the cost of a minor digression. At this moment of obvious relevance it is rarely appreciated that anecdotes are specialized for aptness. As with pat comebacks, standard excuses, and other universal joints of discourse, relevance is to be found not so much in the situation as in the intrinsic organization of the anecdote itself. The little narratives we allow ourselves to interject in a current talk we are likely to have interjected in other talks, too, let alone other presentations of the current one.

May I digress for a moment? Parenthetical elaboration is found in all communication, albeit with differing roles across differing forms. During conversation, a raconteur, lodged in the telling of a story, is likely to kibitz his own telling, breaking narrative frame throughout to interject initially overlooked detail, or provide background whose relevance is only now evident, or warn hearers that a climactic event is imminent. Between songs, pop singers in recital commonly switch into direct address, providing out-of-frame comments as a bridge between offerings, presenting themselves in their "own" name instead of characters in sung dramas. Indeed, they are sometimes so concerned about the figure that they cut while not singing that they develop a stand-up comic's routine in order to linger on the bridges. Giving readings of one's own poetry provides a different sort of case. As with singing, parenthetical transitions from one unit to the next are more or less required by virtue of the segmented character of the offering, but poets must allow themselves less room for what they project during these transitions. Poetry is itself an exploration of the elaborations and asides that the poet can manage in regard to some stated theme; compressed in the text itself there should be allusions to most of what a live commentator might parenthetically elect to say, and preferably this should be rendered to sound spontaneous. To cut a figure talking about a poem is to have failed to cut that figure in the poem.

To return. Bracketing and parenthetical remarks, along with keyings imposed on the ongoing text, seem to bear more than the text does on the situation *in* which the lecture is given, as opposed to the situation *about* which the lecture is given. These remarks can, incidentally, also draw on the biography of experience of the speaker-author in a way that depends upon *this* particular speaker being present, not just *a* particular speaker. And here, of course, is the reason why the printed version of a spoken text is unlikely to contain the introductory and textual asides that enlivened the spoken presentation; what is engagingly relevant for a physically present audience is not likely to be so snugly suitable for a readership. It is not so much that an immediately present audience and a readership are differently circumstanced —although they are—but that a speaker can directly perceive the circumstances of his recipients and a writer cannot. Topical and local matters that a speaker can cite and otherwise respond to are precisely what cannot be addressed in print. And, of course, it is just through such response that the social occasion can be made palpable.

Consider now some words speakers use to describe audiences, words which also happen to be much like those employed by any other type of platform performer. An audience sensed by the speaker to be "unresponsive," an audience that does not pick up on the talker's little gems and doesn't back-channel a chuckle or offer some other sign of appreciation, will tend to freeze him to his script. An audience that is "good" or "warm," that is, one that is audibly quick on the uptake, showing a ready, approving responsiveness, a willingness to take his innuendoes and sarcasms as he intended them to be taken, is likely to induce the speaker to extend each response-evoking phrase or phrasing: he will continue along for a moment extemporaneously where gestured feedback from the audience suggests he has touched home—a playing-by-ear that Albert Lord tells us singers of epic poetry also manage. (If an audience is to be warm, it may have to be "warmed up," a process that is consciously engineered in variety programs, but ordinarily given little thought in lecturing.) Again, note, fresh-talk elaborations that are themselves a response to audience response can little find a place in the printed version of the talk; for where could the writer find the response to trigger these remarks?

One can become aware of the situational work of overlayed keyings, text bracketing, and parenthetical utterances by examining the disphoric effects which result when circumstances require someone other than its author to read the author's talk. Such pinch-hitting can be studded with as many "I's" and other self-references as a normally delivered talk. It can even follow the text in employing a style that is for speaking, not reading. And yet what it can't do is provide the usual kind of keying, bracketing, and parenthetical elaboration. A nonauthorial speaker, that is, someone filling in, can preface his reading with an account of why he is doing it, avow at the beginning that the "I" of the text is obviously not himself (but that he will use it anyway), and even during the reading, break frame and parenthetically add a comment of his own, as does an editor of printed text in an editor's footnote. But to speak a passage with irony or passion would be confusing. Whose irony? Whose passion? To employ parenthetical expressions introduces the same dilemma; for fresh-talk asides can here only encode the thoughts of a second author. And the stand-in who stands off from a particular passage must appreciate that he will be seen as having too easy a shot. In any case, all of these changes in footing cut too deep; they project the self of the animator all right, but this time not the author of the text, thereby widening a split that is just the one that successful lecturing heals. Such an arrangement, then, strikes at the ritual elements of the presentation. (Understandably this tack is principally found in professional meetings where a session may provide reports on the work of three to five authors who are not eminent, so that the failure of one or two to appear in person does not much reduce the ritual density of the occasion.)

Three places for alternate footings have been mentioned: keyed passages, text brackets, and parenthetical remarks. Finally consider—at the cost of a lengthy digression—a fourth location, this one connected with the management of performance contingencies.

Every transmission of signals through a channel is necessarily subject to "noise," namely, transmissions that aren't part of the intended signal and reduce its clarity. In telephonic communication, this interference will involve sound; in TV, by easy extension of the term, sound and sight. (I suppose those who read braille can also suffer noise by touch.)

To those who watch TV it is abundantly clear that a disturbance to reception can come from radically different sources: from the studio's transmission; from malfunction in one's own set; from neighborhood electronic effects, such as spark-coil transmissions; and so on. There are, of course, quite practical reasons why source discrimination should be made; indeed, when a station is at fault it may employ a special visual or sound signal to so inform audiences. Now look at the telephone. In ordinary telephonic communication, the fit of the earpiece to the ear is such that a concern for noise at that interface in the system is unnecessary; at worst, one need only cover the other ear. With TV (and speaker phones) it becomes evident that considerable noise can enter the communication system between the point of signal output and the receiver, as when one tries to listen to a car radio over the noise of an uninsulated engine, or tries to tape radio programs "on air." It is also evident that speaker and hearer can fail to effectively communicate over the phone for physical reasons internal to either, as when the one has laryngitis or the other is hard of hearing. By extending the term "noise," all such constraints on transmission can also be included for consideration.

I elaborate these obvious points to warrant the following formulation: that when communication occurs, noise will also; that a communication system can be seen as a layered composite structure—electronic, physical, biological, and so forth; and that effective communication is vulnerable to noise sources from different layerings in the structure of the system that sustains it.

The next point to note is that the recipients in every communication system develop tolerance for a range of noise, in the sense that they can disattend such sound with little distraction. Recipients doing so, senders can afford to follow their lead. In addition, both recipients and senders deal with some noise by affecting unconcern, treating it as if it were not present even though they are distracted by it. Further, whether a particular source of noise is distracting or not, participants in the communication system can elect to engage in physical actions calculated to improve reception.

To complete the picture it need only be said that senders have another course of action open to them. Whether or not they make a physical effort to improve transmission, they can directly mention the disturbance and their remedial action (if any), employing parenthetical remarks to do so. These remarks necessarily break frame, for instead of transmitting the anticipated text, the sender transmits comments about the transmission. Senders have various motives for such actions. They may not wish the disruption to stand without introducing an account or apology for what has happened to communication, the hope presumably being that they then won't be judged by these failures. Or they may feel that to maintain the appearances of disattendance is itself too distracting for everyone concerned, and that open reference to the difficulty will release hearers from having to fake unconcern. Or they may feel compelled to forestall other interpretations of the disturbance.

Return now to the particular communication system under

consideration—the lecture. It is apparent that the noise associated with lecturing can involve sound or sight, and that its source may be variably located, say in the outside environment surrounding the auditorium, or the interior shell itself, or the audience, or the podium. This latter location is particularly important because noise coming from the podium area will be much more difficult to ignore than noise coming from places where the audience is not obliged to pinpoint its attention.

As a source of potential noise, the podium itself is a many-layered thing. One source we owe to the fact that lecturers come equipped with bodies, and bodies can easily introduce visual and audio effects unconnected with the speech stream, and these may be distracting. A speaker must breathe, fidget a little, scratch occasionally, and may feel cause to cough, brush back his hair, straighten her skirt, sniffle, take a drink of water, finger her pearls, clean his glasses, burp, shift from one foot to another, sway, manneristically button and unbutton a jacket, turn the pages and square them off, and so forth—not to mention tripping over the carpet or appearing not to be entirely zipped up. Observe that these bodily faults can equally plague full-fledged entertainers such as singers, mentalists, and comedians.

Another structural source of noise can be located even closer to the source of transmission: those minor peculiarities of human sound equipment that affect speech production across the board —for example, lisps, harelips, laryngitis, affected speech, "thick accent," a stiff neck, denture whistles, and so forth. One can think here of equipment faults, the human, not the electronic kind. These faults are to be compared to what an improperly tuned instrument brings to a recital, what a wall-eyed person brings to two-person conversation, what misalignment of type brings to the communication occurring on the printed page, what bad lighting brings to the showing of slides, and, of course, to what a malfunctioning microphone brings to any podium.

Human sound-equipment faults as a class have not been much studied systematically, but a closely related source of trouble has: encoding faults bearing differentially on elements of the speech flow itself. Speaking inevitably contains what can be linguistically defined as faults: pauses (filled and otherwise), restarts, redirections, repetitions, mispronunciations, unintended double meanings, word searches, lost lines, and so forth. What will obtrude as a fault varies markedly according to which of the speech forms is involved—fresh, memorized, or read.

During lectures, some equipment and encoding faults are inevitable; they imply that a living body is behind the communication and, correspondingly, a self in terms of which the speaker is present and active, although not relevantly so. A place is made for this self. It is okay to self-correct a word one has begun to mispronounce. It is okay to clear one's throat or even take a drink of water, providing that these side-involvements are performed in speech-segment junctures—except, uniquely, this one, this being the only juncture when so minor a deflection would not be that, but some overcute theatricality, of merit only as a frame-analytical illustration of how to go wrong in performances. In sum, such attention as these various maneuvers get either from speaker or hearer is meant to be dissociated from the main concern. The proper place of this self is a very limited one.

You will note that what is here defined as equipment and encoding noise is meant to be disattended and usually is. Occasionally, however, disturbances from these sources do occur, both visual and aural, which the audience cannot easily ignore, the less so for obligatorily trying to do so. More to the point, there will be noise that the speaker correctly or incorrectly *feels* the audience cannot easily disattend, or shouldn't be allowed to. (This latter occurs, for example, when the speaker misstates a fact that would get by were he not to correct matters.) In response, the speaker may be inclined to briefly introduce accounts, excuses, and apologies. These remedial remarks will have an obvious parenthetical character, something split off from the mainstream of official textual communication yet comprehended nonetheless. One has, then, not merely a disattended stream of events, but sometimes a dissociated stream of verbal communication, too. And this stream of communication, just like the equipment and encoding faults to which it is a response, implies a self, one indeed that has claims upon the audience even if this means minor overridings of other selves that are being projected at the time. After all, an animator not only has a right to cough, but under certain circumstances, to extend the interruption by excusing himself. Indeed, someone serving as a substitute reader (or a language translator) can make precisely the same sort of mistakes, and project the same self in the process of apologizing for them.

Plainly, then, speakers are necessarily in a structural position to betray their obligation to transmit their texts; they can choose instead to intrude comments on the contingencies of transmitting it. Observe that comments on such difficulties, as well as remedial remarks consequent on failing to avoid them, are likely to entail use of the pronouns "I" and "me," but one must be very careful to see that now these terms refer to an individual in his capacity as animator, not the individual in his capacity as author of a prepared text. The fact that the same pronouns are employed, and that indeed they ordinarily refer to the same person makes it very easy to neglect critical differences. When a speaker says, "Excuse me" or, "Let me try that once more" or, "There, I think that will stop the feedback," the author of these remarks is an individual in his capacity as animator, and not an individual in his text-authorial capacity. The person hasn't changed, but his footing certainly has, no less than would be the case were a substitute reader to make a mistake and apologize for it.

I have suggested that when a speaker senses that equipment or encoding troubles have occurred, he may intrude a comment about the difficulty and about any effort to physically correct matters he may undertake. The minor change in footing that ensues as the speaker ceases to transmit his text and instead transmits open reference to his plight as an animator will often be quite acceptable, characteristically attended in a dissociated way. But there are format-specific limits. It is a structurally significant fact of friendly conversations that they are set up to allow for a vast amount of this reflexive frame breaking, and, contrariwise, a crucial condition of prime-time broadcasting to allow for extremely little. Lecturing falls somewhere between. Interestingly, speakers can be optimistic here. Sensing that time is running short, a speaker may change voice and let the hearers in on the fact that the pages he is now turning over are ones he has now decided to summarize in fresh talk or even skip, projecting the rather touching plea that he be given credit for what he *could* have imparted. Finding a page out of order in the script, he may hunt for the right one while candidly describing that this is what he is doing. Reaching for the book he planned to quote from, he may assay a little quip, confiding that he hopes he brought the right one. I believe that once the show has seriously begun, these efforts to frankly project oneself exclusively in one's capacity as an animator are not likely to come off—at least not as frequently as speakers believe. Nonetheless the liberty is often taken.

V

We can now try to put the pieces together. As suggested, from one perspective a lecture is a means through which an author can impart a text to recipients and (from this point of view) is very much like what occurs when any other method of imparting is employed, such as conversational talk or the printed page. The relevant differences among the available methods would presumably have to do with cost, distribution, and the like, that is, constraints on access to the message. But if this imparting were the main point about lecturing, we might only have the university course kind, and even there the matter is in doubt; other means of transmission would probably displace it. Audiences in fact attend because a lecture is more than text transmission; indeed, as suggested, they may feel that listening to text transmission is the price they have to pay for listening to the transmitter. They attend—in part—because of something that is infused into the speaking on the occasion of the text's transmission, an infusion that ties the text into the occasion. Plainly, noise here is a very limited notion. For what is noise from the perspective of the text as such can be the music of the interaction—the very source of the auditors' satisfaction in the occasion, the very difference between reading a lecture at home and attending one. Let me review two aspects of this attendance.

First, there is the issue of access. In any printed work, the writer exposes himself in various ways. Through writing style, biographical detail, intellectual assumptions, mode of publication, and so forth, information about the writer becomes available to readers. Indeed, a book is likely to contain a brief biographical sketch of the author and even a picture on the dust jacket. What readers here learn about the author, they can cross-reference to what, if anything, they had already known about him. Thus, in making himself accessible, and in facilitating their familiarity with him, the writer encourages readers to form something like a one-way social relationship to him.

In the case of live lecturing, all these sources of accessibility (or their equivalent) are present, plus a large number of others. This is especially clear when a speaker is known to his audience through his writings or other activities. Whatever view they may have had of him, this view will be modified when they can see him in the flesh and watch and listen to him handle the transmission of his text over the course of its delivery. Furthermore, however candid and revealing a speaker's written text may be, he can easily render its spoken delivery much more so (or less not so); for vocal keyings and parenthetical admissions not in the text can be added throughout. And all of this opening up and exposing of the self will mean accessibility *only* to the members of the listening audience, a much more exclusive claim than ordinarily can be made by a readership.

To the degree that the speaker is a significant figure in some relevant world or other, to that degree this access has a ritual character, in the Durkheimian, not ethological, sense of affording supplicants preferential contact with an entity held to be of value. May I add that in thus gaining access to an authority, the audience also gains ritual access to the subject matter over which the speaker has command. (Substantive access is quite another matter.) And indeed, this sort of access is the basis of the talk-circuit business. Individuals who come to the attention of the media public because of their association with something in the news can make themselves available in person through a lecture tour. Here authority is not a prerequisite, or the thoughtful development of an academic topic, only association. The subject matter of these talks is exactly and as fully diverse as are the fleeting directions of public attention, the various speakers sharing only the agents and bureaus that arrange their appearances. It is thus that a very heterogeneous band of the famed and ill-famed serve to vivify what is or has recently been noteworthy, each celebrity touching audiences with what he or she has been touched by, each selling association.

So there is the issue of access. (I have mercifully omitted consideration of its final form, the little sociable gathering held by the sponsors for select members of the audience after the talk to "meet" the speaker.) Second, there is the matter of celebrative occasion. The difference between the text as such and the verbal delivery of the text not only supports a sense of preferential access to the speaker, but also gives weight to the uniqueness, the here and now, once only character of the occasion in which the delivery takes place. In thus committing himself to the particular occasion at hand, in thus mobilizing his resources to pay it mind, the speaker is conferring himself on those who are participants.

It might now be worth reviewing and detailing how a printed text that is available to any competent reader can be transformed into a talk that is responsive to the local situation in which it is delivered. Consider, then, some "contextualizing" devices.

First, there is the tacit assumption, an assumption carefully preserved, that what the audience hears was formulated just for them and for this current occasion. A crude token here is the topical reference through which the speaker shows that at least one of his sentences belongs entirely to the particular setting in which the current delivery is taking place. (This is a device of traveling performers which probably antedates even Bob Hope's camp visits.) Introductions, it turns out, are especially likely to be seeded with these topicality tokens.

But there are less obvious devices for producing the effect of responsiveness. When a lecture is given in fresh talk or a simulation of fresh talk, then responsiveness to the current scene seems apparent. And so another kind of tokenism becomes possible. As suggested, bracketing comments and parenthetical remarks delivered in fresh talk can be used to give a coloration of freshness to the whole script. (Where these remarks are not actually in fresh talk, fresh talk can easily be simulated out of memorized bits, simply because only short strips are necessary.)

Another simulation method, standard in aloud reading, is to scan a small chunk and then address the audience with one's eyes while reciting what has just been scanned.

Then there is the effect of "hypersmooth" delivery. As suggested, conversational talk is full of minor hitches—hesitations, repetitions, restarts—that are rarely oriented to as such by speaker or hearers; these little disruptions are simply passed by. On the other hand, it is just such minor hitches that are noticeable when they occur in aloud reading, crudely reminding us that it is aloud reading that is going on. Paradoxically, then, by managing to read aloud without these routine blemishes, we can give the impression that something more than merely aloud reading is occurring, something closer to fresh talk. (Hyperfluency, I might add, is crucial in the illusion of fresh talk that broadcasters achieve.)

Finally, consider the effect of "high style," even if issuing from a patently read address. Elegance of language—turns of phrase, metaphor, parallel structures, aphoristic formulations—can be taken as evidence not only of the speaker's intelligence (which presumably is worth gaining access to), but also of his giving his mind and ability over to the job he is now performing. Indeed, one could argue that "expressive" writing is precisely that which allows a consumer of the text to feel that its producer has lent himself fully to this particular occasion of communication.

Underlying all these devices for localizing or indexicalizing a text is the style or register of spoken discourse itself. What makes for "good" writing is systematically different from what makes for "good" speaking, and the degree to which the lecturer uses the normative spoken form marks the degree to which it will appear he has delivered himself to a speaking event. Some of the differences between written prose and spoken prose are these:

1. In general, writers can use editors' instructions, style sheets of journals, and college writing manuals as a guide for what will and won't be ambiguous, as though the reader, as well as the writer, had an obligation to apply these standards. Readers accept the responsibility of rereading a passage to catch its sense, and seem to be ready to tolerate the difficult more than the "grammatically incorrect." And, of course, readers can reread a passage, whereas hearers can't rehear an utterance—except from a tape. Also, spelling helps to disambiguate what in speech would be homonymous. The reader is further helped by punctuation marks having fixed sets of meanings; most of these marks, observe, have only very rough, ambiguous equivalents in sound. In consequence, a sentence whose head is far away from its feet is much easier to use effectively in print than in speech. In brief, for talk, clauses may have to be changed into sentences. But in compensation, contraction and deletion are favored, as are "left displacement" forms and deictic terms.

2. Print conventions for laying out a text provide for coherence in ways unavailable to oral delivery. Talk has no obvious paragraph markers or section headings. In printed texts, footnotes allow a sharp break in thematic development and can thus accommodate acknowledgments, scholarly elaboration, and parallelisms. (For example, it would be hard for me here, in the speaking that I am doing, to bring in the fact that spoken prose in turn differs very considerably from what occurs in natural conversation, and to cite the source, David Abercrombie's "Studies in Phonetics and Linguistics," but this would be easy and apt as a footnote in the printed form.)
3. Ordinarily, liberties that can be taken with an audience can't be taken with a readership. A speaker correctly senses that there are colloquialisms, irreverences, and the like he can use with his current audience that he would censor in a printed text. In talk, he is likely to feel that he can exaggerate, be dogmatic, say things that obviously aren't quite fully true, and omit documentation. He can employ figures of speech he might feel uncomfortable about in print. For he can rely on people he can see getting the spirit of his remarks, not merely the literal words that carry them. He can also use sarcasm, *sotto voce* asides, and other crude devices which cast him and his audience in some sort of collusion against absent figures, sometimes with the effect of "getting a laugh" (and he can further milk the audience when he gets one) —something that print cannot quite get from a reader. And a speaker can interrupt his own sentence almost anywhere, and with the help of an audible change in voice, interject something that is flagrantly irrelevant.

I need only add that in preparing a text for oral delivery, an author can make an effort to write in spoken prose; indeed he had better. Speakers do sometimes read a chapter from a book or a paper that is ready to be sent to the printer, but they don't keep audiences awake when doing so—at least in contemporary platform performances. Your effective speaker is someone who has written his reading text in the spoken register; he has tied himself in advance to his upcoming audience with a typewritter ribbon.

To write a text in spoken prose and to read it "expertly" is, then, to foster the feeling that something like fresh talk is occurring. But, of course, with illusion goes vulnerability. The prosodic shaping a fresh talker gives to a phrase, clause, or brief sentence is closely guided by his knowing the general drift, if not thematic development, of the argument to follow. So although he may botch a word, or lose one, he remains pointed in the right direction. The worst that can happen is that he can be stopped short momentarily for want of a usable word or because of having lost the point of his own current remark. In aloud reading, however, the speaker tends to commit himself to a particular syntactical interpretation (and therefore prosodic punctuation) of his current phrase by reference mainly to the immediately visible, upcoming line of his text. The sense that informs a fuller portion of his script—the sense that must inevitably emerge—does not much serve the speaker as a check upon what he is currently saying. A simple mistake in perceiving a word or a punctuation mark can therefore send the speaker off on a radically misconstrued aloud reading of his upcoming text. The eventual, and necessary, correction of that reading will expose the speaker as having all along faked the appearance of being in touch with the thoughts his utterances were conveying. As all of you know, this can be a little embarrassing.

VI

Now let me take another try at saying what it is that a speaker brings to the podium. Of course, there is his text. But whatever the intrinsic merit of the text, this would be available to readers of a printed version—as would the reputation of its author. What a lecturer brings to hearers in addition to all this is added access to himself and a commitment to the particular occasion at hand. He exposes himself to the audience. He addresses the occasion. In both ways he gives himself up to the situation. And this ritual work is done under cover of conveying his text. No one need feel that ritual has become an end in itself. As the manifest content of a dream allows a latent meaning to be tolerated, so the transmission of a text allows for the ritual of performance.

Through evident scholarship and fluent delivery the speaker -author demonstrates that such claims to authority as his office, reputation, and auspices imply are warranted. Thus a link is provided between institutional status, reputation, and the occasion at hand. Given warranted claims, parenthetical embroidery provides an example to the audience of how such authority can be worn lightly. The distance that status can exact is here relaxed; the respect that authority can demand is unobtrusively declined. Indeed, the speaker-author shows that although he has external claim to an elevated view of himself, and some currently demonstrated warrant for the claim, he chooses instead to be unimpressed by his own quality. He elects to present himself as just another member of the gathering that is present, someone no different from you or me. He thus provides not only vicarious access to himself but also a model of how to handle oneself in the matter of one's own claims to position (as well as how to cope with performance contingencies). In many ways, this modeling may be the most important thing a speaker does—aligning him, I might say, with TV personalities who provide the same sort of model, but for a wider public. (I only wish such authority existed in the field of face-to-face interaction, and that I had it to handle unassumingly. What I can treat modestly and offhandedly, alas, might not even merit that.)

So the person who delivers a talk can meld himself into the occasion by how, as a speaker, he extemporaneously (or apparently extemporaneously) embellishes his text, using his text as a basis for a situationally sensitive rendition, mingling the living and the read. And in consequence of the way he handles himself, he can render his subject matter something that his listeners feel they can handle. (Which is not to say that he need use anything more broad than donnish vocal qualifiers to gently remove himself from occasional passages.)

But a deeper understanding is to be drawn, an understanding that speaks to the ultimate claims that society makes upon a person who performs. What the audience will sense in an esteemed speaker as intelligence, wit, and charm, what the audience will impute to him as his own internally encompassed character—all this turns out to be generated through what he does to effectively put himself at the disposal of an occasion and hence its participants, opening himself up to it and to them, counting the rest of himself as something to be subordinated for the purpose. If, then, a speaker would encourage the imputation to himself of sterling attributes, he would be advised to display in the way he stands off from his topic and from its textual self that he has rendered both up to the audience. The animator invites the audience to take up this alignment to the text, too — an invitation carried in the intimate and comradely way in which he talks about his material. And lo and behold, this posture to his text is one that members of his audience find they can readily take up, for it gives credit to the world of the text, while showing that people like them are fully equal to the task of appreciation and are not themselves depreciated thereby. And surely this stance to the text is respectful enough, for the speaker himself has modeled it. He who delivers a talk, then, is obliged to be his own go-between, splitting off a self-as-animator who can speak with the voice of the audience although the audience itself is allowed only a rudimentary one. (Indeed, it turns out that the only thing some members of the audience may actually comprehend—let alone take an interest in—is this attitude that has been struck up on their behalf in regard to what is being delivered.) And, to repeat, it isn't merely that the speaker's side-comments are designed for the current context; the self that would utter such comments must be designed for the context, too.

It is here that we can begin to learn about a basic feature of all face-to-face interactions, namely, how the wider world of structures and positions is bled into these occasions. The predetermined text (and its implied authorial self) that the speaker brings to a podium is somewhat like other external matters that present themselves to a local situation: the age, sex, and socioeconomic status that a conversationalist brings to a sociable encounter; the academic and associational credentials that a professional brings to an interview with clients; the corporative organization that a deputy brings to the bargaining table. In all these cases, a translation problem exists. Externally grounded properties whose shape and form have nothing to do with face-to-face interaction must be identified and mapped with such ingredients as are available to and in local settings. The external must be melded to the internal, coupled in some way, if only to be systematically disattended. And just as diplomatic protocol is a transformation function for mapping official position into celebrative occasions, and just as everyday civility is a formula for giving recognition to age, sex, and office in passing social contacts, so, in a deeper way, an author's speaking personality maps his text and his status into a speaking engagement. Observe, no one can better provide a situationally usable construing of the individual than that individual himself. For if liberties must be taken with him, or with what he is identified with, he alone can cause no offense in taking them. If the shoe is to pinch, it is the wearer himself who had best ease it on.

So the individual who has prepared a lecture trumps up an audience-usable self to do the speaking. He performs this self-construing at the podium. Indeed, he can model this self-management for interaction in general. Of course, as any platform performer might remind you, although he is obliged to put out in this way for his audience, he doesn't have to put out for any particular member of it—as he might in personal communication—although, admittedly, at the little reception held in his honor after the talk he will find it more difficult to avoid these person-to-person involvement penalties. And in exchange for this comic song and dance, this stage-limited performance of approachability, this illusion of personal access—in exchange for this, he gets honor, attention, applause, and a fee. For which I thank you.

But that, ladies and gentlemen, is not the end of it. Some there are who would press a final argument.

A text allows a speaker a cover for the rituals of performance. Fair enough. But his shenanigans could be said to produce a reward for him and for the audience that is greater than the ones so far described. For the performance leads the audience and the speaker to treat lecturing, and what is lectured about, as serious, real matters, not less so even when the talk is covertly designed hopefully to be amusing.

The lecturer and the audience join in affirming a single proposition. They join in affirming that organized talking can reflect, express, delineate, portray—if not come to grips with—the real world, and that, finally, there is a real, structured, somewhat unitary world out there to comprehend. (After all, that's what distinguishes lectures from stints at the podium openly designed as entertainments.) And here, surely, we have the lecturer's real contract. Whatever his substantive domain, whatever his school of thought, and whatever his inclination to piety or impiety, he signs the same agreement and he serves the same cause: to protect us from the wind, to stand up and seriously project the assumption that through lecturing, a meaningful picture of some part of the world can be conveyed, and that the talker can have access to a picture worth conveying.

It is in this sense that every lecturer, merely by presuming to lecture before an audience, is a functionary of the cognitive establishment, actively supporting the same position: I repeat, that there is structure to the world, that this structure can be perceived and reported, and therefore, that speaking before an audience and listening to a speaker are reasonable things to be doing, and incidentally, of course, that the auspices of the occasion had warrant for making the whole thing possible. Even when the speaker is tacitly claiming that only *his* academic discipline, *his* methodology, or *his* access to the data can produce a valid picture, the tacit claim behind this tacit claim is that valid pictures are possible.

No doubt some public speakers have broken from the fold, but these, of course, cease to have the opportunity to lecture—although presumably other kinds of podium work might become available to them. Those who remain to speak must claim some kind of intellectual authority in speaking; and however valid or invalid their claim to a specialized authority, their speaking presupposes and supports the notion of intellectual authority in general: that through the statements of a lecturer we can be informed about the world. Give some thought to the possibility that this shared presupposition is only that, and that after a speech, the speaker and the audience rightfully return to the flickering, cross-purposed, messy irresolution of their unknowable circumstances.

REFERENCES

Bauman, Richard. 1975. "Verbal art as performance." *American Anthropologist* 77(2):290–311.

Frake, Charles O. 1977. "Plying frames can be dangerous: Some reflections on methodology in cognitive anthropology." *Quarterly Newsletter of the Institute for Comparative Human Development* 1(3):1–15.

Hymes, Dell. 1975. "Breakthrough into performance." In *Folklore: Communication and performance,* edited by Dan Ben-Amos and Kenneth Goldstein, pp. 9–74. The Hague: Mouton.

5

RADIO TALK

A STUDY OF THE WAYS OF OUR ERRORS

In this paper I want to consider a form of talk that is the central work of a trade—radio announcing—and to consider this talk (and this trade) mainly from the perspective of what audiences can glean by merely listening closely. This allows me to try to bring sociolinguistic concerns to ethnographic ones, all in the name of microsociology.

For the student of talk, the broadcast kind has much to recommend it. It is everywhere available, particularly easy to record, and, because publicly transmitted words are involved, no prior permission for scholarly use seems necessary.[1] Further,

1. The study draws on the following sources: eight of the LP records and three of the books produced by Kermit Schafer from his recording (Jubilee Records) of radio bloopers (to which I am much indebted and for which I offer much thanks); twenty hours of taped programs from two local stations in Philadelphia and one in the San Francisco Bay area; a brief period of observation and interviewing of a classical DJ at work; and informal note-taking from broadcasts over a three-year period. I am grateful to Lee Ann Draud for taping and editing, and to John Carey for reediting the LP recordings. Gillian Sankoff, Anthony Kroch, and Jason Ditton provided critical suggestions, but not enough.

The Schafer sources will be cited as follows: *PB,* for *Pardon My Blooper* (Greenwich, Conn.: Fawcett Crest Books, 1959); *SB,* for *Super Bloopers* (Greenwich, Conn.: Fawcett Gold Medal Books, 1963); *Pr.,* for *Prize Bloopers* (Greenwich, Conn.: Fawcett Gold Medal Books, 1965). I have used the transcriptions presented in the three published books, but where possible have checked them against the LP recordings of the originals. Brackets are employed to mark off my version of Schafer's editorial leads when for brevity I supply only a summary of his own. In a few cases brackets are also used to mark my hearing of

there is no question of the subjects modifying their behavior because they know or suspect they are under study; for after all, announcers in any case are normally very careful to put their best foot forward. Their routine conduct on the air is already wary and self-conscious.

The key contingency in radio announcing (I take it) is to produce the effect of a spontaneous, fluent flow of words—if not a forceful, pleasing personality—under conditions that lay speakers would be unable to manage. What these circumstances are and how they are responded to provide the focus of this study. To properly site the arguments, however, I want to begin very far back in some traditional doctrines of sociology (as enumerated below), work by slow degree through linguistic concerns, and only then consider the problem at hand.

I

1. Once students of social life begin to understand the number of constraints and ends governing each of an individual's acts on every occasion and moment of execution, it becomes natural to shift from considering social practices to considering social competencies. In this way, presumably, appropriate respect can be paid for all the things an individual is managing to do, with or without awareness, on purpose or in effect, when he performs (in the sense of executes) an ordinary act.

A competency, then, can be defined as the capacity to routinely accomplish a given complicated end. An implication is that this end could not have been achieved were the actor unable to accomplish a whole set of slightly different ones, all in the same domain of expertise.

Given this perspective, one can take the traditional line that any occasion of an individual's effort has a double consequence: *substantive,* in terms of the contribution a competent performance would make to some extraneous system of ongoing

"tone of voice" in the recordings when no specification is provided in Schafer's printed transcriptions. No station, times, and dates are provided for transcriptions from my own corpus, although these identifications are available, and announcers' names have been changed.

activity, especially when this activity directly involves the interests of other actors; and *expressive,* in terms of the consequent judgment that failure or success produces concerning the individual's competency and his moral character as a claimant to competency.

Failure at competent execution of an act can initiate the workings of social control, the prospect of which is itself, of course, a means of social control. The failing person ordinarily initiates remedial action of some kind, and if not, others may well remind him to do so.

As might be expected from this formulation, remedial action itself takes two directions. First, there are substantive, restitutive acts of an instrumental sort, sometimes codified in civil law, involving repair, replacement, or monetary compensation—all calculated to restore material matters as much as possible to the way they were before the failure. Here the sentiments of the inept actor are not at issue, merely his reparations. Second, there are ritualistic acts (in the anthropological, not ethological, sense), these being commentarylike and self-referring, designed by the doer to redefine the expressive implications of his own maladroit performance. Through gestural and verbal displays, sentimental relief is attempted; the offender typically tries to establish through disclaimers, excuses, apologies, and accounts that the failing performance is not characteristic, or if it was, that it is no longer, or if it is, that the offender is at least alive to his deficiencies and supports social standards in spirit, if not in deed. In brief, misperformance "expresses" a definition of the actor, one he presumably finds inimical, and the remedial ritual pleads a more favorable way of reading the event.

Ritualistic remedies, more so than substantive ones, have a variable temporal relation to what they comment on. Very crudely speaking, they may be retrospective, occurring immediately after what they are designed to modify the meaning of; or prospective and disclamatory, aimed at controlling the possible implications of something that has not yet occurred; or, finally, concurrent, appearing as an overlay on the ongoing dubious activity.

Observe also that remedial rituals tend to be dialogic in character. Once such a remedy is provided, the provider typically requires some response from recipients so that he can be sure his message has been correctly received and is deemed adequate, effectively redefining the breach. Substantive remedy can also have something of a dialogic flavor, for the individual who provides restitution may need to know that what he has offered is deemed sufficient.

The substantive and ritualistic, of course, can be closely connected. The sequestering of learning from scenes of seriously committed effort allows failure to occur without substantive *or* reputational loss—except, of course, as failure may reflect on rate and prospects of learning. Also, faced with an actor's defective performance, his others will need to know whether this is what can be anticipated from him—ofttimes a very practical concern—and his heartfelt accounting and apology can serve to allay this concern even though at the time the expression itself accomplishes nothing by way of physical restitution for the current loss. Of course, evident effort to restore matters substantively—whether effective or not—provides a ready vehicle for eloquently expressing good intentions.

2. Even at the outset, the application made here of the social control model to competencies must be questioned, at least in one particular. Competencies do indeed fall under the management of normative expectations, but in a special way. Favorable and unfavorable appraisals are certainly involved, but less so moral approval and disapproval. Or, if moral judgment is involved, it is so only in a blunted sense. It is not merely that competence deals with the manner of the performance of an act, rather than its end or purpose; it is that competence is a feature of acts (on the face of it) that is not seen as something intentionally realized. An incompetent act—from the perspective of its incompetency—is in the first instance not something done or do-able against someone with the intent of doing them harm. Of course, falsely claiming a competency whose exercise is vital to the interests of another can seem to qualify; but here in the final analysis the offense is not in the consequence of the incompetent act, but in the false claim to competency. So, too, there is the incompetency sometimes engineered (and more often thought to be) by an actor himself as a cover for insubordinate intent, but this ruse could

hardly serve if we thought an actor should be made responsible in every way for an incompetent endeavor. Thus, although failures to sustain standards of competency can lead to demands for restitution and certainly to disapproving appraisals, failures as such are not standard, full-fledged offenses. In appearance, at least, no wicked intent, no malice, is to be found. *Actus non facit reum nisi mens sit rea.*

3. There is a special family of competencies seen to be common to the human estate by virtue of involving ongoing requisites for living in society: the ability, for example, to walk, see, hear, dress appropriately, manipulate small physical objects and, in literate societies, write, read, and compute with numbers. As a class these abilities exhibit the following properties:

a. Except for the abilities associated with literacy, they are felt to be pancultural.
b. They are in continuous, if not unremittant, exercise throughout the day.
c. With reservations regarding sight and hearing, their acquisition is developmental in character, a product of early socialization.
d. After initial acquisition, they are exercised without apparent effort or focal attention.
e. Their possession is uncredited, lack alone is noteworthy—i.e., "negatively eventful."
f. They are subject to what are perceived as biologically based defects.
g. With reservations for sight, their execution is vulnerable to stress. "Loss of control," "nervousness," "getting rattled," are fundamental possibilities.
h. They are subject to what is seen as incidental, accidental failure in the sense that the foot, hand, and tongue can be said to slip.

As suggested of competencies in general, the anticipation that the individual will perform adequately in these only-human matters can be said to have two different sides. First is the substantive side: failure here can trip up the smooth operation of the business at hand—not merely the actor's, but also the doings of those with whom he is immediately collaborating. Delay, misinformation, confusion, breakage can result. (These substantive costs, as such costs go, tend to be minor on any one occasion of occurrence, but because the capacities involved are exercised repeatedly throughout the course of the day, the summation of cost can be very considerable.) Second, there is the expressive side. Competency in regard to common-human abilities is something we tacitly allot to all adults we meet with, an achievement and qualification they are taken to start with, credit for which they receive in advance. An individual's failure to sustain these "normal" standards is thus taken as evidence not only that he doesn't (or might not) measure up in these respects, but also that as a claimant he has tacitly presented himself in a false light. With reappraisal goes discrediting and an imputation of bad faith.

Speech, of course, is a common-human ability, and to be examined as a competency, as Hymes (1973) has suggested. Moreover, the division between substance and expression applies, albeit the application must be carefully made. When, for example, we unintentionally misinform by emitting *fourteen* instead of *fifteen,* substantive repair for the verbal slip will necessarily be verbal in character, but substantive nonetheless, and not less so because a ritualistic remedy may accompany the substantive one, it, too, involving words.

4. The treatment of speech as just another common-human competency itself raises some questions, one of which bears mentioning now. As suggested, when an actor muffs a nonlinguistic doing in the immediate presence of others, he is likely to shift into words (typically accompanied by gestures) to account, apologize, assure, and (often) avow that restitution or repair will be forthcoming. So words, then, have a special role in the remedial process. Moreover, a well-designed accommodation is implied between the ongoing activity in which the fault occurred (and in which the substantive remedy, if any, will take place), and the activity through which the ritual elements of the remedy are realized; for the latter can be performed without interfering with the nonlinguistic activity at hand. When, however, the fault itself is verbal in character, then a place will have to be found for the remedial action (both substantive and ritualistic) within the very stream of activity in which the fault has occurred. As will be seen, remedy itself can then add to what must be remedied.

II

1. I have argued that competency in speech production would seem to be the proper central concern in the study of announcing. Speech competency itself was placed in the class to which it appears to belong—our constantly exercised mundane abilities. The latter were described in terms of the traditional perspective of social control. This is, I believe, the frame of reference (sometimes well buried) that informs both lay and professional views of speech error; indeed, it is such a framework that gives to speech error its status as a subject matter.

Certainly in our society, competency in speaking, like most other common human competencies, is a matter for lay as well as professional concern. As in the case of other common human capacities, we have a folk notion that speech production will ordinarily be faultless, occurring without hitch. Of the difficulties that do occur, some will strike the hearer as characteristic of the speaker—as when the individual is thought to over- or underemploy the opportunity to take the floor, or is heard to exhibit a lisp or a hesitation in the same phonetic environment across all his words or phrases. Some imperfections will appear to be intermittent, as when a given word is always "misused" or "mispronounced" by a particular individual. And some faults will appear to be accidental or even uncharacteristic, as when a particular word on a particular occasion is tripped over.

We employ a set of fairly well-known folk terms to refer to problems in speech production: speech lapse, stutter, speech defect, speech impediment, gaffe, malapropism, spoonerism, slip of the tongue, and so forth. Students of language behavior have refined these identificatory practices somewhat with such terms as silent pause, filled pause, false start (sentence redirection), dangling sentence, prolongation, influency, sound intrusion, transposition, word change, word repetition, word-segment repetition (stuttering), and the like.

2. Linguistically inclined students have some interesting points to make about imperfections of speech production. For example:

a. "Speech lapses are most likely to occur where conditions of excitement, haste, external distraction, mental confusion, or fatigue are present" (Simonini 1956:253).

b. The production of faults can be progressive. The occurrence of one imperfection increases the chance of another, and that in turn increases the chance of consequent ones—as if, indeed, there were such a thing as getting rattled (ibid.).

c. The mangling that spoken words can suffer turns out to have some orderly linguistic properties characteristic of "normal" speech production (Fromkin 1971). Below the level of the word, one finds that misstating takes the form of the interchange, substitution, addition, or loss of phonemes or groups of phonemes, with retention of syllabic place and stress (Boomer and Laver 1968). Thus, varieties of "phonological disturbance," whether involving consonants or vowels and whether generating nonwords or standard words:

i.	anticipatory interference:	John dropped his cuff of coffee.
ii.	preservative interference:	Spanish-speaping hotel.
iii.	exchange or transposition:	flesh crean water, torn the curner, Hoobert Heever.
iv.	omissions:	He had a fat—flat.[2]

And at a higher level, where whole words are interchanged, the transposition is made in conformance with grammatical constraints ("We now bring you 'Mr. Keene, loser of traced persons' " [*PB:* 12]). Moreover, it has been observed that the vocalization *uh,* used to fill a pause, is partway given the status of a legitimate word, for it induces a preceding *thee* instead of a *the* following the rule for managing vowels in initial position (Jefferson 1974:183–85). And substitution itself is most likely to occur in connection with the stressed, informing word (Boomer and Laver 1968:8) late in what will here be

2. In their "Malapropisms and the Structure of the Mental Lexicon," Fay and Cutler (1977:506) suggest an additional possibility, a "blend" arising when two synonyms are merged, resulting in either a nonword or a real word, as when (to use their examples), gripping is merged with grasping to form grisping, or heritage is merged with legacy to form heresy.

referred to as the "sentential utterance"—or "utterance" for short.[3]

d. Then there is the issue of encoding. Apparently almost all pauses occur at word boundaries, suggesting that words are encoded from thought into speech in whole word clumps (Maclay and Osgood 1959). And because phonological disturbance can be traced forward as well as backward in an utterance, one can only conclude that speakers formulate their upcoming statements before they make them, premonitoring what is formulated. (There is general confirmation for this argument. As Laver [1970:69] suggests, intonational and syntactic choices made at the beginning of an utterance can depend on the choices that will be manifest later, and so must in some way have had prior access to them. A specific phonological example is that thee-the concordance with initial vowels and consonants can apparently be invoked by a word that the speaker does not speak instead of the word that appears as his alternative on occasions of self-censoring [Jefferson 1974:188–89].) Furthermore, because hesitations tend to occur near the beginning of sentential utterances, one can say that the decision work for what is to be said is done here, and once done, a speaking chunk is ready for presentation (Boomer 1965; Dittmann and Llewellyn 1967; but see Beattie 1979:75–76). So, too, when interference or interchange errors occur, the interfering and the interfered-with usually fall within an utterance, not across utterance boundaries (Boomer and Laver 1968:8). Also, hesitation is more likely when novel, thought-requiring formulations are to be employed than when pat, stereotyped phrases are used (Goldman-Eisler 1968).

3. By the term "sentential utterance," I mean to refer to what appears to be a basic unit of speech production, but one for which there are established competing names and overlapping definitions. The American version is the "phonemic clause" (Trager and Smith 1951), definable as a "phonologically marked macrosegment" containing "one and only one stress" and ending in a terminal juncture (Boomer 1965:150). The British version, upon which most current work in the area is being done, is the "tone group" (Halliday 1967): a pause-bounded stretch of speech carrying one major change of pitch, whole units of rhythm, an intended unit of new information, and usually, but not necessarily, coinciding with a syntactic clause (Laver 1970:68–69). The term "sentence fragment" (Morgan 1973) is another candidate.

In pursuing their work on speech error, linguistically oriented students have refined lay notions of imperfection and have evoked a tacit notion of perfect speech production, namely, speech with which a linguistically trained observer could not find fault even when in a position to repeatedly examine an audio tape of the strip of talk in question. At the same time students have come to recognize that lay participants in talk seem to be oblivious to a wide range and number of technically detectable faults which occur during any appreciable period of talk.[4] Thus Boomer and Laver (1968:2) suggest:

> It is important to recognize that in speech "normal" does not mean "perfect." The norm for spontaneous speech is demonstrably imperfect. Conversation is characterized by frequent pauses, hesitation sounds, false starts, misarticulations and corrections. . . . In everyday circumstances we simply do not hear many of our own tongue-slips nor those made by others. They can be discerned in running speech only by adopting a specialized "proofreader" mode of listening. In ordinary conversation it is as though we were bound by a shared, tacit, social agreement, both as listeners and as speakers, to keep the occurrence of tongue-slips out of conscious awareness, to look beyond them, as it were, to the regularized, idealized utterance.

And Patricia Clancy (1972:84):

> One of these factors [influences on the internal structure of sentences] is the speaker's tendency to repeat words or phrases within a sentence. This repetition is extremely difficult to hear without practice. My transcription failed to record almost every one of these repetitions, since at first I did not even hear them. My experience was confirmed by others, who, listening to the recording for the first time, also failed to detect the repetitions. This leads to the hypothesis that the hearer is probably unaware of such repetitions consciously, screening them out unconsciously so that he hears only the message itself.

Accordingly, it would seem reasonable to employ a variant of the term "technical" to qualify references to imperfections a linguistically attuned student would feel he was uncovering by closely

4. George F. Mahl (1956; cited in Kasl and Mahl 1965:425) recommends that, "In terms of absolute frequencies, one of the disturbances occurs, on the average, for every sixteen 'words' spoken; this is equivalent to one disturbance for every 4.6 seconds the individual spends talking."

examining a replayable tape of a strip of talk, this being partly an etic discrimination belonging to the world of linguists. Similarly, a variant of the term "perceived" might be used in referring to the judgment a lay producer or recipient of words makes in orienting to a particular passage as faulty or as unnoteworthy in this respect. (Presumably all perceived faults would be technical ones, too, but not the reverse.) An implication is that a lay listener could be brought along to see that what he heard as talk without imperfections "really" possessed a great number of them, and these he could be trained to detect. Note that insofar as ordinary talk is indeed studded with minor, unnoticed faults, speech competency is different from other common human competencies, for these latter do not seem to incorporate anything like a constancy of minor failings.

3. To these fairly well-established points a few qualifications might be added.

a. There is the tricky issue of how much of a strip of speech is thought to be contaminated by the fault or faults occurring within it—whether these be faults perceived as such by laypersons or merely by linguists. Somehow or other, particular flaws are used as bases for characterizing strips that include more than the actual fault itself, the extension certainly being to the word involved, often to the utterance, and even to the entire stream of words emitted during a turn at talk. But I can say nothing about the conventions involved.

b. Faults should be sorted according to whether they pertain to individual speech production (in the sense of something that occurs once an individual has taken the floor and before he has relinquished it, something that does not appear to directly involve the action of the other participants in the talk) or to turn processing, to be seen, in the first instance at least, as properties of conversations, not conversational utterances. Turn processing faults would include such matters as:

i. overlap—the initiation of next speaker's utterance slightly before the current speaker comes to the ending he was coming to

ii. interruption—the stridently voiced attempt at takeover by a candidate speaker while the current one is still lodged in his utterance

iii. interruption override
iv. interturn gap
v. double uptake
vi. double backoff
vii. double speaking

As with individual speech imperfections, turn processing faults that can be detected by students often are not oriented to as such by participants:

> The most remarkable and frequent occurrence in the change from one speaker to the next is the new speaker's tendency to begin talking before the previous speaker has finished. This causes broken-off unfinished sentences on the part of the previous speaker as well as situations in which the previous speaker completes his sentence while the new speaker is already beginning his. In cases of overlap, the words of both speakers can usually be heard, and the hearer unconsciously interprets the sentences sequentially. In my original transcript, these overlaps were not marked, since I automatically heard them as the first speaker finishing and then the next beginning with no overlap. Other people who listened to the tape also did not hear any overlapping at first. It took much practice to detect this surprisingly frequent occurrence, and numerous replays to hear at what points it actually began. Having detected this pattern, I found that in my own conversations it was impossible for me to listen for or try to refrain from making overlapping interruptions since the effort required made me too tense to continue a normal relaxed conversation. [Clancy 1972:83]

In the case of radio talk, I might add, it is largely individual, not conversational, faults that are at issue.

c. It appears that a working classification of faults can be made—if, indeed, one is not implied in the literature.[5] I divide them into two broad classes, "knows better" and "doesn't know better," according to whether or not the speaker's own hearing (on this or other like occasions) would be likely to inform him of his error, causing him to consider a remedy, which, in turn, he would be competent to provide.

Among "knows better" faults, the following:

5. An earlier version of my own, with team performance as a point of reference, can be found in Goffman (1959:208–12).

i. *Influencies,* namely, hitches in the smooth flow of syntactically connected words, as with restarts, filled pauses, stuttering.

ii. *Slips,* by which I mean words or their parts that have gotten mixed up, or mis-uttered, as in word transposition, phonological disturbance, and the like. I also include those breaches of the canons of "proper" grammar, pronunciation, and word usage that the speaker himself would ordinarily avoid automatically; so, too, one-shot failures of normally rapid access to the corpus of information one would ordinarily be expected to have. Thus, slips are to be seen as a consequence of confused production, accident, carelessness, and one-time muffings—not as ignorance of official standards or underlying incompetence.

Influencies and slips, then, pertain to speech production in a narrow, formal sense—the capacity to draw effectively on the words one knows, put them together in a syntactically acceptable way, and encode them smoothly into well-articulated sound. These are the faults that linguists have tended to focus on. The two classes of faults are obviously allied; I distinguish between them because slips can be, and often are, produced fluently.

There is one type of slip that deserves special attention: utterances which allow for a construing or framing—a reading—that the speaker apparently did not intend. The implication is that the speaker has failed to select sound punctuation, words, phrases, or clauses with an ear to excluding alternative readings. (Examples will be considered later.)

Among "doesn't know better" faults, I include the following:

iii. *Boners,* namely, evidence of some failing in the intellectual grasp and achievement required within official or otherwise cultivated circles, this evidence implied in words spoken or others' words not comprehended. Ignorance of the world (it is felt) may thus be demonstrated, or unfamiliarity with the lore of some specific, prestigeful domain. Language capacity in its own right may be involved—general vocabulary, pronunciation, the fine points of grammar, and the like.

Now it turns out that subgroups of individuals, at least in our complex society, may among themselves employ a speech practice (or fail to) which they ordinarily never attend to as a fault, yet in the face of a cultivated hearer's remarks, are vulnerable to criticism regarding it. The extreme case here is the "incorrect" use of a word (especially a "long" one carrying tacit claims to the user's learnedness)[6] or the formulation of a conversational reply that patently indicates a failure to understand prior speaker's use of a "difficult" word.[7] Nationwide schooling and media-inspired sophistication have given such faults a coercive force in wide populations, in the sense that almost anyone breaching the standards in question can be made to feel ashamed for having done so.[8] With respect to wide coerciveness, then, these faults are like influencies and slips; but unlike these latter, the speaker's own hearing cannot inform him of his error: listeners must tell him—and, in some cases, prove to him with a dictionary—that he is "wrong." Of course, there are boners so subtle that standard-bearing hearers may not be able to specify exactly what they sense to be wrong, and only a specialist—a linguist—may be able clearly to score the point, of which the great example is Labov's (1972) examination of phonological "hypercorrection."

iv. *Gaffes,* that is, unintended and unknowing breaches in "manners" or some norm of "good" conduct—breaches of the kind that are here realized in speech, but can also be perpetrated through other modes of activity. Thus: indiscretions, tactlessness, indelicacy, irreverence, immodesty, intrusiveness, etc.[9] A very

6. The term for it is "malapropism," taking this to refer to the introduction of a whole, meaningful word that is unrelated in meaning to the one apparently intended but sounds somewhat like it (Fay and Cutler, 1977:505), and gives the impression that the speaker is attempting to rise above his lexical station—to use Zwicky's phrase (1978–79:341), but not his argument that the last is not an essential attribute.

7. Although malapropistic speaking has been considered in the literature, malapropistic hearing has not. In the first case, the speaker disavails himself of the opportunity to employ a substitute he can use "properly," and in the second he fails to ask candidly for clarification.)

8. A basic general treatment of the shaming power of prestigeful speech usage is provided by Bourdieu (1975). A useful historical treatment of notions of "proper" English is available in Finegan (1980).

9. See Goffman (1967:36–37). The point has recently been remade well by Lakoff (1973:303):

> One thing I would like to note briefly in passing: the rules of politeness function for speech and actions alike. A polite action is such because it is in accord with the dictates of one or more of Rules 1, 2, 3 [don't impose, give options, be friendly] as in a polite utterance. So covering my mouth when I cough is polite because it prevents me from imposing my

special ignorance is inadvertently displayed, namely, ignorance of what one would have to know about the rights and biography of one's coparticipants in order to conduct oneself with moral sensibility in regard to them.

It is possible, then, to discriminate roughly four kinds of speech faults: influencies, slips, boners, and gaffes.[10] Although these mishaps cover a very wide range of standards and constraints, it appears that somewhat the same sort of embarrassment and chagrin can be felt by the speaker when he discovers he has committed any one of the four, and something of the same sort of spoken corrective action can be taken by him to remedy the matter, the classes of faults merging together as far as their immediate consequences are concerned.

d. In a very useful analysis of error correction, Schegloff et

---

own personal excreta on someone else (quite apart from germs); and standing aside as someone enters a door I am in front of is polite because it leaves him his options, that is, his freedom of movement. This suggests that the rules of language and the rules for other types of cooperative human transactions are all parts of the same system; it is futile to set linguistic behavior apart from other forms of human behavior.

10. Corresponding to the various kinds of speech faults, one finds functionally equivalent handwriting faults. But, of course, there are differences. Speakers can't misspell, writers can't mispronounce. Sentence grammar itself is more strict in the written than the spoken form. No "invisible mending" is possible in the spoken form, some is in the written form. (Taped TV and radio talk, however, does allow for invisible patching.) Multiply interpretable sentences in written texts come under the jurisdiction of formal grammar, and it is my impression that they are held to be an expression of writing incompetency, and thus more to be seen as boners than as slips. The same in the spoken form seem better able to pass as mere slips.

Typing, like handwriting, displays spelling mistakes. Typing mistakes in general seem easier studied than those associated with handwriting. Allowably sloppy penmanship obscures all kinds of errors, whereas typing provides a clear record of mistakes. Typing is learned relatively late in life by learners who can report on themselves with adult sophistication, Interestingly, typing exhibits kinds of faults that are more commonly found in speech than in handwritten texts, perhaps because of the speed of production. One finds lots of misspacing (the equivalent of speech influencies), and the sort of spelling error that corresponds precisely to phonological disturbance—slips which seem much less prevalent in handwriting. In contrast, the misforming of letters in handwriting does not seem to have a close analogue in speech, nor, of course, is this much of a problem ordinarily in typing. (The thorough work on typing errors is due from David Sudnow: the world awaits.)

al. (1977) argue for a distinction between correction as such and the "initiation of a reparative segment" (p. 364), that is, the notification that a correction is or might be called for. And further, that "other-correction" is very rare, "other-initiation" less so ("self-correction" and "self-initiation" being preferred), that remedial work overwhelmingly occurs in one of four possible positions: faulted turn, faulted turn's "transition space," third turn, and (in the case of other-initiation) second turn.[11] In radio talk, of course, "other" has very little direct role in the remedial process, although hearers are sometimes stirred enough to write or phone in a correction.

Taking the lead from Schegloff et al., then, it can be said that upon discovering he has committed what he takes to be a speech fault, a speaker's overt response to his own speech seems to be divisible into two parts: "reaction" (in the form of exhibited

11. Schegloff et al. give much weight to the thesis that there is a preference for self-initiation over other-initiation, and that other-correction is very rare. They recommend the interesting argument that other-initiation can pass as a request for clarification, a side-sequence that does not alter the projected sequence of turn-takings, whereas other-correction among other things can be confused with disagreement (p. 380). They also claim that when other-initiation does occur it is likely to occur after speaker has been given an opportunity during the completion of the turn in which the trouble occurred to initiate and complete his own correcting. Underlying these arguments (insofar as they are valid) would seem to be a general rule of politeness, namely, that the individual be given a chance to correct his own mistakes first, this presumably entailing less threat, less loss of face, than if he must be rescued entirely by other. To which should be added the fact that in many cases the recipient *can't* provide a correction or even a hint that one might be required; not knowing what the speaker had wanted to say (or "should" have said), he may not know that a fault has occurred, or, if he does, what the intended statement was.

Schegloff et al. use "repair" as a covering term for all corrective action. I have not followed their practice because "repair" strikes me as implying the fixing of something that has been broken, and although this nicely covers the substantive reconstructing of a word or phrase, it less happily fits a range of other kinds of work performed in the remedial process. (Of course, no lay term is likely to be satisfactory on all counts.) I have stronger reservations about "initiation" (as a label but not as a concept), for this term can too easily imply the beginning of an actual correction, when in fact—as Schegloff et al. are themselves at pains to point out—no correction at all may follow. What is involved, surely, is a giving of notice that some remedial work might be called for and/or is to be anticipated. "Notification" is a possible choice. Perhaps a better one is the term used by Jordan and Fuller (1975:12): "flag," as in "a trouble-flag."

embarrassment, chagrin, consternation, and the like, externalized as notification or flagging) and "remedy" (in the form of some corrective effort, both substantive and ritualistic).[12]

e. Given a social control perspective—however deeply buried—it seems rather arbitrary to study speech faults without studying the standard techniques for avoiding their occurrence and for remedying the trouble once it has occurred. (As a matter of fact, it seems just as arbitrary to examine production faults and their remedies without also considering the quite parallel subject of speech mishearings,[13] my excuse for which is that the study of radio talk only incidentally raises questions about actual mishearings.) When this more inclusive (and more natural) approach is taken, one can, following Schegloff et al., begin to appreciate that sequences of elements or segments will be involved, and that their delineation is strictly an empirical matter.

In this light consider some of the elementary remedial practices employed by a speaker in response to the issue of speech fault.

First is the simple avoidance of what he assumes might cause trouble. Unsure of the meaning of a word or of his own ability to "properly" pronounce it, he routinely seeks out and employs a safe alternative. Knowing his listener has a particular failing, he tactfully avoids mention of the subject. Speaking in front of a child, he may censor talk of sex and money.

Next the troubles the speaker fails to avert. Some of these neither he nor his listeners catch, and so long as one appreciates

12. I do not mean to imply that this two-part division—reaction and correction—is somehow a "natural" feature of behavior, a reflection of universal human nature. Whatever is biological in this pattern, certainly an important part of the matter consists of individuals acting so as to affirm in their own behavior their own folk theory of human nature.

13. The central work here is Garnes and Bond (1975), where it is shown that hearing errors fairly closely follow speaking ones, that, for example, hearers can: misplace consonantal point of articulation; substitute voicing for stops and fricatives, and l's for r's; delete, add, or shift word boundaries; fail to recover various phonological deletions, simplifications, and neutralizations, or recover these where in fact none had been lost. As typically with speech errors, in all of these hearing errors, only low-level syntactic processes are involved: "Inflectional morphemes are supplied or deleted, as required, and the sentence usually remains intact in terms of NP-VP configuration" (ibid., p. 223). Interestingly, as in production errors, metatheses are commonly found.

that speaker and hearers are subject to realizing or being made to realize what has happened, one need consider the matter no further.

Some problems the speaker will not appreciate but his hearers will. (Doing so, they may tactfully try to give no notice of having done so, or they may flag the fault, or, in some cases, introduce an actual correction.)

Or, knowing that he has gotten himself into trouble, the speaker may try to continue on as though nothing wrong has happened, whether thinking the listeners have not noticed anything wrong (allowing him to sneak by), or that they have noticed, and that drawing attention to the trouble can only make matters worse. The speaker *drives through.* Driving through can be accomplished effectively so that the hearers are unaware of the error (when they hadn't otherwise been); or, being aware, are left not knowing whether the speaker was; or, being aware and sensing that the speaker is, too, are grateful for not having to address the matter further.

It should be immediately apparent that a tricky (and characteristic) problem of interpretation and proof exists here. For in many (but not all) cases there may be no easy way to distinguish between a speaker driving through when this is a strategem, and his driving through "in effect" because he is in fact unaware of his mistake. But I don't think the dilemma is crucial, a question of idiographic, not social analysis. The point is that regardless of the difficulty (or even impossibility) of confidently discriminating the two possibilities in *particular* cases, the two nonetheless occur. As does the possibility that hearers will be left with ambiguity as to actual or feigned obliviousness, as I was in hearing an announcer unfalteringly say:

> She'll be performing selections from the Bach Well-tempered Caviar, Book Two, and also from Beethoven, Sonata in G minor.

Of course, whether a hearer feels sure or unsure of what he has heard, he may be mishearing—a possibility he may appreciate on the occasion.

Sometimes when the speaker essays to drive through, he does not seem to completely believe that the tack is workable or that it should be worked, and during its execution betrays himself with a pause and self-conscious overtone to his voice. (The hesitation or pause can constitute a *negative* notification, as it were: a blank is left where the speaker otherwise would have drawn attention to his error, the slot filled with what can be heard as silent indecision.) The implication is that the speaker is intensely concerned with his predicament and is not in complete control of himself. It is as if he cannot contain his concern for whether or not he will manage himself as he would like; potential disaster seems to be in his mind. Or a speaker may discover a fault in mid-production, pause for a startled moment, give the impression that he is thinking about how to get out of his difficulty, and then make a stab at driving through, as though the other alternative (to frankly draw attention to the embarrassing reading through an apology) had been considered but was found even less acceptable:

> Cooking Show: "So ladies, there is no safer way to insure perfect apple pie each and every time than to use canned sliced apples. . . . So the next time you decide to bake apple pie, go to the can . . . (PAUSE) . . . and you will really enjoy sliced piced apples!" [SB:102]

And throughout, there is the sense that should hearers turn on the speaker and remark on his error, he will have begun to show appropriate shame. The picture, in short, can be one of an individual who isn't really prepared to commit himself fully to appearing to sense that nothing is wrong, and it will always be a close question as to how fully intent the speaker is on concealing *that* impression.

Once the speaker tacitly accepts the strategy of addressing his fault openly, then a standard set of practices—"correction formats"—becomes available to him, these often appearing in combination in various sequences following a notification (if any), the notification itself often taking the form of a nonlexicalized vocal segregate, such as *Uh-oh!* or *Whoops!* Thus, for example, word searches (often associated with filled pauses or prolongation of syllables), restarts, redirections, and perfunctory ritual tags.

These various explicit remedies fall along a continuum with *flat* correction at one end and *strident* correction at the other. In the first extreme, the remedial act is performed apparently unselfconsciously and with no change in pace, as though the correction (and an apology when one is offered) is itself nothing to be ashamed of, nothing to require focal attention. In the other extreme, the speaker gives the impression of suddenly stopping in midstream because of being struck by what he has just heard himself say. Voice is raised and tempo increased. He then seems to redirect his attention to the single-minded task of establishing a corrected statement, as if this could (done quickly and forcefully enough) somehow grind the error into the ground, erase it, obliterate it, and substitute a correct version. If the correction comes in fast and hard enough, presumably the hearer will be saved from registering the mistake and will be able to proceed directly on with the correct version, having been, as it were, overtaken in the receiving process. (The parallel is dropping a breakable pot: move quickly enough and a catch can totally erase the upcoming loss.) The speaker in the act of making such a save often appears momentarily to lose his distance and reserve, flooding into his corrective act. And placed immediately before or after the corrective restatement may be a special tag: *I beg your pardon, I mean, that is,* etc.—the tag itself rendered rapidly so as to minimize the break in what would otherwise be the timing and tempo of the utterance in progress. The stress and rapidity of the correction appears to demonstrate that although the speaker may have been asleep at the switch, he is now more than sufficiently on his toes, fully mobilized to prove that such indiscipline is not characteristic of him, indeed almost as much a surprise to himself as a misguidance to others. I might add that whatever such a save does or doesn't do for what might otherwise have been expressed about the speaker, his text is at least substantively restored to what he had meant it to be:

> "So all you do when you are on your way home is, stop by at Korvette's and leave your odor. . . . ORDER!!!" [*Pr.:* 126]

> Educational Channel: "To me English is an enema . . . enigma!" [*Pr.:* 14]

> Newscaster: "And the Arkansas Senator was injured in a fall when he participated in a turkey toot . . . shoot!" [*Pr.:* 111][14]

14. Whole-word correction is ordinarily treated as a simple editing procedure, much the same as restarts involving self-interruption part-way through a word, followed by a new attempt at providing a whole acceptable word; and I have here done so. But another interpretation is possible. A speaker may wait

. . . performing in nude—in *numerous* musicals . . .

. . . sentenced to one year abortion—*probation* . . .

III

With a few exceptions, the picture sketched of the state of the art regarding speech production faults seems modest in the matter of supplying us with anything of general interest. Pearls are buried here, but linguists and psychologists chiefly undertake to look for strings. (The bearing of error on the issue of how thought is encoded into speech is perhaps the most significant line of inquiry.) A broader approach, it seems to me, can be developed by addressing the social control model that appears to underlie current analyses. For, as suggested, the limits of this model seem especially crucial in the study of speech faults. Consider some of the issues:

1. It appears that the difference between technical faults and perceived ones is not innocent; it is not the difference between trained ears and unconcerned ones; it is not the difference between "picking up" minor blemishes or letting them go by; it is not the difference between careful listening and lax participation. Nor is the difference between radio talk and informal talk the difference between high standards of speech perfection and low. To think simply in terms of differing social norms or sensitivity regarding error is to preserve error as an easily identifiable thing.

---

until he has completed a sentential utterance before providing a redoing of the problematic word, in which case it becomes clear that he might be introducing a new sentential utterance (or something expandable into one), one he had not planned on:

> Disc Jockey: "And now a record by Little Willie John . . . here's 'Sleep-Sleep-Sleep' . . . By the way, did you get any last night? . . . (PAUSE) . . . SLEEP, that is!" (*Pr.*:44)

In hearing these corrections, we automatically read back to their point of application, unconcerned that the surface structure of the new segment may not make grammatical or discursive sense. Of course, what does make sense of the corrective utterance is not the immediately prior discourse, but the *fault* in the prior utterance and the assumption that the speaker's sudden overriding concern would be to correct it. Obviously, it is the mistake, not the discourse, which here provides a meaningful context for the remedy.

In fact, the basic terms employed to designate some sort of imperfection, such as "fault" or "error" (and, of course, "imperfection" itself), cover behavior so heterogeneous as to undermine any unself-conscious analysis of incidental instances, in spite of commonalities of response. This heterogeneity itself must first be addressed before there can be hope that anything analytically coherent will emerge. Thus the need for distinctions such as those among influencies, slips, boners, and gaffes.

2. The two principal responses to a fault—reaction and remedy—can themselves function as faults, indeed are a major source of them. The display of a "reasonable" amount of startle, consternation, and shame over having committed a speech error, and the provision of an appropriate ritual remedy to demonstrate proper aliveness to how matters should have gone, can but add an extraneous note; and if the speaker at the time happens to be obliged to stick to a prescribed text (as in the case of announcing), then this remedial work itself must introduce more to apologize for. So here the very processes of social control must create problems of social control, the workings of social control working against itself. Plainly, in these matters the standard social control approach misses.[15] Thus, for example, a filled pause to cover a word search for an "apt" expression, or a restart to correct a "wrong" choice of word, syllable, or pronunciation must itself constitute a break in presentation, and thus a technical influency, if nothing else.

An underlying issue here is that faults reflect speech production problems, and speech production is apparently not a homogeneous matter. Accessing one's memory for what it is one wants to say seems a different process from encoding accessed thoughts into acceptable speech sounds; but the two are intimately related functionally, in consequence of which a failing in the first will

15. The musical stream presents a more obvious case than the speech stream. While practicing, a musician can stop and start at will and repeat a phrase a thousand times in order to get it right. But during an actual performance, especially in an ensemble, constraints abound. A second violinist in a quartet, missing the moment when he was to reenter the musical stream, cannot hammer home a rapid correction without adding wrong notes to missed ones; for by the time his belated entry occurs, its notes will not fit with the passage the other musicians have come to.

show up as a fault in the second. Given that the speaker will be obliged to have rapid, easy access to a particular corpus of information (in the sense that this corpus will be assumed to be constantly available as a resource for his utterances), his momentary inability to achieve such access will surface as an influency, and this particular source of influency, signalled as such, will be treated as a speech fault. Clearly, then, our subject matter is not speech error but speech *production* error. And admittedly, all that is to be included under "production" cannot readily be itemized.

Perceived influency is itself a special matter in regard to remedy. There is an important sense in which influency is something for which *no* substantive remedy is possible—the best the speaker can hope for is that his remedy itself will be fluently articulated. Some holes, after all, can't be filled, merely dug deeper. (All of this, it will be seen, is a central concern in radio talk.)

3. To say that there are various classes of faults is also to say that quite disparate standards constrain the behavior of speakers; and saying this, it is hardly a step to seeing that these standards need not always be compatible with one another. It should be understandable, then, that the speaker may have a speech task for which *no* unfaultable rendition is possible. The pronunciation of foreign words and names is an example. If a speaker attempts pronunciation native to the foreign word he is employing and has the linguistic capacity to succeed, he can give the impression of immodestly displaying his cultivation and in any case may require a slight break in ordinary rhythm. If he fully anglicizes the term, or translates it, he can give the impression of ignorance. So instead he may elect to compromise—how much, depending on his audience. But how can such a compromise be perfect? And how can it succeed if the audience is itself of mixed degrees of sophistication?[16]

4. Before an action can be treated by speaker or hearer as a fault, it must be regarded as the kind that the speaker would alter

16. Apparently the BBC currently has what is called the Pronunciation Unit (successor to the BBC's Advisory Committee on Spoken English), which establishes desirable compromises between foreign and Anglo-Saxon pronunciation for various foreign place and personal names. On the pronunciation dilemma in general in broadcasting, see Hyde (1959:90).

were he aware of the impression he was creating and was positioned to start anew—the chief distinction being between faults the speaker perceives as such upon committing them and ones he would never see as such unless attention were drawn to them by someone whose judgment is of concern to him. Many gaffes, however, involve actions that at other times are performed with serious intent to affront, or with knowing unconcern, such that the actor cannot be made to feel abashed when the offensive consequences of his deed are brought to his attention. A common example involves breaches of those standards of behavior that apply to the management of conversations as such, as with interruption, turn persistence, unwelcome encounter initiation, unwillingness to close out the talk, abuse by a nonparticipant of accessibility to the talk, and the like. Hearer response to such behavior may start with polite notification of what could be interpreted as an inadvertent lapse, but then be forced to move from there to frank negative sanctions. One is thus required to see that error and its correction can lead imperceptibly to another topic, the social control of full-fledged offense (Humphrey 1978). Similarly, it has been suggested that other notification and correction can become intermingled with the expression of disagreement and argument, so that once again what is available for interpretation as response to error can develop into something else (Pomerantz 1977). In truth, it appears that "error" correction, especially of the other-contributed kind, is part of a complex social control process providing participants with considerable opportunity to negotiate direction, to define and redefine what it is that has been going on.

5. Faults can fade into something else going in the other direction. The format doesn't change, it is just extended. Thus, a speaker who holds up the talk while he fishes for just the right word can be answering to a private ideal, a vaunted expectation regarding self, not necessarily a standard obligation. So, too, a speaker who audibly stops himself from making an erroneous statement in connection with a matter so specialized and recondite that he alone in the present company could possibly catch it; and so, too, the speaker who retracts a thought that had not quite been encoded in speech, alluding to the thought so we will know what it is we were saved from hearing.

6. Now consider the convenience that can be made of the remedial process. Take a speaker who must utter a foreign word in the tortuous circumstances already described. A standard recourse is to break frame and guy the pronunciation, either by affecting an uneducated hyper-Anglicization, or by an articulation flourish that mimics a fully authentic version—in either case providing a response that isn't merely remedial and can't quite be seen simply as corrective social control. Here the danger of making a mistake is not merely avoided, it is "worked," exploited, turned to advantage in the apparent cause of fun.

Or take a speaker who extracts—sometimes by brute force—an unintentional pun from his own discourse in order to break frame and make a little joke. He has found something he can get away with treating as a fault, something he can construe as allowing corrective attention, and simple error correction is no longer an apt description. Even more, the speaker who purposely puns, his sally intoned with prosodic markers to ensure we appreciate that the breach of single-mindedness is under his control: we follow with an answering groan that too openly expresses disgust to be serious, clearing the books, as it were, counterbalancing one deviation with another and thereby presumably returning everyone to the serious business at hand. Here the obligation to speak unambiguously, and the repertoire of standard flutterings and apologies for failing to do so, become something to draw on for play, not serious realization. One deals in all these cases with self-actionable utterances, with bits of what we have said or tried to say that can serve us under pressure as a subject of some sort of remedial-like action. Social control is operative here, but merely as a background model, determining not the ends of actions but the unserious guise in which actions are presented.

7. I have argued that some faults, such as phonemic reversals, are wholly a matter of speech production (although admittedly there are functionally equivalent troubles in nonlinguistic doings), and that other faults, such as tactlessness, are more a matter of *what* is said (fluently and without a slip), as opposed to *getting* it said; and yet that in both cases the fault can be followed by a reaction and correction which can end up as speech faults in their own right.

Now observe that events that lead to verbal fault-flagging reaction and then to verbal correction need not themselves have anything to do with the speech stream, even merely in its capacity as a medium. Being struck silent by what we have just *seen* interferes with smooth speech production in much the same way as being struck silent because of realizing what we have just *said.* Tripping over a companion's feet can cause us to interrupt our talk with a blurted apology, exactly as we might when we trip interruptively over another's turn to talk. And although the list of failings associated intrinsically with speech production might be tractable, the list of those nonlinguistic failings which can occur while we happen to be in talk with others is endless—failings that lead us to feel shame and to interrupt with an apologetic interjection, the interruption itself then constituting a speech fault in its own right. (Indeed, as suggested, it is a central feature of speech that hitches in the nonlinguistic activity of persons who are "together," but not in conversation at the time, produce a shift to speech as the medium for articulating a remedy.)

And, of course, competencies themselves may not be involved, merely unavoidable or unforeseen contingencies, as when, in seeing that the very person we are gossiping about has suddenly and unexpectedly come within earshot, we become acutely embarrassed and our words suffer disarray.

8. Technically perceivable faults not perceived by the speaker may or may not be perceived by his hearers as faults. When speaker and hearer together both fail to perceive a technical fault, it may be because their norms fully sanction the behavior, as in the case of "minor" restarts and certain pronunciations that are contrary to "educated" practice. But in other cases, especially when filled pauses and other sources of technical influency occur, another factor must be considered. Faults not perceived as such by natural talkers can nonetheless be perceived by them in some way (and in ways different from the perception of a technically unfaulted passage) and, thus perceived, can serve a multitude of functions—important ones—unconnected with the notion of speech error itself. It is defined as natural that all of an individual's concerns show up in his speech; and when some of these particular concerns involve him in, say, vacillation or emo-

tional anguish or (as already suggested) the need for sudden apology, then these states will have to be given expression. And one consequence of (if not resource for) this expression is disturbance in the speech stream. Consequently, this disturbance is not to be seen, necessarily, as something that the speaker might want in this context to avoid. After all, in some circumstances calm speech production might impress listeners as evidence that the speaker was, for example, cold or unfeeling or brazen or shameless. We apparently feel there are times when an individual "should" be upset, and speech disturbances are a prime means of "doing" such states. The general point, of course, is that obligations to one's conversation and to one's coparticipants (in their capacity as conversationalists) can hardly be the only claim that we or they recognize as binding on us—and rarely the deepest one. All of which provide good reason why speech is so full of faults, whereas the products of our other everyday competencies are so little faulted. Here, incidentally, radio announcing provides something of a limiting case, for it would appear that the job requires the performer to set aside all other claims upon himself except that of smoothly presenting the script. He is intended to be a perfect speech machine and that alone.

I have suggested that a particular kind of remedial work may itself produce a speech fault, that this work may be occasioned by breaches that are only incidentally manifest in speech, or even not at all. Also that unrepentant offensiveness and intransigently formulated opinions may be greeted initially with the responses that faults generate, the question of just what is to be seen as going on, being a matter of negotiation. Further, that otherwise passable speech production may be canvassed for opportunities it might provide to introduce a remedial format for "fun." So, too, that on occasion, speech fault may be an inevitable result of incompatible constraints on behavior, and that speech disturbances have functions that speaker would be disinclined to forego. Once all of this is accepted, one is in a position to suspect that speech error and speech error correction may not themselves provide us with a neatly circumscribed subject matter for study —a suspicion that would harden were one to proceed to include the entangling effects of mishearings.

Starting, then, with the notion of speech fault and its correction, forms of behavior must be examined that speak to a larger domain; they speak to elements of an individual's verbal performance that he chooses not to be identified with, something he can elect to find fault with, something he finds reasons to take action against. And this can be *almost* anything.[17] And one finds it necessary to take as an initial point of reference not error in any obvious sense but any bit of speech behavior to which the speaker or listener applies a remedy—substantive and/or ritualistic—and to take also any strip that its producer might be or can be made doubtful about, whether through his own hearing or the response of his listeners or by exemplars of socially approved speech whose judgment might carry some weight with him. In a

17. The notion of reserving judgment on the "objective" character of speech error, and attending instead only to how behavior addressed in this way functions in the speech stream was first pressed on me by Emanuel Schegloff. Thus, Schegloff et al. (1977:363) recommend: "In view of the point about repair being initiated with no apparent error, it appears that nothing is, in principle, excludable from the class 'repairable.' " This is a particular example of the basic procedure that the Sacks-Schegloff-Jefferson group of conversation analysts has promoted, a variant of the topic-not-resource theme in ethnomethodology, which principle has, I think, great heuristic value in microanalysis, being perhaps *the* principle of microanalysis. The way to obtain a corpus of errors is not to start with an intuition as to what a quintessential error is and then seek for some prime examples, but to force oneself to collect what gets treated as an error, whatever that might be. But that does not mean that the items in the collection will necessarily share *only* that fact, or that, for example, there are no other qualifications for inclusion in the set. Some errors, for example, will in this way be systematically omitted, such as those that the actual speaker and hearers fail to perceive as such, but which many other individuals in the speech community might; so also the more important errors that speaker and/or hearer perceive but decided to treat as though not happening, and do so effectively. In any case, the argument that anything in principle *can* be defined by speaker or hearer as warranting remedial action, does not, solely in itself, undermine the notion that there are "objective" speech faults, because it does not speak to another issue, namely, whether or not there are phrasings that for all practical purposes *must* be considered to be errors. Such phrasings will be considered later.

A similar set of issues occurs in regard to mishearing, and similar arguments can be made. But there is a further complication—to be considered later. Put crudely, a hearer's hearing of something a speaker did not intend may not only be due to a misspeaking *or* a mishearing, but also, on occasion, to some mixture of both—especially, I believe, in connection with misplaced word boundaries. Discovering an apparent fault, a hearer may try to attribute responsibility, doing so "correctly" or "incorrectly," and if the latter, thereby contributing another fault to the communication stream.

word: *faultables.*[18] As suggested, all technical faults are faultables, if only by virtue of the prestige of grammarians; but not all faultables are technical faults.

Even accepting, then, a focus on individual speech production instead of joint conversational enterprise, and even taking speech producers who are specifically employed to restrict themselves to speech production, speech error can, I claim, carry us far afield in a sociological direction: the microanalysis of how a speaker uses faultables during the course of his speaking, this being an entirely open question that can begin to be closed only by looking to his actual behavior. And for this endeavor the traditional framework of role and social control will be somewhat restrictive.[19] A more microscopic approach is required.

18. My version of Schegloff et al. (1977:363): "We will refer to that which the repair addresses as the 'repairable' or the 'trouble source.' "

19. A purportedly far-reaching critique of the social control model has been introduced as part of the doctrine of ethnomethodology, arguing that the "normative paradigm" should be replaced by the "evaluative" one. The argument is that the social control process is not something that somehow occurs in nature, but rather that participants intentionally perform their roles to produce the effect of there being normative constraints and reactions to breaching them. This requires, among other things, a tacit agreement to perceive the event at hand in terms of that perspective in which a deviant act (or a corrective one) will be isolated as the defining one in the circumstances (Wilson 1970). In brief, participants tacitly collaborate to uphold a *model,* not a norm.

The argument is not persuasive. There is always an issue as to what perspective, what frame, individuals will employ in perceiving an event, but this choosing does not thereby become all that is relevant to study. Similarly, if wide agreement exists about what aspect of events to abstract out for concern (as in games), a consideration of how this consensus is arrived at is not all that need concern the student. So, too, although the social-control perspective can certainly become a conscious framework for some set of individuals—such as those processed by social workers, therapists, enlightened jailers, and sociology textbooks—thereby entering action differently from social control in general, there will remain the fact that these indoctrinated people themselves will be guided by norms and constraints, merely ones that the critic of the social control model has not had the wit, patience, or interest to uncover. And should the "evaluative model" ever become popular as a conscious basis of orientation and brought through that route into everyday action, then its use will itself be subject to the normative framework, an expression of people doing what they feel is "proper," "meaningful," "persuasive," and so forth.

IV

1. The term "speaker" is central to any discussion of word production, and yet the term is used in several senses, often simultaneously and (when so) in varying combinations, with no consistency from use to use. One meaning, perhaps the dominant, is that of *animator,* that is, the sounding box from which utterances come. A second is *author,* the agent who puts together, composes, or scripts the lines that are uttered. A third is that of *principal,* the party to whose position, stand, and belief the words attest. In this latter case, a particular individual is not so much involved as an individual active in some recognized social role or capacity or identity, an identity which may lead him to speak inclusively for an entity of which he is only a part. Now although it is natural to think of these three functions—animator, author, principal—locked together, as when an individual speaks lines that he has composed and which attest to his own position, in fact such congruence will often not be found. In radio talk, for example, although the announcer typically allows the (typically unwarranted) impression to be formed that he himself is the author of his script, usually his words and tone imply that he is speaking not merely in his own name, but for wider principals, such as the station, the sponsor, right-thinking people, Americans-at-large, and so forth, he himself being merely a small, composite part of a larger whole. (A qualification is that on the hours and half-hours, the announcer is likely to announce his own name, identifying himself when he identifies the station, this involving a slight change in stance as he momentarily switches from a voice that speaks for something larger than himself to a voice that speaks—and properly so—in his own name or that of the station, narrowly defined.)

Animator, author, principal together comprise what can be called the production format of an utterance. This basic element in the structure of an utterance is to be distinguished from another: the participation framework, namely, the circle, ratified and unratified, in which the utterance is variously received, and in which individuals have various participation statuses, one of which is that of animator. Just as the character of the production format of a discourse can shift markedly from moment to moment, so, too, can its participation framework, and in fact, the two elements often shift simultaneously. The alignment of an individual to a particular utterance, whether involving a production format, as in the case of the speaker, or solely a participation status, as in the case of a hearer, can be referred to as his *footing* (Goffman 1974:542–44; 1979 and this volume, chap. 3).

The question of footing is systematically complicated by the possibility of embedding. For example, a speaker can quote himself or another directly or indirectly, thereby setting into an utterance with one production format another utterance with its own production format, albeit now merely an embedded one.

2. Singing, chanting, and speaking appear to be the main forms of vocal production. In literate society this production seems to have three bases:

a. memorization
b. reading off from a written text or score that has not itself been memorized
c. the extemporaneous, ongoing assembly and encoding of text under the exigency of immediate response to one's current situation and audience, in a word, "fresh production."

Our concern will not be with singing or chanting, but with speaking, the three production bases of which can be referred to as "recitation," "aloud reading," and "fresh talk."[20] Note, stage acting accordingly involves the open simulation of fresh talk (and very occasionally, of aloud reading), on the basis of a memorized script.

Some qualification of these discriminations is necessary. Insofar as a speaker formulates discourse units such as a sentential utterance before encoding them into sound, then all fresh talk is, in that degree, reciting a prepared text, albeit a very short one prepared a moment ago by the speaker himself. (Observe, just as

20. In *Discourse across Time and Space* (Keenan and Bennett 1977), beginning with Keenan's "Why Look at Unplanned and Planned Discourse" (pp. 1–41), the term "unplanned" is used to refer to spontaneous conversational speech, the contrast being to the various forms of discourse that are thought through before transmission and realized in grammatically formal sentence (and sentence-sequence) structures. This view would seem to slight the "spoken prose" of those practiced public speakers who can provide extemporaneous remarks (and certainly rejoinders) in fluent, well-formed, coherently linked sentences. In any case, it might be argued that the critical issue is scripting, not planning.

we can forget a next line in a memorized text—with the possibility of total derailment—so we can get lodged in uttering a fresh-talk sentence and forget the preformulated strip that was to come next, losing, as is said, our train of thought [Yngve 1973, esp. p. 689].) In the main, however, in fresh talk, what we can do is become "tongue-tied," which is to be at a loss for *any* words, not —as in preformulated texts—*the* words. In aloud reading, of course, we can hardly forget what to say; the worst that can occur (in this connection) is to lose our place.

More important, in some lecturing, aloud reading is closely interwoven with fresh-talked, exegetical asides, which incidentally provide the speaker with a means of heightened responsiveness to the particularities of the occasion of delivery. And of course public addresses can be made from notes, these providing the speaker with a track to stay on and principal stations to pass through, but with little by way of a literal script to repeat. Here the text is in fresh talk and only the thematic development is preformulated. These two styles—elaborated aloud reading and talk from an outline—can be mixed in every proportion.

Finally, many folk traditions provide significant and typical ways in which memorized materials are intermingled with fresh production during audience performances. Prose narratives, songs, and oral poetry can be improvisationally composed during presentation from a blend of formulaic segments, set themes, and traditional plots, the whole artfully tailored to suit the temper of the audience and the specificities of the locale.[21] In which case there is no original or standard text, only a family of equally authentic renditions.

Apparently, then, fresh talk, aloud reading, and recitation can be produced in various blends, with rapid and continuous switching from one form to another, and even mingled with song and recitative. However, it is just in such cases that one most needs to identify and separate out the mingled bases of speech production, for it is likely that the hearers themselves there will obtain an uncertain view of the ingredients.

Just as one can say that there are three bases for speech

21. The classic formulation is by Lord (1960) out of Parry (1971). A critical appraisal of it is available in Finnegan (1977, esp. chap. 3, pp. 52–87).

production, so one might want to argue that there are three types of speech production competency. Plainly, an individual who has one of these competencies may not have another. (An example is the ability of some fresh-talk stutterers to recite or stage-act impeccably.) However, it appears that each of the bases of production is not itself homogeneous with respect to the possession of competency. For example, a speaker's ability with the fresh talk of conversation tells us little about his ability at extemporaneous speech-making. Presumably differences in competency reflect differences in the process of acquiring competency—a comparative subject about which not much seems to be known.

Further, normally competent speech production—that is, speech which strikes the speaker and listeners as something not notably imperfect—will be subject to markedly different standards depending on whether memorization, aloud reading, or fresh talk is involved. The point can be nicely seen when a platform speaker engages in a "production shift," switching, say, from aloud reading to a variety of fresh talk, such as parenthetical elaboration, questions and answers, and so forth. On these occasions it is common for hearers to sense no increase or decrease in competency, and yet examination of a recording is likely to show that a sudden increase in technical faults occurred with the shift. Obviously, corresponding to an increase in fumbling was a decline in defining it as such, but this says very little about what is really involved.

On the face of it, each of the three bases of speech production involves its own characteristic production format. Fresh talk *commonly* presents congruence among animator, author, and principal. Aloud reading can, too, except that in such cases, the person who is author can at best be the "same," in a limited way, as the person who is animator. (After all, the person who was the author necessarily is some past realization of the person who is now the animator.) Memorization seems likely to present an animator who is not the author or principal, although poets (and singers) can present their own work, and moreover be taken to stand behind what gets said. In sum, each of the three bases of speech production is likely to involve a different production format, each such format supporting different grounds for the speaker's relation to his hearers.

A final point. In selecting a phrasing during fresh talk, or managing a scripted phrasing in aloud reading, we seem to have some leeway, some safety margin, with respect to timing, stress, intonation, and so forth. We can therefore find ourselves momentarily distracted or uncertain of what to say or unsure of pronunciation or otherwise needful of special effort at a particular juncture, and yet manage this emergency without the consequent speech flow becoming degraded to technically faulted (when it was technically unfaulted before) or perceivedly faulted (when it was perceivedly unfaulted before). Indeed, this sort of getting things in order in time must be a constant feature of talk not noted for speech faults. One might think here of "production tolerance." Thus, becoming a proficient platform speaker does not so much involve knowing what we are going to say as being able to manage our uncertainties discreetly, that is, within our production tolerance.

3. The various production formats provide a speaker with different relationships to the words he utters, providing, thus, a set of interpretive frameworks in terms of which his words can be understood. (Recitation, aloud reading, and fresh talk are but broad divisions of this potential.) These different possibilities in conjunction with the participation statuses he could enjoy comprise what might be called his *frame space.* In brief, when the individual speaks, he avails himself of certain options and foregoes others, operating within a frame space, but with any moment's footing uses only some of this space. He speaks words formulated by someone in the name of someone, directing these remarks to some set of others in some one of their capacities, and for the moment abjures speaking in all the other ways his resources would allow. And, of course, frame space will be normatively allocated. To speak acceptably is to stay within the frame space allowed one; to speak unacceptably is to take up an alignment that falls outside this space. (A similar statement can be made about the hearer and his frame space.)

As a crude example, take perfunctory accounts and apologies for verbal difficulties, whether presented as disclaimers before an anticipated fault, or, as seems more usual, after. Thus the perfunctory rituals: *Excuse me, I beg your pardon, Let me try that again,* etc.

Such interjections can certainly function as bracket markers, telling listeners where a strip that will be defined as needing attention begins or ends; but apart from this, nothing immediately substantive would seem to be gained. Presumably an aim here is to show, for example, that any deviation from proper standards offends the perpetrator's own sense of propriety and is not to be heard as characteristic of him or as an intended offense to hearers.

Clearly these remedies can be introduced into the stream of talk and executed with utter fluency, aplomb, and unselfconsciousness (which is not to say that in some circumstances they can't have an anxious, blurted character); and in a great deal of verbal interaction, such interjections are hardly noticed at all, by implication being well within the rights of the speaker. Nonetheless, these little rituals require a change in footing. Instead of maintaining the prior blend of animator, principal, and author, the speaker suddenly presents his plight as an animator into his discourse, speaking for himself in his capacity as animator, this capacity typically becoming a protagonist, a character or "figure" in his statement, not merely the engine of its production. At the same time, he becomes (if he wasn't already) the sole principal, and certainly the actual author, of his words—often a sharp contrast to what went before, especially if aloud reading or reciting had been in progress.

As suggested, in much informal talk such changes in footing are perfectly in order, hardly to be oriented to as an event. Nonetheless, there are lots of occasions for animating words where such maneuvers can call attention to themselves, a violation of frame space. When (as, for example, in radio announcing) the individual is speaking in the name of an entity more inclusive than himself, his sudden thrusting of himself (and how he is doing in his animation) as a topic upon our attention, pressing himself thus upon us, can intrude him upon our senses in a way we may not have bargained for. Such remedial work, then, can presume, can strike the hearer as improper. Similarly, even the most perfunctory of hedges—such as "in my opinion" or "I think"—may be perceived as a little self-centering, a little aggrandizing, a little self-intruding, even though apparently the speaker actually hopes in this way to minimize the demands he makes by his expression of opinion.[22] Here, then, a glimpse of another way in which a remedy can itself be an offense, a glimpse of inherent difficulties with the social control model.

V

With the foregoing sketch of sociological and linguistic background and some hints of limitations associated with the social control model, turn finally to a special form of talk: TV and (especially) radio announcing—here using "announcing" broadly to cover all routine talk into a microphone.

1. Announcing comes in different modes, each placing the speaker on a distinctive footing.

First, "action override." At social spectacles of various sorts, an on-the-spot announcer is in a position to observe unfoldings that members of the radio audience can't (or can't as knowledgeably), and can undertake to give a running account of "what" is happening immediately following its happening.[23] Fresh talk is a requisite, if only because in the case of blow-by-blow accounts, presumably no one knows how the blows are going to fall before

22. It is as though speaker believes that by bracketing an assertion with a self-reference and an embedding verb, both the encounter and his reputation can be insulated from any trouble the assertion otherwise might create. Instead of taking up the position implied in the embedded portion of his utterance, the speaker (he can feel) takes the more innocuous position: that it is acceptable to report views including, incidentally, his own. And although hearers might sharply disagree with his view, they are likely to be much less in disagreement with his right to express views circumspectly. Paradoxically enough, then, a self-referencing hedge that thrusts a first-person pronoun before listeners may not strike them as self-centering (at least the speaker feels), for presumably this linguistic device allows them to stand back from the opinion expressed (as the speaker is proving he can), and to relate primarily to that sense of the speaker that is the easiest to accept, being fully shared, the self as a conversationalist offering up an opinion.

23. An interesting contrast and limiting case is the bomb-defuser's performance. He broadcasts a running account, too, but he himself is physically executing the actions that are being covered. His use of "I," then (as in: "I am unscrewing the base and I see that . . ."), has nothing to do with himself as animator, except, say, when first checking out microphonic transmission. So, too, the surgeon who explains to students in the surgical theater what he is doing as he does it.

they do—although admittedly in the case of public rituals, the sequence of events is planned beforehand in detail and ordinarily proceeds accordingly. In consequence, the announcer is in something like a "slave" relation to the events he is reporting. He is free to pick his own phrases, as in other kinds of fresh talk, but not free to stray appreciably from what participants and those familiar with the reported world would see as "what is going on."[24] If the activity in question suddenly breaks down because of fights, assassination, the collapse of physical structures, a cloudburst, or whatever, then this too must be reported as if the announcer were chained to the events before him and obliged to

24. Recently it has been argued that a decision as to what is going on cannot be made apart from understandings of what to attend and what to disattend and how to construe what is attended. Notwithstanding, most public spectacles seem to be put together with a prior agreement about what is to come to be defined as "really" going on, and so perhaps agreement is only to be expected. In any case, remote audience and actual participants are locked together in a common relation to a set of unfolding events—to outcomes—which initiates of the activity would tend to agree were the ones that were occurring. It turns out, then, that different announcers do not select greatly different aspects of what is occurring to describe, nor do they describe them very differently. Whatever arbitrariness is thus exhibited in what is defined as the "thing" going on at the time, whatever selectivity, participants in the occasion tend to concur as to what this should be. They can similarly agree that, for example, a particular announcer has intentionally failed to report something that "actually" occurred, a claim that can be valid even though an infinite number of things could occur which no announcer would bother to report on. And to say that the event as we see it is actually going on is to speak with real meaning, for it is relative to this reality that we can judge descriptions of a less "literal" kind and see them to be fictions—as when advertisers sponsor the delayed relay of a boxing match, mounting a show in which the ultimate outcome is not disclosed until the end, and each round is described sequentially in equivalent amounts of real time, so that listeners will have to sit through the same number of advertisements they would have had to, were the actual match broadcast. Whatever the sense in which a live broadcast is not the real thing, these mock-ups are unreal in an important additional sense.

Admittedly games do have a special status in regard to consensus as to what it is that is going on. The reports provided in hourly news broadcasts offer a considerable contrast; for here from nation to nation, interest group to interest group, and region to region, there is very appreciably difference of opinion as to the kinds of things that are worth reporting on and what should be said about them. And within a nation (or region), most participants are passive, in that they themselves would not necessarily hit upon such topics to report were they determining the matter. Games are designed to bring observers and participants into something of the same world; news broadcasts have to help create these circumstances in the name of reporting "significant" events.

provide live coverage of whatever has become of what he started out describing. In the face of quite unexpected tragedies and shocking surprises, the announcer is obliged to maintain enough composure to continue some sort of reporting, and if (as we might feel reasonable and proper) he does flood into "personal" register, breaching the standard distance between himself and us, we are likely to expect him to reestablish evidence of "full control" rather quickly.

In all these cases, the action in question—presumably something that goes on whether or not a remote audience can follow it—is the primary concern of the audience; the talk of the announcer is only a means to that end, required because the audience would not otherwise be able to follow the action effectively. (In television commentary, only explication and elaboration may be required; in radio announcing, verbal portraiture will be needed.) In consequence, the announcer sustains with his audience something that is equivalent to a "subordinate" encounter —subordinate, that is, to the action being reported—an illusion fostered by the announcer's tone of voice. For example, in reported golf matches, the hush that allows a putter to give undivided attention to his shot is rendered—albeit often with no objective reason—by the announcer's use of a hushed voice. Thus, announcing as action override.

Next, consider the "three-way" mode of announcing. In talk shows and guest interview formats, the master of ceremonies sustains a conversation—ostensibly fresh talk—with one or more others in the studio whilst the remote (and studio) audience is treated as if it were a ratified participant, albeit one that cannot assume the speaking role. Something the same can be said of "on the spot" interviewing. In all these cases, as in ordinarily situated face-to-face talk, the announcer may turn from his fellow participants at the microphone and acquaint the audience with background matters. He may even go so far as to let the audience know what has already transpired between the talkers just prior to the broadcast, thus apparently avoiding the need to fake conversational inquiries concerning matters the guest has already told him about. In these ways the audience can appear to be brought into the conversation as it unfolds, knowing enough to follow the talk, in principle no less knowledgeable than the platform listeners themselves as to what is about to be said. Should the announcer want the guest to repeat a particular story the announcer has already heard, this, too, can be made evident—as it is in natural, multiparty, face-to-face conversation. Thus, instead of saying, "Did you ever meet a shark when you were collecting coral?", the interviewer may say, "We were talking earlier in the green room about the time you met a shark. Would you tell our listeners the story?" (Indeed, in an effort to generate a sense of spontaneity, interviewers recently have been foregoing arranging with their guests beforehand what they are going to cover, reversing ordinary precautions.)

In any case, note that guests and panelists can be said to be present as persons, not officials, and will often be in a position to respond to a statement by an avowal of personal belief, a report of feeling, a review of own experience, and so forth; nor need these interjections be considered in any way a departure from prescribed role. Also, a considerable discrepancy can be sustained between technically faulted and perceivedly faulted discourse—almost as in the case of ordinary conversation.

I have touched on two basic modes of announcing: action override and three-way. Consider now a third, and no doubt the basic kind: "direct" announcing. Here the announcer ostensibly speaks to the audience alone, and, in a sense, speaks as if each individual hearer were the only one. A simulation of two-person conversation is thus attempted, something like a telephone conversation except that no one can answer from the other end of the line. (In television announcing, the simulation is strengthened, of course, by the speaker affecting to look directly at his hearers.) Although we individual remote listeners would certainly allow that persons other than ourselves are listening, these others are for the most part unperceivable and have the same status as we do, having no more access to the speaker than we ourselves. And all of us will ordinarily be kept in the dark about the fact that support personnel are likely to be in close touch with the proceedings. Note, should an announcer address a live studio audience, he will have to change footing, giving up the pretense of talking to an individual for the reality of group focus. (Another variant is found in phone-in shows, where the remote audience is made privy to one or both sides of colloquies that the announcer intermittently has with callers, these two-party talks conducted in the encompassing encounter the announcer is maintaining with his wider audience.)

Given the three modes of announcing—action override, three-way, and direct—it is possible to say that recitation is little used (although short commercials are frequently memorized), the main ingredients being aloud reading and fresh talk. In the case of direct announcing, which is our main concern, aloud reading is principally involved.

2. By the very character of their duties one can anticipate that announcers will be required to change footing frequently. Three-way announcing provides some gross examples. An M.C. maintaining a conversation with a guest must attempt to place the topic, mood, and pace "on hold" during station breaks (much as an interviewer must when he changes tapes, or we all do when we have to leave a telephone conversation for a moment), which can involve addressing a few bridging remarks to the station announcer, thus shifting from one three-party talk to another through temporarily excluding the guest. So, too, there is a special form of ratified by-play: finding official cause to communicate with a member of the off-mike production crew, the announcer holds off his on-mike guests and the remote audience to do so, in no way allowing his voice to suggest that anything furtive or irregular is occurring. Characteristically the addressed recipient of these managerial remarks responds in words that can't be heard by the audience, albeit the announcer may repeat the words, after the bit of business is over, in the interests of "bringing the audience in." Direct announcing involves similar changes in footing. In addition to carrying his "own" show, an M.C. may have the job of helping to switch from the show that was in progress to the one that he will do, and, in turn, from this one to the show that follows. And he will have to hold up his own proceedings with set periodicity for station breaks (call letters, frequency identification), public service announcements, and commercials—interludes which he will have to bridge at both ends, not the least precariously when he himself must do the spot "live." In all of these cases, a momentary change in footing is required.

Less gross changes in footing are easy to cite. It is known, for example, that in reading the news, a practiced announcer will rapidly change tone of voice—along with mood—to reflect sequential changes in subject matter, and even, at the end of the newscast, when he recaps what has been covered, attempt a corresponding run-through of the differential stances he employed. But although this is known, how to transcribe it isn't quite; no convenient notation system is available to enable close description.

3. At the very beginning of this paper it was suggested that the critical task of the announcer is to produce an effect of spontaneous, fluent speech. Here some elaboration is in order.

First, with some systematic exceptions, announcers give the impression that they have a personal belief in what they are saying. The way in which commercials are announced provides the most obvious example.[25] Indeed, the professional literature provides rationalizations for this institutionalized lying (Hyde 1959:35):

> Because the commercial announcer is, after all, a salesman, he has the same problem which has confronted salesmen of all times —to be effective, he must believe in his product. This is not really as difficult as one might expect. Most nationally advertised pro-

25. The western theatrical frame provides that an actor staging a character is himself not to be taken to espouse whatever the part calls for him to avow or do, and this insulation is presumably granted by the audience no matter how convincing and thoroughgoing his performance is. In the reading of commercials something else prevails. The radio or TV announcer may himself believe that such insulation is part of the frame in which he operates, but the audience doesn't necessarily agree. And this applies also to celebrities who appear under their "own" name to endorse a product. (Announcers and especially celebrities can, however, feel doubtful about throwing conviction behind what they say about a product, and [as will be illustrated later] can even betray in various ways their commitment to the sponsor.) In any case, it seems to me that radio and TV audiences are much more likely to assume that the announcer is saying what he himself actually believes than that a stage actor is. After all, actors appear in character in a time, place, role, and costume patently not their "own"; announcers, on the other hand, present themselves in the same guise and name they use in their "own" everyday life. (Professional actors who do commercials but who do not appear in their own name for the occasion are a marginal case. They seem to assume all the rights of self-dissociation from one's character enjoyed by ordinary actors, but they find themselves selling a product, not a dramatist's ideas; therein, of course, lies a very considerable moral difference, albeit one that actors have been able to rise above.

> ducts are of good quality, and although mass production and fair-trade practices have tended to standardize many competing products, each will have some advantages, small or large, over its competitors. The announcer should begin to develop a belief in the products he advertises by buying and trying them. If possible, he should get to know the people who make the products, and should learn how the product is made and what it is made of. As a feeling of kinship is built up between the announcer and the product or the manufacturer, an honest enthusiasm will almost inevitably arise. If, on the other hand, experience with the product and familiarity with the manufacturer work to the opposite result, the announcer is faced with a difficult choice: he must either give up his job, or else attempt to be enthusiastic and convincing about a product in which he does not believe. This is a matter of conscience and must be settled on an individual basis.[26]

Second, if aloud reading is involved, the fact that it is will be somehow downplayed, rendering it easy for the audience to fall into feeling that fresh talk is occurring:

> Even though he works from a script, and even though the audience knows he does, there is yet no worse crime that an announcer can commit than to *sound* as though he is reading. The audience willingly suspends its awareness of the fact that the announcer is reading, but in order to do so, the announcer must play his part. He must *talk* his lines, he must deliver them as though they were thoughts which had just occurred to him. [Ibid.:33]

26. A special problem arises when the same announcer must read the news *and* do the commercials that precede and/or follow. The factual character of the news (such as it is) can carry over to the commercials, which may give to commercial claims even greater credibility than the announcer is comfortable with:

> A question that always arises is the newsman's involvement with commercials. Should a newscaster be permitted to deliver a live commercial within the body of his newscast? Some feel that the newsman's credibility is destroyed when he goes along with heavy world news and then reads a commercial, which obviously must be considered as a partial endorsement at least. [Hoffer 1974:40]

The BBC solves the problem by prohibiting TV announcers from *appearing* in commercials, although they are apparently allowed to do voice-overs.

The implication is that the individual animating has authored his own remarks, indeed, is doing so currently, for fresh talk entails such authorship—except, say, for brief strips of quotation of others' words embedded in the text. All of this can be illustrated by the work that announcers do in obscuring production changes. Thus, the "text-locked" voice: in switching from ordinary text to a strip that is *intended* to be heard as aloud reading (a news quote, author-identified program notes, etc.), the ostensible purpose being to relay the material instead of fully animating it, announcers can employ a voice suggesting that they themselves do not currently figure in any way as author or principal, merely as a voicing machine. In brief, instead of concealing or at least downplaying the preformulated source of what is said, the actual source is played up, its identification openly shared with the audience. (The same text-locked effect can be projected in ordinary talk when relaying what someone else has said or when "bringing to mind" what is presumably contained below the surface of one's memory.) In brief, what is merely a switch from one read text the announcer did not write to another is presented as something more than this. And, of course, the opposite impression can be created. Thus, when changing from a prerecorded spot featuring his own voice to live broadcasting, the announcer may attempt to conceal the production shift, apparently taking some pride in an ability to do this.[27]

I want to add, finally, that stations employ a pattern of "subediting" rules, whereby the surface form of sentences deriving from texts destined for print can be transformed into utterances "easy" to understand when read aloud.[28] And it turns out that sentence structures easy to understand when heard are ones that give a sense of fresh talk.

Two techniques through which the announcer produces a sense of spontaneity have been described: the projection of apparent personal belief in what is said, and the simulation of fresh

27. Reported by Marc Friedman (personal communication). It is, of course, also possible for the announcer to simulate aloud reading when, in fact, he has memorized the text, this being a standard ruse for actors in stage plays when the script calls for the ostensible aloud reading of a text.

28. The leading source here, and probably the most extensive current linguistic examination of radio talk, is Bell (1977).

talk. As a third, consider that characteristically, prime-time national network announcers—newscasters, disc jockeys, program M.C.s—deliver lines that technically speaking are almost flawless, and that they operate under a special obligation to do so, whether fresh talk, aloud reading, or memorization is involved. Indeed, although ordinary talk is full of technical faults that go unnoticed as faults, broadcasters seem to be schooled to realize our cultural stereotypes about speech production, namely, that ordinarily it will be without influencies, slips, boners, and gaffes, i.e., unfaultable. Interestingly, these professional obligations, once established, seem to generate their own underlying norms for hearers as well as speakers, so that faults we would have to be trained linguistically to hear in ordinary talk can be glaringly evident to the untrained ear when encountered in broadcast talk. May I add that what one may here gloss as a "difference in norms" is what I claim to be a difference in prescribed frame space.

Another factor is editorial elaboration. Small additions to a prescribed text, if allowable and if handled under the tonal auspices established for the prescribed text, provide means of giving the whole a fresh-talk feel. More interesting, some printed sources of information can be drawn on quickly—even during the announcer's production tolerance time—thereby allowing the announcer to produce something that is a sort of fresh talk and also to project an impression of considerable knowledgeability. Liner notes provide such a source of material on music programs. In classical music broadcasts, the Schwann catalogue and such books as the *Penguin Dictionary of Music* may also serve, although the announcer may have to cull his information a few minutes before it is to be used. Here the format in which he inserts dates and places will be fresh talk (however oft used as a formula), so the listener tends to hear it all as extemporaneous. Something the same can be said of the use of little formulae preceding the final item in a series (for example, "And last but not least . . ."), which can give a sense that the whole series is one the announcer is more than merely mechanically involved with. In news broadcasts, there is the "kicker," an item that can be read with a change in footing as a funny human interest story upon which a passing (even unscripted) comment may be made, consequently giving the whole news spot (if faintly) a fresh-talk character. Observe, too, that when an announcer openly quotes a text as a means of elaborating his own, he can omit from expression the fact that what he culled was *itself* quoted in liner notes or another source. A lamination is slipped, and an impression of both authority and freshness results.

Finally, consider that whatever else an announcer does, he must talk to listeners who are not there in the flesh. Because talk is learned, developed, and ordinarily practiced in connection with the visual and audible response of immediately present recipients, a radio announcer must inevitably talk *as if* responsive others were before his eyes and ears. (Television announcers are even more deeply committed to this condition than are radio announcers.) In brief, announcers must conjure up in their mind's eye the notion of listeners, and act as though these phantoms were physically present to be addressed through gaze, body orientation, voice calibrated for distance, and the like. In a fundamental sense, then, broadcasting (whether announcing news, giving a political address, or whatever) involves self-constructed talk projected under the demands, gaze, and responsiveness of listeners who aren't there. Of course, here a live studio audience can help, but often (in radio, at least) its presence must be downplayed or acknowledged as a second audience different from the invisible one.

So announcers must not only watch the birdie; they must talk to it. Under these circumstances, it is understandable that they will often slip into a simulation of talking *with* it. Thus, after a suitable pause, an announcer can verbally respond to what he can assume is the response his prior statement evoked, his prior statement itself having been selected as one to which a particular response was only to be expected. Or, by switching voices, he himself can reply to his own statement and then respond to the reply, thereby shifting from monologue to the enactment of dialogue. In both cases the timing characteristics of dialogue are simulated. In short (and to be considered later), announcing is response constructive,[29] and this apart from the fact that ordinar-

29. Stage acting employs a somewhat different timing adjustment. Ostensibly exhibiting the temporal sequencing of natural conversation, actors in fact

ily a relatively "formal" style is sustained, one that is characteristic of public addresses, not intimate conversation.

VI

One starts, then, with the announcer's commitment to maintaining what is heard as fresh talk no more than ordinarily unfaulted, but which is nearly unfaultable aloud reading. This work obligation distinguishes announcers' delivery from that of laypersons in ordinary day-to-day talk. Announcers must not only face many of the contingencies of everyday speech production (and, as will be seen, at greater cost), but also many contingencies specific to broadcasting. Consider now the special features of broadcasting work insofar as they condition the realization of the broadcaster's central task—the production of seemingly faultless fresh talk.[30]

It should be said first that it is true of radio broadcasting, as it is true of any communication system, that trouble enters from different points, these points located at different levels or layers in the organizational structure of the undertaking. For example, a power failure and a voice failure can equally lead to a breakdown in transmission, but obviously these two possibilities should be traced back to different layers in the structure of the communication system, here reflected in the kind of remedial work that is undertaken. Indeed, one of the values of examining troubles is as a reminder that communication systems are vulnerable from different layerings of their structure.

1. Consider first the special character of broadcast audiences. Plainly, the announcer has little specific control over who joins his audience, and often little knowledge of who has elected to do so. So, except in the case of "special-interest" stations and programs, and, say, the age/sex slant of morning and afternoon TV shows, the audience must be addressed as though it were the public-at-large. And, of course, broadcast audiences are typically

inhibit the overlapping found in such talk and build in pauses between turns to allow audiences to "respond" without this response interfering with audibility.

30. Here, for want of proper field work, I draw mainly on the Kermit Schafer corpus of troubles that broadcasters have gotten into.

large compared to auditorium audiences. It follows that any display of faultable conduct will be very widely witnessed, thereby constituting a threat unique to the electronic age. Influencies and slips will disseminate a picture of incompetency. Any factual error that is imparted can mislead a vast number, such that however small the cost to the individual listener, the sum across all listeners can be enormous. (Thus, a strong imperative to provide factual corrections no matter what this does to text delivery.) Any gaffe, any lapse from appropriate respect for ordinary sensibilities —religious, moral, political, etc.—can be considered an impiety at a national level. Any boner, any failure to sustain educational standards, any failure to indicate possession of a respectable corpus of knowledge attesting to familiarity with the world, awareness of recent public events, historical knowledgeability, and so forth, is not likely to be missed; and even ones that aren't fully "obvious" will be caught by some, if only Kermit Schafer:[31]

> [Madison Square Garden announcer just before fight]: "May the winner emerge victorious." [*PB:*53]

Moreover, radio and television audiences are not only large but also heterogeneous in regard to "sensitivities": ethnicity, race, religion, political belief, gender, regional loyalties, and all the physical and mental stigmata. The announcer's inadvertent or intended disparagement of almost any category of person or almost any article of belief is likely to find some angry ears. And, of course, an announcer cannot offend his audience without also incurring the displeasure of the station management and the sponsor (if any). In consequence, announcers—like politicians—have traditionally maintained strict decorum in mentioning sex, motherhood, the lame, the blind, and, not the least, the station and its sponsors.

Further, the delicacy of the announcer's position is not accounted for by patently faulted strips or even technically faultable ones. It is as if the sensitivities of sectionalist audiences, special-interest groups, and presumably the station management

31. And apparently not only Kermit Schafer. The British magazine *Private Eye,* in response to the blooperisms of David Coleman (a sports TV commentator), has established a regular column called "Colemanballs" to record such on the part of both radio and TV announcers.

and sponsors provided the general listener with a discovery device for uncovering risible mistakes. As though the audience sympathized with the position of the announcer merely to find out what he would find embarrassing. The issue, then, is not what

offends the listener, but what a listener assumes *might* offend *some* listener or other. Furthermore, error in any obvious sense—lay or linguistic—need not be involved. It appears that listeners seem primed for and oriented to alternative readings of what is said, that is, to the reframing of texts, and in this an obvious "error" is not essential. What is required is listeners skilled in, and oriented to, rereadings.[32] And where an announcer falls short is not only in failing to maintain the usual requirements of word production, but also in failing to canvas every possible reading of his words and phrases before uttering them, thereby correcting for potential alternatives, no matter how far-fetched. Thus, the progression from faults to faultables must be extended to the risibly interpretable, and this last appears to be the broadest category of all. And yet, however "forced" a second reading, it introduces much the same sort of issues for the announcer as do obvious faults. Thus lexically based ambiguity:

> "Men, when it's time to shave, you have a date with our two-headed model." [*PB:* 10]

> "Stay tuned to this station for your evening's entertainment. Immediately following Walter Winchell, hear the current dope in Hollywood—Listen to Louella Parsons." [*SB:* 134]

Contextual "unfreezing" of formulaic figurative phrases:

> Announcer: "Folks, try our comfortable beds. I personally stand behind every bed we sell." [*PB:* 128]

> [Jim McKay, describing the World Barrel-Jumping Championship on ABC's "Wide World of Sports"]: Leo Lebel has been competing with a pulled stomach muscle, showing a lot of guts!" [*Pr.:* 42]

32. A parallel is to be marked here to the practice in informal talk of punning playfulness in which participants vie with one another to see who can best transform the other's innocent words into ones with a "suggestive," unintended meaning. On unintended puns in general, see Sherzer (1978).

Pragmatic referential ambiguity bearing on the elision of noun or verb:

> "And just received is a new stock of Ries Sanforized Sports Shirts for men with 15 or 17 necks." [*PB:* 19]

> Commercial: "So, friends, if you're looking for frequent deliveries direct to your home, their driver will deliver as many cases of bottled water as you wish. Think of the many conveniences this service offers . . . no empty bottles to return to the store. Look for the nearest delivery man in the yellow pages of your phone book . . . you'll find him under water!" [*Pr.:* 81]

> "It's a nine pound boy born at Memorial Hospital for Mr. and Mrs. Jack Jason of Elm Road. Mrs. Jason was the former Susan Mulhaney. Services will be held tomorrow at 2 P.M. at Morton's Funeral Chapel for Jasper Howard, age 91, who passed on in his sleep yesterday. I'm sorry, our time is running out, so several deaths and births will have to be postponed until next week at the same time." [*PB:* 69]

Questions of syntactic structure—anaphoric reference, word order, and the like:

> Newscaster: "The loot and the car were listed as stolen by the Los Angeles Police Department." [*SB:* 30]

> "Your Masterwork Concert Hour will now present Boris Goudonov, the only opera Mussorgsky ever wrote on Friday evening." [*PB:* 100]

> Want Ads of the Air: "Our next TV want ad comes from a Mrs. Agnes Cooper. She is an elderly single lady looking for a small room where she can bake herself on a small electric stove." [*SB:* 64]

> Louella Parsons: "And here in Hollywood it is rumored that the former movie starlet is expecting her fifth child in a month!" [*Pr.:* 59]

> Local News: "And here is an item of local interest. Calvin Johnson, age 47, was booked for drunken driving in the county jail!" [*SB:* 31]

Ambiguities such as these would ordinarily go unnoticed in everyday face-to-face talk. The "context" would ordinarily make the speaker's intent clear, and speaker's intent would somehow be allowed to inhibit competing interpretations. But it seems that broadcast talk (as with some written discourse) cannot rely on hearers' good will as a means of discouraging alternate framings. Whereas in conversation ambiguity ordinarily seems to be an issue only when listeners are actually uncertain as to how the speaker meant his words to be taken, in broadcast talk there is a different issue. As suggested, it is not that the audience is left unclear about what could possibly be meant, or uncertain as to which of two possible meanings was correct, or whether or not the announcer wanted a double meaning to be taken. Almost always the audience is certain enough as to how the broadcaster meant his references to be interpreted and his remarks framed. (Nor is there a question of "keying," that is, a correct assessment of what was "literally" said, but a misjudgment of how the speaker intended this to be taken—for example, jokingly, sarcastically, quotatively, theatrically, and so forth; for it seems that in radio talk, actual miskeying is rather effectively guarded against.) Indeed, without this understanding there could be no fun and games, no pleasure taken in vicariously twitting the speaker.[33] It is the announcer's failure to arrange his words so that no obviously unintended, additional reading is discoverable that is at point. (Which is not to say, of course, that in some environments, such as schoolrooms and prisons, alternate readings, especially of a sexual kind, aren't even more imaginatively construed than is the case in public broadcasting.) Frame ambiguities, then, even more than other kinds of faults, must be defined in terms of the tendency of various audiences to look for such possibilities, and by and large (at least in the case of ambiguities) it is only

33. It should be apparent that risible announcer faultables could be treated as one department of a general subject matter—the effects, functions, and uses of multiple framings—another department of which is the riddles and jokes intentionally set up in the language play of children. (In this connection, see the useful linguistic classification of sources of ambiguity—to which I am much indebted—in Hirsh-Pasek, Gleitman, and Gleitman [1978:118]: phonological, lexical, surface structure, deep structure, morpheme boundary without phonological distortion, morpheme boundary with distortion. See also Shultz and Horibe [1974] and Shultz and Pilon [1973].) Indeed, as will be illustrated later, upon discovering that he has inadvertently allowed a risible framing to occur, an announcer may try to save a little face by following up with a remark that is to be perceived as intentionally continuing in the same interpretive frame.

relative to such tendencies that one can refer to objective faults.

I have suggested that broadcast audiences are not only personally offendable by faults, but that they actively seek out faults that might be offensive to someone. Typically this means that once attention is focused, say, on a slip, an alternate framing of what was intended will be searched out simultaneously. Nor need the audience wait for an "obvious" fault to occur; by a stretch of interpretation, a well-delivered, apparently innocent, utterance will often do. It should now be obvious that very often what is found in these various circumstances will not be just *any* alternative—an alternative, such as the ones illustrated, that takes its significance from the sheer fact that it *is* an alternative—but one which calls up meanings that are specifically embarrassing in their own right to the line the announcer is obliged to sustain. And announcers occasionally appear to help in this connection. Perhaps a psychoanalytical argument is sometimes warranted here, namely, that what the announcer would be most embarrassed to say he somehow feels compelled to say in spite of himself. Certainly some members of the audience are alive to this "overdetermination" interpretation of slips (whether believing it or not), and having it in mind leave the announcer needful of having it in mind, too. Two matters are to be considered here.

First, the unintended reading can be seen, occasionally, as "only too true," discrediting not merely the assumption that the announcer will control for a single course of meaning, but also the very sentiments it was his duty to convey. The audience may be generally suspicious that the announcer is in league with the station's commercial interests and is mouthing statements he could not himself believe; in any case, second readings can ironically belie innocent, intended ones.[34]

Thus, whole-word reversal can be involved with retention of original structure:

34. Slips that are seen as all too meaningful cause risible notice during informal talk, but it appears that such occurrences are not frequent, the fit having to be too good. I might add that some ironic reversals depend upon a shift from the "dominant" meaning of a word to a vernacular one, thereby involving two principles, not one:

> Religious Program: "In closing our TV CHURCH OF THE AIR, let me remind all of our listeners that time wounds all heals!" [*SB:* 126]

Commercial: "Summer is here, and with it those lazy days at the beach; and don't forget your Tartan sun lotion. Tartan is the lotion that lets you burn but never lets you tan." [*SB:* 66]

Station Break: "This is Station WELL, Battle Creek, where listening is by chance, not by choice." [*SB:* 25]

Announcer: Try this lovely four-piece starter set in your home for seven days. If you are not satisfied, return it to us. So you see you have everything to lose and nothing to gain. [*PB:* 44]

"It's low overhead that does it, so always shop at Robert Hall where prices are high and quality is low." [*PB:* 126]

Commercial: "For the best in glass work, metal work or upholstering, see Hastin Glass, where every department is a sideline, not a business!" [*Pr.:* 39]

Or whole word substitution (or whole word change due to phonological distortion of one segment of the original), again without structural change:

"Viceroys—if you want a good choke." [*PB:* 49]

Sportscaster: "And now coming into the ball game for the Reds is number forty-four, Frank Fuller, futility infielder." [*SB:* 76]

[Local Newscast]: "Credit for the discovery of the stolen automobile was given to Lieutenant Blank, a defective of the Los Angeles force." [*PB:* 92]

[NBC News]: "Word comes to us from usually reliable White House Souses." [*PB:* 93]

"You are listening to the mucous of Clyde Lucas." [*PB:* 33]

Or matters of word order involving agents in passivization, adverbial phrases modifying an understood higher sentence, placement of adverbs and of adverbial phrases, or other such sources of structural ambiguity:

"Here's a house for sale that won't last long." [*PB:* 86]

Commercial: "So drive your old car down to our showroom, come in, and we will show you how little you need to own a brand-new car." [*SB:* 82]

Sportscaster: "Jack Kachave, with a bad knee, limps back to the huddle. He wants to play this game in the worst way . . . and that's exactly what he is doing!" [*Pr.:* 8]

Or pragmatically based referential ambiguity:

Newsman: "And it is felt in Washington that we have been most fortunate in having Nikita Khrushchev with us, and when he leaves we will be most grateful!" [*SB:* 98]

"We note with regrettable sorrow that Mrs. Vandermeer is recovering from a bad fall on the ice." [*PB:* 95]

[Laundry Commercial]: "When your clothing is returned there is little left to iron." [*PB:* 89]

Second, observe that listeners will not only be on the lookout for ironically apt readings, but also of course for prurient, "off-color" ones. Thus, phonological distortion resulting in a conventional word, but an inopportune one:

Local News: "Tonight will be the last night of the charity card party and bridge tournament. As of Friday night, Mrs. Updyke of the Springfield Women's Club is ahead by two pints." [*SB:* 83]

Louella Parsons: "It is rumored here in Hollywood that the film company bought the rights to a new navel for Audrey Hepburn!" [*Pr.:* 16]

"Word has just reached us that a home-made blonde exploded in the Roxy Theater this morning." [*PB:* 139]

"And Dad will love Wonder Bread's delicious flavor too. Remember it's Wonder Bread for the breast in bed." [*PB:* 9]

Or phonological disturbance resulting in a "suggestive" nonword —often along with an inopportune real one:

"This is KTIW, Sexas Titty er, Texas City." [*PB:* 74]

"This is the Dominion network of the Canadian Broad Corping Castration." [*PB:* 105]

Or lexical ambiguity:

Announcer: "Ladies who care to drive by and drop off their clothes will receive prompt attention." [*PB:* 48]

Commercial: "And all you women will love these sheer stockings. This hosiery is dressy enough for any fancy wear, and is so serviceable for every day that many women wear nothing else!" [*SB:* 109]

[Mutual Network announcer]: "The nation was glad to learn that, in the cold of winter, John L. Lewis dropped his union suit." [*PB:* 94]

Commercial: "Ladies, go to Richard's Variety Store today. . . . Richard is cleaning out ladies' panties for 29¢—be sure to get in on this special deal." [*SB:* 32]

Or structural ambiguity:

Announcer: "At Heitman's you will find a variety of fine foods, expertly served by experienced waitresses in appetizing forms." [*PB:* 56]

"Good afternoon, this is your department store TV counselor—Here's news for those who have little time for your Christmas shopping. Tonight, after working hours on the sixth floor, models will display gowns half off." [*PB:* 72]

Less commonly, prurient readings may be allowed by inopportune word boundaries:[35]

[Louis Armstrong, on the Dorsey's "Stage Show"]: "Okay, you cats, now just play the simple mustard jazz not too slow and not too fast . . . just half fast." [*PB:* 132]

[BBC]: "Here's an all time favorite made popular by the famous Miss Jessie Matthews several years back, *Dancing on the Ceiling.* This one surely deserves to be on every British Hit List." [*PB:* 124]

Disc Jockey: "Well, rock 'n rollers, it's time for our mystery-guest contest. If you guess the name of our next artist, our sponsors will send you two tickets to the RKO theatre in your neighborhood. Now the clue to this singer, and this is the only clue I'm going to give you, is that she had two of the biggest hits in the country." [*SB:* 86]

Or by word pronunciation producing homophonic ambiguity:

35. It has been suggested by Garnes and Bond (1975:222) that boundary assignment (addition, shifting, and especially deletion) is a principal source of hearing slips but a minor source of speaking slips.

"Final results of the FFA contest are: Apple picking won by Dick Jones, Tractor driving award to Jack Davis. One of our own girls, Miss Betty Smith, was chosen the best hoer." [*PB:* 43]

Salacious rereadings are especially difficult to guard against in regard to a class of words and phrases which can be called "leaky." Even without benefit of phonological disturbance, word interchange or structural ambiguity, such terms are treacherous, unstabilizing single meanings. Examples: *balls, can, behind, gas, parts, come, lay, globes, big ones, fanny,*[36] *piece, erection, business, rubbers, make, drawers, nuts, sleep with.* (A feature of leaky words is that each usually has a widely employed innocent meaning, whilst the salacious meaning is part of widely accepted, non-"literal" vernacular.) And as with any other source of prurient rereading, the audience can feel that they have caught out the announcer in an inadvertent breach of the moral standards set for broadcasting, that his efforts to avoid this have come to naught comically, and that he is "one down":[37]

[BBC announcer at the launching of the Queen Mary]: "From where I am standing, I can see the Queen's bottom sticking out just over her water line." [*PB:* 120]

Contestant: "How much time do I have to answer my question?" Quizmaster: "Lady, yours is a little behind, so we'd better try to squeeze it in within five seconds." [*SB:* 118]

Cooking Program: "Good morning. Today we are going to bake a spice cake, with special emphasis on how to flour your nuts!" [*SB:* 32]

[OPA spot announcement] "Ladies, take your fat cans down to the corner butcher." [*PB:* 131]

"It's a laugh riot, it's a musical treat, it's the film version of the hit broadway show, *Gentlemen Prefer Blondes,* starring Jane Russell and Marilyn Monroe. Yes sir, the big ones come to R.K.O." [*PB:* 111]

36. Does not leak in Britain.

37. In the collections of leaky utterances I have seen, my impression is that the referent-person leaked on is more likely to be a woman than a man, whereas, in the case of announcing, the perpetrator is usually a man—if only on occupational grounds. I assume the underlying reason is to be found in our traditional sex roles, not our humor.

"Starting next week at the Paramount Theater you will see that rollicking comedy smash hit, *Pale Face,* starring Bob Hope, America's favorite comedian, and lovely Jane Russell. Boy, what a pair!" [*PB:* 103]

"Calling all parents, calling all kids! Here's your chance to buy a Davey Crockett bed—yes, friends, Hunt's Furniture Store has Davey Crockett beds—it's a twin size bed, just right for the kids —with scenes of Davey Crockett in action on the mattress!" [*PB:* 109]

Newscaster: "Plans were announced for the parade which will follow the Governors' Conference. At two P.M. the cars will leave their headquarters just as soon as the Governors are loaded!" [*Pr.:* 55]

Announcer: "At Moe's Esso Station, you can get gassed, charged up, and your parts lubricated in 30 minutes!" [*PB:* 36]

So announcers can fall into saying something that not only allows for unintended reframing, but also a reading that is either all-too-true or risqué. Here again, note, one faces a problem connected with the social control model. Second readings, whether a result of word inversion, mispronunciation, homonymous forms, ambiguous pronominal or clausal reference, or whatever, confront the perpetrator with a dilemma. The more unfortunate the unplanned reading, the more extended and substantial will be the apology that is in order; but the more elaborate and pointed the apology, the more attention will be focused on the difficulty, and in consequence, the more embarrassing will be the misfortune and the more needful of apology.

Moreover, there is this. Whether or not an error is itself interpretable as risqué or ironically apt, the attention that is focused on a corrected replay carries its own special vulnerabilities, and these too reflect on the peculiarities of the social control process. For in the heat of the moment, the announcer will more than usually flub the correction, and thus be stuck with having drawn attention not only to an error already made, but now to the making of an error—an error sometimes more risqué or ironic than the original fault:

Newscaster: "It is beginning to look here, that the Canadian Prime Minister is going to have difficulty with his dame luck cabinet . . . I mean his lame dick cabinet!" [*SB:* 124]

Disc Jockey: "And that was 'South Town' sung by the Blue Bellies . . . I mean, the Blue Balls . . . the Blue Belles!" [*Pr.:* 30]

Weather Forecaster: "Well, many of you who awakened early saw the dreary-looking, foreboding black clouds which indicate that we are in for a long rainy bleakened . . . I mean a long blainey leakend!!!" [*Pr.:* 75]

Once it is seen that audiences take an active interest (and often a delight) in uncovering imperfections in the announcer's word production, it should be evident that the social control response—in this case, snickers and laughs the announcer can't hear unless he has a studio audience—can become something of an end in itself—indeed, an official one—here again pointing to the limitation of the social control model. This is clear in contestant shows and variety talk shows where persons quite inexperienced in broadcast talk find themselves required to perform verbally before a microphone. It appears that the very considerable amount of technical influency they produce is allowed to pass without particular notice (much as it would in ordinary conversation), but the slips, boners, and gaffes they produce are another matter. A studio audience is likely to be available and will establish through its open laughter that laughing at "incompetence" is part of what the show is all about:

[Anna Moffo, on Carson's "Tonight Show"] discussing her role as Brunhilde, stated, "In order to sing Brunhilde, all you need to wear is a pair of comfortable shoes and nothing else (AUDIENCE LAUGHTER). You know what I mean." [*Pr.:* 80]

Quizmaster: "All right now, for twenty-five silver dollars: Who were the Big Four? Contestant: "Er . . . let's see . . . Jane Russell, Jayne Mansfield . . ." (AUDIENCE LAUGHTER) [*Pr.:* 63]

"Laughing at" as an end in itself can also be clearly seen in the "What's My Line?" format, where unintended *double entendre* are automatically generated by the structure of the show. Panelists are required to guess the occupation of persons brought before them. The audience is informed beforehand so that it will be able to appreciate what the panelists can't. And, of course, the presented persons are selected for the show with embarrassments in mind.

"Is your product used by one sex over the other?" (*PB:* 111) becomes an inadvertent but facilitated fault when the respondent has been selected because of being a mattress stuffer.

Here, incidentally, is another complication in regard to social control. When a speaker addressing a live audience learns from the sound of sudden laughter that he has made an error, he may feel compelled to jump in quickly with a strident candidate correction. This remedial utterance will inhabit the focus of attention created by audience response to the defective utterance. When it turns out that the speaker has hit upon the wrong aspect of his faulty utterance to correct, he will inevitably provide his listeners with a second breach and second opportunity for laughter, but this time at the critical moment when they have already started to roll downhill:

> Announcer: "Here's your question. There was a famous French author, who wrote many, many famous stories. He is the man who wrote 'The Black Tulip' and 'The Three Musketeers.' What is the name of this famous French author?"
> Contestant: "Oh golly . . . I'm nervous . . . let me see . . . OH! Alexandre Dumb-ass! (LAUGHTER) OH! Henry Dumb-ass!"

> Here's a question from *Double or Nothing,* CBS, that rocked the studio audience with laughter: Question: Where is the Orange Free State? Answer: California! I mean Florida! [PB:66]

2. We have considered the treacherousness of broadcast audiences. Consider how that the fact that listeners are on the prowl for faultables is worsened by a technical feature of broadcasts, namely, that very often the text is formulated totally in advance, and, of course, very often by someone other than the individual who is to read it aloud. Although one might think that pre-scripting merely eases the announcer's burden in this connection (giving him an opportunity to check through his text before delivering it), there are considerations on the other side.

In everyday fresh talk, whatever impression of speech competency the speaker manages to give is a product of his having a choice of words and phrases with which to realize his thoughts. As suggested, words he can't pronounce "correctly" without special thought, or whose meaning is not quite clear to him, he tends to avoid, and in such a fashion that there is no indication that a lapse has been averted. A favorable impression of competence can thus be generalized from the words that do get spoken. (One might therefore argue that speakers in general appear to be more competent than they actually are.) These avoidance techniques cannot readily be applied when a pre-fixed text must be read, or even when paraphrasing is allowed but certain personal names and place names must be mentioned. (Practice runs help, but are not always possible.)

> "And stay tuned for the late movie, Alexander Dumas' immortal classic *The Count of Monte Crisco,* starring Robert Donut." [*PB:* 133]

> Announcer: "And now to conclude our program of Christmas Carols, our guest star will sing 'Come All Ye Faithful,' by Adeste Fidelis." [*PB:* 13]

> "Now here's an interesting looking record—it's got a classical label, sung by a trio, John, Charles and Thomas." [*PB:* 71]

> "And now back to our all-request recorded program. We've had a request for a record by that popular Irish tenor, Mari O'Lanza." [*PB:* 127]

Indeed, freedom to embed required names in extemporaneous (albeit formulaic) elaboration can make matters worse:

> Disc Jockey: Now we hear one of my favorite selections by George Gershwin, with lyrics by his lovely wife, Ira. [*PB:* 41]

Also, fresh talkers—especially in face-to-face everyday talk—are in a position to take the local environment and the local hearership into consideration in preselecting words and phrases so that likely alternative readings are ruled out. (Of course, in face-to-face talk, the social and personal identity of the listeners will oblige the speaker to preselect on the basis of a whole range of fundamental factors—propriety being at issue, not merely disambiguation. He will have to consider their age, sex, ethnicity, and religion relative to his, their "personal feelings," the information it can be assumed they possess, and so forth.) However, when someone other than the animator prepares a text out of the context of the animation, then, apparently, alternative frames are hard to avoid, even apparently by writers who are acutely alive to the need of doing so. As though the premonitoring which serves as a check in fresh talk can't be employed away from occasions of delivery. Thus, for example, the frequency of "leaky" words in spite of editorial vigilance.

3. I have suggested that prewritten texts have less flexibility than fresh talk, less of what permits the speaker to avoid words he can't use or pronounce "correctly," and avoid phrasings that aren't the best suited to the audience at hand. Consider now another problem associated with scripted texts. Without any failing other than not checking the script, an announcer may find himself lodged cold in a text that is incomplete, jumbled, or in some other way nonsensical. The embarrassment can be deep, speaking to the way we assemble things to say. In actual fresh talk, the speaker's thought or theme seems to serve as a running guide, ensuring that his statements don't run too far off the mark, even though he may have to search for a word or retract one he has spoken. If the speaker does "lose the thought" of a statement in midstream, he can make this evident with a trailing intonation, a ritualized expression of his situation. Reading a prepared text is a considerably different matter. Instead of constantly appealing to the overall thought behind the text as a guide, an aloud reader can rely on upcoming bits of the text itself. Announcers use these upcoming passages to determine how to parse what is currently being read, and thence to provide through stress, juncture, "feeling," pitch, and other prosodic markers a speaking that displays a plausible interpretation of the text. When, however, an announcer loses his text, or, rather, is lost by it, his effort to provide a usable interpretation prosodically can carry him in a direction that cannot be sustained by what turns out to follow. The fresh-talk speaker can warn us of losing his thought while at the same time reducing his claim to meaningful speech, but the announcer has ordinarily foregone such measures, for he has read what he takes to be the line in a confident, committed, "full" voice. In consequence he not only can create the impression that he is not in mental touch with the thought he was to have been expressing, but also that he is intentionally faking fresh talk. Here, then, a fault is discrediting:

> Weather forecaster: "The Mid West is suffering from one of the worst cold-spells in years, with temperatures dropping as low as twenty degrees below zero. Tomorrow's forecast is for continued mild!" [*PB:* 71]

Commercial: "So remember . . . National Airlines has ten flights daily to Miami and also Florida!" [*Pr.:* 59]

[Newscaster reading unchecked item]: "In the head-on collision of the two passenger cars, five people were killed in the crash, two seriously." [*SB:* 68]

4. Another source of trouble, this time not restricted to texts that the announcer has not written himself: track error. Here is a frame problem, pure and simple. An editor—or the announcer himself during a practice run-through—interlards a text with cue signs, reading instructions, and other stage directions; and the announcer, during the "live" reading, construes these comments as part of the text and reads them along with it[38] (of the three forms of production—memorization, aloud reading, and fresh talk—only aloud reading seems vulnerable to this particular kind of confusion):

When Pat Adelman, program director of Station KNOW, Texas, finished preparing the day's schedule, he left it in the control room. Later he made a change—instead of Les Brown's orchestra, he substituted a religious program which was to originate from New York. He scratched out Les Brown's name and wrote over it, Yom Kippur. When the new announcer came on shift, he picked up the schedule and exhorted his listeners to "Stay tuned for the dance music of Yom Kippur's Orchestra." [*PB:* 9]

Bess Meyerson, former Miss America and co-MC on *The Big Payoff,* popular network TV program, was interviewing a contestant on the program. She was handed a note from one of the members of the production staff, which told her that the contestant was London-bound, so as to get this added color into her interview. Believing that this note was an added reminder of the contestant's name,

38. Goffman (1974:320). Some of these instructions, such as the Spanish inverted question mark at the beginning of interrogative sentences, provide help without introducing the possibility of misframing. But other devices, such as the use of parentheses to mark out-of-frame comments, can lead to misinterpretation, in this case reading the comments as if they were parenthetical statements *in* the text instead of *about* it.

A similar problem occurs in *lingua franca* talk ("two parties speaking different native languages communicate via a third language"), where "What happens in fact is that questions about language (metaquestions) get taken as questions about meaning (object questions)" (Jordan and Fuller 1975:11, 22), a confusion, in short, between "mention" and "use."

she introduced him thusly: "Ladies and gentlemen, I would like you to meet Mr. London Bound." [*PB:*62]

"It's 8 P.M. Bulova Watch Time. On Christmas say Merry Christmas, and on New Year's, say Happy New Year." [*SB:*36]

5. Consider the framing issue arising because announcers must frequently cite the title of songs, movies, and the like. Such titles, of course, are meant to be treated as "frozen" wholes, set off from the utterance in which they are embedded; the constituent words of the title are meant to have their standard meanings *within* the title, not outside it. In terms of the work titled, a title can cannote something, presumably touching off a general theme to be found in what is titled. In terms of the utterance in which the title in embedded, the title can only mean what any other title might, namely, the name of some work. In effect, in the embedding or "higher" sentence or clause, a title's words are being *mentioned,* not *used.* However, announcers find that the titles they mention may be interpreted "literally," as words or phrases having the same status as the others in the utterance and readable in a single syntactic sequence:

Station Break: "Stay tuned for our regular Sunday Broadcast by Reverend R. J. Ryan, who will speak on In Spite of Everything." [*Pr.:*63]

"And now, Nelson Eddy sings *While My Lady Sleeps* with the men's chorus." [*PB:*93]

Station Break: "Be sure not to miss THE COMING OF CHRIST, Wednesday, 8:30 P.M., 7:30 Central Time." [*SB:*11]

"There's excitement in store on our *Million Dollar Movie* tonight with Ann Sheridan—stay tuned as Philips Milk of Magnesia brings you *Woman on the Run."* [*PB:*108]

And, indeed, titles may be read off against each other, as though both were part of a single, extendable sequence:

Commercial: "Starting Thursday for four days only, see Betty Davis in *The Virgin Queen* and *Tonight's the Night* . . . Starting next Monday be sure to see *Breakthrough* and *Emergency Wedding!"* [*Pr.:*15]

Announcer: "Your city station now brings you a program of piano music, played by Liberace, in a program titled 'MUSIC YOU

WANT', followed by 'MUSIC YOU'LL REALLY ENJOY' on Melody Theatre." [*SB:* 112]

Disc Jockey: "Our HAPPY DAYS musical show continues with a medley; we will now hear, 'I'm Walking Behind You,' 'Finger of Suspicion,' and 'The Call of the Wild Goose!' " [*Pr.:* 23]

6. Next is the problem of page transitions. Studio "copy" that is two or more pages long requires the aloud reader to finish the last line of one page and start the first line of the next page in a time that can be encompassed by production margins. And this is routinely achieved with opposing pages. When, however, a page must be *turned,* an overheld pause or an overheld syllable may be required, which can intrude on the impression of fresh talk that is otherwise being sustained.[39] Very occasionally at this moment an unintended risible meaning also becomes available to listeners:

Commercial: "So stop by our downtown store and visit our fashion center. You will see our lovely models in heat . . . (PAUSE, TURNS PAGE) . . . resistant fabrics which will keep you cooler this summer." [*SB:* 14]

"Tums will give you instant relief and assure you no indigestion or distress during the night . . . So try Tums and go to sleep with a broad . . ." (turns page) ". . . smile." [*PB:* 137]

7. There is the issue of "juncture readings," an issue structurally similar to the page transition problem already considered. Program management tends to focus on the content of particular segments of the day's broadcasting, and upon fluent

39. When an individual reads to a physically present audience, it seems that pauses at page transitions—including ones involving the turning of a page—are "read out" by listeners, indeed so effectively disattended as to not be heard at all. Radio reading systematically disallows this collaboration, although televised reading might not. Interestingly, in music performances for live audiences, page-turn delays apparently can't be managed by means of the collaborative disattendance of the hearers, presumably because timing is much more fixed in music than in talk—in music being in effect semantic in character. Furthermore, a musician who turns his own pages cannot use that hand for music-making, this not being a problem when the mouth, not the hands, are the source of animation. (Of course, in singing and horn-blowing the timing of breath intake becomes very much an issue, the mechanics of animation here having to be made somehow compatible with the sustaining of sound.)

temporal linkage of one segment to the preceding and following ones. But this very smoothness creates its own problems. Any review of copy that editors, writers, and announcers have time for tends to be limited to the internal content of particular segments, that being the substantive unit of production. In consequence, unanticipated (and thus almost certainly undesired) readings are possible across the ending of one segment and beginning of another. Apparently these possibilities are not sufficiently considered in advance to avoid all juncture readability. Given the tendency for the audience to look for risible readings no matter how obviously unintended, segment junctures can produce faultables.[40]

> On the Arthur Godfrey program, time was running short, therefore two commercials were thrown together back to back. This was the dialogue that resulted from the rushed commercials. "Lipton Soup is what you will want for dinner tonight." (NEXT COMMERCIAL) "Thank goodness I brought an Alka Seltzer!" [*Pr.:* 8]

> [Announcer, in solemn voice] "So, remember friends, Parker's Funeral Home at 4th and Maple for the finest in funeral arrangements . . . and now the lucky winner of our deep freeze." [*PB:* 135]

> ". . . And the United Nations will adjourn until next week. And now here's a local news item: A lot of villagers were very startled today when a pack of dogs broke loose from a dog catcher's wagon and raced crazily through the field of a well known tobacco plantation . . . Friends does your cigarette taste different lately?" [*PB:* 70]

As they can in conjunction with titles:

> Announcer: "So folks, now is a good time to spend planning your Christmas holiday. . . . Take your youngsters to the Radio City Music Hall to see 'Snow White and the Seven Dwarfs'. . . . We now pause for a short sponsor's message!" [*SB:* 95]

> "Before our next recorded selection, here's an item of interest—last night at the Municipal Hospital there were 42 babies born . . . and now . . . *Don't Blame Me.*" [*PB:* 92]

40. What one has here, of course, is an example at a higher (utterance) level of the unexpected reading that is possible across morphemic boundaries.

Formulaic broadcaster phrases for satisfying program requirements such as continuity, timing, and identification, can themselves allow for unanticipated readings:

> Announcer: (After having mike trouble) "Now due to a mistake, The City Light Company presents your garden lady, Peggy Mahaffay." [*SB:* 114]

> Newscast: "This is DIMENSION, Allen Jackson reporting on the CBS Radio Network from New York. Today's big news story is the national spreading of the flu epidemic . . . brought to you by the Mennen Company!" [*Pr.* :29]

> Announcer: "Due to circumstances beyond our control we bring you a recorded program featuring the Beatles!" [*Pr.:* 11]

> Announcer: "Excuse me, Senator . . . I am sure that our listening audience would like to hear more about the fine work that your important Congressional committee is doing . . . but unfortunately, Margaret Truman is about to sing." [*Pr.:* 22]

And indeed, the news format can call for a succinct review of vital facts, which in turn requires a disconnectedness, and "implication block," across adjacent utterances which hearers may not allow:

> Newscaster: "And word has just reached us of the passing of Mrs. Angela Cirrilio, who died at the age of eighty-seven. Mrs. Cirrilio was a noted amateur chef who specialized in Italian cooking. There are no survivors." [*Pr.:* 58]

> Local News: "Mr. Baker, who applied for the job, seemed to be very well qualified. He is obviously a man of sound judgment and intelligence. Mr. Baker is not married." [*SB:* 82]

> "And in the world of sports, Yogi Berra the great Yankee catcher was accidentally hit on the head by a pitched ball. Yogi was taken to Fordham Hospital for X-rays of the head. The X-ray showed nothing." [*PB:* 127]

8. As already suggested, a radio station's broadcast output is planned as a continuous flow of sound production across all of the hours the station transmits. This requires that most segments will begin at a predetermined moment in chronological time and end at another, similarly predetermined. Only in this way can a

particular program be fitted to the one just preceding and the one to follow to produce a continuous ribbon of broadcasting—a functional equivalent of the conversational ideal of no-gap/no-overlap. Yet different announcers, different authors, different sponsors, and different support personnel will be involved—in fact, with "remotes," even different program sources.

It follows that because the content of a segment is usually itself predetermined, in order to maintain required continuity an announcer must not only begin any given segment at the right moment, but also pace his aloud reading to end his text exactly when his allotted time is up. This fitting of reading time to allotted time whilst not breaching production margins is an important part of the professional competence of announcers. But, of course, contingencies can arise, requiring more slowing down or speeding up of reading pace than will be overlooked by hearers.

9. The "ribbon effect" raises some other questions. Modern technology makes it possible to construct a smooth flow of words (and images, in the case of TV) out of small strips that are of greatly disparate origin. For example, a beginning-of-hour news program can involve a local announcer's introduction, a sound-jingle "logo" from a cassette, a cutting into a national hookup precisely in time for a time beep, then four minutes of national news. The news itself may be broken up into three sections to allow for interspersed commercials, each news portion in turn broken up by "remotes" involving taped on-the-scene comments introduced by an on-the-scene announcer, and leading into the excerpted comments of an official or other actual participant. Following the national hookup news, there may be a minute or two of local news and weather, finally closing with a recorded sound logo. Although heard as a continuous stream of sound, with no gaps or overlaps, a few such minutes can be made up of a great number of small segments, each of which has to be very nicely timed and patched in and out if coherence is to be maintained. Here in the extreme is the way in which technology and planning bring to a traditional mold—the expectation of no gap, no overlap—an artificial filling that is more variegated and compacted than could be expected to occur in nature. And, of course, the technology that allows disparately produced strips of talk to be orchestrated so that a unitary flow of words results, also opens

up the possibility that the "wrong" segment will be brought in at a juncture, or that an ongoing segment will be "cut into" by another accidentally. In consequence, the possibility of unplanned and undesired readings across properly unrelated strips:[41]

> Our lovely model, Susan Dalrymple, is wearing a lovely two-piece ensemble . . . *(Station Cut-In)* . . . with a rear engine in the back!" [*SB:* 28]

> "It's time now, ladies and gentlemen, for our featured guest, the prominent lecturer and social leader, Mrs. Elma Dodge . . ." *(Superman cut in)* ". . . who is able to leap tall buildings in a single bound. SWISHHHH!" [*PB:* 16]

> "The recipe this afternoon is for potato pancakes. I'm sure you will enjoy them. You take six medium sized potatoes, deep fat . . . and I am sure your guests will just love them." *(Cut in)* "Funeral services will be held promptly at two o'clock." [*PB:* 79]

> "So remember, use Pepsodent toothpaste, and brush your teeth . . ." (CUT IN [to a cleansing product commercial]) ". . . right down the drain!" [*Pr.:* 26]

> Emcee: "You are quite a large man . . . how much do you weigh?" Man: "About two hundred eighty-five pounds, and I . . ." (COMMERCIAL CUT IN) ". . . have trouble with hemorrhoids." [*Pr.:* 32]

As might be expected, unanticipated boundary readings seem especially likely when an ongoing program must be interrupted for an unscheduled special news bulletin:

> A local TV station carrying a network telecast of a prize fight from Madison Square Garden in New York, interrupted its coverage to inform its audience of the death of a local politician. Upon cutting back to the fight, the announcer was heard to say, "That wasn't much of a blow folks!" [*Pr.:* 48]

> On the Ed Sullivan program, movie actor Van Johnson was singing a spirited song about the pitfalls of show business, which highlighted such problems as mikes breaking down, poor lighting, the show must go on, etc., when a CBS news bulletin broke in, inter-

41. There is a children's game that efficiently accomplishes much the same effect. The adverbial phrase *between the sheets* is added by one player to the end of every sentential utterance of the other.

> rupting his song. After Harry Reasoner finished his bulletin about the Greek-Turkish Cypriot crisis, the station cut back to Johnson, who was singing, "It's just one of those things!" [*Pr.:* 105]

> Wild Bill Hickok had his program interrupted by a newscaster just after four shots were fired by the program's sound effects man. "We interrupt this program to bring you a bulletin from the Mutual News Room. L.P. Beria has just been executed, according to an announcement from Moscow Radio. We now return you to *Wild Bill Hickok.*" At that moment, Guy Madison was reading this line: "Well, that should hold him for awhile." [*PB:* 42]

10. Consider the contingencies of "modality integration." Much radio announcing involves only the spoken voice, but radio drama involves the simulation of the sound associated with various physical events and actions.[42] And, of course, sound effects can be introduced at the wrong time, or the wrong ones at the right time:

> "Beyond the head waters of the Nile, Stanley continued his search for Livingston. Dense jungle growth and the ever-present danger of the Tse-Tse fly made the journey more hazardous. Supplies were

42. The technological vicissitudes of staging a radio drama can, of course, be much greater even than those of staging a multisource newscast. When in real life lovers sit in the park in season, they themselves don't have to secure the services of birds, brooks, and falling leaves to ensure a parklike effect; for what we mean by parklike is what occurs there without particular users' help. The problem of coordinating the various effects is no problem at all for the lovers: the prior effort of the park authorities in conjunction with mother nature does it all—parks being (like the real forests Turner painted) social constructions based on community resources expended over a certain period of time. But if you are to make a radio drama of all this, sound-alternatives to visual effects and sound-mimicry of actual sounds will have to come from different sound-makers. Production conventions allow the show's producer to severely limit the number of these streams of sound required to set the scene, and he will also be allowed to play them down once he has played them up, so that ongoing interference won't have to be tolerated. But when sound effects *are* scheduled to appear, they have to appear on time. It is just this coordination that can break down, so that the sound counterpart to action comes too late or too early or fails to come or is of the wrong kind. (I might add that in addition to communally constructed ongoing backgrounds for action, there are extensive scenes set up with one celebrative occasion or affair in mind: specially constructed reviewing stands for an inauguration are one example; tent facilities for a large garden party are another. Radio dramas can involve scenic resources that are also occasion-constructed, but, of course, here one deals with a simulation of a social occasion, not the real thing.)

getting low, the natives had almost reached the breaking point, when suddenly, in the distance, they heard the sounds of a village . . . (HORNS, TRAFFIC SOUNDS, CITY SOUNDS)." [*SB:* 56]

The issue is even more acute in television. TV commercials are likely to involve the close interweaving of scripted words and visual demonstration of the working of the sponsor's product. Should a hitch develop in the physical manipulation of the product, the product itself can lose credibility, and in addition all the cues for the scripted words can be thrown off, resulting in confusion. Here, incidentally, one can see in paradigmatic form the intimate bearing a nonlinguistic fault can have upon the speech stream:

"There's no reason to be satisfied with old-styled refrigerators. This Westinghouse is completely automatic—a self-defrosting feature takes care of that. Let's look inside—just the slightest push on this snap-open door and uh! wait a minute—just push—wait a minute. Oh, this opens—I guess you'll just have to take my word for it." [*PB:* 76]

"Well, now, you can have this model plane all for yourself, and it's a lot of fun. You just take the kit and it comes completely set up for you. All the parts are ready to put together. You take the part and you well—now you—well, this section here is—well it's—just a minute now. It must be a little stiff and you—this is a very educational toy . . . It teaches children how to cuss!" [*PB:* 108]

11. For technological reasons in broadcasting in general, and radio broadcasting in particular, single-point transmission prevails; quite small sounds occurring at this point and very little of what occurs away from this point are transmitted. If a single meaningful stream of sound does not issue from this point, then the interaction fails in a way that the informal face-to-face variety cannot, in that the latter is unlikely to be so pinpoint dependent. (For example, a fellow conversationalist in a somewhat different microecological position can easily take over should a speaker be struck dumb.) One manifestation of this issue is the dead air problem: if no transmission occurs—that is, if the announcer or other source of meaningful sound is for any reason silent for more than a few seconds—then audiences are left hanging. They may be inclined to think that the station has ceased to

function, and in consequence turn to another; and other listeners, searching their dials, won't know that they have passed through a station.[43] Another expression of the single point problem is the high cost of extended overlaps at turn changes, and, especially, the high cost of interruptions. (In everyday conversational interaction, of course, simultaneous sounds coming from sources even slightly separated in space can be sorted to a degree binaurally to avoid confusion; multiple sound sources in radio can't be separated in this fashion except under special stereo conditions.) On the same grounds, "creature releases," such as burps, hiccups, sneezes, and coughs can be magnified, becoming something the announcer is likely to recognize as disruptively noticeable. (Thus the remedial practice of using a power potentiometer [the "pot"] to cut out [by "back-cueing"] disruptive sounds, such as coughing, page-turning, the slow first revolution of a record, the clicking of the mike key, and so forth, the resulting moment of silence being more manageable than the sound alternative.) So, too, if the announcer draws back from the microphone or turns his head slightly, the consequence in sound will be very great, to avoid which the announcer must maintain a fixity of posture while "on" that is rarely required in ordinary face-to-face interaction.

12. Just as the microphone generates a small zone in which any sound present gets broadcast, the recipient then being unable to pick and choose among the sounds, so the microphone's power source introduces the condition that when the power is known to be off, it can be confidently assumed that nothing in the vicinity will be transmitted. And, of course, it will always be possible for an announcer to err in his belief as to which state the micro-

43. In ordinary, informal face-to-face talk, the sudden stopping of a speaker's words *can* cause the listener bewilderment and even alarm, but the local scene is likely to provide the listener with a million cues as to why a sudden pause should be taken in stride—merely a reflection of the fact that a multitude of legitimate claims will impinge upon the person speaking in addition to the one obliging him to complete whatever utterance he is in the middle of. Many of the "good reasons" the speaker has for suddenly stopping will be visible to the listeners; other reasons, part of what the speaker alone has in mind at the moment, can be "externalized," as when a speaker in midspeech stops, *then* slaps his forehead, *then* says, "My God, I forgot to bring the letter." These visual presentations being available to the speaker, he can afford to suddenly stop; these sources not being available to the radio announcer, he can't.

phone is in, alive or dead, open or shut. Thinking that he is merely talking aloud to himself or to nearby station personnel or into the off-air, broadcaster to control-room hookup, he can find that the mike is open and that his words are being "carried." Similarly, he can think he is out of range of the microphone when he isn't. Broadcasting live from the site of some action, he may inadvertently pick up utterances from nearby participants that violate FCC standards. Here, simply on technological grounds, is a frontstage, backstage problem of awesome proportions:

> ["Uncle Don," after closing his children's program and wrongly assuming the microphone was off]: "I guess that will hold the little bastards." [*PB:* 18]

> After he [an announcer filling in on the "board" during a bad cold epidemic] cut off the mike switch and put on a musical recording, someone asked him how he felt. He said, "I feel like hell, and I'm full of Anacin." A few minutes later the phone rang, and a fan requested that he repeat that recording, "I Feel Like Hell, and I'm Full of Anacin." [*PB:* 23]

> "It's nice to see we have such a nice crowd here tonight. It's a great turnout; we've got some wonderful matches for you. Now the main event of the evening is gonna be two falls out of three. Chief Bender is going to wrestle with Sando Kovacs—promises to be real exciting. First let's get a word in from our sponsor." (OFF MIKE) "Hey, Mac! Where's the can?" [*SB:* 63]

> [Arlene Francis, doing a studio audience warmup on *What's My Line,* miscalculated her allotted warmup time and said]: "There are thirty seconds to go, if anyone has to." This advice was heard by millions of her listeners. [*PB:* 26]

Nor is the announcer alone in having to contend with this issue. Associated collaboratively with the radio announcer will be a circle of technical support figures who may be monitoring his words (directly or electronically) and watching his gestures, but who—so far as the audience is concerned—are ostensibly not present at all. Speaker's collusion with them is thus technically facilitated, if not required—as when a DJ announces records that are played by the studio engineer. And just as an announcer may find himself broadcasting when he least expects it, so may support personnel find that the words they thought were private, or restricted to a nonbroadcast ("talk-back") channel, are heard by all the station's listeners:

> "In Pall Malls, the smoke is traveled over and under, around and through the tobacco; thereby giving you a better tasting smoke . . ." (ENGINEER FLIPS WRONG SWITCH AND PICKS UP UNSUSPECTING DISC JOCKEY) ". . . How the hell can smoke go through a cigarette, if it don't go over, under, around and through the tobacco?" [*Pr.:*98]

> [As Frank McGee, NBC-TV commentator, announced a switch of cameras from one city to another, his director was heard through what should have been only McGee's earphone]: "Oh, yeah, the line isn't ready yet and you're stuck with a five-minute ad-lib job." [*Pr.:*57]

> [Singer on local high school amateur hour]: "For my old Kentucky home far away." [She hits high, off-key note, and announcer, believing he was off-mike, says]: "Oh God, who goosed the soprano?" [*SB:*60]

As suggested, when TV, not radio, is considered, the discrediting event can be visual, not aural, but no less an embarrassment to what has been said:

> Upon finishing a commercial for a nationally advertised beer, an announcer took a drink of this "wonderfully tasting beer," and a roving camera picked him up spitting his mouthful into a trash can. [*SB:*46]

13. Note, finally, the vulnerability of the announcer to technological faults that have nothing to do with a script or its sound presentation per se, but only with the efficacy of its nonhuman transmission. Power and equipment failures which entirely cut off an announcer's words tend not to be attributed to his own incompetency, whereas weakened or overlayed transmission can be. So, too, music records that get stuck, crudely reminding listeners that it is a record they are listening to, and providing them also with an accurate gauge as to how closely the announcer is attending his duties—the measure being how long the repetitions continue. (In fact, of course, it is often the studio engineer who is responsible here and whose attentiveness is actually being measured.) Cartridge ("carts") voice segments can also get stuck,

but here the embarrassment is less easily assigned to the mechanics of reproduction, for apparently we are more ready to keep in mind that radio music comes from records and tapes than that speech does.

One general point should be made in connection with the speech faults that have been reviewed here. Although the linguistically oriented literature devoted to what seems to be taken as "speech in general" is quite helpful, an analysis deriving from what are essentially ad hoc examples (or, even worse, traditional views of sentence grammar) cannot be expected to carry one very far. A significant amount of the speech trouble that announcers get into is to be traced to such matters as transmission technology, staff division of labor, format and editing practices, sponsorship, FCC regulations, and audience reach, and cannot be analyzed without reference to the ethnographic details of the announcer's work.

VII

Having considered some basic sources of speech faults in broadcasting, one could go on to consider the announcer's means of managing them. And this in a sense is what I propose to do. However, this task is very much complicated by the precarious nature of the concept of speech fault itself, regarding which some general strictures have already been reviewed. Before proceeding to the management of faults, then, I want to raise again the question of their nature, and document from radio talk the reasons already considered as to why the conventional view is too restrictive.

The mission of the professional announcer is to follow consistently a very narrow course. Whether engaged in fresh talk, memorization, or aloud reading he must be able to do so with very little stumbling or mumbling. Unexpected hitches, from whatever source, must be managed inaudibly. Unintended framings must be avoided. When there is a set text, the announcer must be able to stick to it quite fully and at the same time fit its delivery precisely into the time slot alloted to it. He is obliged to stay in role and not, through word or inflection, intentionally or inadvertently betray his tacit support for what he is saying in whoever's name he is saying it. Finally, he is obliged to provide meaningful sound no matter what happens, dead air and nonlexical eruptions being unacceptable. Observe, the maintenance of these standards does not require that no hitch in transmission occurs, only that such as do are not readily identifiable as his responsibility, and in the event of a hitch, that he provide a coherent account whilst sustaining his customary calm delivery.

When things are going well, that is, when performance obligations are being satisfied, the announcer is presumably projecting an image of himself as a competent professional, this being an image he can seemingly live with. A prearranged harmony will then exist among station, sponsor, audience, and the announcer's own self-image. And the work that the announcer is doing to carry off this "normal" competency will be hidden from us.

Now it appears that in lieu of a proper participation study of job socialization, one way to open up to view what the announcer is accomplishing when we think he is achieving nothing noteworthy is to examine the talk of radio performers whose ability is marginal. It is from them that one can most readily learn what it is that professional announcers have learned not to do and aren't doing. Incidentally, as will be seen, what one finds buried thus in the ontology of professional socialization will help us characterize ordinary informal talk.

And here again is a limitation of the social control model. Professional announcing, that is, network announcing that will strike the listener as unnoticeable as a thing in itself, allows announcers to commit themselves projectively to their profession. They can afford to project a self that would be embarrassed by a hitch in the proceedings because, indeed, they (and incidentally, the station's equipment and support staff) are unlikely to produce such a hitch. Given the prestige hierarchy of stations, it is apparent that an announcer who starts out on lesser stations by making mistakes or by being rambunctious will either leave this line of work or acquire "self-discipline," in this case the ways and habits necessary to produce professional broadcasting.

And yet whatever course a neophyte is destined to take, it will still be understandable that he currently holds the professional model at a distance and in emergencies try to save himself, not the program. For if a beginner's effort to maintain sober and faultless speech production is doomed to lead to a considerable number of failures, the effort in the first place may have to be undertaken self-defensively. Especially so in that even on its own, failure here is self-breeding. Once unnerved, the announcer is likely to err, which in turn may unnerve him more, which in turn leads to more error, this time as the center of attention. And once a remedy has been introduced, this remedy will be something that breaks the flow itself and may itself require remedy. Once started out in error, then, announcing can quickly unravel, and the announcer finds it costly—often apparently too costly—to present himself as taking the whole job seriously, or at least the part of it obliging him to speak faultlessly. On the other hand, once errors are consistently avoided, announcing quickly rolls itself up into tight production, for the announcer then can afford to play it straight. Thus, for the announcer, both failure and success have adaptive consequences as circular effects.

I admit now that not only unskilled or alienated announcers or those faced with transmission breakdowns provide us with material. There are also those announcers who are apparently concerned to "broaden" their role, bring "color" to their show, and come through as interesting, vital, unique persons—in brief, as "radio personalities." This they attempt to achieve by allowing more of what will be thought of as their integrity and individuality to show through, more, that is, than would show were they to adhere to the scripted forms. And, as already suggested, that announcers might be concerned to make their words compatible with their sense of who and what they are personally is to open up rather fully what it is that any one of them might consider a fault, that is, an utterance that allows for (if not warrants) some standing back from, some qualification, if not correction, on his part. In shows formatted to be "informal," such correction becomes a mainstay, for an announcer can take some sort of exception to almost any of his own statements if he is of a mind to do so. Indeed, a DJ who is shifting into becoming a stand-up comic and is guiding his show accordingly may define the standard information provided in spot announcements, recordings, weather reports, and time checks merely as an opportunity (and one he better seize) to elaborate and digress, to adumbrate in a manner approximating free association. His reputation and his market value will depend on his being able to qualify and extend required announcements—in effect, to correct them—with remarks that no one else would choose because no one else would have hit upon just these remarks as something whose corrective relevance could be shown.[44] Here something like a Freudian view begins to have appeal. If an announcer speaks a word or phrase that could easily have been misuttered, with consequent production of an embarrassing second reading, then he can assume that such an eventuality might be in his hearers' minds even in absence of the misuttering; and if not actually in their minds, then certainly recallable thereto. And so after successfully avoiding the slip, the announcer is in a position to make something out of what would have happened had he not. There being no real error to remedy, the announcer can address remarks to a latent one. In sum, having broadened analysis from faults to faultables and from faultables to the risibly interpretable, one must broaden analysis still a little more to include *remark-ables.*

It follows that no two announcers will be in total agreement as to what calls for correction and what doesn't. Thus, on the same station on successive airings of the same program, one announcer will say:

> This is John Nisbet, filling in for the vacationing Bob Ross.

and a second, with somewhat different sensibilities, that is, with a somewhat different image to sustain, will say:

44. Public service station DJs of classical music programs, alas, provide a good example here. On first taking on the program (which sometimes means when the station is first beginning *and* the DJ is first acquiring basic competencies), he will tend to stick to music, often long selections, with brief comments in between identifying performers, title, composer, and record company. As the DJ acquires more ease with his duties and more musical lore, however, he seems doomed to begin to extend the spoken bridge—culling from liner notes, proferring personal opinions, remarking on past local performances, and so forth—until eventually the program becomes a showcase for the display of his frame space, and only brief pieces of music can be aired or single movements from larger works. Listeners in search of music must then turn to stations that are less public spirited and ostensibly provide less service. In a word, classical music programs seem to have a natural history; they begin with music bridged with words and end with words bridged with music.

This is Mike Gordon, filling in for the vacationing Bob Ross—as we say in radioland.

Or, faced with the final item in the hourly news, an item often selected to provide a light, if not comic, note to end on, the second announcer will say:

And finally, in what news people call the kicker . . .

in this way again giving the impression that it is not only discriminating members of the audience who feel uneasy with media jargon.

What a particular announcer "lets go by," then, is not merely something he did not perceive as an error but listeners might, or something he observed to be an error but hopes listeners might not notice, or something obviously noticeable but too embarrassing to try to correct; rather he may let something go by simply because according to his own standards and interests nothing has occurred upon which to hang a qualifying comment. Yet what he sees as something to pass over without further thought, another announcer can hang his career upon. Moreover, the individual announcer and his personality need not be the fundamental unit here. Certainly a sense of characteristic practice is generated, and certainly in the close study of any one announcer's verbal production over time personal and habitual locutions can be uncovered; but variability is also uncovered. What an announcer lets go by one day or week, he may elect to distantiate himself from the next. The basic unit, then, is not the person but the set of stances available during any given moment. And although it may appear that the tack taken by an announcer is an expression of his personality, in fact one finds that the choice was necessarily made from a handful of established possibilities, and that what should impress is not the idiosyncrasy of the choice, but the conventionality and paucity of the options.

Return to the argument, then, that very often one can learn that a fault has occurred only after the announcer has displayed an effort to draw attention through comment to it, and that in many cases nothing "objective" exists in what has occurred to account for its ultimate treatment as something to remedy.

The argument must be qualified. Just as some announcers

will find grounds (or rather opportunity) for correction and adumbration where no such reworking of the prior utterance could be anticipated, so it is plain that some words and phrases receiving remedial treatment were glaringly obvious candidates for it by virtue of broadly based cultural understandings. Some slips produce an alternative reading that is so widely evident in our society, and some assertions are so contrary to the way we know the world to be, that these acts provide reasonable grounds for saying that a "fault" is objectively present. Even had the speaker been unaware of the risible or erroneous implications of what he had said, large numbers of listeners could still be depended on to be more observant, and, being observant, to observe the same thing:

> Weather forecast: "Of the 29 days in February, 126 were clear." [*PB:* 97]
>
> Newscaster: "Word has just reached us from London, that England's Queen Elizabeth has given birth to a baby boy. The infant son weighs seven pounds, fifteen inches!" [*Pr.:* 5]
>
> Commercial: "So, dad, it's time for that new dinette set for your ever-growing family . . . and at Travers for only $99.00 you can now buy a seven-piece set consisting of six tables and a large-sized chair!!!" [*Pr.:* 7]
>
> Newscaster: "The only way the man could be identified was by the fact that he was standing in the road alongside his stalled automobile with a cool tit in his hand." [*SB:* 41]
>
> "This is a final warning! Failure to report to your alien officer may result in your deportation or prostitution!" [*PB:* 68]
>
> "It's 9:00 P.M. B-U-L-O-V-A. Bulova Watch Time. This Christmas, buy the new Bulova President: curved to fit the foot!" [*PB:* 93]

Indeed, in these cases were both the speaker and his hearers to have noticed nothing out of line, there would still be good grounds for saying that they had all "overlooked" a fault that was "really" present. After all, a great many other members of their speech community—both announcers and station listeners—would certainly feel that something had gone wrong. Further, speaker and hearers would themselves be subject to being told later what they had "missed," and could then be counted on to "realize" that they had missed something, and what it was they had missed. Even in the case of errors that whole populations within a language community would miss (as when most Britons and some Americans would fail to appreciate that "futility outfielder" is "obviously" an all-too-true version of "utility outfielder"), there would still be the possibility that they could readily be shown why other sectors of the community would hear an "obvious" slip.[45]

And so too with the question of not being able to tell always whether an announcer is genuinely unaware of the error he has committed or has merely given the appearance that this is the case in order to avoid drawing more attention to his unfortunate lapse. This is a genuine question, sometimes, answerable, incidentally, by listening in on what the announcer says to his support personnel as soon as he is off the air. But the question itself presupposes (and I think with warrant) that within a broadly based speech community *certain* verbal constructions would inevitably be judged to be faults.

Here the question of perspective must be addressed. I believe it is perfectly sound to distinguish between faults in speaking and faults in hearing, and that lots of "objective" faults can be found that are clearly one or the other, not either or both. And that like the student, speaker and hearer know these possibilities exist. When one focuses on only one of the two sources of trouble (in this case, on speaker faults), one can still attempt an inclusive approach that tacitly treats such faults from both speaker's and hearer's point of view. Doing so, however, one should be clear that the bearing of one point of view on the other—the "interaction" between the two—is a problem in its own right.

Thus one can say that in the face of an utterance that makes no sense or only improper sense, a hearer may correctly attribute the cause to his own mishearing or to speaker's misstating, or incorrectly do so, where "correctly" and "incorrectly" derive

45. Something of the same line of argument can be made about the "objective" character of some slips of the ear, and about the possibility, in principle, of distinguishing speech production faults from hearing produced faults, in spite of some obvious complications. Here, see Garnes and Bond (1975).

from the encompassing perspective of the analyst, not the hearer.

The hearer, of course, may sometimes find himself quite unable to decide whether it is he or the speaker who is at fault. Here an encompassing view can lead one to say that hearer may be deficient in this connection, for on various grounds it is sometimes possible to show that responsibility can be "correctly" attributed in such cases. But in other settings it can be shown that the hearer's doubt has better warrant, for some troubles, it appears, are objectively indivisible. Thus, if hearer turns away at the moment speaker drops his voice, a mishearing can be *jointly* accomplished. Whether speakers and hearers appreciate that in principle such joint responsibility is possible, is, however, another matter, and a social fact in its own right. As is the possibility that on particular occasions, the hearer may perceive himself or the speaker to be solely at fault, when in fact joint responsibility is at work.

Announcing provides useful illustrations of these perspectival issues. As already considered at length, listeners eagerly search for alternate readings they know weren't intended. The announcer knows this, attempts to guard against it, and treats such interpretive opportunities as he fails to block as faults on his part. And this is the interpretation (however labored) required for the unintended meaning. Presuming that he has tried to block such framings, listeners can jump on any that occur and snicker at his failure—a failure they see from his point of view—even though in fact he may never discover that they have caught him out on this occasion. But of course, the possibility of being put down in this way is built back into the announcer's general conduct, a stimulus to his routine precautions. So each of the two parties takes the other's point of view and each—in a way—takes it that this is taken.

A somewhat different possibility is presented in regard to full-fledged misunderstandings, that is, hearings that fail to grasp what the speaker had intended. Knowing that listeners are prone to err by deleting word boundaries, an announcer may make a special effort to check his copy for such junctures, and speak very carefully when he broadcasts these passages. He incorporates an anticipation of audience tendencies. Failing in this, their error becomes his fault. Again there is a collapsing of the two points of view, but here the speaker is doing the collapsing, not the listener.

All in all, then, the point of view of speaker and hearer must be kept separate, but each point of view involves close, although perhaps different, commitment to the other's point of view. Divided by an obvious barrier, announcer and listener are yet intimately joined, the announcer to the situation of the listener, and vice versa. All of which an encompassing view must find a place for. Incidentally, it is this interpenetration of points of view which provides one reason (but not the only reason) why a single individual (such as Kermit Schafer) can collect apparent troubles with some confidence that other hearers *and* announcers will agree that something had gone wrong.

A final point. When an announcer makes an all too obvious slip of the kind considered here, the chronicler and the student, like the members of the audience, apparently feel no need to explain in detail what feature of the world is violated by the slip, the assumption being that the matter is self-evident and can be taken for granted. And by and large it can be. Admittedly it would be worthwhile to try to formulate the underlying presuppositions that inform wide arrays of "evident" errors, especially insofar as these understandings are of a generalized character and not themselves made explicit by those who employ them. But that, surely, would be a separate study whose findings could in no way deny that certain errors were widely perceivable, and perceived as "obvious." (Which is not to deny that a cultural group will have its own beliefs about the workings of the world, and thus its own relativistic bases for "obvious, objective" error.)

The required reorientation is now evident. Although many faults stand out in a very obvious way—clearly a fault to nearly everyone in the speech community—other faults are very much a question of discretion, namely, what the announcer himself wants to disaffiliate himself from. Differently put, because it turns out that when an obvious fault is committed, one apparent consequence for, if not intent of, the announcer is to distance himself from the event—from the image of incompetence it might imply—one can take this disaffiliation as the key matter and go on to address anything the speaker attempts to dissociate himself from, including, but only incidentally, errors in the obvious sense. An utterance, like any other personal act, projects an image of the actor; and actors, act by act, endeavor to maintain a personally acceptable relation to what they may be taken to be exhibiting about themselves. And given the circumstances of the action, the personally acceptable can be extended upward to the personally desired, or downward to the personally least unacceptable.

As suggested, instances of this remedial behavior usually will not come from fully professional, network announcers of news and commercials (especially not from those who are happy with their role), but rather from those who have frequent cause for remedial action: incompetent announcers, alienated announcers, and announcers on special interest stations. Along with these there is reason to include those who have (or are trying to acquire) an M.C. role on an informal "personal" show. It is the conduct of these performers that will be our guide.

VIII

I turn now to an examination of the practices announcers employ to manage faults that have not been avoided and, not having been avoided, are treated by them as something to openly address. But on analytical grounds, this concern now resolves into a larger one: namely, what announcers do to project a self different from the one they have apparently just projected, whether projected through their own speech faults, their own official text, or the comments, prerecorded or live, of anyone else whose contribution to what gets broadcast they might be partly identified with. Differently put, I will now examine announcers' frame space, apart, that is, from the standard alignments allotted to them. What we will thus consider, incidentally, is what professional announcers in the main have learned never to need. "Role distance" is involved or, more accurately, "event distance."

1. AD HOC ELABORATION. While aloud-reading a text, the announcer may briefly assume the authorial function and extend his copy, drawing on what is to be taken as his own fund

of knowledge or personal experience, amplifying, specifying, and so forth. Transition into and out of this parenthetical elaboration (and the consequent switching between aloud reading and fresh talk) will commonly be marked by a change in voice and tempo. A similar license can be taken when the main text is itself in fresh talk, the asides departing from what would ordinarily be the routinely required development. Note, whether it is a fully scripted text or a planned fresh talk that he extends, the announcer need not openly betray the spirit of the anticipated presentation, that is, the line it was intended to develop. But however much his ad libs are in keeping with his official theme, they suggest, if only faintly and fleetingly, that he is not completely bound by his duties, and that his standard voice is not his only one.

Personal elaboration can occur through minor (and formulaic) parenthetical insertions within an utterance:

> The time in our fair city is . . .
>
> . . . directed by a man with the unlikely name of Victor Ewell . . .
>
> . . . no less than Frederick the Great . . .
>
> . . . now unfortunately out of the catalogue . . .
>
> . . . that really wonderful music by . . .
>
> . . . directed, of course, by Neville Mariner . . .

or as a tag at the end of a segment of the expected text:

> . . . well, actually it opened last night.
>
> [After reading the closing human interest note in the news]: Sort of does your heart good, doesn't it?
>
> I might mention in passing something about the piano Glenn Gould uses.
>
> . . . 5 percent chance of rain. [Dryly] So leave your umbrella in its stand. You do have an umbrella stand, don't you? No home should be without one.

Observe again that the significance of such elaborations will vary greatly depending on initial tacit assumptions concerning the rightful place in the talk of the personal resources of the speaker. In much everyday talk, of course, participants seem to be accorded the right to dip into their fund of knowledge and experience at will, providing only that canons of tact and relevance be sustained, and these sometimes minimally. An academic lecturer, speaking from notes, develops a text that can fully intermingle elaborative parenthetical comments with thematic development. In contrast, in court proceedings, counsel's questioning (especially "cross-questioning") can be held to a rule of strict relevance; what the judge chooses to consider irrelevant, he can openly characterize as such.

Broadcasts themselves display a wide range of definitions regarding extraneous, unscripted, "personal" elaboration. In those talk shows and interview programs in which the M.C. is concerned to develop an attractive "air personality" and is allowed to use a format that is not "tight," parenthetical extensions of any current thematic line may be perfectly standard, and well within both the rights and competence of the speaker. Popular DJs may feel that free association is the mainstay of their reputation, and are much motivated to dredge up incidental comments about almost everything they are obliged to talk about. (Probably they could not become "popular" without doing so.) In national hourly news broadcasts, a closely timed text is likely to be adhered to, and the reading rate tends to be high, with silences considerably compressed. Here the speaker, however professional, may be unable (and in a sense unwilling) to shift smoothly to fresh talk when necessary—say, to cover the failure of a remote commentary to come in. On such occasions the announcer can be expected to stumble a little, inadvertently change tone, slow up the tempo, and speak his ad-libbed filler with less than usual conviction.

2. METACOMMUNICATING. I refer to the ways in which the announcer may—whilst retaining the two-party character of direct announcing—change footing at points not scheduled for this, shifting from speaking in a collective "station editorial" voice to one in which he speaks more specifically for himself, and himself in his capacity as animator of the text he is delivering.

a. Central here is the shift in footing necessarily involved when a strident correction is employed, the stress projecting the image of a speaker struggling to get his words right. The image that was supposed to be projected, namely, a self that merges with the voice of the station, is undermined:

> . . . at Temple Cit . . . Temple University Center City Cinema . . .

> Station Break: "Stay tuned for WOODY'S PECKER SHOW . . . WOODY'S WOODPECKER SHOW!" [*Pr.:* 33]

Apology tags employing "I" in their construction, which sometimes follow such corrections, make the change in footing explicit, for here the personal pronoun underscores the fact that the plea is being presented solely in the speaker's own name.

b. Consider now some variants of the "pronunciation frame." For example, the "phonetic trial" approach. Instead of treating a word (or phrase) in the usual way—as an unthinkingly available resource to say something with—the speaker seriously reframes the bit of text as something to try to pronounce, much as a child might for whom trying pronunciation was an appropriate developmental task. The speaker picks his way through the word's pronunciation, often with the help of some sort of letter-by-letter, syllable-by-syllable articulation, and often giving a sense of self-oriented, self-directed rehearsal or experimentation:

> . . . played by (slowing up) Ań át́ ólé Fisá oó lárié.

> . . . and as pianist Lydia Pé trá skí yah́ . . .

Sometimes the rising intonation of a question is employed, as if the announcer were openly underscoring that the "correct" pronunciation is unknown, the one employed being offered merely as a possibility—a possibility that seems to await what can't be delivered, namely, confirmation or correction by the hearer. These gambits, note, shift the attention of hearers from the sense of what is being said to production contingencies involved in saying it, a metalinguistic shift from the semantic reference of an utterance to the mechanics of its animation.

Note, too, that the question of ritualization is involved—in a somewhat ethological sense. Although for any speaker the prosodic features of these utterances may originally have been simply a by-product of having to piece out the course of the pronunciation syllable by syllable, no doubt the sound pattern becomes a format in its own right, something a speaker can employ when for a whole range of reasons his intent is to reduce tacit claims to his knowing what he is doing.

c. In the same way that an announcer can direct attention to the requirements of pronunciation, he can change footing and display the pleasure he takes in the word's sound when he himself seems not to have a problem with pronunciation. Again, the pronunciation frame, and the implicating of the animating process as a subject matter in its own right:

> . . . playing the hurdy-gurdy. Delightful sound. Hurdy-gurdist, if that's what you call him.

> That was Benjamin Britten's Simple Symphony. Try saying that fast—Simple Sympathy . . .

> Similarly. Sim/a/l/ar/ly [as if savoring the sound of the correct pronunciation] . . .

And as suggested, in the face of foreign words, an articulation flourish may be employed, an overrounded, slightly unserious venturing of native pronunciation, sometimes followed by an accounting:

> Ber nar do pas qui na. I love to pronounce those Italian names.

As with "phonetic trials" a switch is here involved from use to mention.[46]

d. When an announcer reads a text other than one prepared by himself or his coworkers, he is likely to provide a clarifying and identifying "connective," tying what is being said to the party originally saying it, as in the phrase, "according to an AP release." In brief, a certain scrupulosity is observed in the matter

46. Mock uneducated hyper-Anglicization is another example of the pronunciation frame. But although its use is not uncommon in face-to-face talk (sometimes, of course, as a strategic cover for felt ignorance of both the native and standard Anglicization forms), no instance appears in my radio sample. There is one example of a translation played straight, but then followed up by a guyed apology that is probably more stereotyped in its unserious ironic form than in the literal: "Well, here's his *Waltzes Noble* and *Sentimental*—pardon my French."

of tacit claims to authorship. Sometimes a connective may have to be parenthetically introduced when the text is meant to be heard as a quoted one and contains anaphorical expressions which might not otherwise be properly interpreted. (For example, when the liner notes on a record jacket cite Mahler's wife's biographical comment on Strauss's behavior after the premier of the Sixth, and uses "we" to refer to the persons backstage at the time, the announcer must make sure that hearers won't take *him* to be saying that he was among those present.) During the reading of such a quoted text, or when a long, cited passage might possibly cause listeners to forget initial authorship disclaimers, a "reconnective" may be parenthetically injected, as in, ". . . caused the explosion, Chief Wilson goes on to say." The point here is that by injecting unscripted connectives and reconnectives, an announcer may show extra circumspection, taking added care not to be attributed with the knowledge and experience implied in what is about to be, or just has been, heard. As though the requirements of modesty forced the announcer to break the illusion of his discourse at an unexpected point—a Brechtian technique.

Interestingly, announcers are sometimes faced with a text whose reading might give the impression that they themselves have introduced stylistic license. In such cases they need an equivalent to *sic,* the sign a writer can use following a quoted word or phrase to indicate that the apparent imperfection belongs to the original text, not to its transcription. Here the announcer can discreetly employ an interjected connective:

> . . . while speaking at the podium Judge Sirica just keeled over, UP states, and was taken to the hospital suffering a massive heart attack.

Scrupulosity, and the slight change in footing its maintenance can require, may involve more than the insertion of a connective. The reading of excerpts from liner notes of a recording is a standard way in which DJs generate something relevant and informative to say. And presumably because such citations can easily pass as an expression of the announcer's own knowledgeability, some speakers are careful to introduce authorial disclaimers:

I have Paul Cleb, who wrote the liner note for this particular recording, to thank for that.

[Regarding Schubert's age when he wrote his posthumous trio]: It's very easy to sound erudite, but I learned this from the liner notes.

We are grateful to a Mr. Bent for a brief life of Chausson. In the liner notes he says . . .

D'Indy is said to have said . . .

This sort of nicety can be carried to the point where backstage secrets of the broadcast are revealed—all presumably in the interests of avoiding pretense. For example, in reporting the weather forecast, an announcer can gratuitously inform on how the station receives the forecast:

. . . according to the National Weather Bureau [change in voice] and Ma Bell . . .

while incidentally employing an ironic tone throughout to convey his personal belief that there is reason to be a little skeptical of the reliability of the prediction.

In ordinary conversation the unqualified expression of an intention or belief can readily be interpreted in self-aggrandizing terms—an act that is immodest, intractable, demanding, presumptuous—and further, can restrict the maneuverability of listeners who might disagree, leaving them no easy way to present a contrary view. A very standard strategy, then, is the perfunctory hedge that hopefully mitigates some aspect of avowing, these forms being almost as common in broadcast talk as in the everyday kind. As already suggested, however retiring a maker of such comments is, he nevertheless must draw attention to the production format of his statement—that is, to himself in his personal capacity as animator, author, and principal—and this in its own right constitutes an intrusion of self. Thus, a broadcaster's hedges may question his own belief or competency (and thereby, of course, reduce the potential discrediting of a mistake):

. . . piece played, if I'm not mistaken, by . . .

. . . Burgemeister, if I pronounced that correctly.

. . . that tune was a hit around 1965, 67—I think.

or the right to inject a personal opinion:

> If you ask me . . .
>
> If I may say . . .
>
> If I may express an opinion . . .
>
> And I must say, Bob Ross really outdid himself in that one.

or the implication that anyone other than himself might hold with the personal opinion he has interjected:

> . . . played the harpsichord with a very subtle touch, it seems to me.
>
> . . . what is for me my favorite Bruckner symphony, for what that's worth.
>
> [After saying you can learn a lot about a period from its history]: That's sort of an armchair musicologist's note. I don't know. At twenty-five after seven I guess . . .

But, of course, the cost of these modest disclaimers is the addition of yet another extraneous utterance, another utterance in which the announcer vents a personal view—even though this second departure can provide something of a bridge back to format duties.

There are other sources of broadcaster hedge. The announcer may feel that standard industry phrases for covering standard items may commit him to pretentions he is uneasy with, so he will ad lib some self-disclaiming, dis-identifying comment:

> . . . the probability of precipitation—or the chance of rain, as we say in the street . . .
>
> . . . and the glass, as they say, is rising . . .
>
> And the barometric pressure—for those of you who are fans of barometric pressure—is . . .

Even the title of a composition can provide warrant for an ironic remark:

> And we're going to continue now with a composition by Roger Sessions written in 1935 called Concerto for Violin—pretty basic simple title there—with Paul Zukofsky performing on violin.

A similar self-dissociation can occur when available materials, such as liner notes, lead the announcer to convey obscure, technical, or learned facts, recital of which might be taken to imply pedantry, traditionalism, pomposity, and so forth:

> . . . born in 1757—for those who care.
>
> . . . Brandenburg Concerto no. 1 in F, BVW 1046, if you're interested.
>
> I know you want to know John Stanley's dates. They are . . .
>
> . . . Wolfgang Amadeus Mozart [lightly], to give you his full name.

One has here what is sometimes called self-consciousness—an individual's readiness to turn on his own acts to question their propriety, originality, sincerity, modesty, and so forth. This self-consciousness, as already suggested, is also found on occasions when an announcer discovers that his own extemporaneous formulations have led him to employ what might be heard as a stereotyped phrase, these being the circumstances in which he may respond to his own words with an ironic phrase of self-dissociation:

> . . . without further ado, as they say . . .
>
> . . . who could ask for anything more—to coin a phrase . . .
>
> Time marches on, inexorably, if you will—if you can handle that kind of language this early in the morning.

A repertoire of ironic, self-dissociating phrases not only allows an announcer to counteract self-projections he feels might be questionable, but also frees him from finding unobjectionable phrasings in the first place. A remedy being available, the fault that calls it forth can be indulged without danger. And on occasion it appears that a self-alien word or phrase may be introduced just so colorful disclaimers can be brought into play. Indeed, mock, unserious immodesties can be employed, the assumption apparently being that because these acts are not seriously assayed, their doer must certainly know how to conduct himself modestly. So to cut a modest figure, modesty itself is hardly a qualification, being something that its possessor might not frequently be in a position to demonstrate the possession of; in any case, such demonstrations would remove him from the center of attention where evidence of character can be efficiently conveyed.

e. The parenthetical remarks that have been considered so far follow rather closely upon the faultable for which they are meant to provide a remedy. Disclaimers can, however, reach back further for their reference, providing the speaker with a special basis for intruding himself as animator into the discourse. To open up the matter, consider the question of "textual constraints."

Whether starting with a word, phrase, clause, or sentence, and whether the unit is written or spoken, one can move from there to some larger segment of discourse of which the instance unit is but one part. Attempts can be made to try to uncover the constraints and license that apply to the instance unit by virtue of its being part of a larger whole.

One issue, presumably, is that of topical coherence, namely, the requirement that a theme, once established, be adhered to throughout a segment of discourse; thus, "digression," and the obligation to curtail it. Another issue is repetition. For example, no matter how long a book is, the writer is obliged to be concerned about the repetition of ideas (except by way of summary), and about using the same expressive phrase "too often," the same descriptor in close sequence, and any particular illustration more than once. So, too, in the case of news columns, the initial mention of a subject tends to spell out his full name and place him socially, whereas each succeeding mention will employ more abbreviated forms, with some stylistic obligation to use different ones.

An interesting point about these textual constraints is, apparently, how readily repair of their breach can be attempted by means of some sort of remark; for example, the ubiquitous, "As already suggested" and "To repeat an earlier argument." So, too, digression excuses: "Not to change the subject, but. . . ." An explanation, I think, is that many of these constraints seem to be aimed at showing that the writer (or speaker) is alive to, and mindful of, the whole course of his communication. Consequently, his showing that he is aware of his lapses even as he commits them is to employ an alternative means of demonstrating that he is awake to his communication obligations. Repetition constraints also seem to be designed to sustain the notion that something fresh and unique is occurring with each word and phrase; here, however, excuses and apologies for too quickly repeating an expression can only provide a partial remedy.

Textual constraints have a special bearing on broadcast talk, for in the ordinary course of affairs there seems to be very little "segmental depth" to the announcer's obligations. It is almost as if he assumes his audience is constantly changing, and therefore that anything he says one moment need not constrain (or, contrariwise, provide much anaphoric background for) what is to follow. (Thus, new listeners are not likely to feel for very long that they are out of touch with what is going on; after no more than a sentence or two, they are likely to be able to follow fully what the announcer is talking about.) Nonetheless, some constraints do apply, especially on shows that run for an hour or more. When these constraints are breached, remedies require the announcer to step out of role momentarily and address his own text in his capacity as the formulator of it. Thus, coherence excuses:

> . . . what those three facts [culled from liner notes] have in common, I don't know, but there you are.

And, of course, repetition excuses:

> That was the ubiquitous J. P. Rampal—if we may use that expression twice in one morning.

> . . . that incredible—and I use that word again . . .

> . . . delightful, if I may be permitted to use that word again.

Interestingly enough, announcers may make a back-reaching reference that implies more listener continuity than might be considered conventional, and by this very breach, mark what they say as an unserious, self-referential break in frame, drawing attention to the discourse as discourse:

> We will continue with some . . . pre-nineteenth-century music—for want of a better name. [Then, after the recording in question]: We have been listening to "pre"-nineteenth-century music [this time the neologism being uttered unseriously, presupposing the prior accounting].

[After playing Milhaud's four-piano sonata, the announcer goes on to say with an ironic touch]: Now a piece for only two pianos.

And indeed, because announcers must routinely repeat some of the same information before and after a record, or periodically repeat the same advertisement or public service notice, they are in a position to "play" their own speech errors, repeating a difficulty, but this time in quotes, as it were—presupposing that the listener will appreciate that the announcer is not making a mistake but mimicking a mistake already made. And once again, the process of animation itself becomes an object of reference, not merely the vehicle for reference:[47]

. . . an eight-minute walk from the Haverford station, not an eight-mile walk, as I believe I said yesterday [laugh].

f. Consider "counterdisplays." Immediately following an erroneous statement, doubtful pronunciation, or misconstructed word, an announcer may do more than merely respond with a flat correction (or even a strident one) and a perfunctory apology. At whatever cost to timing and prescribed text, he can break his pace and, in an openly self-admissive tone, unhurriedly introduce a rather extensive redoing of the faulted passage, the repair work requiring a clause or sentence. The new addition often includes a self-reference and, much to the point, is executed with fluency and control, a display of aplomb presumably supplying immediate evidence that the announcer is now (and characteristically) in control of himself and his situation, admittedly guilty but yet unabashed. The old animator is cast off, as it were, carried right into the talk by "I," leaving a new animator in full charge of matters—the one able to fluently intone the correction. In any case, the attention of listeners is turned for a moment from the text to a consideration of the individual animating the text.

Counterdisplays can be achieved merely by executing in a

47. This raises the issue of the "topical life" of a fault: when a speech fault occurs, and after appropriate notice is given it by the speaker, at what point in remove will he find it inappropriate to make a joking reference to his difficulty, and how many such references can the original contretemps bear? Note, this is a different life from the more significant one distinguished by Schegloff et al., where the issue is how many turns from the turn in trouble can speaker or hearer allow before remedy is referentially ambiguous and therefore inappropriate.

well-enunciated, well-rounded manner what might otherwise be a correction and a perfunctory apology:

> . . . a three-record set. I *beg* your pardon. A two-record set.

> Sportscaster: "The proceeds of the Annual All-Star Game goes to indignant players—I beg your pardon, that is indigent ballplayers." [*PB:* 82]

Formulaic phrases may also be involved as part of the controlling action:

> Did I say Tuesday? It's Wednesday I mean, of course.

> . . . at 31 . . . make that 3200 East Charleston . . .

> . . . low to mid-thirties. Did I say low to mid-thirties? I meant low to mid-fifties. Not in the low thirties, for heaven's sake . . . and at night . . . that's when it'll be in the low thirties.

> The time is sixteen minutes, make that fourteen minutes to twelve.

> Short-līved or short-lived, if you prefer.

> . . . not rubber workers but rather auto workers, I should say.

> Seventy-two degrees Celsius. I beg your pardon. Seventeen degrees Celsius. Seventy-two would be a little warm.

And, of course, a quip can be essayed, the aptness of the remark functioning to demonstrate how fully the speaker can bring his mind into gear in spite of his apparent confusion:

> . . . if I can get my tongue straightened out.

> Excuse me . . . get the frog out of my throat.

> . . . Gilbert . . . let me try that again. Wait till I get my false teeth in here again.

> My tongue is not cooperating this morning.

> One of the listeners said I said January instead of February. Oh, it's going to be one of those days.

Observe, irony can be injected into a counterdisplay by the pat metalinguistic device of referring to self in third person, this reflexive frame break presumably further distancing the current animator from the one under criticism:[48]

> . . . well deserves your enjoyable listening to, he says in a not very well-expressed way.

> . . . and now, he says as he catches his breath . . .

Counterdisplays—like other correction strategies—involve a special risk, namely, that having openly directed the full attention of the audience to the correction, a counterdisplay may itself contain a garbled version of what was meant to have been the correct version. But here there is the further embarrassment of projecting a pointed claim to self-control which discredits itself, and under concertedly audible conditions:

> "Place the sports and foons on the . . ." "I mean the sporks and sphoons . . . !" "Of course I mean the porks and soons." [*PB:* 50]

> Announcer: "And now, Van Cliburn playing Tchaikovsky's Piano Concerto Number One in Blee Fat Minor . . . I beg your pardon, that should be Fee Blat Minor!!!" [*Pr.:* 36]

g. Perfunctory apologies and excuses always seem to have a self-reference, explicit or elided, and can thus be taken as providing a brief report by the speaker on his state of mind and his feelings. So, too, the little flourishes contained in counterdisplay reports on the speaker's intentions, proper purpose, and actions. Now consider self-reporting as a practice in its own right.

One way an announcer can face a production hitch *and* comply with the norm that there should be no dead time, is to constitute his own situation—his actions, obligations, predicament, feelings, opinions—as the subject matter to describe, this being a source of copy always at hand. After all, as a source of emergency fill, the individual animating is in a special relationship to himself. If he is willing to change footing and introduce references to his own circumstances at the moment, then he need never be at a loss for something to say; for inevitably on occasion

48. The device can also be used by an announcer to deal with questionable comment insertions: ". . . he added, parenthetically."

of unexpected crisis, he will be experiencing something, if only shock. (Perhaps one exception should be made, namely, that although in face-to-face life we sometimes elect to report that we are bored or have nothing to talk about, such an admission might hardly serve as something to mention in broadcast talk.)

Some hitches responded to by self-reports can clearly be attributed to agencies beyond the announcer himself:

> This has taken me rather by surprise, but I want to say that the sound should certainly be soon restored.

> I don't like to make such announcements, but there you are.

Further, the announcer can report on his efforts to set matters right, even while he executes them:

> However, we don't seem to be getting through. Can you tell me the situation, Chuck? Will we get through? No? Well, then, let's turn instead to . . .

The price, of course, is that the speaker must thrust himself into the content of the program as part of its subject matter, adding to what may already be a deviation from expected text. It should be noted that biographical self-reports delivered in response to an emergency can themselves be delivered calmly and fluently, showing that the speaker is in command of at least one part of himself—whatever has happened to the rest of the world.

Self-reports can also be used in reference to a hitch that the announcer can only questionably treat as beyond his responsibility; indeed, the self-report can be a means of establishing reduced responsibility:

> For more information—no I don't have a number for that.

> It doesn't say exactly when these classes will start.

> I can't quite make it out, but I think the name of the pianist is . . .

> For more information about this festival . . . and there is no address; it doesn't even tell you where it takes place. But this is the festival . . .

Of special interest are those hitches in continuous broadcast flow that are apparently clearly traceable to the behavior of the announcer himself. Here, too, as in less blameworthy confusions, he may introduce a running report of his own remedial actions and his own predicament as someone trying to assemble a proper production, including references to the mechanics of show production, these being backstage matters ordinarily concealed from listeners. The minimal case here is the standard "filled pause," whereby the speaker, momentarily unable or unwilling to produce the required word or phrase, gives audible evidence that he is engaged in speech-productive labor.[49] Although the sound involved doesn't appear in itself to suggest much organization, it seems at least to convey that the speaker is still at the microphone addressing himself to the subject matter at hand, that transmission and reception are still in working order, and that words will soon return to the air.[50] But, of course, this minimal effort is not

49. In everyday conversation, filled pauses occur when the speaker needs time to think through an issue, or to find words to encode a thought already arrived at, or to choose from an array of encodings already brought to mind; and so also when his intent is to insure that listeners obtain the impression, warranted or not, that any of the above is the case (see James 1978). Thus a speaker can use a filled pause to convey that he himself is having no trouble with a thought or its direct encoding, but rather must give attention to finding a phrase that exactly matches his recipients socially—given their assumed knowledge of the subject at hand, their right to full disclosure, their relationship to him, and so forth. Filled pauses, of course, also function "to perceptually segment the speech stream for the listener and/or to allow the listener time for processing the speech at such points" (Beattie 1979:64), to mark a "turn transition relevant" place, and, contrariwise (as suggested), to hold the floor after finishing a point when wanting to continue on with a different one.

50. Although it might seem that announcers who have recourse to filled pauses as a means of holding the floor (or, rather, the air) are not overly conscious of what they are doing, the practice can, of course, be guyed. For example, there is a West Coast announcer, well loved by many of her station's subscribers, who uses a long string of nonsense syllables where an unobtrusive filled pause would otherwise be. She uses a similar string of sounds to exaggerate the mess created when a word is garbled:

> Yesterday, noted criminal lawyer ah F. Lee Bailey who had joined Miss Hearst, de Miss Hearst, defec defibbabab. Let me try it again. Take it from the top. Yesterday, noted criminal lawyer F. Lee Bailey . . .

> The crimes include a series of roba bab a booble—a series of bombings in San Francisco.

> An article in Pravda which is described by a-authorities in Moscow who work for Reuters as a comment from the very highest level of Soviet foreign . . . policy . . . or something like that . . . baoobaalaboodal . . . In Angola . . .

all that is found. Well-articulated verbal statements are not uncommon:

> I've lost my place, I'll have it for you in a moment.
>
> The U.S. government is urging American, British, and Canadian residents to leave Angola because the fighting is going to spread. The . . . very briefly . . . Oi boy it's after nine o'clock . . . in the Middle East there's been another message sent from Israel through the United States . . .
>
> PUBLIC SERVICE ANNOUNCEMENT: "So be sure to think of our less fortunate friends overseas. They will appreciate anything that you can give. A few cents a day will feed a Korean elephant, so send your money to Care, care of your local postoffice—Did I say elephant? I don't know where I got that. I mean orphan." [*SB:* 99]
>
> Now what else can I tell you . . . Oh yes. I will give you I will tell you that . . . lots of folks have subscribed today.
>
> I was going to say it was a nice name before I tripped over a syllable.
>
> . . . first since 19 . . . since 1757. I almost said 1957. Of the Masque by . . .
>
> Let me look at this for a moment.
>
> A ride is offered on October 2nd. Let's see when is that, it's oh, next week sometime, it's Thursday.
>
> This is by . . . let me see if I can get the right section here.
>
> I would like to refrain from announcing the name of the songs in that they are German and I can't pronounce German very well.
>
> . . . although Saudi Arabia opposes it. This according to the Iraqi oil minister after the opening session [sound of paper rattling] and rattling all this paper here [more rattling, this time as a demonstration of rattling].
>
> Stay tuned for Aeolia where they will be reading—if you wait a moment I'll be able to tell you . . . here it is . . .
>
> I just got lost in the liner notes.

Next. Someone is trying to tickle me here. We'll have the . . .

Well, let's see. Okay, that's about it.

. . . in . . . let me see here, in 1932 . . . the number is . . . here we are . . . it's . . .

Let me see who the performer was.

Disc Jockey: "Before I bring you the hurt record by trumpeter Al Hit, 'The Girl from Ipana' . . . here's a word about Ipanema toothpaste . . . wait a minute, I got that all fouled up . . . that should be Al Hirt and 'The Girl from Ipanema'!!!" [*Pr.:* 128]

Okay—we've seen all that before *(sotto voce)* ahh here is another news story which I should . . . around here in this great mess of papers here and I don't know what to . . . I know there's something here—I ought to remember to staple them next time. Well, would I be offending anyone if I said, well, that's the news for now.

It looks like—seem to have run out. I know there was something else I was going to read on. Pardon the shuffling of papers. Okay. The forty-nation Islamic conference . . .

Franklin P. Zimmerman, musical director . . . Oh yeah, here we go. On the final concert on the steps of the art museum . . .

Local News: "And the farmers of Boynton County have banded together to form a protective chicken-stealing association . . . (PAUSE) . . . that sounds like they are doing the stealing . . . of course, you know that is not what I mean!" [*Pr.:* 43]

Self-reporting can be tied to the pronunciation frame, both involving deviation from scripted projection:

In German that's Ver Clar ta Nacht. That's as far as I can get.

Niels W. Gade. I guess that's the way it's pronounced. It's spelled G-A-D-E.

Theatre de [slows up] well, I don't think I'll attempt that in French. It's the Theatre Orchestra of the Champs Elysees.

Here's that word again. I have to look at it for a moment to make sure I can pronounce it.

It should now be clear that self-reporting is not to be considered merely as a desperate measure to which resort is taken in a crisis. During informal face-to-face talk, its role is central, and no conversational mishap is necessary to warrant calling it into use. On some programs (and some stations) a similar impression is given; the speaker seems licensed to tap in at will into what would ordinarily be taken to be his silent backstage thoughts concerning his current situation:

> Gee, that was an awful joke. I shouldn't have told it on the air. Someone dared me.

and these may involve production matters about which he has cause to be pleased, not chagrined:

> [At the end of a show that runs till twelve]: Talk about timing. It's exactly twelve o'clock.

I have cited many examples of self-reporting because I believe that each of them has something to teach us about a fundamental feature of all speech, namely, the continuous decisions every individual must make regarding what to report of his passing thoughts, feelings, and concerns at any moment when he is talking or could talk. The self-reporting resorted to by marginal announcers when they get into a bind points not only to the kinds of trouble that major-station announcers are likely to avoid, but also—and more important—to remedies they might not employ were they to fail to avoid such predicaments. The obligation and right to restrict one's self-reporting, appears, then, to be a significant feature of formality. The self-reporting essayed by marginal announcers establishes informality, and links their style of talk to what is characteristic of everyday conversation. Which fact, in turn, leads to a critical question: What self-concerns, fleeting or otherwise, do conversationalists have in mind but forebear reporting, and this on the various grounds described as "self respect"? Which question, in turn, suggests a general conclusion: To do informal talk is to walk a very narrow line, often with no appreciation of how carefully one is walking; it is to blithely use self-reports up to a point, and silently foreswear such autobiography thereafter.

3. SUBVERSION. In various circumstances an announcer in effect betrays the different interests and entities in whose name

he ordinarily speaks. It is as if (on these occasions) he were under self-imposed pressure to stand up and be counted, that is, to express his "own" personal feelings and views about what it is he is obliged to utter, whether or not this expression comports with the stand he is supposed to take. And it seems that in maintaining a required line, a speaker finds himself admirably placed to infiltrate a contrary one simultaneously, modifying the original two-party, direct-announcing format to do so. Observe, in creating a clear contrast between official voice and "personal" voice, the announcer makes very evident that what we have been listening to until now is not a spontaneous expression of his full inner self. Note also that because an individual has more than one set of self-defining loyalties, he can feel obliged to convey reservations regarding what he has already established as a line that is opposed to the official one.

a. A common technique for subverting station commitment is to override a "personally" unacceptable strip of the text with phonological markers—tempo, voice articulation, intonation contour—which have the effect of "keying" the strip, giving it sarcastic or ironic implications. Standard, too, is the overt collusive aside, an unscripted, frame-breaking editorial comment conveyed *sotto voce* and rendered just before or after the derided strip. The two techniques—often combined—allow the announcer to align himself collusively with the audience against a third party: the station management, the source of the copy, individuals or groups mentioned in a news text, indeed, even society at large:

> [In progress is a commercial for a Florida hotel]: We're up to our armpits in people. [Aside to audience] One of the more elegant statements of our time.
>
> . . . what the weather forecast calls a dusting of snow . . .
>
> . . . snow flurries, or as it says here, slurries.
>
> . . . by, well, as the liner notes say anyway, the dean of the American musicians, Wallingford Riegger.
>
> A hostile Izvestia article said today [and then into singsong] twenty-six years after the victory of the people's revolution a great country has ended up in a economic and political wilderness. Okay.

> But his remarks according to the Associated Press indicate that he [Frank Church] has personally seen a copy of a letter on CIA file [and then with shock], that he had written to his mother. Hmm. [And then in *sotto voce* singsong] They got nothing better to do than . . . Okay. Senate Republican leader Hugh Scott said . . .

> He examined the crew of the Pueblo, the U.S. spy ship which was captured by North Korea. [And then sarcastically] So that's what's happening there . . .

May I add that we have here a nice example of the kind of ritualization that speaking is full of (Goffman 1979:23–24, and this volume, pp. 153–54): the speech markers announcers employ to establish collusive communication with their invisible audience are an integral part of intimate face-to-face talk; their use in broadcasting involves a transplantation.

b. Consider the role of punning. Distinguish "self-punning" (use of one's own utterance as the object of one's own pun) from "other-punning" (use of another's utterance as the object of one's own pun). Announcers when alone at the microphone are, of course, restricted to self-punning. By dint of a pun, an announcer can arbitrarily introduce an editorializing line where none might otherwise be available to him. He can momentarily betray his text and textual role, displaying a self that puts little weight on the duties at hand. It is as though a "joke" were being used as a cover for departure from the script:[51]

> . . . that was the music of Johann Wilhelm Hertel to open our program this morning as we go hurtling along.

Another connection in which self-punning occurs is worth noting. The announcer makes a "serious" blunder, one which introduces an unintended reading that is readily evident and improper. Apparently he then wants to show that he has not been completely thrown off balance by the mishap. So he continues in the vein he has inadvertently established, adding what is in effect an intentional pun (overloaded with a leering sound, presumably so that the key—and his purpose—will not be mistaken). Here,

51. In face-to-face talk, other-puns, of course, are possible, and there have characteristic functions, one of which is to allow the punster to be heard from, without his having to get the floor (or take the floor) to accomplish this.

it seems to me, the announcer sacrifices the line he was meant to maintain in order to save himself. Having accidentally started his listeners down the wrong path, he gives them a further shove in the same direction. He demonstrates that he not only knows what it is they might find risible, but also that he has sufficient distance from his official task and sufficient wit to organize additional remarks in accordance with the unanticipated interpretation. One has, then, a sort of counterdisplay, but one that follows from an unintended second meaning, intentionally extending it:

> . . . rain and possibly peet . . . Pete who? . . . ah, ah . . . Rain and possibly sleet.
>
> Commercial: "So, men, be sure to visit Handleman's hardware store on the mall for the finest in tools for your tool kit. Our special for today only is precision wenches for only two dollars each . . . (GIGGLING) . . . Of course I don't mean that you can get a wench for two dollars . . . I mean that you can get a wrench for two dollars!!!" [*Pr.:* 119]
>
> Disc Jockey: "We hear now a song from the new Columbia album featuring Very Jail . . . Oops, I ought to be in jail for that slip . . . of course, I mean JERRY VALE!!" [*Pr.:* 120]
>
> Commercial: "So, friends, be sure to visit Frankie's restaurant for elephant food and dining . . . The portions may be elephant size . . . but I meant to say *elegant* food and dining!" [*Pr.:* 11]

Elaboration of the unscheduled reading is sometimes managed with an off-mike aside, as though listeners were now being addressed in a different capacity—a different "participation status" —half-acknowledged overhearers of remarks that are to stand as partly self-directed:

> Political Program: "Everybody is watching the new incumbent with a great deal of interest. They are watching his every move, and are wondering where he will stand when he takes his seat! . . . That sounds like a nice trick if you can do it." [*SB:* 85]
>
> Newscaster: "And the FBI is expecting to make an announcement shortly, linking their newly discovered cues to the Clue Kux Klan . . . that should be, kooks to the Koo Klux Klan . . . clues to the Ku Ku . . . I'm sorry . . . I never liked the organization anyway!" [*Pr.:* 104]

[Bess Meyerson narrating TV fashion show]: "Our next model is shoed with the latest high hells . . . I mean, is wearing high hell . . . well, sometimes they may feel like hell . . . but what I meant to say is, high heels!!!"[*Pr.:* 76]

[Announcer doing Rem Cough Medicine commercial]: "So when you have a cough due to a cold, always keep some Rum on hand!" . . . "This may be good cough medicine, but I don't think it was what the sponsor had in mind." [*SB:* 20]

As a device for displaying control in a situation, extending one's own unintentional pun carries a price: to take this tack is to forego leaving open the possibility that one has not seen one's own *double entendre* (due, hopefully, to having a pure mind), as well as the possibility that at least some hearers have missed it, too. Thus, the following, an actual error and a hypothetical correction, has a chance of getting by some hearers:

Hillbilly Disc Jockey: "And now, Zeke Parker sings 'My Hole Has a Bucket In It.' . . . Sorry . . . 'My Bucket Has a Hole In It.' "

The actual correction played it less safely:

Hillbilly Disc Jockey: "And now, Zeke Parker sings 'My Hole Has a Bucket In It.' . . . Sorry . . . wrong number . . . that should be, 'My Bucket Has a Hole In It.'—That's quite a difference!" [*SB:* 13]

Note also that although second-reading extensions—like all other overt remedies—have the undesired effect of drawing attention to the fault, announcers seem almost always careful to leave something unstated. Something is usually left to the imagination. Therefore, no absolutely incontrovertible evidence is provided that they have "caught" the worst implications of the unsought interpretation or that they consider the audience able to do so. Leaving something unsaid here seems to ensure a tacit character to the communication, and it is just this tacitness in this context that produces a sense of collusion with the audience, a covert coalition against the official copy.

c. It is thinkable, and it sometimes occurs, that an announcer openly turns against his sponsors and his text and presents reservations without employing mitigation, indirection, or cover of any kind. A collusive tone or register is not employed, the announcer showing unwillingness to credit the official line sufficiently to be sly or prudent in his rejection of it, incidentally disavailing himself of the opportunity to use expressions whose distancing implications he could deny were he to be directly questioned by station authorities.[52]

> Portugal's main rival parties today stepped up their pressure for radical solutions to the present political deadlock. Following anti-Communist rioting throughout the conservative north last night, the Communist Party leader Alvaro Cunhal said uncertainty about who rules the country, how, and with what backing was at the heart of the crisis. The Socialists meanwhile brought thousands of people out into the streets of the capital, the North and the South to demand the removal of Communist-backed prime minister Vasco Gonçalves. This Alvaro Cunhal statement, coming shortly after the appointment of three generals to rule the country and the formation of a . . . of a . . . excuse me, folks, this is what happens when you get in the middle of a paragraph that you don't want to finish, and I do not want to finish the paragraph and I will explain to you [ironically] that occasionally even Reuters' wire service tends to be biased. Reuters reports that . . .
>
> Gonçalves spoke to the five thousand laborers in Lisbon last night. One member of the Communist Party was shot dead and up to one hundred persons were wounded in an anti-Communist riot, or so-called by Reuters, in the northern town of Ponte de Lima.

There is an environment which seems to strongly incline the announcer to subvert his text: when he reads the text itself without prior check, that is, "cold," and finds, while doing so, that it contains an "impossible" statement—one that any listener could be expected to judge as senseless and contrary to the working of the world. At such times there is an appreciable possibility that the announcer will openly break frame and comment to his hearers candidly about the copy he was given, saving what he can of his own image at whatever cost to station programming:

> Sportscaster: "And in the world of baseball: The Los Angeles Dodgers lead the San Francisco Giants 3–3 after eleven innings!

52. The movie *Network,* a lamentable 1978 effort to provide something of an exposé of the broadcasting industry, featured a newscaster who, on the occasion of his last broadcast, decides to say what he "really" believes. Pandemonium and a high rating result.

> . . . I've got two words for this report . . . im-possible!!!" [*Pr.:* 35]

> Political Program: "The 67-year-old candidate for the Senate, now of Peoria, was born on a farm in Columbia County 58 years ago. That doesn't sound right but that's what it says in my script!" [*SB:* 84]

> Commercial: "Try this wonderful new bra . . . you'll especially love the softly lined cups that are so comfortable to wear. You gals who need a little something extra should try model 718. It's lightly padded and I'm sure you'll love it. I do! . . . I mean I like the looks of it . . . Well . . . what I am trying to say is that I don't need one myself naturally, as a man . . . but if you do, I recommend it . . . How do I know? I really don't . . . I'm just reading the commercial for Mary Patterson who is ill at home with a cold!" [*Pr.:* 92]

> If you're confused by that [weather report] well so am I and I'm looking at it.

d. Consider next the possibility that an announcer may momentarily "flood out" into speech that seems to have broken free from the special circumstances of its production, namely, broadcasting. If the announcer's involvement is great enough, what we can hear is something like the "direct register" (Goffman 1974:361–62):

> [Sportscaster during a Newark Bears' ball game when Ernie Koy hit a home run]: "Jesus Christ! It's over the wall!" [*SB:* 114]

e. A related possibility is "exposed" collusion. Support personnel (never meant to speak on the air) are ordinarily available close at hand and/or through an off-air earphone channel. And, of course, a switch can totally cut the announcer off from the broadcast audience, while making staff auditors immediately available. Any urge the announcer might have to make undercutting, collusive comments about the audience is thus organizationally facilitated. Therefore, as already illustrated, there will be occasions when an announcer *thinks* that his staff-directed remarks are not being broadcast when indeed they are. At point here, however, is a further possibility: under no misapprehension that the microphone is closed, the announcer can blurt out a behind-the-scenes comment to technicians present, using a "rough," informal voice, as if momentarily blind to—or uncaring about—its wide reception:

> Stay tuned. At a quarter to nine there'll possibly be somebody in here who can read news better than I with a more updated and more ah understandable newscast. This is [to off-mike personnel] —did I do an ID? Well, I'll do another one anyway. This is KPFA in Berkeley at 94 . . .

> Newscaster: "And rumor has it that the North Dakota lawmaker has been ill for quite some time and this illness was caused by his death. We tried to reach him but we were told at the Executive Mansion that he is away at present on a little vacation. (FRUSTRATED, OFF MIKE) Who typed this goddamn thing?" [*SB:* 88]

I might add that given the vulnerability of announcers to impossible texts, one might expect that on occasion copywriters and editors will purposely set up an announcer (or be thought by the announcer to have done so), a blurted remonstrance being a possible consequence:

> [Cardinal baseball network]: "Our sponsors today are Lucky Strike cigarettes, Camel cigarettes and Chesterfields . . . (CONFUSED AT THE COMPETITIVE PRODUCTS) . . . All right now, who's the wise guy?" [*Pr.:* 45]

All of these blurted communications, note, are to be distinguished from talk the announcer openly directs to support personnel by way of officially bringing them into the talk already in progress with the distal audience—albeit, like the latter, only as recipients.

4. SELF-COMMUNICATION. One of the basic resources of the announcer (perhaps even more than of the ordinary speaker) is that of conveying something that listeners will be privy to but which cannot stand as something they openly have been given access to. The audience is, as it were, forced into the role of overhearers, but of messages the announcer is sending only to himself or not to anyone at all. Several varieties of this self-communication are to be found.

a. Caught in the middle of reading something that doesn't quite make sense, or that makes all too much sense of a wrong kind, the announcer can allow his concern about what is happening to invade his words, much as if he were addressing a query to himself, this expression providing "notification" that a fault of some kind is occurring. Indeed, because the eye can take in an upcoming segment before the segment itself is encoded into speech (a sort of forward monitoring), the aloud reader can know that a mistake is imminent even though none has yet been transmitted; so self-directed concern and doubt can seep into his words well in advance of what will shortly show why such alarm is warranted. This seems to be an enactment—an "externalization"—of self-monitoring, the latter being a function that is ordinarily unobtrusively sustained. And with this ritualized expression, the work of animation becomes the subject of attention instead of the means for organizing it:

> Fashion Commentator: "And now for the latest from the fashion world. It is good news for men. Women are not going to wear their dresses any longer . . . [self-questioningly] this year." [*SB:* 51]

Interestingly, an announcer may extend this self-querying practice, casting his speech production deeper and deeper into the shadow of doubt and wonderment, until his speech peters out into silence. We are allowed first to catch only a glimmer of the speaker as animator, but gradually we see more and more, until finally a complete change of footing has occurred and the speaker is present before us solely as someone whose audible self-concern has been made available for our overhearing:

> Musician: "For my next selection, I would like to play a medley of Old Stephen Foster favorites; among them will be 'Jeannie with the Light Brown Hair,' 'My Old Kentucky Home,' and 'My Ass Is In the Cold . . . Cold . . . Ground.' " [With the last word, speaker's voice fades entirely away.] [*SB:* 56, and recording]

These dwindlings are sometimes followed by a hedge:

> That tune was a hit around 19–60–5?–6?–4? *I think* [this last said as if talking to himself].

These means of displaying self-doubt are not presented as subject much to conscious control, and yet, of course, they can serve an obvious function. Although they advertise the speaker's predicament, this exposure specifically saves him from "announcer's leap"—namely, throwing himself into a statement as though he were fully alive to what would end up as its meaning (and moreover was enormously convinced of its validity), only to find out too late that the utterance made no sense.

b. The self-communicative expressions so far considered involve "tone of voice," and are carried across word boundaries. They are to be considered along with segmented interjections, these blurtings constituting self-communication in a more obvious sense. Thus, consider "response cries" (Goffman 1978, and this volume, chap. 2)—imprecations and semiwords such as *Uh-oh!, Eek!, Yipe!*—which appear to be directed to no one, not even the self. Through these blurtings, the announcer ostensibly leaks evidence of his alignment to what is occurring, which expression has the form of something that is beyond self-control. In this way the announcer makes his audience privy to his own feelings (not the station's or sponsor's or any generalized "we"), shifting the audience's status to that of overhearers. Because response cries employ standard sounds, well-articulated and properly pronounced (even if not official lexical items), and do so right at the moment of crisis, they provide evidence that the speaker is fully alive to what has happened and, moreover, has not been completely disorganized by it. Paradoxically, then, these vocalizations are ritualized indicators of incapacity for verbal expression, whilst at the same time uttering them demonstrates (and apparently often intendedly so) that all control has not been lost:

> "Stay tuned now for a dramatization of Dickens' immortal *Sale of Two Titties.* Uh! I mean *Tale of Two Cities.*" [*PB:* 77]

Allied to response cries are interjective expletives of various strengths, which rather clearly display what is presumably the announcer's own personal "response" to a source of trouble, in these examples his own animating:

> Newscast: "We switch you now for a report from CBS's Dallas Texas . . . I mean Texas Townsend . . . Good Lord, I mean Dallas Townsend." [*Pr.:* 6]

> Commercial: "So ladies, we urge you to shave at Cook's . . . I mean shake at Cook's. What I really mean is that you can shave at Cook's . . . Lordy, I mean save at Cook's!" [*SB:* 8]

Commercial: "So remember, for the finest in profane gas . . . I mean propane gas . . . darn it . . . remember the Federal Profane Gas Company . . . Propane Gas Company!" [*Pr.:* 30]

[Film Commentator]: "Hollywood stars as well as those here in London are usually faced with the problem of losing weight before starting a new picture. But not in the case of the talented Shelley Winters, who in her latest picture, *The Diarrhea of Anne . . .* oh! . . . *The Diary of Anne Frank,* found that she had to gain 53 pounds. When asked how this was done, she replied she had to go on a very strict high colonic diet . . . Oh, mercy. [*PB:* 138, and recording]

Self-directed interjections, I might add, sometimes precede another, and fuller, change of voice, namely a shift into exposed comments to support personnel:

Sportscaster: "And in the Eastern Playoffs of the NBA tonight, it was Philadelphia 122, Cincinnati 114, with Cincinnati winning that one . . . (Off Mike) . . . I'll be goddamned . . . now how the hell is that possible! Hey, Charlie . . . who the hell typed this!" [*Pr.:* 95]

c. Along with response cries, consider less formulaic, often more extended strips of communication that the audience is made privy to, but that aren't openly addressed to them. For an under-the-breath delivery is available to the announcer, a sort of non-theatrical aside through which he can momentarily take up a footing radically different from the one he has been otherwise maintaining. Here, then, self-talk—remarks of an interjective character the speaker apparently addresses to himself. Through this arrangement, the speaker can employ self-accusations, showing in his response to his own error that he is, for example, surprised, shocked, and chagrined at making the mistake, and, at the very least, is perfectly aware of what the audience may think he has done. And with the proper modulation of his wonderment, he can indicate that he is really well organized and self-possessed, in a word, bemused. Note, this kind of self-communication can also be employed by the announcer to cut himself off from responsibility for faultables attributable to the station's equipment, the sponsor's advertising agency, the presumably prepared copy, and so forth:

. . . overnight lows . . . what am I saying . . . the highs today will be in the low 80s and the overnight lows [laugh] will be in the mid 60s.

No, that can't be right.

Now what have I done?

. . . for more information . . . no, I don't have a number for that.

. . . send a stamped . . . no, that doesn't apply.

. . . narrated by Leonard Bernstein and performed . . . is that the right version, yeah . . . by the New York Philharmonic . . .

Announcer: "Our next selection to be sung by our great baritone soloist is Rachmaninoff's 'Oh, Cease Thy Sinning, Maidenform.' . . . That should be, 'Oh, Cease Thy Sinning, Maiden Fair' . . . Oh, great, Maidenform is a bra!" [*SB:* 112]

"Beat the egg yolk and then add the milk, then slowly blend in the sifted flour. As you do you can see how the mixture is sickening. I beg your pardon, I didn't mean sickening I meant thickening" *(Off mike)* "Oh, I goofed there, I know." [*PB:* 81]

Commercial: "This is KECK, Odessa, Texas. When you think of air conditioning, think of Air-Temp at a price everyone can't afford . . . so if you don't want to pinch tit . . . (FLUSTERED) . . . pitch a tent on the front yawn . . . lawn—buy Frigi-King . . . er, Air-Temp, for your home. (OFF MIKE) God damn, I'm glad that's over!" [*Pr.:* 91]

"And now, audience, here is our special TV Matinee guest that we've all been waiting for—world famous author, lecturer, and world traveler, a man about town. Mr. er—er, Mr. . . . Oh! What the hell is his name?" [*PB:* 111]

d. An announcer can use the verbal channel to address his own faultables, as would a critical member of the audience. He can use the perspective of the audience not merely as a guide in formulating excuses and accounts, but also as the substance of a self, a self that is, for example, amused at the mishap that has occurred and is ready to mock the speaker who caused it.

In the mild and most common form, the announcer allows an override of laughter to creep into his voice, betraying that he himself feels what he is saying is risible[53]—perhaps even beating the listener to the punch:

> We'll confine, we'll continue [laugh] . . .

Such self-amusement may be carried to the point where the announcer frankly "breaks up" into privately directed laughter over what the speaker (who happens to be himself) has said:

> Disc Jockey: "And now it's time for another record by that svelte, smooth singer of songs . . . slinky Pinky Lee . . . (BREAKS UP) . . . of course, I mean PEGGY LEE!!" [*Pr.:* 124]

> Announcer: "And as I stand here at my vantage point overlooking the Hudson River on this historical Fourth of July night, I can see the fireworks eliminating the entire Riverside Drive . . . (Laughing) . . . I mean illuminating!!!" [*Pr.:* 96]

Indeed, laughter may build upon itself until the announcer appears to give up all effort at self-containment, all effort to provide any text:

> "In the wonder of science, the Hayden Planetarium has heard from a Minnesota man who claims that the shape of the aurora borealis can be changed by flapping a bed sheet at it from the ground. The Planetarium doubts this but the man says he did successfully flap sheets in his backyard one midnight, although his wife kept hollering at him to cut out the foolishness and get back in the house! . . . [The announcer gives up trying to maintain a newscasting register, breaks up with laughter, and then, barely containing himself, attempts to continue.] This Sunday evening be sure to hear Drew Pearson on ABC. Pearson has received many awards for his work, and one of his treasures is the *Saturday* Revoo *of Literature* . . . [The last error is too much and he floods out again, a few moments later regains enough composure to continue on, and

53. There is an interesting transformation of this practice. After a "humorous" commercial skit taped by professional actors, the announcer coming in may allow the initial moments of his talk to carry a self-laughter override, half in collusion with the audience, as if thereby to add to the realism of the skit. The implication is that he, too, thinks it funny (presumably because this is the first time he has heard it) and is so close to his audience that he need not forebear allowing his appreciation to be sensed—which implication is quite beyond belief.

finishes with a mock slip.] . . . This is ABC, the American *Broad* Company." [*Pr.*:15, and recording]

It would be wrong here to present too simple a picture of the footings—the frame space—available to the announcer. Finding that he has committed a hopeless error—hopeless in the sense that the unanticipated reading is very obvious and all too meaningful—the announcer may present a corrected reading in a tone of voice to suggest that he tacitly admits to the audience the impropriety he has called to mind and indeed, is not so station-minded as to deny the relevance and humor of the reading he has inadvertently allowed. And yet by refraining from laughing outright, and by adhering to what would otherwise be a standard correction format, he can carefully manage his subversion so as to convey self-respect *and* station discipline.

It would also be wrong to assume that because a distinction can be drawn (and certainly heard) between collusive asides to the audience, and aloud asides to self, to no one, or to station personnel, any given formulaic remedy will be employed in only one of these participation frameworks. For example, upon making an "error," an announcer may repeat it in wonderment, as if holding it up so he himself can get a better look at what he somehow said, projecting thus a little dialogue of self-communication:

> . . . mostly skunny.
> Mostly skunny?
> No, mostly sunny.

> Good Wednesday morning.
> Good Wednesday morning?
> Good Tuesday morning.

However, self-quoted errors (like the pun extensions already considered), can be presented not as overhearable self-communications, but as collusive asides to the audience:

> . . . vins of . . . winds, not vins—vindows . . . must be those new false teeth of mine.

> . . . no, not an eight-mile walk, my goodness, just an eight-minute walk from the [laugh] just an eight-mile walk—no, no, just an eight-minute walk.

In the meantime I want to tell you about a very live [laugh] *live* . . . very good program of . . .

A second example. It was suggested that when an announcer discovers that he is lodged into the reading of an "impossible" text, he can allow his voice to dwindle as he gives increasingly candid (and increasingly self-directed) expression of his bewilderment over what is happening (see 4a, above). A somewhat similar sequence, but perhaps even more ritualized, is the "despairing give-up." An announcer utters a "wrongly" constructed word or phrase, attempts a standard correction (flat or strident), fails to get it right—indeed, may worsen the product—tries once again, fails once again (all the while with increasing stridency) until finally, as if in angered resignation, he changes footing, transforms his audience into overhearers, and utters his final words on the matter aloud and uncaring, half to himself.

Newscaster: "This is your eleven o'clock newscaster bringing you an on the pot report . . . I mean on the spot retort . . . I mean on the tot resort . . . oh, well, let's just skip it!" [*SB:6*]

Sportscaster: "That was a great game that Drysdale pitched last night. Now wait a minute, it wasn't last night, it was the night before, and it wasn't Drysdale it was Koufax. Or was it? Wait a minute. (OFF MIKE) Hey, Joe. Oh, yeah. No! Wait a minute, now I'm all fouled up over here. Now I don't remember if it was night before last . . . (EXASPERATED) . . . to hell with it!" [*SB:* 51]

Announcer: "Our music-appreciation hour continues as we hear an instrumental selection by a well-known flautist. We hear now a sloat flulu . . . a fluke solo . . . I mean a sloat flulu . . . Nuts—I'm back to where I started!!" [*SB:* 33]

The ritualized, patterned character of this response is suggested by the fact that it is not merely announcers who employ it; others fall back on the device, too:

[Contestant on CBS musical quiz program, asked to identify a recorded musical composition]: "It sounds like Smetana's Buttered Bride . . . er . . . Battered Bride, oh the hell with it." [*SB:* 25]

And as might be expected, much the same ritualization can be employed in collusive asides to the audience:

Local News: And this station is glad to be the first to bring you news of our mayor's death . . . that is, we are glad to be the first station to bring you news of the mayor's death, not that we are glad of the mayor's death . . . You know what I mean." [*SB:* 98]

[Actress during interview asked for her reaction to the opportunity to appear in the TV series "77 Sunset Strip"]: "I'm delighted to appear in a SUNSET STRIP . . . I mean I'm delighted to strip . . . Oh, my goodness, you know what I mean!!!" [*Pr.:* 123]

All of which forces a further conclusion. What is heard, say, as self-communication must depend on more than the actual formulaic words the speaker employs; prosodic features (in the absence of visual cues) are critical. Thus, to repeat a previous example, "Oh! What the hell is his name?" is an utterance that clearly breaks frame, involving a change of footing in which the announcer comes to speak wholly in his capacity as an animator; but whether self-communication is presented, or an aside that is rather openly directed to the audience that isn't present or to the support personnel who are, depends entirely upon intonation, "phrasing," and sound cues of head orientation. (In consequence, the illustrations I have provided of collusive asides and of self-communication are not, as printed, self-sufficient, although the LP and tape transcriptions almost always are; the reader must take my word for the frame in which they are to be "heard.") Nor, in many cases, would currently available transcription techniques for limning in prosodic features be discriminating enough to establish how the utterance is to be framed; a gloss in the form of bracketed stage directions would have to be employed. Thus, although an announcer may orient off-mike interjections in four different directions—to no one, to himself, to the remote audience, to support personnel—and be clearly so heard, no convenient notation for such facts is available. I might add that these issues cannot be adequately considered unless one appreciates that participation framework will always be a structural presupposition of our hearing of an utterance.

IX

So far in reviewing the frame space of announcers, I have limited the discussion to occasions when an announcer serves as the sole official speaker. Many of the remedial practices described, however, are also to be found when two announcers share the speaking duties, as in some newscasting and record-playing programs. In these formats, one finds that instead of one announcer splitting himself into two voices (an official one which utters a faultable, and an unofficial one which contributes a remedial comment), the job can be split between the two participants, sometimes one announcer carrying the remedial (and distancing) comments, sometimes the other:

> First announcer: "It's Thursday, October the twenty-first."
> Second announcer: "Hold it, Cameron, it's Tuesday."
> First announcer: "You're right, I'm wrong. It's Tuesday."

> First announcer: ". . . and it will be a nippy forty-two degrees tonight."
> Second announcer: [*Sotto voce*] "I could stand a nip."
> First announcer: "Get away from here."

Indeed, the two-person, speaker and kibitzer format may be the underlying structure in all of this communication, the one-announcer form being an adaptation.[54]

From the examples given, it is plain that when a dialogue is conducted before the microphone, a straightforward statement said in good faith by one speaker may be reframed by the other in an apparent spirit of raillery and fun:

> Bennett Cerf: "Is the product made in Hollywood?"
> Arlene Francis: "Isn't everybody?" [*SB:* 78]

> On *Name That Tune,* on NBC-TV, a contestant was asked to identify *Hail to the Chief,* which was played by the orchestra. MC Bill Cullen tried helping the girl by hinting, "What do they play whenever the President's around?" She answered, "Golf." [*PB:* 92]

54. Certainly a two-party model is required in the vast number of childhood jokes, riddles, and snappy comebacks that work by inducing a standard interpretation of an utterance and, once induced, provide the uncommon verbal environment that neatly establishes an unexpected but cogent interpretation.

> The late Marilyn Monroe was asked if she had anything on when she posed for that famous calendar photo. She told her radio and TV interviewers, "I had the radio on!" [*Pr.:* 49]

> In a television interview several years ago, Senator Margaret Chase Smith of Maine was questioned about her Presidential aspirations. Asked what she would do if she woke up one morning and found herself in the White House, she replied, "I would go straight downstairs and apologize to Mrs. Eisenhower, and then I would go right home." [*Pr.:* 52]

> On the popular Art Linkletter program, a youngster was asked what he wanted to be when he grew up. He replied, "A space man." He was then asked what he would do if he ran into a Martian. The youngster snapped back with, "I would say, 'Excuse me.' " [*Pr.:* 56]

In brief, "quipping" or "snapping back" is possible, the provision of a response that admittedly derives from a misframed interpretation of the other's remarks. All of which leaves open the question of how frequently an announcer covertly sets himself up for his own misframing of his own remarks, allowing one part of him to produce a dually interpretable utterance so that another part of him can get a quip off by humorously extending the initial error, serving then as his own straight man. (Again, what seems generic to two-person play can be managed by one person.) And from here it is only a step to seeing that an announcer may intentionally phrase a statement so that hearers can construe the phrasing in an officially unintended way, to the disparagement of the subject matter.[55] Or, learning that he has inadvertently al-

55. This possibility must itself be distinguished from two other keyings: the serious citation of faults and corrections in talks on speech behavior, and the unserious introduction of faults and corrections when these happen to be the topic under consideration:

> When I [Kermit Schafer] was interviewed by Maggie McNellis over NBC Radio in connection with the release of my new book, *Your Slip is Showing,* Maggie came out with the following: "It now gives me great pleasure to introduce to you the author of that hilariously funny book, *Your Show is Slipping*—radio-TV producer Kermit Schafer!!! . . . er, I'm sorry, Kermit . . . I got the name of your book wrong . . . please excuse the shlip-sod introduction." [*Pr.:* 127]

On the next page, the last in his book, Schafer concludes with, "This conclues . . . this conclees . . . that is all!!!" [*Pr.:* 128].

lowed a double meaning, the announcer may attempt after the fact to give the impression that he had slyly intended it. In consequence of which, hearers may be left uncertain as to whether the risible ambiguity was or wasn't intentional.

X

The notions of speech fault and self-correction imply a simple sequential, remedial model basic to the traditional notion of social control. Starting from a baseline of acceptable talk, a fault then occurs, a correction is made, and the speaker returns to the baseline of talk unnoteworthy for its blemishes. Or, schematically:

baseline → fault → remedy → baseline

To which the standard variation could be added, namely, a sequence in which the remedy appears immediately *preceding* the trouble, the better to deal with it:

baseline → remedy → fault → baseline

For announcers, the schema would read something like this: The text an announcer must read, recite, or extemporaneously formulate sets the task. Ordinarily his competence at delivery, along with technical support from the station's equipment and staff, ensures that a flow of words is sustained that is acceptable to the station, provides a single, clear line for the audience to follow, and implies an image of the particular announcer he is prepared to accept. This, then, is the baseline. Then a fault occurs in speech production that the announcer feels he can't handle simply by passing over, whether the fault is an influency, slip, boner, or gaffe, whether the responsibility is to be attributed to himself or to station programming. Presumably something has been evoked that he feels is incompatible with the station's requirements or with his own reputation as an announcer. A remedy is then attempted and, typically, the announcer is thereafter free to return to the base line he had been maintaining before the trouble occurred.

This paper has argued that such a framework is inadequate to handle error in radio talk. Several grounds were suggested for extending the basic social control sequence, the aim being to make the formula fit the facts.

First, when a speaker is obliged to adhere closely to a script, or at least a format, any self-correction will itself constitute a deviation from what is prescribed as the text, and will itself establish a need for remedial action, with consequent prolongment of the remedial sequence. The following is therefore found:

baseline → fault → remedy → remedy for remedy → baseline

the question being open as to how any remedy can be the last one.

Second, as argued repeatedly, the notion of fault must be broadened to include "remark-ables," namely, anything the announcer might treat as something to not let stand. He can editorially extend what has been under discussion, deride in various ways what he has been obliged to say, and provide a risible alternative reading—one that listeners themselves may not have thought of. And if neither an obvious error nor an opportunity for skittishness arises, nor even a latent error, then a determined announcer can allow himself to commit an error with malice aforethought, just in order to be able to make something out of it.[56] And the point is that —more than in the case of ordinary self-correction— *these* makings-something-out-of-it, these remedial actions that other announcers might not be venturing at all, themselves provide deviations from the base line. Thus they are themselves candidates for remedy, even as the individual who produced them is already someone who has demonstrated a taste for working deviations for what can be gotten from them. For the more an announcer must coerce a faultable from what has just occurred, the more the remedy is likely to display an attempt at wit; the less the remedy is likely to be merely remedial, the more it will itself be questionable. So the shift from fault to faultable, and from faultable to remark-able, increases the likelihood that

56. A possibility perhaps even more exploited in face-to-face talk. Thus, for example, it has been recommended that individuals who begin to use an untactful descriptor for someone present, then catch themselves and rush in with a more acceptable alternative, will sometimes be acting tactically, committing the error for what can be safely leaked in this manner (Jefferson 1974:-192–93).

the social control sequence will be extended by an extra step or two:

> . . . rain and possibly sleet. They're not treating us well in the weather department. That's all I can say. [Dropping voice] That's all I should say.

Third, the simple remedial sequence can be complicated by the question of framing. Some elaboration is required. When an "obvious" fault occurs in announcing, it tends to occur in a nicely self-bounded fashion, the words just before and after it providing discernible contrasts and hence brackets for the spoiled strip. The prospective or retrospective correction then presents no problem with respect to what it refers to. By and large, no corroboration from the audience is required in order to ensure that they have gotten the point and will have correctly referred the remedy to what was in need of it. It will be clear to them that the remedy is not part of the copy, but the speaker's out-of-frame correction, and clear, too, when the correcting is complete and the speaker has reverted to his prescribed text.[57] The unavailability of listener back-channel response—a response which helps stabilize frames in face-to-face talk—is here not damaging.

When, however, the speaker elects to provide an editorial-like comment about a remedy he has provided, or, even more so, chooses to betray his prescribed text in the absence of evident error, then framing problems can arise. Hearers may not know whether a strip of talk is an out-of-frame comment on the text or a part of the text itself; and if they do appreciate that the announcer is not delivering his copy but commenting on what he is required to deliver, they still may not know precisely where this side-remarking ends and the official text begins again. In turn, because back-channel cues from hearers are not available, the announcer will not know whether or not his listeners know how he wants them to take what he is saying, or, if they do sense how he wants his comments to be taken, whether or not they are ready to do so.

A general solution for this framing problem is for the speaker

57. A more refined treatment of correction placement position is to be found in Schegloff et al. (1977:366 and 377), and Schegloff (1979).

to assume the role of his hearers and provide an approximation of their response, were they present in the flesh to provide the feedback he needs. The dialogic character of remedial work is thus maintained, but the announcer performs both parts of it. Thus, the "bracket laugh," a standard frame cue announcers employ to show that what they had been saying is not part of the text proper but a comment on it, and that now this commentative aside is terminated and the official text is about to be resumed.[58] The bracket laugh is in fact not unlike the laugh that members of a live audience might give to show that they have gotten the point and find it funny, the announcer often inserting his version at just the juncture the live audience would have selected. The difference is that he runs the risk of appearing to laugh at his own jokes. (But he does get a chance to imply by tone that he admits his remark might have been a little uncalled for, and that he makes no claim to a sure right to carry on in this fashion.) Observe, the availability of framing cues itself allows the announcer to venture a remark about aspects of his copy that other broadcasters would find no need to make something of, and to offer such remedies playfully in a tone of voice that might otherwise be miskeyed as serious:

> . . . that's the longest sentence I've ever read from an AP release [laugh].
>
> [During a weather forecast, wind speed is announced in a hoarse voice]: I think my voice left with those winds this morning [laugh].
>
> . . . Mozart composed while playing skittles. It doesn't say whether he was drinking beer or not, be that as it may and all that [laugh].
>
> . . . an Argo record—to give the British their due [laugh].
>
> [Transmission noise]: No, a bee didn't get loose in your receiver [laugh].
>
> [From the liner notes]: Music to entertain a king. In this case, King Henry VIII, in fact, his whole entourage [laugh].

Announcers seem particularly concerned that a hearer might miskey the enactment of pretension, and here they seem particularly

58. See the comment on "joking openers" in Goffman (1971:182). A close treatment of the placement of laughter is provided in Jefferson (1979).

prone to employ a bracket laugh to ensure proper framing. For example, after a straight reading of liner notes (on Buxtehude) that could be considered overbearing, an announcer may display his view of such erudition by means of mock personal elaboration of the notes, and then use a laugh (apparently) to make sure he isn't misinterpreted:

> One doesn't hear much of Buxtehude's chamber music [laugh], does one now?

Just as bracket laughs are often found after questionable remedies, so they are found after a remedy (serious or not) has been itself remedied:

> . . . by Karl Maria von Weber. That was pretty lively music, not to say bumptious—and I don't know why anyone would, except me [heh heh].

> One of the slogans flying at the park read, "Be prepared against war, be prepared against natural disasters, and do everything for the people. Dig tunnels deep, store grain everywhere, and never seek heg, heg, hegomany"—I should learn to read these things beforehand. Hegemony [laugh].

Interestingly, if the speaker's laugh comes right at the juncture between out-of-frame remark and the resumed text, a break in fluency is chanced. To deal with this issue, announcers sometimes delay their bracket laugh, displacing it until just after the prescribed text has been resumed, the laugh taking the characteristic form of a slight swelling of the initial words of the reestablished text:

> . . . barometer stands at twenty-eight degrees and
> falling. Crash. We turn . . .
> [laugh]

> That's soprano, comma, trumpet, not soprano trumpet
> on this record.
> [laugh]

> How do you like that? He [meaning himself] got through
> the weather forecast without making a mistake. The next . . .
> [laugh]

> And now that you're awake, this is . . .
> [laugh]

In sum, once an announcer undertakes a digression, or ad libs a remark, or takes exception to a phrasing that would otherwise have passed unnoticed, he has the problem of getting back to base; so, whether or not he provides a mitigating comment on his comment, he may add a bracket cue to ensure that his hearers find their way back to his text. A full expansion of the remedial cycle in the case of announcer's self-correction would then be:

baseline → remark-able → remedial work ↗ bracket cue → baseline
↘ reworking → bracket cue → baseline

I want only to add that a frame bracket laugh can also appear at the *beginning* of an utterance that is not to be taken literally but keyed, for example, as irony, sarcasm, quotation, or mock pretension:

> If my [laugh] if my memory serves, yes, Thomas Weelkes [a very, very obscure composer] was born in 1575.

—which would require a slight reordering of the elements of the remedial cycle.

As already argued, the less an announcer is in control of his circumstances, the more, it seems, he must be poised for these remedial sequences, these little essays in compensation, recompensation, and reconnection. He must, indeed, be ready in relatively serious shows to engage in just those shticks that professional announcers engage in when emceeing an informal show. In any case, these little remedial sequences turn out to be extremely well patterned, extremely stereotyped. The path of words along which the announcer retreats is likely to be one that is well worn. That is, the verbal and expressive rituals he employs to get himself back into countenance are relatively standardized and common to the trade. Indeed, many are common to talk in general. The individual who uses these devices in announcing is likely to have used them in off-mike hours. And when an individual does use these moves while announcing, he or she is not using them *qua* announcer but as a person who is stuck with a particular job and therefore stuck with the particular ways in which this work can go wrong. Social (indeed formulaic) this behavior is, and certainly it is displayed *during* the performance of an occupational role; but in the last analysis it speaks to the job of being a person, not an announcer. Which is not to say, of course, that just such a display of personhood may not become the mainstay of a radio or TV show.

XI

CONCLUSIONS

1. Take it that a standard in much broadcasting is that the speaker will render his prepared text with faultless articulation, pronunciation, tempo, and stress, and restrict himself entirely to the copy. He is to appear to us only in the guise that his prepared material has planned for him, almost as though he were to hold himself to the character allotted to him in a play. And whether aloud reading or fresh talk is required of him, he is obliged to compress or stretch his talk so that it lasts exactly as long as the time allotted, just filling up the space between his "on" and "off" cues. Given this ideal, any noticed faultable may not only introduce irrelevant associations (if not misinforming us), but also divert the obligatory stream, presenting a view of someone stumbling—indeed a view of a stumbler—instead of a view of the person who has been programmed for the occasion. Further, remedies themselves necessarily add further diversion, further introducing a difference between what was to have occurred and what is occurring. More to the point, corrective actions can intrude the speaker upon us in a way we hadn't bargained for: his plight as a speaker of words. Substantive repairs, self-reports, and apologies—remedial acts of all kinds—thrust the person making them upon us in a more rounded and intimate way than the role that was meant to emerge for him might recommend. He becomes fleshier than he was to have been. After all, the very efficacy of an apology is due to its capacity to convince us that the person making it is a somewhat different person from the one who committed the offense in the first place, and how can this evidence be presented without deflecting attention from the original text to the announcer in his capacity as animator?

It was argued that announcers on small and on special-interest stations, and announcers employing a comic format, do not merely make errors and employ remedies for them, betraying their own role obligations to do so, but also make unscripted comments about strips of their performed text that otherwise would have passed by with no special attention. So, too, they may choose to treat error correction itself as requiring remedial comments. It was suggested that here repair work might be seen as merely one example of maintaining a dual voice, of commenting on one's own production even while producing it. And that at the heart of it is the characterizing, self-projective implication of any stream of activity and the capacity and license to introduce contrary images during its flow. Here role is a rough gloss, for it is really multiple voices and changes of footing that are at work. With marginal announcers, then, the shift is from errors in talk and their correction to definitions of the self that talk projects and the means of escaping these definitions—and then escaping the escape. And the study of speech faults and what is done about them proves to be an integral part of a larger matter: the study of how a speaker can construe a strip of his own speech to provide himself with something upon which to base a remark. How, in effect, a speaker can transform a linear text into a mono-dialogue. What starts with a consideration of error correction should end with an analysis of sequential movements within frame space.

2. Now finally I want to review the argument that an examination of radio talk, especially the differences between the formal and informal kind, can direct our attention to critical features of everyday face-to-face talk that might otherwise remain invisible to us.

As suggested, there are obvious differences between ordinary talk and radio talk of any kind, all a consequence of the presence in radio talk of absent addressees. Correction in radio talk is almost all of the self-administered variety; correction in everyday talk is considerably other-noticed, if not other-administered (Schegloff et al. 1977). (A member of an audience can write or phone in a correction, but the remedy will ordinarily have to be transmitted considerably after the error has occurred, by which time the announcer's subject matter and audience will have changed somewhat; if he is to make a public acknowledgment, he will have to replay the original context of the error to be sure his comments will be understood.) Radio listeners are free to laugh derisively and openly when a faultable occurs, not being bound by the tact that leads face-to-face listeners to pass over some of the faults to which a speaker seems oblivious.[59] Also as suggested, nonbroadcast talk would seem to allow for subtler changes in footing than does radio talk, in part because a speaker in everyday talk can obtain ongoing, back-channel evidence that his intention—his frame and its keying—is understood.

But there are deeper issues. The fresh talk to be found in informal conversation, and the simulated fresh talk to be found in network announcing, are similar on the surface but different underneath. Both tend to be heard as faultless and spontaneous, the first because the sort of technical faults that routinely occur are routinely disattended or flatly corrected (in any case, lots of warrant is available for them), the second because special skill has been applied to eliminate such faults in spite of very treacherous conditions.

In everyday informal talk, the conception of individual-as-animator that seems to prevail allows speakers a considerable margin of error and imperfection. They have the right to break down in minor ways; they can cough, sneeze, yawn, pause to wipe their glasses, glance at passing objects of interest, and so forth. Speakers can disattend these interruptions and assume that their listeners have done likewise. Further, conversational talk allows not only the disattendance of many minor faultables but also the introduction of candid corrections—restarts, filled pauses, redirections—as well as perfunctory excuses and apologies. In addition, stressed corrections abound. Corrections in general, then, whether flat or strident, themselves don't much require excuse and remedy. And many priorities are accepted as taking precedence over smooth speech production by virtue of the fact that many claims in addition to that of coparticipant in talk are recognized as legitimately bearing on the individual, even if he happens to be in the role of speaker at the time.

Informal talk allows still other liberties. Often a participant can forego speaking in favor of mere back-channel evidence of

59. Studio audiences are in a similar position. On various grounds they can behave like an absent audience, tittering and laughing in the face of the person who is the target of this response; indeed, they may be encouraged by a show's M.C. to do so (see Goffman 1974:372–73).

participation that passes the right and obligation of speaking back to prior speaker. If more than two participants are involved, there are circumstances in which one of them may move in and out of effective participation. A participant also has the right to generate discourse by referring to his own situation, including his situation as animator, telling us, for example, of the difficulty he is having remembering what he knows he knows, or finding the right words for what he has in mind—a form of self-involvement that need not be heard as a particularly eventful change in footing; after all, the speaker in any case is likely to have been uttering his own formulations in his own name. (It is as if the biography and officially irrelevant concerns of a talker are always accorded the right to some attention from listeners; that claim is presumably a feature of the way we are in informal, natural talk.) Also, he may be able to pun at will, responding with alternative interpretations, playfully reframing what he or another has said.

All of these deviations from a fixed role can themselves be of small moment because informal talk is defined as presenting the individual participant in this fuller way. No particular voice or footing is fixed for the speaker, so shifting from one to another voice needs no apology or excuse. Insofar as the speaker can claim the right to report on his own fugitive feelings, his own responses and passing concerns, then shifting from a wonted concern to a "personal" one requires no excuse; and what would be perceived as an abrupt change of footing in formal circumstances is here hardly perceived at all. And because no fixed, continuous script is involved, unexpected pauses and introjections are not disorganizing.

I am suggesting that the very license to employ these stratagems freely, very appreciably defines what informal talk is. To repeat: The right to disattend a multitude of minor faultables, to apologize easily in passing for ones that one elects not to disattend, to report self-concerns widely, indeed, to turn upon one's own words or the words of another in order to discover something to remark on—all these flexibilities are not generic to communication as such, but particular to the multiple selves we are allowed to project during informal talk. The right to shift topic either with a crude bridge for coherence or a perfunctory excuse for its total absence, to inject "side sequences" of long duration, to take physical leave of the conversational circle temporarily or permanently on any of a wide range of grounds—all these possibilities speak to the same looseness of demand. So, too, does the right to split voice and employ sarcasm, irony, innuendo in a rather open play of multiple address and behind this, multiple selves. A fixed footing is not required. In short, a wide frame space is legitimately available, albeit a formal stance is disallowed. It need only be added that this license in conversational talk is so much taken for granted by us that it is only by looking at such things as delicts in broadcast talk that the liberty we conversationalists have been enjoying becomes obvious. And it is through a microanalysis of these varieties of talk and the frame space they employ that we can begin to learn just what informality and formality specifically consist of.

Contrasting broadcast talk with the ordinary kind thus allows a glimpse of the distinguishing structural features of everyday discourse. However, at least one similarity between the two genres of talk is worth considering, too. Clearly, professional aloud reading of fully worded copy tends to produce a mere illusion of fresh talk. But then how fresh is everyday face-to-face talk?

Competent announcers with the permission of their stations editorially elaborate on their copy extemporaneously in the course of reading it, thus appreciably strengthening the impression of fresh talk overall. A lay speaker (or even a neophyte announcer), thrust before a microphone, likely would not have the ability to do this. Yet when one examines how this editorial elaboration is accomplished, it appears that a relatively small number of formulaic sentences and tag phrases are all that is needed. Providing that any one use of a particular remark does not immediately follow another use of the same remark, the illusion of spontaneous, creative, novel flow is engendered.[60] When one shifts from copy that is merely elaborated somewhat by extemporaneous remarks, to shows that are fully unscripted,

60. A structurally similar effect is found in gesticulation. Professional pop singers ordinarily employ a small repertoire of hand-arm gestures—perhaps six or eight—but so long as the same gesture is not repeated before others have been interspersed, the illusion is created that a uniquely developing flow of feeling is occurring.

fresh talk would seem to be a reality, not an illusion. But here again it appears that each performer has a limited resource of formulaic remarks out of which to build a line of patter. A DJ's talk may be heard as unscripted, but it tends to be built up out of a relatively small number of set comments, much as it is said epic oral poetry was recomposed during each delivery.[61] A lay speaker suddenly given the task of providing patter between records would no doubt be struck dumb—but this for a want of tag lines, not for a want of words.

Surely, the ability to engage in face-to-face "small talk" in natural settings depends on a similar resource, merely one that is widely distributed. No doubt grammar generates a near infinite set of sentences, but that does not mean that talk is novel in the same way. It would seem that a reason we can bring a phrase or sentence to mind before encoding it in speech (so that once we start encoding, the task can be finished without much thought) is that we draw on a limited compendium of pat utterances in doing so. The mind of the lay speaker is a repertoire of sayings —large when compared to the gesticulatory stereotypes of pop singers, but small and manageable in other respects.

However, even as a model this approach to the mind of the speaker is simplistic. The mind may contain files of formulaic expressions, but speakers are not engaged merely in culling from the roster. The underlying framework of talk production is less a matter of phrase repertoire than frame space. A speaker's budget of standard utterances can be divided into function classes, each class providing expressions through which he can exhibit an alignment he takes to the events at hand, a footing, a combination of production format and participation status. What the speaker is engaged in doing, then, moment to moment through the course of the discourse in which he finds himself, is to meet whatever occurs by sustaining or changing footing. And by and large, it seems he selects that footing which provides him the least self-threatening position in the circumstances, or, differently phrased, the most defensible alignment he can muster.

During his stint before the microphone, a professional's footing may be considerably set in advance; changes may not be

61. As considered by Parry (1971) and Lord (1960).

frequent and may occur at preestablished junctures—for example, station breaks. But for the announcers in some program formats and some announcers in most of their programs, local responsiveness will be considerable, the performer not knowing in advance what alignment he will find it desirable to take to what is happening currently. And certainly during ordinary informal talk, the speaker must be ready moment to moment to change footing in a way he hadn't planned for, else he will not be able to continuously sustain such viability as his position offers him. And error correction and apology introduces one such locally responsive change in footing, as does the remedial work sometimes then performed upon the first remedy. But this local responsiveness must not be misperceived. The predicaments a speaker is likely to find himself facing during the course of his talk cannot be established in advance. However, given the predicaments that do arise, his response to them plays itself out within the limited frame space available to him, and this space of alignment possibilities is itself not generated moment to moment, nor are the phrases and gestures through which he will represent the alignment he has selected. From moment to moment, unanticipated junctures at which interaction moves must be made will occur; but each move is selected from a limited and predetermined framework. (Even when an announcer follows the novel course of remarking on a latent error, an error that wasn't made but could have been, he must choose an utterance that could indeed stir the audience to some concern in this regard, and either has, or will, be seen as a likely candidate in this respect when he remarks on what he escaped doing. Perhaps even more than is ordinarily the case, the announcer here depends on standard understandings.) If what thereby occurs is something like a game, it is less like chess than like tic-tac-toe. But no less than tic-tac-toe, this game can hold attention; for the illusion is allowed that at every moment new responses are revealed.

Learning about the little maneuvers that announcers employ to keep themselves in countenance, and learning about the participation framework and production format in which these moves are grounded, is what gives warrant for something so trivial as the close analysis of radio talk. Catching in this way at what broadcasters do, and do not do, before a microphone catches at what we do, and do not do, before our friends. These little momentary changes in footing bespeak a trivial game, but our conversational life is spent in playing it.

REFERENCES

Baker, Charlotte. 1975. "This is just a first approximation, but . . ." In *Papers from the Eleventh Regional Meeting of the Chicago Linguistic Society,* pp. 37–47.

Beattie, Geoffrey W. 1979. "Planning units in spontaneous speech: Some evidence from hesitation in speech and speaker gaze direction in conversation." *Linguistics* 17:61–78.

Bell, Allan. 1977. "The language of radio news in Auckland." Ph.D. dissertation, University of Auckland, New Zealand.

Boomer, Donald S. 1965. "Hesitation and grammatical encoding." *Language and Speech* 8:148–58.

Boomer, Donald S., and Laver, John D. M. 1968. "Slips of the tongue." *British Journal of Disorders of Communication* 3:2–11.

Bourdieu, Pierre. 1975. "Le fétichisme de la langue." *Actes de la recherche en sciences sociales* 4 (Juillet): 2–32.

Clancy, Patricia. 1972. "Analysis of a conversation." *Anthropological Linguistics* 14(3):78–86.

Corum, Claudia. 1975. "A pragmatic analysis of parenthetic adjuncts." In *Papers from the Eleventh Regional Meeting of the Chicago Linguistic Society,* pp. 133–41.

Dittmann, Allen T., and Llewellyn, Lynn G. 1967. "The phonemic clause as a unit of speech decoding." *Journal of Personality and Social Psychology* 6:341–49.

Fay, David, and Cutler, Anne. 1977. "Malapropisms and the structure of the mental lexicon." *Linguistic Inquiry* 8: 505–20.

Finegan, Edward. 1980. *Attitudes toward English usage.* New York: Teachers College Press.

Finnegan, Ruth. 1977. *Oral poetry.* Cambridge: Cambridge University Press.

Fraser, Bruce. 1975. "Hedged performatives." In *Syntax and semantics: Speech acts,* vol. 3, edited by Peter Cole and Jerry L. Morgan, pp. 187–210. New York: Academic Press.

Friedman, Marc. 1970. Personal communication.

Fromkin, Victoria A. 1971. "The non-anomalous nature of anomalous utterances." *Language* 47:27–52.

Garnes, Sara, and Bond, Zinny S. 1975. "Slips of the ear: Errors in perception of casual speech." In *Papers from the Eleventh Regional Meeting of the Chicago Linguistic Society,* pp. 214–225.

Goffman, Erving. 1959. *Presentation of self in everyday life.* New York: Anchor Books.

———. 1967. *Interaction ritual.* New York: Anchor Books.
———. 1971. *Relations in public.* New York: Harper and Row.
———. 1974. *Frame analysis.* New York: Harper and Row.
———. 1978. "Response cries." *Language* 54(4):787–815.
———. 1979. "Footing." *Semiotica* 25(1/2):1–29.

Goldman-Eisler, Frieda. 1968. *Psycholinguistics: Experiments in spontaneous speech.* London: Academic Press.

Halliday, M. A. K. 1967. "Notes on transitivity and theme in English (Part 2)." *Journal of Linguistics* 3:177–274.

Hirsh-Pasek, Kathy; Gleitman, Lila R.; and Gleitman, Henry. 1978. "What did the brain say to the mind? A study of the detection and report of ambiguity by young children." In *The child's conception of language,* edited by A. Sinclair, R. J. Jarvella, and W. J. M. Levelt, pp. 97–132. Berlin: Springer-Verlag.

Hoffer, Jay. 1974. *Radio production techniques.* Blue Ridge Summit, Pa.: Tab Books.

Humphrey, Frank. 1978. *"Shh::!"* Unpublished paper presented at the Seventh Annual Colloquium on New Ways of Analyzing Variation, Georgetown University, Washington, D.C.

Hyde, Stuart W. 1959. *Television and radio announcing.* Boston: Houghton Mifflin Co.

James, Deborah. 1978. "The use of oh, ah, say and well in relation to a number of grammatical phenomena." *Papers in Linguistics* 11:517–535.

Jefferson, Gail. 1974. "Error correction as an interactional resource." *Language in Society* 3:181–200.

———. 1979. "A technique for inviting laughter and its subsequent acceptance declination." In *Everyday language: Studies in ethnomethodology,* edited by George Psthas, pp. 74–96. New York: Irvington Publishers.

Jordan, Brigitte, and Fuller, Nancy. 1975. "On the non-fatal nature of trouble: Sense-making and trouble-managing in *lingua franca* talk." *Semiotica* 13:-11–31.

Kasl, Stanislav V., and Mahl, George F. 1965. "The relationship of disturbances and hesitations in spontaneous speech to anxiety." *Journal of Personality and Social Psychology* 1(5):425–33.

Keenan, Elinor. 1977. "Why look at unplanned and planned discourse." in *Discourse across Time and Space,* edited by Elinor Keenan and Tina Bennett, pp. 1–41, Los Angeles: Southern California Occasional Papers in Linguistics, no. 5.

Labov, William. 1972. "Hypercorrection by the lower middle class as a factor in linguistic change. In William Labov, *Sociolinguistic Patterns,* pp. 122–42. Philadelphia: University of Pennsylvania Press.

Lakoff, Robin. 1973. "The logic of politeness; or minding your P's and Q's." In *Papers from the Ninth Regional Meeting, Chicago Linguistic Society,* edited by Claudia Corum et al., pp. 292–305. Chicago: Department of Linguistics, University of Chicago.

Laver, John D. M. 1970. "The production of speech." In *New horizons in linguistics,* edited by John Lyons. Middlesex: Penguin Books.

Lord, Albert, B. 1960. *The singer of tales.* New York: Atheneum.

Maclay, Howard, and Osgood, Charles E. 1959. "Hesitation phenomena in spontaneous English speech." *Word* 15:19–44.

Morgan, J. L. 1973. "Sentence fragments and the notion 'sentence.' " In *Issues in linguistics,* edited by Braj B. Kachru et al., pp. 719–51. Urbana: University of Illinois Press.

Parry, Adam, ed. 1971. *The making of Homeric verse: The collected papers of Milman Parry.* Oxford: The Clarendon Press.

Pomerantz, Anita. 1977. "Agreeing and disagreeing with assessments: Some features of preferred/dispreferred turn shapes." Unpublished paper (reported in part at the American Anthropological Association Meetings, San Francisco, November 1978).

Schafer, Kermit. 1959. *Pardon my blooper.* Greenwich, Conn.: Fawcett Crest Books.

———. 1963. *Super bloopers.* Greenwich, Conn.: Fawcett Gold Medal Books.

———. 1965. *Prize bloopers.* Greenwich, Conn.: Fawcett Gold Medal Books.

Schegloff, Emanuel. 1979. "The relevance of repair to syntax-for-conversation." In *Syntax and semantics: Discourse and syntax,* vol. 12, edited by T. Givon and C. Li, pp. 261–86. New York: Academic Press.

Schegloff, Emanuel; Jefferson, Gail; and Sacks, Harvey. 1977. "The preference for self-correction in the organization of repair in conversation." *Language* 53(2):361–82.

Sherzer, Joel. 1978. " 'Oh! That's a pun and I didn't mean it.' " *Semiotica* 22(3/4): 335–50.

Shultz, Thomas R., and Horibe, Frances. 1974. "Development of the appreciation of verbal jokes." *Developmental Psychology* 10:13–20.

Shultz, Thomas R., and Pilon, Robert. 1973. "Development of the ability to detect linguistic ambiguity." *Child Development* 44:728–33.

Simonini, R.C., Jr. 1956. "Phonemic and analogic lapses in radio and television speech." *American Speech* 31:252–63.

Trager, George, and Smith, Henry L. 1951. *An outline of English structure.* Studies in Linguistics: Occasional Papers, no. 3. Norman, Okla.: Battenberg Press. (Republished, New York: American Council of Learned Societies, 1965.)

Urmson, J. O. 1952. "Parenthetical verbs." *Mind* 61:480–96.

Wilson, Thomas P. 1970. "Normative and interpretive paradigms in sociology." In *Understanding everyday life,* edited by Jack D. Douglas, pp. 57–79. Chicago: Aldine.

Yngve, Victor H. 1973. "I forgot what I was going to say." *Papers from the Ninth Regional Meeting, Chicago Linguistic Society,* edited by Claudia Corum et al., pp. 688–99. Chicago: Department of Linguistics, University of Chicago.

Zwicky, Arnold M. 1977. "Classical malapropisms." *Language Sciences* 1 (2): 339–48.

INDEX